D1498253

STAR OCEAN®

Integrity and Faithlessness™

INTRODUCTION

Star Ocean V: Integrity and Faithlessness follows the globetrotting adventures of Fidel of Sthal and his friends. Gameplay involves exploring the countryside, undertaking various tasks, and looking for clues to progress the story. There are monsters afield to fight for EXP and Fol (the local currency), harvesting points and treasure chests to seek out for loot, and side quests in addition to the main events that place the heroes in motion. Naturally, there's also a stock of both console-wide trophies and in-game battle trophies, which unlock as you complete many overarching objectives.

As an RPG, the game is also brimming with different items to collect and craft, and hundreds of hostile entities to seek out and subjugate. The game itself does a very good job of ramping up players to the combat and controls of *Star Ocean V*, so this section and several other peripheral sections serve as data reference for all of the sights and tasks in and around Resulia. The walkthrough here functions as the meat of the guide, going through every main objective and side quest of the game, including every secret and the bonus dungeons near the end.

Fidel Camuze

Sex: Male
Age: 23
Height: 5'9"
Weight: 152 lb.

Fidel Camuze is the son of a renowned Resulian swordsman and the main protagonist of *Star Ocean: Integrity and Faithlessness*. Fidel transformed the chore of swordsmanship training into his passion and quickly became one of the most talented fighters in the region.

While his father is preoccupied as an advisor to the Resulian military, Fidel protects their hometown of Sthal, proving himself to be an invaluable pillar of the community.

Miki Sauvester

Sex: Female

Age: 18

Height: 5'2"

Weight: 99 lb.

Orphaned at a young age due to a tragic incident, Miki grew up with Fidel as a long-time childhood friend. Miki considers Fidel an older brother rather than just a family friend.

As a signeturge, she has signets imbued on her back, which activate seemingly magical powers. Her strengths lie in defense-based signeturgical spells, and she acts as a selfless healer to her allies. Although her primary practice is in curing wounds, she's no slouch when it comes to attack-oriented spell usage.

Victor Oakville

Sex: Male

Age: 32

Height: 6'2"

Weight: 170 lb.

Victor is the leader of the King's Chosen, an elite squadron of the Central Resulian Army. His time in the military earned him training under Daril, Fidel's father, so his fighting style closely resembles those of the Camuze men.

Although he possesses a serious demeanor, Victor values the lives of others deeply, and he only resorts to violence when necessary. With a strong sense of justice and duty, Victor is a valuable ally.

Fiore Brunelli

Sex: Female

Age: 25

Height: 5'3"

Weight: 97 lb.

Fiore, also known as Lady Brunelli, is a signeturge hailing from the eastern lands. She was born and raised in Santeroule, the capital of signeturgy.

As a researcher for the Royal Institute of Signetary Studies, she's one of the most gifted signeturges in the known world. Her proficiency is mainly in the offense-oriented arts, able to engulf her enemies in elemental destruction.

Her extravagant fashion style tells myriads about her personality and talents, with her imbued signets peeking through her leggings and mini-skirt.

Emmerson

Sex: Male

Age: 41

Height: 6'2"

Weight: 154 lb.

Emmerson blends in by wielding crossbows. Eventually, though, he starts using other weaponry once the group learns more about him.

Although he's seen as a womanizing wildcard, Emmerson is a caring and passionate friend to the group, particularly when it comes to Relia.

Anne

Sex: Female
Age: 28
Height: 5'8"
Weight: 108 lb.

Anne is a realist and is the ego to Emmerson's id, constantly keeping him in check.

While she earned much of her martial arts prowess from military training, Anne attributes most of her brawling skills to her grandmother. Her résumé doesn't end with her fighting skills, either. She graduated top of her class, making her a fierce combination of brains and brawn.

Relia

Sex: Female
Age: 12
Height: 4'1"
Weight: 55 lb.

Relia is a young girl dropped into Fidel and Miki's care after a mysterious incident in the Dakaav Footpath. It becomes evident that Relia is an amnesiac with no recollection of her origins, so the group sets out to uncover the mysteries surrounding her dormant powers.

Relia is a timid little girl, but she eventually opens up to the rest of the group. As a hobby, she likes to humorously imitate her friends' mannerisms.

Welch Vineyard

Sex: Female
Age: 18
Height: 5'2"
Weight: 105 lb.

This eccentric inventor has all of the passion of inventing with none of the work ethic. She often bursts out into self-praising soliloquys that may or may not be delusions of grandeur. Regardless, she's a valuable resource for the crew.

Gunter

Sex: Male
Age: 26
Height: 5'7"
Weight: 172 lb.

Gunter is the muscle of the King's Chosen and is considered "Victor's little brother" among the other soldiers. Unlike Victor, Gunter prefers to fight with his fists, out-muscling the opposition. Although he may seem like a meathead, he's an extremely calculating operative. He's part of the King's Chosen for a reason, after all.

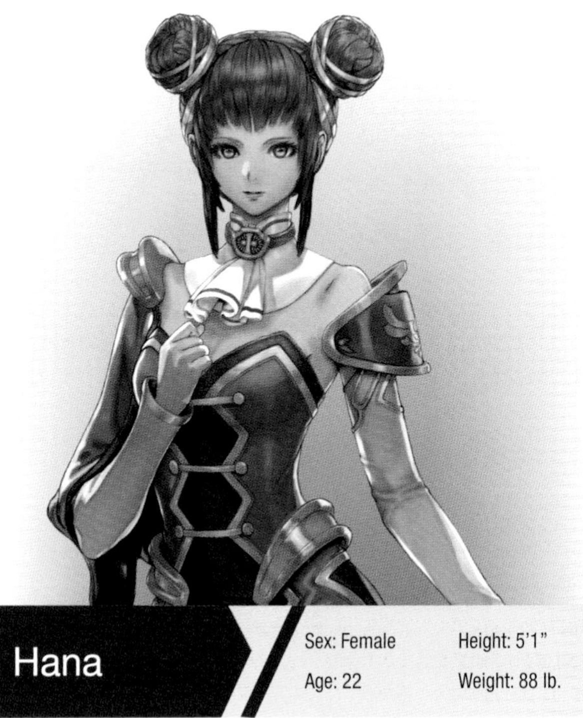

Hana

Sex: Female
Age: 22
Height: 5'1"
Weight: 88 lb.

As a former employee of the Royal Institute of Signetary Studies, Hana is an adept signeturge and an acquaintance of Fiore Brunelli. She's currently the supporting signeturge of the King's Chosen, led by Victor Oakville. Though she was born with a silver spoon in her mouth, she's grown into a down-to-earth soldier.

Daks

Sex: Male
Age: 40
Height: 5'11"
Weight: 143 lb.

Daks is an older member of the King's Chosen, being almost 10 years Victor's senior. He's the group's spymaster, and his work revolves around espionage and intelligence. Not only does he provide invaluable reconnaissance data, but he also provides supporting cover fire with his skills in the crossbow.

Difficulty Levels

Difficulty levels affect basic attributes for all the game's enemies, as well as a few system trophies.

Difficulty Level Multipliers

DIFFICULTY	HP	MP	ATK	INT
Earth	x0.8	x1	x0.8	x0.8
Galaxy	x1	x1	x1	x1
Universe	x1.5	x1.2	x1.2	x1.2
Chaos	x2	x1.5	x1.5	x1.5

At **Earth** difficulty, everything is slightly gentler than normal, with mildly reduced max health and offensive power. The game can be very challenging even on "normal" Galaxy difficulty, so this setting is encouraged for players who want to experience the sweeping story and charming characters with minimal frustration along the way. It isn't vastly easier, but a little bit of the edge is taken off the enemy blade.

Galaxy is the standard *Star Ocean V: Integrity and Faithlessness* experience—adversaries have the parameters listed throughout this guide. Aside from trophies acquired through repeat playthroughs or higher difficulties, most console system trophies are available on Galaxy difficulty, along with all of the in-game battle trophies, which are user-wide unlockables. (Acquired battle trophies are shared between all characters and save files for a given PlayStation user account.)

Universe, unlocked after an initial successful playthrough, is about as much a step up from Galaxy difficulty as the Earth setting is a step down. Foes have 150% their normal listed HP, while dealing out 20% extra damage to Fidel and friends. A system trophy unlocks for game completion on Universe. For completionists and passionate *Star Ocean* fans, this is also a good set of training wheels before taking on Chaos mode.

The **Chaos** setting is the game at its most brutal. Attackers deal 150% their normal output, while having twice as much HP as usual. Success in Universe and Chaos difficulties requires game familiarity, mastery of combat pace and positioning, and thoughtful assignment of battle roles. A system trophy unlocks for game completion on Chaos.

Battles

Of course, as an action-RPG, much of *Star Ocean V: Integrity and Faithlessness* takes place locked in combat against lots of aggressive, vile creatures. In the spirit of previous tri-Ace/Square-Enix spiritual antecedents *Infinite Undiscovery* and previous *Star Ocean* adventures, the action is grounded in RPG stat-driven mechanics, but with combat that is a mix of turn-based and real time. Characters (besides Relia) can each be controlled individually and made to act with action-oriented commands (dodge, weak/strong attack, guard, counterattack, etc.). However, you can also pause the action, and more calculated, turn-based actions can be queued up (using items or signeturgy to restore allies, using offensive signeturgy against monster groups, targeting a particular character's battle skill against a particular enemy, and so on).

Tapping attack buttons during combat initiates normal attacks, whether weak or strong; holding the attack buttons initiates battle skills or signeturgy, as assigned in each character's skill menus off the Main Menu. You learn new battle skills and signeturgy spells by finding new spell books. These abilities expend MP for powerful attacks that add up lots of hits and often inflict negative effects on foes, launch them into the air, or knock them down. Normal attacks and guarding work with a rock-paper-scissors-like system, with weak attacks interrupting strong attacks, strong attacks breaking guard, and guard defending against weak attacks. Successfully playing with this system, guarding against weak attacks (enabling potent counterattack moves), strong attacking through the enemy's shields, and jabbing them out of slow attack windup with weak strikes, builds up Reserve Gauge, which allows access to Reserve Rushes, each character's ultimate attack.

Often, in combat afield, the preferred character can be controlled and battle treated as an action-adventure game, with allies being taken over by AI. From the same temporary battle pause screen where you can queue up actions, you can also toggle the AI on or off so that characters won't act on their own if total micromanagement is preferred. This is great (or even necessary) on nasty bosses that have expansive, lethal area attacks that AI-controlled party members won't necessarily be wise about dodging. The harder the battle, the more micromanagement is usually required. Don't be afraid to pause and think things through.

Character AI is determined mostly by battle roles, equippable combat assignments. At first, only a few battle roles are accessible, but through story progress and optional content completion, many more battle roles are eventually unlocked, over 100 in all. You can assign up to four battle roles on each character. These determine whether computer-controlled allies will be aggressive or reserved; whether they'll go after beefy, full-health enemies or attempt to pick off low-HP, weak ones; whether they'll cut loose with MP consumption or be parsimonious with resources; and on and on. The combination of assigning skills and signeturgy along with battle roles and accessories lends a huge amount of flexibility to party purpose in fights. There's no restriction on what you try to do; just because Fidel, Victor, and Anne are the competent melee fighters, nothing's stopping you from attempting to make Fiore and Miki charge in close. (It just might not work out as planned!)

This chapter contains a full list of each character's battle skills, as well as each signeturgical spell available for Miki and Fiore, the signet-imbued among the party. Initially, each skill caps out at a skill level of 5, once the skill has been used enough in battle (and/or enough spell books applicable to that skill have been expended on it, which greatly speeds up the skill mastery process). With the ultimate specialty skill, though, this limit can be transcended and skills leveled all the way up to 9, unlocking vastly stronger power levels and sometimes new skill effects.

Specialty skills are like skills for the party at large. They involve things like more ways to gather resources in the field, new features for the minimap, the ability to increase resell prices to merchants, and so on.

Battle skills and specialties must be unlocked first (the discovery method differs for each skill), but then also purchased with skill points, or SP, from the Skills portion of the Main Menu. Only then will the skill become usable. A complete list of specialty skills accompanies the battle skill and battle role lists in this chapter.

Attributes

Attributes determine the combat prowess of a given character or enemy.

Lv.	An overall gauge of a character's power level.
HP	The amount of health points a character has. If this is depleted, they're incapacitated (or, for enemies, defeated). Signeturgy like Healing restores health, but other items and skills do, too.
MP	Mana points, which determines how many battle skills and signeturgical abilities a character can use. When MP is low, use of skills is limited. Make use of items or abilities to replenish MP.
ATK	Attack power, strength with martial arts and other physical abilities. This checks against the target's DEF. Some attacks will deal the brunt of their damage through ATK power, but with a supplemental magical INT kicker.
INT	Signeturgical/magical power. Strength with spiritual arts. Although only signet-bearers can use fully fledged, INT-driven signeturgy, each character has skills that deal at least some of their damage in elemental INT form.
DEF	Physical defense. Sturdiness against ATK-driven strikes and skills.
MEN	Mental defense. Resistance against INT-driven spiritual attacks and signeturgy.

Elements

Among magic attacks and signeturgy, there are three pairs of opposed elements that power the spiritual forces in the land. These are fire, ice, earth, wind, light, and darkness. Each pair represents opposing poles of that force. Each enemy has different resistance levels to each element. This guide's bestiary contains these ratings to help optimize party makeup for challenging fights. Positive values for elemental resistance mean that that a target will take reduced damage from that elemental damage source. Negative values for elemental resistance mean you should fire away. That monster won't be able to withstand that element for long and will take extra damage.

Remember that it's not just signeturgical skills that bear elements. Many martial arts have an elemental portion to their damage, as do some weapons.

Status Ailments

Some attacks have certain noxious or debilitating properties aside from elemental damage. Victims may be inflicted with certain debuffing effects that range from annoying to crippling until they're removed via certain curative items or the Cure Condition signeturgy. Temporary percentage-based reductions to base attributes are possible; some allied battle skills also have a chance to inflict attribute-reducing effects to enemies (for example, ATK or DEF -10% for 30 seconds). Beyond momentary alterations to base stats, more specific enfeebles are also possible:

Poison	HP damage is taken at intervals. Poison eventually dissipates after a while if it isn't cured beforehand. Poison's base duration is 50 seconds.
Freeze	Characters move very slowly and are quite brittle, taking extra damage. Being frozen wears off after battle if it isn't removed earlier. Freeze's duration is five seconds.
Paralysis	All actions are restricted by paralysis. Have another character assist in removing paralysis, or it will also expire at a battle's conclusion. Paralysis lasts 50 seconds.

Silence	MP cannot be used, which means battle skills and signeturgy are off-limits. The character can still use normal attacks or items until silence is removed. Silence lasts 50 seconds.
Curse	Like poison for MP, periodically reducing mana points. Like poison, curse eventually wears off on its own, though it can be addressed sooner. Curse lasts 50 seconds.
Fog	Clouded vision prevents target selection from long range, or attacks from far away. Fog lasts 50 seconds.
Stun	A temporary groggy period caused by certain pulverizing attacks. Victim is dizzied and cannot act for three seconds.

CHARACTER SKILLS — FIDEL

Fidel's Attributes

Fidel's Attribute Ranks

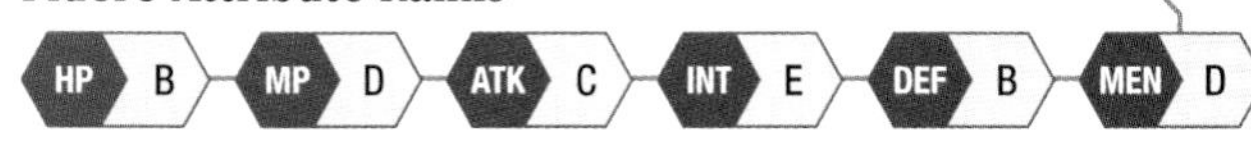

Fidel's Attribute Scaling

LV.	HP	MP	ATK	INT	DEF	MEN
1	234	89	17	8	11	10
25	3674	555	88	47	80	57
50	12240	1416	203	110	190	133
75	21998	2753	364	198	345	240
99	28437	4024	550	300	523	364
125	35652	5739	753	410	717	498
150	40692	7203	914	498	872	605
175	44498	8667	1029	561	982	681
200	53797	10488	1103	601	1053	730
225	63718	12021	1146	625	1094	758
255	74209	13840	1174	640	1121	777

FIDEL'S ATTACKS

Fidel's Normal Attacks

NORMAL ATTACKS	POWER—WEAK ATTACK	HITS—WEAK ATTACK	POWER—STRONG ATTACK	HITS—STRONG ATTACK
Short Range	ATK 100	2	ATK 120	2
Long Range	ATK 100	2	ATK 120	1

Fidel's Counterattack

COUNTERATTACK POWER	COUNTERATTACK HITS
ATK 216	3

Fidel's Reserve Rush

LV.	ATTACK POWER	HITS
1	1800	15
2	3780	15
3	5760	15
4	7740	15
5	9720	15

FIDEL'S SKILLS

Mirror Blade

DESCRIPTION	SKILL BOOK	ELEMENT	ATTRIBUTE
Slice and dice an enemy with five instantaneous strikes, the final one of which may knock the foe into the air.	Swordsman's Manual III	Non-elemental	ATK

LV.	POWER—WEAK SKILL	POWER—STRONG SKILL	HITS	MP COST—WEAK SKILL	MP COST—STRONG SKILL	NOTES
1	290	348	5	18	22	—
2	305	366	5	20	24	—
3	320	384	5	22	26	—
4	335	402	5	24	29	—
5	350	420	5	26	31	—
6	365	438	5	28	34	—
7	380	456	5	30	36	—
8	395	474	5	32	38	—
9	410	492	5	34	41	—

Air Slash

DESCRIPTION	SKILL BOOK	ELEMENT	ATTRIBUTE
Unleash a shock wave that barrels straight toward the enemy.	Swordsman's Manual I	Non-elemental	ATK primary, INT secondary

LV.	POWER—WEAK SKILL	POWER—STRONG SKILL	HITS	MP COST—WEAK SKILL	MP COST—STRONG SKILL	NOTES
1	73	87	1	6	7	INT damage 7%/8% (weak/strong)
2	82	98	1	8	10	INT damage 8%/10% (weak/strong)
3	91	109	1	10	12	INT damage 9%/11% (weak/strong)
4	100	120	1	12	14	INT damage 10%/12% (weak/strong)
5	109	130	1	14	17	INT damage 11%/13% (weak/strong)
6	118	141	1	16	19	INT damage 12%/14% (weak/strong)
7	127	152	1	18	22	INT damage 13%/16% (weak/strong)
8	136	163	1	20	24	INT damage 14%/17% (weak/strong)
9	145	174	1	22	26	INT damage 15%/18% (weak/strong)

Double Slash

DESCRIPTION	SKILL BOOK	ELEMENT	ATTRIBUTE
Perform a two-stage attack by slashing up and then down, the second slash of which slams the opponent into the ground.	Swordsman's Manual II	Non-elemental	ATK

LV.	POWER—WEAK SKILL	POWER—STRONG SKILL	HITS	MP COST—WEAK SKILL	MP COST—STRONG SKILL	NOTES
1	240	288	2	4	5	—
2	250	300	2	7	8	—
3	260	312	2	10	12	—
4	270	324	2	13	16	—
5	280	336	2	16	19	—
6	290	348	2	19	23	—
7	300	360	2	22	26	—
8	310	372	2	25	30	—
9	320	384	2	28	34	—

Shotgun Blast

DESCRIPTION	SKILL BOOK	ELEMENT	ATTRIBUTE
Unleash a lightning strike that explosively shoots forward. Enemies hit may have their vision clouded.	Swordsman's Manual IV	Light	ATK primary, INT secondary

LV.	POWER—WEAK SKILL	POWER—STRONG SKILL	HITS	MP COST—WEAK SKILL	MP COST—STRONG SKILL	NOTES
1	225	270	3	15	18	INT damage 25%/30% (weak/strong)
2	225	270	3	17	20	INT damage 28%/34% (weak/strong)
3	245	294	4	19	23	INT damage 35%/42% (weak/strong)
4	245	294	4	21	25	INT damage 38%/46% (weak/strong)
5	265	318	5	23	28	INT damage 46%/55% (weak/strong)
6	265	318	5	25	30	INT damage 49%/59% (weak/strong)
7	285	342	6	27	32	INT damage 56%/67% (weak/strong)
8	285	342	6	29	35	INT damage 59%/71% (weak/strong)
9	305	366	7	31	37	INT damage 65%/78% (weak/strong)

Death Palm

DESCRIPTION	SKILL BOOK	ELEMENT	ATTRIBUTE
Unleash the power of channeled energy from the palm of Fidel's hand. The blast continues in a straight line after piercing enemies.	Swordsman's Manual V	Non-elemental	ATK primary, INT secondary

LV.	POWER—WEAK SKILL	POWER—STRONG SKILL	HITS	MP COST—WEAK SKILL	MP COST—STRONG SKILL	NOTES
1	180	216	3	10	12	INT damage 20%/24% (weak/strong)
2	180	216	3	12	14	INT damage 23%/28% (weak/strong)
3	190	228	4	14	17	INT damage 30%/36% (weak/strong)
4	190	228	4	16	19	INT damage 33%/40% (weak/strong)
5	200	240	5	18	22	INT damage 40%/48% (weak/strong)
6	200	240	5	20	24	INT damage 43%/52% (weak/strong)
7	210	252	6	22	26	INT damage 50%/60% (weak/strong)
8	210	252	6	24	29	INT damage 53%/64% (weak/strong)
9	220	264	7	26	31	INT damage 60%/72% (weak/strong)

Cyclone Blade

DESCRIPTION	SKILL BOOK	ELEMENT	ATTRIBUTE
Spring into the air while spinning to cut down surrounding enemies. Those caught in the attack will be launched helplessly into the air.	Swordsman's Manual VII	Non-elemental	ATK

LV.	POWER—WEAK SKILL	POWER—STRONG SKILL	HITS	MP COST—WEAK SKILL	MP COST—STRONG SKILL	NOTES
1	340	408	5	28	34	—
2	360	432	5	30	36	—
3	380	456	5	32	38	—
4	400	480	5	34	41	—
5	420	504	5	36	43	—
6	440	528	5	38	46	—
7	460	552	5	40	48	—
8	480	576	5	42	50	—
9	500	600	5	44	53	—

Abyssal Gate

DESCRIPTION	SKILL BOOK	ELEMENT	ATTRIBUTE
Gather energy, then charge toward an enemy and deliver a merciless blow. The aura enveloping Fidel's body may damage the foe, as well.	Swordsman's Manual VI	Non-elemental	ATK primary, INT secondary

LV.	POWER—WEAK SKILL	POWER—STRONG SKILL	HITS	MP COST—WEAK SKILL	MP COST—STRONG SKILL	NOTES
1	205	246	6	22	26	INT damage 75%/90% (weak/strong)
2	220	264	6	24	29	INT damage 75%/90% (weak/strong)
3	235	282	6	26	31	INT damage 75%/90% (weak/strong)
4	250	300	6	28	34	INT damage 75%/90% (weak/strong)
5	265	318	6	30	36	INT damage 75%/90% (weak/strong)
6	280	336	6	32	38	INT damage 75%/90% (weak/strong)
7	295	354	6	34	41	INT damage 75%/90% (weak/strong)
8	310	372	6	36	43	INT damage 75%/90% (weak/strong)
9	325	390	6	38	46	INT damage 75%/90% (weak/strong)

Air Raid

DESCRIPTION	SKILL BOOK	ELEMENT	ATTRIBUTE
Raise an enemy into the air, and then let loose a wave of energy that both slams him to the ground and blasts nearby foes.	Swordsman's Manual VIII	Non-elemental	ATK primary, INT secondary

LV.	POWER—WEAK SKILL	POWER—STRONG SKILL	HITS	MP COST—WEAK SKILL	MP COST—STRONG SKILL	NOTES
1	270	324	8	34	41	INT damage 80%/96% (weak/strong)
2	295	354	8	36	43	INT damage 80%/96% (weak/strong)
3	320	384	8	38	46	INT damage 80%/96% (weak/strong)
4	345	414	8	40	48	INT damage 80%/96% (weak/strong)
5	370	444	8	42	50	INT damage 80%/96% (weak/strong)
6	395	474	8	44	53	INT damage 80%/96% (weak/strong)
7	420	504	8	46	55	INT damage 80%/96% (weak/strong)
8	445	534	8	48	58	INT damage 80%/96% (weak/strong)
9	470	564	8	50	60	INT damage 80%/96% (weak/strong)

Miki's Attributes

Miki's Attribute Ranks

HP E · MP B · ATK E · INT C · DEF F · MEN A

Miki's Attribute Scaling

LV.	HP	MP	ATK	INT	DEF	MEN
1	192	131	12	15	9	17
25	3012	821	66	86	61	98
50	10036	2096	152	200	146	229
75	18038	4075	273	360	266	413
99	23318	5955	413	545	403	626
125	29235	8493	565	746	552	856
150	33368	10660	686	907	672	1040
175	36488	12827	772	1021	756	1171
200	44113	15522	827	1094	811	1255
225	52249	17791	860	1137	843	1304
255	60851	20483	880	1164	863	1336

MIKI'S ATTACKS

Miki's Normal Attacks

NORMAL ATTACKS	POWER— WEAK ATTACK	HITS— WEAK ATTACK	POWER— STRONG ATTACK	HITS— STRONG ATTACK
Short Range	ATK 90, INT 10	1	ATK 108, INT 12	1
Long Range	INT 100	1	INT 120	1

Miki's Counterattack

COUNTERATTACK POWER	COUNTERATTACK HITS
INT 216	1

Miki's Reserve Rush

LV.	NOTES
1	Heals 20% of party HP
2	Heals 40% of party HP
3	Heals 60% of party HP
4	Heals 80% of party HP
5	Fully heals party HP

MIKI'S SKILLS

Earth Glaive

DESCRIPTION	SKILL BOOK	ELEMENT	ATTRIBUTE
Cause earthen spears to burst forth from under the enemy's feet. All enemies hit are launched into the air.	Cerulean Orb Signets, Vol. 1	Earth	INT

LV.	POWER— WEAK SKILL	POWER— STRONG SKILL	HITS	MP COST— WEAK SKILL	MP COST— STRONG SKILL	NOTES
1	260	312	1	10	12	—
2	275	330	1	13	16	—
3	290	348	1	16	19	—
4	305	366	1	19	23	—
5	320	384	1	22	26	—
6	335	402	1	25	30	—
7	350	420	1	28	34	—
8	365	438	1	31	37	—
9	380	456	1	34	41	—

Stone Rain

DESCRIPTION	SKILL BOOK	ELEMENT	ATTRIBUTE
Cause massive boulders to descend from the sky that may temporarily stun the adversaries they strike.	Cerulean Orb Signets, Vol. 2	Earth	INT

LV.	POWER— WEAK SKILL	POWER— STRONG SKILL	HITS	MP COST— WEAK SKILL	MP COST— STRONG SKILL	NOTES
1	320	384	4	20	24	5% stun chance
2	340	408	4	23	28	5% stun chance
3	360	432	4	26	31	6% stun chance
4	380	456	4	29	35	6% stun chance
5	400	480	4	32	38	7% stun chance
6	420	504	4	35	42	7% stun chance
7	440	528	4	38	46	8% stun chance
8	460	552	4	41	49	8% stun chance
9	480	576	4	44	53	10% stun chance

Terra Hammer

DESCRIPTION	SKILL BOOK	ELEMENT	ATTRIBUTE
Drop gigantic jagged boulders onto and around the target. All enemies hit will have their DEF temporarily lowered.	Cerulean Orb Signets, Vol. 3	Earth	INT

LV.	POWER—WEAK SKILL	POWER—STRONG SKILL	HITS	MP COST—WEAK SKILL	MP COST—STRONG SKILL	NOTES
1	350	420	15	30	36	2% chance for 30 seconds of DEF -10%
2	354	424	15	33	40	3% chance for 30 seconds of DEF -10%
3	414	496	20	36	43	4% chance for 30 seconds of DEF -10%
4	418	501	20	39	47	5% chance for 30 seconds of DEF -10%
5	423	507	20	42	50	6% chance for 30 seconds of DEF -10%
6	482	578	25	45	54	7% chance for 30 seconds of DEF -10%
7	486	583	25	48	58	8% chance for 30 seconds of DEF -10%
8	491	589	25	51	61	9% chance for 30 seconds of DEF -10%
9	550	660	30	54	65	10% chance for 30 seconds of DEF -10%

Fire Bolt

DESCRIPTION	SKILL BOOK	ELEMENT	ATTRIBUTE
Unleash scorching balls of flame that tenaciously follow their target.	Solar Signets, Vol. 1	Fire	INT

LV.	POWER—WEAK SKILL	POWER—STRONG SKILL	HITS	MP COST—WEAK SKILL	MP COST—STRONG SKILL	NOTES
1	240	288	3	7	8	—
2	242	290	3	10	12	—
3	279	334	4	13	16	—
4	281	337	4	16	19	—
5	283	339	4	19	23	—
6	319	382	5	22	26	—
7	321	385	5	25	30	—
8	323	387	5	28	34	—
9	360	432	6	31	37	—

Explosion

DESCRIPTION	SKILL BOOK	ELEMENT	ATTRIBUTE
Drop a seething, blazing rondure down onto the target and have it violently detonate, incinerating enemies over a wide swath.	Solar Signets, Vol. 4	Fire	INT

LV.	POWER—WEAK SKILL	POWER—STRONG SKILL	HITS	MP COST—WEAK SKILL	MP COST—STRONG SKILL	NOTES
1	400	480	9	42	50	—
2	425	510	9	45	54	—
3	450	540	9	48	58	—
4	475	570	9	51	61	—
5	500	600	9	54	65	—
6	525	630	9	57	68	—
7	550	660	9	60	72	—
8	575	690	9	63	76	—
9	600	720	9	66	79	—

Volcanic Burst

DESCRIPTION	SKILL BOOK	ELEMENT	ATTRIBUTE
Generate a flaming vortex that emerges under the target, launching all enemies within it into the air.	Solar Signets, Vol. 2	Fire	INT

LV.	POWER—WEAK SKILL	POWER—STRONG SKILL	HITS	MP COST—WEAK SKILL	MP COST—STRONG SKILL	NOTES
1	300	360	7	16	19	—
2	313	375	7	19	23	—
3	345	414	8	22	26	—
4	370	444	8	25	30	—
5	378	453	8	28	34	—
6	403	483	9	31	37	—
7	415	498	9	34	41	—
8	428	513	9	37	44	—
9	460	552	10	40	48	—

Radiant Lancer

DESCRIPTION	SKILL BOOK	ELEMENT	ATTRIBUTE
Rain down manifold spears of light that always pierce their target.	Moonlight Signets, Vol. 1	Light	INT

LV.	POWER—WEAK SKILL	POWER—STRONG SKILL	HITS	MP COST—WEAK SKILL	MP COST—STRONG SKILL	NOTES
1	310	372	5	23	28	—
2	313	375	5	26	31	—
3	340	408	6	29	35	—
4	343	411	6	32	38	—
5	370	444	7	35	42	—
6	373	447	7	38	46	—
7	400	480	8	41	49	—
8	403	483	8	44	53	—
9	430	516	9	47	56	—

Aurora Rings

DESCRIPTION	SKILL BOOK	ELEMENT	ATTRIBUTE
Cause multiple columns of light to rise around the target and perhaps temporarily cloud the vision of enemies encased within them.	The Founder's Signets, Vol. 1	Light	INT

LV.	POWER—WEAK SKILL	POWER—STRONG SKILL	HITS	MP COST—WEAK SKILL	MP COST—STRONG SKILL	NOTES
1	270	324	3	11	13	—
2	272	326	3	14	17	—
3	309	370	4	17	20	—
4	311	373	4	20	24	—
5	313	375	4	23	28	—
6	349	418	5	26	31	—
7	351	421	5	29	35	—
8	353	423	5	32	38	—
9	390	468	6	35	42	—

Sunflare

DESCRIPTION	SKILL BOOK	ELEMENT	ATTRIBUTE
Radiate focused beams of sunlight down from the sky that temporarily lower the INT for all enemies they strike.	Solar Signets, Vol. 2	Light	INT

LV.	POWER—WEAK SKILL	POWER—STRONG SKILL	HITS	MP COST—WEAK SKILL	MP COST—STRONG SKILL	NOTES
1	360	432	6	32	38	1% chance for 30 seconds of INT -5%
2	363	435	6	35	42	2% chance for 30 seconds of INT -5%
3	425	510	8	38	46	2% chance for 30 seconds of INT -5%
4	426	511	8	41	49	3% chance for 30 seconds of INT -5%
5	430	516	8	44	53	4% chance for 30 seconds of INT -5%
6	493	591	10	47	56	4% chance for 30 seconds of INT -5%
7	495	594	10	50	60	5% chance for 30 seconds of INT -5%
8	498	597	10	53	64	6% chance for 30 seconds of INT -5%
9	560	672	12	56	67	7% chance for 30 seconds of INT -5%

Divine Wave

DESCRIPTION	SKILL BOOK	ELEMENT	ATTRIBUTE
Erect a wall of light around Miki that emanates outward and knocks back any enemies in its path.	Moonlight Signets, Vol. 3	Non-elemental	INT

LV.	POWER—WEAK SKILL	POWER—STRONG SKILL	HITS	MP COST—WEAK SKILL	MP COST—STRONG SKILL	NOTES
1	380	456	12	45	54	—
2	405	486	12	48	58	—
3	430	516	12	51	61	—
4	455	546	12	54	65	—
5	480	576	12	57	68	—
6	505	606	12	60	72	—
7	530	636	12	63	76	—
8	555	666	12	66	79	—
9	580	696	12	69	83	—

Silence

DESCRIPTION	SKILL BOOK	ELEMENT	ATTRIBUTE
Silence a target enemy and nearby foes.	Signeturgical Book of Quietude	Non-Elemental	INT

LV.	POWER—WEAK SKILL	POWER—STRONG SKILL	HITS	MP COST—WEAK SKILL	MP COST—STRONG SKILL	NOTES
1	—	—	—	22	26	10% silence chance
2	—	—	—	23	28	11% silence chance
3	—	—	—	24	29	12% silence chance
4	—	—	—	25	30	13% silence chance
5	—	—	—	26	31	14% silence chance
6	—	—	—	27	32	15% silence chance
7	—	—	—	28	34	16% silence chance
8	—	—	—	29	35	18& silence chance
9	—	—	—	30	36	20% silence chance

MIKI'S SIGNETURGY

Healing

DESCRIPTION	SKILL BOOK	ELEMENT	ATTRIBUTE
Restore the HP of one party member.	Restorative Signets, Vol. 1	Non-elemental	—

LV.	MP COST	NOTES
1	6	HP +30%
2	7	HP +32%
3	8	HP +34%
4	9	HP +35%
5	10	HP +36%
6	11	HP +37%
7	12	HP +38%
8	13	HP +39%
9	14	HP +40%

Ex Healing

DESCRIPTION	SKILL BOOK	ELEMENT	ATTRIBUTE
Drastically restore the HP of one party member.	Restorative Signets, Vol. 2	Non-elemental	—

LV.	MP COST	NOTES
1	13	HP +70%
2	15	HP +72%
3	17	HP +74%
4	19	HP +75%
5	21	HP +76%
6	23	HP +77%
7	25	HP +78%
8	27	HP +79%
9	29	HP +80%

Faerie Healing

DESCRIPTION	SKILL BOOK	ELEMENT	ATTRIBUTE
Slightly restore the HP of all party members.	Fae Signets, Vol. 1	Non-elemental	—

LV.	MP COST	NOTES
1	18	HP +25%
2	20	HP +27%
3	22	HP +29%
4	24	HP +30%
5	26	HP +31%
6	28	HP +32%
7	30	HP +33%
8	32	HP +34%
9	34	HP +35%

Faerie Light

DESCRIPTION	SKILL BOOK	ELEMENT	ATTRIBUTE
Restore the HP of all party members.	Fae Signets, Vol. 2	Non-elemental	—

LV.	MP COST	NOTES
1	30	HP +50%
2	32	HP +52%
3	34	HP +54%
4	36	HP +55%
5	38	HP +56%
6	40	HP +57%
7	42	HP +58%
8	44	HP +59%
9	46	HP +60%

Faerie Star

DESCRIPTION	SKILL BOOK	ELEMENT	ATTRIBUTE
Drastically restore the HP of all party members.	Fae Signets, Vol. 3	Non-elemental	—

LV.	MP COST	NOTES
1	52	HP +71%
2	54	HP +72%
3	56	HP +73%
4	58	HP +75%
5	60	HP +77%
6	62	HP +79%
7	64	HP +81%
8	66	HP +83%
9	68	HP +85%

Antidote

DESCRIPTION	SKILL BOOK	ELEMENT	ATTRIBUTE
Cure all party members of poison.	Purification Signets, Vol. 1	Non-elemental	—

LV.	MP COST	NOTES
1-9	8	—

Cure Condition

DESCRIPTION	SKILL BOOK	ELEMENT	ATTRIBUTE
Cure all of the following status ailments afflicting all party members: poison, paralysis, freeze, curse, silence, fog, and stun.	Purification Signets, Vol. 2	Non-elemental	—

LV.	MP COST	NOTES
1-9	18	—

Raise Dead

DESCRIPTION	SKILL BOOK	ELEMENT	ATTRIBUTE
Revive an incapacitated party member.	Pneuma Signets, Vol. 1	Non-elemental	—

LV.	MP COST	NOTES
1	24	HP +30%
2	26	HP +32%
3	28	HP +34%
4	30	HP +35%
5	32	HP +36%
6	34	HP +37%
7	36	HP +38%
8	38	HP +39%
9	40	HP +40%

Resurrection

DESCRIPTION	SKILL BOOK	ELEMENT	ATTRIBUTE
Revive and fully heal an incapacitated party member.	Pneuma Signets, Vol. 2	Non-elemental	—

LV.	MP COST—STRONG SKILL	NOTES
1	56	HP +100%
2	55	HP +100%
3	54	HP +100%
4	53	HP +100%
5	52	HP +100%
6	51	HP +100%
7	50	HP +100%
8	49	HP +100%
9	48	HP +100%

Arcane Weapon

DESCRIPTION	SKILL BOOK	ELEMENT	ATTRIBUTE
Allow one party member to absorb enemy MP through normal attacks.	Moonlight Signets, Vol. 2	Non-elemental	—

LV.	MP COST	NOTES
1	25	1% normal attack damage converted to MP for 35 seconds
2	26	1.1% normal attack damage converted to MP for 38 seconds
3	27	1.2% normal attack damage converted to MP for 41 seconds
4	28	1.3% normal attack damage converted to MP for 44 seconds
5	29	1.4% normal attack damage converted to MP for 47 seconds
6	30	1.5% normal attack damage converted to MP for 50 seconds
7	31	1.6% normal attack damage converted to MP for 53 seconds
8	32	1.8% normal attack damage converted to MP for 56 seconds
9	33	2% normal attack damage converted to MP for 60 seconds

CHARACTER SKILLS — VICTOR

Victor's Attributes

Victor's Attribute Ranks

HP	MP	ATK	INT	DEF	MEN
A	G	B	F	A	G

Victor's Attribute Scaling

LV.	HP	MP	ATK	INT	DEF	MEN
1	550	128	28	7	22	9
25	4114	438	95	39	86	44
50	13708	1119	219	90	205	103
75	24638	2175	393	162	372	185
99	31849	3179	595	246	565	280
125	39931	4534	813	336	775	383
150	45575	5690	987	408	942	466
175	49838	6847	1112	460	1061	524
200	60252	8285	1191	493	1137	562
225	71364	9496	1238	512	1182	584
255	83114	10934	1268	525	1211	598

VICTOR'S ATTACKS

Victor's Normal Attacks

NORMAL ATTACKS	POWER—WEAK ATTACK	HITS—WEAK ATTACK	POWER—STRONG ATTACK	HITS—STRONG ATTACK
Short Range	ATK 100	2	ATK 120	1
Long Range	ATK 100	1	ATK 180	3

Victor's Counterattack

COUNTERATTACK POWER	COUNTERATTACK HITS
ATK 216	1

Victor's Reserve Rush

LV.	ATTACK POWER	HITS
1	1800	10
2	3780	10
3	5760	10
4	7740	10
5	9720	10

Air Slash

DESCRIPTION	SKILL BOOK	ELEMENT	ATTRIBUTE
Unleash a shock wave that barrels straight toward the enemy.	Swordsman's Manual I	Non-elemental	ATK primary, INT secondary

LV.	POWER—WEAK SKILL	POWER—STRONG SKILL	HITS	MP COST—WEAK SKILL	MP COST—STRONG SKILL	NOTES
1	73	87	1	6	7	INT damage 7%/8% (weak/strong)
2	87	98	1	9	11	INT damage 8%/10% (weak/strong)
3	91	109	1	12	14	INT damage 9%/11% (weak/strong)
4	100	120	1	15	18	INT damage 10%/12% (weak/strong)
5	109	130	1	18	22	INT damage 11%/13% (weak/strong)
6	118	141	1	21	25	INT damage 12%/14% (weak/strong)
7	127	152	1	24	29	INT damage 13%/16% (weak/strong)
8	136	163	1	27	32	INT damage 14%/17% (weak/strong)
9	145	174	1	30	36	INT damage 15%/18% (weak/strong)

Dragon Roar

DESCRIPTION	SKILL BOOK	ELEMENT	ATTRIBUTE
Summon a furious dragon to attack an enemy in front of Victor. The dragon will let out a bloodcurdling roar as it charges forward.	Swordsman's Manual VIII	Non-elemental	ATK primary, INT secondary

LV.	POWER—WEAK SKILL	POWER—STRONG SKILL	HITS	MP COST—WEAK SKILL	MP COST—STRONG SKILL	NOTES
1	315	378	7	29	35	INT damage 35%/42% (weak/strong)
2	328	393	7	31	37	INT damage 42%/50% (weak/strong)
3	341	409	7	33	40	INT damage 49%/59% (weak/strong)
4	354	424	7	35	42	INT damage 56%/67% (weak/strong)
5	367	440	7	37	44	INT damage 63%/76% (weak/strong)
6	380	456	7	39	47	INT damage 70%/84% (weak/strong)
7	393	471	7	41	49	INT damage 77%/92% (weak/strong)
8	406	487	7	43	52	INT damage 84%/101% (weak/strong)
9	419	502	7	45	54	INT damage 91%/109% (weak/strong)

Mirror Blade

DESCRIPTION	SKILL BOOK	ELEMENT	ATTRIBUTE
Slice and dice an enemy with five instantaneous strikes, during the last of which Victor rushes forward to smite his falling foe.	Swordsman's Manual III	Non-elemental	ATK

LV.	POWER—WEAK SKILL	POWER—STRONG SKILL	HITS	MP COST—WEAK SKILL	MP COST—STRONG SKILL	NOTES
1	290	348	5	18	22	—
2	305	366	5	20	24	—
3	320	384	5	22	26	—
4	335	402	5	24	29	—
5	350	420	5	26	31	—
6	365	438	5	28	34	—
7	380	456	5	30	36	—
8	395	474	5	32	38	—
9	410	492	5	34	41	—

Bloodstorm Revolution

DESCRIPTION	SKILL BOOK	ELEMENT	ATTRIBUTE
Swing Victor's weapon around to generate a whirlwind that draws foes toward it and then lacerates them.	Swordsman's Manual VIII	Non-elemental	ATK

LV.	POWER—WEAK SKILL	POWER—STRONG SKILL	HITS	MP COST—WEAK SKILL	MP COST—STRONG SKILL	NOTES
1	340	408	10	25	30	—
2	360	432	10	27	32	—
3	380	456	10	29	35	—
4	400	480	10	31	37	—
5	420	504	10	33	40	—
6	440	528	10	35	42	—
7	460	552	10	37	44	—
8	480	576	10	39	47	—
9	500	600	10	41	49	—

Diabolic Edge

DESCRIPTION	SKILL BOOK	ELEMENT	ATTRIBUTE
Attack in rapid succession while charging forward. You will send enemies flying as Victor continues his charge.	Swordsman's Manual VI	Non-elemental	ATK

LV.	POWER—WEAK SKILL	POWER—STRONG SKILL	HITS	MP COST—WEAK SKILL	MP COST—STRONG SKILL	NOTES
1	330	396	5	23	28	2% chance for 30 seconds of DEF -10%
2	345	414	5	25	30	3% chance for 30 seconds of DEF -10%
3	360	432	5	27	32	4% chance for 30 seconds of DEF -10%
4	375	450	5	29	35	5% chance for 30 seconds of DEF -10%
5	390	468	5	31	37	6% chance for 30 seconds of DEF -10%
6	405	486	5	33	40	7% chance for 30 seconds of DEF -10%
7	420	504	5	35	42	8% chance for 30 seconds of DEF -10%
8	435	522	5	37	44	9% chance for 30 seconds of DEF -10%
9	450	540	5	39	47	10% chance for 30 seconds of DEF -10%

Nether Strike

DESCRIPTION	SKILL BOOK	ELEMENT	ATTRIBUTE
Release a war cry as Victor channels his fighting spirit into his sword, summons the fires of the netherworld, and incinerates the enemy.	Swordsman's Manual IV	Darkness	ATK primary, INT secondary

LV.	POWER—WEAK SKILL	POWER—STRONG SKILL	HITS	MP COST—WEAK SKILL	MP COST—STRONG SKILL	NOTES
1	160	192	1	5	6	INT damage 20%/24% (weak/strong)
2	161	193	1	8	10	INT damage 21%/25% (weak/strong)
3	162	194	1	11	13	INT damage 22%/26% (weak/strong)
4	193	231	2	14	17	INT damage 32%/38% (weak/strong)
5	194	232	2	17	20	INT damage 33%/40% (weak/strong)
6	195	234	2	20	24	INT damage 33%/40% (weak/strong)
7	216	259	3	23	28	INT damage 38%/46% (weak/strong)
8	218	261	3	26	31	INT damage 39%/47% (weak/strong)
9	220	264	3	29	35	INT damage 40%/48% (weak/strong)

Double Slash

DESCRIPTION	SKILL BOOK	ELEMENT	ATTRIBUTE
Perform a two-stage attack by slashing up and then down. The second slash slams the opponent into the ground.	Swordsman's Manual II	Non-elemental	ATK

LV.	POWER—WEAK SKILL	POWER—STRONG SKILL	HITS	MP COST—WEAK SKILL	MP COST—STRONG SKILL	NOTES
1	240	288	2	4	5	—
2	250	300	2	6	7	—
3	260	312	2	8	10	—
4	270	324	2	10	12	—
5	280	336	2	12	14	—
6	290	348	2	14	17	—
7	300	360	2	16	19	—
8	310	372	2	18	22	—
9	320	384	2	20	24	—

Flying Guillotine

DESCRIPTION	SKILL BOOK	ELEMENT	ATTRIBUTE
Hurl a blade encased in a stygian aura at the enemy. The blade will return, as if somehow bound to Victor.	Swordsman's Manual V	Non-elemental	ATK primary, INT secondary

LV.	POWER—WEAK SKILL	POWER—STRONG SKILL	HITS	MP COST—WEAK SKILL	MP COST—STRONG SKILL	NOTES
1	190	228	2+	11	13	INT damage 10%/12% (weak/strong)
2	198	237	2+	13	16	INT damage 12%/14% (weak/strong)
3	206	247	2+	15	18	INT damage 14%/17% (weak/strong)
4	214	256	2+	17	20	INT damage 16%/19% (weak/strong)
5	222	266	2+	19	23	INT damage 18%/22% (weak/strong)
6	230	276	2+	21	25	INT damage 20%/24% (weak/strong)
7	238	285	2+	23	28	INT damage 22%/26% (weak/strong)
8	246	295	2+	25	30	INT damage 24%/29% (weak/strong)
9	254	304	2+	27	32	INT damage 26%/31% (weak/strong)

Fiore's Attribute Ranks

Fiore's Attribute Ranks

Fiore's Attribute Scaling

LV.	HP	MP	ATK	INT	DEF	MEN
1	412	278	16	28	17	27
25	2865	871	60	92	68	90
50	9547	2223	140	214	163	209
75	17158	4322	251	386	297	377
99	22181	6317	380	584	450	571
125	27809	9010	519	799	617	781
150	31740	11308	631	971	750	949
175	34709	13607	710	1094	845	1069
200	41962	16465	761	1172	905	1145
225	49700	18873	791	1218	941	1190
255	57883	21729	810	1248	964	1219

FIORE'S ATTACKS

Fiore's Normal Attacks

NORMAL ATTACKS	POWER—WEAK ATTACK	HITS—WEAK ATTACK	POWER—STRONG ATTACK	HITS—STRONG ATTACK
Short Range	ATK 50, INT 50	1	ATK 60, INT 60	1
Long Range	ATK 50, INT 50	1	ATK 60, ATK 60	1

Fiore's Counterattack

COUNTERATTACK POWER	COUNTERATTACK HITS
ATK 168, INT 24	2

Fiore's Reserve Rush

LV.	ATTACK POWER	HITS	NOTES
1	900	1	—
2	1890	1	15% chance for 30 seconds of ATK/INT -5%
3	2880	1	30% chance for 30 seconds of ATK/INT -5
4	3870	1	50% chance for 30 seconds of ATK/INT/DEF/MEN -5%
5	4860	1	50% chance for 30 seconds of ATK/INT/DEF/MEN -10%

Ice Needles

DESCRIPTION	SKILL BOOK	ELEMENT	ATTRIBUTE
Summon myriad razor-sharp icicles that hurl toward an enemy at breakneck speeds.	Cerulean Orb Signets, Vol. 1	Ice	INT

LV.	POWER—WEAK SKILL	POWER—STRONG SKILL	HITS	MP COST—WEAK SKILL	MP COST—STRONG SKILL	NOTES
1	250	300	3	6	7	—
2	252	302	3	9	11	—
3	289	346	4	12	14	—
4	291	349	4	15	18	—
5	293	351	4	18	22	—
6	329	394	5	21	25	—
7	331	397	5	24	29	—
8	333	399	5	27	32	—
9	370	444	6	30	36	—

Deep Freeze

DESCRIPTION	SKILL BOOK	ELEMENT	ATTRIBUTE
Generate an area of frigid air centered on the target that may also cause all enemies within it to freeze.	Cerulean Orb Signets, Vol. 2	Ice	INT

LV.	POWER—WEAK SKILL	POWER—STRONG SKILL	HITS	MP COST—WEAK SKILL	MP COST—STRONG SKILL	NOTES
1	290	348	7	23	28	2% freeze chance
2	310	372	7	26	31	3% freeze chance
3	330	396	7	29	35	4% freeze chance
4	350	420	7	32	38	5% freeze chance
5	370	444	7	35	42	6% freeze chance
6	390	468	7	38	46	7% freeze chance
7	410	492	7	41	49	8% freeze chance
8	430	516	7	44	53	9% freeze chance
9	450	540	7	47	56	10% freeze chance

FIORE'S SKILLS

Arctic Impact

DESCRIPTION	SKILL BOOK	ELEMENT	ATTRIBUTE
Encase enemies in a giant pillar of ice, which fragments into shards. The extreme cold within it will temporarily lower MEN.	Cerulean Orb Signets, Vol. 3	Ice	INT

LV.	POWER—WEAK SKILL	POWER—STRONG SKILL	HITS	MP COST—WEAK SKILL	MP COST—STRONG SKILL	NOTES
1	330	396	2	32	38	5% chance for 30 seconds of MEN -10%
2	355	426	2	35	42	7% chance for 30 seconds of MEN -10%
3	380	456	2	38	46	10% chance for 30 seconds of MEN -10%
4	405	486	2	41	49	12% chance for 30 seconds of MEN -10%
5	430	516	2	44	53	15% chance for 30 seconds of MEN -10%
6	455	546	2	47	56	17% chance for 30 seconds of MEN -10%
7	480	576	2	50	60	20% chance for 30 seconds of MEN -10%
8	505	606	2	53	64	22% chance for 30 seconds of MEN -10%
9	530	636	2	56	67	25% chance for 30 seconds of MEN -10%

Wind Blade

DESCRIPTION	SKILL BOOK	ELEMENT	ATTRIBUTE
Unleash a gale that swirls so incredibly fast, its currents form blades that slice their target and those in their path to shreds.	Solar Signets, Vol. 1	Wind	INT

LV.	POWER—WEAK SKILL	POWER—STRONG SKILL	HITS	MP COST—WEAK SKILL	MP COST—STRONG SKILL	NOTES
1	230	276	3	8	10	—
2	234	280	3	11	13	—
3	268	321	4	14	17	—
4	271	325	4	17	20	—
5	275	330	4	20	24	—
6	309	370	5	23	28	—
7	313	375	5	26	31	—
8	316	379	5	29	35	—
9	350	420	6	32	38	—

Tornado

DESCRIPTION	SKILL BOOK	ELEMENT	ATTRIBUTE
Form a colossal tornado that torpidly creeps along. All enemies sucked into its funnel will be sent flying.	Solar Signets, Vol. 3	Wind	INT

LV.	POWER—WEAK SKILL	POWER—STRONG SKILL	HITS	MP COST—WEAK SKILL	MP COST—STRONG SKILL	NOTES
1	300	360	10	31	37	—
2	325	390	10	34	41	—
3	350	420	10	37	44	—
4	375	450	10	40	48	—
5	400	480	10	43	52	—
6	425	510	10	46	55	—
7	450	540	10	49	59	—
8	475	570	10	52	62	—
9	500	600	10	55	66	—

Lightning Blast

DESCRIPTION	SKILL BOOK	ELEMENT	ATTRIBUTE
Call forth a burst of lightning that streaks forward and may also temporarily paralyze the enemies it hits.	Solar Signets, Vol. 2	Wind	INT

LV.	POWER—WEAK SKILL	POWER—STRONG SKILL	HITS	MP COST—WEAK SKILL	MP COST—STRONG SKILL	NOTES
1	280	336	5	18	22	1% paralysis chance
2	295	354	5	21	25	1% paralysis chance
3	310	372	5	24	29	2% paralysis chance
4	325	390	5	27	32	2% paralysis chance
5	340	408	5	30	36	3% paralysis chance
6	355	426	5	33	40	3% paralysis chance
7	370	444	5	36	43	4% paralysis chance
8	385	462	5	39	47	4% paralysis chance
9	400	480	5	42	50	5% paralysis chance

Thunder Flare

DESCRIPTION	SKILL BOOK	ELEMENT	ATTRIBUTE
Create a cage of lightning around the target that temporarily lowers the ATK of enemies it surrounds.	Solar Signets, Vol. 4	Wind	INT

LV.	POWER—WEAK SKILL	POWER—STRONG SKILL	HITS	MP COST—WEAK SKILL	MP COST—STRONG SKILL	NOTES
1	400	480	8	43	52	2% chance for 30 seconds of ATK -10%
2	425	510	8	46	55	3% chance for 30 seconds of ATK -10%
3	450	540	8	49	59	4% chance for 30 seconds of ATK -10%
4	475	570	8	52	62	5% chance for 30 seconds of ATK -10%
5	500	600	8	55	66	6% chance for 30 seconds of ATK -10%
6	525	630	8	58	70	7% chance for 30 seconds of ATK -10%
7	550	660	8	61	73	8% chance for 30 seconds of ATK -10%
8	575	690	8	64	77	9% chance for 30 seconds of ATK -10%
9	600	720	8	67	80	10% chance for 30 seconds of ATK -10%

Shadow Needles

DESCRIPTION	SKILL BOOK	ELEMENT	ATTRIBUTE
Send down briery needles of stygian tenebrosity that may also temporarily curse the enemies they strike.	Moonlight Signets, Vol. 1	Darkness	INT

LV.	POWER—WEAK SKILL	POWER—STRONG SKILL	HITS	MP COST—WEAK SKILL	MP COST—STRONG SKILL	NOTES
1	270	324	3	16	19	3% curse chance
2	272	326	3	19	23	4% curse chance
3	309	370	4	22	26	4% curse chance
4	311	373	4	25	30	5% curse chance
5	313	375	4	28	34	6% curse chance
6	349	418	5	31	37	6% curse chance
7	351	421	5	34	41	7% curse chance
8	353	423	5	37	44	8% curse chance
9	390	468	6	40	48	8% curse chance

Dark Devourer

DESCRIPTION	SKILL BOOK	ELEMENT	ATTRIBUTE
Summon a creature from the depths of the netherworld that drags its targets helplessly around while feasting upon them.	Moonlight Signets, Vol. 3	Darkness	INT

LV.	POWER—WEAK SKILL	POWER—STRONG SKILL	HITS	MP COST—WEAK SKILL	MP COST—STRONG SKILL	NOTES
1	350	420	5	39	47	—
2	375	450	5	42	50	—
3	400	480	5	45	54	—
4	425	510	5	48	58	—
5	450	540	5	51	61	—
6	475	570	5	54	65	—
7	500	600	5	57	68	—
8	525	630	5	60	72	—
9	550	660	5	63	76	—

Vampiric Blade

DESCRIPTION	SKILL BOOK	ELEMENT	ATTRIBUTE
Mow down enemies surrounding Fiore with lacerating shadows that absorb MP from each foe they scar.	Moonlight Signets, Vol. 2	Darkness	INT

LV.	HITS	MP COST—WEAK SKILL	MP COST—STRONG SKILL	NOTES
1	4	20	24	—
2	4	23	28	—
3	5	26	31	—
4	6	29	35	—
5	7	32	38	—
6	7	35	42	—
7	8	38	46	—
8	8	41	49	—
9	9	44	53	—

Extinction

DESCRIPTION	SKILL BOOK	ELEMENT	ATTRIBUTE
Seal an enemy under an enigmatic dome that explodes, engulfing anyone unfortunate enough to be in its vicinity.	The Founder's Signets, Vol. 2	Non-elemental	INT

LV.	POWER—WEAK SKILL	POWER—STRONG SKILL	HITS	MP COST—WEAK SKILL	MP COST—STRONG SKILL	NOTES
1	380	456	2	41	49	—
2	405	486	2	44	53	—
3	430	516	2	47	56	—
4	455	546	2	50	60	—
5	480	576	2	53	64	—
6	505	606	2	56	67	—
7	530	636	2	59	71	—
8	555	666	2	62	74	—
9	580	696	2	65	78	—

Reaping Spark

DESCRIPTION	SKILL BOOK	ELEMENT	ATTRIBUTE
Cause distortions in the space around the target that swallow up any enemies with whom they come into contact.	The Founder's Signets, Vol. 1	Non-elemental	INT

LV.	POWER—WEAK SKILL	POWER—STRONG SKILL	HITS	MP COST—WEAK SKILL	MP COST—STRONG SKILL	NOTES
1	260	312	8	14	17	—
2	264	316	8	17	20	—
3	298	357	10	20	24	—
4	301	361	10	23	28	—
5	305	366	10	26	31	—
6	339	406	12	29	35	—
7	343	411	12	32	38	—
8	346	415	12	35	42	—
9	380	456	14	38	46	—

Sacred Pain

DESCRIPTION	SKILL BOOK	ELEMENT	ATTRIBUTE
Lower all elemental resistances of one enemy.	Signeturgical Book of Quietude	Non-elemental	—

LV.	MP COST—WEAK SKILL	MP COST—STRONG SKILL	NOTES
1	24	29	35 seconds of elemental resistance -15
2	25	30	38 seconds of elemental resistance -15
3	26	31	41 seconds of elemental resistance -15
4	27	32	44 seconds of elemental resistance -15
5	28	34	47 seconds of elemental resistance -15
6	29	35	50 seconds of elemental resistance -15
7	30	36	53 seconds of elemental resistance -15
8	31	37	56 seconds of elemental resistance -15
9	32	38	60 seconds of elemental resistance -15

Void

DESCRIPTION	SKILL BOOK	ELEMENT	ATTRIBUTE
Negate all of the beneficial effects currently on every enemy.	Purification Signets, Vol. 2	Non-elemental	—

LV.	MP COST—WEAK SKILL	MP COST—STRONG SKILL	NOTES
1-9	30	36	—

FIORE'S SIGNETURGY

Healing

DESCRIPTION	SKILL BOOK	ELEMENT	ATTRIBUTE
Restore the HP of one party member.	Restorative Signets, Vol. 1	Non-elemental	—

LV.	MP COST	NOTES
1	6	HP +30%
2	7	HP +32%
3	8	HP +34%
4	9	HP +35%
5	10	HP +36%
6	11	HP +37%
7	12	HP +38%
8	13	HP +39%
9	14	HP +40%

Antidote

DESCRIPTION	SKILL BOOK	ELEMENT	ATTRIBUTE
Cure all party members of poison.	Purification Signets, Vol. 1	Non-elemental	—

LV.	MP COST	NOTES
1-9	8	—

Raise Dead

DESCRIPTION	SKILL BOOK	ELEMENT	ATTRIBUTE
Revive an incapacitated party member.	Pneuma Signets, Vol. 1	Non-elemental	—

LV.	MP COST	NOTES
1	24	HP +30%
2	26	HP +32%
3	28	HP +34%
4	30	HP +35%
5	32	HP +36%
6	34	HP +37%
7	36	HP +38%
8	38	HP +39%
9	40	HP +40%

Emmerson's Attribute Ranks

Emmerson's Attribute Ranks

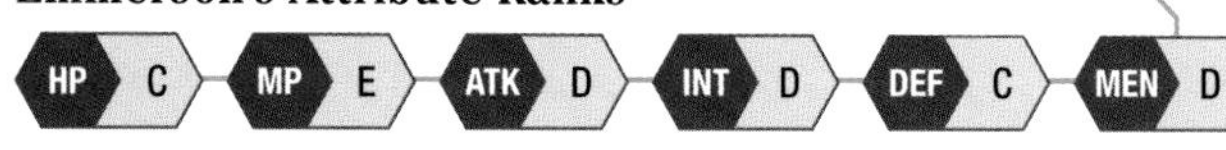

Emmerson's Attribute Scaling

LV.	HP	MP	ATK	INT	DEF	MEN
1	3508	441	33	36	31	26
25	3736	513	81	60	79	74
50	11505	1260	184	136	184	171
75	20678	2450	332	246	334	308
99	26731	3581	501	372	508	466
125	33513	5107	685	508	696	637
150	38251	6410	832	618	846	774
175	41828	7713	937	696	953	872
200	50569	9334	1003	745	1021	934
225	59895	10698	1043	774	1061	971
255	69756	12318	1068	793	1087	994

EMMERSON'S ATTACKS

Emmerson's Normal Attacks

NORMAL ATTACKS	POWER—WEAK ATTACK	HITS—WEAK ATTACK	POWER—STRONG ATTACK	HITS—STRONG ATTACK
Short Range	ATK 100	2	ATK 120	1
Long Range	ATK 100	1	ATK 120	1

Emmerson's Counterattack

COUNTERATTACK POWER	COUNTERATTACK HITS
ATK 216	1

Emmerson's Reserve Rush

LV.	ATTACK POWER	HITS	NOTES
1	6000	10	—
2	18900	15	—
3	38400	20	—
4	64500	25	—
5	97200	30	—

Sound Spike

DESCRIPTION	SKILL BOOK	ELEMENT	ATTRIBUTE
Shoot an arrow-shaped projectile formed from untold amounts of energy that flies straight and true through any victims in its path.	CQC Program Alpha	Non-elemental	ATK primary, INT secondary

LV.	POWER—WEAK SKILL	POWER—STRONG SKILL	HITS	MP COST—WEAK SKILL	MP COST—STRONG SKILL	NOTES
1	140	168	4	7	8	INT damage 20%/24% (weak/strong)
2	143	171	4	9	11	INT damage 20%/24% (weak/strong)
3	165	198	5	11	13	INT damage 25%/30% (weak/strong)
4	168	201	5	13	16	INT damage 25%/30% (weak/strong)
5	170	204	5	15	18	INT damage 25%/30% (weak/strong)
6	187	224	6	17	20	INT damage 30%/36% (weak/strong)
7	190	228	6	19	23	INT damage 30%/36% (weak/strong)
8	193	231	6	21	25	INT damage 30%/36% (weak/strong)
9	205	246	7	23	28	INT damage 35%/42% (weak/strong)

Seraphic Thunder

DESCRIPTION	SKILL BOOK	ELEMENT	ATTRIBUTE
Let loose an arrow into the sky, causing countless bolts of lightning to descend upon the surrounding area and possibly paralyze enemies.	CQC Program Beta	Wind	ATK primary, INT secondary

LV.	POWER—WEAK SKILL	POWER—STRONG SKILL	HITS	MP COST—WEAK SKILL	MP COST—STRONG SKILL	NOTES
1	185	222	3	9	11	—
2	186	223	3	11	13	—
3	187	224	3	13	16	—
4	207	248	4	15	18	—
5	208	249	4	17	20	—
6	229	274	5	21	25	—
7	230	276	5	23	28	—
8	230	276	5	23	28	—
9	250	300	6	25	30	—

EMMERSON'S SKILLS

Red Rain

DESCRIPTION	SKILL BOOK	ELEMENT	ATTRIBUTE
Let loose myriad arrows in rapid succession that burn with crimson fury. The resulting projectile hail strikes all enemies within a straight line.	CQC Program Gamma	Non-elemental	ATK primary, INT secondary

LV.	POWER—WEAK SKILL	POWER—STRONG SKILL	HITS	MP COST—WEAK SKILL	MP COST—STRONG SKILL	NOTES
1	185	222	5	13	16	INT damage 25%/30% (weak/strong)
2	186	223	5	15	18	INT damage 26%/31% (weak/strong)
3	208	249	6	17	20	INT damage 31%/37% (weak/strong)
4	210	252	6	19	23	INT damage 32%/38% (weak/strong)
5	232	278	7	21	25	INT damage 37%/44% (weak/strong)
6	234	280	7	23	28	INT damage 38%/46% (weak/strong)
7	256	307	8	25	30	INT damage 43%/52% (weak/strong)
8	258	309	8	27	32	INT damage 44%/53% (weak/strong)
9	280	336	9	29	35	INT damage 50%/60% (weak/strong)

Avian Rage

DESCRIPTION	SKILL BOOK	ELEMENT	ATTRIBUTE
Uncage projectile concentrations of acrimony that relentlessly track their target like a flock of enraged sparrows.	CQC Program Theta	Non-elemental	ATK

LV.	POWER—WEAK SKILL	POWER—STRONG SKILL	HITS	MP COST—WEAK SKILL	MP COST—STRONG SKILL	NOTES
1	360	432	9	30	36	—
2	362	434	9	32	38	—
3	380	456	10	34	41	—
4	382	458	10	36	43	—
5	400	480	11	38	46	—
6	402	484	11	40	48	—
7	420	504	12	42	50	—
8	423	507	12	44	53	—
9	440	528	13	46	55	—

Hunter's Moon

DESCRIPTION	SKILL BOOK	ELEMENT	ATTRIBUTE
Fire a projectile that causes the target to flinch, and then morphs into a scad of arrows that all strike the foe at once.	CQC Program Epsilon	Non-elemental	ATK

LV.	POWER—WEAK SKILL	POWER—STRONG SKILL	HITS	MP COST—WEAK SKILL	MP COST—STRONG SKILL	NOTES
1	230	276	10	18	22	—
2	245	294	10	20	24	—
3	260	312	10	22	26	—
4	275	330	10	24	29	—
5	290	348	10	26	31	—
6	305	366	10	28	34	—
7	320	384	10	30	36	—
8	335	402	10	32	38	—
9	350	420	10	34	41	—

Crescent Wings

DESCRIPTION	SKILL BOOK	ELEMENT	ATTRIBUTE
Crouch and then unleash a wide, crescent-shaped projection that slices enemies to shreds.	CQC Program Zeta	Non-elemental	ATK primary, INT secondary

LV.	POWER—WEAK SKILL	POWER—STRONG SKILL	HITS	MP COST—WEAK SKILL	MP COST—STRONG SKILL	NOTES
1	216	259	4	21	25	INT damage 24%/29% (weak/strong)
2	218	261	4	23	28	INT damage 24%/29% (weak/strong)
3	235	282	5	25	30	INT damage 30%/36% (weak/strong)
4	237	284	5	27	32	INT damage 30%/36% (weak/strong)
5	240	288	5	29	35	INT damage 30%/36% (weak/strong)
6	256	307	6	31	37	INT damage 36%/43% (weak/strong)
7	259	310	6	33	40	INT damage 36%/43% (weak/strong)
8	262	314	6	35	42	INT damage 36%/43% (weak/strong)
9	278	333	7	37	44	INT damage 42%/50% (weak/strong)

Heavenly Flight

DESCRIPTION	SKILL BOOK	ELEMENT	ATTRIBUTE
Jump high into the air and shoot a beam of light at the ground below. The beam will explode upon impact, injuring any nearby enemies.	CQC Program Eta	Non-elemental	ATK primary, INT secondary

LV.	POWER—WEAK SKILL	POWER—STRONG SKILL	HITS	MP COST—WEAK SKILL	MP COST—STRONG SKILL	NOTES
1	270	324	1	27	32	INT damage 30%/36% (weak/strong)
2	288	345	1	29	35	INT damage 32%/38% (weak/strong)
3	306	367	1	31	37	INT damage 34%/41% (weak/strong)
4	324	388	1	33	40	INT damage 36%/43% (weak/strong)
5	342	410	1	35	42	INT damage 38%/46% (weak/strong)
6	360	432	1	37	44	INT damage 40%/48% (weak/strong)
7	378	453	1	39	47	INT damage 42%/50% (weak/strong)
8	396	475	1	41	49	INT damage 44%/53% (weak/strong)
9	414	496	1	43	52	INT damage 46%/55% (weak/strong)

Gravity Bullet

DESCRIPTION	SKILL BOOK	ELEMENT	ATTRIBUTE
Fire an extremely dense, slowly moving projectile that draws nearby enemies toward it as it plods forward.	CQC Program Delta	Darkness	ATK primary, INT secondary

LV.	POWER—WEAK SKILL	POWER—STRONG SKILL	HITS	MP COST—WEAK SKILL	MP COST—STRONG SKILL	NOTES
1	224	268	7	24	29	INT damage 56%/67% (weak/strong)
2	232	278	7	26	31	INT damage 63%/76% (weak/strong)
3	240	288	7	38	34	INT damage 70%/84% (weak/strong)
4	249	298	7	30	36	INT damage 76%/91% (weak/strong)
5	257	308	7	32	38	INT damage 83%/100% (weak/strong)
6	265	318	7	34	41	INT damage 90%/108% (weak/strong)
7	274	328	7	36	43	INT damage 97%/116% (weak/strong)
8	282	338	7	38	46	INT damage 103%/124% (weak/strong)
9	290	348	7	40	48	INT damage 110%/132% (weak/strong)

CHARACTER SKILLS — ANNE

Anne's Attribute Ranks

Anne's Attribute Ranks

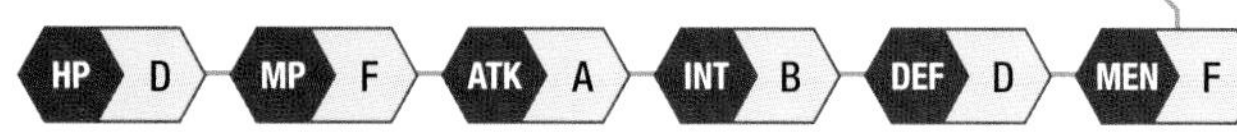

Anne's Attribute Scaling

LV.	HP	MP	ATK	INT	DEF	MEN
1	3268	401	52	51	26	23
25	3496	473	100	75	74	48
50	10771	1161	227	169	175	111
75	19358	2258	408	305	317	199
99	25024	3300	617	461	481	302
125	31374	4706	843	631	660	413
150	35809	5906	1024	767	802	502
175	39158	7107	1153	864	904	565
200	47341	8600	1235	925	968	606
225	56072	9857	1284	962	1007	629
255	65304	11349	1315	985	1031	645

ANNE'S ATTACKS

Anne's Normal Attacks

NORMAL ATTACKS	POWER—WEAK ATTACK	HITS—WEAK ATTACK	POWER—STRONG ATTACK	HITS—STRONG ATTACK
Short Range	ATK 100	1	ATK 120	1
Long Range	ATK 100	2	ATK 120	1

Anne's Counterattack

COUNTERATTACK POWER	COUNTERATTACK HITS
ATK 192, INT 24	4

Anne's Reserve Rush

LV.	ATTACK POWER	HITS	NOTES
1	1800	6	—
2	3780	6	—
3	5760	6	—
4	7740	6	—
5	9720	6	—

ANNE'S SKILLS

Hammer of Might

DESCRIPTION	SKILL BOOK	ELEMENT	ATTRIBUTE
Clasp Anne's hands over her head while airborne and slam them down to send the enemy flying with a wave of compressed air.	CQC Program Beta	Non-elemental	ATK primary, INT secondary

LV.	POWER—WEAK SKILL	POWER—STRONG SKILL	HITS	MP COST—WEAK SKILL	MP COST—STRONG SKILL	NOTES
1	180	216	1	8	10	INT damage 20%/24% (weak/strong)
2	189	226	1	10	12	INT damage 21%/25% (weak/strong)
3	198	237	1	12	14	INT damage 22%/26% (weak/strong)
4	207	248	1	14	17	INT damage 23%/28% (weak/strong)
5	216	259	1	16	19	INT damage 24%/29% (weak/strong)
6	225	270	1	18	22	INT damage 25%/30% (weak/strong)
7	234	280	1	20	24	INT damage 26%/31% (weak/strong)
8	243	291	1	22	26	INT damage 27%/32% (weak/strong)
9	252	302	1	24	29	INT damage 28%/34% (weak/strong)

Crescent Locus

DESCRIPTION	SKILL BOOK	ELEMENT	ATTRIBUTE
Unleash a kick so powerful that it not only flings an enemy into the air to be struck by a wave of energy, but it also leaves a trail of upturned soil.	CQC Program Gamma	Non-elemental	ATK primary, INT secondary

LV.	POWER—WEAK SKILL	POWER—STRONG SKILL	HITS	MP COST—WEAK SKILL	MP COST—STRONG SKILL	NOTES
1	185	222	4	10	12	INT damage 60%/72% (weak/strong)
2	191	229	4	11	13	INT damage 64%/77% (weak/strong)
3	198	237	4	12	14	INT damage 68%/82% (weak/strong)
4	204	244	4	13	16	INT damage 71%/85% (weak/strong)
5	210	252	4	14	17	INT damage 75%/90% (weak/strong)
6	216	259	4	15	18	INT damage 79%/95% (weak/strong)
7	223	267	4	16	19	INT damage 83%/100% (weak/strong)
8	229	274	4	17	20	INT damage 86%/103% (weak/strong)
9	235	282	4	18	22	INT damage 90%/108% (weak/strong)

Triple Kick

DESCRIPTION	SKILL BOOK	ELEMENT	ATTRIBUTE
Bombard an enemy with a series of three debilitating kicks that temporarily lower his ATK and leave him crying for his mother.	CQC Program Delta	Non-elemental	ATK primary, INT secondary

LV.	POWER—WEAK SKILL	POWER—STRONG SKILL	HITS	MP COST—WEAK SKILL	MP COST—STRONG SKILL	NOTES
1	315	378	3	28	34	2% chance for 30 seconds of ATK -10%
2	333	399	3	30	36	3% chance for 30 seconds of ATK -10%
3	350	420	3	32	38	4% chance for 30 seconds of ATK -10%
4	368	441	3	34	41	5% chance for 30 seconds of ATK -10%
5	385	462	3	36	43	6% chance for 30 seconds of ATK -10%
6	403	483	3	38	46	7% chance for 30 seconds of ATK -10%
7	420	504	3	40	48	8% chance for 30 seconds of ATK -10%
8	438	525	3	42	50	9% chance for 30 seconds of ATK -10%
9	455	546	3	44	53	10% chance for 30 seconds of ATK -10%

Fists of Fury

DESCRIPTION	SKILL BOOK	ELEMENT	ATTRIBUTE
Strike the enemy so rapidly that streaks of light trail Anne's punches. The penultimate strike knocks the foe in the air to set up the finishing blow.	CQC Program Theta	Non-elemental	ATK

LV.	POWER—WEAK SKILL	POWER—STRONG SKILL	HITS	MP COST—WEAK SKILL	MP COST—STRONG SKILL	NOTES
1	390	468	26	33	40	—
2	406	487	26	35	42	—
3	422	506	26	27	44	—
4	439	526	26	39	47	—
5	455	546	26	41	49	—
6	471	565	26	43	52	—
7	487	584	26	45	54	—
8	504	604	26	47	56	—
9	520	624	26	49	59	—

Electric Fists

DESCRIPTION	SKILL BOOK	ELEMENT	ATTRIBUTE
Besiege an enemy with three unmitigated punches: one that allows Anne to approach him quickly, and two that send him flying.	CQC Program Alpha	Non-elemental	ATK

LV.	POWER—WEAK SKILL	POWER—STRONG SKILL	HITS	MP COST—WEAK SKILL	MP COST—STRONG SKILL	NOTES
1	265	318	3	12	14	—
2	378	333	3	14	17	—
3	290	348	3	16	19	—
4	303	363	3	18	22	—
5	315	378	3	20	24	—
6	328	393	3	22	26	—
7	340	408	3	24	29	—
8	353	423	3	26	31	—
9	365	438	3	28	34	—

Shockwave

DESCRIPTION	SKILL BOOK	ELEMENT	ATTRIBUTE
Jump into the air, descend upon the target, and slam Anne's fist into the ground, thus fracturing it and causing an explosive shock wave.	CQC Program Epsilon	Non-elemental	ATK

LV.	POWER—WEAK SKILL	POWER—STRONG SKILL	HITS	MP COST—WEAK SKILL	MP COST—STRONG SKILL	NOTES
1	270	324	1	16	19	—
2	385	342	1	18	22	—
3	300	360	1	20	24	—
4	315	378	1	22	26	—
5	330	396	1	24	29	—
6	345	414	1	26	31	—
7	360	432	1	28	34	—
8	375	450	1	30	36	—
9	390	468	1	32	38	—

Acrobat Locus

DESCRIPTION	SKILL BOOK	ELEMENT	ATTRIBUTE
Kick an enemy skyward and pummel him with various attacks before slamming him into the ground and stomping on his immobile body.	CQC Program Zeta	Non-elemental	ATK

LV.	POWER—WEAK SKILL	POWER—STRONG SKILL	HITS	MP COST—WEAK SKILL	MP COST—STRONG SKILL	NOTES
1	290	348	7	22	26	—
2	305	366	7	24	29	—
3	320	384	7	26	31	—
4	335	402	7	28	34	—
5	350	420	7	30	36	—
6	365	438	7	32	38	—
7	380	456	7	34	41	—
8	395	474	7	36	43	—
9	410	492	7	38	46	—

Infinity Kick

DESCRIPTION	SKILL BOOK	ELEMENT	ATTRIBUTE
Perform a variety of kicks in rapid succession that are strong enough to occasionally pierce armor and inflict large amounts of damage.	CQC Program Eta	Non-elemental	ATK

LV.	POWER—WEAK SKILL	POWER—STRONG SKILL	HITS	MP COST—WEAK SKILL	MP COST—STRONG SKILL	NOTES
1	340	408	11	28	34	2% chance to ignore DEF
2	360	432	11	30	36	3% chance to ignore DEF
3	380	456	11	32	38	4% chance to ignore DEF
4	400	480	11	34	41	5% chance to ignore DEF
5	420	504	11	36	43	6% chance to ignore DEF
6	440	528	11	38	46	7% chance to ignore DEF
7	460	552	11	40	48	8% chance to ignore DEF
8	480	576	11	42	50	9% chance to ignore DEF
9	500	600	11	44	53	10% chance to ignore DEF

Relia's Attributes

Relia's Attribute Ranks

HP	MP	ATK	INT	DEF	MEN
G	C	G	G	G	C

Relia's Attribute Scaling

LV.	HP	MP	ATK	INT	DEF	MEN
1	863	122	3	7	20	20
25	2388	766	27	34	54	76
50	7956	1954	63	80	129	177
75	14299	3799	113	145	234	320
99	18484	5553	171	219	356	484
125	23174	7919	233	299	488	662
150	26450	9940	283	364	593	804
175	28924	11960	319	409	668	906
200	34968	14473	342	439	716	970
225	41417	16589	355	456	744	1008
255	48236	19099	364	467	762	1033

Relia is not a playable character, but after joining, she accompanies the party, sticking close during exploration and battle. Unraveling the mystery of her presence and powers is one of the central threads of *Star Ocean V.*

Specialties (Party Skills)

While battle skills are abilities that party members execute in battle, specialty skills are more general traits that determine a lot of little things about what the party can do. Various crafts are mastered through unlocking and leveling up specialties, allowing item creation and augmentation. Spoils received at the end of encounters with specific enemy types can be increased, extra minimap functionality can be added, and new field abilities can be accessed.

New specialties are unlocked through quest completion. Specialties must be unlocked and then purchased from the Skills menu with SP before they're activated. Most specialties can also be leveled up several times, increasing the effects in some way.

HARVESTING SPECIALTIES

NAME	DESCRIPTION	ACQUISITION	LV.1 SP COST	LV.2	LV.3	LV.4	LV.5	LV.6	LV.7	LV.8
Harvesting	Harvest nature's bounty from certain locations. Your likelihood of success increases with the level of this skill.	Chapter 1 progress	25	100	225	400	625	900	1225	1600
Excavation	Extract minerals, ore, and more from excavation locations. Your likelihood of success increases with the level of this skill.	Quest 003: Brute Strength of Blacksmithing	25	100	225	400	625	900	1225	1600
Fishing	Fish for catches at fishing holes. Your likelihood of success increases with the level of this skill.	Quest 002: Drunk on Creation	25	100	225	400	625	900	1225	1600

Harvesting Results Bonus

LV.1	LV.2	LV.3	LV.4	LV.5	LV.6	LV.7	LV.8
—	+3%	+5%	+7%	+9%	+11%	+13%	+15%

These specialties allow for collection of various spoils afield. Harvesting points appear in grassy fields, excavation points appear along rocky cliff faces, and fishing points appear along various bodies of water. After these specialties are unlocked and harvesting is possible, you can improve harvesting rewards by spending SP to level up these specialties.

ITEM CREATION SPECIALTIES

NAME	DESCRIPTION	ACQUISITION	LV.1 SP COST	LV.2	LV.3	LV.4	LV.5	LV.6	LV.7	LV.8
Compounding	Fuse materials together to create items. The number of items you can create increases with the level of this skill.	Quest 001: If It Tastes like Blueberries, It Must Be Good For You	25	100	225	400	625	900	1225	1600
Engineering	Tinker with gadgets to create items. The number of items you can create increases with the level of this skill.	Quest 007: Of Weapons and Womanizers	25	100	225	400	625	900	1225	1600
Smithery	Forge materials to create items. The number of items you can create increases with the level of this skill.	Quest 003: Brute Strength of Blacksmithing	25	100	225	400	625	900	1225	1600
Crafting	Craft new items from materials. The number of items you can create increases with the level of this skill.	Quest 005: Grand Designs	25	100	225	400	625	900	1225	1600

NAME	DESCRIPTION	ACQUISITION	LV.1 SP COST	LV.2	LV.3	LV.4	LV.5	LV.6	LV.7	LV.8
Cooking	Cook ingredients to create items. The number of items you can create increases with the level of this skill.	Quest 002: Drunk on Creation	25	100	225	400	625	900	1225	1600
Authoring	Put pen to paper to create items. The number of items you can create increases with the level of this skill.	Quest 008: Behavioral Study	25	100	225	400	625	900	1225	1600
Alchemy	Use alchemical processes to create items. The number of items you can create increases with the level of this skill.	Quest 004: The End of Welch's Laboratory!?	25	100	225	400	625	900	1225	1600

These specialties enable the creation of all kinds of items. Some items can only be accessed through item crafting. When an item creation specialty is unlocked, visit the Creation submenu off the Main Menu to explore potential material fusion combinations. At first, before a recipe has been attempted, only the required raw materials are visible—the result is not, at least not until the object has been made the first time.

Crafting attempts cannot fail; item creation success is assured. It's just a matter of having the proper skill level and materials.

Increasing the level of item creation specialties opens up more potential recipes. At a skill level of 8, all recipes for a given item creation specialty are available; it's just a matter of collecting the items needed.

You can always check out the Item Creation tables toward the back of this guide, where all recipes are included. This can remove the guesswork from going through new recipes or targeting particular results.

SYNTHESIS AND AUGMENTATION SPECIALTIES

NAME	DESCRIPTION	ACQUISITION	LV.1 SP COST	LV.2	LV.3	LV.4
Synthesis	Synthesize materials to create items. The number of items you can create increases with the level of this skill.	Quest 006: Happy Fun Bunny Time	250	1000	2250	4000

Beyond item creation, synthesis and augmentation specialties allow other means to produce new and powerful items.

With synthesis, items are fused into a surprise result. At first, you can only combine a couple of items, but you can eventually mash up to six items together in one synthesis attempt. Synthesis will always succeed, but unlike item creation, there's no way to be certain about what results.

Before a synthesis is undertaken, the synthesis result's "quality" and "impurity" levels are listed. Synthesis results basically pull from two very large pools of potential drops, one being the "quality" pile and the other the "impure" pile. (A synthesis result being "impure" is not necessarily a commentary on usefulness or rarity; some impurities-derived synthesis results are rare and sought after just the same.) These two reward pools both have values ranging from 0 to 50. These ratings reveal the range of potential results the synthesis will draw from. Generalizing, the listed value is the top end of the potential drop pool, with the spectrum extending 10-15+ levels down in value.

For example, attempt a Quality 39, Impurities 25 synthesis, and the result will be one item pulled from Quality results 25 to 39, and Impurities results 10 to 25.

If this sounds complex, just imagine rolling a pair of dice, but the numbers listed on them are different, and only one of them ends up counting. For more details on the synthesis system, as well as guidelines to synthesize all of the rarest synthesis results, see the Creation appendix near the end of the book.

NAME	DESCRIPTION	ACQUISITION	LV.1 SP COST	LV.2	LV.3	LV.4	LV.5
Whetting	Enhance weapons via equipment augmentation. The number of items you can augment increases with the level of this skill.	Quest 009: Keys to the Present in the Past	200	800	1800	3200	5000
Fortification	Enhance armor via equipment augmentation. The number of items you can augment increases with the level of this skill.	Quest 009: Keys to the Present in the Past	200	800	1800	3200	5000
Ornamentation	Enhance accessories via equipment augmentation. The number of items you can augment increases with the level of this skill.	Quest 005: Grand Designs	100	400	900	1600	2500

Augmentation is more straightforward. Once you've earned the ability, item lists can be scanned, and the effects they can apply to equipment are simply listed. Items can be used as raw materials for augments to permanently increase items' stats and even add new factors. What's nice about augmentation is that there's no guesswork or mystery. Check the Augmentation submenu under Creation regularly to see which surplus items can meaningfully juice up useful weapons and armor.

Naturally, any items used as raw materials in augmentation are destroyed. There are no surprises, but there are still consequences.

Each item also has a limit on how often it can be augmented, which is the other bottleneck on improving gear through item cannibalization. Augmentations can't just be performed whenever extra items are lying around and might give marginal boosts to useful gear. The number of total augmentations left must be considered. In other words, make augmentation shots count. The augmentation limit differs for each piece of equipment. These values are listed in the equipment tables of this guide and can also be found in the Augmentation submenu under Creation.

COMBAT DROP RATE SPECIALTIES

NAME	DESCRIPTION	ACQUISITION	LV.1 SP COST	LV.2	LV.3	LV.4	LV.5	LV.6	LV.7	LV.8
Anthropology	Raise the chance of getting spoils from fallen humanoid enemies. The higher your level, the higher the chance of getting them.	Quest 040: The Four Stooges Strike Again	40	160	360	640	1000	1440	1960	2560
Zoology	Raise the chance of getting spoils from fallen bestial enemies. The higher your level, the higher the chance of getting them.	Quest 024: Subjugation Directive: Gargans	40	160	360	640	1000	1440	1960	2560

NAME	DESCRIPTION	ACQUISITION	LV.1 SP COST	LV.2	LV.3	LV.4	LV.5	LV.6	LV.7	LV.8
Ornithology	Raise the chance of getting spoils from fallen avian enemies. The higher your level, the higher the chance of getting them.	Quest 042: Subjugation Directive: Moogmorts	40	160	360	640	1000	1440	1960	2560
Entomology	Raise the chance of getting spoils from fallen insect enemies. The higher your level, the higher the chance of getting them.	Quest 021: Subjugation Directive: Gileeghas	40	160	360	640	1000	1440	1960	2560
Botany	Raise the chance of getting spoils from fallen plant enemies. The higher your level, the higher the chance of getting them.	Quest 025: Subjugation Directive: Magvors	40	160	360	640	1000	1440	1960	2560
Corruptology	Raise the chance of getting spoils from fallen corrupt enemies. The higher your level, the higher the chance of getting them.	Quest 114: Subjugation Directive: Sandra	40	160	360	640	1000	1440	1960	2560
Mechanology	Raise the chance of getting spoils from fallen machine enemies. The higher your level, the higher the chance of getting them.	Quest 032: Reconstructing an Enigma	40	160	360	640	1000	1440	1960	2560

Drop Rate Specialty Bonus

LV.1	LV.2	LV.3	LV.4	LV.5	LV.6	LV.7	LV.8
+3%	+4%	+5%	+7%	+9%	+11%	+12%	+15%

These specialties slightly boost the spoils you receive after defeating enemies from particular monster categories. The bonus increases the more you level up the specialty with SP. On one hand, the faster you invest as much as possible into these categories, the longer you'll benefit from them. After all, once they're on, they're on forever. On the other hand, SP can easily be spent elsewhere, where the impact on abilities might be more directly felt.

MISCELLANEOUS SPECIALTIES

Minimap and Treasure Chests

NAME	DESCRIPTION	ACQUISITION	LV.1 SP COST
Lookout	Display enemy positions on the minimap.	Quest 023: Subjugation Directive: Dek	250
Treasure Sense	Display treasure chest positions on the minimap.	Quest 016: Shiny, Shiny Scales!	500
Lockpicking	Open locked chests.	Quest 039: Survive This!	500

The minimap becomes significantly more useful when extra pieces of information are placed on it. The Lookout specialty adds the positions of hostile creatures to the map, while the Treasure Sense specialty does the same for treasure chests. Treasure chests afield are usually locked—they're treasure chests, after all—but the Lockpicking specialty eventually allows access to the booty within.

These specialties are basically toggles, either unlocked or still hidden away, and they don't level up beyond their initial activation.

Haggling Specialty

NAME	DESCRIPTION	ACQUISITION	LV.1 SP COST	LV.2	LV.3	LV.4	LV.5	LV.6	LV.7	LV.8
Haggling	Increase the prices of goods you sell to shops.	Quest 083: Quiet Down in There!	100	400	900	1600	2500	3600	4900	6400

Sell Price Boost

LV.1	LV.2	LV.3	LV.4	LV.5	LV.6	LV.7	LV.8
+5%	+8%	+10%	+15%	+20%	+25%	+30%	+40%

In some of this guide's item lists, values (in Fol) are included. These values indicate what a shop can be expected to sell the item for. Items that aren't sold anywhere still have a value listed, in parentheses. Either way, you can sell items in hand to shops for 10 percent of their listed value. Thus, an item with a listed value of 1000 or (1000) can be sold for 100 Fol.

The Haggling specialty buffs this amount. Like the specialties that benefit combat rewards, the faster this is leveled up as much as possible, the better, so the boost is bigger for longer. (There wouldn't be much point to waiting until near the end of *Star Ocean V* and then finally spending the SP to begin leveling up specialties for combat drop rate specialties and resale prices.) But this depends on preference, too. Combat is inevitable, but haggling with vendors isn't. It's perfectly reasonable and encouraged to keep most spare items around as fodder for item creation, synthesis, and augmentation. In that case, it doesn't provide much benefit to invest a lot of SP into maximizing sale value. Whether to invest SP in leveling up creation categories or Haggling can be seen as an either/or decision, coming down to playstyle.

Ocarina

NAME	DESCRIPTION	ACQUISITION	LV.1 SP COST
Ocarina	Attract enemies on the map to you by playing the ocarina.	Quest 074: Collecting the Metal that Plays Second Fiddle	2000

Once unlocked, you can use the ocarina afield to attract local monsters to the location of the music. When combat is desired, this is a big help for removing the tedium of locating prey repeatedly. The ocarina is played from the Specialties submenu from the Main Menu and cannot be used in locations where combat isn't possible.

Express Yourself!

NAME	DESCRIPTION	ACQUISITION	LV.1 SP COST	LV.2	LV.3	LV.4	LV.5
Emoter	React to the world around you. The number of reactions you can have increases with the level of this skill.	Quest 033: By the Skin of His False Teeth	50	200	450	800	1250

This specialty unlocks many gestures that add a lot of flavor to Fidel, with way more of these to unlock and play with than one might expect from a single-player RPG. At Lv. 1, eight emote gestures are available, and more are added to the total when this skill is leveled up. Emotes are accessed with the R2 button—hold it down to access the emote quick menu, then use the D-Pad to toggle between available emotes, four on each D-Pad pane. Eight new emotes are unlocked at each level-up, until Lv. 5 adds a baker's dozen.

LV. 1, PANE 1	LV. 1, PANE 2	LV. 2, PANE 1	LV. 2, PANE 2	LV. 3, PANE 1	LV. 3, PANE 2	LV. 4, PANE 1	LV. 4, PANE 2	LV. 5, PANE 1	LV. 5, PANE 2	LV. 5, PANE 3	LV. 5, PANE 4
Bow Head	Deny Something	Point	Salute	Sit in Chair	Console	Attack Something Invisible	Pound the Ground	Pound on Wall	Turn Around and Give Thumbs Up	"Everything, Everything, EVERYTHING!"	"No Good" Pose
Pray	Get Mad	Relax on Ground	Taunt	Lie Down	Be Suspicious	Be Overjoyed	Cover Ears	Grovel	Strike Bodybuilder Pose	Introduce	
Think	Cry	Be Surprised	Sit on Feet	"Safe" Gesture	Cheer	Hold Head in Distress	Reach Out	Blow a Kiss	Dance Happily About	Stretch	
Affirm Something	Laugh Heartily	Clap	Crouch	Call Over	Snap Fingers	Stamp Foot in Frustration	Explain Something	Slip	Throw Something	Stretch Your Back	

PART 02

The Augury and the Hare

NAME	DESCRIPTION	ACQUISITION	LV.1 SP COST	LV.2	LV.3	LV.4	LV.5	LV.6	LV.7	LV.8
Augury	Listen to Tria's sage advice whenever you want.	Quest 028: Batting 1.000 Against Luck Suckers	80	320	720	1280	2000	2880	3920	5120
Familiar Spirit	Send a bunny familiar on an errand.	Quest 067: Runaround Ruddle	100	400	900	1600	2500	3600	4900	6400

SPECIALTY SKILL LEVEL	ITEM	PRICE
1	Blueberries	40
1	Blackberries	80
2	Fresh Sage	160
2	Mint	90
2	Basil	90
3	Chamomile	180
3	Cinnamon	300

SPECIALTY SKILL LEVEL	ITEM	PRICE
4	Spring Water	240
5	Red Fruit	300
5	Green Fruit	360
6	Nectar	120
6	Gunpowder	240
6	Signet Card	300
6	Signet Card: Enshelter +	1600

SPECIALTY SKILL LEVEL	ITEM	PRICE
7	High-Grade Ink	1200
7	Signet Card: Angel Feather +	6400
8	Jasmine	90
8	Lavender	300
8	Signet Card: Reflection +	1600
8	Diffusion Device	1080

Like with the ocarina, a couple of other specialties add new functions to the Specialties menu. You unlock these by completing quests later on in the story.

The Augury specialty allows consultation with Tria straight from the menu. Tria has more than 100 different cryptic pieces of wisdom she can dispense. Increasing the skill level of Augury increases the amount of wise comments Tria will utter, with 15~20 added for each skill level up to Lv. 6. Eight more pieces of wisdom are added at Lv. 7, and a final three tokens of wisdom from the sage emerge at Lv. 8.

Familiar Spirit adds a lot of convenience since it summons a bunny familiar directly from Specialties in the Main Menu. At first, the bunny arrives only selling Blueberries and Blackberries, but its wares increase as SP is invested into leveling up the specialty.

Transcending Your Limits

NAME	DESCRIPTION	ACQUISITION	LV.1 SP COST
Limit Break	Increase your maximum character and skill levels beyond their normal limits.	Late-game progress	10000

The ultimate specialty is unlocked late in the game. Once Limit Break is available during Chapter 12, its benefits can be conferred to the party permanently for the low price of 10,000 SP. The bonuses are incredible: the party's level cap is boosted from 99 to 255, and the cap on individual battle skills is increased from Lv. 5 to Lv. 9.

Battle Roles

Battle roles determine character behavior when computer-controlled, and up to four can be equipped on each ally. A few battle roles are initially available, and several others are acquired when new characters join, but most battle roles are accessed by mastering other ones. You gain level mastery by having a battle role equipped during combat, so unlocking occurs organically. New battle roles unlocked must also be learned with SP before being equipped. You earn the most exclusive battle roles by completing some battle trophies, which are specific hidden goals in-game. Toward the end of this guide, you can find a full list of battle trophies. Role acquisition methods are also listed here.

ATTACK ROLES

NAME	PREREQS	TACTICS	FACTORS	LV.1 FACTOR VARIABLE	LV.2	LV.3	LV.4	LV.5	LV.6	LV.7	LV.8	LV.9
Machine Slayer	Warrior Slayer Lv. 3	Prioritize attacks on mechanical foes.	Damage to machines +#%, damage from machines -#%	10	15	20	25	30	35	40	45	50
Raven Slayer	Insect Slayer Lv. 3	Prioritize attacks on avian foes.	Damage to avians +#%, damage from avians -#%	10	15	20	25	30	35	40	45	50
Beast Slayer	Plant Slayer Lv. 3	Prioritize attacks on beast foes.	Damage to beasts +#%, damage from beasts -#%	10	15	20	25	30	35	40	45	50
Plant Slayer	Base Role	Prioritize attacks on plant foes.	Damage to plants +#%, damage from plants -#%	10	15	20	25	30	35	40	45	50
Insect Slayer	Base Role	Prioritize attacks on insect foes.	Damage to insects +#%, damage from insects -#%	10	15	20	25	30	35	40	45	50
Mutant Slayer	Raven/Beast/Plant/ Insect Slayer Lv. 9	Prioritize attacks on corrupt foes.	Damage to corrupt +#% / damage from corrupt -#%	10/10	15/20	20/30	25/40	30/50	—	—	—	—
Warrior Slayer	Raven Slayer Lv. 3, Beast Slayer Lv. 3	Prioritize attacks on humanoid foes.	Damage to humanoids +#%, damage from humanoids -#%	10	15	20	25	30	35	40	45	50
God Slayer	Mutant Slayer Lv. 5, Warrior Slayer Lv. 9	Prioritize attacks on divine foes.	Damage to divinities +#%, damage from divinities -#%	50	—	—	—	—	—	—	—	—
Attacker	Base Role	Attack aggressively and often.	ATK +#, perform more automatic attacks	4	6	8	10	12	14	16	18	20
Ace	Attacker Lv. 3	Prioritize attacks on weakened foes.	Fill Reserve Gauge by # unit	1	2	3	4	5	6	7	—	—
Invoker	Fiore Joins Party	Attack often using skill attacks.	INT +#, use attack skills more often	4	6	8	10	12	14	16	18	20
Shrewd Overseer	Invoker Lv. 3	Use powerful skill attacks indiscriminately.	MP cost -#%, use strong attack skills more often	15	17	19	21	24	27	30	—	—
Menace	Emmerson Joins Party	Prioritize using quick attacks on foes.	Take more actions +#, perform more auto, weak attacks and fewer auto, strong attacks	1	2	3	4	5	6	7	8	9

ATTACK ROLES (continued)

NAME	PREREQS	TACTICS	FACTORS	LV.1 FACTOR VARIABLE	LV.2	LV.3	LV.4	LV.5	LV.6	LV.7	LV.8	LV.9
Sharpshooter	Menace Lv. 3	Use precision attacks from long range.	Critical hit rate +#% / take fewer actions +6 / perform more attacks from long range and move more often	3	5	7	9	11	13	15	—	—
Brawler	Anne Joins Party	Forgo defense and focus on attacking.	Take more actions +#, perform more automatic attacks and guard less	1	2	3	4	5	6	7	8	9
Pulverizer	Brawler Lv. 3	Break through foes' defenses with single blows.	Receive #% HP when break guard, perform more strong attacks and fewer weak attacks	4	5	6	7	8	9	10	—	—
Executioner	Ace Lv. 3, Pulverizer Lv. 3	Focus attacks on foes with low HP and status ailments.	#% chance to ignore target's DEF and MEN	1	2	3	4	5	—	—	—	—
Fringe Fighter	Shrewd Overseer Lv. 3, Sharpshooter Lv. 3	Focus on attacking foes with lots of HP from long range.	Normal attack: +#% chance to silence, perform more attacks from long range and move more often	2	4	6	8	10	—	—	—	—
Enforcer	Sharpshooter Lv. 3, Pulverizer Lv. 3	Focus attacks on nearby foes with high HP.	Normal attack: +#% chance to paralyze, more short-range attacks, fewer long-range attacks, and move more from long range	2	4	6	8	10	—	—	—	—
Necromancer	Shrewd Overseer Lv. 3, Pulverizer Lv. 3	Turn damage from foes' darkness-based attacks into life force.	Normal attack: +#% chance to curse, absorb 100% darkness damage	2	4	6	8	10	—	—	—	—
Elementalist	Shrewd Overseer Lv. 3, Savior Lv. 3	Turn enemies' elemental attacks into signeturgical power.	Turn #% of fire/ice/wind/earth damage to MP	4	8	12	16	20	—	—	—	—
Assassin	Ace Lv. 3, Sharpshooter Lv. 3	Hit your target's blind spot with one devastating attack.	Normal attack: +#% chance to instant kill, less likely to be targeted	1	2	3	4	5	—	—	—	—
Daemon	Executioner Lv. 3, Fringe Fighter Lv. 3, Enforcer Lv. 3	Break foes' wills with an intensely hateful gaze.	Normal attacks: #% chance foe's DEF or MEN reduced by #%	5/10	7/15	10/20	—	—	—	—	—	—
Berserker	Brawler Lv. 5	Focus on slaughtering foes, not defense or healing.	ATK +#%, DEF -#%, greatly impair own judgment	50	65	80	95	110	135	150	—	—
Terror Knight	Berserker Lv. 3	Spread fear through the enemy's ranks with your aura.	All foes take fewer actions +#, impairs foes' judgment	1	2	3	4	5	—	—	—	—
Daredevil	Ace Lv. 5, Table Turner Lv. 3	Draw upon your inner reserves in a crisis.	10% HP or less: ATK and INT +#%	20	25	30	35	40	45	50	—	—
Enchanter	Sage Lv. 3	Focus on using skill attacks.	INT +#% / MEN +#% / MP cost +#%	20/5/ 100	40/10/ 125	60/15/ 150	80/20/ 175	100/25/ 200	—	—	—	—
Whirlwind	Daredevil Lv. 5	Enhance your physical power to prepare for combat.	Fight: ATK and DEF +#% (Temporary)	20	30	40	—	—	—	—	—	—
Lightning Strike	Enchanter Lv. 5	Enhance your signeturgical power to prepare for combat.	Fight: INT and MEN +#% (Temporary)	20	30	40	—	—	—	—	—	—
Pervader	Sharpshooter Lv. 5	Exploit the gaps in your opponent's defenses.	Damage +#% when guarded	20	40	60	80	100	—	—	—	—
Aggressor	Pulverizer Lv. 5	Focus on weak points in opponents' armor.	#% chance to ignore target's DEF and MEN	2	4	6	8	10	—	—	—	—
Rampager	Berserker Lv. 7	Show no mercy to those who harm your allies.	Rage activation rate +#%, impair own judgment	10	20	30	40	50	—	—	—	—
Asura	Rampager Lv. 3	Feed off your anger, but do not succumb to it.	Rage duration +#%, impair own judgment	30	90	150	—	—	—	—	—	—
Bridge Burner	Daredevil Lv. 3	Unleash the totality of your power in times of crisis.	20% HP or less: Critical +#%	10	30	50	—	—	—	—	—	—
Survivalist	Invoker Lv. 7	Avoid using non-healing skills once your MP is low.	Enhance own judgment	—	—	—	—	—	—	—	—	—
Table Turner	Attacker Lv. 5	Exert your full power against more powerful foes.	#% chance to ignore target's DEF and MEN	1	2	3	—	—	—	—	—	—
Purveyor of Pity	Menace Lv. 5	Refrain from trying hard against weaker foes.	Hang back against foes weaker than you +#, enhance own judgment	1	2	3	—	—	—	—	—	—

DEFENSE ROLES

NAME	PREREQS	TACTICS	FACTORS	LV.1 FACTOR VARIABLE	LV.2	LV.3	LV.4	LV.5	LV.6	LV.7	LV.8	LV.9
Vainglory Alpha	Guardian Lv. 5	Refuse to flinch when taking physical damage.	No flinch when ATK damage is under #% of max HP	2	4	6	8	10	—	—	—	—
Vainglory Beta	Sage Lv. 5	Refuse to flinch when taking signeturgical damage.	No flinch when INT damage is under #% of max HP	2	4	6	8	10	—	—	—	—
Vainglory Omega	Vainglory Alpha Lv. 3, Vainglory Beta Lv. 3	Refuse to flinch when taking damage from foes.	No flinch when damage is under #% of max HP	3	4	5	—	—	—	—	—	—
Evasionist	Battle Trophy 049, 25 consecutive critical hits	Outmaneuver foes to avoid severe blows.	Foe critical hit rate -#%	10	12	14	16	18	21	24	27	30
Chevalier	Defender Lv. 5	Focus on foes targeting weakened allies.	DEF +#	8	10	12	14	16	18	20	—	—
Royal Guard	Chevalier Lv. 3	Show no mercy to those who harm the princess.	DEF +#%, MEN +#%	1	2	3	4	5	—	—	—	—
Defender	Base Role	Target tough foes while defending yourself.	Take more actions +#, guard more often	1	2	3	4	5	6	7	8	9
Guardian	Defender Lv. 3	Deflect attacks to reduce damage.	Successful guard: damage taken -#%	20	25	30	35	40	45	50	—	—
Paladin	Ace Lv. 3, Savior Lv. 3	Analyze and suppress light- and darkness-based attacks.	#% chance to nullify light or darkness damage	5	10	15	20	25	—	—	—	—
Vanguard	Ace Lv. 3, Guardian Lv. 3	Overflow with energy while fending off foes.	Max HP +#% / Successful guard: recover #% HP, guard more often	2/1	4/2	6/3	8/4	10/5	—	—	—	—
Avenger	Pulverizer Lv. 3, Guardian Lv. 3	Counter aggressively upon successful blocks.	MEN +#%, guard more often / Counter +100%	2	4	6	8	10	—	—	—	—
Marshal	Shrewd Overseer Lv. 3, Guardian Lv. 3	Analyze elemental signets to suppress their powers.	#% chance to nullify fire/ice/wind/earth damage	5	10	15	20	25	—	—	—	—
War God	Vanguard Lv. 3, Avenger Lv. 3, Marshal Lv. 3	Use defensive techniques to wear down your foes.	Successful guard: #% chance foe's ATK or INT -#%, guard more often	5/10	7/15	10/20	—	—	—	—	—	—

DEFENSE ROLES (continued)

NAME	PREREQS	TACTICS	FACTORS	LV.1 FACTOR VARIABLE	LV.2	LV.3	LV.4	LV.5	LV.6	LV.7	LV.8	LV.9
Dead Man Walking	Necromancer Lv. 3	Use your own life force to create a tough suit of armor.	Invincible during battle, but damage occurs constantly at intervals	Short interval	Medium interval	Long interval	—	—	—	—	—	—
tri-Ace	Daemon Lv. 3, War God Lv. 3, Holy Mother Lv. 3	Repel and reject disasters that may beset you.	5% chance to nullify damage from foes, vastly enhance own judgment	—	—	—	—	—	—	—	—	—
Emissary of the Blue Sphere	Elementalist Lv. 5	Become more militant when hit with ice or earth spells.	Ice and earth damage dealt +#%, 5% ice and earth damage taken becomes MP	20	30	40	—	—	—	—	—	—
Solar Emissary	Elementalist Lv. 5	Become more militant when hit with fire or wind spells.	Fire and wind damage health +#%, 5% fire and wind damage taken becomes MP	20	30	40	—	—	—	—	—	—
Moonlight Emissary	Necromancer Lv. 5, Princess Lv. 5	Become more militant when hit with light or darkness spells.	Light and dark damage dealt +#%, 5% light and darkness damage taken becomes MP	20	30	40	—	—	—	—	—	—
Turtle	Defender Lv. 7	Redouble defensive efforts when near death.	10% HP or less: DEF +#%	20	30	40	—	—	—	—	—	—
Suckerpuncher	Turtle Lv. 3, Warmonger Lv. 3	Become more aggressive after countering.	Guard more often / Counter +10%	—	—	—	—	—	—	—	—	—
Half-Butterfly, Half-Bee	Turtle Lv. 3, Pacifist Lv. 3	Put distance between you and your target after countering.	Guard more often / Counter +10%	—	—	—	—	—	—	—	—	—

HEALING ROLES

NAME	PREREQS	TACTICS	FACTORS	LV.1 FACTOR VARIABLE	LV.2	LV.3	LV.4	LV.5	LV.6	LV.7	LV.8	LV.9
First Responder	Healer Lv. 5	Perform first aid after taking projectile damage.	Hit: #% chance to recover 2% HP	2	3	4	5	6	7	8	9	10
Gritty Warrior	Complete Bounty 64, 100,000 total hits	Survive a fatal blow by your enthusiasm alone.	#% chance to avoid dying	4	6	8	10	12	14	16	18	20
Dauntless	Gritty Warrior Lv. 3	Survive a fatal blow by your fighting spirit alone.	Battle: avoid dying once	—	—	—	—	—	—	—	—	—
Princess	Chevalier Lv. 3	Stop actively fighting.	Battle: periodically recover #% HP, periodically recover #% MP, hang back +5	1	2	3	4	5	—	—	—	—
Healer	Base Role	Concentrate on healing quickly.	Max MP +#%	2	3	4	5	6	7	8	9	10
Savior	Healer Lv. 3	Pour all energy into life-saving measures.	Curative spell potency +#%	4	5	6	7	8	9	10	—	—
Crusader	Guardian Lv. 3, Savior Lv. 5	Heal or revive allies while focusing on curing their ailments.	Battle: periodically recover #% HP, remove status ailments and revive others more often	1	2	3	4	5	—	—	—	—
Holy Mother	Elementalist Lv. 3, Paladin Lv. 3, Crusader Lv. 3	Watch lovingly over the battlefield.	Battle: periodically recover #% MP, foes take fewer actions +10	1	2	3	—	—	—	—	—	—
Draugr Monarch	Dead Man Walking Lv. 3, Vainglory Omega Lv. 3	Attack aggressively as long as you do not take light-based damage.	Normal attack: absorb 5% HP, attack more often	—	—	—	—	—	—	—	—	—
Mindbreaker	Enchanter Lv. 3	Lie in wait to release your soul-siphoning power.	Normal attack: absorb #% MP, ATK -50%	5	7	10	—	—	—	—	—	—
Shock Therapist	Crusader Lv. 5	Pain is your friend and wounds are your sustenance.	Hit: #% chance to cure ailment	10	30	50	—	—	—	—	—	—

SUPPORT ROLES

NAME	PREREQS	TACTICS	FACTORS	LV.1 FACTOR VARIABLE	LV.2	LV.3	LV.4	LV.5	LV.6	LV.7	LV.8	LV.9
Sage	Invoker Lv. 5, Healer Lv. 5	Use more concise incantations to cast signeturgy faster.	Signeturgy casting time -#%, enhance own judgment	10	20	30	40	50	60	70	—	—
Skulker	Poltroon Lv. 3	Act inconspicuous and figuratively disappear.	Less likely targeted +#	1	2	3	4	5	6	7	—	—
Instigator	Complete Bounty 11, defeat 5 foes at once	Draw attention to yourself in battle.	More likely targeted +#	1	2	3	4	5	6	7	8	9
Boon Companion	Unlocks via "Stances Like Daril's" PA	Target the same foes as your party leader.	—	—	—	—	—	—	—	—	—	—
Rival	Unlocked via "Leader by Proxy" PA	Target different foes from your party leader.	—	—	—	—	—	—	—	—	—	—
Interceptor	Menace Lv. 7	Actively counter foes you find particularly hostile.	Normal attack: Stun rate +#%	4	5	6	7	8	9	10	—	—
Spendthrift	Unlocked via "Tipping the Scales When Tipsy" PA	Go all-out using attack skills.	Use attack skills more often	—	—	—	—	—	—	—	—	—
Pinchfist	Unlocked via "Patch Conversion" PA	Attack without using many skill attacks.	Enhance own judgment, use attack skills less often	—	—	—	—	—	—	—	—	—
Vivifier	Unlocked via "The Plague" PA	Inspire allies with rousing words.	Allies take more actions +6, DEF -20%, MEN -20%	—	—	—	—	—	—	—	—	—
Master Tactician	Complete Bounty 92, 500 victories	Assess the situation and issue appropriate orders.	Enhance all allies' judgment, greatly enhance own judgment, INT +10%	—	—	—	—	—	—	—	—	—
Eccentric	Complete Bounty 05, 25,000 damage from a single hit	Assess the situation poorly and issue idiotic orders.	Impair all allies' judgment, greatly impair own judgment, ATK +30%	—	—	—	—	—	—	—	—	—
Betrayer	Complete Bounty 41, 100-hit long-range chain	Hinder allies so that foes can move more freely.	Allies act less, foes more +6, enhance own judgment, EXP +50%	—	—	—	—	—	—	—	—	—

SUPPORT ROLES (continued)

NAME	PREREQS	TACTICS	FACTORS	LV.1 FACTOR VARIABLE	LV.2	LV.3	LV.4	LV.5	LV.6	LV.7	LV.8	LV.9
Charlatan	Interceptor Lv. 3	Confuse your opponent with unconventional ploys.	Normal attack: fog rate +#%	2	4	6	8	10	—	—	—	—
Warmonger	Complete Bounty 51, defeat 5 consecutive foes with 1 blow each	Actively participate in combat.	Critical hit rate +#%, take more actions +10	2	4	6	8	10	—	—	—	—
Pacifist	Complete Bounty 45, block 30 consecutive attacks	Refrain from participating in combat unless required.	Take fewer actions +10, guard more often, counter +#	10	15	20	25	30	—	—	—	—
Barbarian	Berserker Lv. 5	Actively use skill attacks when many foes are present.	—	—	—	—	—	—	—	—	—	—
Slouch	Purveyor of Pity Lv. 3	Forgo using skill attacks when few foes are present.	—	—	—	—	—	—	—	—	—	—
Poltroon	Unlocks via "Bad Dream" PA	Distance yourself from your foes when you take damage.	DEF +#%, MEN +#%	5	7	10	—	—	—	—	—	—
Hothead	Complete Bounty 72, take 100,000 total damage	Counter with a skill attack when you are shot.	ATK +#%, INT +#%	5	7	10	—	—	—	—	—	—
Late Bloomer	Warmonger Lv. 5	Actively use skill attacks when afflicted with ailments.	—	—	—	—	—	—	—	—	—	—
Conservative	Pacifist Lv. 5	Adopt conservative tactics when afflicted with ailments.	—	—	—	—	—	—	—	—	—	—
Archivist	Blue Sphere/Solar/ Moonlight Emissary Lv. 3	Analyze weak points for precise attacks.	MP cost -70%, cast signeturgy more often	—	—	—	—	—	—	—	—	—

MISCELLANEOUS ROLES

NAME	PREREQS	TACTICS	FACTORS	LV.1 FACTOR VARIABLE	LV.2	LV.3	LV.4	LV.5	LV.6	LV.7	LV.8	LV.9
Stamina Stockpiler	Base Role	Convert your fighting spirit to stamina.	Max HP +%	10	15	20	25	30	35	40	45	50
Mana Maverick	Base Role	Convert your fighting spirit to mana.	Max MP +%	10	15	20	25	30	35	40	45	50
Attack Advocate	Base Role	Convert your fighting spirit to attack power.	ATK +#%	4	6	8	10	12	14	16	18	20
Intelligence Indulger	Base Role	Turn your fighting spirit to offensive signeturgical power.	INT +#%	4	6	8	10	12	14	16	18	20
Defensive Devotee	Base Role	Convert your fighting spirit to defensive prowess.	DEF +#%	4	6	8	10	12	14	16	18	20
Mentality Maven	Base Role	Convert your fighting spirit to signeturgical defensive prowess.	MEN +#%	4	6	8	10	12	14	16	18	20
Critical Combatant	Complete Bounty 75, 1000 critical hits	Use your fighting spirit to enhance your accuracy.	Critical hit rate +#%	10	12	14	16	18	21	24	27	30
Stun Supporter	Complete Bounty 36, chain 100 hits with an attack	Convert your fighting spirit to a stupefying power.	Normal attack: Stun rate +#%	4	6	8	10	12	14	16	18	20
Scavenger	Complete "First Steps as a Collector" quest	Refrain from attacking and think only of money.	Fol +#%, impair own judgment, hang back +4	10	15	20	25	30	35	40	45	50
Instructor	Unlocked via "Anne's First Mission" PA	Enlighten your allies.	EXP +#%	10	15	20	25	30	35	40	45	50
Minstrel	Unlocked via "Miki's Grandiose Dream" PA	Regale allies with stories of bravery, boosting their skills.	+5% SP per level	10	15	20	25	30	35	40	45	50
Miser	Scavenger Lv. 3	Sell off experience for money.	Gain Fol, not EXP, at #% conversion rate	120	125	130	135	140	145	150	—	—
Altruist	Unlocked via "Find Ruddle!" quest	Inspire your allies to become more skilled.	Gain SP, not EXP, at #% conversion rate	1	1.5	2	2.5	3	3.5	4	4.5	5
Item Expender	Complete Bounty 99, use 500 items in combat	Use items efficiently.	Item cooldown reduction +#	1	2	3	4	5	6	7	8	9
Unfortunate Soul	Unlocked via "An Unmatchable Piece of Technology" PA	Rouse your fighting spirit in preparation for battle.	ATK +30%, DEF +30%, critical rate increased, foe critical rate decreased	—	—	—	—	—	—	—	—	—
Equal Opportunist	Unlocked via "Happy Together" PA	Fight as if every battle has something new to offer.	Normal attack: remove self buff, remove foe buff, reduce critical hit rate	—	—	—	—	—	—	—	—	—
Bunny	Complete "Happy Fun Bunny Time" quest	Raise escape speed.	Be ready to flee at any moment.	—	—	—	—	—	—	—	—	—

HOW TO USE THIS WALKTHROUGH

Welcome to the main story walkthrough for *Star Ocean: Integrity and Faithlessness*. This guide focuses on taking you through the game's primary missions while also indicating optional objectives on the way. Most optional tasks can be done at any point in the game. However, there are a few pieces of missable content (mainly Private Actions and role unlocks). This guide warns you at these points in the story so you don't miss out.

Additionally, while combat strategy is highlighted for particularly difficult encounters, most in-depth battle tactics can be found in the **Game Mechanics** section of this book.

Optional Tasks

SIDE QUESTS

There are two types of side quests in *Star Ocean: Integrity and Faithlessness*: bulletin board quests and the Welch line of quests. All of these quests can be completed at your leisure and are not missable. Generally, quests are unlocked depending on your progress in the main storyline.

A few bulletin board quests are unlocked after you complete prerequisite ones. If you follow this guide thoroughly and complete all of the side quests listed, this ensures the unlocking of subsequent ones. It's important to note that many Specialty skills are obtained through completing these quests. Refer to the **Side Quests** section of this book for reward details as well as quest prerequisites.

The Welch line of quests is particularly important if you're into crafting items, so make sure to undertake and complete these when you can (these are noted in the walkthrough at the earliest point you can pick them up).

CATHEDRAL OF OBLIVION

During your adventure, you'll come across distortion points that warp you to a mysterious establishment known as the Cathedral of Oblivion. These can be completed for bonus equipment and are noted throughout this walkthrough. You can obtain the chests in these dungeons at any point in the game, so don't worry if you miss a few of them. If you like a good challenge, it's recommended that you try your hand at these when you come across them. You can find enemy details and rewards in the **Cathedral of Oblivion** section within the **Optional Tasks** part of this book.

Private Actions and Affinity

As with most *Star Ocean* games, you can view Private Actions for additional insight into the game's interesting characters. Triggered Private Actions are available whenever you see a "whistle" icon on the in-game map, with a designated area to start the Private Actions event. The maps in this walkthrough have these points listed, while the walkthrough itself notes when you can trigger them. Note that Private Actions are randomized (within a specific time period), so you may experience a different set of Private Actions than ones listed in this walkthrough. However, it's possible to trigger all of them with enough adventuring.

Not only do you get to experience each character's quirks and personality traits, but triggering Private Actions also affects a hidden affinity value between Fidel and his allies. This affinity value results in minor changes in the game's cutscenes, particularly the ending, so keep this in mind if you're exceptionally fond of one character over another. You might not want to trigger everyone's Private Actions! You can find details about manipulating this value at the end of Chapter 12 (albeit with spoilers), so *be warned*!

Furthermore, there are random Private Actions that are triggered at certain points of a map. These differ from the aforementioned triggered ones because they can occur in almost any area of the game, and as the name suggests, they are generated randomly. The in-game map won't show you these points, but the maps in this book will show the general vicinity where these random Private Actions can be triggered. Some of these random Private Actions will unlock normal Private Actions, so the more adventuring you do, the more likely you are to access normal Private Action events.

Map Legend

Harvest Node	Chest	Restore Point
Excavation Point	Locked Chest	Teleport Pad
Fishing Node	Save	Cathedral of Oblivion

CHAPTER 1

FATHER'S FOOTSTEPS

The story begins in the seaside village of Sthal, where a young swordsman named Fidel Camuze routinely spars with Ted, his childhood friend. While on patrol, the two companions overhear rumors from the worried townsfolk of an incoming invasion on the village. With aspirations of creating a legacy as grand as his father's, Fidel decides to investigate the potential threat.

PART 03

MISSION: INVESTIGATE THE INVASION

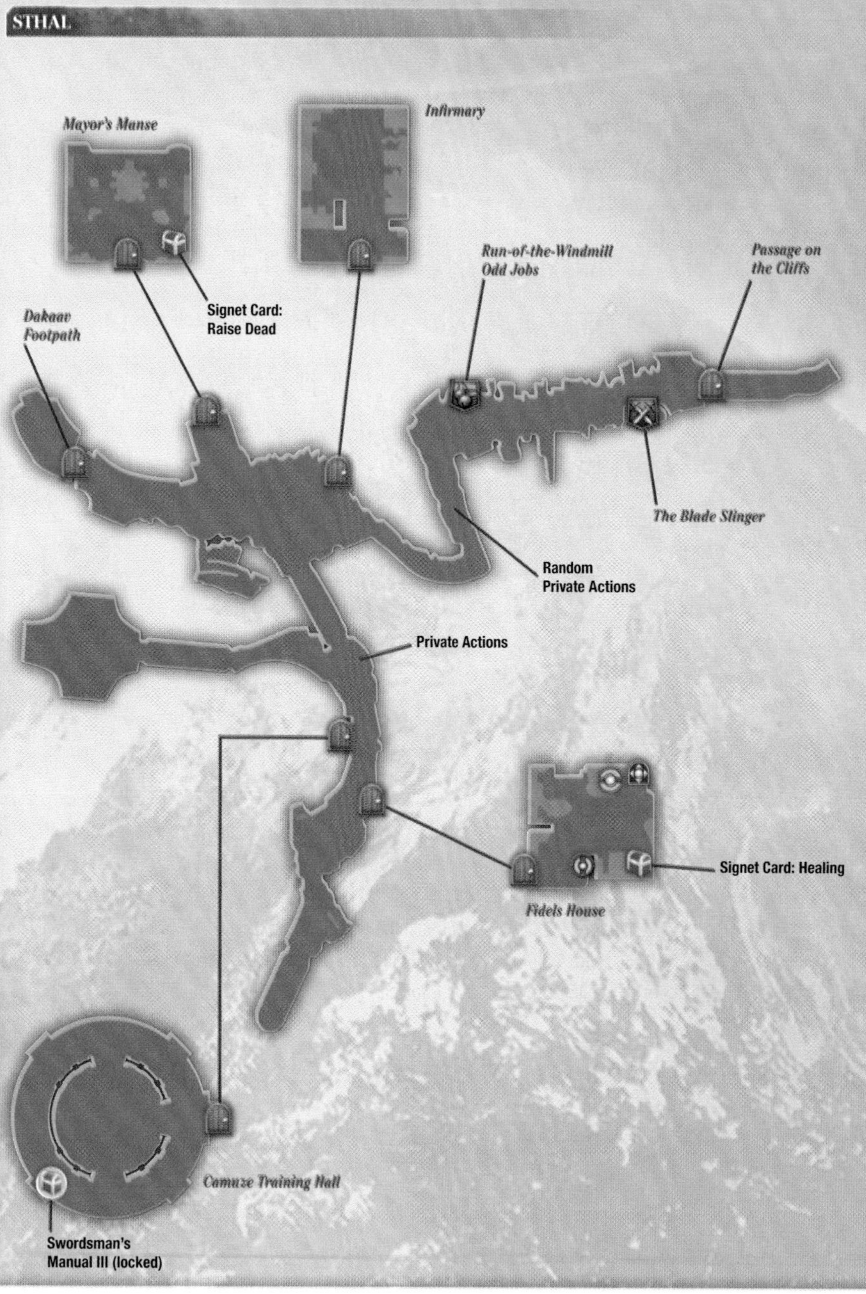

STHAL

Mayor's Manse

Infirmary

Signet Card: Raise Dead

Dakaav Footpath

Run-of-the-Windmill Odd Jobs

Passage on the Cliffs

The Blade Slinger

Random Private Actions

Private Actions

Signet Card: Healing

Fidels House

Camuze Training Hall

Swordsman's Manual III (locked)

Fidel and Ted set out to investigate the rumors of an attack on Sthal. During their investigation, they come across another mutual friend of theirs. Miki Sauvester, orphaned when she was a child, grew up with Fidel's family and looks up to him as an older brother.

Action Checklist

1. Optional: Take the in-game battle tutorial
2. Optional: Explore the area and talk to concerned villagers
3. Meet up with Miki
4. Enter the Mayor's Manse
5. Meet with Ted
6. Defeat the intruders

Shops

Run-of-the-Windmill Odd Jobs

ITEM	COST	TYPE
Fresh Vegetables	180	Food
Raw Fish	240	Food
Shellfish Meat	240	Material
White Rice	180	Material
Basil	90	Usable
Blackberries	80	Usable
Blueberries	40	Usable
Fresh Sage	160	Usable
Mint	90	Usable

The Blade Slinger

ITEM	COST	TYPE
Rudimentary Protector	140	Armor
Sthal Cloak	150	Armor
Longsword	200	Weapon
Petaline Wand	160	Weapon

Mission Walkthrough

Having finished his training with Ted, Fidel begins his first mission: investigating the rumors of an invasion plot on the village of Sthal. Your objective is to find out what's shaking up the townspeople and to defend Sthal from the looming threat.

SPAR WITH TED

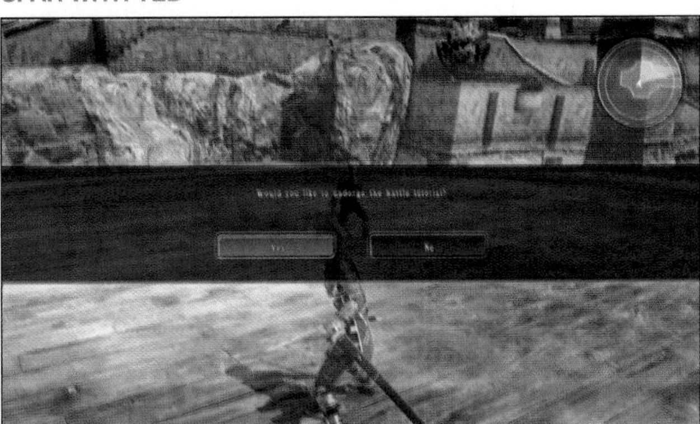

Before you survey the area, opt into taking the game's battle tutorial. This consists of several instructional pages teaching you how attacking and guarding work. Practice these concepts on Ted, then proceed with your investigation. Remember, you can always review these lessons in the game's Glossary menu (under Resources).

> **TALK OF THE TOWN**
>
> While you patrol the village, you can talk to other townsfolk by walking up and interacting with them (default ⊗ button) to see what they're saying about the invasion rumors. Talking to various people in the *Star Ocean* world is a good way to gather information about current events taking place.

MEET WITH MIKI AND WARN THE MAYOR

While touring the town, Ted will notice Miki off in the distance to the west. Go see what she's up to! Both the minimap and the main map (viewed with the OPTIONS or START button) will have a red star indicating a waypoint for progressing the main storyline. When you get close enough to her, a cutscene triggers, with Miki pointing out some scouts in the horizon. Those guys look like they're up to no good. After you've reunited Fidel with his longtime friend, go warn the mayor of the impending invasion. You can find the Mayor's Manse in the northernmost section of Sthal. There's a chest containing a **Signet Card: Raise Dead** inside the mayor's house, just to the right of the entrance.

ELIMINATE THE EITALONS

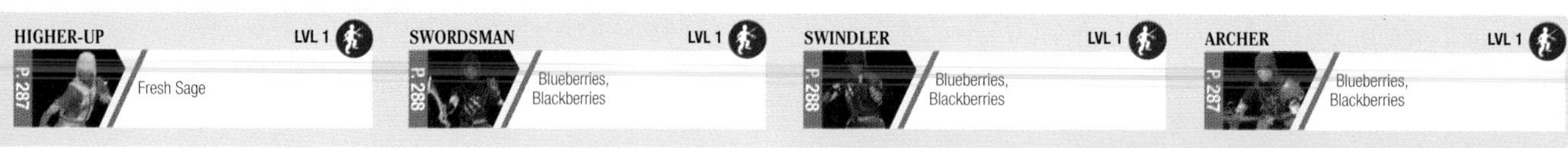

Enemy	Level	Page	Drops
HIGHER-UP	LVL 1	P. 287	Fresh Sage
SWORDSMAN	LVL 1	P. 288	Blueberries, Blackberries
SWINDLER	LVL 1	P. 288	Blueberries, Blackberries
ARCHER	LVL 1	P. 287	Blueberries, Blackberries

It's nightfall. Meet up with Ted in the middle of the village—a flaming arrow flies by, signaling an attack as Eitalon troops storm into the village. Prepare for your first real fight! Target incoming Eitalon soldiers with **L1** or **R1**, and press the Attack buttons to fend off these interlopers!

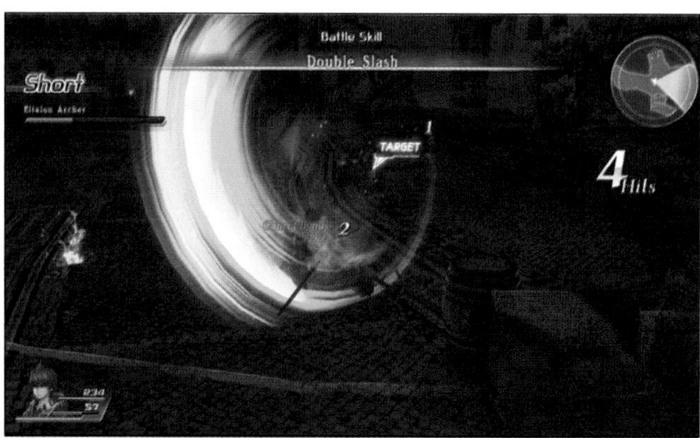

Apply what you've learned through the tutorial in the fight against these intruders. Remember to time your attacks accordingly for a multiplicative boost in damage (indicated by the Cancel Bonus percentage pop-up). Also, make sure to guard and counter your enemies' weaker attacks to minimize damage taken. Halfway through the battle, Miki joins and helps you with her signeturgical healing prowess. After you defeat the first set of Eitalons, head south to suppress the rest of the terrorists. Once the Eitalons are forced out and the villains vanquished, a cutscene between Fidel and the mayor plays.

MISSION: MAKE WAY TO MYIDDOK

PASSAGE ON THE CLIFFS

Worried that it won't be the only attack on the village, Fidel decides to embark on a voyage to the capital of Central Resulia in order to request reinforcements. First, he'll have to navigate across the Passage on the Cliffs and the Coast of Minoz to the trade city of Myiddok.

Action Checklist

1. Optional: Rest up and save your game
2. Traverse the Passage on the Cliffs
3. Optional: Learn the Harvesting specialty
4. Take a walk along the beaches in the Coast of Minoz
5. Defeat the Discord Gerel and recruit Victor Oakville
6. Enter Myiddok

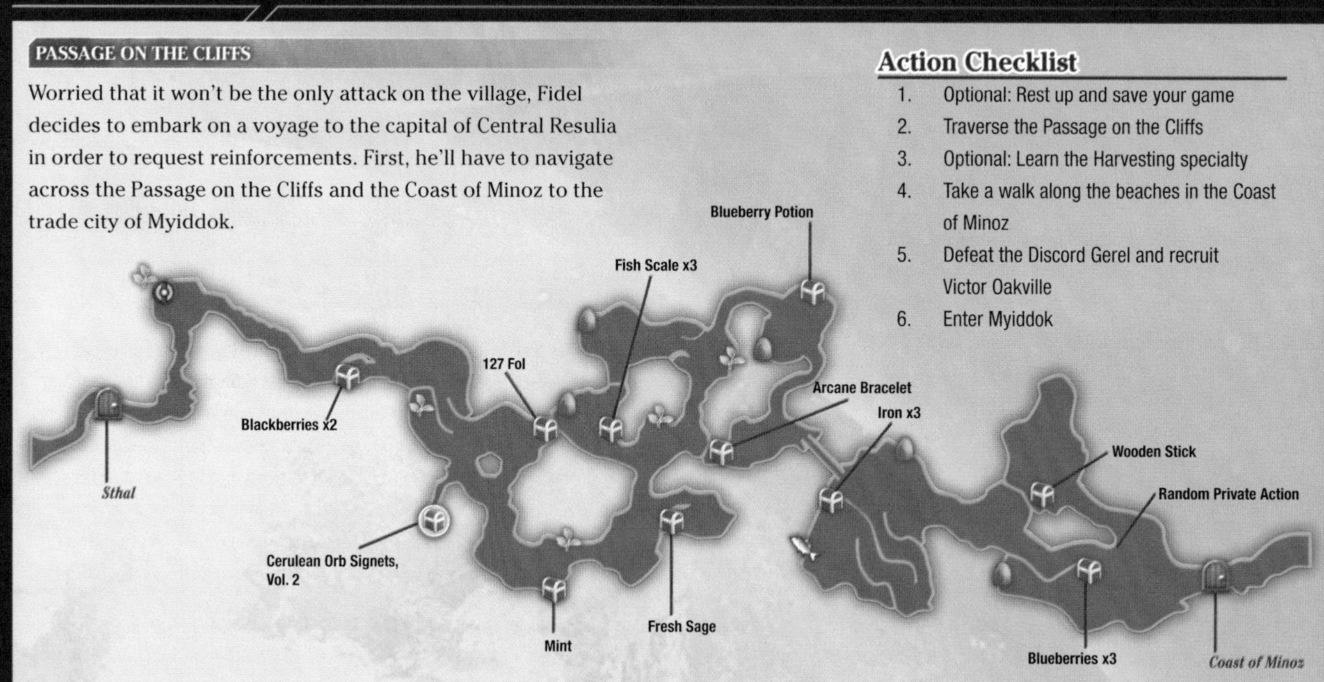

Mission Walkthrough

You're now free to leave Sthal's east exit to the Passage on the Cliffs. You'll need to trek through this passage leading to another area called the Coast of Minoz. On your journey to the capital, the team encounters many hostile creatures that you can practice your battle techniques on.

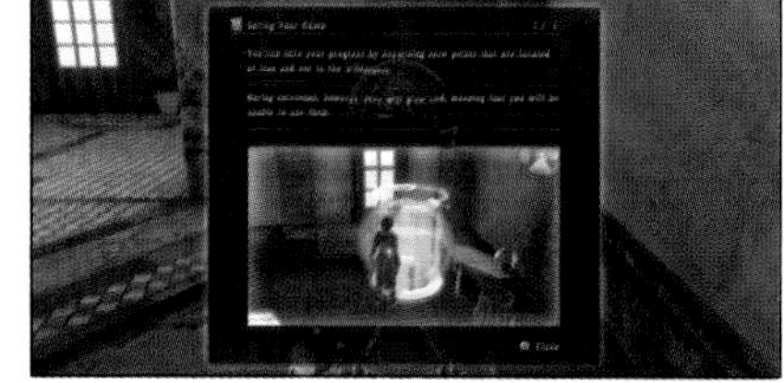

RESTING AND SAVING

Before you leave, you can make a visit to Fidel's House for a tutorial on saving your progress. After you save, you should rest up in bed to restore lost HP and MP. Sleeping here doesn't cost anything, but when you're away from home, you'll usually be charged a few hundred Fol to stay at an inn. There's also a **Signet Card: Healing** in a chest behind a room divider in the southeast corner of the house. Pick it up before you leave.

LOCKED CHESTS

If you enter the Camuze Training Hall, you'll notice a locked chest. Expect to encounter several of these if you're fond of exploring every nook and cranny in the environment. However, you won't be able to open these until later on in the game because you need to have the Lock Picking specialty skill unlocked.

MIKI TAGS ALONG

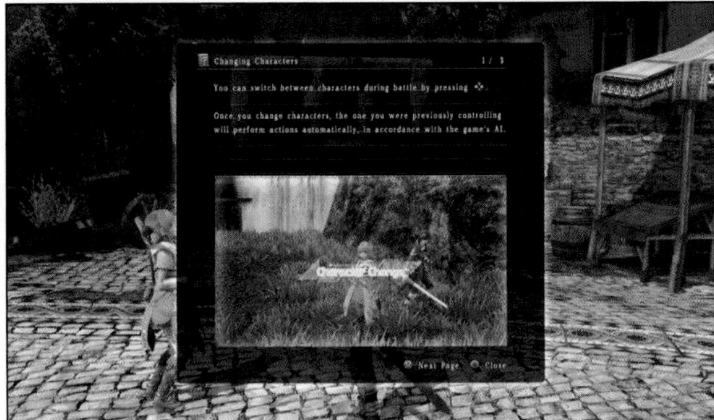

As you head for the Passage to the Cliffs, you'll encounter a roadblock in the form of Fidel's childhood friend Miki. She insists on coming along, but Fidel is reluctant to let her put herself in danger. He could sure use some signeturgical support, though. After she convinces Fidel to let her help, you're then introduced to several tutorials: one on selecting and controlling characters in battle, one on setting roles, one on pausing to the menu during battle, and one on casting signeturgy. Read these carefully to learn the game's various battle mechanics. You can also consult this guide's Game Mechanics chapter for more in-depth discussion on various systems in the game.

PASSAGE ON THE CLIFFS

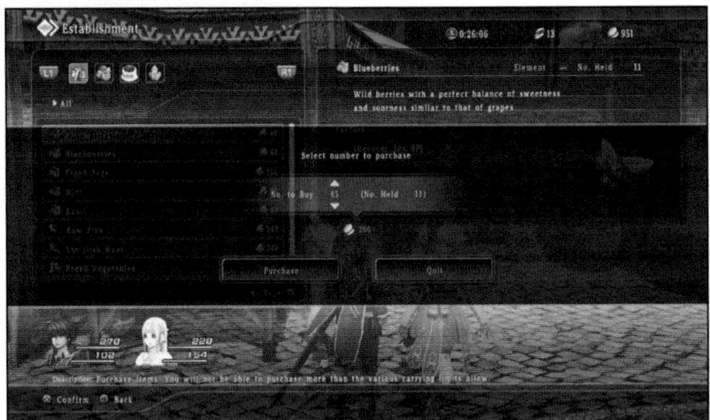

Before you make your trek to the capital, visit the general goods store on the way out of Sthal if you want to bring some restorative supplies with you. It never hurts to have some extra healing supplies, so buy a few Blueberries and Blackberries, just in case.

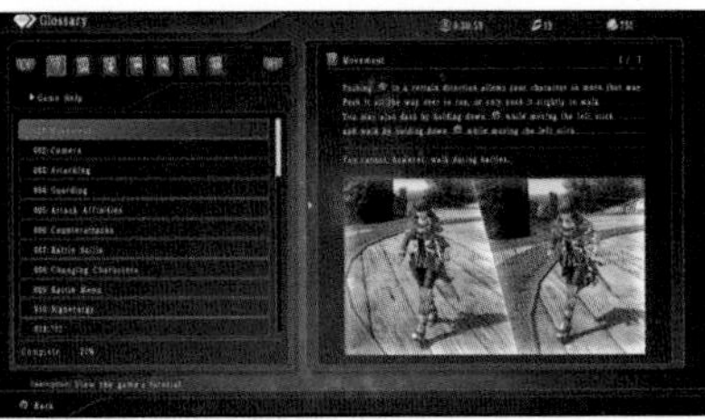

Now, exit Sthal to the east by interacting with the gate. You'll be introduced to yet even more tutorials involving skill points, learning roles, specialty skills, and harvesting. You can always refer to the Game Help glossary if you forget any of this information—which there is a ton of!

Once that's all out of the way, get ready for your first adventure into the wilderness! Wait, there's one more tutorial regarding encounters just up ahead. Check it out to learn how to perform preemptive attacks on your enemies and how to escape battles.

PREEMPTIVE ATTACKS

While exploring, you can get the jump on your enemies before they engage with you for a preemptive attack, boosting your ATK and INT attributes. When you have a foe targeted that hasn't noticed you yet, quickly press either of your Attack buttons for a boost in ATK and INT in battle. However, if the adversary succeeds in attacking you first, you'll be surprised, resulting in a party-wide DEF debuff for a short time.

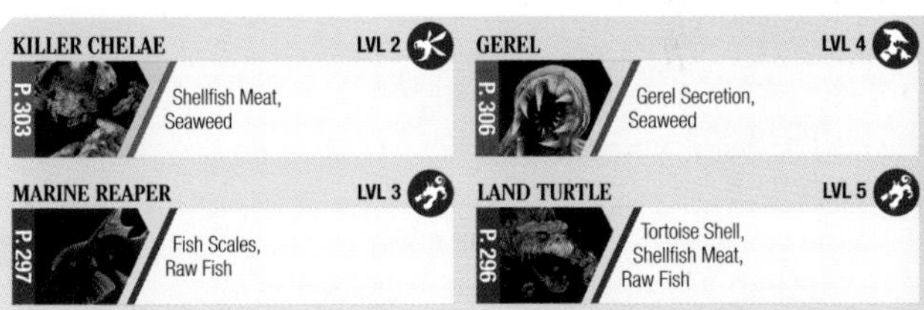

Okay, now it's time to do some hiking. Head east, and slay the crab and plant enemies in your way. There's a chest containing **Blackberries x 2** close to the ledge to the west of the slope near the crab enemies you've just slain. Grab them, and continue on south. When you've collected 25 SP, you should invest it into the Harvesting specialty, unlocked through the Specialties menu. Unlocking this will allow you to see harvest nodes on your minimap. Run to any harvest points you see and interact with them to collect valuable resources you may need later on. Slightly east of the south path you just took, you'll find a chest with **127 Fol** in it.

Now, go south until you reach the water's edge. In the south central area of the map, there's a chest containing a **Mint**. Pick it up, and continue east into another inset. There's another chest here containing **Fresh Sage**, an essential curative item that raises knocked-out allies.

DON'T LET YOUR GUARD DOWN

The Gerel enemies here will only use normal attacks when you're in melee range. If you keep your guard up, you can unlock one of many battle trophies. By guarding 30 consecutive attacks, you'll unlock the Pacifist role. This is a great time to do so, as these slimy monsters don't particularly care for going for guard crush attacks! Accomplish this by killing off all but one Gerel. Then, set both of your party members to the manual AI setting (by pressing UP or DOWN on the D-Pad). Finally, hold down the Guard button in front of a Gerel until you get the "Block 30 Consecutive Attacks" battle trophy. When you finish off the monster, a message displays, indicating that a new role was unlocked.

Go north, taking the trail up to an alcove to the left. There's a chest here with **Fish Scales x 3** in it. You can fight the residents in here for extra EXP and SP, too. Turn north from here to enter the maw of a short tunnel. As you exit the tunnel, there's a **Blueberry Potion** waiting for you in a chest northwest of the structure you're in. Now, start traveling southbound. From here, go south through a path and to the west near a ledge to find a chest containing an **Arcane Bracelet**.

KILLING EFFICIENCY

If you have enough SP, you can start investing them into your roles. It's recommended that you work at leveling up the "slayer" roles when you can, as they not only increase your damage to certain monsters, but also reduce damage taken from them. Leveling up these roles will eventually unlock more slayer roles, which are extremely helpful in defeating some of the more difficult enemies you'll face.

Keep traveling east and across a bridge. You'll meet some new enemies called Land Turtles. These enemies love to guard attacks, so use your strong attack to penetrate their defenses. There's a southbound path leading to a chest after a bending trail. Collect **Iron x 3**, then return north, then east, heading down to the shore. A chest near the water's edge contains **Blueberries x 3**.

From here, you can head north into another alcove with some enemies and a chest holding a **Wooden Stick**. Take the stick, and exit to the east path into the Coast of Minoz.

Save your game at the entrance here, and continue onwards to the destination marked with a star on your map, toward Myiddok.

The path splits in two: one directly east and one that goes south to an expansive shoreline. Go south if you want to explore the scenery and pick up some goodies while earning more EXP and SP from the coast's various monsters. There are a couple of harvest nodes on your way down to the beach, too.

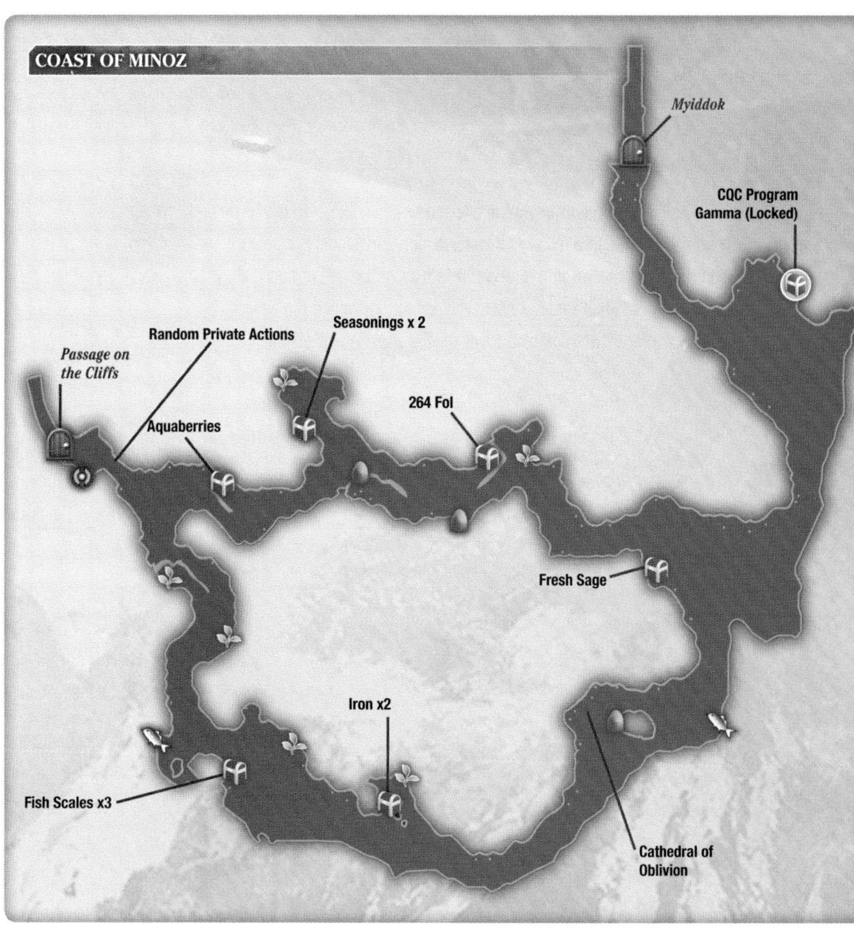

When you get to the sandy shores, near the west part of the beach will be a chest with **Fish Scales x 3** in it. Then, at an inset just north of the center of the beach, there's a chest containing **Iron x 2**. As you continue east down the coast, Miki makes a remark about hearing something creepy…it's probably nothing, right? Keep going, and you'll run into the creepy thing she was talking about: Discord Gerel, a huge plant-type creature. Heal up and restore your HP and MP with Blueberries and Blackberries if you need to (press the Menu button and use your items within the Items menu), then attack the group of slimes.

This is one tough puddle of slime. Defeat its smaller friends before taking it on. Like the smaller slimes, you can guard and counter most of its attacks. Fidel's Side Kick counter is particularly useful since it inflicts a stun effect on its victims. Partway into the battle, a mysterious knight joins the fray to help you defeat the giant pile of ooze.

The soldier introduces himself as Victor Oakville, a friend and apprentice of Fidel's renowned father. The Resulian officer volunteers to escort the party to Central Resulia. He comes with the Defender role, so he makes for an excellent close-range combatant, especially considering his high base HP.

NEW ROSTER, NEW ROLES

You'll notice that new party members bring new roles with them. These roles aren't exclusive to them, so you can mix and match if you want to change things up. For instance, if you want to make Victor an Attacker and Fidel a Defender, you can swap their roles as desired.

Now that you have a new knightly companion, you can make your way north to Myiddok. Alternately, if you want to explore the path not taken to pick up some chests, head back west along the north path toward the Passage on the Cliffs. There's a chest containing **Fresh Sage** before you enter the north path from the east side. Pick it up, and then enter the path. On a ledge to the north, you discover a chest with some **Fol** in it. Keep going west to find an alcove to the north with some enemies and another chest containing **Seasonings x 2**. Go a bit farther, and there will be a ledge with some **Aquaberries** inside. Once you've obtained all of those items, you can turn around and go back east and into Myiddok.

Near the entrance to the city, there's a locked chest to the east near the water's edge. Don't worry about this until you've obtained the Lock Picking specialty. Go north, and enter Myiddok for a well-deserved moment of respite.

MISSION: THE JOURNEY TO THE CAPITAL

MYIDDOK

The three adventurers reach the trade center town of Myiddok for some rest and relaxation after their hard-fought battle with the Discord Gerel. Here, they will bump into a pair of interesting foreigners, meet an eccentric inventor, and befriend a prodigy of signeturgy.

Action Checklist

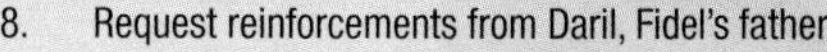

1. Optional: Upgrade equipment
2. Optional: Meet Welch, the inventor
3. Optional: Fulfill some of Welch's quest line and learn specialty skills
4. Sleep at the inn
5. Find Victor and meet Fiore Brunelli
6. Head to Central Resulia through the Resulian Plains
7. Optional: Undertake and complete bulletin board quests
8. Request reinforcements from Daril, Fidel's father

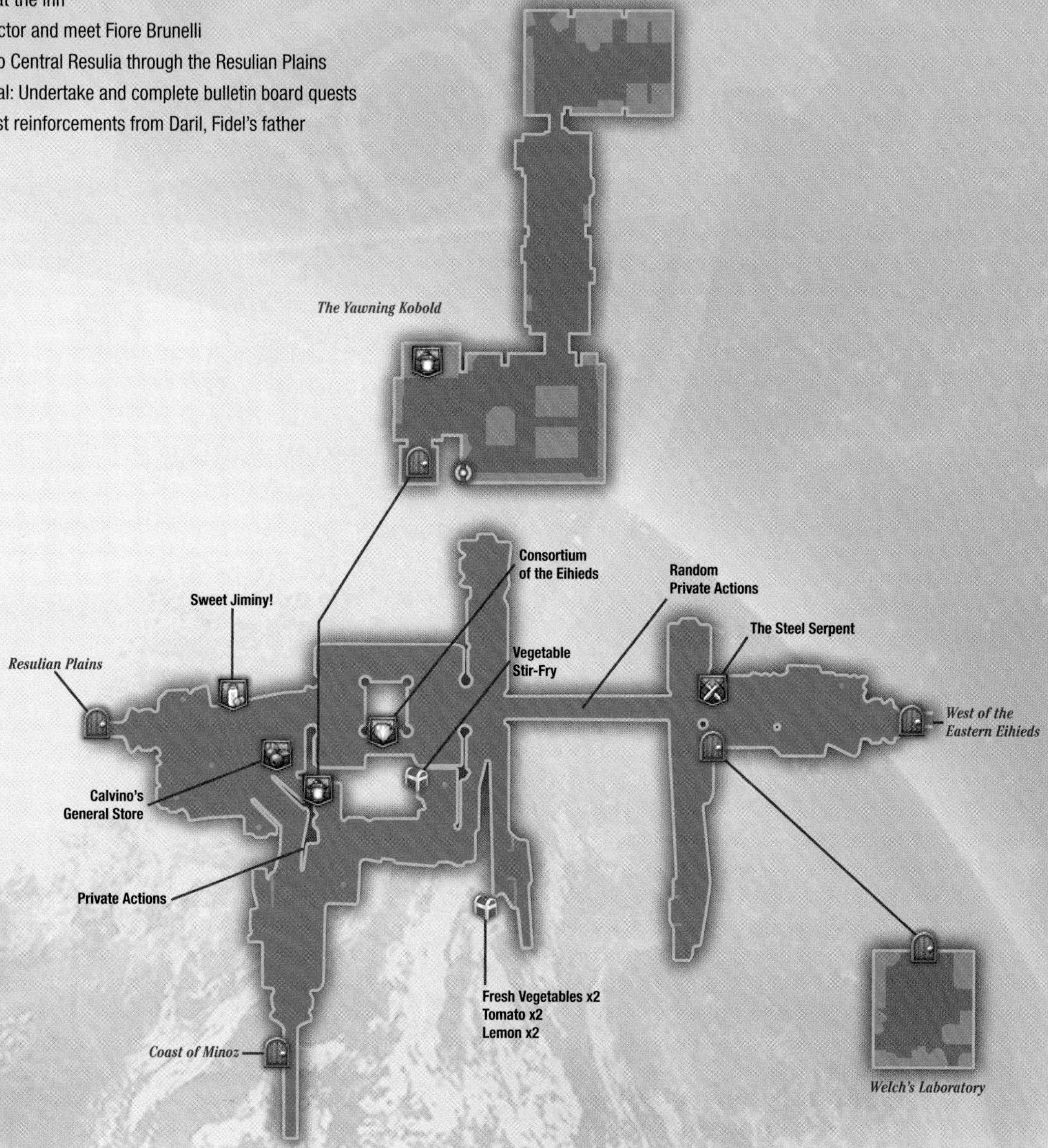

The Yawning Kobold

Consortium of the Eihieds

Random Private Actions

Sweet Jiminy!

The Steel Serpent

Resulian Plains

Vegetable Stir-Fry

West of the Eastern Eihieds

Calvino's General Store

Private Actions

Fresh Vegetables x2
Tomato x2
Lemon x2

Coast of Minoz

Welch's Laboratory

Shops

Sweet Jiminy!

ITEM	COST	TYPE
Common Eggs	90	Food
Fresh Vegetables	180	Food
Lemon	90	Food
Nectar	120	Food
Raw Fish	240	Food
Seaweed	90	Food
Spring Water	240	Food
Tasty Mushrooms	240	Food
Shellfish Meat	240	Material
Soy Sauce	90	Material
Vinegar	120	Material
White Rice	180	Material

Calvino's General Store

ITEM	COST	TYPE
Basil	90	Usable
Blackberries	80	Usable
Blueberries	40	Usable
Chamomile	180	Usable
Cinnamon	300	Usable
Fresh Sage	160	Usable
Jasmine	90	Usable
Lavender	300	Usable
Mint	90	Usable

Consortium of the Eihieds

ITEM	COST	TYPE
Empty Bottle	120	Material
Hand-Spun Thread	300	Material
Silk	1200	Material
Taffeta Ribbon	600	Material
Wooden Stick	300	Material
Wool	600	Material

The Steel Serpent

ITEM	COST	TYPE
Arcane Crest	1500	Accessory
Energy Crest	1500	Accessory
Leather Armor	350	Armor
Signeturge's Garb	400	Armor
Broadsword	600	Weapon
Knight's Saber	600	Weapon
Longsword	200	Weapon
Petaline Wand	160	Weapon
Rod of Jewels	400	Weapon

SIDE QUESTS

WELCH'S LABORATORY
If It Tastes like Blueberries, It Must Be Good for You
Drunk on Creation
Brute Strength of Blacksmithing

Mission Walkthrough

Once you enter Myiddok, you can tackle several optional tasks. Your objectives here are to gear up, learn the ways of invention, and get a good night's sleep in preparation for the rest of your voyage to the Resulian capital city.

MYIDDOK MERCHANDISE

Toward the east side of town, there's a weapons merchant shop with some upgrades if you have the cash to spend (which you should if you've been slaying most of the enemies you've encountered). If you can afford it, go ahead and buy the upgrades for all of your characters; Fidel and Victor's weapons are particularly useful.

EQUIPMENT LOGISTICS

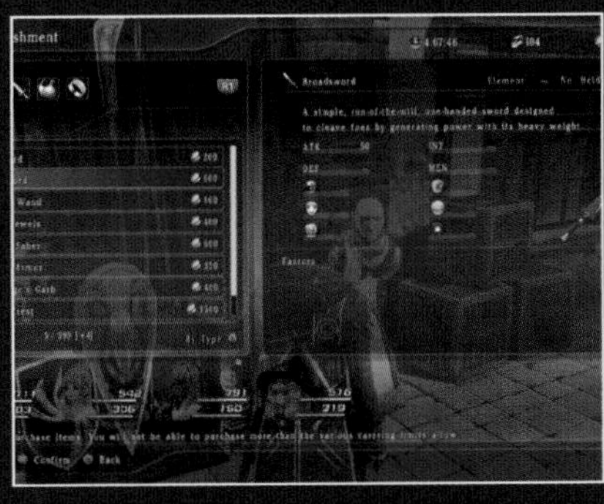

Throughout your adventure, you should be diligently upgrading the equipment of your party members. Don't worry—if anyone leaves your party, they'll leave behind any accessories they have equipped while retaining the weapon and armor they had on. Each character uses a specific type of weapon, so weapons are never shared between characters (and therefore, it's never an issue if one leaves temporarily). Some characters do share armor types, but you should be making enough Fol to sustain two sets of armor.

Stop by any armory shops that you find to check if there are upgrades for your party. When a weapon or an armor piece is selected, an indicator by the character portrait will show you whether it's an upgrade or a downgrade for that party member.

WELCH THE BEAUTIFUL AND GENIUS INVENTOR, PART I

Just south of **The Steel Serpent**, there's a door to **Welch's Laboratory**. It's highly recommended that you visit the flamboyant inventor because she gives you important quests that unlock various specialty skills. After her introduction, you receive a tutorial on quests.

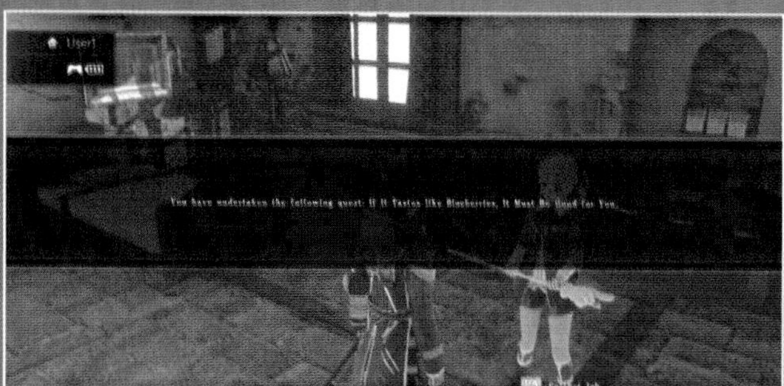

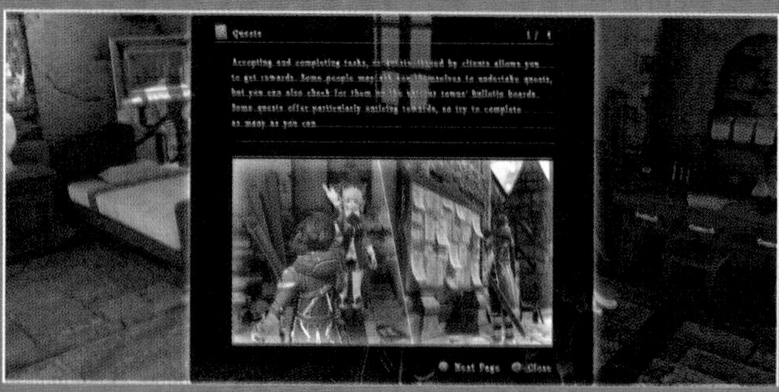

Welch's first quest, **If It Tastes like Blueberries, It Must Be Good for You**, only requires you to hand over five **Blueberries**. If you have them on you, go ahead and give them away. Otherwise, you can head to the general goods shop in town to purchase them. After Welch thanks you for your services, another tutorial regarding item creation is shown. You can now learn the Compounding skill by spending SP within the Specialties Skills menu.

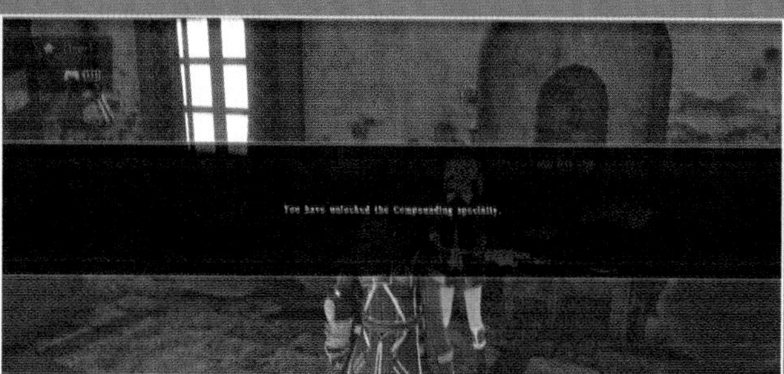

If you leave the laboratory and return, Welch will have another quest lined up for you, **Drunk on Creation**. However, you'll need a **Lemon** and a bottle of **Spring Water**, which you probably don't have yet. Go over to the local grocer at the west end of Myiddok (called **Sweet Jiminy!**) to buy a bottle of Spring Water. On the way back to Welch's Laboratory, you can pick up **Fresh Vegetables x 2**, **Tomato x 2**, and **Lemon x 2** from a chest near the dock south of the bridge. Now that you have both required quest items, take them to Welch to unlock the Cooking and Fishing specialties.

Again, leave the laboratory and re-enter to queue up another crafting-related quest. This time, Welch needs three pieces of **Iron** and five **Wooden Sticks**. During your travel from Sthal, you may have collected enough Iron (hopefully, you plundered the chest containing **Iron x 3** in the Passage on the Cliffs). If so, you can buy the Wooden Sticks required from the material vendor just west of the central bridge in Myiddok. Return to Welch to complete **Brute Strength of Blacksmithing**. This unlocks the Excavation and Smithery specialty skills. If you have enough SP and want to collect resources while you're out adventuring, consider investing into Excavation and Fishing so that you have access to all resource nodes.

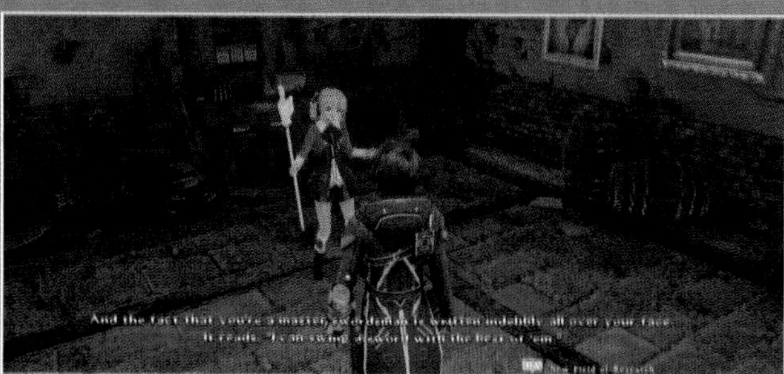

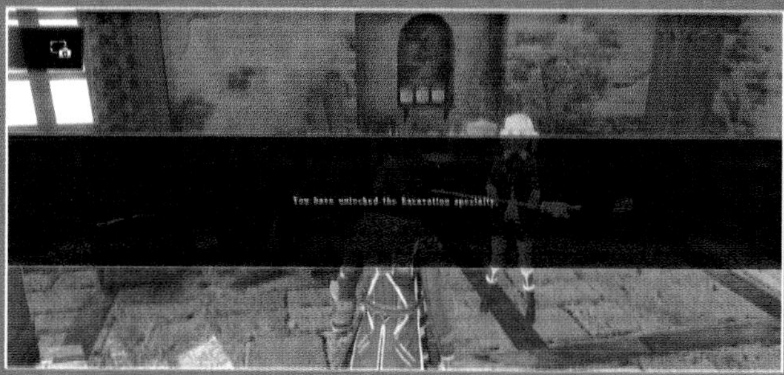

That's all for her quest line for now. She won't give you more quests until later on as you progress through the story, so remember to come back!

REST UP, AND MEET LADY BRUNELLI

After all of your item-fetching for the eccentric inventor, you can rest up at the inn (for free!). On your way into the inn, you'll bump into a rather interesting-looking woman. Nevertheless, go ahead and enter the inn. Talk to the innkeeper for a good night's rest in preparation for the trek to Central Resulia.

In the morning, Miki gives Fidel a rude (and endearing) awakening while Victor waits near the western gate of Myiddok.

Head west and meet up with Victor, where you'll notice an extravagantly dressed woman. Victor introduces her as Fiore Brunelli, a signeturge from Langdauq's capital city of Santeroule. Evidently, Victor's primary mission was to escort the lady to Central Resulia. With Fiore joining the party, you can now exit to the Resulian Plains via the western gate.

TRAVERSE THE RESULIAN PLAINS

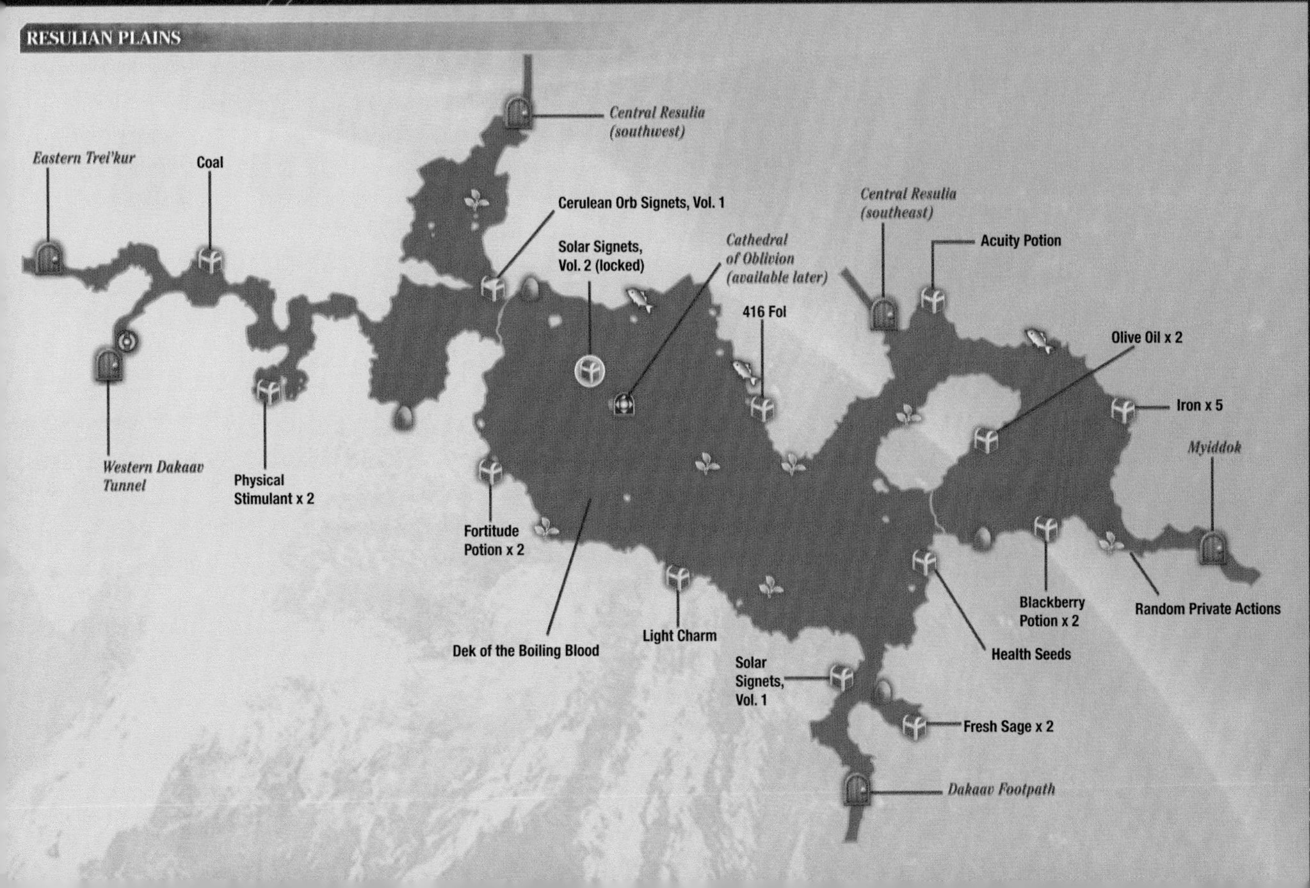

RESULIAN PLAINS

Central Resulia (southwest)
Eastern Trei'kur
Coal
Cerulean Orb Signets, Vol. 1
Solar Signets, Vol. 2 (locked)
Cathedral of Oblivion (available later)
Central Resulia (southeast)
Acuity Potion
416 Fol
Olive Oil x 2
Iron x 5
Myiddok
Western Dakaav Tunnel
Physical Stimulant x 2
Fortitude Potion x 2
Dek of the Boiling Blood
Light Charm
Solar Signets, Vol. 1
Blackberry Potion x 2
Health Seeds
Random Private Actions
Fresh Sage x 2
Dakaav Footpath

CHAPTER 1

Monster	Level	Page	Drops
KILLER WASP	LVL 8	P. 304	Bee Stinger
DRYAD	LVL 9	P. 305	Nectar, Mint, Lemon
PERYTON	LVL 9	P. 300	Peryton Droppings, Common Eggs
PYGMY GLAIVE	LVL 8	P. 305	Tasty Mushroom, Colorful Mushrooms
MIST GRAVE	LVL 10	P. 307	Tasty Mushroom, Colorful Mushrooms
LIZARD SOLDIER	LVL 10	P. 297	Iron, Blueberries

As you leave, Victor gives the party a synopsis of the war between the two kingdoms of Resulia and Trei'kur. He also mentions that Trei'kur has procured a new weapon of war, which Fiore has been sent to investigate.

Your destination is marked with a red star on your map, and it's relatively close.

However, now's a good time to explore the scenery while collecting treasure and resources, especially if you've unlocked the Harvesting, Fishing, and Excavation specialties.

Most of the chests and harvest points lie along the edges of the map, so run along the mountainsides picking up anything you find. Notable loot includes **Blackberry Potion x 2**, **Olive Oil x 2**, **Iron x 5**, an **Acuity Potion**, **416 Fol**, **Fortitude Potion x 2**, a **Light Charm**, a copy of **Solar Signets, Vol. 1**, **Fresh Sage x 2**, and some **Health Seeds**. Refer to the map preceding this text for exact locations of items.

This is also a convenient time to farm up some EXP and SP while you have Fiore in your party. She's most likely the strongest character in your group in terms of damage output, so take advantage of this while you can before you escort her back to the capital.

When you've collected everything that there is to collect on this side of the plains, you can finish escorting Fiore into Central Resulia.

CENTRAL RESULIA

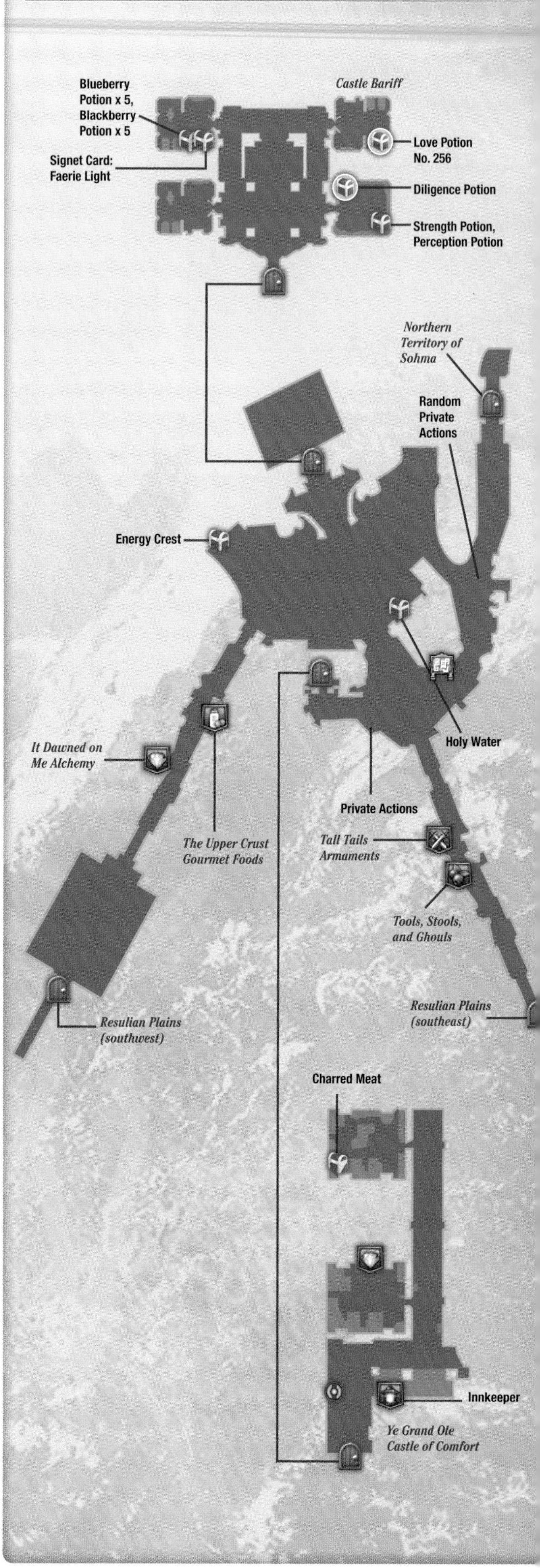

Blueberry Potion x 5, Blackberry Potion x 5
Signet Card: Faerie Light
Castle Bariff
Love Potion No. 256
Diligence Potion
Strength Potion, Perception Potion
Northern Territory of Sohma
Random Private Actions
Energy Crest
Holy Water
It Dawned on Me Alchemy
Private Actions
The Upper Crust Gourmet Foods
Tall Tails Armaments
Tools, Stools, and Ghouls
Resulian Plains (southwest)
Resulian Plains (southeast)
Charred Meat
Innkeeper
Ye Grand Ole Castle of Comfort

OPTIONAL HELP WANTED: BULLETIN BOARD QUESTS

You'll find your first bulletin board in Central Resulia, just across from the inn near the center of the city. The quests listed on the boards can be done at any point in the game, with more popping up as you progress further into the story. If you're eager to unlock specialty skills while earning EXP, Fol, and SP, be sure to complete all of these mini quests during your travels around Faykreed! These side objectives generally consist of item-collecting and monster-hunting tasks. Many of the collection tasks can be turned in as soon as you undertake them (provided that you have the items), like the two initial quests here in the capital.

SIDE QUESTS

CENTRAL RESULIA
The Things We Do for Beauty
First Steps as a Collector

QUESTING ADVENTURER

Several side quests offer hidden rewards, such as new battle roles. For instance, the first bulletin board quest in Central Resulia, **The Things We Do for Beauty,** rewards you with the Scavenger role upon completion. You should undertake as many as you can and complete them at your convenience. Of course, a job well done should be its own reward!

SEE DARIL, RESULIAN MILITARY ADVISER

Head to the destination near the castle steps to trigger a cutscene with Fidel's father, Daril. He refuses Fidel's request for aid because of the need for troops in Resulia and pleads with his son to return home to defend Sthal. Fidel and Miki have no choice but to turn back empty-handed. Victor suggests that they take a shorter route home, through the Dakaav Footpath. After the cutscene, you'll see a tutorial message regarding characters leaving the party. Fiore and Victor depart from the group, so Fidel and Miki are left to make a trek back to the seaside village, bearing the bad news.

There are a couple of chests lying around in plain sight here in Resulia. Just west of the castle steps is a chest containing an **Energy Crest**. Just southeast from the castle is another chest, hosting a bottle of **Holy Water**. There's one more chest inside the Ye Grand Ole Castle of Comfort inn, inside the northern guest room. You'll find a piece of **Charred Meat** in it. This is the only one in the entire game, and it's required for a quest you can undertake later on. *Do not* eat it if you want to complete the **Revenge is a Dish Best Served Burnt** quest!

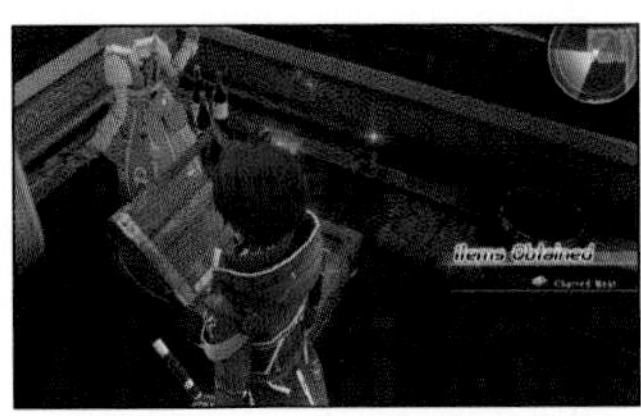

Additionally, if you enter and leave the inn, you'll see a whistle icon floating within a golden circle just outside of the inn. Stepping into the gold circle triggers the Private Actions event. Go ahead and step into it, prompting a Private Actions tutorial (If this is your first Private Actions event). Looks like you only have one with Miki in Central Resulia so far, indicated by the diamonds in the lower-right corner of the screen. When you're done, look for the golden circle again and step inside it to end the Private Actions event.

PRIVATE ACTIONS

CENTRAL RESULIA
Practical Applications of Signeturgy

ACQUAINT YOURSELF WITH THE PARTY

Private Actions are interactions between party members that help develop the character. You'll get to see interesting details within your party members' lives and get to know much more about them than you would just going around slaying monsters.

Most Private Actions are **not** missable, but a few are (which you'll be warned of if you follow this guide). Private Actions will queue up into a "stack" if you don't access them at the earliest point they're unlocked. If you have many Private Actions waiting to be viewed, you can visit various towns to view them, then transition into a new area (like the inn of the town), and then re-enter the town to access a new set of Private Actions.

Some Private Actions require a specific set of party members to be present, but they will become viewable when those party members return.

Taking part in Private Actions is a nice way to take a break from adventuring while getting to know your party members. Additionally, a select few will reward you with valuable role unlocks!

There's not much else to do here, so leave Central Resulia the way you came and make your way south, toward the Dakaav Footpath. You can equip any roles the departing members left behind on to Fidel and Miki for a slight boost in battle efficiency. You can also gather any chests and harvest points you've missed in the Resulian Plains before leaving.

CHAPTER 2

ESCALATION

PART 03

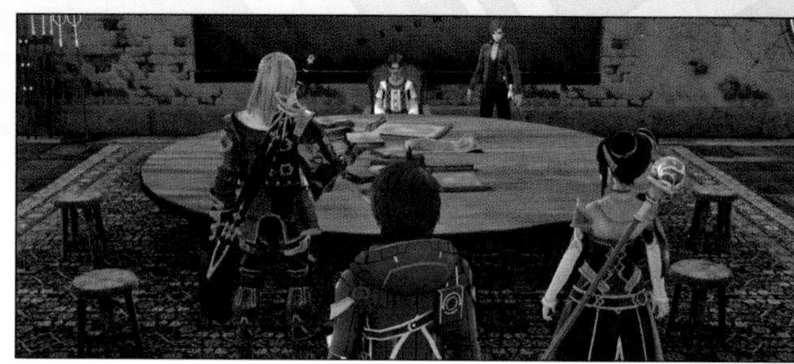

Turned away by his father, Fidel has no choice but to return home. With only his childhood friend in tow, the two leave the capital to check on the situation at home.

MISSION: RETURN TO STHAL

DAKAAV FOOTPATH

Fidel makes his way back home with Miki through the Dakaav Footpath in order to defend another potential attack on their seaside village. However, they're in for a few surprises along the way...

Dakaav Footpath

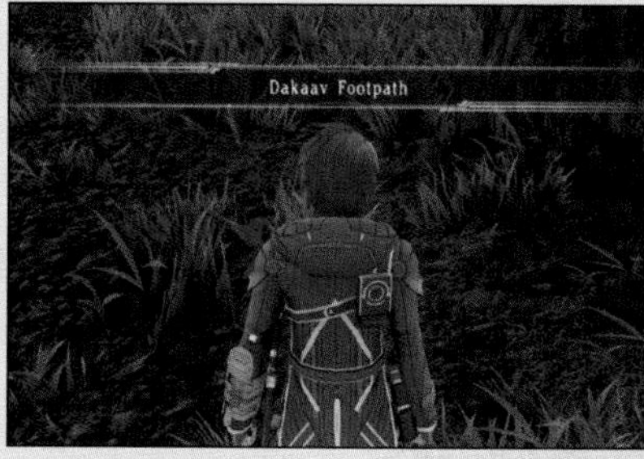

Action Checklist

1. Optional: Explore the Dakaav Footpath
2. Fight off Eitalon forces
3. Save the mysterious girl
4. Enter Sthal

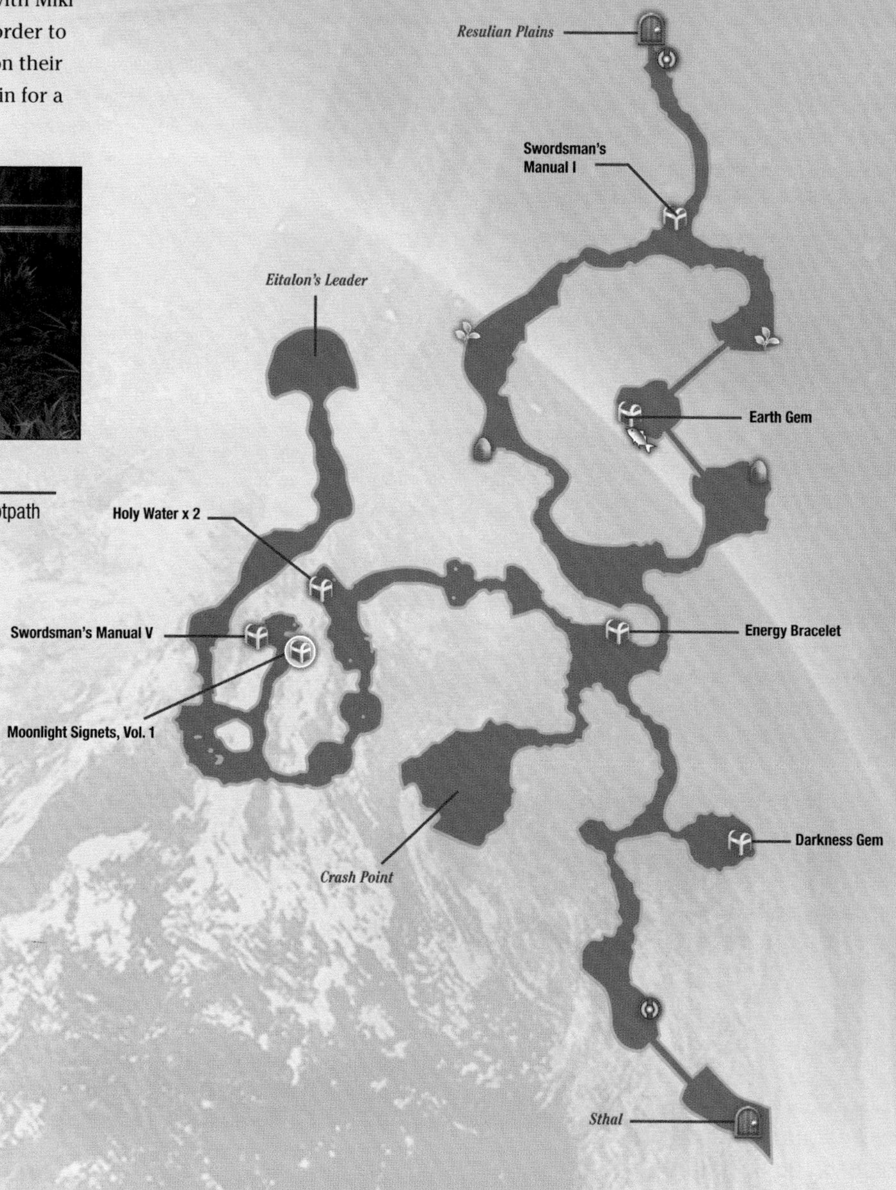
Resulian Plains
Swordsman's Manual I
Eitalon's Leader
Earth Gem
Holy Water x 2
Swordsman's Manual V
Energy Bracelet
Moonlight Signets, Vol. 1
Darkness Gem
Crash Point
Sthal

Mission Walkthrough

You'll need to trek back south to Sthal through the Dakaav Footpath. Here, you must survive an Eitalon attack, face off against some enigmatic enemies, and save an innocent girl from harm.

HIKING THE DAKAAV FOOTPATH

Enemy	Level	Page	Drops
ARMORED LIZARD	LVL 13	P. 298	Dragon Scales
ADEPHAGA	LVL 12	P. 302	Basil, Green Fruit
GIANT BAT	LVL 11	P. 299	Jasmine, Mint

You start at the north end of the Dakaav Footpath, with your destination at the south end. Sthal is not too far away, judging by the map. There's a divergence near your starting point, along with a chest containing a copy of **Swordsman's Manual I**. You can take either path from here because they eventually converge, or you can explore both paths to pick up chests and harvest resources. The east trail across a bridge takes you to an island with a chest containing an **Earth Gem**.

Fight any enemies along the way, and remember to restore your HP and MP between battles if your party members are low. There's only the two of you, and the foes here are plentiful and more difficult than the ones in the plains.

After the path converges and you arrive at the middle of the Dakaav Footpath, Miki mentions hearing something strange. She then spots several Eitalon soldiers in the distance. Before you two can escape, you are ambushed! You'll have to fight off a seemingly endless amount of bandits. Slash away at the ambushers, and keep Miki safe. She's your primary source of healing, after all.

BRIGANDS, BANDITS, AND... SPACEMEN?

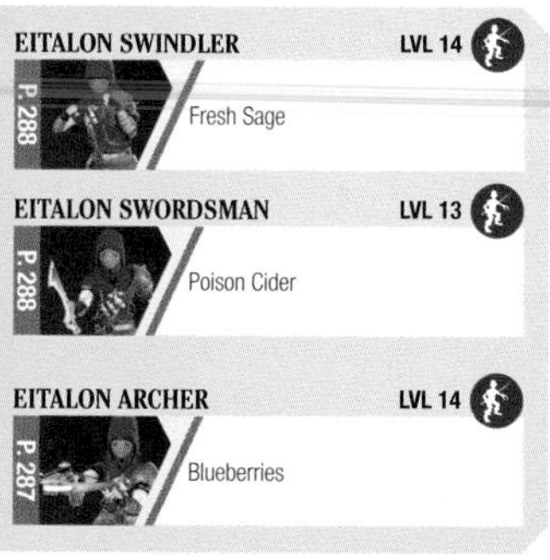

Once you've finished them off, a crash is heard nearby. Fidel and Miki go to investigate and find an enigmatic young girl emerge from the wreckage of what looks to be a spacecraft with cloaking technology. Two mysterious men wielding light-emitting weapons also emerge and demand that the Sthalians return the young girl to them.

It's time to protect the apparently defenseless girl from these soldiers.

These mysterious spacemen have peculiar but powerful phaser weapons. Avoid their gunfire as best as possible by sidestepping with the Guard button plus LEFT or RIGHT on the analog stick. When you've depleted their health low enough, they'll become immune to your attacks.

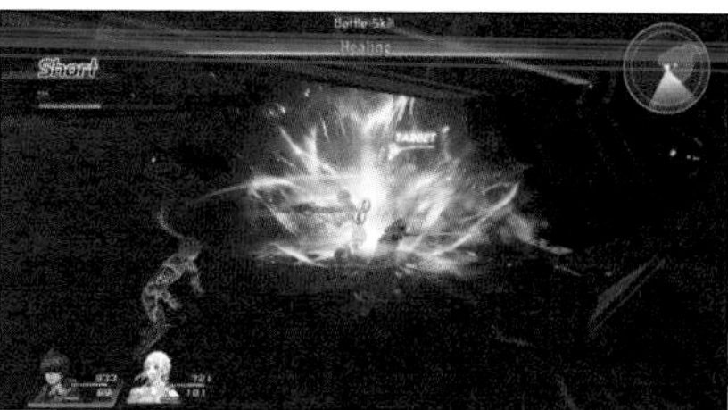

However, the girl begins to cast some sort of signeturgical spell, eventually unleashing a torrent of power that freezes the hostiles in place. After the cutscene, you'll need to carry the girl with you down to Sthal.

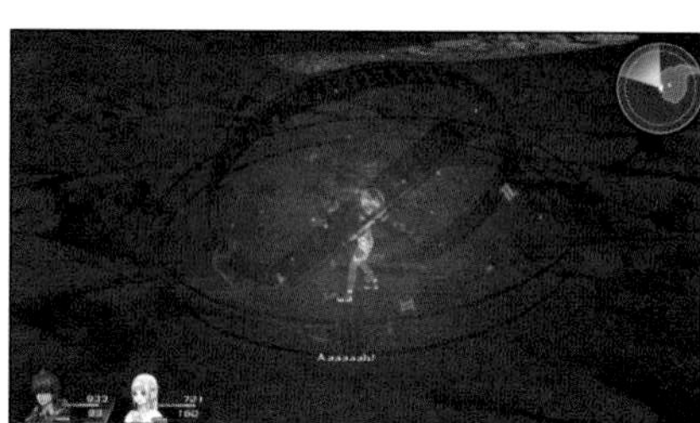

Upon entering Sthal, Fidel and Miki realize they're too late to help defend their people. The inevitable Eitalon invasion dealt significant damage to the village, leaving much of it in ruins. To make matters worse, the party still has a young girl to care for. Make your way to Fidel's House to let the unconscious girl rest awhile.

MISSION: INFILTRATE THE EITALON BASE

As the mysterious girl sleeps, Fidel sets out to brief the mayor with details of his journey and the apparent refusal of Resulian aid. However, Daril has decided to send Victor and the King's Chosen to help his son and the village of Sthal. The aid consists of an infiltration operation on the Eitalon base.

Action Checklist

1. Report to the mayor
2. Join Victor's infiltration mission
3. Optional: Witness a random Private Action
4. Defeat the Eitalons and their leader
5. Return home and prepare for a return trip to the capital

SHOPS—STHAL (UPDATE)

Run-of-the-Windmill Odd Jobs

ITEM	COST	TYPE
Fresh Vegetables	180	Food
Raw Fish	240	Food
Shellfish Meat	240	Material
White Rice	180	Material
Basil	90	Usable
Blackberries	80	Usable
Blueberries	40	Usable
Fresh Sage	160	Usable
Mint	90	Usable

The Blade Slinger

ITEM	COST	TYPE
Arcane Crest	1500	Accessory
Energy Crest	1500	Accessory
Leather Armor	350	Armor
Rudimentary Protector	140	Armor
Signeturge's Garb	400	Armor
Sthal Cloak	150	Armor
Broadsword	600	Weapon
Longsword	200	Weapon
Petaline Wand	160	Weapon
Rod of Jewels	400	Weapon

Mission Walkthrough

THE KING'S CHOSEN

It's time to report in to the mayor to tell him what's transpired so far over the course of your journey to the capital. Head north into the Mayor's Manse.

It seems that Victor beat you to it. He's here with his elite Resulian squad, the King's Chosen, who were ordered by Daril to provide aid to Sthal. After leaving the Mayor's Manse, meet up with Victor and his officers to the west to join the King's Chosen in infiltrating the Eitalon base.

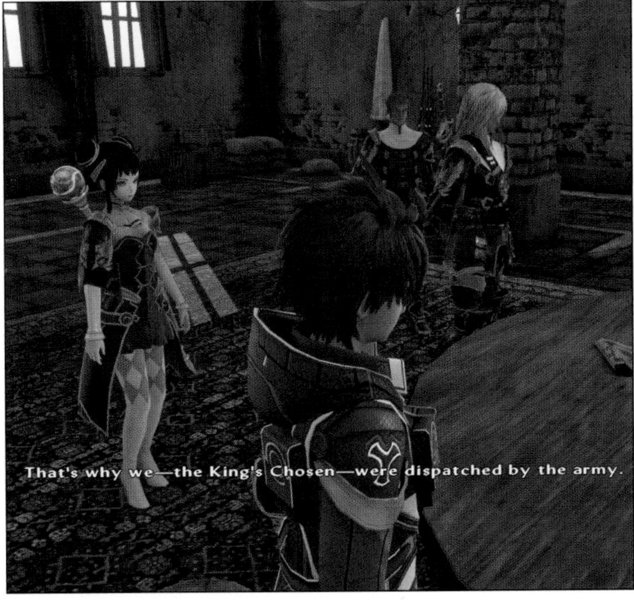

RANDOM PRIVATE ACTIONS

There's a separate set of Private Actions you can witness during your travels that doesn't involve activating the Private Action event whistle. These generally trigger in certain areas of towns as you walk by them, and some even reward you with role unlocks. When you rejoin with Victor, you might activate one by heading northeast toward the general goods store in Sthal. If you trigger the Leader by Proxy Private Action, you'll gain access to the Rival role.

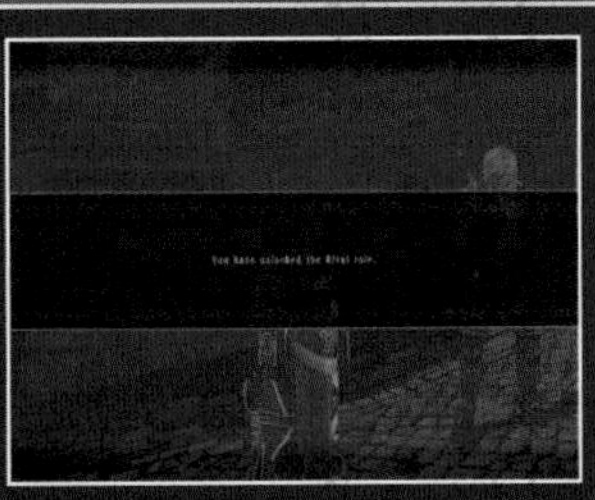

Head back out to the Dakaav Footpath, where you're introduced to a tutorial on Reserve Rushes. Read these carefully because the Reserve Rush system is an extremely useful mechanic to take advantage of. Not only can you unleash devastating combos on your enemies with Fidel and Victor, but you can flip a losing battle on its head by unleashing party-wide heals and raises (with Miki's Arcadia).

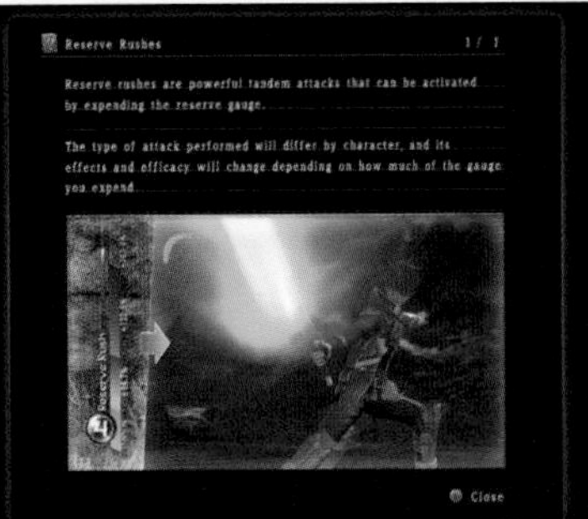

RESERVE RUSH SETTINGS

Now that you have Reserve Rushes unlocked, you can change its settings under the Settings menu. There are two settings that you might want to change, depending on your preferences.

The default scheme (labeled as Set Independently) keeps the Reserve Rush user separate from the currently controlled party member, which lets you command one of the AI-controlled characters to perform their Reserve Rush. The other setting (labeled as Character You Control Activates) simply uses the currently controlled party member as the Reserve Rush user. This method can make it slightly easier to perform Reserve Rush Cancel Combos. (You can still do them with the independent setting, but you just have to be mindful of which character it's set to.)

Performing a Reserve Rush Cancel Combo can be done by performing combos as you normally would, then tacking on a well-timed Reserve Rush at the end of it. A 200% Cancel Bonus Reserve Rush attack deals twice as much damage!

You can turn off the Reserve Rush Performances setting if you don't want to see the initial Reserve Rush cutscene animation.

After the tutorial, Victor introduces the party to his subordinates, Hana and Gunter. If you haven't saved your game yet, do so now at the save point across the bridge. Trek along north until Victor mentions his spymaster running a reconnaissance mission.

You'll meet Daks, who leads you to the Eitalon base. Follow him northbound. If you haven't looted the chest here in the middle of the area, there's an **Energy Bracelet** inside. Pick it up, and then follow Daks northwest into an alcove, where he opens a secret entrance to the Eitalon base.

EITALON EXTERMINATION

Deeper into the base, there's a chest containing **Holy Water x 2** if you look to your right. Follow the tunnel south, defeating any Eitalons and lizards in the way. The path eventually bends westward, where you'll encounter an empty enemy encampment.

Seems that there's another hidden door somewhere; the only way the Eitalons could have escaped is through an escape route. In the northwest area of the room, it looks like Miki's on to something. As she opens a secret passage, Eitalon troops flee from the scene.

Before chasing the Eitalons, if you enter a thin tunnel northeast of the empty encampment, you'll find two chests here: one locked and one unlocked. Open the unlocked one for a copy of **Swordsman's Manual V**, which you can use to unlock Death Palm for Fidel or Flying Guillotine for Victor. You can come back for the locked chest later when you have the Lock Picking specialty available. There are several Eitalon forces here, along with a new type of enemy, the Eitalon Spellslinger. Defeat these forces until you reach the waterfall at the end of the path.

Now go back to the hidden escape path and prepare to fight your way north!

Here, you face off with the Eitalon Leader. Before you engage, heal up if you need to.

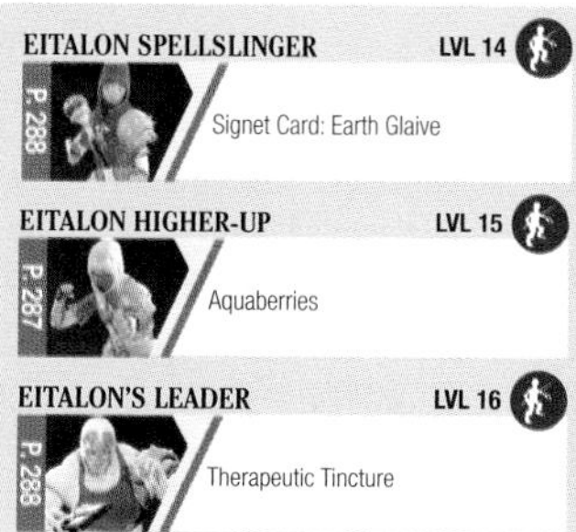

Enemy	Level	Page	Drop
EITALON SPELLSLINGER	LVL 14	P. 288	Signet Card: Earth Glaive
EITALON HIGHER-UP	LVL 15	P. 287	Aquaberries
EITALON'S LEADER	LVL 16	P. 288	Therapeutic Tincture

EITALON'S LEADER

LVL 16

The leader has a powerful firearm that you should avoid as best as possible. Keep moving, using your guard-dash to maneuver around while your other party members, including the ever-so-helpful King's Chosen, eliminate the Eitalon underlings. You can take control of either Fidel or Victor to flank Eitalon's Leader. He'll take aim and try to unleash his blasts at you, but if you sidestep often enough, you should make it difficult for him to land his shots.

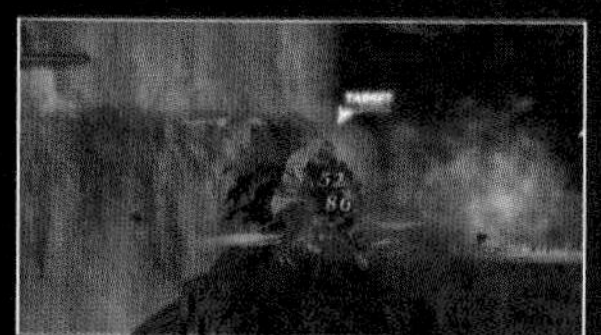

Once your team members cull the weaker Eitalons, they'll focus their efforts on the leader, and you'll eventually be successful in liberating your hometown from danger. Congratulations on a mission well executed! Now to head on home.

Head back to Sthal the same way you came. The mayor, Ted, and the other villagers welcome your return and rejoice when they hear of the good news. Additionally, the strange girl you saved earlier has regained consciousness, so go check on her. Aside from her name, she seems to have lost her memory of everything else. Maybe Fiore can help. Leave Fidel's House and make your way toward the Dakaav Footpath, where you'll run into Victor. He accepts the request to escort the party to Central Resulia in hopes of reuniting with Fiore. Go back to Fidel's House, where Miki, of course, insists on coming along.

After she gathers her things and the party leaves Fidel's home, a tutorial is displayed regarding Relia.

You can meet up with Victor again by the west exit, where he rejoins your party as an escort back to the capital. After your farewell to Ted, you can take the Dakaav Footpath back to Central Resulia. But first, go back to Fidel's House to rest up and save your game. When you leave the house, you can witness some available Private Actions.

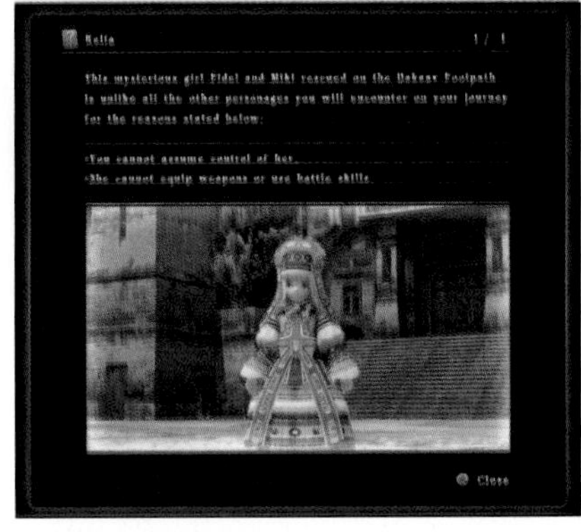

RELIA'S ROLES

As you've read in the tutorial, Relia can't be used in battle and won't attack enemies. However, she's still an immensely helpful member of the party. Like everyone else, she can equip up to four roles. Although combat-related roles are useless to her, she can make full use of quite a few supportive roles, such as those that boost EXP and SP gain or boost the party's morale. You might not have any of these roles this early in the game, but keep this in mind.

PRIVATE ACTIONS

STHAL
Miki's Hatred of Gambling
Eat Your Vegetables

CHAPTER 3

UNSOLVED MYSTERIES

PART 03

With the threat of the Eitalons nullified, Fidel and friends can focus their efforts on unraveling the inexplicable origins of Relia's enigmatic power and reuniting her with her parents.

MISSION: FINDING FIORE

Lady Brunelli seems to be their best bet for figuring out what to do next. The party sets out for another voyage across Faykreed to Fiore's last known location, Central Resulia.

Action Checklist

1. Optional: Take the long route back to the capital
2. Optional: Complete the Cathedral of Oblivion in the Coast of Minoz
3. Optional: Stop by Myiddok to upgrade equipment
4. Optional: Trigger Private Actions
5. Find Lady Brunelli in Central Resulia

Mission Walkthrough

With the young girl awake from her coma and the Eitalon threat extinguished, your new task is to find Fiore in hopes that she can help you solve the mystery that is Relia. Fiore should still be at the capital, so make your way back to Central Resulia.

THE SCENIC ROUTE

On your way back to the capital, you can either take the short route through the Dakaav Footpath, or the long route through the Passage on the Cliffs and the Coast of Minoz. Weaker enemies inhabit the west path through the Dakaav Footpath. However, the longer route through the Passage on the Cliffs has new tougher enemies, which means more potential EXP and SP gain for your party. Additionally, you can access an optional dungeon when you reach the Coast of Minoz. This walkthrough takes you to Myiddok via the long route.

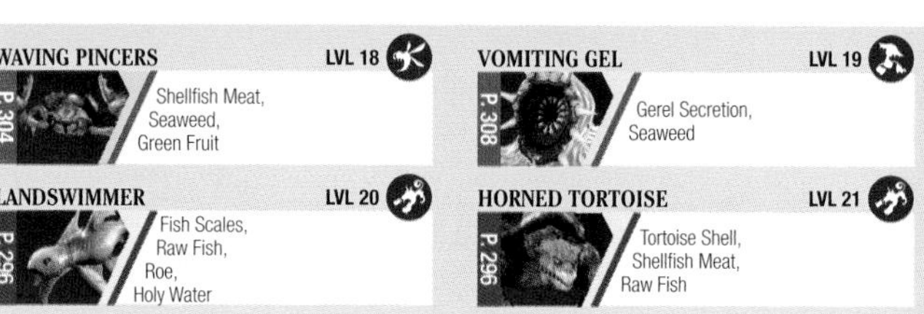

Exit Sthal from the east gate to traverse through the Passage on the Cliffs again. As you travel eastward, fight any enemies you encounter and collect any chests you missed the first time through this area (refer to the provided map preceding this text for chest locations). Foes here hover around Lv. 20; they might pose a nice challenge because your party will probably be around Lv. 17 or 18 at this point, if you have been following this walkthrough.

ENEMY EVOLUTION

As you progress through the story, monsters in certain areas are replaced with stronger ones. This lets you constantly improve your skills and overall power level, rewarding you with appropriate amounts of EXP and SP. For instance, the Lv. 1-5 enemies in the Passage on the Cliffs are now replaced by adversaries around Lv. 20 on your return trip to Central Resulia after eradicating the Eitalons.

This is a convenient time to harvest resources among the cliffs, especially if you've been putting SP into all three harvesting specialties.

When you reach the Coast of Minoz, there's an optional dungeon that has a *chance* to spawn in this location each time you enter the area. When you enter the area, press the OPTIONS/START button, and take a look at the map. If you see a warp point icon in the southeast area, then you can access the Cathedral of Oblivion. If it doesn't appear, simply exit back into the Passage on the Cliffs, and then re-enter the Coast of Minoz to check your map again. When it appears, fight your way to the dimensional rift to enter the dungeon.

At this point in the game, the cathedral instance dungeons have three rooms of enemies. Restore any lost HP and MP before you enter, then take on your first group of opponents.

Make sure that you're prepared for a few tough battles, particularly in the second and third rounds. The second-round enemies are Lv. 24 to 25.

Enemy	Level	Page	Drops
APPRENTICE SCUMBAG	LVL 19	P. 286	Scrap, Wooden Stick, Rivets, Iron
AXE BEAK	LVL 24	P. 299	Peryton Droppings, Giant Bird Feather, Common Eggs
STONE GOLEM	LVL 25	P. 314	Iron, Fire Gem

When you've dispatched them, get ready for a difficult boss battle in the third round.

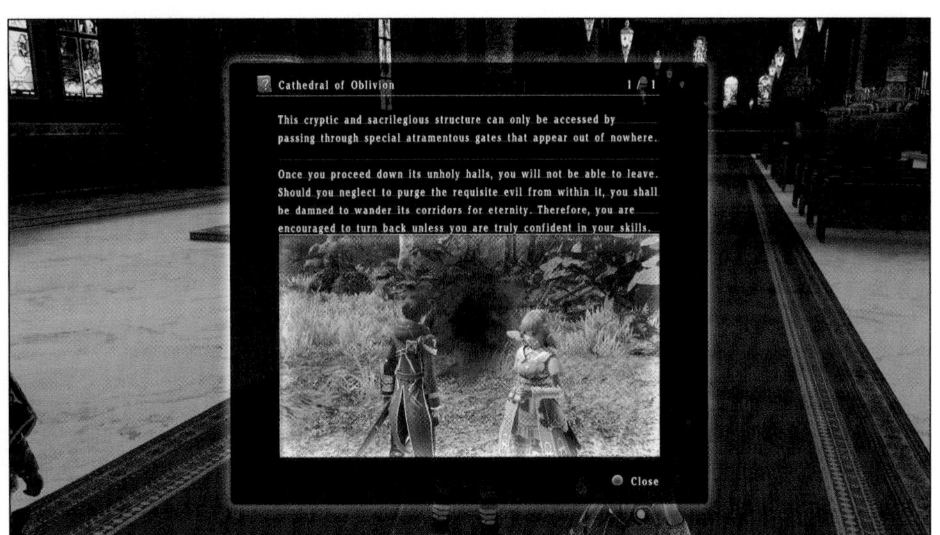

EYEBALONE

LV. 25

Eyebalone is a Corrupted-type flying monstrosity with eye beam attacks. It occasionally begins charging up an attack skill, telegraphing one of its powerful beams. You need to move out of the way as soon as you see it readying its laser, Dry Eye.

Its other eye beam attack is Eye of the Beholder, which can be difficult to avoid, but possible as long as you're mobile. It only targets a single member, so heal up its victim as quickly as you can.

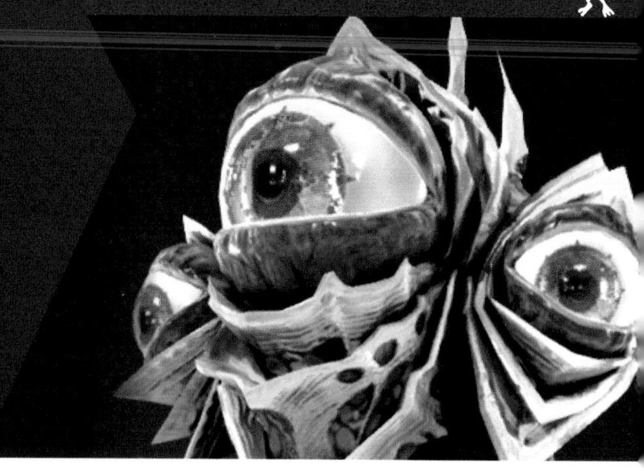

Eyebalone also performs a long-range spell called Radiant Lancer, usually targeted at Miki. If you open the battle menu when it's starting the attack, you can pause combat and take control of Miki to dodge the lance that falls from a warp portal above.

Its physical attack can be extremely annoying, as well. The eye slams into the ground and performs a whirling area-of-effect attack, damaging and breaking the guard of your nearby fighters with a chance of inflicting paralysis (which you can remedy with Basil).

If you see the abomination make a beeline toward Miki, open the battle menu and assume control of her to run away. She can't heal your party members if she's knocked out!

Don't be afraid to unleash your Reserve Rush abilities, especially at the end of a 175% Cancel Bonus combo. This technique does massive damage, especially with Fidel's Ethereal Blast.

Once you've defeated the monster, you're rewarded with an incredible amount of Fol. You can use it to go shopping later and upgrade equipment, or you can dabble in Item Creation if you've been investing in those specialty skills.

Just north of the boss is a chest that contains a **Blue Talisman**. Pick it up, and then exit the cathedral through the final warp point.

THE CATHEDRAL OF OBLIVION

You can access this optional dungeon crawl at any point in the game. The first iteration of the dungeon only has three rounds. As you progress through the story, the number of rooms per dungeon increases, with even more difficult monsters lurking about. Don't worry too much if you miss out on the first or second iterations of these dungeons; the chests in the earlier rounds are a constant, so you can pick them up later in the game if you missed entering an earlier instance of a cathedral.

Now, finish your trek to Myiddok to rest at the inn and save your progress. This is a good time to spend your money, so head over to **The Steel Serpent** to buy new equipment for your party. (Alternately, wait until you get to Central Resulia.)

SHOPS—MYIDDOK (UPDATE)

The Steel Serpent

ITEM	COST	TYPE
Arcane Crest	1500	Accessory
Energy Crest	1500	Accessory
Chainmail	700	Armor
Cuirass	850	Armor
Leather Armor	350	Armor
Signeturge's Garb	400	Armor
Traveler's Cloak	750	Armor
Broadsword	600	Weapon
Crescent Rod	800	Weapon
Falchion	1000	Weapon
Knight's Saber	600	Weapon
Longsword	200	Weapon
Pallasch	1100	Weapon
Petaline Wand	160	Weapon
Refulgent Orb	1250	Weapon
Rod of Jewels	400	Weapon

YOU WANT IT? I GOT IT

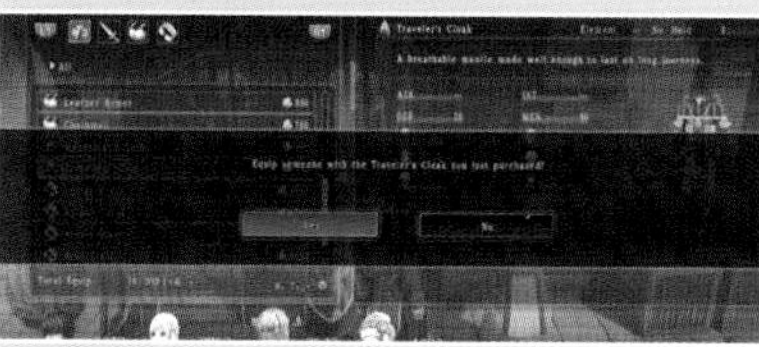

As you progress through the story, the various shopkeepers you encounter keep up with your needs, providing better equipment as you continue your journey. For instance, the shop here in Myiddok now carries upgrades for all of your members, so be sure to check stores you've already visited for new items.

MYIDDOK

Terrible Dining in Myiddok

That should be it for your rest stop. Now, exit from the west end of Myiddok and proceed into Central Resulia. Fight your way to the capital, and harvest any resources you come by. You can also run around to pick up any missed chests or to farm up EXP and SP from the new monsters here.

When you're ready, enter southeast Central Resulia from the plains. Head to the castle steps to view a short cutscene between Victor and a Resulian major. It seems that Lady Brunelli isn't here. Your new primary objective is to head to an outpost west of Resulia, toward the Trei'kuran border.

POISONOUS PLANTS

Some of the new plant-type enemies in this location can inflict poison on your party members, which persists even after battle. It's important to keep curatives on hand at all times. Items like Mint, Jasmine, and Chamomile can be lifesavers!

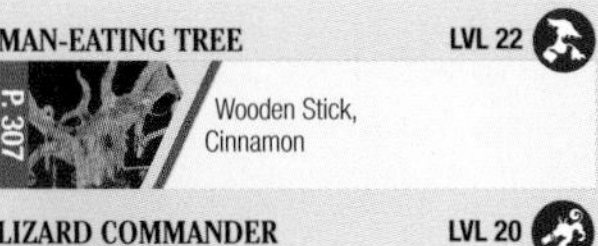

MAN-EATING TREE LVL 22
P. 307 — Wooden Stick, Cinnamon

LIZARD COMMANDER LVL 20
P. 297 — Lizardskin, Longsword, Blueberries

MANDRAGORA LVL 19
P. 306 — Nectar, Mint, Lemon

BLIGHTCAP LVL 20
P. 305 — Tasty Mushroom, Colorful Mushrooms, Wind Gem

APPRENTICE SCUMBAG LVL 19
P. 286 — Scrap, Wooden Stick, Rivets, Iron

TINYCAP LVL 18
P. 308 — Tasty Mushroom, Colorful Mushrooms, Wind Gem

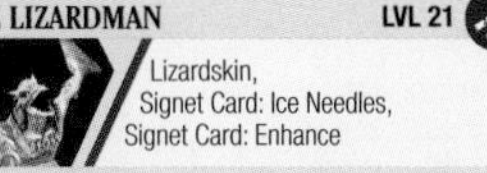

WISE LIZARDMAN LVL 21
P. 298 — Lizardskin, Signet Card: Ice Needles, Signet Card: Enhance

MISSION: REINFORCE THE RESULIAN ARMY

Upon reaching the castle steps, Fidel and his cohorts discover that Lady Brunelli has joined the Resulian efforts against the Trei'kuran military, which has breached the Sortevue border. If they want answers, they'll have to make their way to the Resulian encampment and join the fray.

OPTIONAL QUESTS

There are several new side quests at the bulletin board in Central Resulia that you can undertake before heading off. You can complete them now before heading to the Trei'kuran battlegrounds, or save them for later.

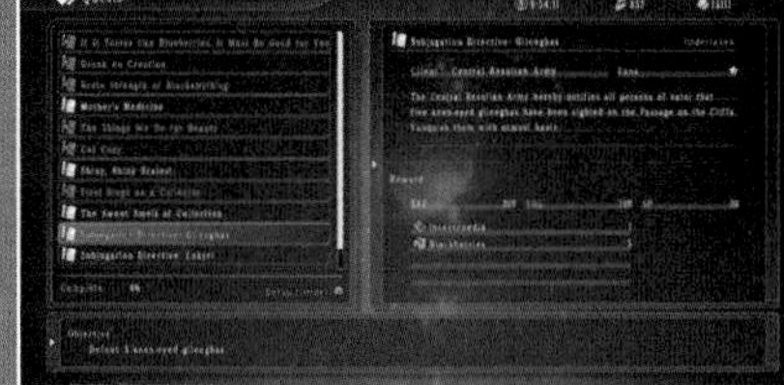

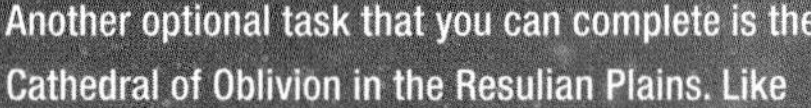

Another optional task that you can complete is the Cathedral of Oblivion in the Resulian Plains. Like the one in the Coast of Minoz, you can get it to spawn by repeatedly entering the Resulian Plains and checking for a warp point on the in-game map. The dimensional warp point is located near the center of the plains.

FOR THE COMPLETIONIST

If you want to take a break from the main storyline, here's a good point to do it. There are multiple optional quests you can pursue from the bulletin board, as well as a quest for Welch in Myiddok. However, these can be done at virtually any point in the game, so don't be afraid of missing out on side quests if you're itching to progress the story further.

If you travel back to Sthal and Myiddok (while completing the subjugation quests), you can get a few Private Actions and Welch quests out of the way. If you've completed her previous quests, Welch will have a new quest in her quest line called **The End of Welch's Laboratory!?**. It's recommended that you complete this quest early since it unlocks the Alchemy specialty. Alchemy allows you to create complex materials used in other crafting recipes.

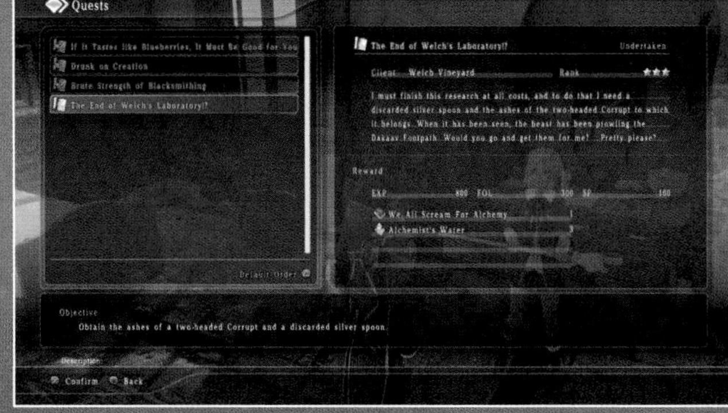

Action Checklist

1. Optional: Undertake and complete bulletin board quests
2. Optional: Complete the Cathedral of Oblivion in the Resulian Plains
3. Optional: Undertake and complete quests for Welch, the inventor
4. Optional: Trigger Private Actions
5. Meet with the Resulian army west of the Resulian Plains

Mission Walkthrough

Your primary objective here is to head westbound from Central Resulia, where Daril is leading war efforts against the intrusive Trei'kuran military. At this point, you can choose to complete several optional tasks before embarking on the excursion. When you're ready, make your way toward the Western Dakaav Tunnel.

WELCH THE END OF WELCH'S LABORATORY!?

This quest consists of two named monsters in the Dakaav Footpath that need to be slain.

TINAT OF THE DAWNING LIGHT LVL 22

One is on an island connected by two bridges in the northeastern region of the area.

UEN OF THE MIDNIGHT WAIL LVL 22

The other is hidden in the former Eitalon base, where you defeated the Eitalon's Leader. Each of these mini bosses drops a key item that Welch requires from you.

SUBJUGATION DIRECTIVES

Side quests prefixed with "Subjugation Directive:" and "Open Season on" are monster-hunting quests. These monsters can always be found in the designated areas if you have undertaken the quest. If you save these quests for later, you won't have to worry about your target enemies not spawning, since they'll always be present while the quest is active.

TREASURE HUNTER

The **Shiny, Shiny Scales!** bulletin board quest rewards you with the Treasure Sense specialty. This skill populates your minimap with icons of any nearby chests, including locked ones. It's an invaluable tool for hunting loot!

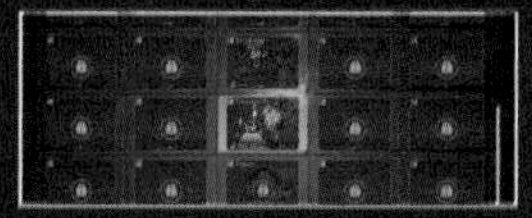

MISSING IN ACTION

Although most Private Actions are queued and can be viewed at a later time, you might want to trigger them as soon as you see them listed here, since your party members tend to cycle in and out throughout the story.

SIDE QUESTS

CENTRAL RESULIA
Mother's Medicine
Cat Cozy
Shiny, Shiny Scales!
The Sweet Smell of Collection
Subjugation Directive: Gileeghas
Subjugation Directive: Lnkyri
Give Back that Bonus
Batting 1.000 Against Luck Suckers

WELCH'S LABORATORY
The End of Welch's Laboratory!?

PRIVATE ACTIONS

CENTRAL RESULIA
The Phantom Malko

Why Signeturgy?
Another Chance at Life
The ABCs of Dining in Resulia
Malko Strikes Back
A New Hopeless Malko

MYIDDOK
Fidel and Fighting Styles

STHAL
Miki's Hatred of Frogs
Into the Wild with Fidel

Miki's Hatred of Surprises

MILITARY SERVICE

When you're ready to take on the Trei'kuran forces, take the southwest exit from Central Resulia. This gate leads you to the western section of the Resulian Plains, which is divided by a tall cliff. You can drop down the cliff to get to the east half, but the only way back up is through Central Resulia's southeast entrance.

Head toward the red star marked on your map to trigger a cutscene where Victor departs from the party to search for the rest of the King's Chosen.

A roaring battle can be heard in the distance. Enter the valley, and help the Resulian troops fend off the Trei'kuran soldiers!

Deeper into the valley, you'll meet up with Fidel's father, Daril, and the King's Chosen. There's a chest containing **Physical Stimulant x 2** in a corner, southwest of where you find Daril. Save one of these curatives for the **Mother's Medicine** quest.

Fight your way westward until you run into a familiar signeturge casting luminescent spells at the Trei'kuran enemies. Fiore immediately rejoins the party—a welcome addition. As the situation becomes dire, with hordes of Trei'kuran troops rushing into the battle, Relia activates her time-freezing powers for the second time, saving the Resulian army from further casualties. Smash the frozen interlopers to end the battle, forcing the rest of their reinforcements to retreat.

MISSION: ONWARD TO SANTEROULE

While Relia recovers from the exhaustion caused by the use of her heroic powers, Fiore examines the girl. She concludes that it's signeturgy, but none that she's ever seen. She suggests there's someone even more qualified than her who can help solve the mystery, and that someone resides in the capital of Langdauq. Daril, believing Relia to be an answer to the war, asks Fidel to escort Fiore and Relia to Santeroule.

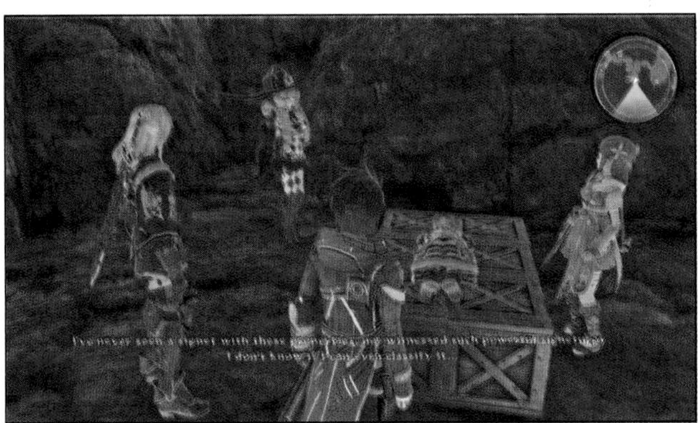

Action Checklist

1. Optional: Undertake and complete side quests
2. Optional: Begin the **Find Ruddle!** quest
3. Optional: Accept the **Grand Designs** quest from Welch
4. Travel east to Myiddok and sleep at the inn
5. Traverse the West of the Eastern Eihieds zone

Mission Walkthrough

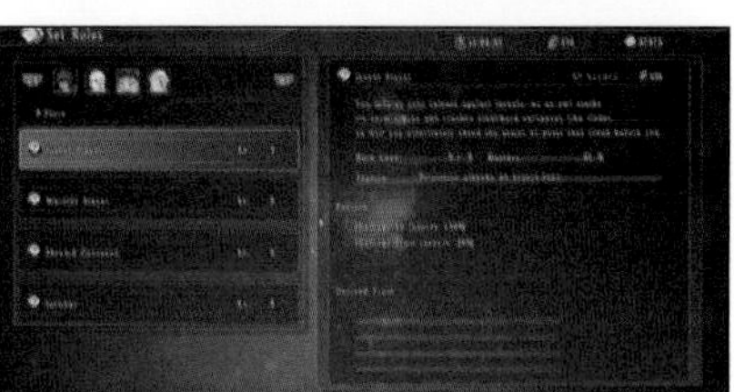

After some time, Relia wakes up from her signeturgy-induced coma. Your next mission is to take Relia and Fiore to Santeroule, where Fiore believes a genius scholar of signeturgy can identify the nature of Relia's power.

EASTBOUND

You've lost some physical firepower with Victor leaving the party, but you've gained an excellent spell-caster in Fiore. Make sure to equip her with a new set of roles, including Shrewd Overseer and Invoker. These roles significantly enhance offensive-based signeturgical attacks.

Before returning east, venture west and farther into the valley to open a chest with **Coal** in it. Turn around and head back to Central Resulia to rest up and save your progress.

Remember those Physical Stimulants that you picked up earlier? You can turn one in at the bulletin board for the **Mother's Medicine** quest. In return, you're rewarded with an Energy Amulet—an accessory that boosts max HP by 500! There are a few more side quests here you can undertake, as well.

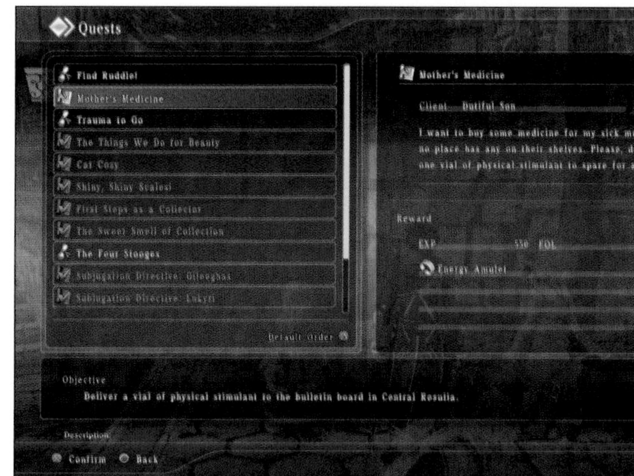

A notable quest to accept here is **Find Ruddle!**. It's the first quest in a series of quests throughout the game. When the entire quest line is completed, an invaluable merchant becomes available. However, this manhunt can be a serious pain, considering Ruddle's elusiveness.

OPTIONAL TASKS

WHERE'S RUDDLE?

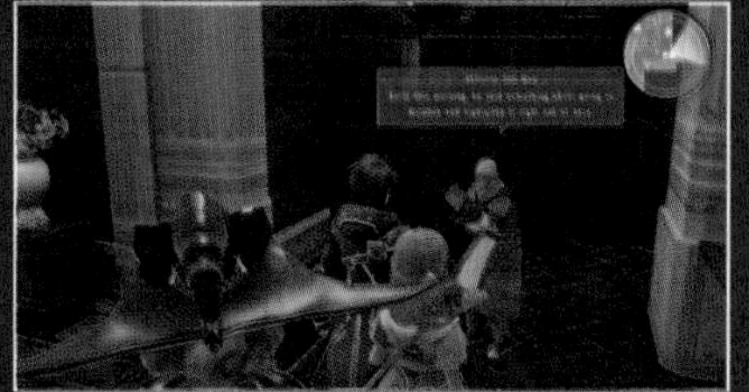

The Ruddle quest line is a bit different than the other bulletin board quests you're given. For whatever reason, someone is always looking for this particular individual. To make things more difficult, he has a problem with staying still! The first clue to finding Ruddle lies within the Central Resulian inn, Ye Grand Ole Castle of Comfort. When someone has information about Ruddle, you'll see a yellow star on your minimap. Talk to these people to find out what Ruddle's been up to and where he's going, then follow his trail.

RECON MADE EASY

Completing the **Subjugation Directive: Dek** side quest rewards you with the Lookout specialty. When unlocked, this specialty displays enemy positions on your minimap. It's an exceptionally convenient tool to have as you explore new areas, allowing you to plan ahead for preemptive attacks.

SIDE QUESTS

CENTRAL RESULIA
Find Ruddle!
Trauma to Go
The Four Stooges
Subjugation Directive: Dek

WELCH'S LABORATORY
Grand Designs

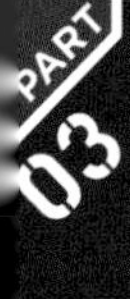

When you're ready for the expedition to Santeroule, make your way to Myiddok. As you approach the trade city, Fiore mentions an arduous mountain climb ahead and insists that the party takes a moment to rest in Myiddok.

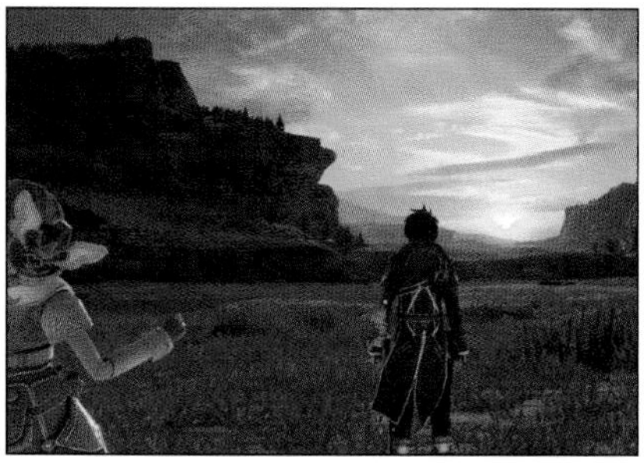

If you're caught up in Welch's crafting quest line, you can accept a new one before you visit the inn. With Fiore in the party, you can undertake **Grand Designs**.

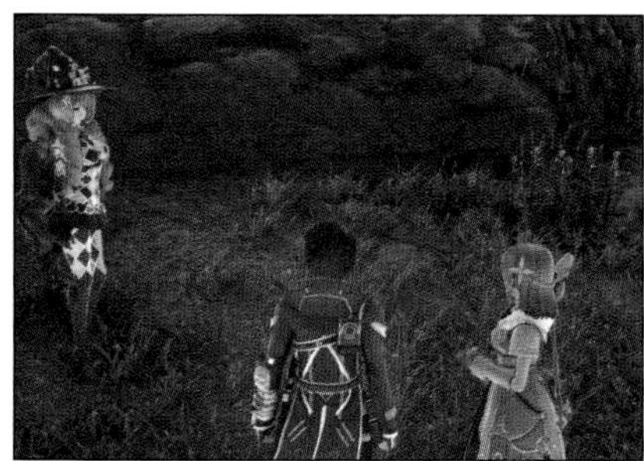

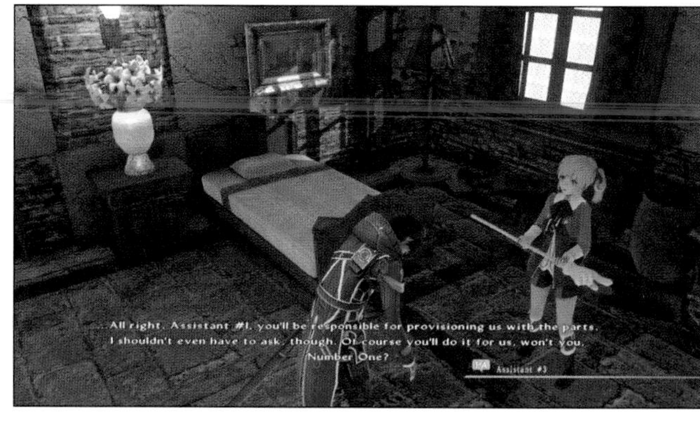

Unfortunately, most side quests are blocked off for now; the Dakaav Footpath and Coast of Minoz are inaccessible until you finish your business in Santeroule.

...All right. Assistant #1, you'll be responsible for provisioning us with the parts.
I shouldn't even have to ask, though. Of course you'll do it for us, won't you, Number One?

In the meantime, enter Myiddok and rest up at the inn, courtesy of Fiore. This triggers a cutscene with some mysterious men attempting to ambush the crew. The party escapes through the window, and you're forced to exit to the east of Myiddok. Seems like your assailants are connected to the two spacemen who were trying to take Relia.

When we first met Relia, there were two guys with her...

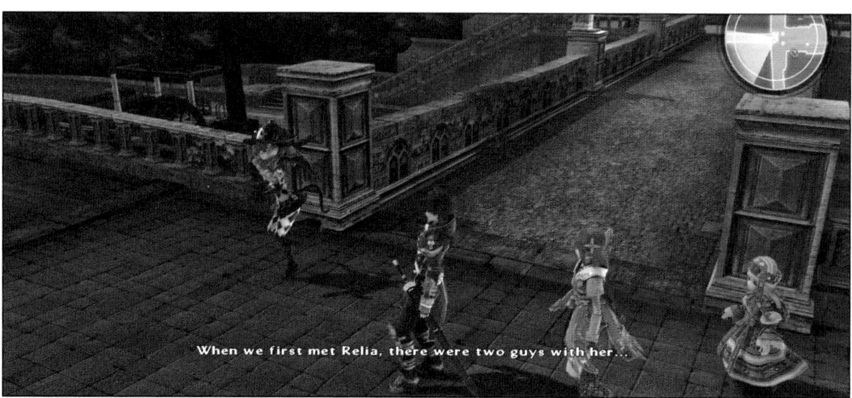

ASCEND THE MOUNTAIN

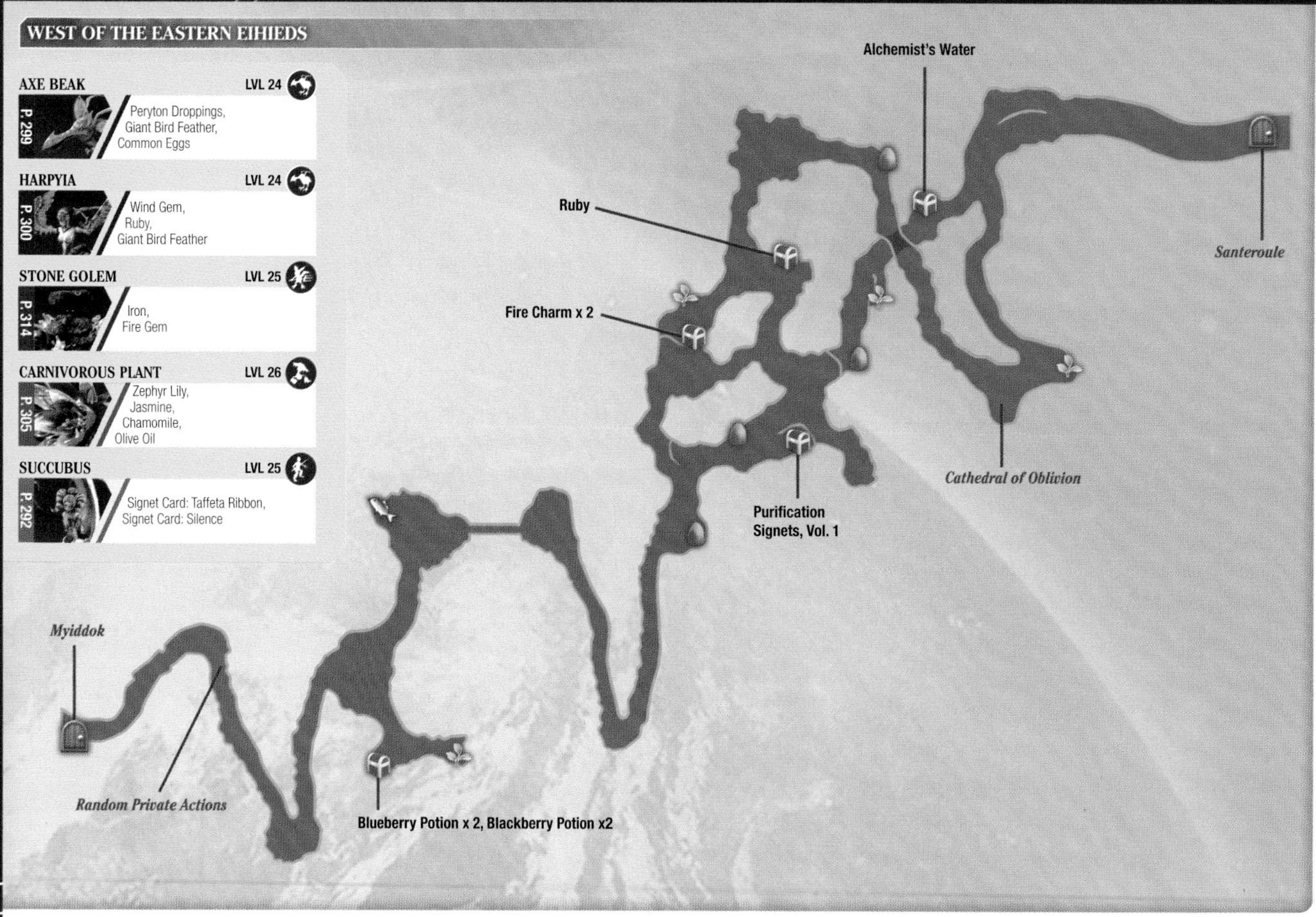

WEST OF THE EASTERN EIHIEDS
AXE BEAK LVL 24
P 299
Peryton Droppings, Giant Bird Feather, Common Eggs
HARPYIA LVL 24
P 300
Wind Gem, Ruby, Giant Bird Feather
STONE GOLEM LVL 25
P 314
Iron, Fire Gem
CARNIVOROUS PLANT LVL 26
P 305
Zephyr Lily, Jasmine, Chamomile, Olive Oil
SUCCUBUS LVL 25
P 292
Signet Card: Taffeta Ribbon, Signet Card: Silence
Alchemist's Water
Ruby
Santeroule
Fire Charm x 2
Cathedral of Oblivion
Purification Signets, Vol. 1
Myiddok
Random Private Actions
Blueberry Potion x 2, Blackberry Potion x2

Climb the linear trail up the mountain until you reach a small path leading to an inlet to the south. You can find a chest containing **Blueberry Potion x 2** and **Blackberry Potion x 2** in the inlet, along with a harvest point nearby. Keep hiking up the mountain, and the party will conclude that the men have stopped chasing them.

Cross the bridge and continue climbing the steep mountain. When you reach the center of the area, there's a chest containing a copy of **Purification Signets, Vol. 1** inside. Grab it, and then just east of the chest, find a restoration point, along with a save point. Fill up your HP and MP and save your progress.

YOU GET A ROLE. YOU GET A ROLE. EVERYONE GETS A ROLE!

Choosing what to spend your SP on can be a difficult decision because there are so many SP-related unlockables. If you want to unlock the greatest number of roles, it's best to level up as many roles as you can to at least Lv. 3. This is a common break point for unlocking more advanced roles, giving you many more options, so it's okay to spread your SP thin. Eventually, you'll have seven party members who can each equip four roles, so you'll want to at least be able to fill each role slot.

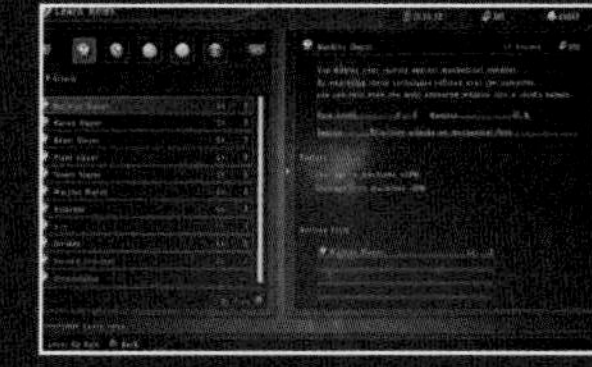

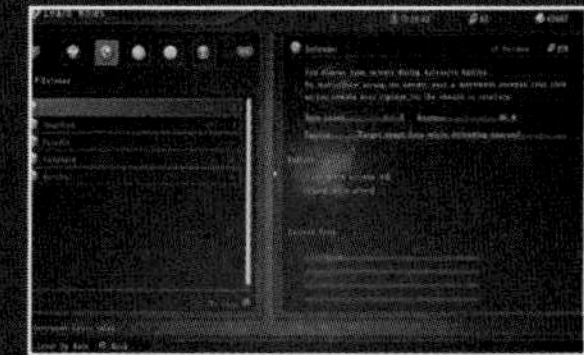

From the save and restoration points, head north until you reach a chest with a **Ruby** in it. From there, if you go west and into an alcove to the south, there's a harvest point and a chest with **Fire Charm x 2** waiting for you. Now, keep going north to trigger a cutscene—three of the mysterious men teleport in to ambush the group yet again! When the battle starts, you won't be able to damage them, just like in your first encounter with these spacemen.

However, a pair of strangers (albeit, familiar ones) arrives to save the day. The woman seems to have some sort of device that disables the enemies' force fields. The fight is now fair since you're able to whittle down their HP. These guys are still quite powerful, though, due to their advanced weaponry and high amount of health. Thankfully, your new friends join the fight by your side.

Focus on the mysterious men one by one, making sure they're not ganging up on Miki. If you see them going after her, peel them off of her using Fidel's Double Slash attack skill. When you're victorious, a cutscene triggers. Your two saviors introduce themselves as Emmerson and Anne, and they ask to come along with the group to Santeroule. They seem to be hiding something from the party… nevertheless, they're lifesavers.

EMMERSON AND ANNE

Your two new party members are exceptional combatants. Emmerson specializes in ranged attacks with his crossbow (an interesting choice of weapon, considering what kind of technology you've seen the two possess). Anne is an expert in martial arts, so she prefers fighting with her fists in close-quarters combat.

Make sure to spread out your combat roles among these two accordingly. For example, you can opt to equip more defensive roles on Fidel and more offensive ones on Emmerson and Anne.

Once you've set up Emmerson and Anne's roles, keep following the path east, where you'll get to witness a beautiful view of Santeroule.

Continue hiking down the mountain until you reach a path that bends west. Before you take the west trail, open the chest that's against the north wall to pick up a bottle of **Alchemist's Water**. Continue down that path to collect some resources from a harvest point and an excavation node if you have these specialties unlocked.

You can now take the north path, leading you downhill into Santeroule.

PART 03

CHAPTER 4

INTERGALACTIC PLANETARY

As Miki marvels at the sight of the incredible signeturgical symbols decorating the city of Santeroule, Fiore leads the party into the Royal Institute of Signetary Studies. Hopefully, they will find answers to Relia's mysterious power here.

MISSION: THE ANCIENT INSTITUTE

SANTEROULE

Being a renowned signeturge herself, Fiore has no answers to Relia's situation. However, she introduces the party to someone who might—a child prodigy within the Royal Institute of Signetary Studies.

Action Checklist

1. Follow Fiore into the Royal Institute of Signetary Studies
2. Talk to Ceisus
3. Optional: Undertake side quests
4. Optional: Trigger Private Actions
5. Optional: Upgrade equipment
6. Traverse North of the Eastern Eihieds
7. Investigate the Ancient Institute

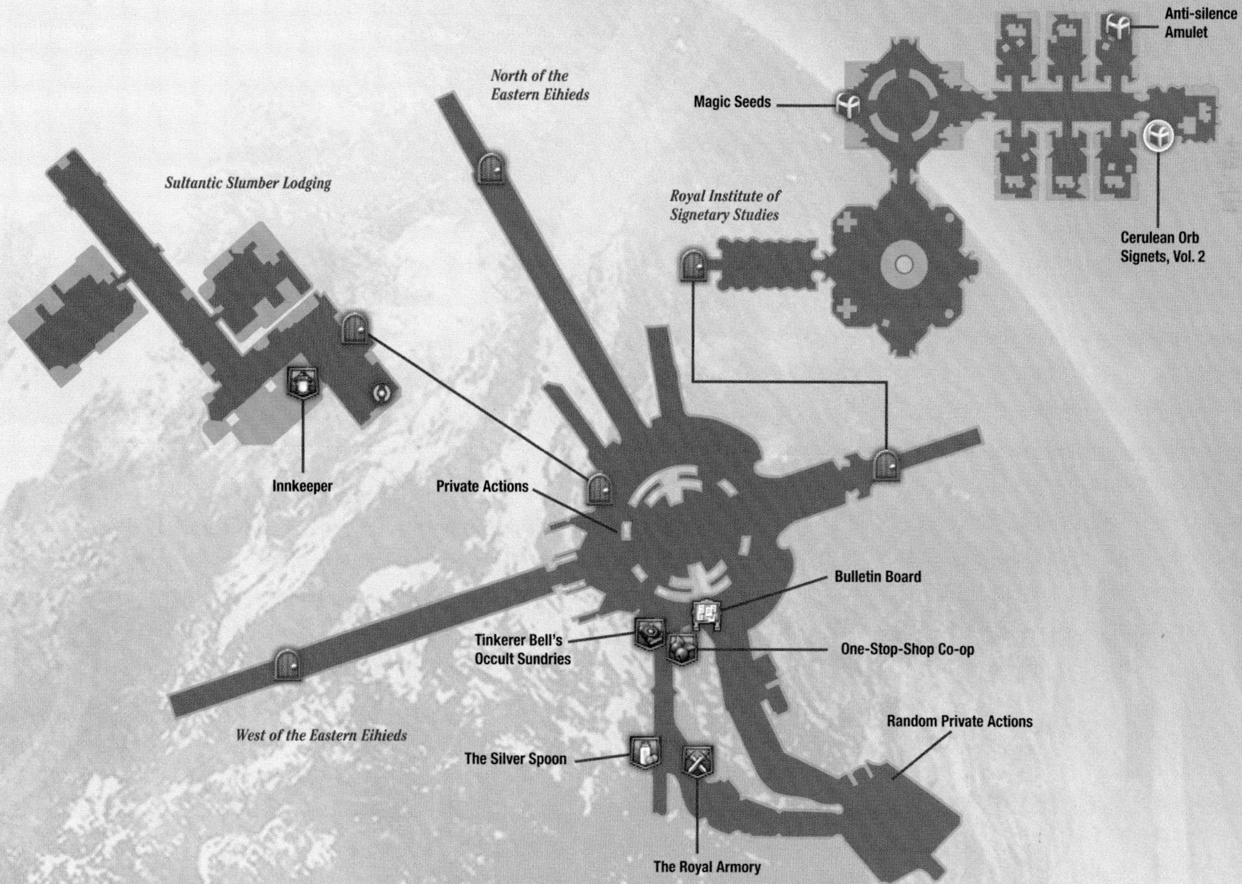

Anti-silence Amulet
Magic Seeds
North of the Eastern Eihieds
Sultantic Slumber Lodging
Royal Institute of Signetary Studies
Cerulean Orb Signets, Vol. 2
Innkeeper
Private Actions
Bulletin Board
Tinkerer Bell's Occult Sundries
One-Stop-Shop Co-op
Random Private Actions
West of the Eastern Eihieds
The Silver Spoon
The Royal Armory

Mission Walkthrough

This mission requires you to delve deeper into the source of Relia's mysterious powers. Fiore escorts you to meet Santeroule's top signeturgical scholar. He should have a lead for you to follow.

Shops

Tinkerer Bell's Occult Sundries

ITEM	COST	TYPE
Empty Bottle	120	Material
Gunpowder	240	Material
Mercury	600	Material
Signet Card	300	Material
Signet Card: Earth Glaive	800	Usable
Signet Card: Enhance	800	Usable
Signet Card: Enlighten	800	Usable
Signet Card: Enshelter	800	Usable
Signet Card: Faerie Healing	1500	Usable
Signet Card: Fire Bolt	800	Usable
Signet Card: Healing	400	Usable
Signet Card: Ice Needles	800	Usable
Signet Card: Reflection	800	Usable
Signet Card: Sacred Pain	800	Usable
Signet Card: Wind Blade	800	Usable

The Silver Spoon

ITEM	COST	TYPE
Common Eggs	90	Food
Fresh Vegetables	180	Food
Lemon	90	Food
Nectar	120	Food
Prehistoric Meat	180	Food
Spring Water	240	Food
Tomato	240	Food
Well-Aged Cheese	360	Food
Whole Milk	360	Food
Olive Oil	240	Material
Vanilla Beans	360	Material
Wheat Flower	240	Material

The Royal Armory

ITEM	COST	TYPE
Acuity Bracelet	10000	Accessory
Arcane Bracelet	5000	Accessory
Attack Bracelet	10000	Accessory
Energy Bracelet	5000	Accessory
Fortitude Bracelet	10000	Accessory
Mind Bracelet	10000	Accessory
Banded Mail	1400	Armor
Chainmail	700	Armor
Crest Mail	1050	Armor
Crest Robe	1150	Armor
Cuirass	850	Armor
Traveler's Cloak	750	Armor
Blessed Sword	1500	Weapon
Crescent Rod	800	Weapon
Falchion	1000	Weapon
Gelid Orb	1850	Weapon
Magus Staff	1200	Weapon
Metal Knuckles	1350	Weapon
Pallasch	1100	Weapon
Refulgent Orb	1250	Weapon
Short Crossbow	1500	Weapon

One-Stop-Shop Co-op

ITEM	COST	TYPE
Basil	90	Usable
Blackberries	80	Usable
Blueberries	40	Usable
Chamomile	180	Usable
Cinnamon	300	Usable
Fresh Sage	160	Usable
Jasmine	90	Usable
Lavender	300	Usable
Mint	90	Usable

OPTIONAL

SIDE-TRACKED

At this point in the game, there are many new side quests and Private Actions available from the various towns you've traveled to. However, a few will be difficult to finish since some of the collection items aren't easily accessible. Also, some quests ask you to go to areas that you don't yet have access to.

It's highly recommended that you progress through the story more until a more convenient method of travel becomes available so that backtracking is less of an issue.

But, if you are going to backtrack, a great quest to get out of the way is **Find Ruddle!**.

The reward for finishing it is the Altruist role, which significantly enhances SP gain at the cost of EXP.

SIDE QUESTS

SANTEROULE
Revenge is a Dish Best Served Burnt
Collecting the Metal that Plays Second Fiddle
Open Season on Ostharks
Open Season on Hados

CENTRAL RESULIA
Birthday Boy
Collection: The Cure for Youthful Fears
Subjugation Directive: Gargans
Subjugation Directive: Magvors
Corruption of the Land
Wanted: The Skoudde Brothers
By the Skin of His False Teeth
Wanted: Chaos Corpse Corporals

PRIVATE ACTIONS

SANTEROULE
Signeturgical Tools
Caught in the Act
The Daily Lives of Signeturgical Researchers
Family Ties
Who's Most Popular?
Spicy or Sweet?

MYIDDOK
Warm Places
Here, Kitty, Kitty
Watching Miki
It's the Thought that Counts
Miki the Patissiere

PRIVATE ACTIONS

CENTRAL RESULIA
Technologically-Advanced Country Mouse
Are You My Friend?
Mundane Magic Trick
Anne's Priorities
Has Love Blossomed?
Love Is in the Hair?

STHAL
Unsupported Assumption
You Can Only Save One
Fun with Frogs
The Benefit of Being a Snake
Fidel's Angels
Watching Fidel
Barrage of Questions
Mom and Dad
Someone

PRIVATE ACTION PROGRESS

Several of the Private Actions above are only unlocked when other Private Actions in other towns are triggered. You can view them now if you want to make a round between towns or take a tour before you return to Central Resulia later.

MEET CEISUS, SIGNETURGICAL PRODIGY

Follow Fiore into the Royal Institute of Signetary Studies. She'll give you a tour of the extraordinary establishment. Meanwhile, Emmerson and Anne whisper to each other, seemingly amazed by the advanced technology they're bearing witness to.

As you follow Fiore, you'll enter a room with shelves placed in a circular pattern. There's a chest containing **Magic Seeds** lying at the west end. Grab the seeds, and continue following Fiore east into a hallway. In the room at the end of the hall, you're introduced to Ceisus, Santeroule's most talented scholar.

Seems like even the child prodigy is bewildered by Relia's form of signeturgy. Nevertheless, he suggests that the party should check the archaic documents held within the Ancient Institute that may hold answers to Relia's mysterious signets. Before you leave the Royal Institute of Signetary Studies, when leaving Ceisus's office, immediately turn right to go north, find an **Anti-silence Amulet**.

Head back out to Santeroule. You can now rest at the inn and save your progress. Additionally, Santeroule is one of three quest hubs with a bulletin board. You can pick up a few side quests and view any available Private Actions here if you want to get some optional objectives out of the way. If you've been diligent in slaying enemies on your way up the mountain, you might have excess cash to spend on upgrading your equipment and buying items; feel free to go shopping.

ANSWERS IN THE ANCIENT INSTITUTE

Once you're all set to go, exit Santeroule from the north gate, to North of the Eastern Eihieds.

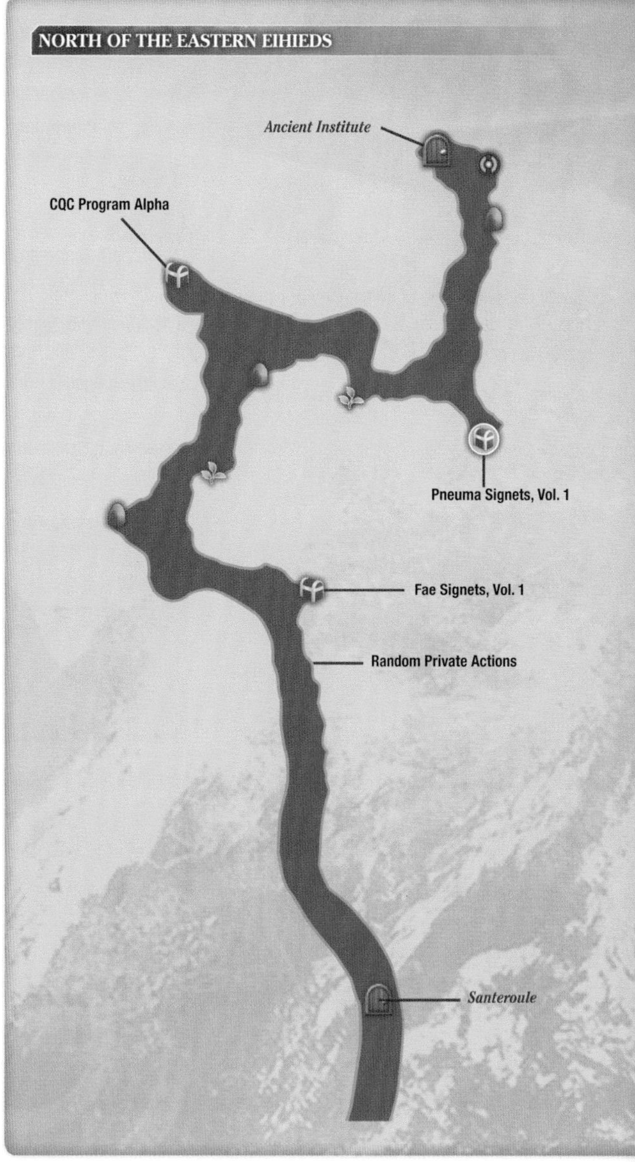

Enemy	Level	Page	Drops
AXE BEAK	LVL 24	P. 299	Peryton Droppings, Giant Bird Feather, Common Eggs
HARPYIA	LVL 24	P. 300	Wind Gem, Ruby, Giant Bird Feather
STONE GOLEM	LVL 25	P. 314	Iron, Fire Gem
CARNIVOROUS PLANT	LVL 26	P. 305	Zephyr Lily, Jasmine, Chamomile, Olive Oil
DEMON IMP	LVL 27	P. 310	Demon's Tail, Wolf Fang, Signet Card
THUNDERSTRUCK OSTHARK	LVL 28	P. 293	Scrap, Wooden Stick, Rivets, Iron

Your destination from here is straightforward. Take the linear path north until the road takes a left turn. Before the turn, there's a chest with a copy of the **Fae Signets, Vol. 1** book in it. This is one of Miki's best healing spells, so make sure to have her read it right away (through the Learn Battle Skills menu).

Follow the trail west and then north, while battling any enemies in your way. There are a couple of harvest points in the area, too. When you reach the northwest portion of the map, you find a chest containing a disk copy of **CQC Program Alpha**.

If you accepted the Open Season on Ostharks quest ("Open Season" quests are just like Central Resulia's "Subjugation Directives" quests), you'll find Thunderstruck Ostharks on your way to the Ancient Institute. Defeat any you see to complete the quest.

Continue eastward until you see a locked chest. You won't be able to open it yet, but make sure to come back for it later once you've gained the Lock Picking specialty. Now, go north and save your game at the save point, and then enter the Ancient Institute. With any luck, you'll finally get some answers.

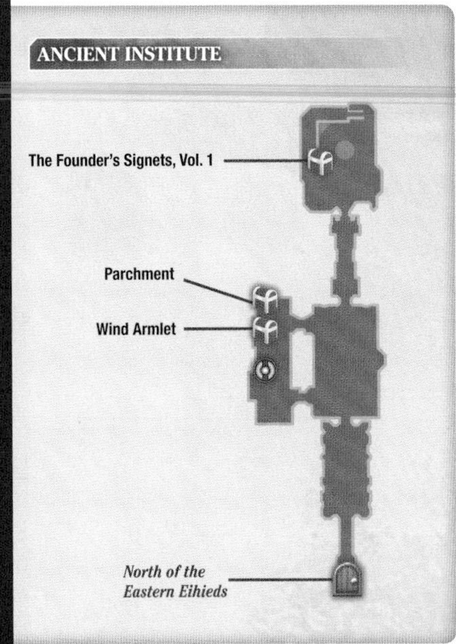

Inside the institute, continue following Fiore up until the second automatic door. You can find a couple of chests in the room to the left, by a save point. Grab the piece of **Parchment** and a **Wind Armlet**, then catch up with Fiore to the north.

Entering the northernmost room triggers a cutscene with Relia. The area seems to have a negative effect on her, but it also sparks a memory recollection. She mentions sand and a laboratory—maybe a clue about her origins. Emmerson deduces that Relia may be talking about dunes in Trei'kur. Since the government has sanctioned off Trei'kur, the party must request help from Victor in Central Resulia.

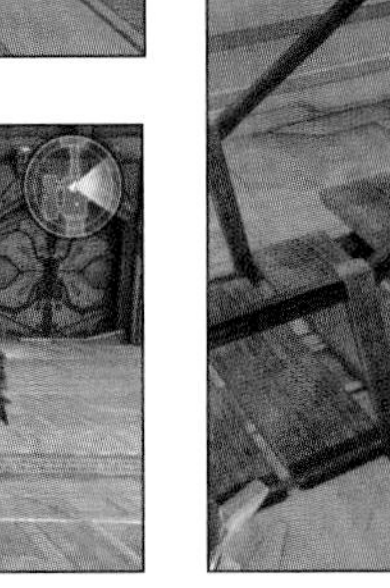

After the cutscene, open the chest in the room. Its contents consist of **The Founder's Signets, Vol. 1** book. Turn around and head back to Santeroule the way you came.

MISSION: SEEK OUT VICTOR

While they don't have all of the answers, Fidel and company have gained some ground, since Relia now recalls growing up in a sandy area. Maybe her parents were scientists in Trei'kur? But before they can cross the border, the party needs to catch up with Victor at Castle Bariff.

Action Checklist

1. Optional: Trigger additional Private Actions
2. Optional: Clear the Cathedral of Oblivion in West of the Eastern Eihieds
3. Optional: Stop at Myiddok to complete Welch quests and view Private Actions
4. Optional: Stop by Sthal to trigger Private Actions, visit the Infirmary (**Find Ruddle!**), and complete any outstanding quests
5. Return to Central Resulia
6. Optional: Upgrade equipment
7. Optional: Complete **Find Ruddle!**
8. Find Victor at the Castle Bariff steps
9. Defend Castle Bariff

Mission Walkthrough

Your primary goal now is to find Victor in Central Resulia to get permission to cross into Trei'kuran territory. Finish up any optional tasks in the area and then leave Santeroule, making your descent down the mountain back to Myiddok.

SIDE QUESTS

WELCH'S LABORATORY
Grand Designs
Happy Fun Bunny Time

PRIVATE ACTIONS

SANTEROULE
From Prodigious to Pedestrian
One Has Smarm, the Other Charm
Fidel as a Kid
Figment of Anne's Imagination
Bird Watching

OPTIONAL

CULINARY CLOUT

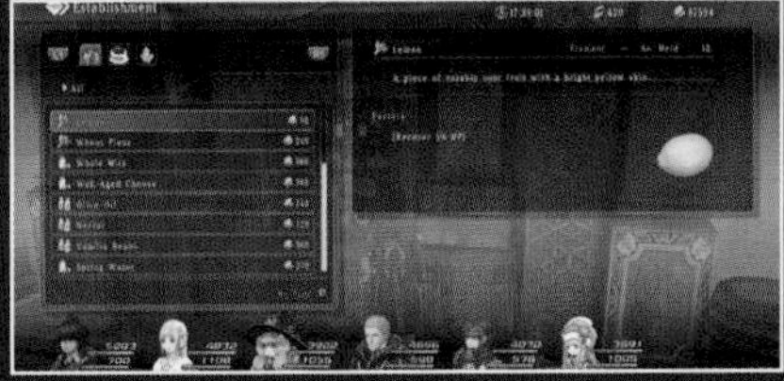

If there's any one crafting specialty to spend SP on early in the game, it's Cooking. Eating food gives your *entire* party a temporary buff over a certain amount of battles. Check out the grocery stores in various towns and purchase any ingredients you need to make your favorite foods so you'll have access to unique bonuses while you're out exploring.

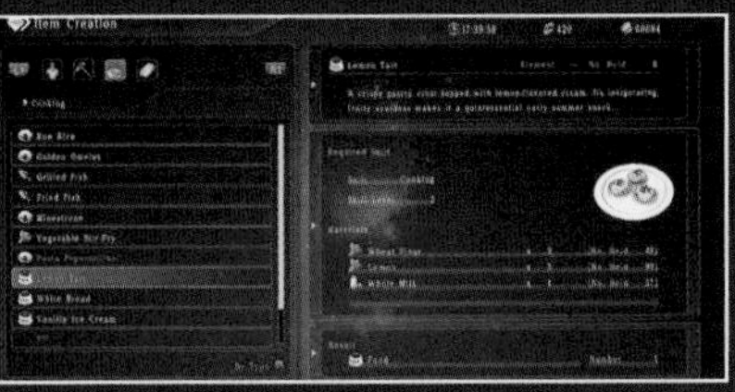

For instance, **The Upper Crust Gourmet Foods** in Central Resulia and **The Silver Spoon** in Santeroule carry all of the ingredients you need to create **Lemon Tarts.** This food item gives you +20% EXP earned in battle over three battles. You can easily bake up a stack of 20 of these, expediting level-ups while you're out exploring.

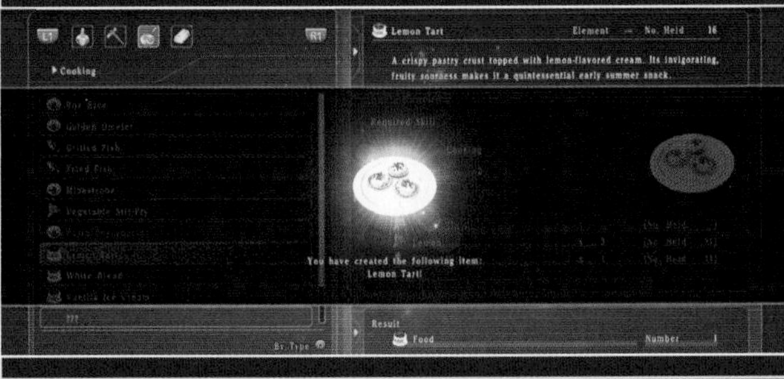

MONSTER MASH

If you're fortunate enough to have gathered five chunks of **Silver** at this point (which can be mined from excavation nodes in West of the Eastern Eihieds), you can turn them in during the **Collecting the Metal that Plays Second Fiddle** quest to obtain the Ocarina specialty. This skill lets you respawn all monsters in an area, allowing you to repeatedly defeat them for EXP, SP, and item drops.

This is particularly useful for gathering quest items. Look through the in-game bestiary (or the bestiary provided in the encyclopedia portion of this guide) to see which items you need for a given quest. Find the foe and defeat it, then go to your Specialties menu and activate the Ocarina skill (default ◉ button). The monsters you've just defeated will conveniently return, allowing you to quickly find the items that you need.

MAJOR MINER

You might have noticed that many quests involve gathering materials from harvest points. Whenever you interact with a resource point, there's only a chance of actually collecting material from it. To repopulate resource nodes, all you need to do is sleep at an inn. For example, if you're looking for chunks of **Silver** from the mining points in West of the Eastern Eihieds, go through and mine all of the excavation points, sleep in Santeroule or Myiddok, and then return to the area. You'll find that all of the resource points are back up and ready to be farmed!

RETURN TO RESULIA

If you cleared the Private Actions in Santeroule before visiting the Ancient Institute, you can trigger a few more of these special events.

Once you're all set to go, return to West of the Eastern Eihieds. There's a Cathedral of Oblivion warp point here, just off the south path from Santeroule. As before, if you want to get it to spawn, enter the area and check your map with the OPTIONS/START button. If it doesn't appear on the map, return to Santeroule and re-enter West of the Eastern Eihieds until it does.

Now, make your way back down the mountain and enter Myiddok. There are a couple of Private Actions to view here. If you've been vigilantly completing Welch quests, you can finish a few more while you're here, too.

PRIVATE ACTIONS

MYIDDOK
Can't Find Kitty
The Most Bitter Drink Is Life
In the Mood for Sweets

STHAL
Emmerson's Reconnaissance Methods
A Skirt for Fidel
Selfish Children

WELCH THE BEAUTIFUL AND GENIUS INVENTOR, PART II

If you have two hunks of **Silver**, a **Ruby**, and two sheets of **Silk**, you can complete **Grand Designs** during your stop in Myiddok. This quest unlocks two specialty skills, Crafting and Augmentation, with an in-game tutorial about Augmentation following it.

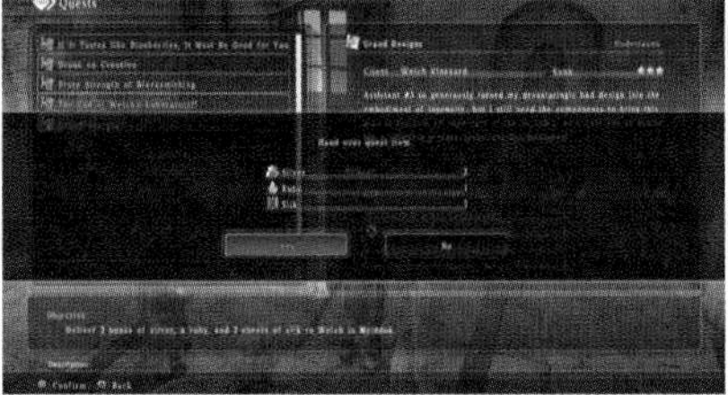

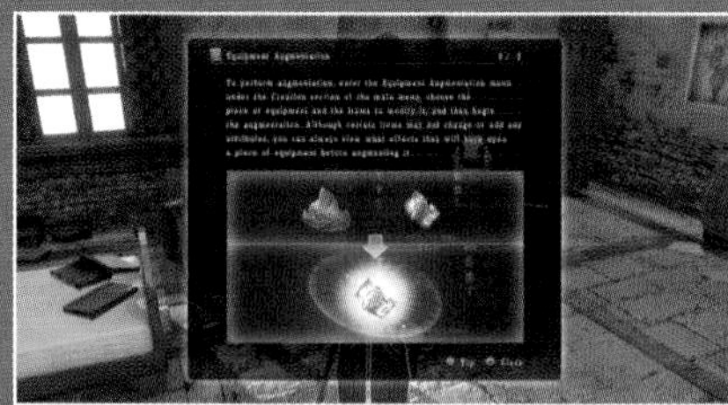

AUGMENTATION

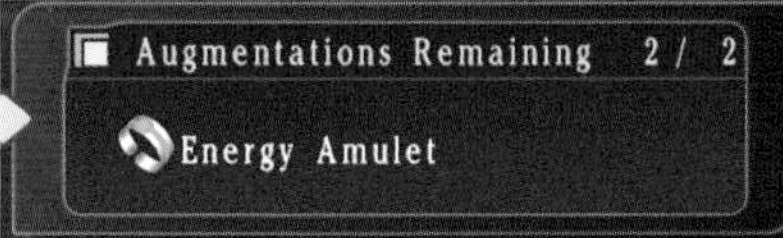

The Augmentation specialties are invaluable tools for modifying your weapons, armor, and accessories. Each piece of equippable gear you have has its own amount of total augmentations (shown at the bottom-right of the Augmentation menu, labeled "Augmentations Remaining").

You can upgrade the basic attributes (ATK, DEF, INT, MEN) of an item as many times as you want, provided you have augmentations for that item remaining. The special "Factors" attributes associated with an item have a limit of four.

For now, you'll only be able to augment accessories through learning the Ornamentation specialty. Later on in the game, you'll gain access to augmentation specialties for weapons and armor.

Exit Welch's Laboratory and re-enter it to take on the **Happy Fun Bunny Time** quest. This quest requires the Cooking skill specialty to complete since you need to create five **Bunnylicious Pies.** Two of the ingredients, **Wheat Flour** and **Nectar,** can be found at the grocer in Santeroule. You can find **Red Fruit** and **Green Fruit** on enemies or from harvesting points.

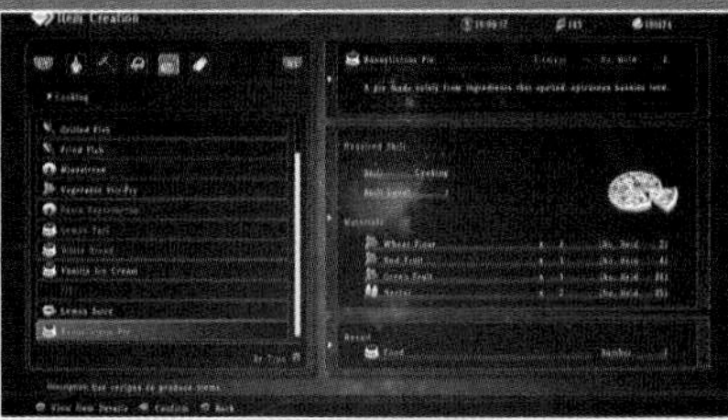

When this quest is completed, you'll earn the Bunny role and the Synthesis specialty. Synthesis allows you to combine almost any mixture of items in the game to produce other items.

SYNTHESIS

Synthesis can be quite costly early on in the game when you don't have access to many spare items. However, it's the only way to obtain the rarest equipment later in the game, especially post-ending. The higher you level up your Synthesis specialty, the more items you're able to toss into the synthesis blender.

The basic principle behind synthesis is the quality of the result, plus another piece of modifier material (which will alter the impurity factor). The higher the quality of the result, the better the result. There are hundreds of possibilities, but for the most part, you can control the outcome.

Generally, the resulting type of item is a combination of two similar items thrown into the synthesis. For instance, if you put in two food-type items, the result will usually be food. If you add two random material-type items into the mix, it will still be food, but with added impurity, slightly altering the results (usually, this means that the result can be less than ideal).

If you have the **Find Ruddle!** quest, you can find more clues about his whereabouts from a couple of people just west of the bridge in Myiddok. Otherwise, head out to the Resulian Plains.

At this juncture, you can take a detour and go home to Sthal to view some Private Actions or complete any quests involving the Dakaav Footpath. You can also visit the Infirmary in Sthal to progress the Ruddle quest, which you can then finish when you return to Central Resulia.

When you're ready, travel to Central Resulia. As you walk into the capital, the city folk all seem perturbed by something.

Before you visit Castle Bariff, it's a good idea to upgrade some of your equipment here for the upcoming battle. **Tall Tails Armaments** carries better weapons, armor, and accessories now, so stop in and buy whatever you need.

You can also complete the **Find Ruddle!** quest if you've been keeping up with it.

SHOPS—CENTRAL RESULIA (UPDATE)

Tall Tails Armaments

ITEM	COST	TYPE
Acuity Crest	3000	Accessory
Arcane Amulet	25000	Accessory
Arcane Bracelet	5000	Accessory
Attack Crest	3000	Accessory
Energy Amulet	25000	Accessory
Energy Bracelet	5000	Accessory
Fortitude Crest	3000	Accessory
Mind Crest	3000	Accessory
Chainmail	700	Armor
Cuirass	850	Armor
Plate Armor	2150	Armor
Traveler's Cloak	750	Armor
Bastard Sword	2500	Weapon
Conflagrant Soul	3200	Weapon
Cordon Scepter	2000	Weapon
Crescent Rod	800	Weapon
Falchion	1000	Weapon
Gauntlets	2250	Weapon
Hunting Bow	2700	Weapon
Pallasch	1100	Weapon
Refulgent Orb	1250	Weapon
Sinclair	2750	Weapon

Now, find out what's disturbing the city by making your way to the castle steps.

During the cutscene here, Victor greets the party and gives you the unfortunate news of Sortevue's demise.

CENTRAL RESULIA - CASTLE BARIFF

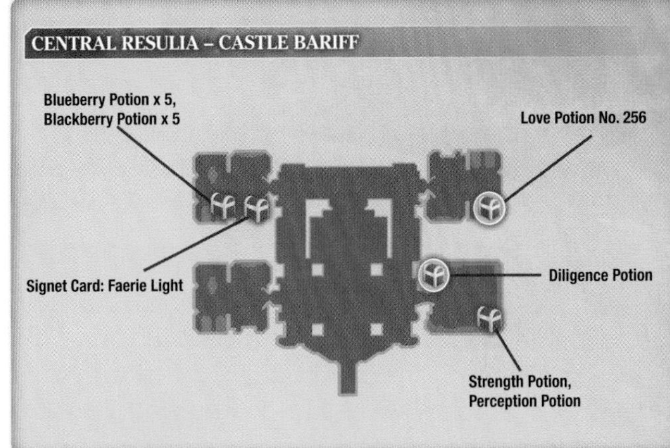

Afterward, you're finally welcome into Castle Bariff. Follow Victor upstairs into a room on the left, where he insists that you take some provisions. Open the chests to retrieve **Blueberry Potion x 5**, **Blackberry Potion x 5**, and **Signet Card: Faerie Light**.

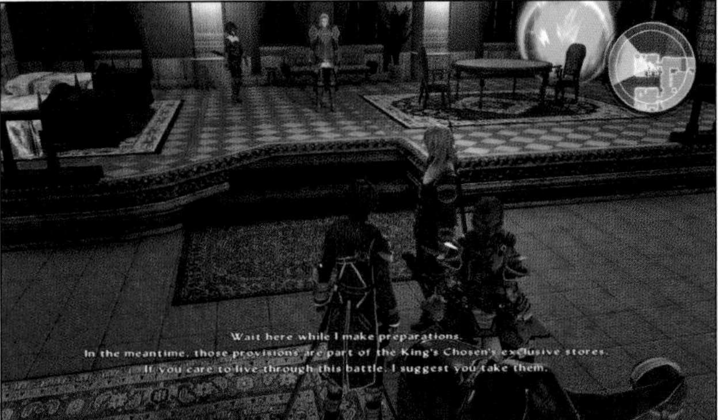

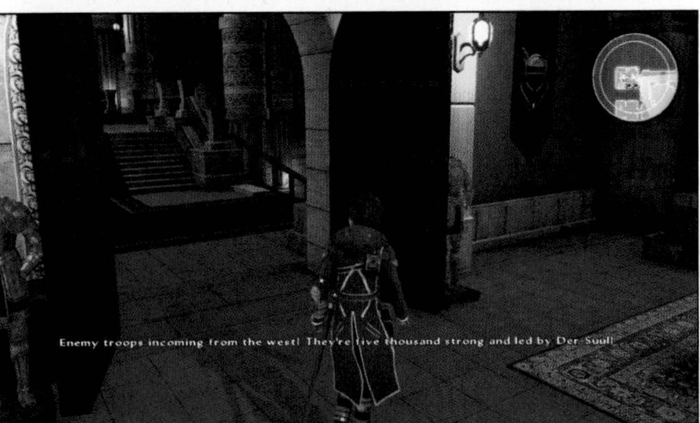

As you talk to Victor and your other companions about the situation, a horde of enemies attacks! Go downstairs into the southeast room to pick up some more items, including a **Strength Potion** and **Perception Potion**. You can also restock on consumables here if you talk to the nearby Supply Corps Soldier who mans the Call of the Desert Traders shop. When you're ready, gather with Victor and exit the castle. Prepare to defend the city!

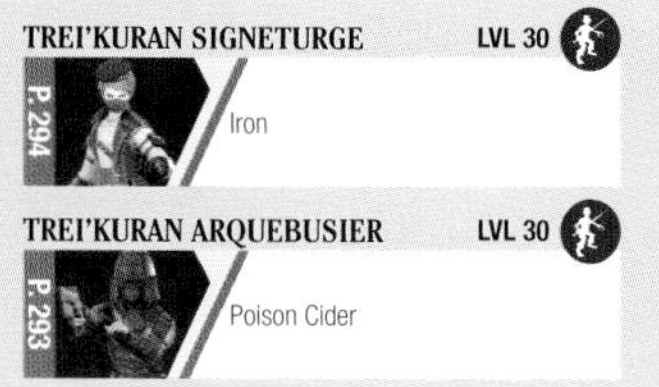

Here you're confronted with several groups of Trei'kuran Signeturges. However, when defeated, endless waves continuously replace them, so ignore them and make your way to the southwest section of the city. Get ready for a difficult battle with a group of Trei'kuran gunmen in the middle of the street. It seems they have obtained extraordinary weaponry similar to those equipped by the Eitalons. Take caution, and make sure to heal up any allies taking gunfire.

WARRIOR SLAYER

The enemies here are humanoids, so it's a good idea to equip one of your members with the Warrior Slayer role. It increases the damage done to your foes while reducing the damage taken by your ally. Hopefully, you've unlocked it by now (it requires Raven Slayer and Beast Slayer Lv. 3).

After a seemingly endless amount of Trei'kuran forces is defeated, you'll be introduced to Pavine, a ruthless soldier whose mission is to take Relia.

The plot thickens when Fidel realizes that things aren't what they seem. Emmerson and Anne reveal some information, including the fact that external forces are interfering with the war between Resulia and Trei'kur.

As Pavine orders his men to take Relia, she activates an incredible signeturgical technique, teleporting Fidel and his company away from danger—but to where?

The party ends up far north of Resulia, in a snowy tundra called the Northern Territory of Sohma. Head south and follow a path until you reach a save and restoration point. As the crew gathers their thoughts under the natural mountainside shelter, talk to your companions for extra dialogue. When you're ready, exit the cavern to the northwest. You can turn around and activate the save point now that it's blue.

PART 03

CHAPTER 5

ENERGIZE

After a close call with their Kronos pursuers, Fidel and his company find refuge in the arctic tundra of Sohma. They need to figure out a way to get to Trei'kur while Victor makes haste back to the capital.

MISSION: TRAVERSE THE TUNDRA

A few of the travelers are still mistrustful of Emmerson and Anne. Although they raise well-reasoned questions, the secretive pair's protectiveness over Relia doesn't go unnoticed. Together, they make their way toward Trei'kur through the harsh conditions of the Sohma mountains.

NORTHERN TERRITORY OF SOHMA

Action Checklist

1. Optional: Visit the merchant at The Stray Sheep to upgrade equipment
2. Travel west toward Trei'kur
3. Defeat Pavine

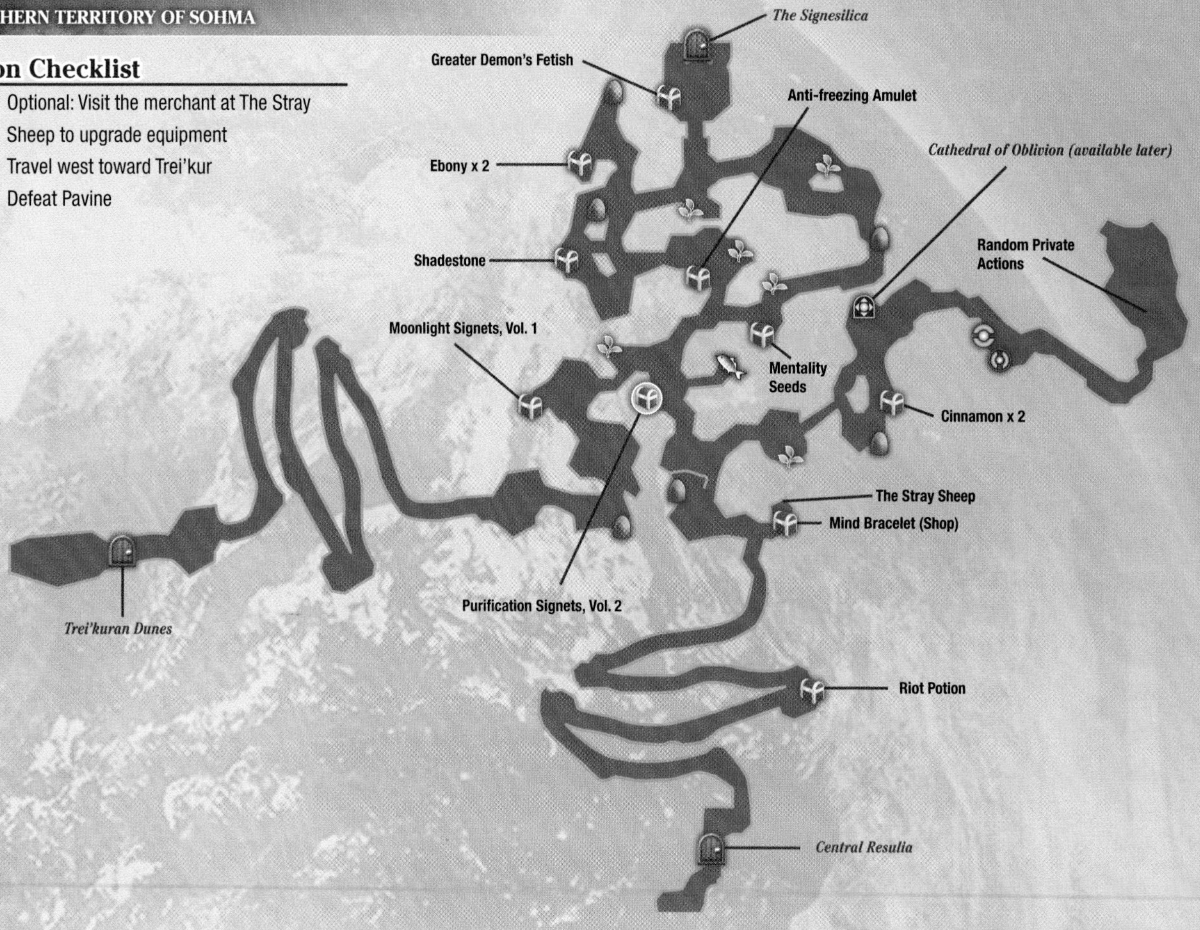

The Signesilica
Greater Demon's Fetish
Anti-freezing Amulet
Cathedral of Oblivion (available later)
Ebony x 2
Random Private Actions
Shadestone
Moonlight Signets, Vol. 1
Mentality Seeds
Cinnamon x 2
The Stray Sheep
Mind Bracelet (Shop)
Trei'kuran Dunes
Purification Signets, Vol. 2
Riot Potion
Central Resulia

Mission Walkthrough

Your main goal is to hike your way across the snowy mountains and into Trei'kur. Prepare yourself for a final confrontation with one of your pursuers.

SNOW MERMAID LVL 30

P.313 — Ice Gem, Fish Scales

SABER-TOOTHED TIGER LVL 30

P.297 — Wolf Fang

Shops

The Stray Sheep

ITEM	COST	TYPE
Acuity Crest	3000	Accessory
Arcane Amulet	25000	Accessory
Arcane Bracelet	5000	Accessory
Attack Crest	3000	Accessory
Energy Amulet	25000	Accessory
Energy Bracelet	5000	Accessory
Fortitude Crest	3000	Accessory
Mind Crest	3000	Accessory
Banded Mail	1400	Armor
Crest Mail	1050	Armor
Crest Robe	1150	Armor
Plate Armor	2150	Armor
Basil	90	Usable
Blackberries	80	Usable
Blueberries	40	Usable
Chamomile	180	Usable
Cinnamon	300	Usable
Fresh Sage	160	Usable
Jasmine	90	Usable
Lavender	300	Usable
Mint	90	Usable
Bastard Sword	2500	Weapon
Conflagrant Soul	3200	Weapon
Cordon Scepter	2000	Weapon
Crescent Rod	800	Weapon
Falchion	1000	Weapon
Gauntlets	2250	Weapon
Hunting Bow	2700	Weapon
Pallasch	1100	Weapon
Refulgent Orb	1250	Weapon
Sinclair	2750	Weapon

NAVIGATE THROUGH THE ARCTIC

From the save point, make your way west and then south. Before you encounter a group of Snow Mermaids, there's a chest containing **Cinnamon x 2** in it. Open it, and then continue west, fighting any enemies you find. The monsters here are primarily ice-based, so naturally, they're weak to fire-based attacks.

Upon reaching the center of the area, Victor leaves the party to check on the results of the attack on Central Resulia, trusting Emmerson to keep his friends safe.

FOG OF WAR

Snow Mermaids can inflict fog, a severely debilitating ailment, especially for range-based members. You don't have access to a curative spell to cure it just yet, but you can use the Jasmine item as a remedy. Otherwise, you can wait out the Fog effect while you're not in combat. Interestingly, Emmerson's special attack, Avian Rage, is still effective while he's fogged.

There's an unfortunate merchant located in an inlet just southeast from the center of the map (which is fortunate for you). As perilous as his situation seems, he has valuable stock, with up-to—date upgrades if you happened to miss the shopping opportunity in Central Resulia. Alternatively, you can wait until the next mission for even better upgrades if you'd like to save your hard-earned Fol. There's also a chest holding a **Mind Bracelet** next to the merchant.

As nice as it would be to explore the area, you're blocked off from the north and south paths, forced to trek west toward Trei'kur.

Enter and follow the western trail northwest of the center of the map. Don't forget to grab the **Moonlight Signets, Vol. 1** book from the chest before heading south along the path.

PUMMEL PAVINE

Along the trail, Pavine, who's been patiently waiting for his second chance at snatching Relia, confronts the party. He calls for backup from his mothership, but unfortunately for him, he won't be receiving any. Friendly troops (presumably with Emmerson) beam down to help fight against Pavine and his henchmen, and a battle ensues. Get ready to defend Relia from Pavine!

PAVINE

LVL 33

The ruthless Kronos soldier wields an exceptionally powerful firearm. Many of his attacks deal damage over a large area, so be careful of how your party is positioned. Try to keep your allies separated and out of the way of his gunfire while dealing with his underlings. An effective strategy against Pavine is to take control of Anne to unleash repeated Hammer of Might attacks on him. This attack has a chance of stunning an enemy, particularly humanoids.

Enemy	Level	Page	Item
PAVINE 	LVL 33	P. 292	CQC Program Gamma
KRONOS SOLDIER 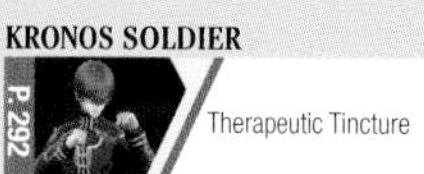	LVL 32	P. 292	Therapeutic Tincture
KRONOS RANGER  	LVL 32	P. 291	Blueberry Potion

Note that Miki won't be controllable for this fight. Additionally, she's a primary target for many of the enemies, so peel any aggressors off of her so she can heal up hurt allies uninterrupted. Don't spare your usable items if you need to heal, either; this can be a tough battle because of Pavine's damage output. Once you've dealt with the weaker soldiers, you can unleash a Reserve Rush combo to take Pavine's health down quickly. When his health drops to 25%, a cutscene triggers. In a fit of rage, Pavine callously unleashes a barrage of bullets, leaving Miki in critical condition.

Since you'll need to finish off Pavine without Miki's healing spells, it's imperative that you heal your party with Blueberries and Blueberry Potions.

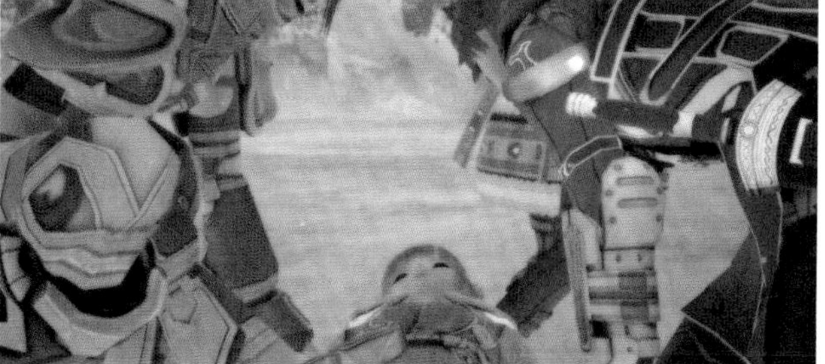

After you avenge Miki, Emmerson calls for a transport from his starship, and the team is beamed up to safety.

On board the Charles D. Goale's transport room, there's a treasure sphere containing a copy of **Restorative Signets, Vol. 1** to your immediate left. Pick it up, and have Fiore learn the Healing battle skill. She'll need it since Miki's out of commission. Before you can do anything else, you'll need to escort Miki to the Sick Bay, so head to the north exit of the transport room to the turbo lift.

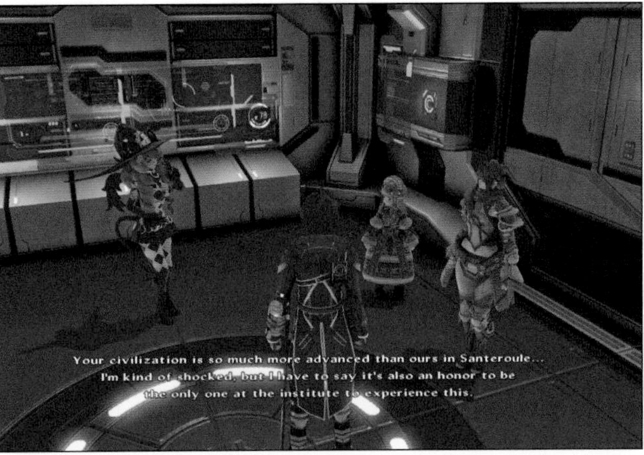

The sick bay doctors are able to stabilize Miki's condition, revealing to the party that she'll make a recovery in a few days. With Miki in good care, the party is summoned to the ship's bridge. Follow Anne to the lift to meet with Emmerson. On the way there, Anne explains that she and Emmerson are from a world far, far away from Faykreed.

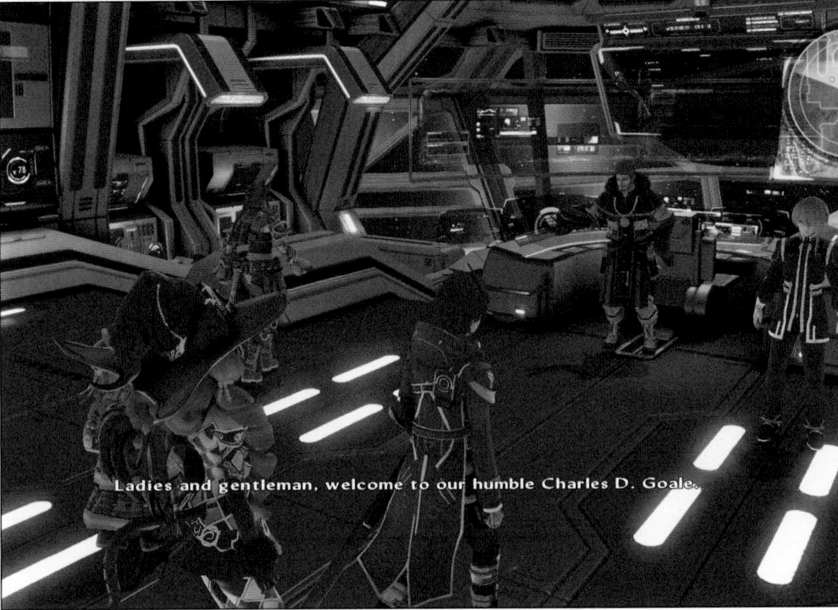

There's no time to waste, though. Emmerson brings up a map of Trei'kur and surmises that Relia originates from there. Follow him to the transport room, where you'll be beamed down to the Trei'kuran Dunes.

MISSION: FIND RELIA'S ORIGINS

As Miki recovers from the devastating wounds she suffered from the encounter with Pavine, Fidel and the others go on the hunt for answers without her. Their next destination is located somewhere in the dusty dunes of Trei'kur.

Action Checklist

1. Optional: Complete side quests and view Private Actions with your new teleportation capabilities
2. Uncover the secret entrance of the Cryptic Research Facility
3. Find Relia's origins and escape the facility

PART 03

Mission Walkthrough

Now that you have a lead to follow (thanks to the starship's advanced technology), your next mission is to find the laboratory that Relia mentioned during her memory recollection. The location you're looking for is suspected to be masked with a cloaking field. You'll need to explore the dunes and find anything that looks suspicious.

You're also given a new key item, the **Communicator**. Using this through the Item menu allows you to instantly transport the party back to the Charles D. Goale. From there, you can be beamed to any locations on Faykreed that you've visited.

For now, use the **Communicator** to return to Emmerson's starship to save your progress and do some shopping.

SHOPS—CHARLES D GOALE

Myth & Weston Outfitters

ITEM	COST	TYPE
Acuity Crest	3000	Accessory
Arcane Crest	1500	Accessory
Attack Crest	3000	Accessory
Energy Crest	1500	Accessory
Fortitude Crest	3000	Accessory
Mind Crest	3000	Accessory
Resistance Suit	2650	Armor
Riot Gear	2450	Armor
Booster Wand	2800	Weapon
Ceramic Sword	3500	Weapon
Mechanical Fists	3150	Weapon
Mekhanesphere	4400	Weapon
Microblaster	3700	Weapon

Atoms R Us Provisions

ITEM	COST	TYPE
Diffusion Device	1080	Material
Micro Circuit	1200	Material
Rivets	360	Material
Wire	900	Material
Basil	90	Usable
Blackberries	80	Usable
Blueberries	40	Usable
Chamomile	180	Usable
Cinnamon	300	Usable
Fresh Sage	160	Usable
Jasmine	90	Usable
Lavender	300	Usable
Mint	90	Usable

The Future Is Now

ITEM	COST	TYPE
Common Eggs	90	Food
Fresh Vegetables	180	Food
Prehistoric Meat	180	Food
Spring Water	240	Food
Whole Milk	360	Food
Olive Oil	240	Material
Seasonings	60	Material
Wheat Flour	240	Material
White Rice	180	Material

BEAM ME UP!

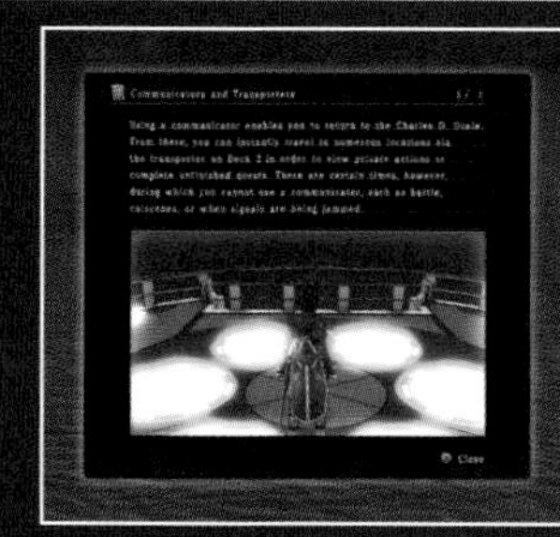

Thanks to the Charles D. Goale's transport functionality, this is an excellent point in the story to complete any side quests you've undertaken; take advantage of your newfound physical displacement technology while you can. You won't always have this luxury!

Consider completing any Welch's Laboratory quests and viewing the various Private Actions across the five hubs you've been to so far: Sthal, Central Resulia, Myiddok, Santeroule, and the Charles D. Goale.

OPTIONAL

PRIVATE ACTIONS

CHARLES D. GOALE

Resulian Fruit Wine

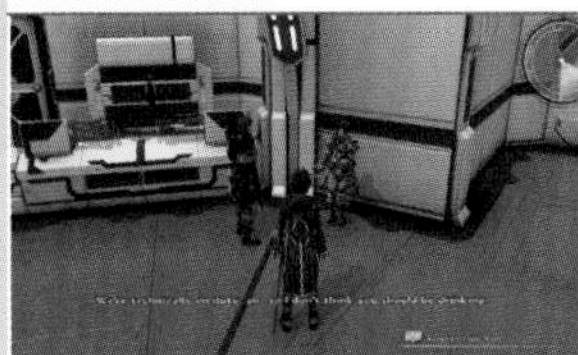

Fiore's Mentor Waxes Inspirational

Fiore's Mentor Waxes Admonitory

STHAL

Mom and Dad for Fidel

Climate Change

MYIDDOK

Mistaken Identity

Fidel's Relationship Status

Survey on Singing

Fidel's Type

Fidel's First Love

CENTRAL RESULIA

Seemingly Unattainable

Faykreedian Beauty

Stuffed Full of Kindness

Return to Sender

Picking Presents

Outstretched Hand

The Joy of Giving

Gift Guidance

SANTEROULE

Different Frame of Reference

Different Perspectives

Emotionally Distant

Mr. Rabbit's Change of Clothes

SIDE QUESTS

CENTRAL RESULIA

Building Character into Your Crafts

Collecting Coal for the Fire

Subjugation Directive: Napto

Subjugation Directive: Moogmorts

Death to the Dine-and-Dasher

Subjugation Directive: Walking Conflagrations

SANTEROULE

Of Vital Importance After Hours

Sexy Little Devil

Building a House Takes a Collective Effort

Open Season on Fran

TREI'KURAN DUNES

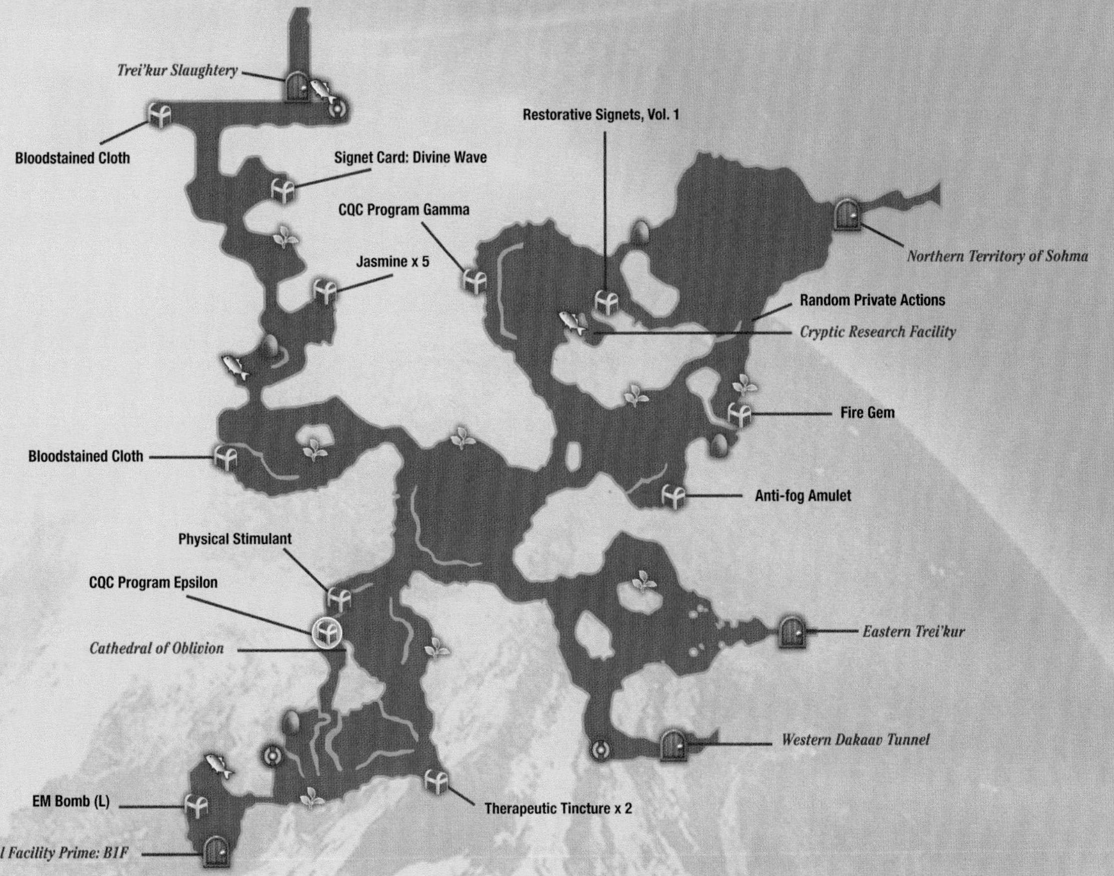

KOBOLD BANDIT LVL 30

P. 296 — Ruby, Hand-Spun Thread Wool, Wolf Fang

TERARIN LVL 32

P. 301 — Wind Gem, Giant Bird Feather

SANDEATER LVL 30

P. 304 — Shellfish Meat, Seaweed, Springwater

ROCK HERMIT LVL 31

P. 313 — Earth Gem, Mercury

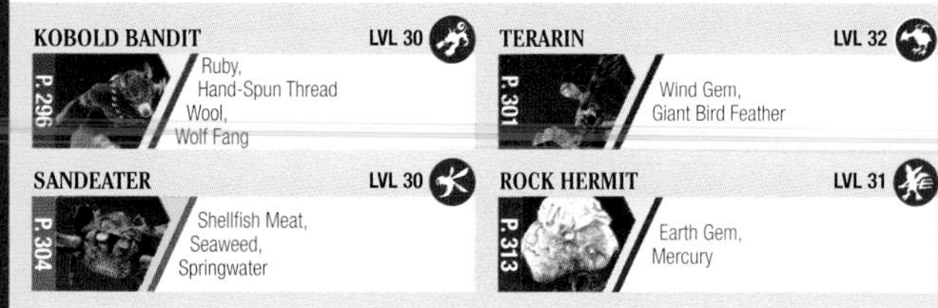

UNCLOAK THE LABORATORY

When you're ready to continue, teleport back out to the Trei'kuran Dunes. Since the northeast exit and the southwest portions of the map are blocked off, you won't be able to do much exploring here.

We have no business that way.

Nuh-uh. Not that way.

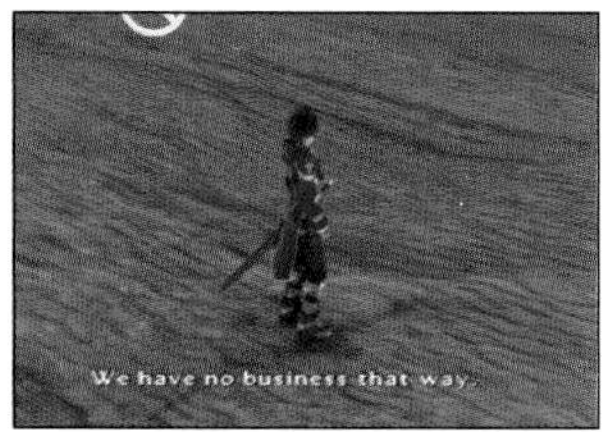

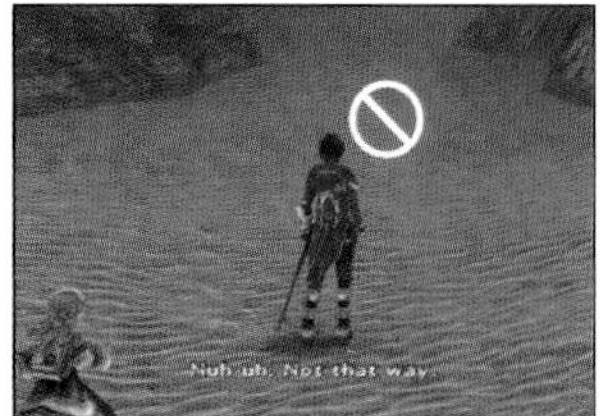

Your destination is north from your starting position, inside an alcove by a chest. Before you head there, collect some items from chests in the area. Just west from your initial teleport position, you can find an **Anti-fog Amulet** in a chest on a ledge. To the northeast up a cliff, there's another chest containing a **Fire Gem**. Then, northwest of that one, you'll find a chest close to your destination with the **Restorative Signets, Vol. 1** book. Before you enter the alcove, grab a copy of **CQC Program Gamma** in the western corner of the immediate area.

After you've opened all of the chests, go into the inlet next to the Restorative Signets, Vol. 1 chest, where Anne uncloaks the entrance of a building.

It looks like the facility itself is buried underground, and this is the entrance to the place.

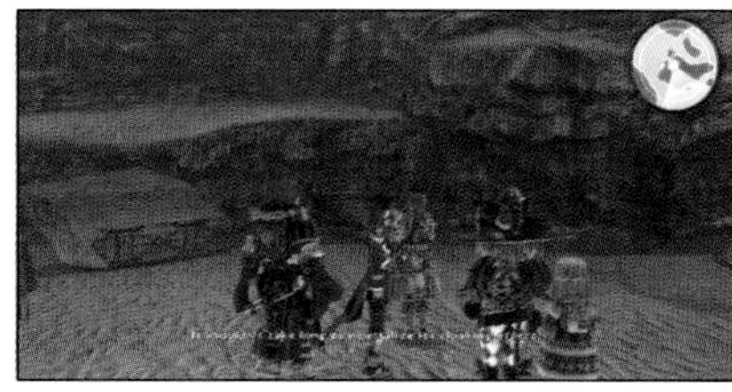

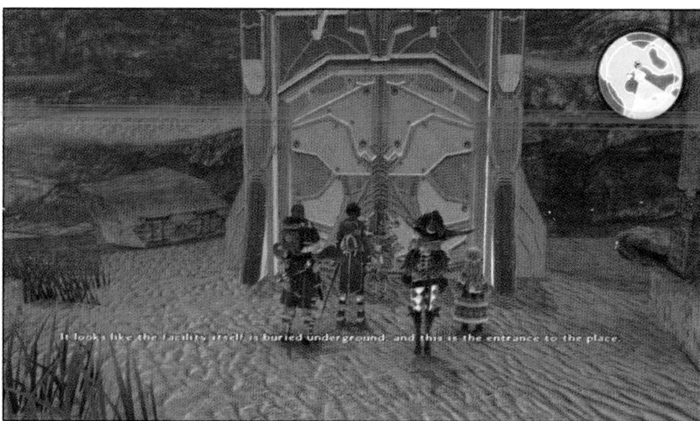

Relia runs inside ahead of everyone else. Follow her into the Cryptic Research Facility. Turns out that this is where Relia used to live, as she recognizes the institute. After the party's short dialogue sequence, save your progress, and then prepare to delve into the facility to find out more about Relia's past.

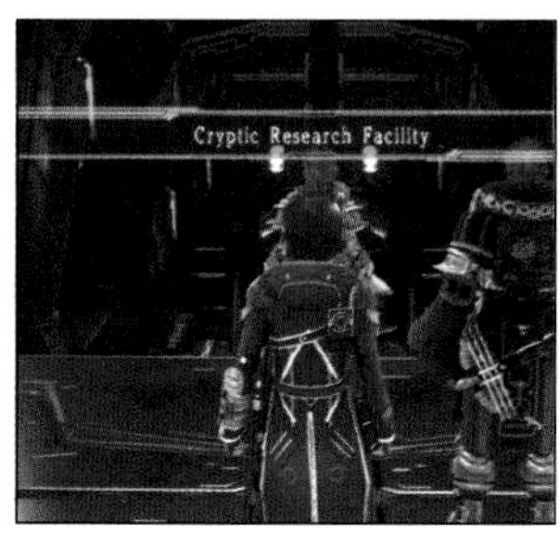

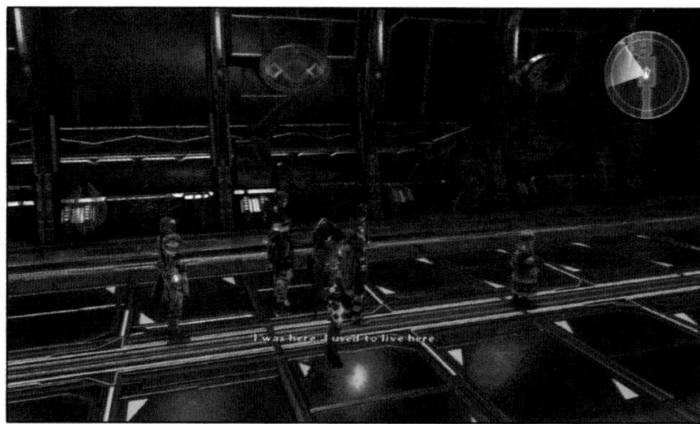

Cryptic Research Facility

I was here. I used to live here.

CRYPTIC RESEARCH FACILITY

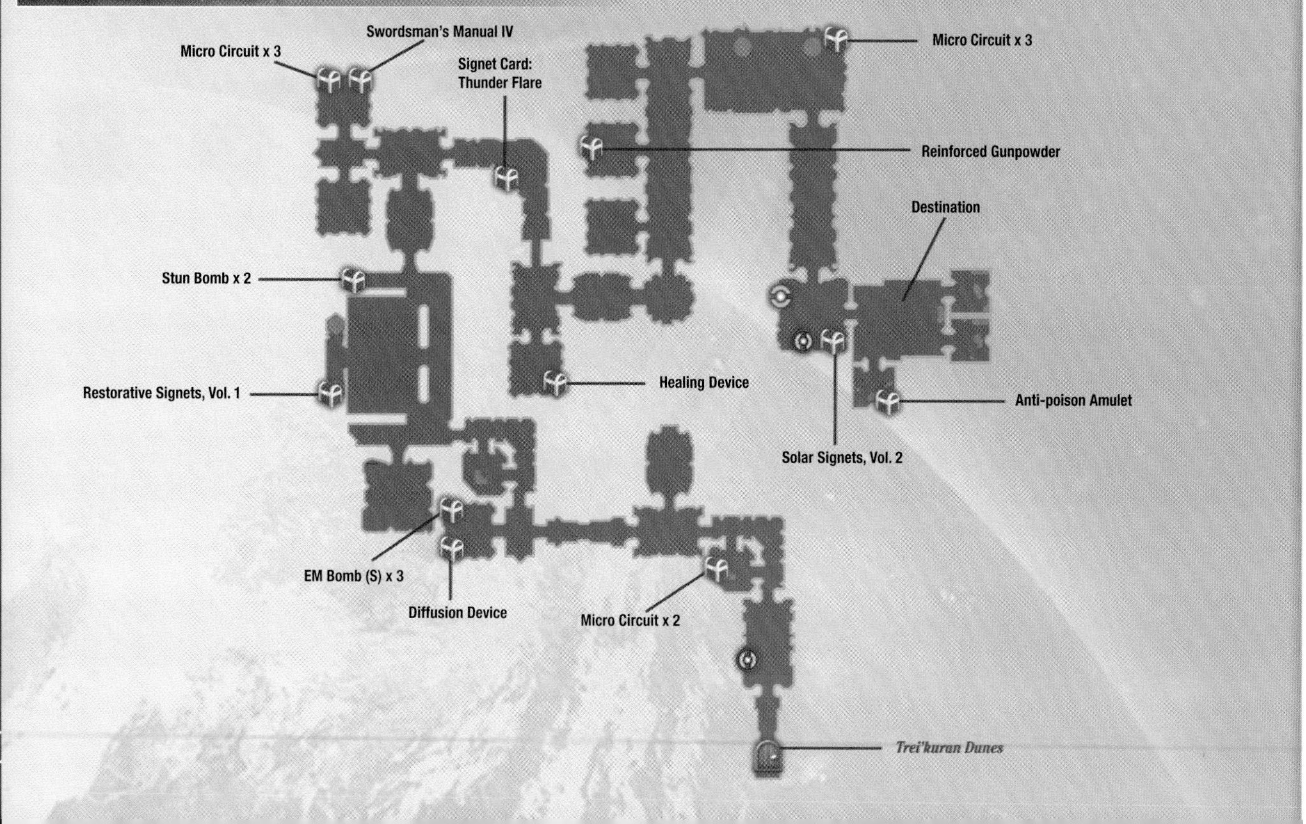
Micro Circuit x 3
Swordsman's Manual IV
Signet Card: Thunder Flare
Micro Circuit x 3
Reinforced Gunpowder
Destination
Stun Bomb x 2
Restorative Signets, Vol. 1
Healing Device
Anti-poison Amulet
Solar Signets, Vol. 2
EM Bomb (S) x 3
Diffusion Device
Micro Circuit x 2
Trei'kuran Dunes

EXPLORE THE RESEARCH FACILITY

From the save point, go north and make a left into a connecting room with a workstation in it. Open the treasure sphere with **Micro Circuit x 2** inside, and then make your way out into the hallway, traveling westward.

Keep going west until you reach a room with two spheres in it, containing **EM Bomb (S) x 3** and a **Diffusion Device**. Pick these up, then leave the room and continue north and west. In the large room, you'll see some amazing machinery. There's a treasure sphere close to it in the west end, containing another **Restorative Signets, Vol. 1**. This should be your third copy of this book if you've been following this guide, so Fiore should really have learned the Healing spell by now!

MOONLIGHT MEDIC

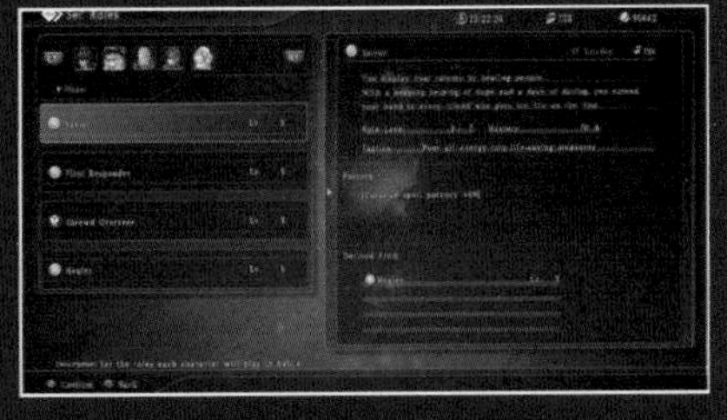

With the lack of Miki's healing powers, you'll need to rely on Fiore and restorative items like Blueberries and Blueberry Potions to heal your party. It's recommended that you equip Fiore with healing roles such as Healer and Savior to encourage the AI-controlled signeturge to prioritize healing your party members instead of casting offense-based spells. Additionally, you can disable her other spells by going into the Set Battle Skills menu and then pressing ◉ to get into the Set Signeturgy menu, where you can turn her signeturgies ON or OFF.

Don't forget to have her learn the Healing signeturgy from reading a **Restorative Signets, Vol. 1** book, too!

In the northwest corner of the room, there's another sphere containing **Stun Bomb x 2**. You're finding a lot of these things... there might be a use for them soon.

Fight through more Polyhedron enemies through the north, and make a left turn into a room to the west. Enter the north room from here to find a group of foes and two spheres that hold **Micro Circuit x 3** and **Swordsman's Manual IV**.

Turn around and go east until the path bends south. Around the corner here is a sphere with **Signet Card: Thunder Flare** in it. Go straight south from here until you hit a dead end with a treasure sphere containing a **Healing Device**.

Turn around and take the east path through more automatic doors. Make a left, heading north, when you reach the small circular room. You find three rooms to your left in the hallway here. In the second room, you'll find a sphere containing **Reinforced Gunpowder** in it.

Head back out to the hallway, and take a right at the north end. There's more interesting research technology here, along with some comments from Emmerson and Fiore.

In the northeast corner of this room, pick up **Micro Circuit x 3** from a sphere there. Go south into a room with restore and save points, including another treasure sphere with a **Solar Signets, Vol. 2** book inside. Restore your HP and MP here, and save your progress. Consider using some stat-boosting food here if you have some. Either Pasta Peperoncino or Golden Omelet works nicely. You can equip Anne with HP-enhancing accessories to make the next encounter more manageable, too.

When you're ready, enter the next room. It seems to be an observation room where Relia grew up, with a toy room and a research workstation nearby. After some party dialogue, Anne attempts to gather data from the computer console.

It trips off security measures, and enemies beam in to stop her! Get ready to protect Anne at all costs!

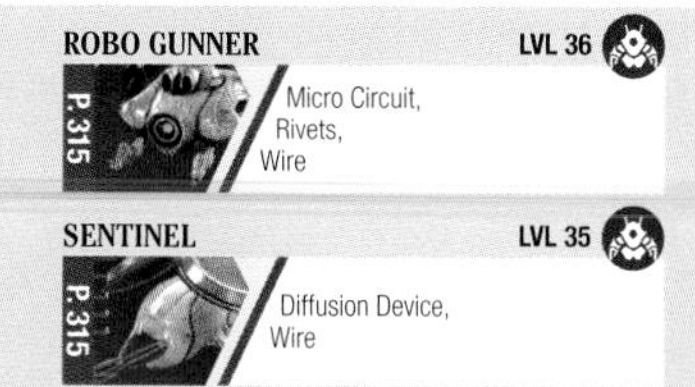

PROTECTION DUTY

A few fights in the game have an additional "game over" condition. For instance, in this fight against the security robots, if Anne goes down, the game immediately ends since she fails to perform her data-mining duties. To make matters more difficult, the enemies will almost always attack her, ignoring the rest of your party members. You'll need to be vigilant in keeping her health full while focusing on eliminating one foe at a time.

Use any items that you need to keep her safe, including any of the **Stun Bombs** and consumable items you've picked up on your way here. Either debilitate the machines, or use your Reserve Rush gauge to finish them off quickly. You should also have the Machine Slayer role unlocked at this point, so have Fidel or Emmerson equip it to make the fight a bit easier.

After you dismantle the robots, a self-destruct sequence commences, and you'll need to hightail it out of there!

ESCAPE

Before you leave the room, open the treasure sphere in Relia's room to the south to find an **Anti-poison Amulet**. Now, fight your way back to the entrance of the research facility to escape. You have around 18 minutes to do so. You can restore your HP and MP at the restore point if any of your allies were knocked out from the boss encounter.

On your way out, there are several security bots roaming the halls. If you've opened all of the chests on your way to Relia's observation room, you shouldn't need to go out of your way to collect anything while you escape. However, you should have enough time to do so in case you missed any. Refer to your map frequently. Pausing the game with the OPTIONS/START button also pauses the timer, so check your map to plan out your exit route.

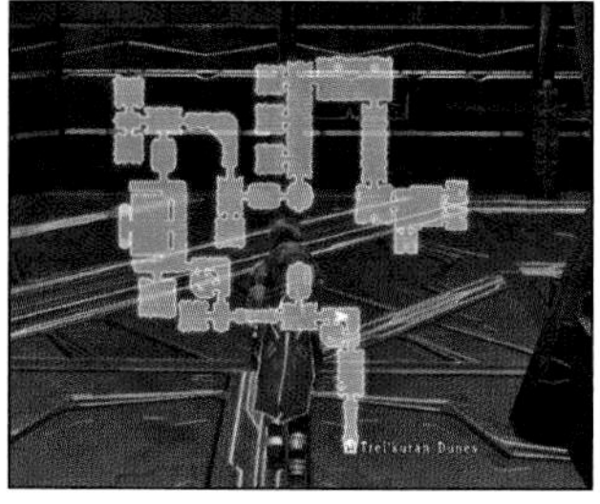

Once you've exited the compound, Emmerson calls in a transport to have the party beamed up to safety.

Before you check up on Miki's condition, save your progress aboard the starship. Head to the lift to the sick bay, where Emmerson discloses pertinent information about his origins and the situation between the Pangalactic Federation and Kronos.

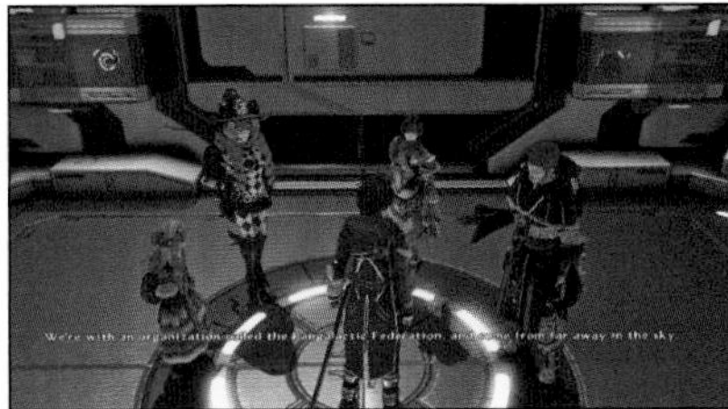

When you enter the sick bay, a lengthy cutscene plays out. Miki has recovered, and plans have changed.

Emmerson insists that Relia stay with him and Anne to prevent Kronos from pursuing the group, as well as to put an end to the attacks on Resulia. After Fidel, Miki, and Fiore beam back to their home planet, Kronos ships begin an assault on the Charles D. Goale. With his quick wit and acuity, Emmerson devises a plan to escape with Relia from his pursuers.

After the cutscene, you'll gain control of Relia. Follow Emmerson and Anne into the lift to commence Emmerson's escape ruse. After exiting the elevator, you can save your progress at the save point before entering the transport area. Get into position on the transport pads to play out another cutscene showing Emmerson and Anne following through with their ploy. The three safely board an escape pod. With the Charles D. Goale sacrificed, they land on Faykreed IV to wait for a rescue team. Unfortunately, their plan didn't go as smoothly as they had hoped. A shielded Kronos ship was able to lock on to Relia's coordinates, kidnapping her with a remote teleportation sequence.

PART 03

CHAPTER 6

GONE BABY GONE

Fidel, Miki, Victor, and Fiore gather inside the Resulian fortress, Castle Bariff. Victor informs the others that the Kronos military has rescinded its troops from the war, leaving the Trei'kurans no choice but to retreat. In response, the Resulian army has issued a mission involving an invasion into Trei'kuran territory. Fidel, Miki, and Fiore volunteer their help with the mission.

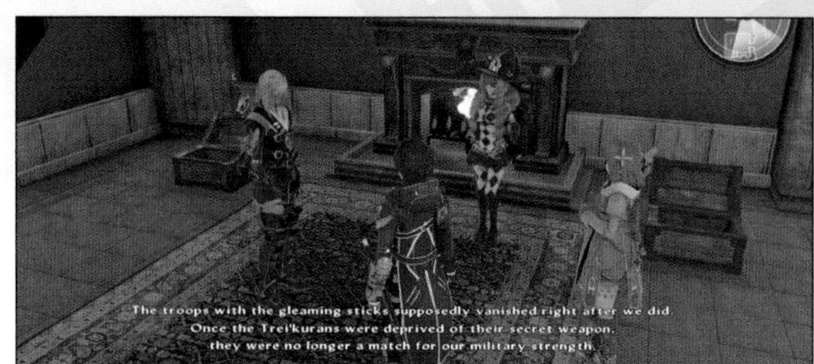

MISSION: OPERATION SNAKE EYES

The four are ready to make their way to Eastern Trei'kur, where the Resulian military is planning an assault to take over the area in order to set up a base of operations. They'll need to traverse the Western Dakaav Tunnel to join the invasion with a subversive rear attack.

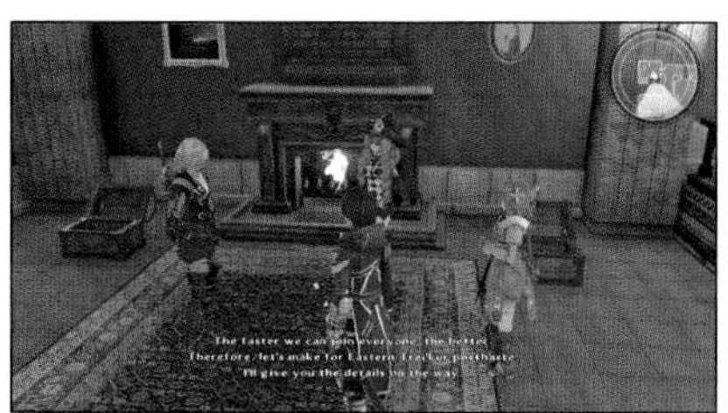

Action Checklist

1. Optional: Upgrade equipment
2. Optional: Undertake and complete side quests
3. Optional: Take a tour around various towns to view Private Actions
4. Take the southwest exit from Central Resulia and travel to the Western Dakaav Tunnel
5. Fight through the Western Dakaav Tunnel and into Trei'kuran Dunes
6. Enter the Eastern Trei'kur outpost

Mission Walkthrough

Your next mission involves joining a small task force at the west end of Eastern Trei'kur while the rest of the Resulian military creates a diversion from the east. Do so by traveling through the dangerous Western Dakaav Tunnel, fighting through its corrupted inhabitants.

THE TUNNEL TO TREI'KUR

With your party consisting of Fidel, Miki, Victor, and Fiore, your next task is to head toward Trei'kur, through the Western Dakaav Tunnel. Enter the inn to rest up and save your progress. When you exit, there should be new Private Actions that you can trigger. New side quests are available at the bulletin board in Central Resulia, too. If you have extra Fol, you can upgrade your equipment at **Tall Tails Armaments** before leaving town.

SHOPS —CENTRAL RESULIA (UPDATE)

Tall Tails Armaments

ITEM	COST	TYPE
Acuity Crest	3000	Accessory
Arcane Amulet	25000	Accessory
Attack Crest	3000	Accessory
Energy Amulet	25000	Accessory
Fortitude Crest	3000	Accessory
Mind Crest	3000	Accessory
Amber Robe	3750	Armor
Chainmail	700	Armor
Plate Armor	2150	Armor
Streaked Chainmail	3500	Armor
Superior Armor Plate	4250	Armor
Traveler's Cloak	750	Armor
Bastard Sword	2500	Weapon
Conflagrant Soul	3200	Weapon
Cordon Scepter	2000	Weapon
Deadly Edge	5500	Weapon
Gauntlets	2250	Weapon
Hunting Bow	2700	Weapon
Rune Wand	4000	Weapon
Sinclair	2750	Weapon
Slasher Claws	4500	Weapon
Sunsylph Orb	6250	Weapon
Walloon Sword	5000	Weapon
Wild Arc	5250	Weapon

OPTIONAL

SIDE QUESTS

CENTRAL RESULIA

- Enrollment Gift
- Feeling Fuzzy All Over
- Resulian Beauty: Collector's Edition
- The Four Stooges Strike Again

SANTEROULE

- Runaround Ruddle
- Sweet on the Outside...
- Steel Yourself for the Future
- Collecting the Fungus among Us
- Open Season on Karacins

PRIVATE ACTIONS

CENTRAL RESULIA

- Cheeky Spot for a Signet

PRIVATE ACTIONS

MYIDDOK

- The Luxury of Eating
- Fidel and Outer Space

SANTEROULE

- Aptitude for Ambiguity

- Suspicions Arise over Baths
- Chez Miki
- Suspicions Arise over the Male Form

- Fidel and Fish: Dining in Santeroule

STHAL

- While Fidel's Away, Ted Plays
- Dueling a Vicious Beast

- Dueling a Trained Professional

RUNAROUND RUDDLE

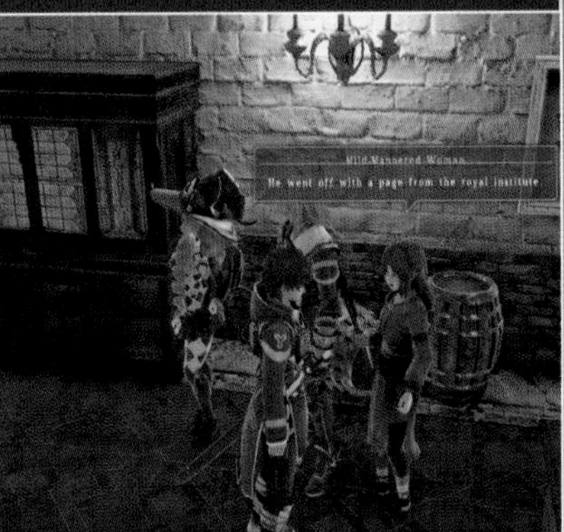

Part two of the Ruddle quest line can be found in Santeroule. Accept the Runaround Ruddle quest, and you can find your first tip in the Sultantic Slumber Lodging inn. Talk to the guests at the inn to find your next clue toward finding the elusive Ruddle!

Finish this quest by finding Ruddle near the pier in Myiddok. This unlocks the Familiar Spirit specialty skill.

ENEMY DATA

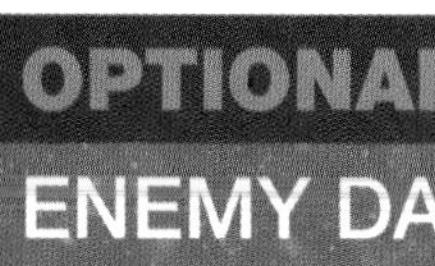

West of the Eastern Eihieds:

DEVIL CHILD LVL 40
P. 310
Demon's Tail, Wolf Fang, Signet Card, Darkness Gem

CRATER PERYTON LVL 38
P. 299
Peryton Droppings, Remex, Common Eggs

RIDICULER LVL 39
P. 292
Parchment, Velvet Ribbon, Signet Card: Sacred Pain +, Blue Roses

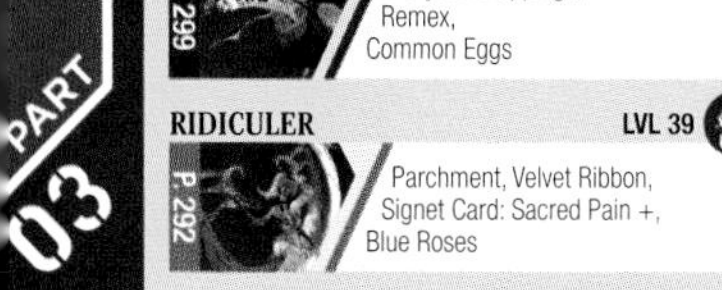

Passage on the Cliffs and Coast of Minoz:

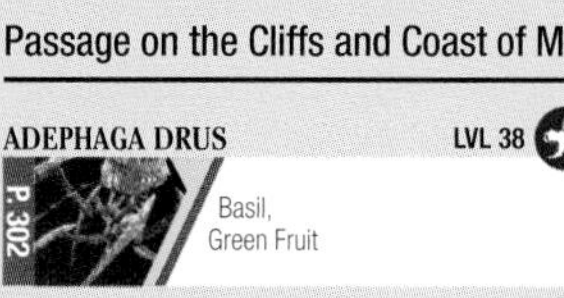

ADEPHAGA DRUS LVL 38
P. 302
Basil, Green Fruit

DEEP ONE LVL 39 
P. 295
Fish Scales, Raw Fish, Roe, Holy Water

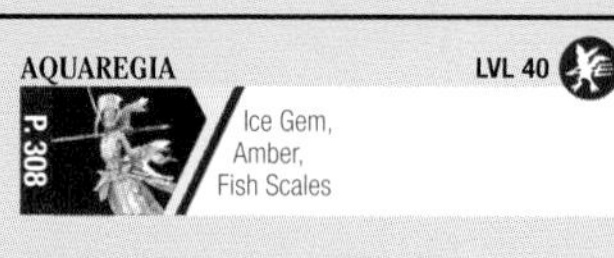

AQUAREGIA LVL 40
P. 308
Ice Gem, Amber, Fish Scales

Dakaav Footpath:

CORPSE BAT LVL 37
P. 299
Jasmine, Basil, Darkness Gem

When you're ready to progress the story, start by exiting the capital of Central Resulia through the southwest exit. Since you now have access to the Western Dakaav Tunnel, make sure to undertake any quests involving the area, such as **Collecting Coal for the Fire**, **Wanted: Chaos Corpse Corporals**, and **Steel Yourself for the Future**.

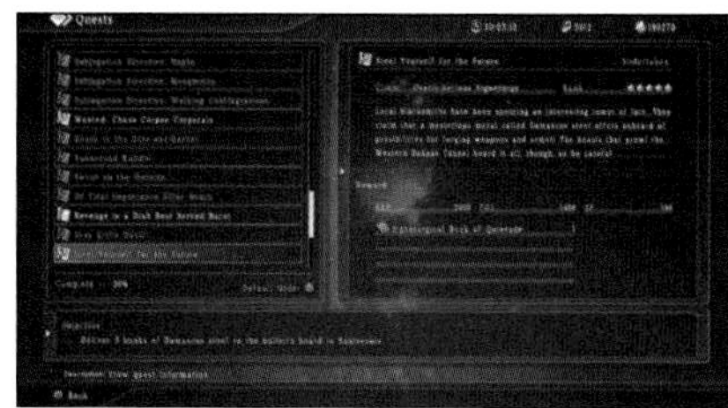

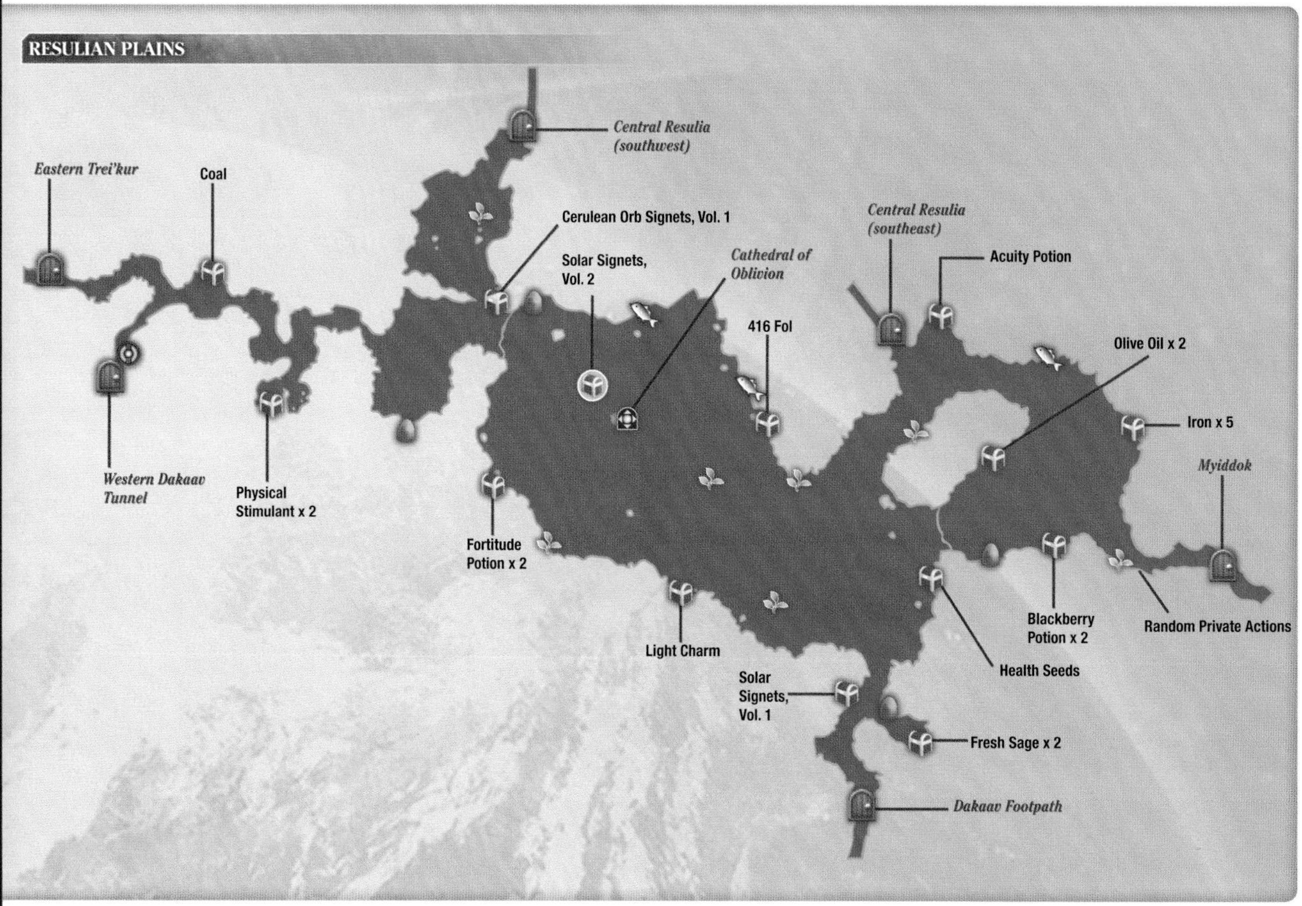

RESULIAN PLAINS

Central Resulia (southwest)
Eastern Trei'kur
Coal
Cerulean Orb Signets, Vol. 1
Solar Signets, Vol. 2
Cathedral of Oblivion
Central Resulia (southeast)
Acuity Potion
416 Fol
Olive Oil x 2
Iron x 5
Myiddok
Western Dakaav Tunnel
Physical Stimulant x 2
Fortitude Potion x 2
Light Charm
Blackberry Potion x 2
Random Private Actions
Health Seeds
Solar Signets, Vol. 1
Fresh Sage x 2
Dakaav Footpath

UNICORN WOLF LVL 37
P. 298
Wolf Fang, Bushy Fur, Fire Gem

THIEVING SCUMBAG LVL 36
P. 293
Well-Aged Cheese, Tomato, Fresh Vegetables, Dwarven Embroidery Thread

ALBERO DI ANIMA LVL 38
P. 305
Wooden Stick, Ebony, Oak, Cinnamon

HONEYBEE LVL 36
P. 303
Bee Stinger, Nectar

DIMINUTIVE FUNGUS LVL 34
P. 305
Tasty Mushroom, Colorful Mushrooms, Mint

GIANT FUNGUS LVL 36
P. 306
Tasty Mushroom, Colorful Mushrooms, Mint

Traverse through the plains to the west, toward the Resulian outpost set up earlier for the encounter with the Trei'kuran army. There are two entrances to Trei'kur, one directly west of the encampment and one southwest. Save your progress at the save point near the east end of the Resulian Plains, then take the southwest exit, as it's the only one accessible for now. This takes you to an indirect passage into Trei'kur, through the Western Dakaav Tunnel. This is an excellent area for excavating valuable ores to smith—like Silver, Coal, and Gold. Make sure to have your Excavation specialty leveled up if you want to take advantage of the mining nodes here.

WESTERN DAKAAV TUNNEL

Trei'kuran Dunes

Niflhel and Niflheim

Diligence Potion x 2

Resulian Plains

Ruby x 2

Swordsman's Manual I

Williwaw Bow

Signeturgical Book of Quietude

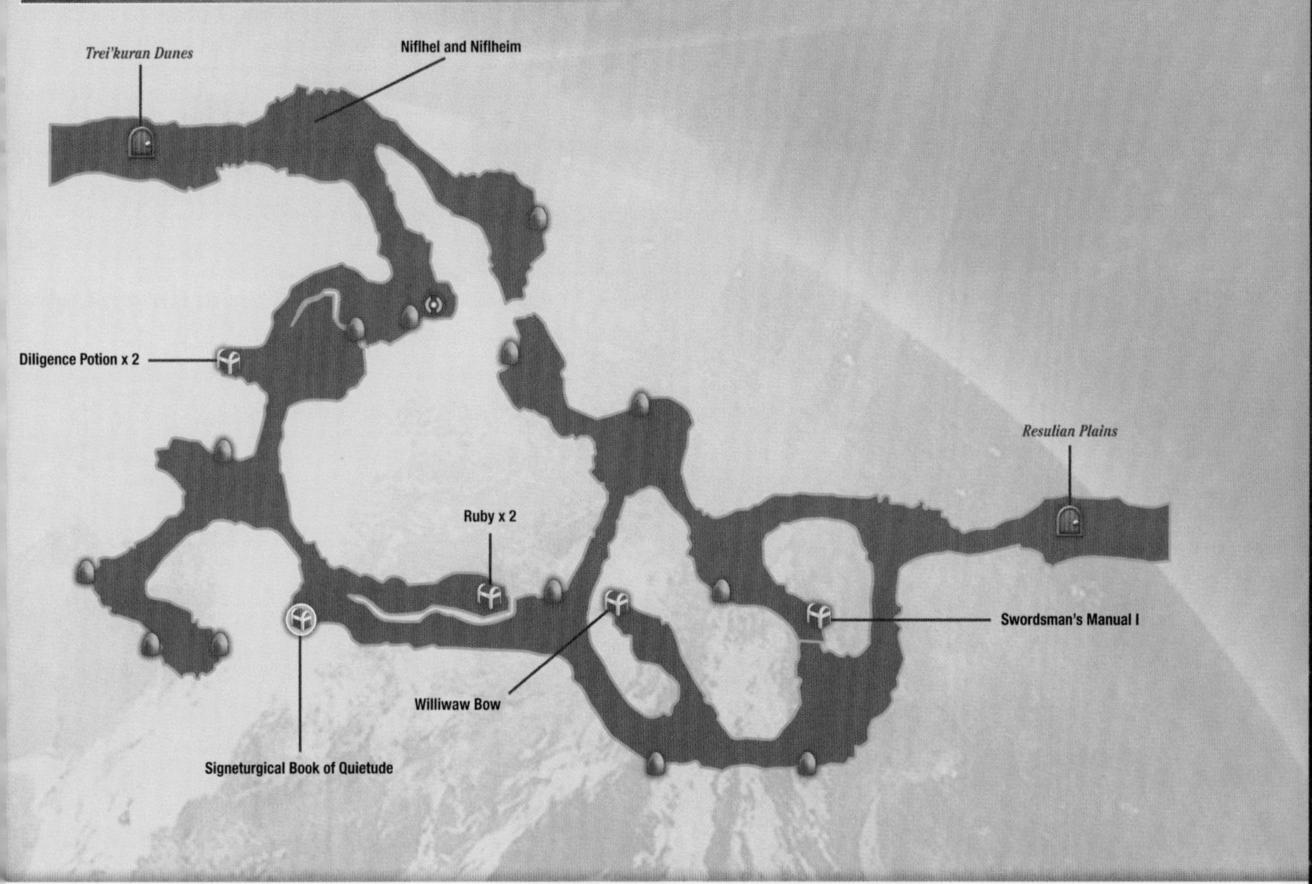

ON THE WAY TO THE DUNES

Once inside the tunnel, take the path west and defeat any enemies you encounter (many of the monsters here drop valuable crafting materials).In the path to the south of the three skeletons enemies is a chest with a copy of **Swordsman's Manual I** inside. Open it, and then head into the northwest area with more foes and excavation points. If you want to pick up a new weapon for Emmerson, you can go south, then east along the southern area. There's a cul-de-sac to the north with a treasure chest containing a **Williwaw Bow** at the end of it.

Exit the cul-de-sac, then keep traveling westward along the southern path. There's a chest in another cul-de-sac that branches to the east around here, containing **Ruby x 2**. Pick it up, and continue west (there's a locked chest on the way, which you can open once you have the Lock Picking specialty). In a corner area southwest of the map, you find three excavation nodes with plenty of Damascus Fort enemies inside. Defeat the enemies for hunks of **Damascus Steel**, and harvest the mining points for extra resources.

Now, continue north from there until you see a chest to your left. Pick up the **Diligence Potion x 2**, and save your game at the save point up ahead. To the north, before you can exit the tunnel, a minor boss battle is awaiting.

NIFLHEL, THE ARMOR THAT WALKS LVL 41

P.312 — Pneuma Signets, Vol. 1

NIFLHEIM, THE ARMOR THAT ROAMS LVL 41

P.312 — Ghost's Soul

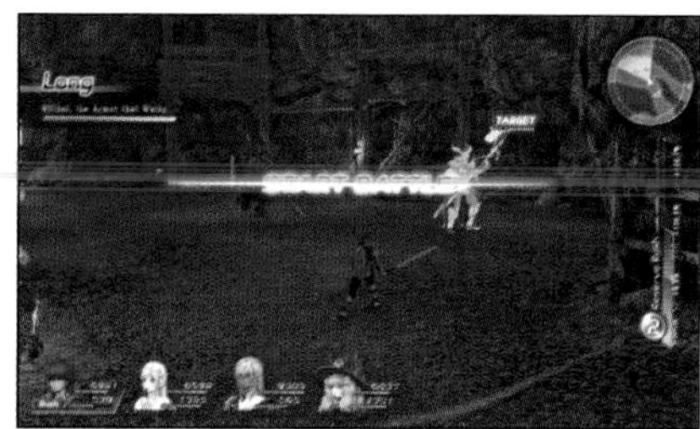

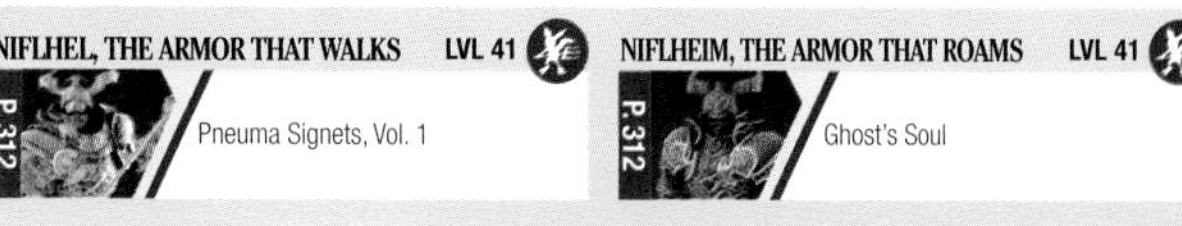

These two suits of possessed armor hit extremely hard. However, they move rather slowly, so your main goal is to keep Miki and Fiore away from them. They can be paralyzed, so if you've learned Fiore's Lightning Blast signeturgy, you can incapacitate them. This makes the fight much easier to manage.

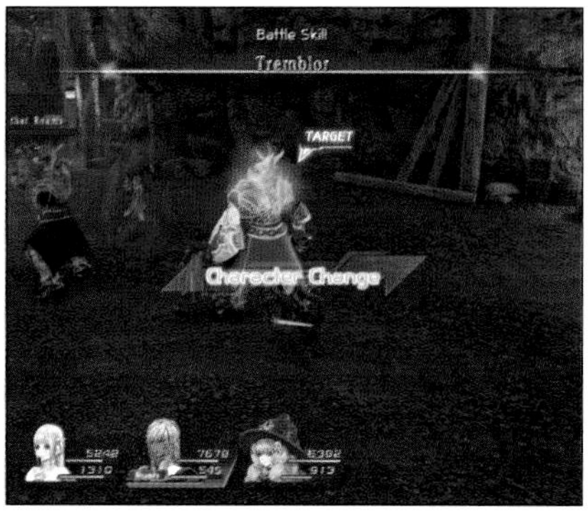
Battle Skill
Tremblor
TARGET
Character Change

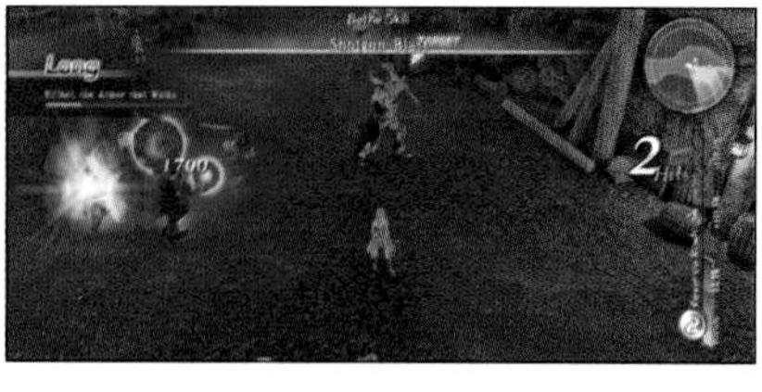

Once you've defeated them, you'll have access to the Trei'kuran Dunes, and you won't have to fight these large armored husks again if you re-enter the tunnels. Additionally, you're rewarded with a copy of **Pneuma Signets, Vol. 1** from slaying the two giants. Have Miki read the book so she can learn the Raise Dead spell.

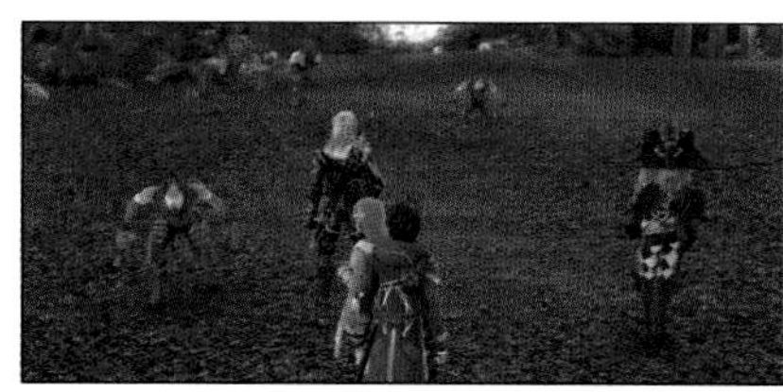

If you have the **Wanted: Chaos Corpse Corporals** quest, you can complete it by clearing out the room just east of the boss area.

When you're done collecting items and mining the tunnels, exit to the west into the Trei'kuran Dunes.

TREI'KURAN DUNES

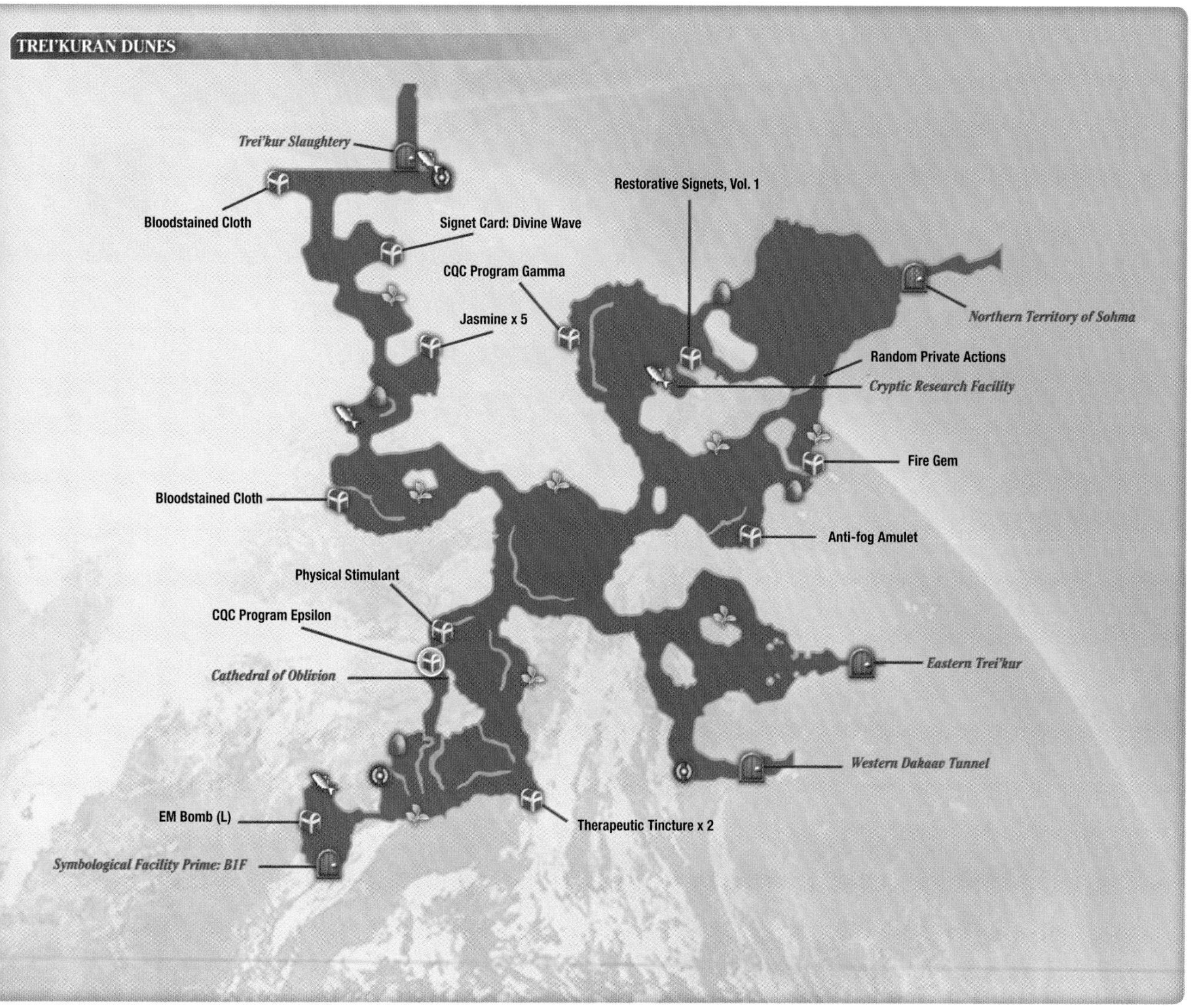
Trei'kur Slaughtery
Bloodstained Cloth
Restorative Signets, Vol. 1
Signet Card: Divine Wave
CQC Program Gamma
Northern Territory of Sohma
Jasmine x 5
Random Private Actions
Cryptic Research Facility
Fire Gem
Bloodstained Cloth
Anti-fog Amulet
Physical Stimulant
CQC Program Epsilon
Eastern Trei'kur
Cathedral of Oblivion
Western Dakaav Tunnel
EM Bomb (L)
Therapeutic Tincture x 2
Symbological Facility Prime: B1F

From here, your destination is Eastern Trei'kur, located northeast from the mouth of the Dakaav tunnels. If you need to refuel on curatives, there's a convenient usable items vendor nearby.

ADEPHAGA MILIES LVL 42

P. 303 — Insect Egg, Basil, Green Fruit

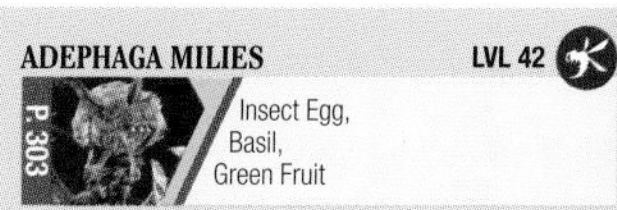

Shops

Call of the Desert Traders

ITEM	COST	TYPE
Basil	90	Usable
Blackberries	80	Usable
Blueberries	40	Usable
Chamomile	180	Usable
Cinnamon	300	Usable

ITEM	COST	TYPE
Fresh Sage	160	Usable
Jasmine	90	Usable
Lavender	300	Usable
Mint	90	Usable

OCCUPY EASTERN TREI'KUR

When you're ready, approach the destination, indicated by the red star on your minimap. Resulian troops soon gather around, with one of the leaders giving you some advice on how to approach the Trei'kuran opposition.

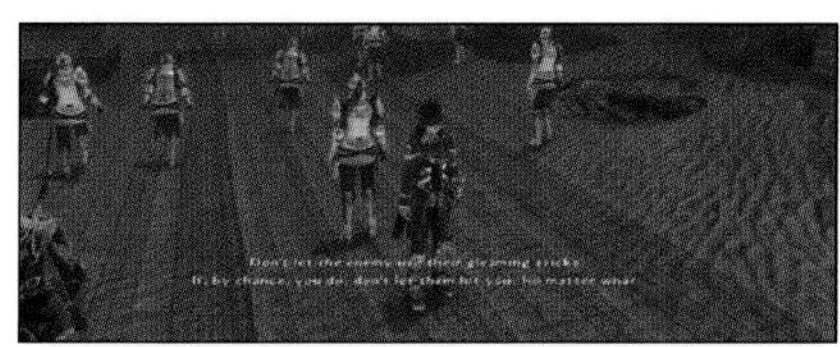

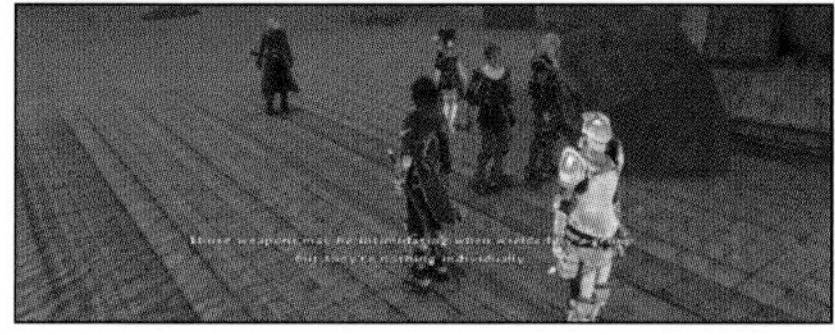

Once again, the King's Chosen joins the party. Save your progress and heal up if you haven't done so already, then enter Eastern Trei'kur to dive into the fray. Victory ensures Resulian occupation of the area.

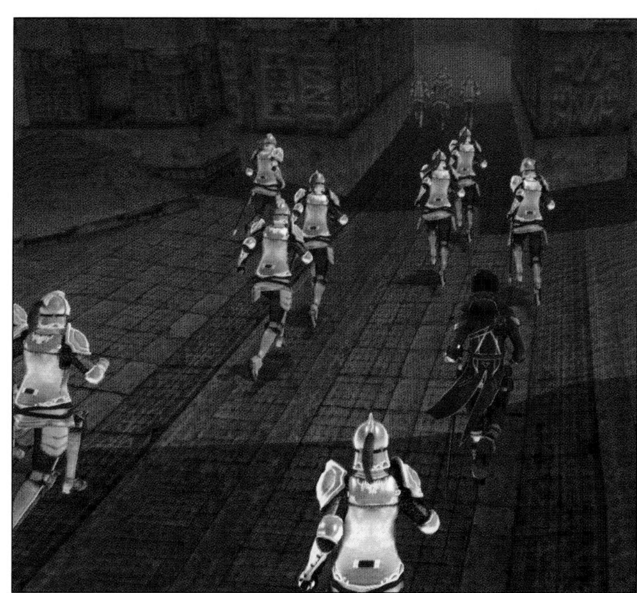

EASTERN TREI'KUR

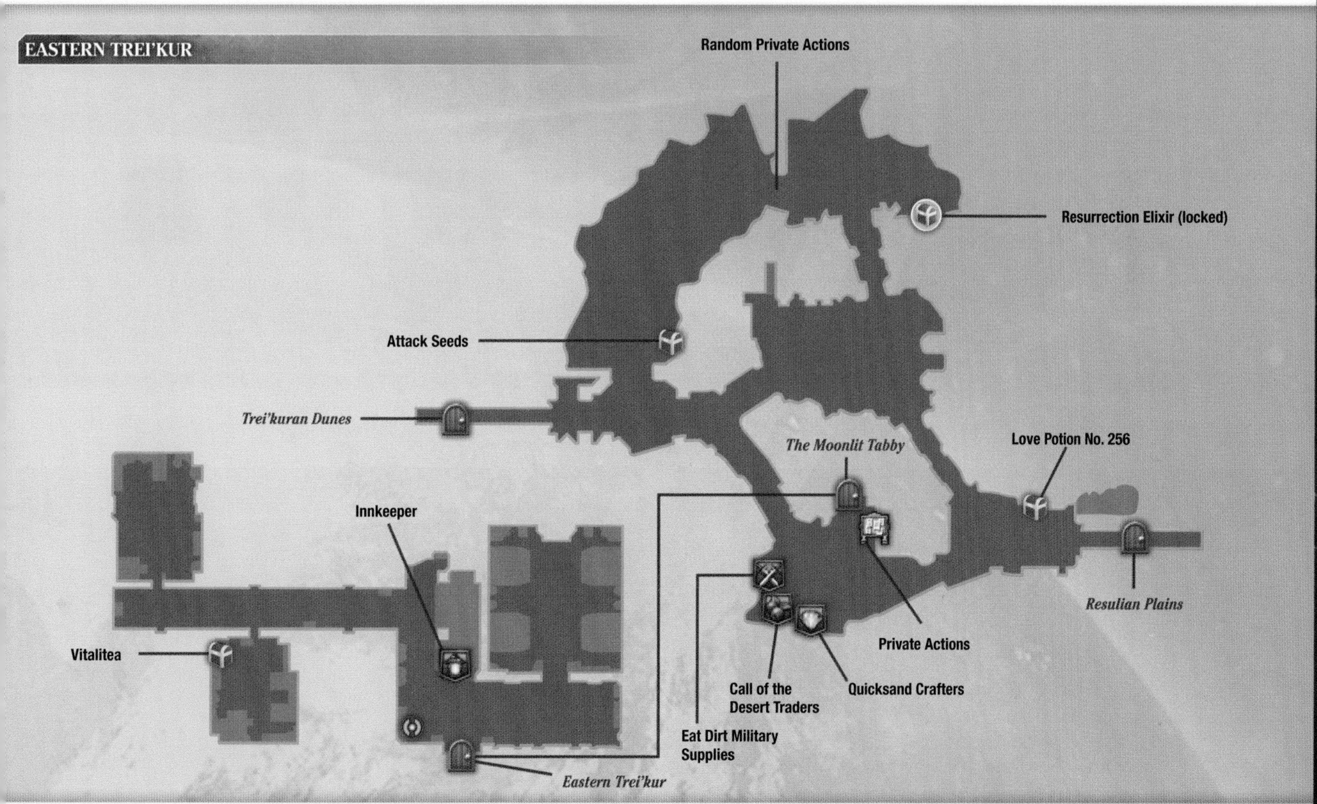

Random Private Actions
Resurrection Elixir (locked)
Attack Seeds
Trei'kuran Dunes
The Moonlit Tabby
Love Potion No. 256
Innkeeper
Resulian Plains
Vitalitea
Private Actions
Call of the Desert Traders
Quicksand Crafters
Eat Dirt Military Supplies
Eastern Trei'kur

TREI'KURAN KNIGHT LVL 41

P. 293 — Iron, Silver

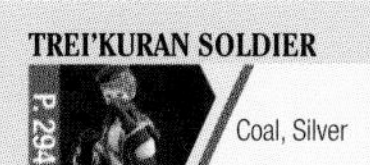

TREI'KURAN ARMORED BOWMAN LVL 41

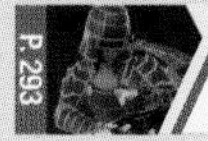

P. 293 — Gravity Bomb

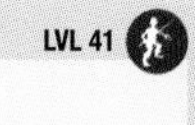

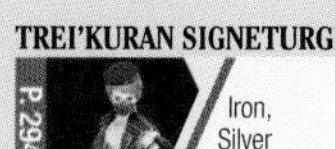

TREI'KURAN SOLDIER LVL 41

P. 294 — Coal, Silver

TREI'KURAN SIGNETURGE LVL 41

P. 294 — Iron, Silver

TREI'KURAN SHARPSHOOTER LVL 41

P. 294 — Stun Bomb, Coal, Silver

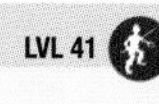

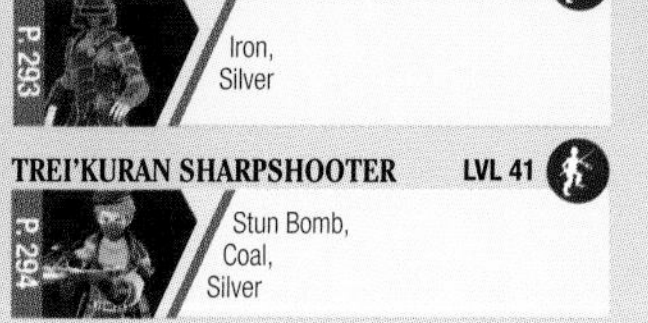

Once inside, head north and defeat the Trei'kuran Knights and Armored Bowmen here. Remember to equip the Warrior Slayer role on either Fidel or Victor since all of the enemies here are humanoids. After you've dealt with this group, open the chest nearby for some **Attack Seeds**. Continue north, and confront the Trei'kuran Soldiers here. During this fight, the crew is reunited with Emmerson and Anne, who will fight alongside you.

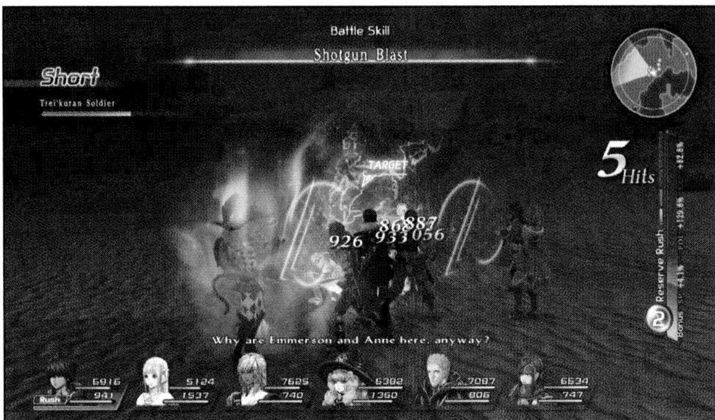

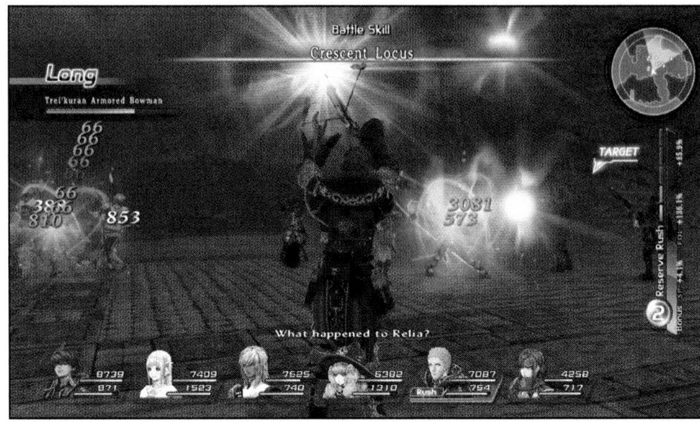

PART 03

Finish off the soldiers, and then make sure to fill out Emmerson and Anne's accessories and role slots (since they're empty).

Continue east, then south, clearing out the Trei'kuran military in your way.

You'll eventually meet their commander, Der-Suul. Take out his underlings before you take him on, making sure to heal up any hurt party members (at this point, an AI-controlled Miki with the proper healing roles can do just fine on her own).

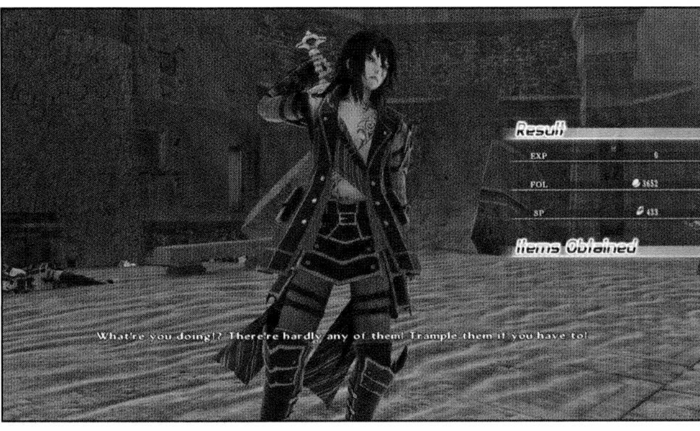

When you take Der-Suul down to 25% HP, he'll retreat to the roof, leaving several waves of his subordinates for you to deal with.

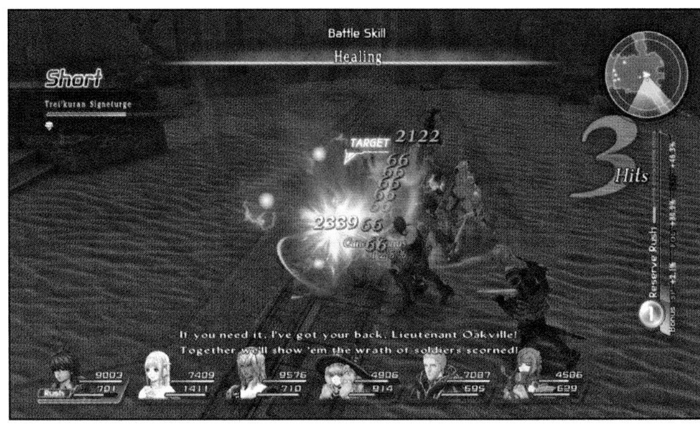

Once they've all been vanquished, a cutscene triggers. Fidel and Miki fume as they discover that Relia's been kidnapped under Emmerson's watch.

However, Fiore reminds Anne about data retrieved from the research facility.

After a brief recess, the group reconvenes and discusses a lead regarding another laboratory Kronos has set up, involving studies in symbometrics. However, further analysis must be done before they can identify its location.

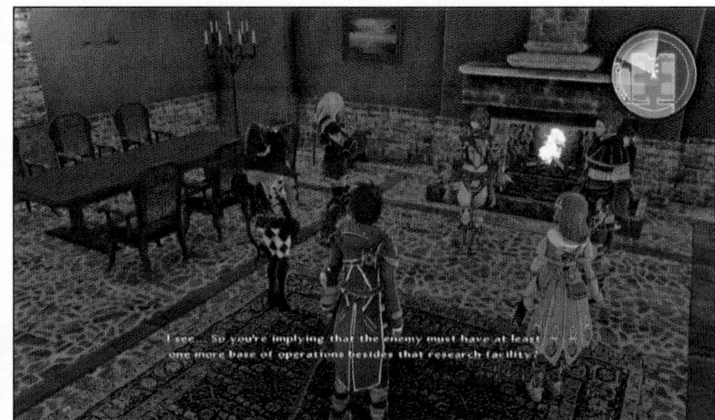

When you're back in control of Fidel in The Moonlit Tabby, talk to the innkeeper to rest for the night.

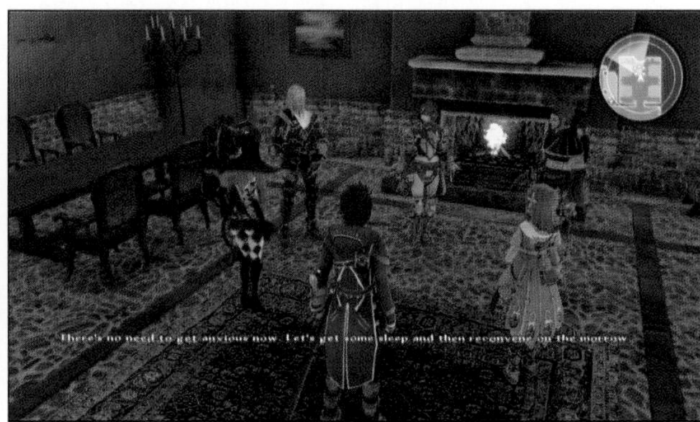

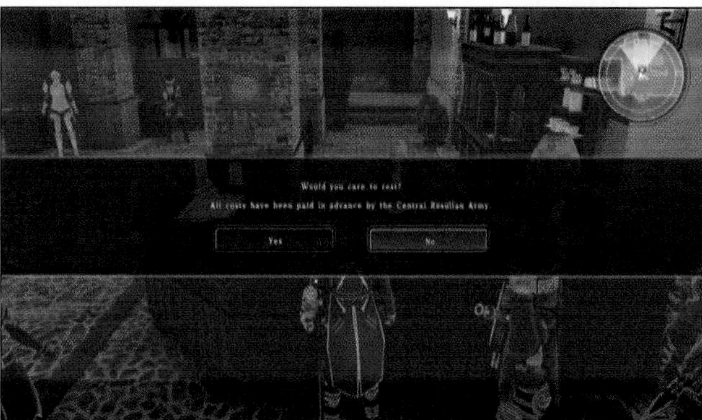

EXTRACTION

After a successful annexation of Eastern Trei'kur, the Resulian military now has a localized base of operations. Fidel, Miki, Victor, and Fiore rejoin Emmerson and Anne to rescue Relia from the clutches of her abductors.

MISSION: CLOAK-AND-DECIPHER

Tensions arise between Emmerson and Fidel. However, no amount of blame can change what has transpired. The Faykreedians need to work with the two federation officers if they want to save the innocent child from Kronos' exploitative practices.

Action Checklist

1. Optional: Upgrade equipment
2. Optional: Undertake new side quests and view Private Actions
3. Optional: Complete Welch quests
4. Optional: Complete Cathedral of Oblivion (second set)
5. Find the cloaked research facility
6. Descend to the bottom floor
7. Rescue Relia

SHOPS—EASTERN TREI'KUR (UPDATES)

Quicksand Crafters

ITEM	COST	TYPE
Common Eggs	90	Food
Fresh Vegetables	180	Food
Lemon	90	Food
Nectar	120	Food
Prehistoric Meat	180	Food
Spring Water	240	Food
Cocoa Powder	240	Material
Fermentation Pot	2400	Material
Seasonings	60	Material
White Rice	180	Material

Eat Dirt Military Supplies

ITEM	COST	TYPE
Acuity Crest	3000	Accessory
Arcane Amulet	25000	Accessory
Attack Crest	3000	Accessory
Energy Amulet	25000	Accessory
Fortitude Crest	3000	Accessory
Mind Crest	3000	Accessory
Amber Robe	3750	Armor
Silver Cloak	5250	Armor
Silver Cuirass	5950	Armor
Silver Mesh	4900	Armor
Streaked Chainmail	3500	Armor
Superior Armor Plate	4250	Armor
Composite Bow	7350	Weapon
Corvine Orb	8750	Weapon
Deadly Edge	5500	Weapon
Farcutter	7700	Weapon
Fragmenters	6300	Weapon
Moonfalx	7000	Weapon
Rune Wand	4000	Weapon
Sacred Scepter	5600	Weapon
Slasher Claws	4500	Weapon
Sunsylph Orb	6250	Weapon
Walloon Sword	5000	Weapon
Wild Arc	5250	Weapon

Mission Walkthrough

With the Resulian occupation of Eastern Trei'kur and the reunion between Fidel and his space-faring allies, your new priority is to search for Relia. Your objective here is to gather any intel you can from Emmerson and Anne, and then follow the leads that you find.

Before you set off on your search, you can take a break from the main story mission to obtain exceptionally powerful equipment and battle skills. A plethora of optional tasks has opened up, including several Private Actions, bulletin board quests, and all-new instances of the Cathedral of Oblivion.

SIDE QUESTS

EASTERN TREI'KUR
Medical Emergency
Grannie Never Rests on Her Laurels

CENTRAL RESULIA
Reconstructing an Enigma
Collection of Romantic Entanglements
Survive This!
Spleen for a Spleen

WELCH'S LABORATORY
Of Weapons and Womanizers

SANTEROULE
Too Little, Too Late
Open Season on Mujas
Wanted: Randaghor
Quiet Down in There!

PRIVATE ACTIONS

EASTERN TREI'KUR
No Two-Timing
Reminiscing with Daril (* Missable Private Action *)
Position of Power
You a Cat Person or Dog Person?
A Fine Young Man
Patch Conversion
No Different
Ask Him Yourself
Crossing the Line
Sweet and Sour Personalities
Combat and Concern
Prepared to Take Lives
Spirited Conversation
Overshadowed by Fear
Only So Much You Can Do
Enter a Mysterious Woman (* Missable Private Action *)

CENTRAL RESULIA
The True Cause of the Corrupt
Trouble Brewing Between Nations
Anne and Canines
Manly Miki
Asking About Accessories

MYIDDOK
Neverending Story of Sweets
The Dutchess of Duking It Out
Fidel and Love
Reverse Psychology
More Cat Capers
Portrait of the Creature as a Young Kitten
Tipping the Scales When Tipsy
No Hangovers, No Reason to Decline
Guzzle It Like Granny

SANTEROULE
Nothing's There
Asceticism over Affections
Conversational Battle of the Sexes
Helping Hand Towel
Fixated on Fiore
Out for Blood
Sneaking Suspicion
Haunted by the Unknown

STHAL
Like Father, Like Son (* Missable Private Action *)
Space Food
High-Stakes Gambling
Over Fidel's Head (* Missable Private Action *)

VICTOR'S MYSTERIOUS PAST

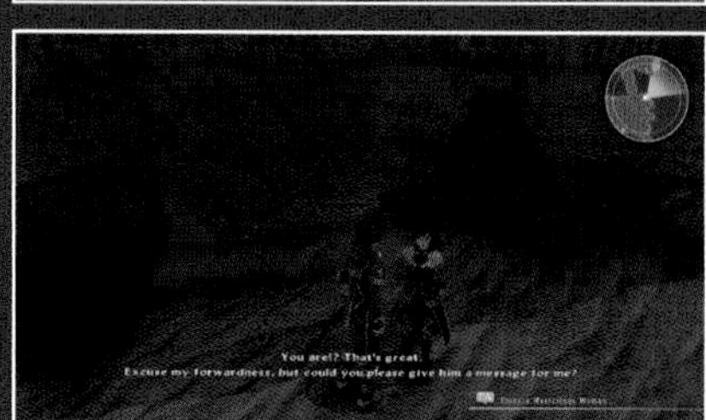

There's a missable series of Private Actions here in Eastern Trei'kur that can be accessed with a specific set of conditions. First, Victor and Fidel will need to have a decent amount of affinity with each other. This can be attained through triggering Private Actions with Victor while responding to him positively (when given a choice). Up to this point in the game, if you've been diligent in viewing all Private Actions, you should have enough affinity between these two characters.

When you've met the affinity requirement, you'll gain access to a **random** Private Action called Victor on Love. To ensure you trigger this Private Action, you can repeatedly trigger random Private Action points (designated on the area maps in this guide) by leaving and re-entering the same zone. The closest one is in Eastern Trei'kur if you're following this walkthrough.

Once Victor on Love is triggered, a unique Private Action will be available in Eastern Trei'kur. Talk to the Mysterious Woman, and she'll give you instructions if Fidel tells her that he's friends with Victor.

This will queue up another Private Action, so enter Eastern Trei'kur's inn (or exit the area). Re-enter Eastern Trei'kur to view the next Private Action in the series, called The Mysterious Woman's Name. Talk to Victor, and he'll tell you her name while revealing a bit of his past.

Seems like he's still hiding something, though. Exit and return to Eastern Trei'kur one more time, and you'll have access to the last in this Private Action series. Talk with Victor's soldiers, the King's Chosen. They'll divulge Rebecca's identity, as well as expose a tragic story regarding Victor and his past love life.

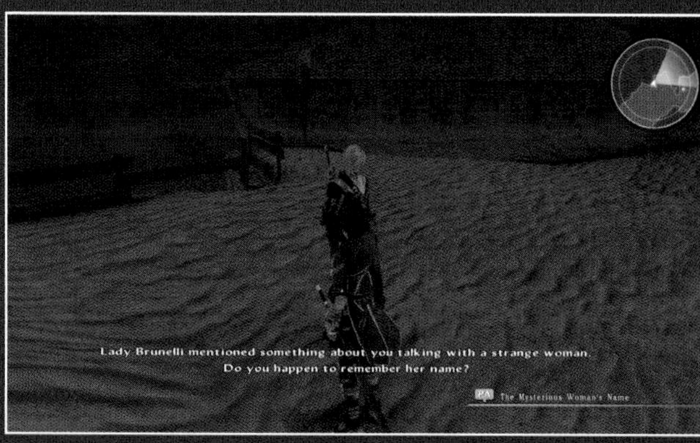

CATHEDRAL OF OBLIVION, EVOLVED

Once you've taken part in the siege of Eastern Trei'kur, more instances of the Cathedral of Oblivion open up. Not only will there be two additional gauntlets (located in the Trei'kuran Dunes and the Northern Territory of Sohma), but the previous ones will have new enemies for you to take on, with even better rewards.

If you want to attempt a challenge, try your hand at some of these dungeons. It's recommended that you complete them in the following order: Coast of Minoz, Resulian Plains, West of the Eastern Eihieds, Trei'kuran Dunes, and the Northern Territory of Sohma. The final boss in each instance is identical, but its power level is much higher in the latter areas. For example, the Coast of Minoz's cathedral boss is Lv. 45, while the one in the Northern Territory of Sohma is Lv. 65!

Start with the cathedral in the Coast of Minoz to familiarize yourself with Vidofnir, the final round boss of this set of dungeons. To get them to appear, simply re-enter the area until the warp point is displayed on your in-game map.

VIDOFNIR

LVL 45

Vidofnir is a phoenix-like avian adept at fire-based spells and attacks. Naturally, it's weak to ice spells, so you'll want to equip your battle sets accordingly. Have Fiore's signeturgies set to Ice Needles (or Deep Freeze, if available). For Miki, don't forget to turn off her offensive spells. You'll need her to focus primarily on healing and raising your allies.

Additionally, because Vidofnir is an avian-type creature, the Raven Slayer role is extremely effective on one of your close-combat fighters (like Fidel, Victor, or Anne).

This infernal phoenix is most likely the hardest boss you've fought up until now if you're running through the cathedral at the earliest point possible, so bring plenty of supplies and food items.

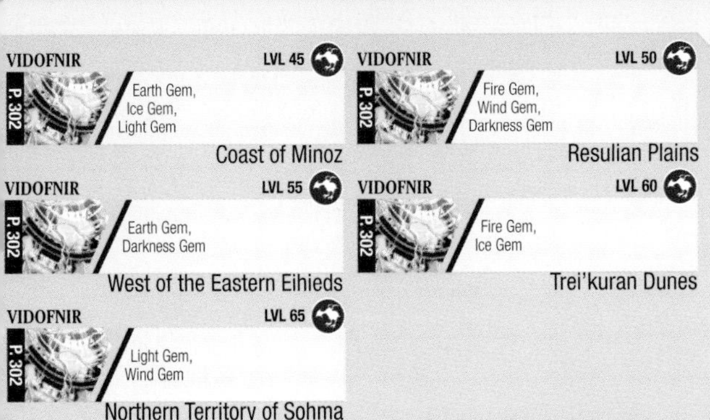

Its main attacks to watch out for are Tornado, Volcanic Burst, and Divergent Shade. Tornado is particularly devastating, as it can knock up and deal extraordinary amounts of damage on Miki and Fiore. Watch out for this spell, open the battle menu, and take control of your back line members to move away from its path or to guard the incoming tornado.

Volcanic Burst is an area-of-effect spell that lays down destruction in a large space. Mitigate its damage by separating your members as best as possible, especially your back line. Vidofnir has a tendency to cast it on Miki, Fiore, and Emmerson.

When Vidofnir casts Divergent Shade, it randomly unleashes a flock of fireballs. These can't be guarded, but they're mostly avoidable.

It's imperative that you keep Miki alive as best as you can, since she's most likely your only reliable way of healing multiple party members. Use Fresh Sage on knocked-out party members immediately.

During the fight with Vidofnir, keep your allies healthy while doing your best to avoid its devastating spells, and you'll eventually be victorious.

If you manage to save up Reserve Rush, don't be afraid to unleash a high-damage 200% ratio Reserve Rush attack on the beast.

WELCH THE BEAUTIFUL AND GENIUS INVENTOR, PART III

At this point in the game, you can undertake another Welch quest if you've been diligently completing the previous ones in the quest line. Visit Welch's Laboratory in Myiddok to trigger a cutscene for the **Of Weapons and Womanizers** quest. If you've saved up five Micro Circuits, you can turn them in immediately. This unlocks the Engineering item creation specialty.

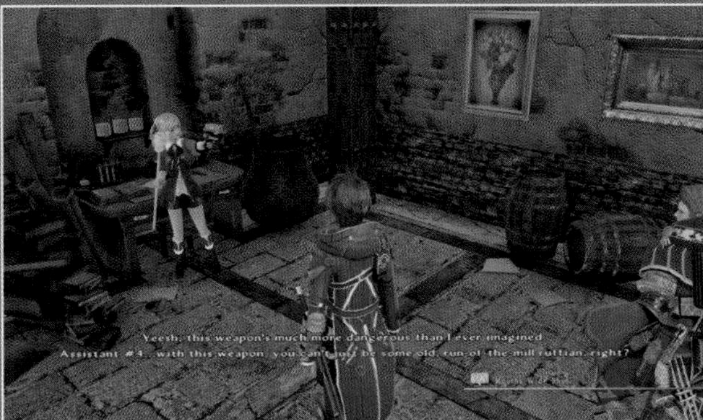

ENGINEERING

Engineering allows you to create various machinery, including phaser weapons, bombs, and skill disks. However, if you obtain this specialty skill early on, you might not be able to utilize it fully— your access to certain electronics is limited until later in the game.

DEAD RAISER

The **Wanted: Randaghor** quest rewards you with a **Pneuma Signets, Vol. 1** skill book. This should be your second copy obtained at this point. Have Fiore read it so she can learn the Raise Dead spell (or Miki, if Fiore already knows it). Having two members able to raise your other party members is extremely valuable, especially during the more challenging boss encounters. Not only can you raise multiple members simultaneously, but it also frees up your item usage cooldown while conserving your Fresh Sage count.

LOCKED STOCK

The **Survive This!** quest unlocks the Lock Picking specialty skill. If you want to start opening the locked chests that you've been finding, finish this quest, and then spend 500 SP into obtaining the Lock Picking specialty. You can refer to the maps provided in this guide for the locations of locked chests, or you can use the data table in the **Optional Tasks** chapter.

You can get access to extremely powerful abilities early on in the game if you make the trek around the world, unlocking these treasures. For instance, you can obtain **Swordsman's Manual III** (Mirror Blade) and **Cerulean Orb Signets, Vol. 2** (Deep Freeze) before you would naturally get them through progressing the story. These special attacks are incredibly strong.

RECOMMENDED ROLES

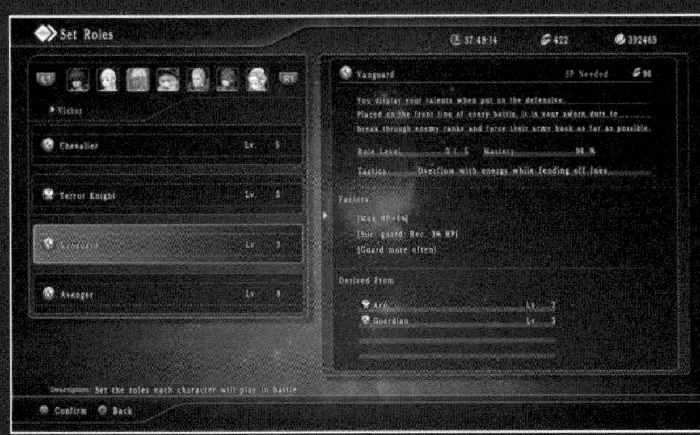

At this point in the game, you should have several roles unlocked and leveled up to around Lv. 4 or 5. Every one of your characters should have their role slots filled out with useful ones that synergize with each other.

Fidel and Victor can make good use of defense-oriented and attack-oriented roles like Vanguard, Avenger, Pulverizer, and Ace. Anne is most efficient when she can be relentlessly aggressive with the slayer roles, which can be equipped during battle according to the type of enemy you're facing. Emmerson does well with the Berserker role since he fights from a distance and doesn't need to put himself at risk often.

Miki should have Healer, Crusader, Savior, and Sage equipped for the majority of the game. These all enhance her healing capabilities drastically. Fiore's spells scale with INT, and there's no shortage of INT-enhancing roles. Therefore, aim to level up Shrewd Overseer, Enchanter, and Elementalist (which eventually unlocks the "emissary" roles).

When you have Relia in the party, she can make use of passive support roles like Altruist and Scavenger.

To plan out role unlock paths, refer to the roles data table in the **Game Mechanics** section of this guide.

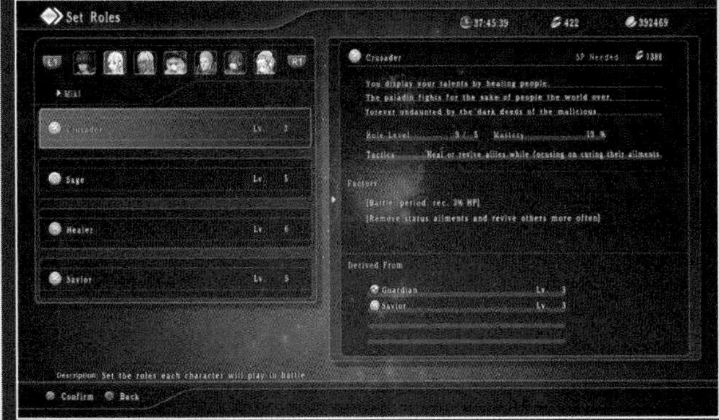

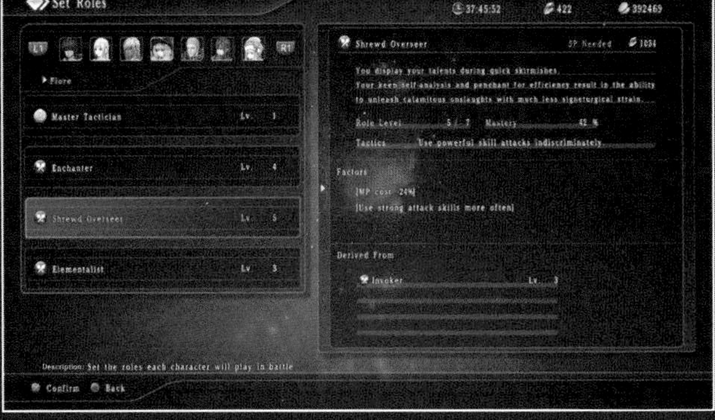

UNCLOAK THE LABORATORY ENTRANCE

Fidel wakes up alone in The Moonlit Tabby. Pick up the **Vitalitea** potion in a chest in the room, and then leave the inn to find out where everyone is.

Explore the Eastern Trei'kur outpost, picking up some side quests from the bulletin board here and upgrading equipment from the armorer. Near the east exit, up a ramp, you can find a chest containing a **Love Potion No. 256**. Next, go to the waypoint in the northern section of the encampment to meet with Emmerson and Anne.

The two federation officers seem to be discussing the mission amongst themselves. After Fidel maturely apologizes for his aggressive behavior toward Emmerson, head back into the inn.

The party reconvenes, with Anne having new information of the whereabouts of another cloaked research facility.

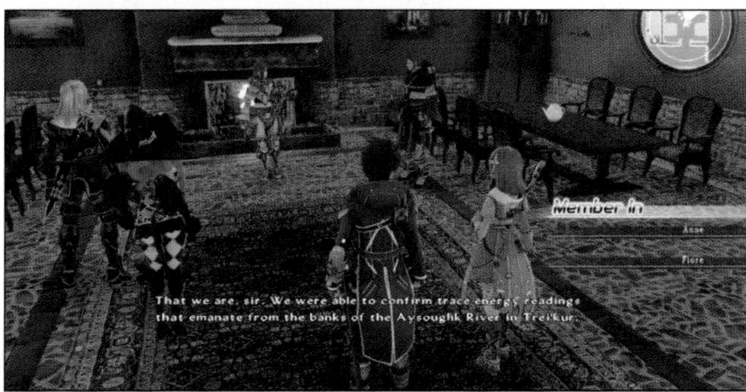

You can now traverse the Trei'kuran Dunes to search for the hidden research facility. Unlike your first visit to the dunes, you'll have access to the entire area. Exit to the dunes through the west exit from Eastern Trei'kur.

TREI'KURAN DUNES

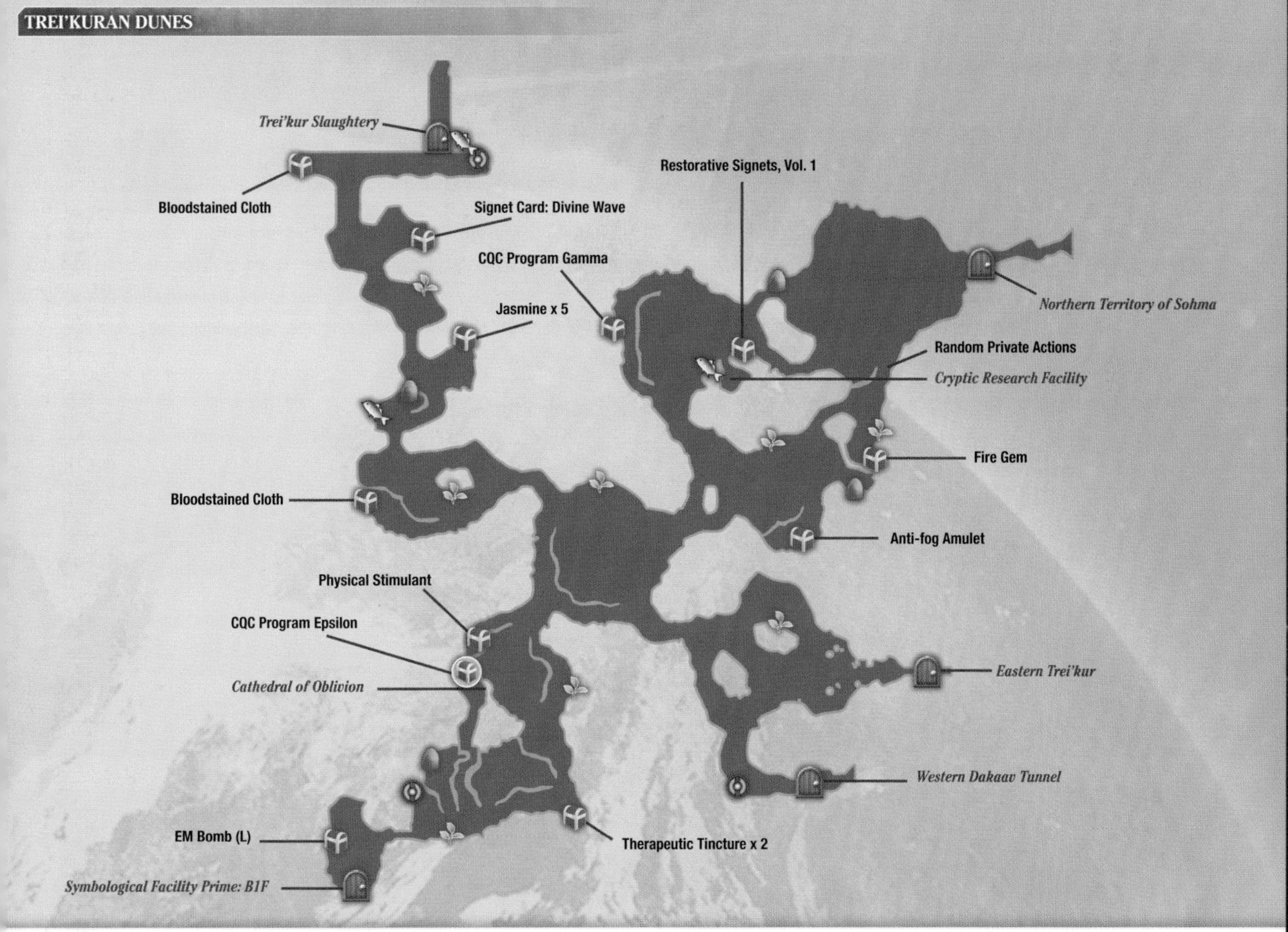

Trei'kur Slaughtery
Bloodstained Cloth
Signet Card: Divine Wave
CQC Program Gamma
Jasmine x 5
Restorative Signets, Vol. 1
Northern Territory of Sohma
Random Private Actions
Cryptic Research Facility
Fire Gem
Bloodstained Cloth
Anti-fog Amulet
Physical Stimulant
CQC Program Epsilon
Cathedral of Oblivion
Eastern Trei'kur
Western Dakaav Tunnel
EM Bomb (L)
Therapeutic Tincture x 2
Symbological Facility Prime: B1F

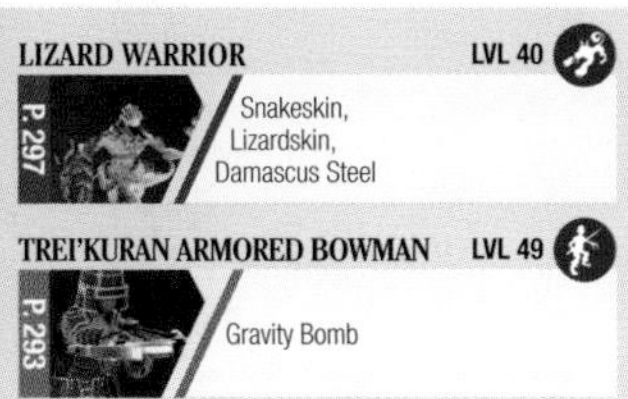

LIZARD WARRIOR LVL 40 — P. 297 — Snakeskin, Lizardskin, Damascus Steel

TREI'KURAN ARMORED BOWMAN LVL 49 — P. 293 — Gravity Bomb

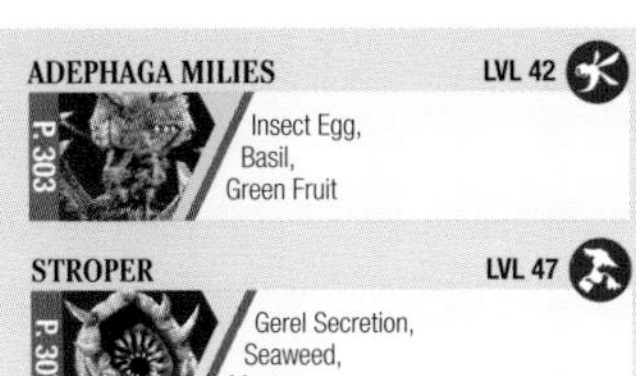

ADEPHAGA MILIES LVL 42 — P. 303 — Insect Egg, Basil, Green Fruit

STROPER LVL 47 — P. 307 — Gerel Secretion, Seaweed, Mercury

TREI'KURAN KNIGHT LVL 48 — P. 293 — Blueberry Potion

VAMPIRE BAT LVL 46 — P. 302 — Jasmine, Chamomile, Crystal, Darkness Gem

TREI'KURAN SIGNETURGE LVL 50 — P. 294 — Blackberry Potion, Signet Card: Earth Glaive +

LIZARD SHAMAN LVL 41 — P. 297 — Snakeskin, Lizardskin, Signet Card: Fire Bolt, Signet Card: Healing

Your objective in the southwest region of the area is marked with a red star. On your way there, you can pick up a few chests. On a ledge to the west is a chest containing a **Physical Stimulant**. After you pick it up, head southeast from there to the other corner of the immediate region, and open a chest with **Therapeutic Tincture x 2** in it. Now, head west until you reach a bridge formation that leads north. If you have the Lock Picking specialty, you can unlock a chest with a **CQC Program Epsilon** disk in it at the end of this bridge. You can also try your hand at the Cathedral of Oblivion here if the warp point has spawned (although it may be difficult if you're under-leveled, so be sure to save your progress first).

Continue into the southwest area, where you'll trigger some dialogue with Anne. Her scanner has picked up something off in this location.

Just like with the Cryptic Research Facility, you're looking for a cloaked entrance. There's a chest with an **EM Bomb (L)** on the edge to the west. Open it, and then to the south of the area, look for an odd distortion near Anne. When you've found it, Anne will attempt a hack into the building's system. This triggers an ambush—protect Anne at all costs!

Similar to the security drones you encountered at the first research facility, you'll need to fight without Anne, as she's busy hacking the security protocols. Furthermore, enemies will relentlessly attempt to take her down; if they're successful, the game ends, and you'll need to reload your save. Do your best to keep her alive. Heal her up with Miki's spells while your other members take out the threats. This can prove very difficult if you're not prepared. The first thing you should do is move Miki out of the foes' line of sight so that she doesn't take collateral damage while they're attacking Anne. Then, you can use the bomb that you picked up earlier to eliminate some of the troops.

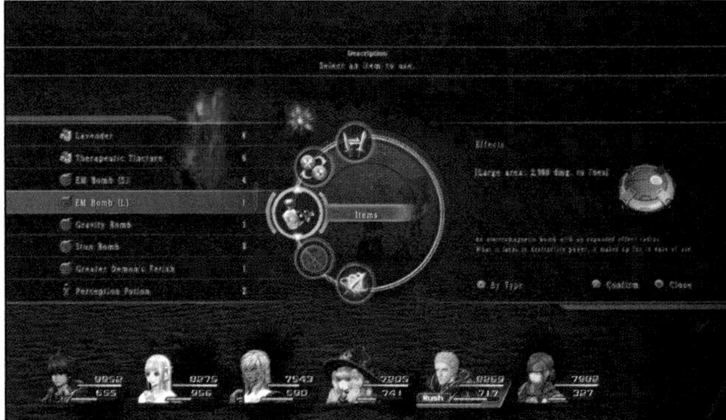

Make sure to heal Anne with items like Blueberry Potions if Miki can't keep her health up. If she's healthy, you can start using debilitating attack skills like Fidel's and Victor's Double Slash techniques to knock out aggressors, mitigating damage done to Anne. After a period of time, she'll successfully open the emergency hatch.

PART 03

SYMBOLOGICAL FACILITY

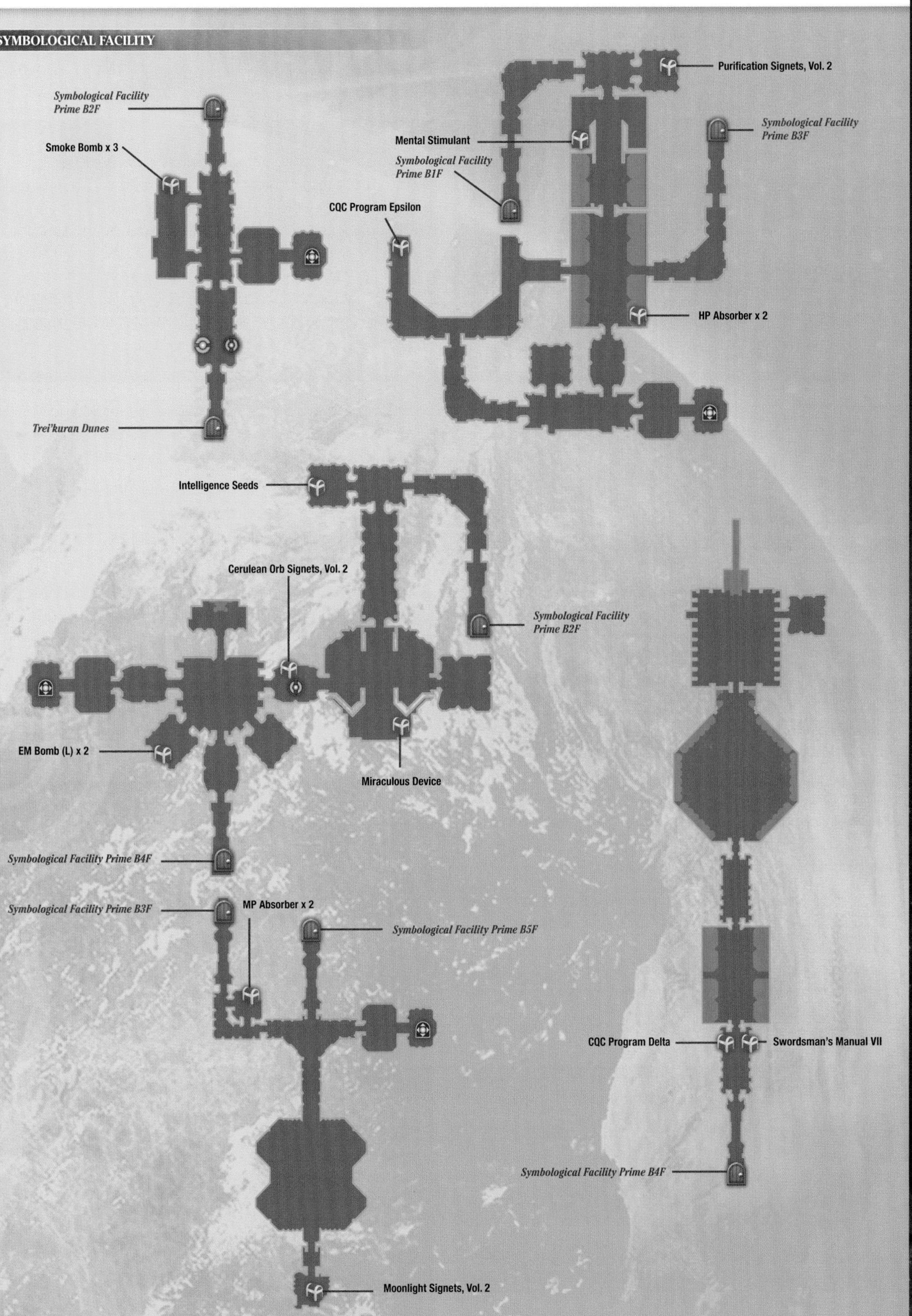

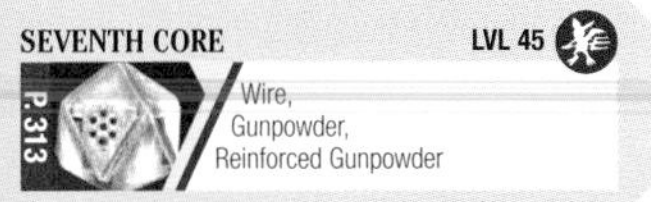

Once you're safely inside the facility, you can use the save and restore points. When you're ready, go north and west into a room with a treasure sphere containing **Smoke Bomb x 3**. Open it, and then continue north to the second basement floor.

From your starting point here, head north, then make a right and continue going straight into the room to the east. Pick up a copy of **Purification Signets, Vol. 2** here, then turn around and enter the large laboratory to the south. There's another treasure sphere here west of the ramp; open it to obtain a **Mental Stimulant**.

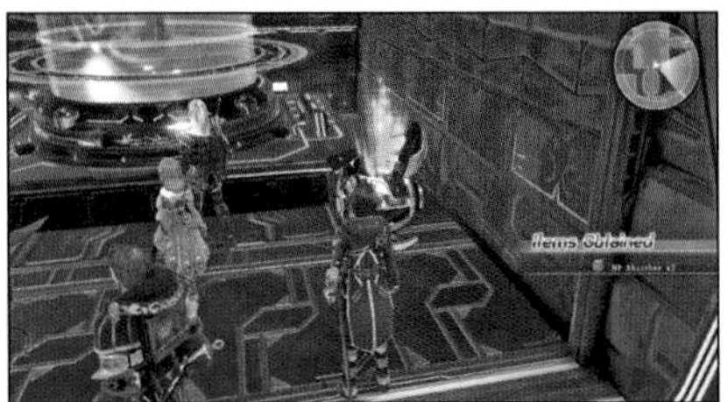

Continue south past the Kronos experimental subjects, then take the door to the west. Across the platform here (at the westernmost end), you'll find a **CQC Program Epsilon** disk in a sphere. Defeat the Phantom Dragoon guarding it, and then open the sphere so you can have Emmerson or Anne learn a new attack skill.

Now, turn around and take the door to your right into the southern region of the floor. Then, travel east, fighting through more Kronos cronies. Take the second door to your left, looping back around into the large lab area. There is a sphere to your immediate right, containing **HP Absorber x 2**. Open it, then take the path to the east from the center of the area, leading to the third basement floor.

On the third floor here, follow the hallway until it bends west. Keep going west, and you'll find a treasure sphere with **Intelligence Seeds** in it. After you pick it up, turn around and take the door south, proceeding past a long hall until you reach a storage unit with what looks to be Relia inside. However, it's not. In the southeast corner of the laboratory, pick up a **Miraculous Device** in the sphere there.

Continue by going west from the Relia-like experiment to a room with a save point and another treasure sphere that has **Cerulean Orb Signets, Vol. 2** inside it. Loot the contents, and then save your progress here. Restore your HP and MP with items if you need to. You'll be on Anne protection duty again soon!

At this point, you should have your party chow down on party-wide stat-boosting food (such as Hamburg Steak or Curry Rice). From the save point, go west and then north into the workstation area. Anne attempts to access the network in hopes of finding more information on Relia's whereabouts. This cues several Kronos security soldiers to attack the party. As before, you'll need to protect Anne again at all costs!

Thankfully, you have a positional advantage here because enemies must funnel into the room to get to Anne. Keep them out with your relentless attacks, making sure to keep Anne healed with items and healing spells.

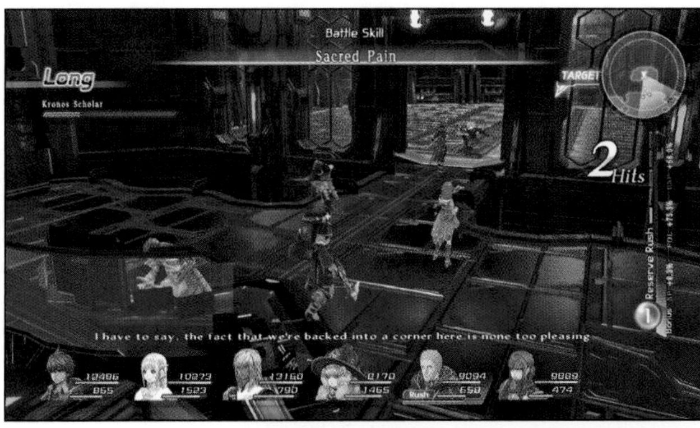

After you defeat several waves of Kronos Gunners and Scholars, Anne successfully finds Relia's location. Before you follow Anne, enter the room to the southwest of the larger main room to pick up **EM Bomb (L) x 2**. Now, head for the south path, taking you to the floor beneath where Relia is supposedly held.

On the fourth floor, make an immediate left into a small workstation room. Open the treasure sphere to pick up **MP Absorber x 2**. Continue east, and then to the south. You arrive at a large area with what looks to be an army of robots and soldiers waiting for you.

COMPLETE THE EXTRACTION MISSION

This mini-boss battle has you up against a massive spider-like machine and several Kronos troops. Start by separating your party members, keeping Miki away from harm. Make sure to equip Fidel, Victor, or Anne with the Machine Slayer role if you have it, and another damage-dealer with the Warrior Slayer role to take care of the Kronos Soldiers. The Destroyer inflicts a ton of damage and can apply a stun effect; it can be especially dangerous if it decides to make a beeline for Miki. Take control of her if necessary to maneuver her away from its physical area-of-effect attacks.

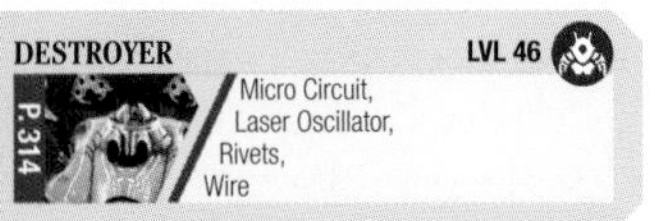

When you've stabilized the situation, unleash your most powerful Reserve Rush combo on it to turn the giant mechanical arthropod to scrap.

Now, move to the room to the south, where a short cutscene triggers. Looks like Relia got a haircut. She'll rejoin your party, so make sure to equip her with supportive roles.

Before you leave, open the treasure sphere here for a copy of **Moonlight Signets, Vol. 2**. Turn back the way you came, and Anne will notify the crew of active transport devices, conveniently located on each floor for easy transport between levels. They're now marked on your map, so head back up north until you get to the divergence, and then make a right into the transport room. Exit the facility by selecting B1F while operating the transport pad.

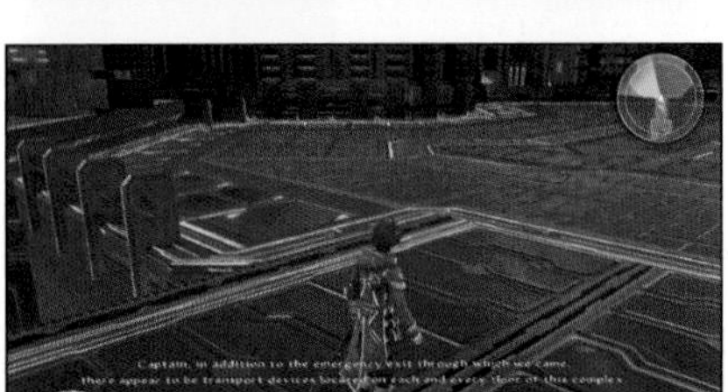

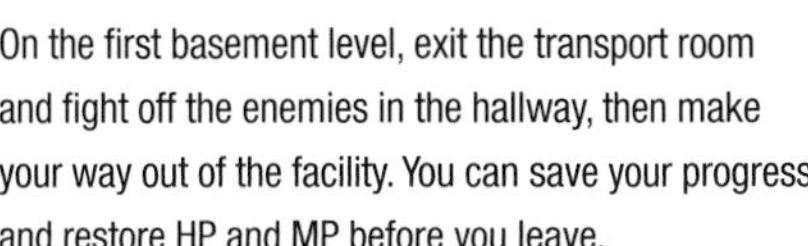

On the first basement level, exit the transport room and fight off the enemies in the hallway, then make your way out of the facility. You can save your progress and restore HP and MP before you leave.

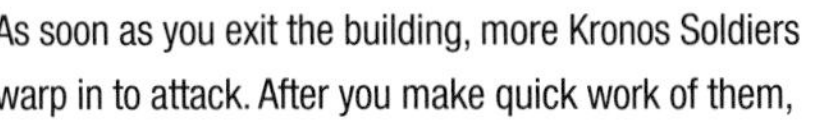

As soon as you exit the building, more Kronos Soldiers warp in to attack. After you make quick work of them, more dialogue between Emmerson, Anne, and Fiore ensues as they talk about removing Relia's signets. Your new mission is to take Relia to Santeroule.

The journey back to Eastern Trei'kur is littered with hostile Kronos troops, so fight through them, and then enter the encampment.

Upon entering Eastern Trei'kur, Victor reports to Daril in a short dialogue sequence. The party is exhausted after the extraction mission, so head to the inn to get some rest.

CHAPTER 8

TRAGEDY IN TREI'KUR

With the recuperation of Relia, Fidel and his allies return to Eastern Trei'kur. While the Resulian operation to occupy the area was successful, it's not without consequences...

PART 03

MISSION: RESCUE

Fidel's acts of nobility and courage don't go unnoticed by his father. In a rare gesture, Daril gives his son a few words of adulation. However, Fidel's elation is cut short when a vengeful villain attacks the now-Resulian encampment.

Action Checklist

1. Meet with Daril
2. Summon Victor and defend the encampment
3. Optional: Upgrade equipment
4. Optional: Unlock Private Action events and random Private Actions by visiting the Trei'kur Slaughtery entrance
5. Optional: Undertake and complete side quests in various towns
6. Find Daril and Relia in the Trei'kur Slaughtery

Mission Walkthrough

Your main objective here is to meet with Daril and defend Eastern Trei'kur from its original proprietors. Then, you'll need to undergo a rescue mission in the Trei'kur Slaughtery.

DEFEND AGAINST DER-SUUL

Again, Fidel wakes up in the middle of the night. Exit The Moonlit Tabby, and take a walk outside for some fresh air. Your destination is in the northern area of Eastern Trei'kur, where you'll meet with Fidel's father. As they have a heart-to-heart talk, Daril feels that something is amiss.

He orders Fidel back to the inn to beckon Victor's aid. Return to The Moonlit Tabby to send Victor on a reconnaissance mission. Before he can go, Trei'kur sieges the encampment.

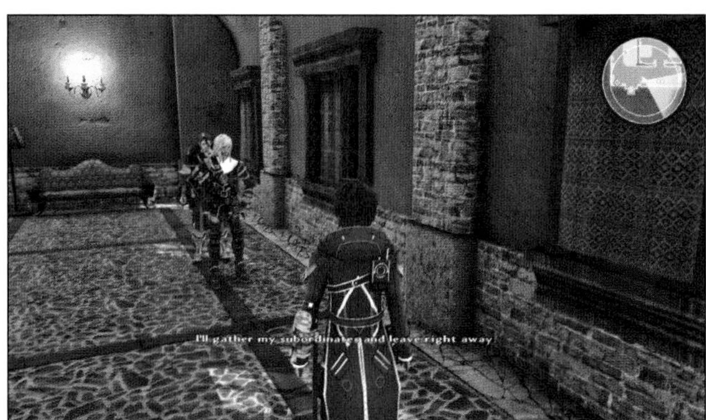

Enemy	Level	Page	Items
DER-SUUL	LVL 42	P. 286	NO ITEMS
TREI'KURAN SHARPSHOOOTER	LVL 49	P. 294	Gravity Bomb
TREI'KURAN SOLDIER	LVL 49	P. 294	Coal, Silver
TREI'KURAN SIGNETURGE	LVL 50	P. 294	Blackberry Potion, Signet Card: Earth Glaive +

With control of the full party, leave the inn to defend the Resulian outpost. Fight your way to the upper area of the map, where you met with Daril earlier. Der-Suul is here, along with several Trei'kuran troops. Since you won't be able to damage Der-Suul, you'll need to work on thinning out the barrage of incoming henchmen. Keep fighting, and Der-Suul's men eventually retreat without him.

In a desperate fit of rage Der-Suul maims Daril with a signeturgical spell. He then abducts both Relia and Fidel's father and demands for Resulian troops to concede the Trei'kuran territory before sunrise. However, Fidel and Victor have different plans: they're going to infiltrate the enemy camp and put an end to Der-Suul.

TO THE OTHER END OF THE DUNES

Looks like plans have changed and you won't be heading to Santeroule after all. Since you only have until sunrise, all of your adventuring from now until you confront Der-Suul will take place at night. You can stop by the military supply shop here in Eastern Trei'kur before making your way toward the Trei'kur Slaughtery.

OPTIONAL

FROM DUSK 'TIL DAWN

With Fidel's father and Relia as Der-Suul's hostages, you only have until sunrise to carry out your rescue mission. Anywhere you go from now until the next story mission is accomplished takes place in a dark and dusky setting. Furthermore, although there's a sense of urgency, there's no real timer. Feel free to explore the world and complete side quests before you make your way to the Trei'kur Slaughtery.

PRIVATE ACTIONS PROGRESS

Further Private Action events and random Private Actions are locked at this point until you visit the Trei'kur Slaughtery. You do *not* have to finish clearing the area or completing the mission, but you do need to at least visit the entrance of the slaughtery. If you want to take a break from the main story, it's advised that you visit the Trei'kur Slaughtery and then return to Eastern Trei'kur. The nighttime setting remains, but you'll be able to access Private Actions again (both stationary and random ones).

SHOPS— EASTERN TREI'KUR (UPGRADES)

Eat Dirt Military Supplies

ITEM	COST	TYPE
Acuity Crest	3000	Accessory
Arcane Amulet	25000	Accessory
Attack Crest	3000	Accessory
Energy Amulet	25000	Accessory
Fortitude Crest	3000	Accessory
Mind Crest	3000	Accessory
Alchemist's Cloak	6750	Armor
Ogre's Armor	7650	Armor
Silver Cloak	5250	Armor
Silver Cuirass	5950	Armor
Silver Mesh	4900	Armor
Superior Armor Plate	4250	Armor
Superior Mesh	6300	Armor
Cesti of Torment	8100	Weapon
Composite Bow	7350	Weapon
Corvine Orb	8750	Weapon
Crystal Wand	7200	Weapon
Farcutter	7700	Weapon
Flamberge	9000	Weapon
Fragmenters	6300	Weapon
Homing Arc	9450	Weapon
Marmoreal Sphere	11250	Weapon
Moonfalx	7000	Weapon
Oriental Blade	9900	Weapon
Rune Wand	4000	Weapon
Sacred Scepter	5600	Weapon
Slasher Claws	4500	Weapon
Sunsylph Orb	6250	Weapon
Walloon Sword	5000	Weapon
Wild Arc	5250	Weapon

SIDE QUESTS

EASTERN TREI'KUR
Collective Parting of the Sands
Subjugation Directive: Sandra
Subjugation Directive: Zurtails

CENTRAL RESULIA
Subjugation Directive: Pargyns
Subjugation Directive: Donadello
Device of the Ancients
It Came from the North
Collection as Innocent as a Valkyrie
Subjugation Directive: Arjain
Subjugation Directive: Shelda
Wanted: Anonnus

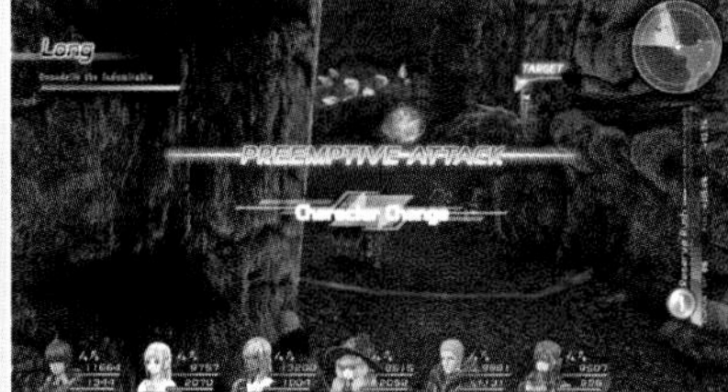

WELCH'S LABORATORY
Behavioral Study

SANTEROULE
For Whom the Bell Tomes
An Inkling for Artistry
Collecting Something Blue
Open Season on Orizons

PRIVATE ACTIONS

EASTERN TREI'KUR
Rendered Speechless while Dining in Trei'kur
Support from his Subordinates
Especially Observant
Bathroom Breakdown

MYIDDOK
Its and Her Circumstances

STHAL
Talking with Ted

WELCH THE BEAUTIFUL AND GENIUS INVENTOR, PART IV

If you return to Welch at this point in the game and you've completed all of her previous quests, you can complete a simple subjugation task for her to unlock the Authoring specialty. You can find the Sanddozer she wants you to hunt down in the Trei'kuran Dunes.

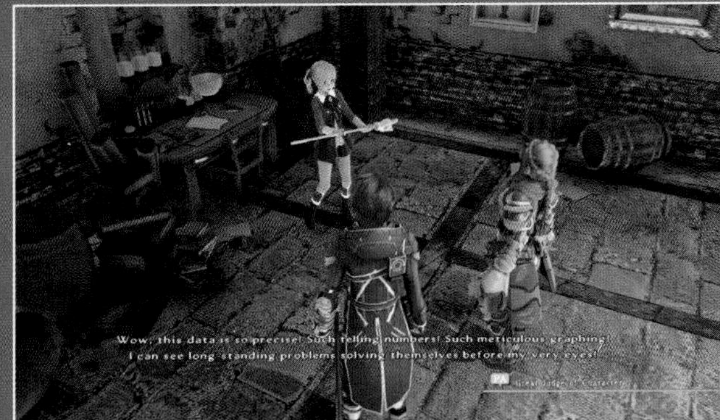

AUTHORING

Authoring allows you to create consumable signet cards, as well as skill books. You most likely won't have the ingredients required to author many of these books yet, but you will later on in the game. Invest SP into Authoring if you'd like to make your own signet cards for use in battle. Signet Card: Raise Dead and Signet Card: Resurrection are particularly useful.

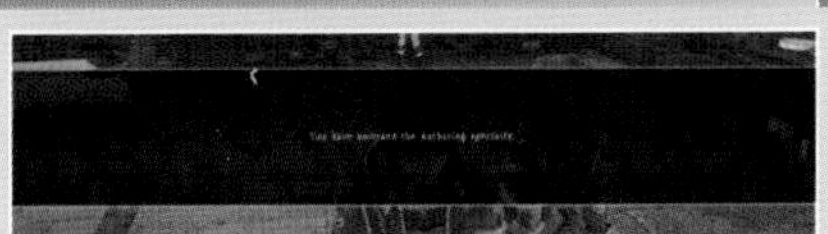

A DARING RESCUE

TREI'KURAN DUNES

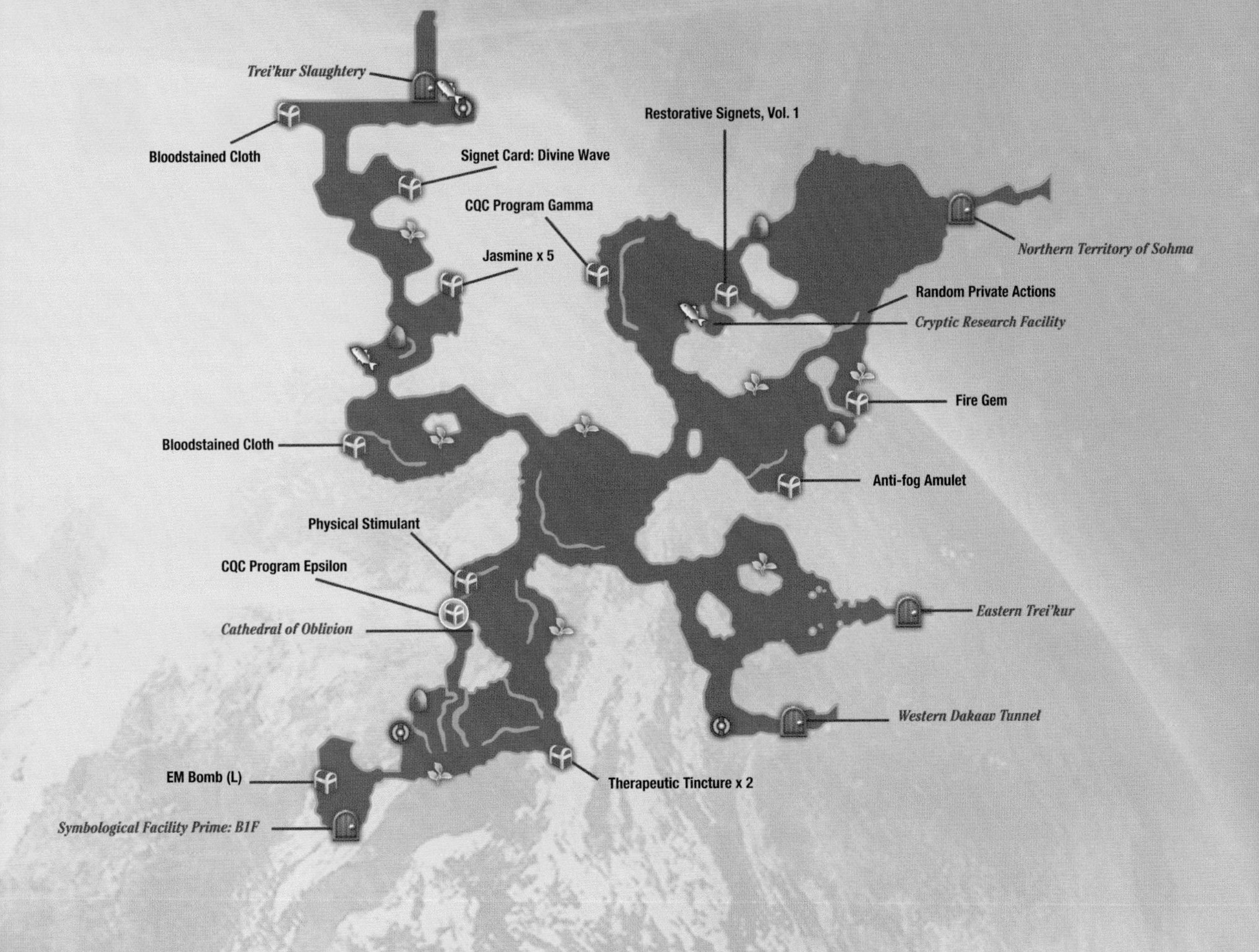

Trei'kur Slaughtery
Bloodstained Cloth
Signet Card: Divine Wave
CQC Program Gamma
Jasmine x 5
Restorative Signets, Vol. 1
Northern Territory of Sohma
Random Private Actions
Cryptic Research Facility
Fire Gem
Bloodstained Cloth
Anti-fog Amulet
Physical Stimulant
CQC Program Epsilon
Cathedral of Oblivion
Eastern Trei'kur
Western Dakaav Tunnel
EM Bomb (L)
Therapeutic Tincture x 2
Symbological Facility Prime: B1F

Before you leave to rescue Daril and Relia, make sure to stock up on restorative supplies like Blueberries and Blackberries. Then, exit Eastern Trei'kur from the west gate, heading into the Trei'kuran Dunes. Your destination here is in the northwest corner of the map, indicated by the red star waypoint of your in-game map. Traverse to the center of the map, then take the path west into another open area with a harvesting node. On a ledge to the west here, there's a chest containing a **Bloodstained Cloth**. Pick it up, then go north into another area, cutting through the Trei'kuran defense troops.

To the northeast of the immediate area, there's a chest that holds **Jasmine x 5**. Open it, then continue north to find another group of Trei'kuran enemies. Defeat them, then retrieve the **Signet Card: Divine Wave** from the chest nearby. Now, go north, and you'll see the Trei'kuran Slaughtery just over its moat. At the west end lies another chest, containing another **Bloodstained Cloth**. After you open the chest, you can save your progress at the point to the east near the slaughtery's bridge. Enter the tower to start the rescue operation.

INSIDE THE TREI'KUR SLAUGHTERY

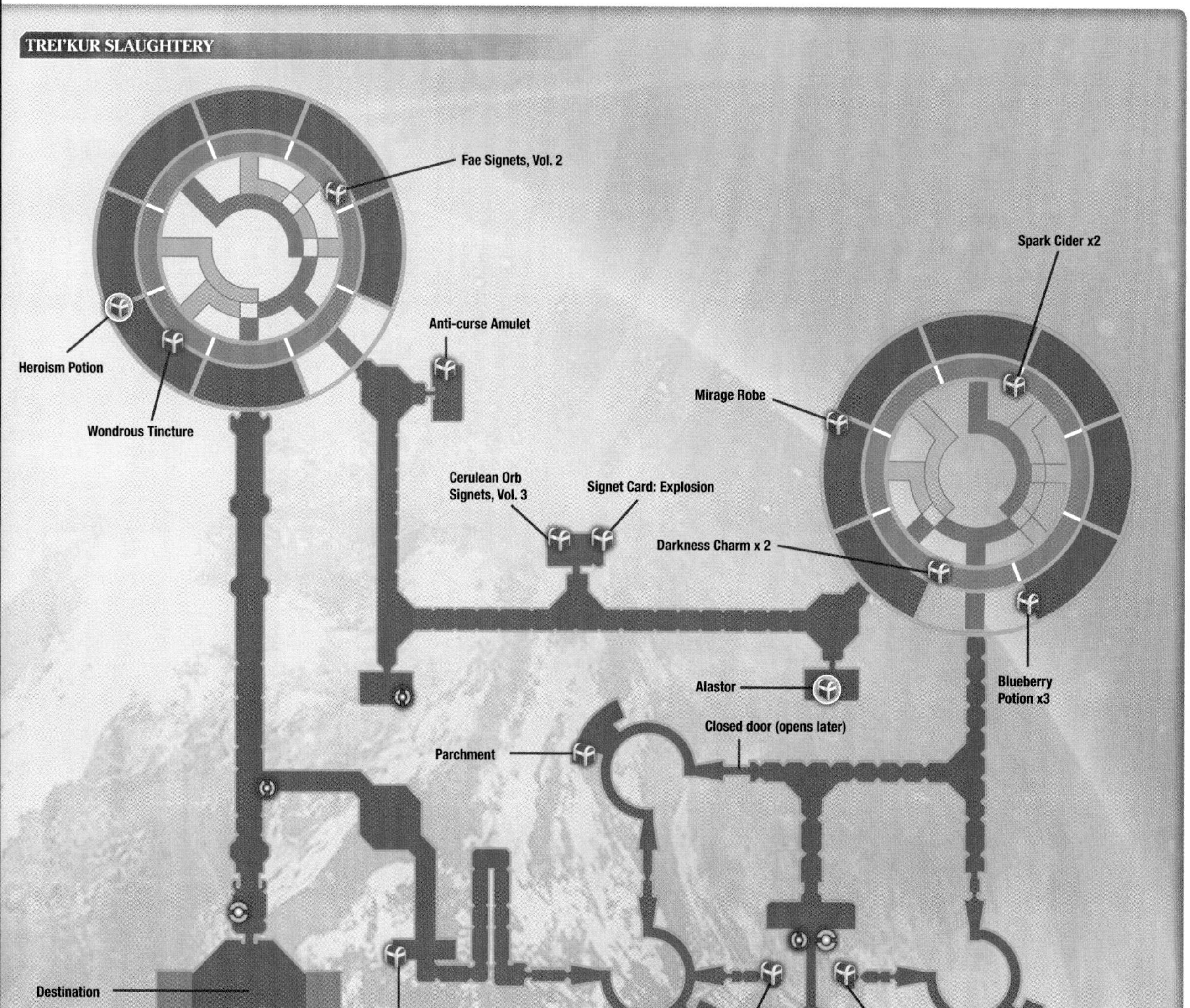

TREI'KUR SLAUGHTERY

Fae Signets, Vol. 2
Spark Cider x2
Heroism Potion
Anti-curse Amulet
Wondrous Tincture
Mirage Robe
Cerulean Orb
Signets, Vol. 3
Signet Card: Explosion
Darkness Charm x 2
Alastor
Blueberry Potion x3
Closed door (opens later)
Parchment
Destination
Defense Seeds
Signet Card: Arctic Impact
Solar Signets, Vol. 3
Trei'kuran Dunes

Once inside, you can refill your HP and MP at the restore point here. You can also save your progress if you haven't already. Your destination on this map is in the southwest corner, but you're going to have to go the long way around since the back door is locked (for now). Make your way north from the save point, then go east and follow the path south. This leads you upstairs to a dead end with a chest containing a copy of **Solar Signets, Vol. 3**. You can have Fiore learn the powerful Tornado signeturgical spell with this skill book.

Now, turn around and take the north path that leads into one of the slaughtery's watchtowers. To your immediate left, just before the tower, there's a chest with **Darkness Charm x 2** inside. These can be used to augment your equipment with darkness elemental resistances. If you have the **Subjugation Directive: Zurtails** quest, you'll encounter Cunning Zurtails foes as you enter the tower.

Before you make the tower climb, take a left at the base of the tower. This takes you to a prison cell with some enemies and a chest with a **Mirage Robe** inside. After you grab it, equip it on one of your signeturges. Then, start climbing the tower by taking the stairs to the east. At the peak of these stairs, there's a chest immediately before a cell entrance. Open it to obtain **Spark Cider x 2**, then enter the cell to the west.

Defeat the adversaries here, and enter the adjacent cell just south of it. Head west from this cell back into the tower. If you take a left inside the tower here, you can enter the southeast cell with a chest containing **Blueberry Potion x 3**.

Continue up the tower by climbing the interior stairs, which lead you to a cell with two armored enemies.

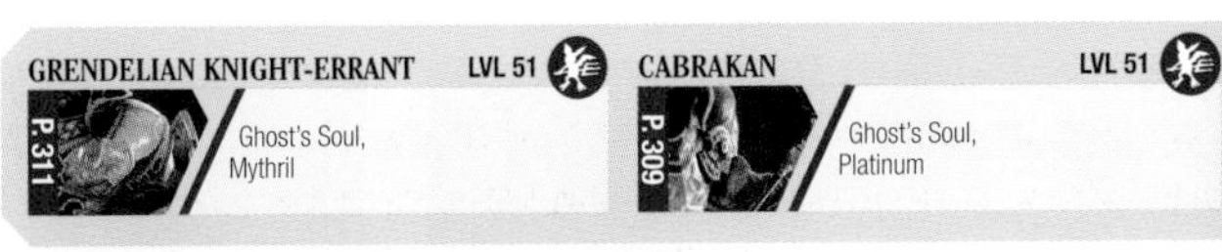

Like the armored mini-bosses from the Western Dakaav Tunnel, these two walking suits of steel can deal large amounts of damage around themselves. Keep Miki and Fiore away from them while healing your front line party members.

After you've banished them, you can make your way into the adjacent cell to the west, which then loops back into the tower, up to the top level. From here, you can make your way east toward another tower. Before you cross the bridge, there's a room to the south with a locked chest inside. If you have the Lock Picking specialty, you can obtain a new weapon for Victor: the **Alastor**.

It should be an upgrade for him at this point, so equip it, and then make your way across the bridge and up another set of stairs to the east. In the room north of the bridge, there are two chests, one with a **Cerulean Orb Signets, Vol. 3** skill book and one with **Signet Card: Explosion**.

Continue eastward. At the divergence, you can make a left turn into a room to the south to save your progress at the save point. Head north from here up two more flights of stairs. Before you enter the second tower, there's a room to your right with a chest containing an **Anti-curse Amulet** inside.

Enter the northwest tower. Take a left down the stairs, leading to a room with some enemies, a locked chest, and an unlocked one. The open chest contains a **Wondrous Tincture**, while the locked one holds a **Heroism Potion**.

Now, climb your way up several stairs, which take you to the north cell. Enter the adjacent cell to the east, clearing the Trei'kuran Soldiers. Just outside of this cell, there's a chest containing **Fae Signets, Vol. 2**. Have Miki read the book to learn Faerie Light, an enhanced version of Faerie Healing.

Re-enter the tower and make a right when you're inside, up a set of stairs. This takes you to the northwest cell, which connects to the western cell. Enter the west cell, then take the connecting path east up two more sets of stairs to the top level. From here, you can exit the tower, going south.

Along this bridge, you'll fight another pair of armored suits, except they have some extra Trei'kuran troops with them. Defeat them, and continue all the way south until you reach a save point along the path. Save your progress, and go follow the path east. Slay the Cursed Horrors here, then keep following the path until you come to a locked door (these doors will be open the next time you visit the slaughtery). There's a chest with **Defense Seeds** in it to your right. Pick them up and return to the save point, then go south into the large room to find Daril and Relia.

Unsurprisingly, you walk into a trap. Der-Suul orders waves of Trei'kuran troops to attack. After you fight off several soldiers, a cutscene triggers where Der-Suul calls for a retreat, but not before he orders his men to fire on the party. Daril heroically embraces Relia to protect her from the gunfire. With the ultimate sacrifice, Daril succumbs to his fatal wounds.

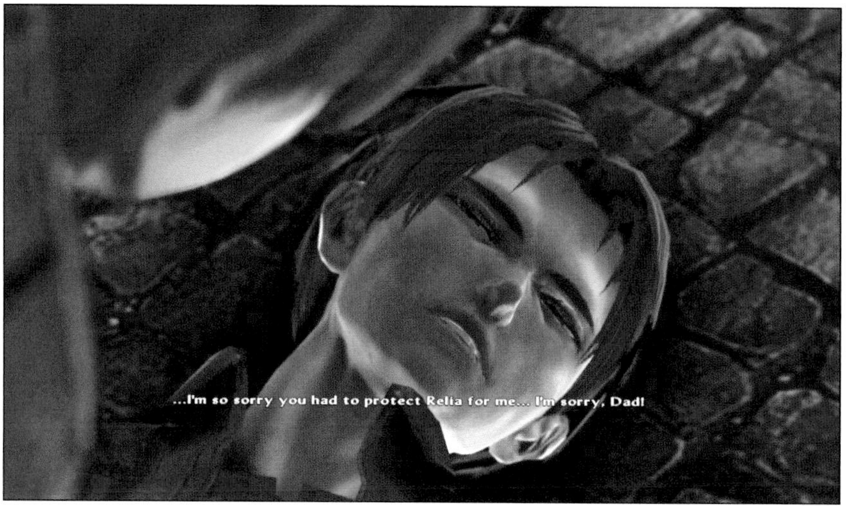

MISSION: TYING UP LOOSE ENDS

Daril's death isn't enough for Der-Suul. His arrogance combined with his ruthlessness means that he'll eventually open himself up for reprisal, which Fidel will gladly deliver.

Action Checklist

1. Destroy Der-Suul
2. Optional: Obtain missable role through Private Actions
3. Optional: View Private Actions in various cities
4. Trek to the Royal Institute of Signetary Studies in Santeroule
5. Get to the Ancient Institute

Mission Walkthrough

Before you can continue your primary mission of reaching Santeroule, you'll have to defeat the arrogant Trei'kuran military commander, Der-Suul. Then, you can make your way back to Santeroule to begin the expunction process on Relia.

AVENGE DARIL

The story continues with Miki consoling Fidel over his tragic loss. However, there's another incoming attack on the Resulian encampment. Looks like Der-Suul is back, doubling down on his efforts to retake the once Trei'kuran outpost.

Make your way out of The Moonlit Tabby to exact revenge. Once outside, cut through the Trei'kurans here, and then meet with Der-Suul in the northern area for a final face-off with Daril's murderer.

DER-SUUL

LVL 42

As usual, start by annihilating Der-Suul's henchmen, and then focus your attacks on Der-Suul. Over the battle, more Trei'kuran Soldiers will flood the area, so make sure to stay on top of eliminating them. Occasionally, Der-Suul switches targets. If you see him run toward Miki, take control of her to get her away from the ruthless leader. He's an adept signeturge, so watch out for his high-damage AoE spells, as well, keeping your party members separated.

When Der-Suul is low on health, he'll gain access to a new devastating attack called Spicule. This is a high-damage AoE attack that can instantly kill anyone around him. Keep Miki, Fiore, and Emmerson positioned well away from Der-Suul at all times to prevent as much destruction as possible. With Miki's Faerie Light spell, you should be able to heal up your party accordingly.

If you've built up enough reserve gauge, unleash your strongest Reserve Rush gauge combo on Der-Suul to finish off the ruthless villain.

After defeating Der-Suul, Victor gives Fidel Daril's sword, **Insignivon**. When you're back in control of Fidel, equip the sword. Then, meet up with the rest of the crew to the east of the area, as marked on the map. With Der-Suul out of the way and Fidel's father avenged, you can now make way to your original destination—Santeroule.

WARNING: MISSABLE ROLE UNLOCK

After you defeat Der-Suul, a few new Private Actions unlock here in Eastern Trei'kur. You'll need to enter the inn or exit the area, then re-enter Eastern Trei'kur to trigger the Private Action whistle spawn point.

One of a few missable Private Actions can be viewed here (the reason becomes clear later on in the story). The **Happy Together** Private Action unlocks the Equal Opportunist role and becomes available after you've viewed all of the other Private Actions here. View the first set of Private Actions, enter the inn, then exit the inn. Repeat this process after viewing all available Private Actions. Eventually, you'll earn the Equal Opportunist role after speaking with Relia.

PRIVATE ACTIONS

EASTERN TREI'KUR

- Hold Hands
- Time for Remembrance
- Can't Wind Back the Clock

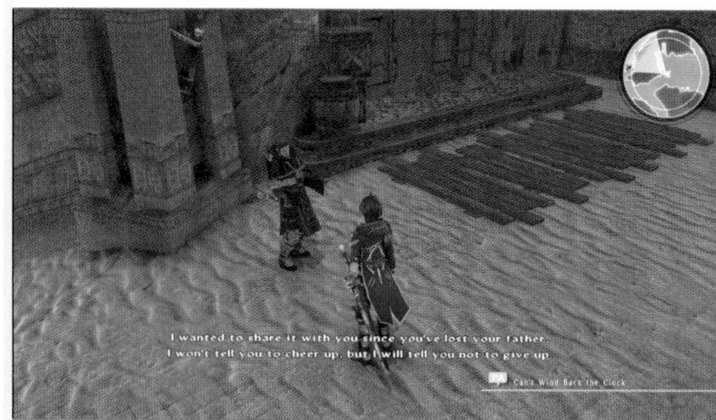

- More Mundane Magic
- Happy Together (missable role unlock)

CENTRAL RESULIA

- Anything You Want?

- Reason to Smile

STHAL

- Fastidious about Food
- Singing
- The Apple
- Imitating Fidel Poorly

- Warmth

MYIDDOK

- Mutterings
- More Mutterings

SANTEROULE

- Condolences Cut Short
- Girls' Hair
- Mother and Child
- Finding Fidel
- The Nut

You can stop by Sthal, Myiddok, and Central Resulia before returning to Santeroule if you want to view a few more missable Private Actions with Relia (none of which unlocks roles, however). Otherwise, trek all the way back to Santeroule, completing any side objectives you might have undertaken. On your way there, Emmerson receives a transmission with a warning that Kronos ships are en route to their destination, so they need to hurry.

Once you're in Santeroule, enter the Royal Institute of Signetary Studies. Inside, Ceisus informs the party that the expunction device there isn't functioning, so you'll have to use the original one in the Ancient Institute. If you have the Lock Picking specialty, you can open the locked chest in Ceisus' office for a copy of **Cerulean Orb Signets, Vol. 2**.

Now, leave Santeroule from the north gate, into North of the Eastern Eihieds. Oddly enough, there are no enemies in the area.

Continue north to the Ancient Institute. On your way there, a cutscene triggers where you'll meet General Alma, the Kronos mastermind behind the dastardly plots.

You find out that the Relia you have is actually Feria, Relia's twin sister. To make matters worse, the Kronos Soldiers were able to abduct her with the help of a neutralization device.

To get the twins back, the party must wait for the federation to send Emmerson's new ship. Furthermore, if the Faykreedians decide to take part in the intergalactic rescue mission, they may never come back to their home planet. The party disbands in the meantime to contemplate their futures.

CHAPTER 9

UNCERTAIN DESTINIES

PART 03

Fidel and his companions take a moment of respite to ruminate on the events they've endured and what their futures hold. Each one of them has a life-altering decision to make. Will they risk losing everything to save a child from an intergalactic war?

MISSION: ALL ABOARD THE CHARLES D. GOALE G

Fidel and Miki decide to mature their relationship beyond just being sibling-like friends. Together, they commit to the responsibility of saving Feria and Relia and set off to Santeroule to meet with their new space-faring pals.

Action Checklist

1. Travel to Santeroule through the Dakaav Footpath or the Passage on the Cliffs
2. Rendezvous with Emmerson and Anne in the southern area of Santeroule
3. Optional: Clear Private Actions aboard the Charles D. Goale G
4. Optional: Undertake and complete side quests and Private Actions on Faykreed with the starship's teleport functionality
5. Infiltrate the Cavaliero

Mission Walkthrough

Here, you'll need to meet with Emmerson, Anne, and the rest of your allies, where you'll gain access to an upgraded Charles D. Goale. Your primary objective is to prepare your party for an intergalactic rescue mission.

RETURN TO SANTEROULE

With only Fidel and Miki in your party, your next destination is Santeroule. At this point in the game, all of the enemies have evolved to around Lv. 60. Fortunately, you'll only face them in singles until you gather with the rest of your allies.

You can get to Santeroule through either the Dakaav Footpath into the Resulian Plains or through the Passage on the Cliffs to Coast of Minoz route. Both lead into Myiddok, which you can exit to the east into West of the Eastern Eihieds, then Santeroule.

Fight through either path. When you get to Santeroule, your destination is marked with a red star on the map, located to the south of the capital of signeturgy. Head to the rendezvous point, and your whole party comes together, committing to the cause.

Dakaav Footpath Route:

Enemy	Level	Page	Drops
LESSER DRAGON	LVL 60	P. 300	Dragon Scales, Dragon Hide
POLYPHAGA DRUS	LVL 59	P. 304	Insect Egg, Silk, Red Fruit
ADEPHAGA PROX	LVL 57	P. 303	Insect Egg, Basil, Gold, Green Fruit
LEONBLADE	LVL 54	P. 297	Wolf Fang, Bushy Fur, Prehistoric Meat, Fire Gem
MYCONID	LVL 53	P. 307	Tasty Mushroom, Colorful Mushrooms, Caterpillar Fungus
ELDER TREANT	LVL 54	P. 305	Wooden Stick, Ebony, Oak, Ash
GREAT SCUMBAG	LVL 53	P. 289	Alchemist's Water, Fermentation Pot, High-Strength Adhesive, Faerie Embroidery Thread
LAMIA RADIX	LVL 54	P. 306	Nectar, Mint, Poison Hemlock, Laurel Tree
STINGER	LVL 53	P. 304	Bee Stinger, Nectar, Amber

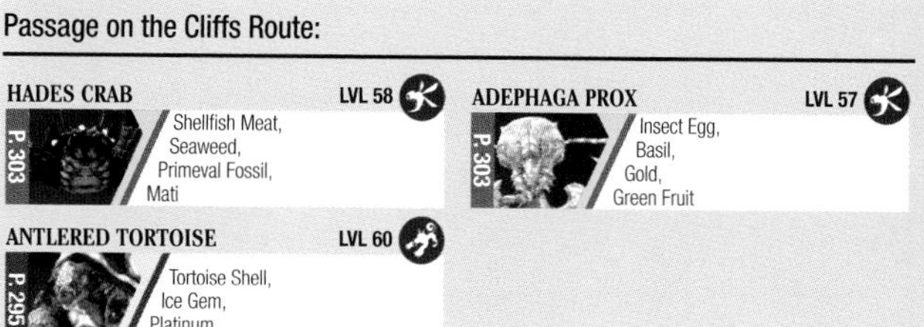

Passage on the Cliffs Route:

Enemy	Level	Page	Drops
HADES CRAB	LVL 58	P. 303	Shellfish Meat, Seaweed, Primeval Fossil, Mati
ADEPHAGA PROX	LVL 57	P. 303	Insect Egg, Basil, Gold, Green Fruit
ANTLERED TORTOISE	LVL 60	P. 295	Tortoise Shell, Ice Gem, Platinum

West of the Eastern Eihieds:

Enemy	Level	Page	Drops
ANCIENT PERYTON	LVL 55	P. 298	Peryton Droppings, Remex, Common Eggs, Egg Paragon
WINGED NIGHTMARE	LVL 55	P. 302	Wind Gem, Giant Bird Feather, Remex, Velvet Ribbon
DEMON SERVANT	LVL 56	P. 310	Demon's Tail, Lesser Fiend's Tail, Signet Card +, Darkness Gem
JADE GOLEM	LVL 56	P. 311	Silver, Gold, Platinum, Shadestone
BONE KNIGHT	LVL 55	P. 309	Blessed Sword, Ghost's Soul, Alchemist's Water

Once you're in control of Fidel, you'll be given the **Communicator Model G** key item. You can now teleport freely around Faykreed again! The onboard quartermaster here has equipment upgrades, as well. After you're done shopping, take the lift to the north to get to the Bridge.

Shops—Charles D. Goale G (Upgrades)

Myth & Weston Outfitters

ITEM	COST	TYPE
Acuity Crest	3000	Accessory
Arcane Amulet	25000	Accessory
Attack Crest	3000	Accessory
Energy Amulet	25000	Accessory
Fortitude Crest	3000	Accessory
Mind Crest	3000	Accessory
Bronto Armor	17000	Armor
Cloak of the Stars	15000	Armor
Resistance Suit	2650	Armor
Riot Gear	2450	Armor
Solid Protector	14000	Armor
Amalgametal Blade	22000	Weapon
Booster Wand	2800	Weapon
Ceramic Sword	3500	Weapon
Gatling Gauntlets	18000	Weapon
Mechanical Fists	3150	Weapon
Mekhanesphere	4400	Weapon
Microblaster	3700	Weapon
Photonic Blaster	21000	Weapon
Resonance Scepter	16000	Weapon
Sybilline Orb	25000	Weapon
Titan's Nail	20000	Weapon

IMBUE THE GRAVITIC WARP ENGINE

Looks like Kronos is one step ahead of the Pangalactic Federation when it comes to warp drive technology. Anne's data shows that with the help of symbometrics, the starship's warp drive can exceed its speed limit. Ceisus may be able to help, so Fiore and Anne leave for Santeroule.

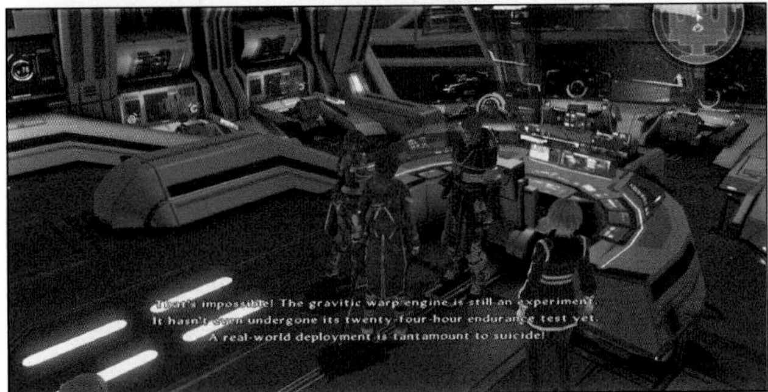

In the meantime, you're free to explore the new and improved Charles D. Goale. This is a good time to collect items from various treasure spheres on the ship.

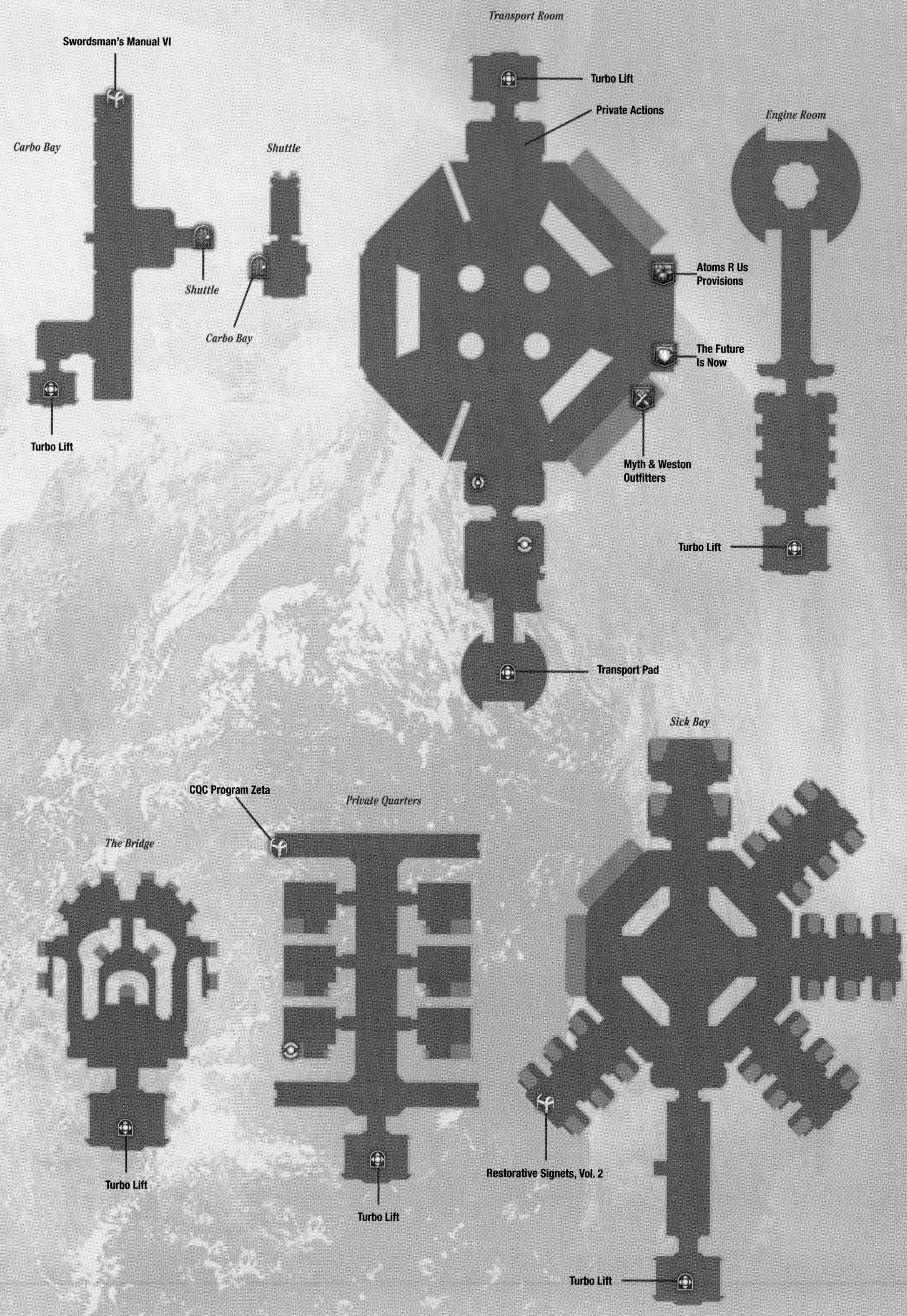

Carbo Bay
Swordsman's Manual VI
Shuttle
Turbo Lift
Shuttle
Carbo Bay
Transport Room
Turbo Lift
Private Actions
Atoms R Us Provisions
The Future Is Now
Myth & Weston Outfitters
Transport Pad
Engine Room
Turbo Lift
The Bridge
Turbo Lift
Private Quarters
CQC Program Zeta
Turbo Lift
Sick Bay
Restorative Signets, Vol. 2
Turbo Lift

In the Cargo Bay, you can find a copy of **Swordsman's Manual VI** to the north of the area. On the Private Quarters level, there's a **CQC Program Zeta** skill disk in the northwest corner. In the Sick Bay, pick up **Restorative Signets, Vol. 2** in the southwest section of the map. Once you've collected all of the battle skill items, there won't be much else to do, so return to the Bridge to trigger another cutscene.

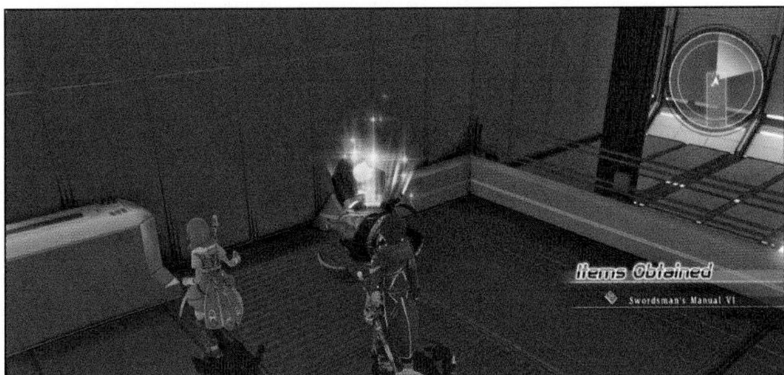

Thanks to Ceisus and Dr. Krupp, Fiore has all the information she needs to be able to imbue symbols onto the gravitic warp drive. Follow her into the engine room to watch her perform her magic.

Then, return to the Bridge for the moment of truth.

With the Charles D. Goale G flying at warp fifteen, Fidel and his crew will just have to wait to catch up to the Kronos ship holding Relia. Before you take a nap, you can view some new Private Actions available in the Transport Room. Note that there is a plethora on the starship, so it may take many visits into the Transport Room to exhaust them all. You can clear them now if you'd like to experience the interesting quips and stories your party members have to share, or save them for later since they aren't missable.

Additionally, the transporter in the Transport Room is now available for use, which continues for the remainder of the game. You can conveniently travel around the world at your leisure, completing side quests and viewing Private Actions.

OPTIONAL

PARTY LOOKING FOR A BARD

At this point in the game, you can obtain one of the best support roles by witnessing the **Miki's Grandiose Dream** Private Action in Myiddok.

The Minstrel role can potentially boost SP gain by an additional 50% when the role is leveled up fully. It also stacks with the Altruist role! It's highly recommended that you max out these two roles to expedite unlocking the rest of your SP-related abilities.

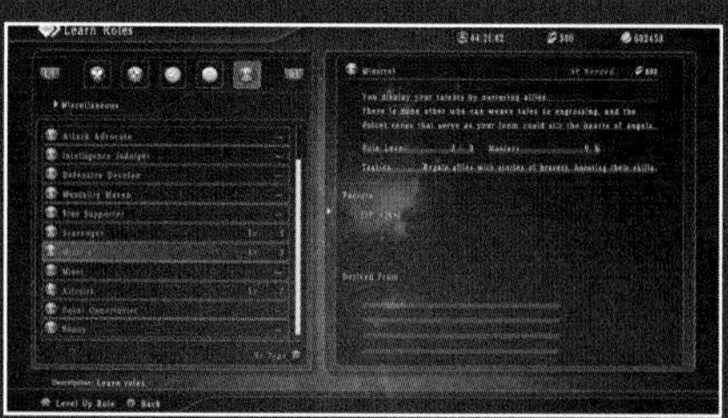

PRIVATE ACTIONS

CHARLES D. GOALE G
Mechanical Marvel
He's a Good Man...and Thorough
Faykreed's Exquisite Scenery
The Military Elite
Clueless Cupid

Difficulty with Directories
Ghost Story

Feelings for Emmerson
No Rest for the Storyteller
Another Peaceful Day on the Bridge
Threat to Society
A Gift for Anne
Punctuality's Imperative

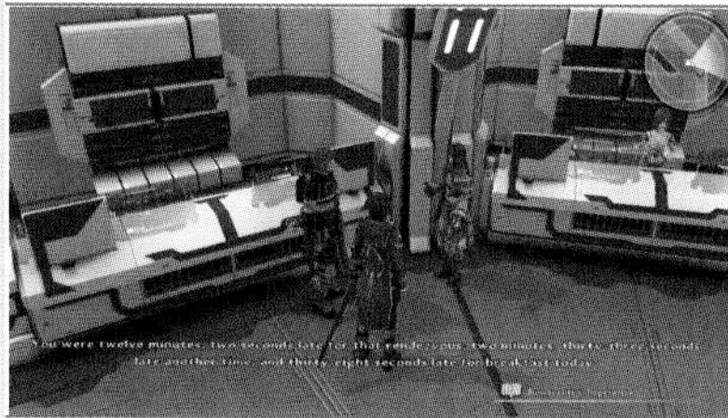

Every Second Counts
Much to Learn
Latest in a Long Line of Heroes

STHAL
Introspective Fidel

MYIDDOK
Miki's Grandiose Dream
Alcohol Appreciation

Brains of the Family
The Consensus on Anne's Grandmother

CENTRAL RESULIA
Like Brother and Sister

Return of the Jocular Malko
Hitting on Hana

Resulia's in Good Hands
When to Trust

EASTERN TREI'KUR
The Path They've Tread

The Horror of War
Cleaning for Klutzes
Yearning for Home
Kronos's Namesake

The Plague

Work Within the System

SIDE QUESTS

CENTRAL RESULIA
Emblematic of Knighthood
Showdown at the Training Hall

Medal of Honor
Eggcellent Haul

Lurking in the Shadows of Collection
Subjugation Directive: Vejheerits

Subjugation Directive: Hoodini

Subjugation Directive: Rihvnauts

SANTEROULE
Cloaked in Mistakes
The Enchanted Quill
Open Season on Hourigh

Airing Out a Collection

EASTERN TREI'KUR
Taste of Home
Processing the Possibilities
Mouth-Watering Collection
Subjugation Directive: Vlad

Wanted: Hannah

A Peeping Golem!

When you're ready, take the turbo lift on board the Charles D. Goale G to the Private Quarters to get some rest. Fidel awakens to a red alert, where he'll be notified to get to the Bridge immediately.

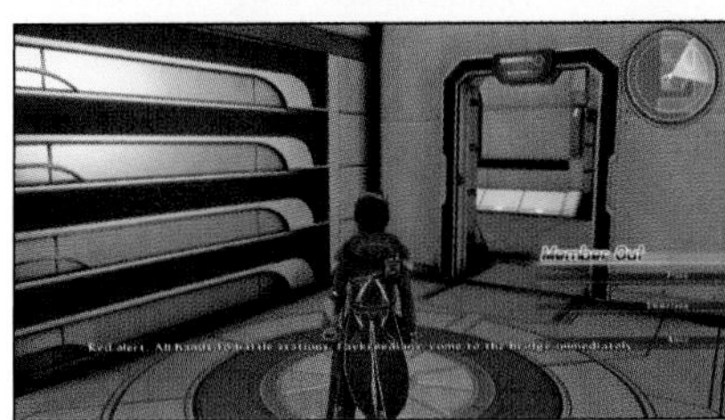

Take the lift to the Bridge for a cutscene. Emmerson's ship has caught up with the Kronos spacecraft, and a dogfight ensues. With Captain Kenny's tactical ingenuity, the Charles D. Goale G successfully disables the enemy ship, binding it with a tractor beam.

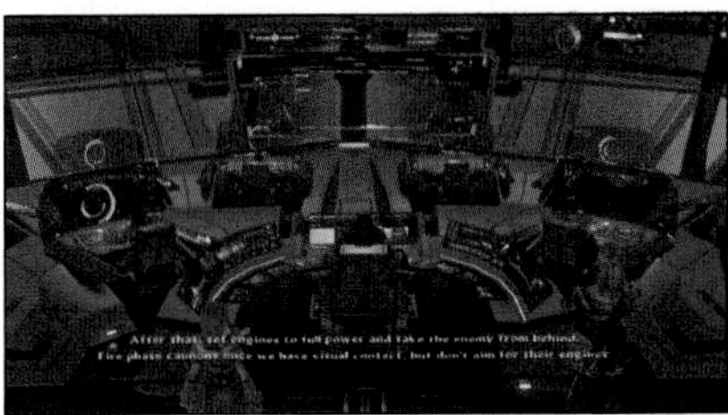

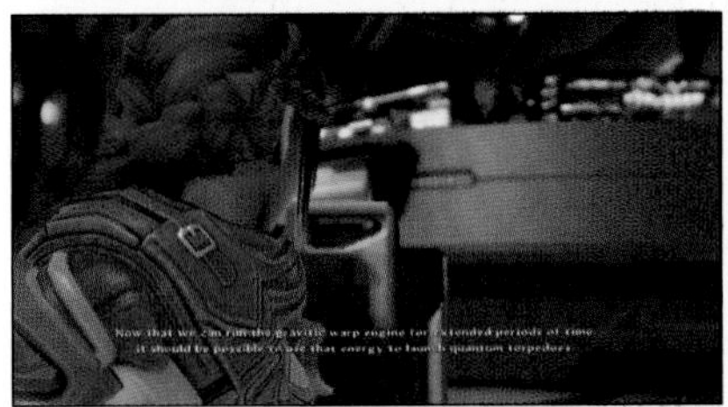

MISSION: ENERGIZE AND ENGAGE

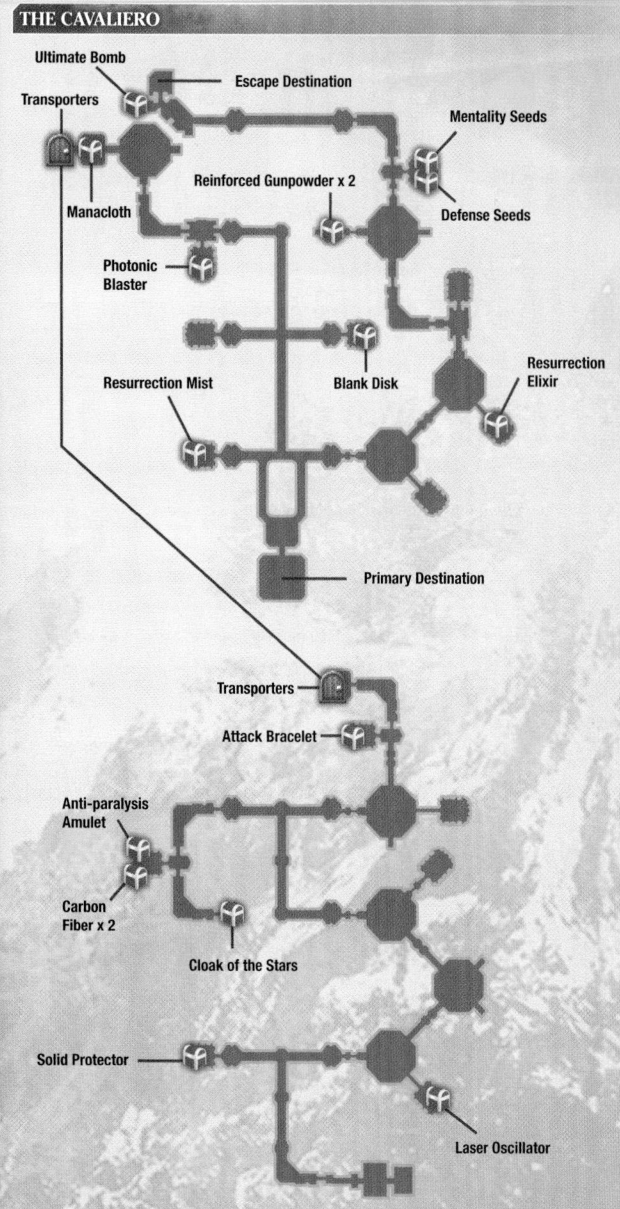

Thanks to Fiore's symbological prowess, the Charles D. Goale G gains access to warp speeds exceeding any other Pangalactic Federation vessel. The Charles D. Goale G catches up to the Cavaliero, allowing the heroes to formulate a rescue operation.

Action Checklist

1. Infiltrate the Kronos vessel, the Cavaliero
2. Fight through Kronos defenses to rescue the twins
3. Escape the Cavaliero

BOARD THE ENEMY SHIP

The party can now embark on a rescue mission, so head to the Transport Room to infiltrate the Kronos battleship, the Cavaliero. Before you energize, save your progress here.

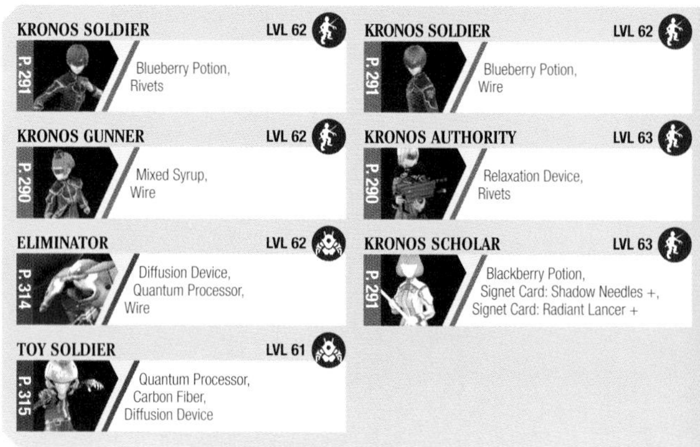

As soon as you board the Cavaliero, a welcoming party consisting of several hostile Kronos Soldiers ambushes you. This battle can be particularly difficult, so prepare to defend yourself from all angles. Make Miki your party leader so she can stay safe from enemies at the flank. Once you've defeated them, you can make way to the east of your starting position to access restore and save points.

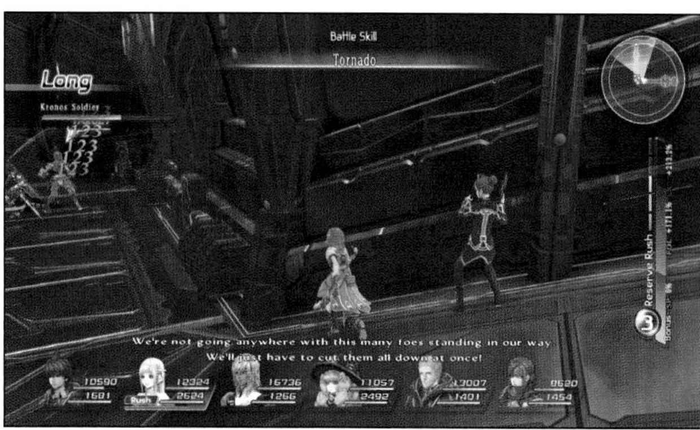

The Cavaliero is composed of two areas. Starting from the southern section, you'll need to traverse your way to the north to get to the transport to the northern area. Begin by crossing the bridge to the north, then head west into a room with a treasure sphere containing a **Solid Protector**. Pick it up, then cross the bridge east into a room with more soldiers and a dangerous sentry robot called Eliminator. Take out the Eliminator before the less threatening soldiers. It has relatively low HP, but it deals a large amount of damage

The room southeast of here has a sphere with a **Laser Oscillator** in it. You can collect three of these for the **Reconstructing an Enigma** quest. Continue north through two more circular areas, leading into a center bridge going west and north. The bridge eventually splits into two paths. Take the left one, leading to several treasure spheres. The two spheres in the west room contain an **Anti-paralysis Amulet** and **Carbon Fiber x 2**. Keep following the path south and east to get to another sphere with a **Cloak of the Stars** in it.

Now, return to the center bridge and continue east into a room with two Eliminators and some Kronos Scholars. Take them out, then head north into a hallway. Before you take the teleport to the northern half of the ship, enter the small room to the west to pick up an **Attack Bracelet** in the sphere there.

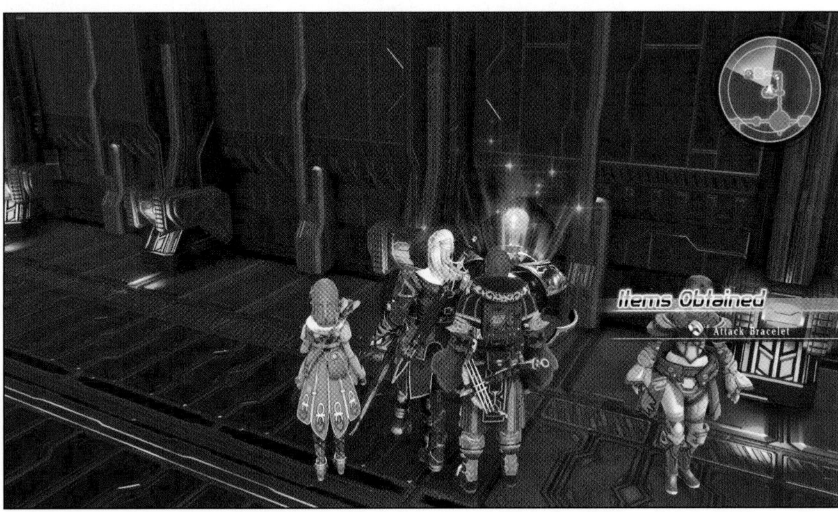

Continue north, and operate the teleporter pad to get to the next area. You begin at the northwest portion of the area with a treasure sphere nearby containing a **Manacloth**.

In the adjacent room to the east, you'll encounter a Guardian Beast, a powerful beast-type monster. Be careful of its high-damage Crystal Ray attack. Not only does it deal a massive amount of damage, it also breaks guard. Move out of its line of sight to avoid the damage.

SEARCH FOR RELIA AND FERIA

Slay the beast, then continue south and then west. There's a small room to the south on your way to the main bridge area. Enter the room and pick up the **Photonic Blaster** inside. Proceed across the bridge, defeating any Kronos enemies in your way. In the middle of the bridge is a save point. Before you save your progress, take the west path at the intersection on the bridge to get to a treasure sphere with a **Blank Disk** in it. Grab it, then save your game. Head south to trigger a short cutscene indicating that one of the girls is nearby.

Before entering the large room to the south, go inside the room to the west to obtain a **Resurrection Mist** from a sphere there. Now, make your way south, where you'll encounter a large number of Kronos Soldiers guarding a room.

Defeat them, and then restore your HP and MP with curative items or foods. When you enter the room, there will be a standoff between Fidel and a Kronos Commander, with Relia as hostage.

CHAPTER 9

While the commander is distracted, Victor leaps in from behind the enemy troops and heroically rescues Relia. A battle with the commander and his cronies ensues.

The commander isn't much stronger than his subordinates, but he does have a high HP total. Naturally, you'll want to eliminate his underlings before taking him on, all while keeping Miki safe. You can make the fight much more manageable by burning your Reserve Rush on the Kronos Rangers.

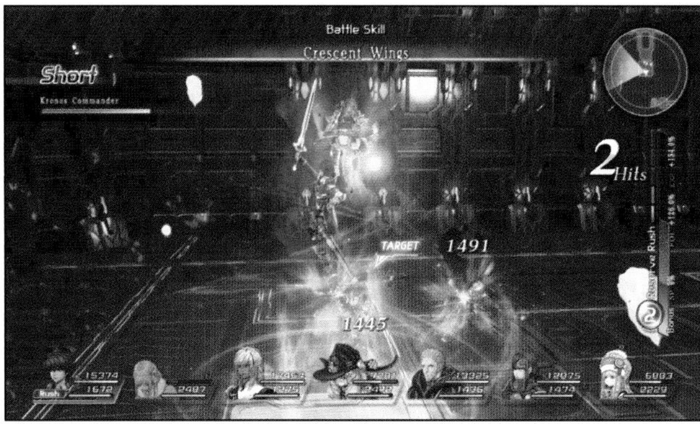

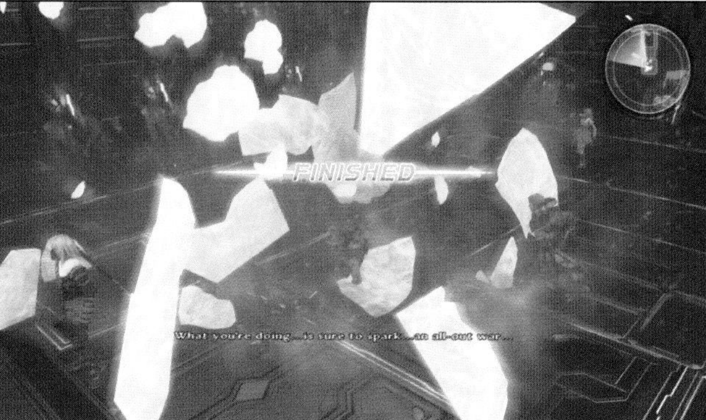

After you defeat the commander, a short cutscene triggers. The real Relia is now permanently a part of your group. Don't forget to equip her with supportive accessories and roles before making your escape from the Cavaliero.

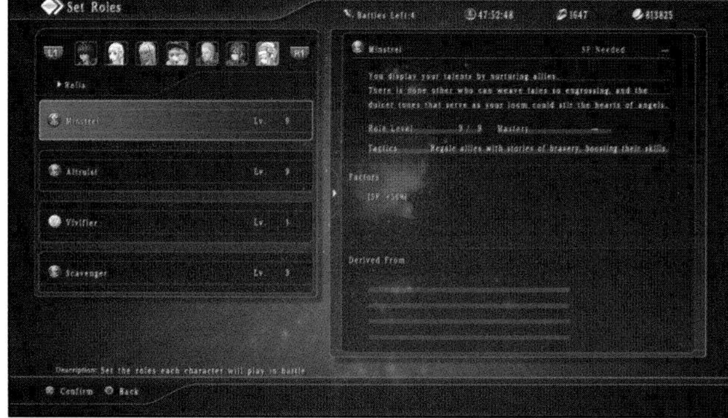

With Relia safe, leave the room. Emmerson calls in for a transport, but the tracking signal is jammed by the Cavaliero's force fields. Furthermore, killing the commander has caused a self-destruct sequence to initiate. You have roughly 27 minutes to get to the Cargo Bay for a physical extraction from the Cavaliero.

BEAT THE CLOCK

To get to your destination, take the path east from the save point into a circular room with an Eliminator enemy and more Kronos Soldiers. Clear them, and then enter the adjacent room to the northeast and take care of more foes here. To the southeast of this room is a treasure sphere with a **Resurrection Elixir** in it. Grab it, then continue north into a small room. From here, make a left going west and then north into another circular area with more Kronos assault troops.

You should have plenty of time left to pick up more items on the way out, so after you take care of the enemies here, go into the room to the west to obtain **Reinforced Gunpowder x 2**. Then, go north, and then turn right into another small room with two treasure spheres holding **Mentality Seeds** and **Defense Seeds**. After you pick up the seeds, finish escaping the area by returning to the hallway and traveling north, then all the way west, where you'll see another treasure sphere with an **Ultimate Bomb** inside it. Open the sphere, then go north to the Cavaliero's Cargo Bay for an escape cutscene.

CHAPTER 10

REJOINED TWINS

PART 03

After narrowly escaping the self-destructing blast caused by the Kronos starship, Fidel and company return safely to the Charles D. Goale. Although Relia is safe and sound aboard Emmerson's ship, Feria is still being held in enemy hands.

MISSION: RETURN TO THE SYMBOLOGICAL RESEARCH FACILITY

Worried about Feria, Fidel wakes up in his Private Quarters aboard the Charles D. Goale G. Feeling obligated for the well-being of his new dependents, he resolves to do anything it takes to rescue Feria from her abductors. Meanwhile, a troubled Emmerson can't help but feel powerless and disgusted by Kronos' depraved scientific methods.

Action Checklist

1. Find Relia in the Transport Room
2. Rendezvous with Emmerson and Anne on the Bridge
3. Find Relia in the Cargo Bay
4. Optional: Undertake and complete side quests
5. Optional: View new Private Actions
6. Follow Anne's lead on Feria's whereabouts
7. Rescue the remaining twin from her abductors

Mission Walkthrough

Now that you have access to your entire party, your primary concern is finding Feria and unraveling General Alma's motives. Gather the crew to take on one more rescue operation.

HOW'S RELIA DOING?

The first order of business is to check on Relia in the Transport Room. She and Miki can be found gazing at the stars near the west window. Head over, and they'll volunteer to join you.

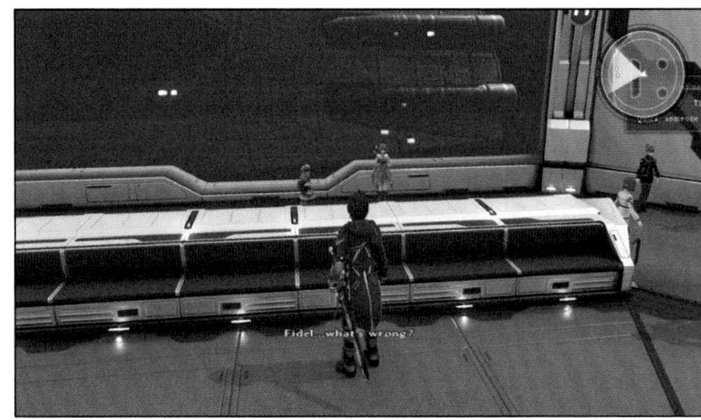

Next, visit Emmerson and Anne on the starship's Bridge. Unfortunately, Relia walks in at a bad time and overhears a frustrated Emmerson make an insensitive remark.

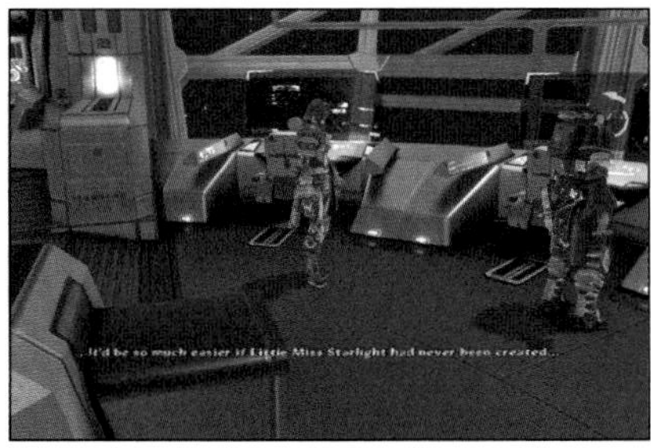

Take the turbo lift to the Cargo Bay to find Relia by the dock.

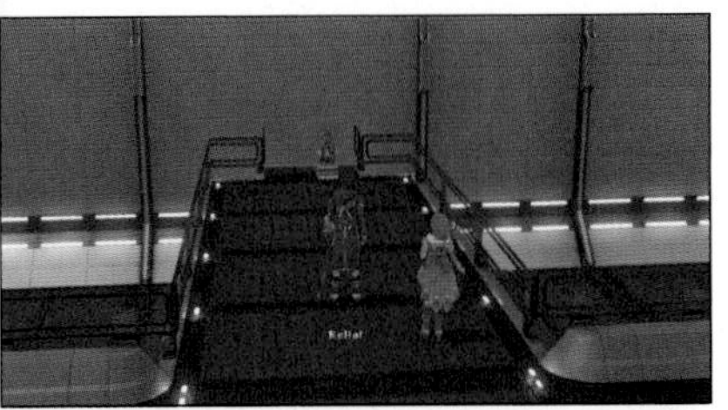

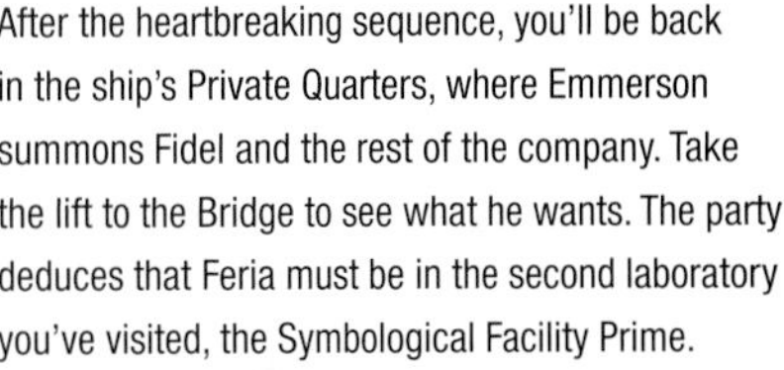

After the heartbreaking sequence, you'll be back in the ship's Private Quarters, where Emmerson summons Fidel and the rest of the company. Take the lift to the Bridge to see what he wants. The party deduces that Feria must be in the second laboratory you've visited, the Symbological Facility Prime.

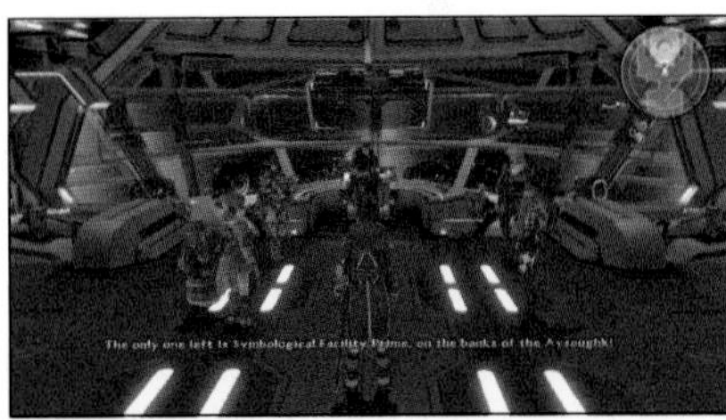

With control of a full party, you can use the teleporter to travel back to Faykreed to search for Feria. Before you leave, you can view new Private Actions on the Charles D. Goale G, assuming you've exhausted the ones prior. There are also several new side quests available at this point, most of which you can complete before venturing into the Symbological Facility Prime.

OPTIONAL

SIDE QUESTS

WELCH'S LABORATORY
Keys to the Present in the Past

CENTRAL RESULIA
Always Be Prepared

Heavyweight Champion of the Insect World

Collecting a Taste from the Heavens

Subjugation Directive: Mojangos

SANTEROULE
Changing History: Young Women, Power, and Pets

Sylph-Sewn Robes

Open Season on Ouyeits

Wanted: Abigail

An Emotional Gift Idea

On the Trail of Eitalon Stragglers

The Golden Rule of Collecting

EASTERN TREI'KUR
Empty Shelves, Empty Coffers

Reaping Bloody Benefits

The Collective Gift of Giving

Subjugation Directive: Sythwas

Garrote the Guerillas

PRIVATE ACTIONS

CHARLES D. GOALE G
Turbo Lift Luddite

Whipped

Heart Says Yes

STHAL
Thoughts on the Military

Thank You

Remembering Feria

CENTRAL RESULIA
Love Is Pain?

Parents and Loneliness

Watching Victor

Easily Understandable Animals

EASTERN TREI'KUR
Miki the Matron

Thanks for All You Do

Bye-Bye, Sanity

Drawing a Blank

WELCH THE BEAUTIFUL AND GENIUS INVENTOR, PART V

If you've completed all of Welch's quests, including **Behavioral Study**, she'll have one final job for you to do. Visit her in her laboratory in Myiddok to undertake the **Keys to the Present in the Past** mission.

The enemy that you need to defeat for the Erstwhile Ultimate Sword is in the Northern Territory of Sohma, near the Trei'kuran Dunes exit.

Defeat the Revenant Swordmaster Daeus along with its polyhedron helpers to obtain the **Erstwhile Ultimate Sword** key item. When you return the item to Welch, you'll be rewarded with the Whetting and Fortification specialties, allowing you to augment weapons and armor. Congratulations on completing the entire line of Welch quests!

CONVERTING TRASH INTO TREASURE

With the weapons and armor augments, you can now assimilate other pieces of gear and items into your equipment to enhance their effects. If you've been saving your old weapons, armor, and accessories up to this point, you can enhance your current loadout by consuming the unused ones. Generally, weapons and armor used as materials will effectively add appropriate stats. For instance, if you were to augment your currently equipped weapon with an older weapon, it will add either ATK or INT (depending on weapon type).

Make use of this feature to get the most out of your unwanted gear!

CATHEDRAL OF OBLIVION (SECOND ITERATION)

Before you undertake the next portion of the main story, consider completing the Cathedral of Oblivion if you haven't yet. The dungeon will evolve into its final iteration after your second visit to the Symbological Facility Prime. Although you won't miss out on items (since the chests inside remain constant throughout the game), you might want to clear them anyway to face off with the challenging Vidofnir boss.

When you're ready to rescue Feria, use the Communicator Model G device to teleport back to the Charles D. Goale G's Transport Room. Then, take the transporter to the Aysoughk River Bank in Trei'kur.

KOBOLD KNAVE LVL 59

P.296 — Platinum, Hand-Spun Thread, Wool, Cashmere

LAVA GOLEM LVL 62

P.311 — Silver, Platinum, Ruby, Gnomestone

MAN TRAP LVL 61

P.307 — Zephyr Lily, Laurel Tree, Blue Roses, Poison Hemlock

MISFORTUNER LVL 60

P.312 — Bloodstained Cloth, Ghost's Soul

Your destination from the starting point is just to the west, indicated by the red star on the map. With the help of the Charles D. Goale G's processing power, Anne easily hacks the laboratory's security mainframe, energizing the party directly into the third basement floor.

SYMBOLOGICAL FACILITY PRIME B3F

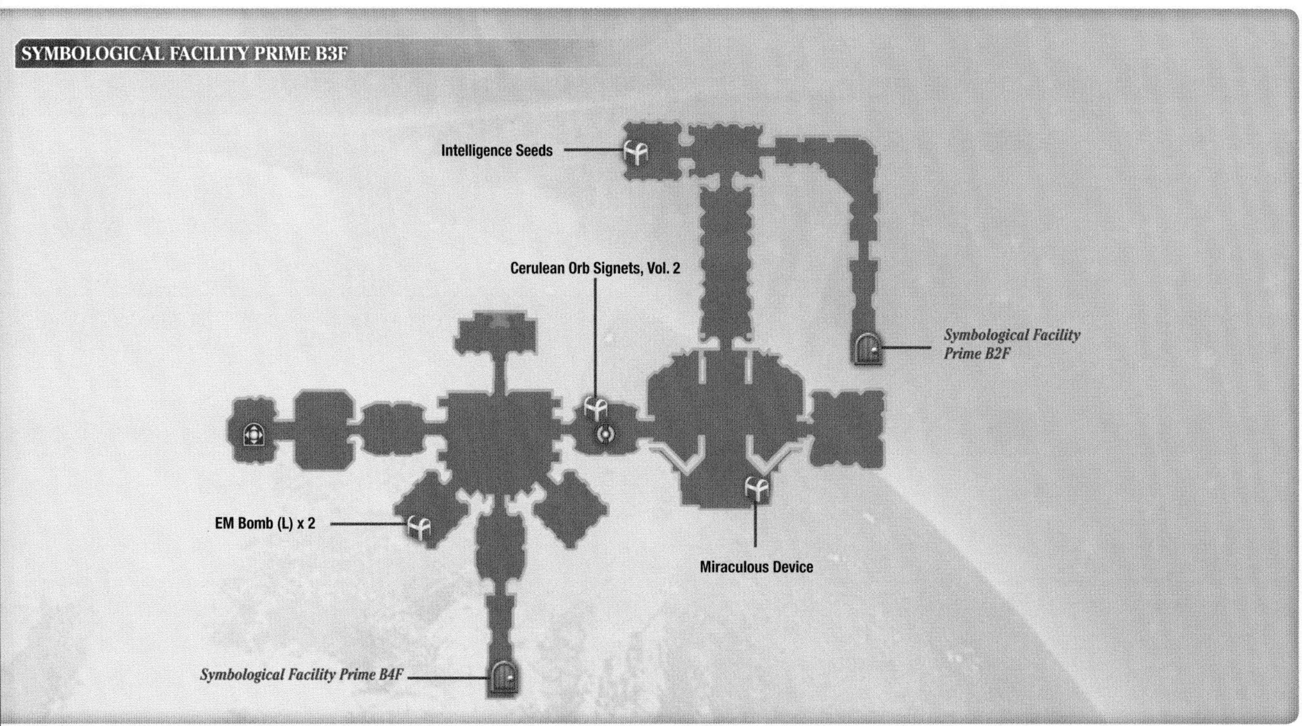

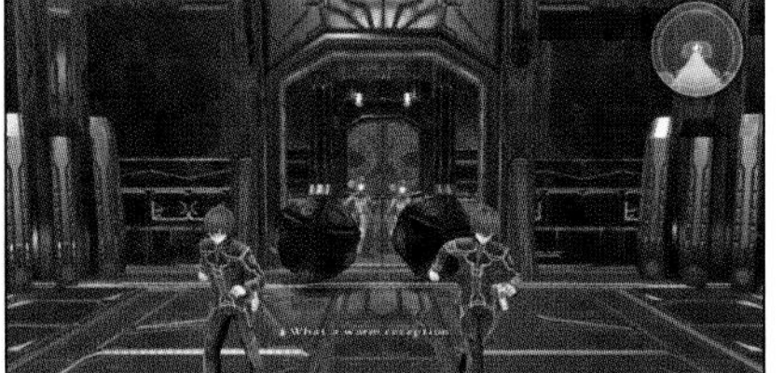

From here, check out the main computer terminal, which is north of the large room where you fought off hordes of foes during your first visit.

Déjà vu. Enemies are alerted to your presence, so get ready to defend yourself. During the fight, a few of your party members give you a hint at where to look.

The adversaries came from the southern exit, leading down into the fourth basement floor, so head there after you clean up the Kronos troops.

PART 03

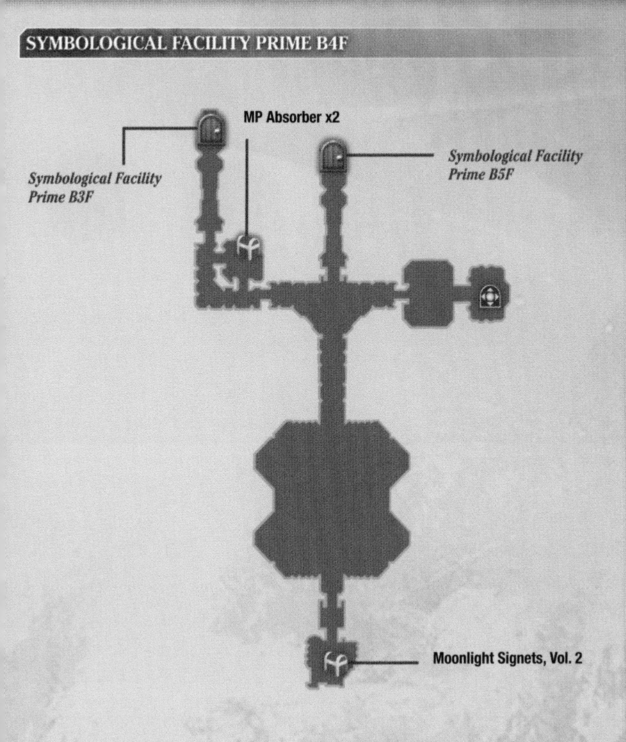

On the fourth floor, you'll notice that a new path is accessible north from the center of the map. Go down one more floor to see what Kronos is putting so much effort into protecting.

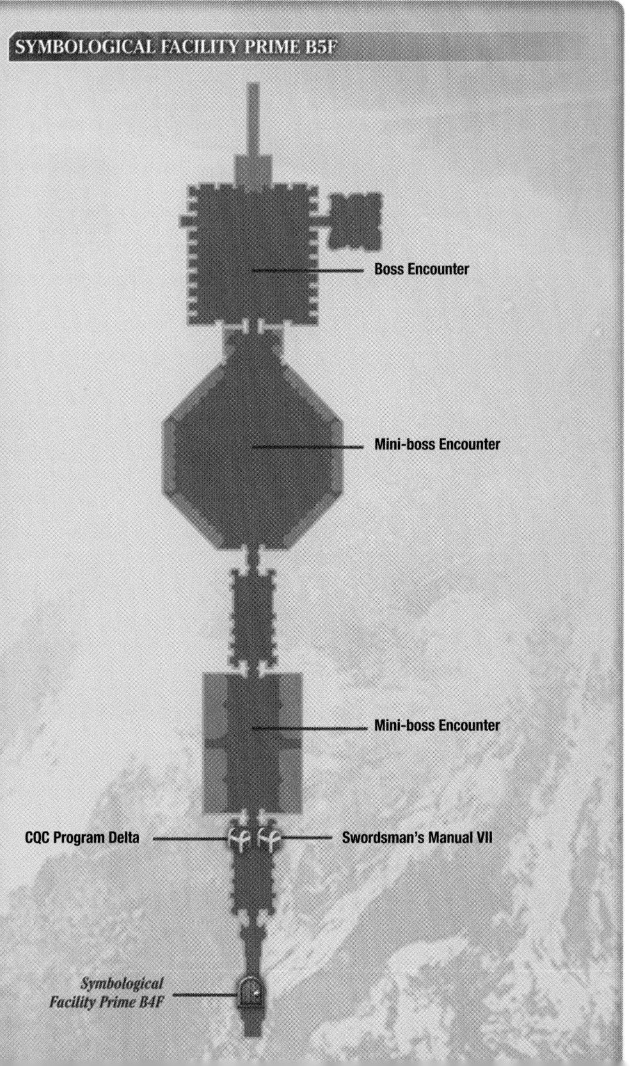

Here, you meet Raffine, a Kronos scientist who seems eager to help you find Feria.

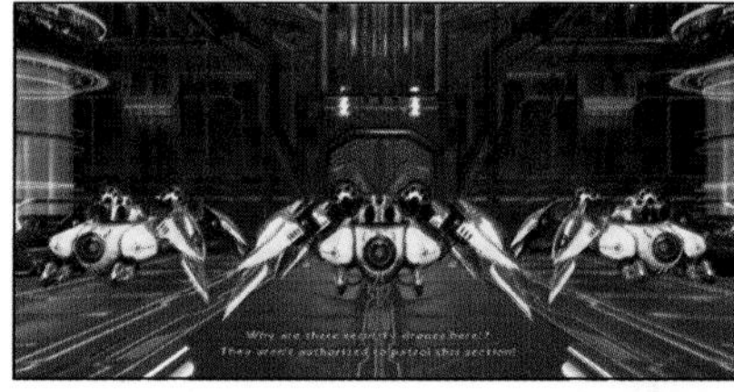

Open up the two treasure spheres nearby, containing a **CQC Program Delta** disk and a copy of **Swordsman's Manual VII**, then follow Raffine into the next room.

Another set of security forces soon interrupts Fidel and company.

These spider bots are machine-type enemies, so equip one of your damage-dealing members with the Machine Slayer role to help make quick work of them.

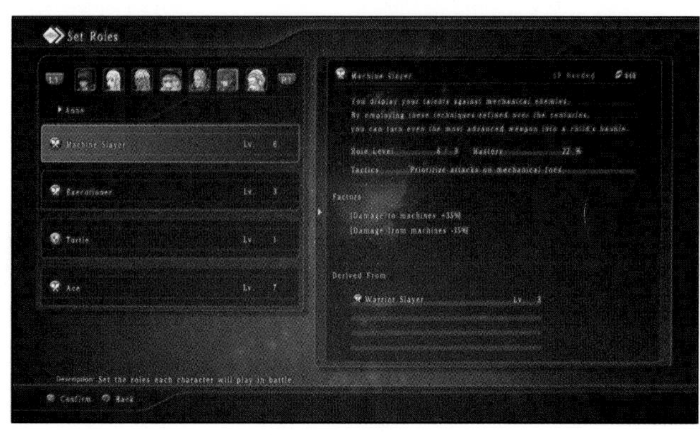

CHAPTER 10

After you destroy the Kronos assault bots, continue north, past a hallway and into an even larger room. Three plant-type monsters called Welwitschia greet you there.

WELWITSCHIA LVL 64
P. 308
Zephyr Lily, Laurel Tree, Shadow Roses, Poison Hemlock

As before, you can cut down these enemies more easily if you have the Plant Slayer role. These repulsive plants primarily use melee attacks, but they can also inflict poison; make sure to cast Antidote on anyone afflicted.

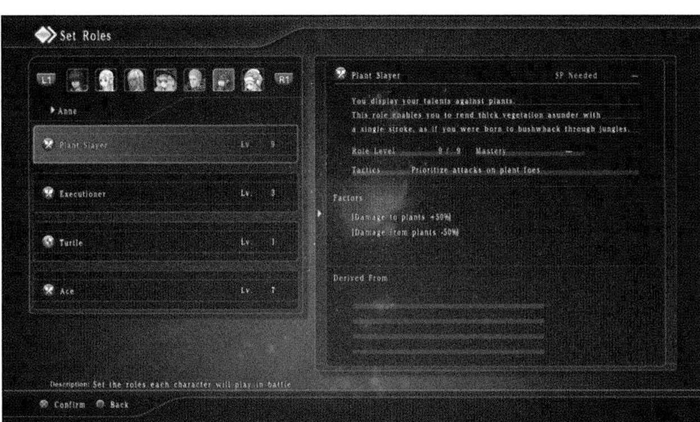

After taking them out, continue north for a boss battle with a mutated Manticore.

ILLUSTRIOUS MANTICORE LVL 66
P. 311
Parchment, Moonlight Signets, Vol. 3

Your first priority should be to change your party leader to Miki and run away from the mutant.

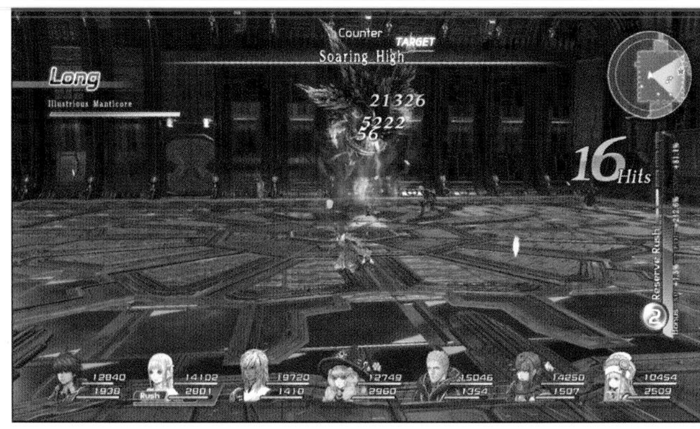

The monster has devastating area-of-effect attacks but primarily targets Fidel. Additionally, any damage you do to it is nullified by a constant healing effect.

It's a good idea to equip Fidel with defense-based roles like Royal Guard or Vanguard to mitigate damage. Keep him healed up with Miki's Ex Healing spell. Eventually, Relia casts a powerful signeturgical spell, halting its healing effect and slowing it down to a crawl.

This is your chance to take the flying Manticore down. Although it's tremendously incapacitated, it can still deal a large amount of damage around itself, so make sure that Miki is at a safe distance while you deplete its health.

You can deal more damage to it with the Mutant Slayer role, as well (it's a Corrupt-type, although it may seem like a beast).

After you slay the Illustrious Manticore, a cutscene triggers. You're greeted by General Alma and his villainous subordinate Thoras, with Feria in captivity.

Relia finally gets to meet her parents: a pair of scientists forced to work furtively for the Kronos government to produce humanoid clones made for war.

Unfortunately, her reunion with her caretakers is short-lived, as they're certain that they'll have to face inevitable consequences for their betrayal.

CHAPTER 10

CHAPTER 11

PROGENITOR OF SIGNETURGY

The exposition from the confrontation with General Alma and Thoras confirmed that Relia and Feria were created as human clones, birthed with symbological powers and cultivated as weaponry. Relia's guardians, whom she knows as her parents, were found to be ordinary scientists forced into the unethical Kronos research.

MISSION: INVESTIGATE THE SIGNESILICA

Before departing the Symbological Research Facility, Fidel and crew are given a clue into Relia's past and the reason for her existence on Faykreed IV. In a redeeming act, Relia's parents hand over an enigmatic card to the party, used to access a mystery within the Signesilica.

Action Checklist

1. Optional: Undertake and complete side quests
2. Optional: View Private Actions around various towns and the Charles D. Goale G
3. Optional: Complete the final set of Cathedral of Oblivion challenges
4. Head to the Signesilica, through Northern Territory of Sohma
5. Find the statue of Palafytos
6. Return to the Charles D. Goale G

OPTIONAL

SIDE QUESTS

CENTRAL RESULIA

Indecent Exposure

SANTEROULE

Open Season on Ruphin

Open Season on Bordnaks

Open Season on Pyekards

Open Season on Douxrah

Uprooting Families

EASTERN TREI'KUR

That Darn Ruddle

Subjugation Directive: Dante and Mateo

War and Peace

PRIVATE ACTIONS

CHARLES D. GOALE G

Relia's Fate

CENTRAL RESULIA

Under My Thumb?

New Friend

Friends for Now

SANTEROULE

The Letter

EASTERN TREI'KUR

Far from Home

Remembering Mom and Dad

Mission Walkthrough

With the mystery behind Relia's origin unraveled, there's one final piece of the puzzle to investigate. Why was she raised on Faykreed IV, of all planets? To find out, you'll need to take a plunge into the birthplace of signeturgy, the Signesilica.

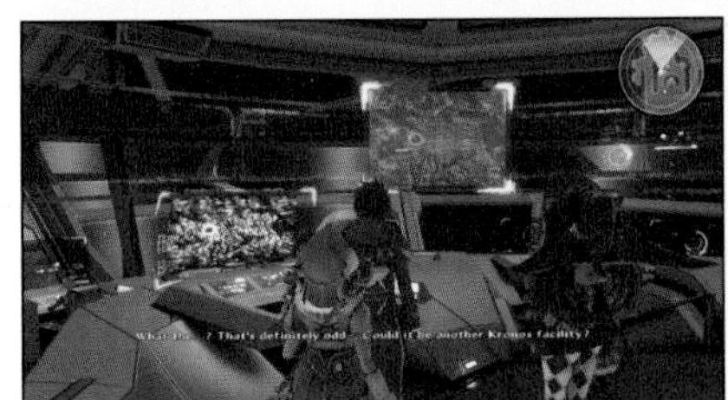

THE MANHUNT FINALE

You can undertake the last in the Ruddle line of quests at the bulletin board in Eastern Trei'kur. Finishing this quest grants access to a vast variety of crafting materials that would normally be obtained through harvesting or slaying monsters. Start the quest, then talk to the guard next to the bulletin board for the first clue of Ruddle's whereabouts.

Thanks to your starship's teleportation technology, hunting down Ruddle is made simple. Use the Communicator Model G, then teleport to the Coast of Minoz, in front of the Myiddok entrance. Talk to the steward of Myiddok's inn for another lead.

Next, teleport to West of the Eastern Eihieds and enter Santeroule. In the center of the town square, talk to the elderly woman for yet another tip. Looks like Ruddle's gone back to Central Resulia.

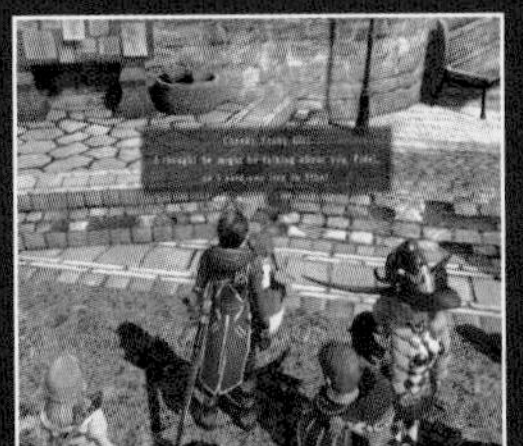

Now teleport to the Resulian Plains, and talk to the cheeky young girl by the bulletin board. Unsurprisingly, Ruddle isn't here, either. He's gone to look for Fidel in Sthal.

Finally, teleport to the Passage on the Cliffs to enter Sthal, where you'll find Ruddle waiting for you in Fidel's home. He'll tell you that he's done gathering stock for his business and that he's setting up shop in Central Resulia.

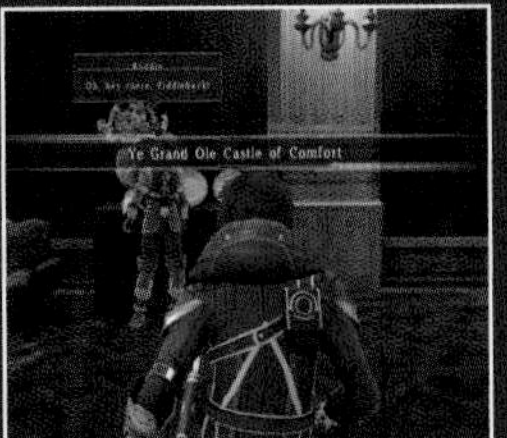

After you turn in the quest at the Eastern Trei'kur bulletin board, you'll gain access to Ruddle's new shop in the capital's inn. Congratulations! You now have an unlimited supply of valuable crafting materials like Alchemist's Water and High-Strength Adhesive!

SHOP—RUDDLE, CENTRAL RESULIA

Ruddle the Wanderer

ITEM	COST	TYPE
Alchemist's Water	3600	Material
Blue Roses	1200	Material
Cashmere	2800	Material
Demon's Tail	200	Material
Dwarven Embroidery Thread	1800	Material
Fish Scales	160	Material
Giant Bird Feather	400	Material
Green Fruit	360	Material
High-Strength Adhesive	1200	Material
Iron	400	Material
Red Fruit	300	Material
Ruby	1400	Material
Silver	800	Material
Velvet Ribbon	2400	Material

CATHEDRAL OF OBLIVION, FINAL

At this point in the story, the final iteration of the Cathedral of Oblivion is available. You can complete the previous five areas, plus an additional one that becomes accessible later on. For completing each skirmish, you're rewarded with the second strongest weapon, one for each of your controllable party members. The upgrade from your current equipment is drastic—so drastic that obtaining these weapons may make the rest of the main story battles seem trivial! However, the boss found in these final cathedrals can be incredibly difficult.

You can access the cathedral through the same warp points you entered from before. From easiest to hardest, the order is Coast of Minoz, Central Resulia, West of the Eastern Eihieds, Eastern Trei'kur, Northern Territory of Sohma, and then one final challenge that you can enter later as you progress through the story.

Your party should be at least around Level 60 to 70 since the minimum level of the cathedral's main boss is 80 (in the Coast of Minoz). Additionally, the final iteration consists of seven rounds (whereas the previous iteration consisted of five): six with groups of enemies that become increasingly difficult, and then a final boss—the mighty Storm Dragon.

You can save these dungeons to complete for post-ending content, or you can give yourself a challenge in order to obtain incredible weaponry. When you're ready for the trial, head to the Coast of Minoz and look for the warp point on your map. If it doesn't spawn, simply exit the zone and re-enter it until it does.

STORM DRAGON

LVL 80

The Storm Dragon is most likely your toughest encounter yet, especially if you're going into the fight under Level 70. However, it's manageable with the correct preparations.

Your equipment should consist of the latest possible purchases, either from locked chests or from crafting and synthesis. They don't need to be augmented fully, but it helps if you have Ornamentation, Fortification, and Whetting unlocked to boost your combat attributes.

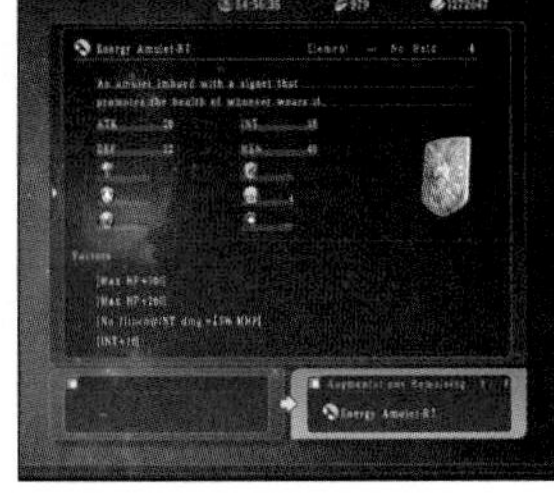

For roles, you'll want to have the following healer types leveled: Crusader, Sage, Healer, and Savior. For offense, suggested roles include: Berserker, Daemon, Raven Slayer, Enchanter, and Emissary of the Blue Sphere. Equip Miki with the healer roles, Emmerson with Daemon and Berserker, and Anne with Raven Slayer and any other offense-enhancing roles. Raven Slayer is crucial because it increases damage done to and reduces damage taken from avians by 50% (at max level). On your swordsmen, Fidel and Victor, you can equip guard-boosting roles to help them survive the dragon's melee onslaught. Having Vanguard, Marshal, and Avenger leveled is ideal. Relia should have at least the Vivifier support role equipped to keep your AI-controlled members active.

For food, you should either eat ATK- or INT-boosting food before engaging with the dragon. Grilled Steak works well, especially considering the dragon's high DEF rating. Hopefully, you have Fiore's Void spell learned at this point, as well. You should also disable all of Miki's offensive signeturgies so that she can focus on raising and healing other party members when you're not controlling her.

The actual fight can be hectic. Your primary concern is to separate your party members to avoid multiple casualties from the devastating Tornado spell.

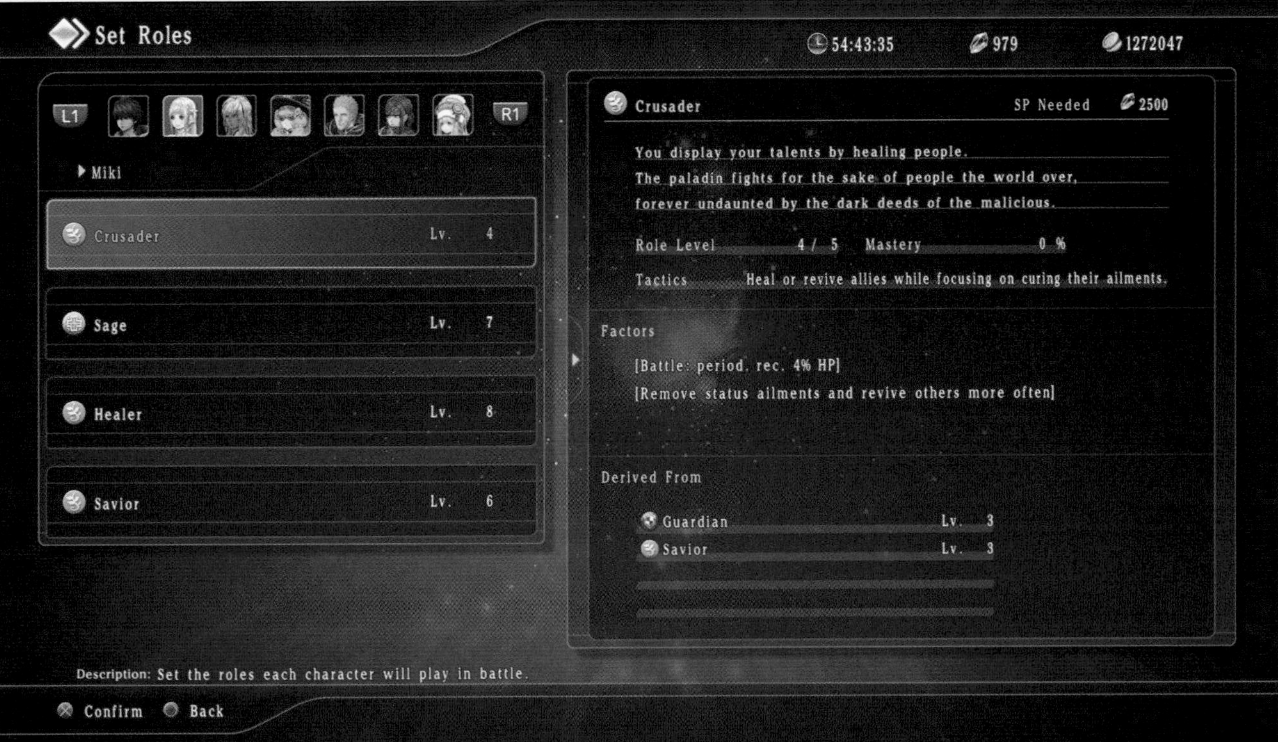

When you engage, take control of Miki and move her as far away from the dragon as possible. If the dragon starts casting Tornado, make sure to open the battle menu (default △ button), assess where the attack is projected, and then move anyone in danger out of the way. If your party is set up properly, the AI-controlled Miki should be able to keep everyone's health up with Ex Healing and Faerie Light. Try to keep Emmerson and Fiore far away, too. The dragon frequently changes its target and chases after your other party members, so keep a lookout and move them accordingly.

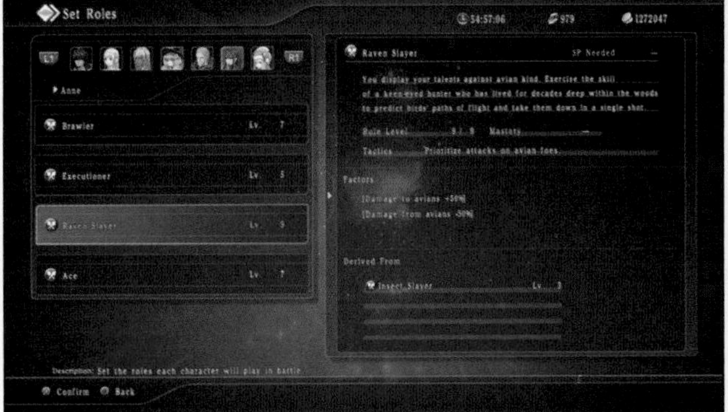

Anyone hit by Tornado, especially at close range, can potentially die instantly because it deals a devastating amount of damage. If this happens, raise your party members up as soon as possible. If Miki goes down, have Fiore cast her Raise Dead spell on her, or have one of your other members use the Fresh Sage item. If you're positioning correctly, you'll most likely be able to raise your knocked-out members without risk of wiping out.

Another aspect of the dragon to watch out for is Enshelter, the buff it casts on itself. This boosts its DEF drastically, so you'll need to make sure to dispel it with Fiore's Void signeturgy. Watch for the DEF UP icon beneath the Storm Dragon's status bar, and react accordingly. When it has this buff on, you'll notice that your attacks deal significantly less damage, even from your strongest members.

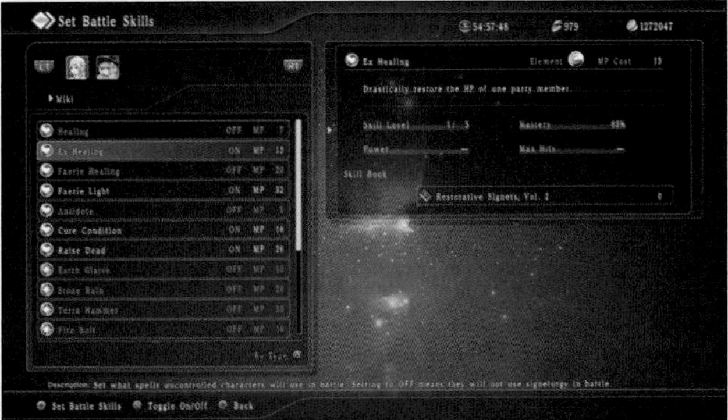

As its name implies, the Storm Dragon is not only immune to wind- and lightning-based attacks, but it absorbs them. Make sure to turn off any wind-based spells to prevent this (Emmerson's Seraphic Thunder is also wind-based, so change his battle set if you need to).

Although the Storm Dragon absorbs Wind-based spells, Ice magic (and other non-Wind based ones) does well against it, so when you have time, you can control Fiore to combo cast repeated Ice Needles. Remember to unleash your high-damage Reserve Rush cancel combos with your ATK-based damage dealers, too.

To summarize, keep your back line members away from Tornado, pausing the game when necessary. Cast Void whenever the Storm Dragon buffs itself with Enshelter, and spend your Reserve Rush liberally. Eventually, the dragon goes down, rewarding you with an epic weapon for one of your party members in the nearby treasure chest.

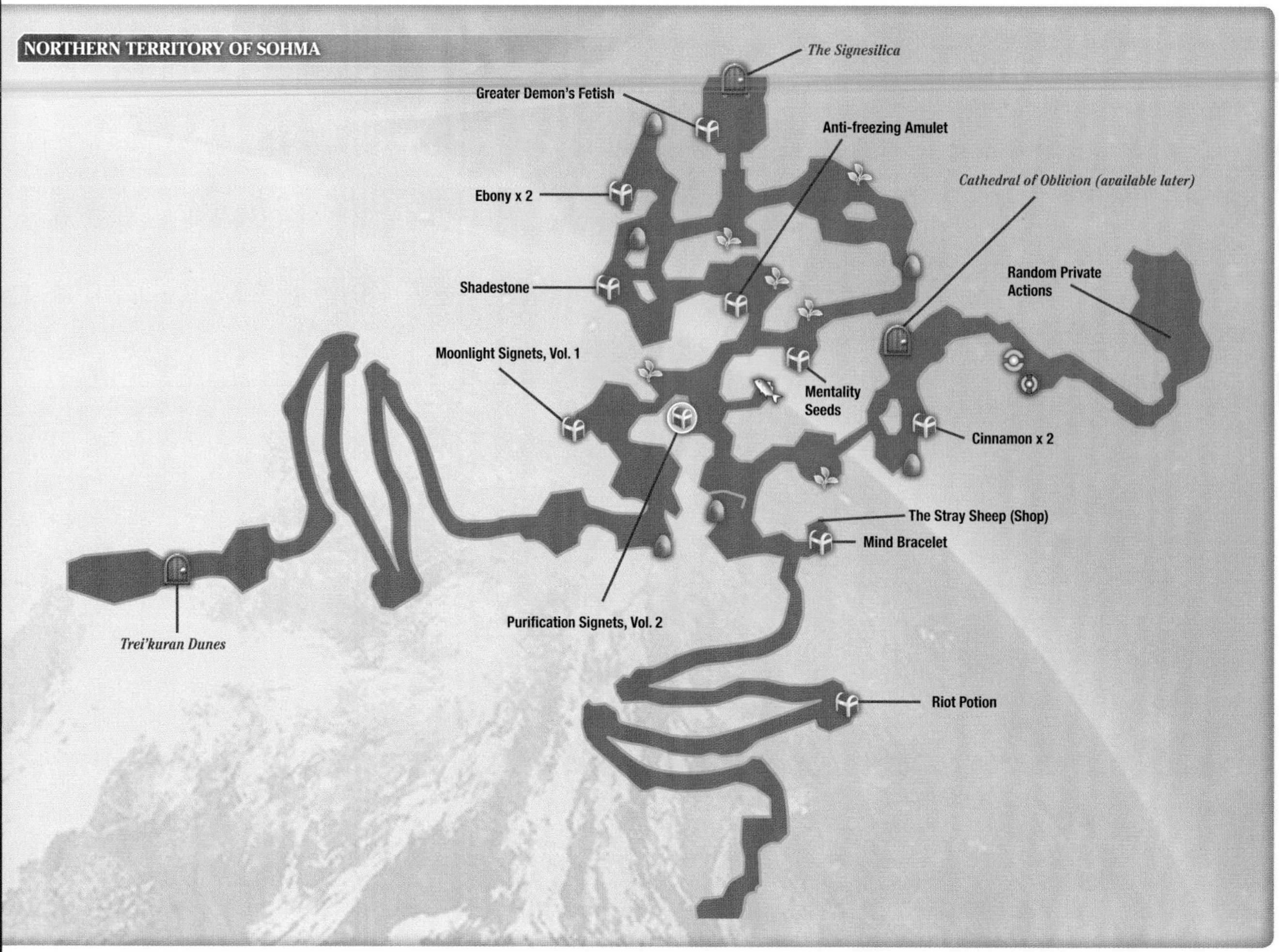

NORTHERN TERRITORY OF SOHMA

The Signesilica
Greater Demon's Fetish
Anti-freezing Amulet
Ebony x 2
Cathedral of Oblivion (available later)
Shadestone
Random Private Actions
Moonlight Signets, Vol. 1
Mentality Seeds
Cinnamon x 2
The Stray Sheep (Shop)
Mind Bracelet
Purification Signets, Vol. 2
Trei'kuran Dunes
Riot Potion

Enemy	Level	Page	Drops
SKELETON SOLDIER	LVL 65	P.313	Falchion, Ghost's Soul, Alchemist's Water, Nereidstone
AMBER PRINCESS	LVL 66	P.308	Earth Gem, Moon Pearl, Fish Scales
JATAYU	LVL 67	P.300	Egg Paragon, Gigantavian Egg, Angelstone, Nereidstone
DINOSAURUS	LVL 75	P.299	Dragon Scales, Dragon Hide, Meteorite

RETURN TO THE NORTHERN TERRITORY OF SOHMA

When you're ready to dive into the Signesilica, take the Charles D. Goale's transporter to the Northern Territory of Sohma. Your starting point is at the west end, near the Trei'kuran Dunes, with your destination at the north end of the map.

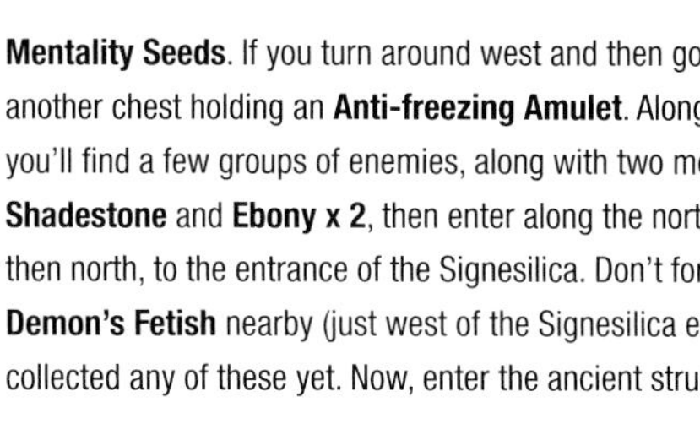

If you haven't picked up the chests in the northern region of the map, you can do so now. Head north from the center of the area; to your immediate east, you can find a chest containing some **Mentality Seeds**. If you turn around west and then go north a few steps, there's another chest holding an **Anti-freezing Amulet**. Along the west side of the area, you'll find a few groups of enemies, along with two more chests. Pick up the **Shadestone** and **Ebony x 2**, then enter along the northern path heading east, then north, to the entrance of the Signesilica. Don't forget to grab the **Greater Demon's Fetish** nearby (just west of the Signesilica entrance) if you haven't collected any of these yet. Now, enter the ancient structure to the north.

THE SIGNESILICA

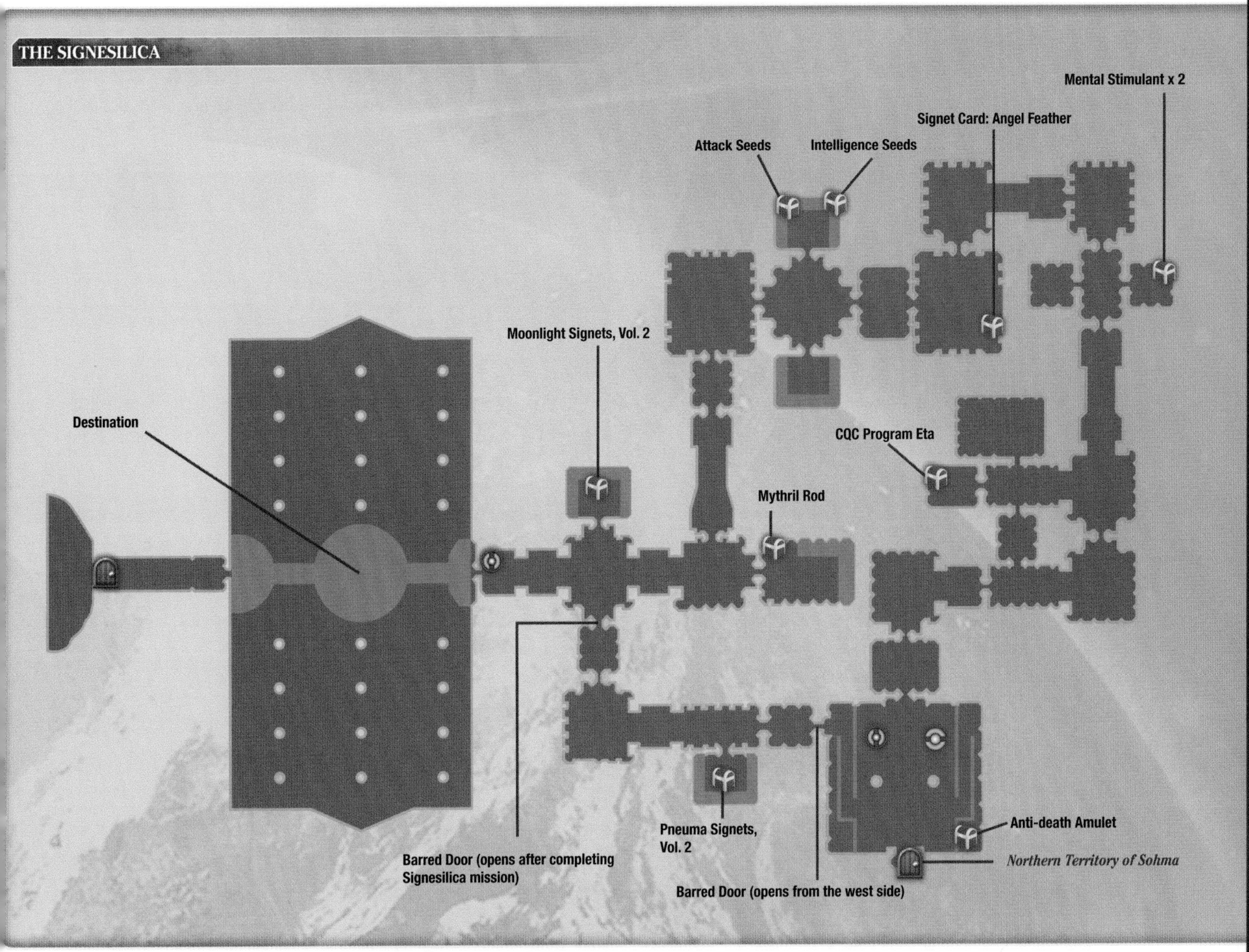

Mental Stimulant x 2
Signet Card: Angel Feather
Attack Seeds
Intelligence Seeds
Moonlight Signets, Vol. 2
Destination
CQC Program Eta
Mythril Rod
Anti-death Amulet
Northern Territory of Sohma
Pneuma Signets, Vol. 2
Barred Door (opens after completing Signesilica mission)
Barred Door (opens from the west side)

Monster	Level	Page	Drops
LITTLE SATAN	LVL 68	P.311	Shadow Roses, Lesser Fiend's Tail, Signet Card +, Darkness Gem
DARK MATERIAL	LVL 68	P.309	Darkness Gem, Crystal, Mythril, Platinum
CHAOTIC CELL	LVL 69	P.305	Gerel Secretion, Gelatinous Slime, Alchemist's Water
SACRED GUARD	LVL 69	P.318	Silver, Gold, Platinum, Mythril
RAVENNE	LVL 70	P.301	Egg Paragon, Salamanderstone, Sylphstone, Nereidstone

Once you are inside, there are save and restore points in the main hall. Refill your HP and MP, then save your progress here. If you take a look at the map, there's a door up the stairs to the west that's barred. This is a shortcut you can take later if you want to return for quests or to pick up anything you might have missed.

First, go up the stairs on to the east balcony in the main hall. At the southeast end lies a treasure chest with an **Anti-death Amulet** inside.

Pick it up, then take the door to the north from the main hall, fighting through the Signesilica's Corrupt-type monsters. Your path here is fairly straightforward. Travel east, then make the first left you can make, going north. Eventually, you find a door to your left. Head west inside to open a treasure chest containing a **CQC Program Eta** skill disk.

Use the disk to learn a new skill for one of the federation officers, then turn around and continue all the way east until you can go north. Continue north until you come to a hall with three doors. Enter the one to the east to pick up **Mental Stimulant x 2** from a chest in there.

Return to the hallway and take the north door, entering a room full of Sacred Guards. Dispatch them, then continue along the path westward.

In the room to the south from here resides an avian-type enemy called Ravenne. Defeat it, then open up the chest in the room to obtain **Signet Card: Angel Feather**. Keep going west until you reach an intersection room. Through to the door to the north, there are two chests in a room that hold **Attack Seeds** and **Intelligence Seeds**. Grab them, then return to the intersection room. Open the door to the west, and you'll see a giant Ash Dragon just waiting to get its teeth in you.

Before you fight it, you might want to prepare by eating stat-boosting food; HP-enhancing food can be helpful. While the Ash Dragon doesn't have an amazing amount of hit points, it does dish out a large amount of damage. Slay it, then proceed all the way south. If you've undertaken the **Open Season on Ruphin** quest, enter the room to the east here to defeat Ruphin the Imperious, a Corrupt-type enemy. In the same room, open the chest to obtain a **Mythril Rod**.

Continue west, and you'll see a save point ahead. Before the save point, enter the room to your right, going north, to pick up a copy of **Moonlight Signets, Vol. 2** in the treasure chest. Now, save your game and prepare for a boss battle in the west wing of the Signesilica.

The Crystal Guardian is a Corrupt-type enemy, so Mutant Slayer works well against it on one of your damage-dealing party members. It's also capable of casting powerful signeturgical spells at your back line heroes, so watch out for things like Radiant Lancer. The guardian also uses a full-screen lunge attack, as well as an extremely powerful triple beam attack skill. This causes devastating damage, so make sure to run out of its line of fire.

THE FLOATING DESERT BENEATH

When you've defeated it, continue west down a flight of stairs, where you'll find a statue of Palafytos, the founder of signeturgy. Although it's seemingly a dead end, Anne senses an electrical field emanating from behind the statue. She takes the card that Relia's caretakers gave to Fidel and scans it at the statue's base. A hidden doorway appears.

Relia runs ahead. Follow her down into the mysterious dimension.

Relia! Wait!

What in the world is this place?

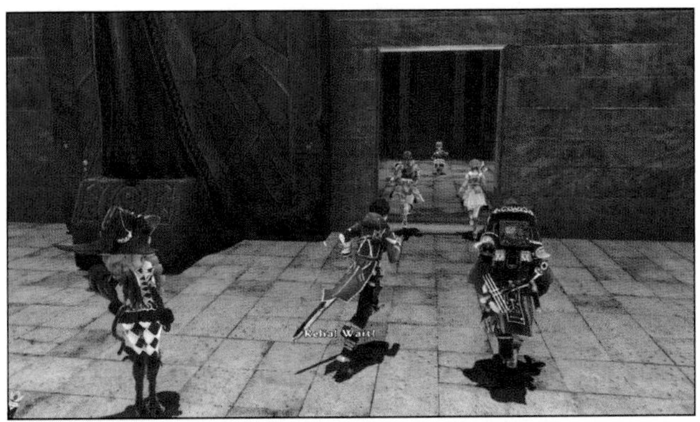

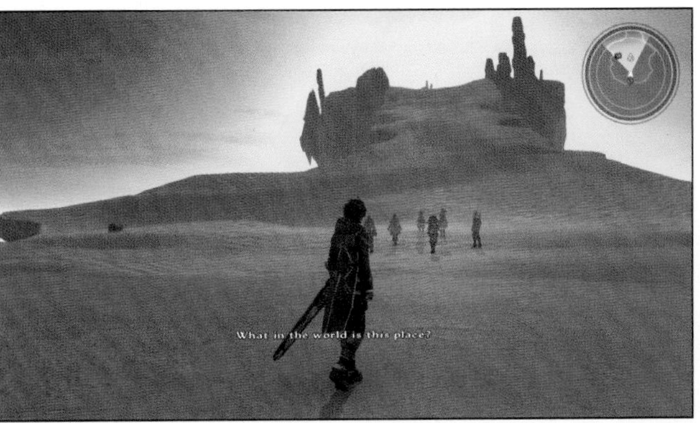

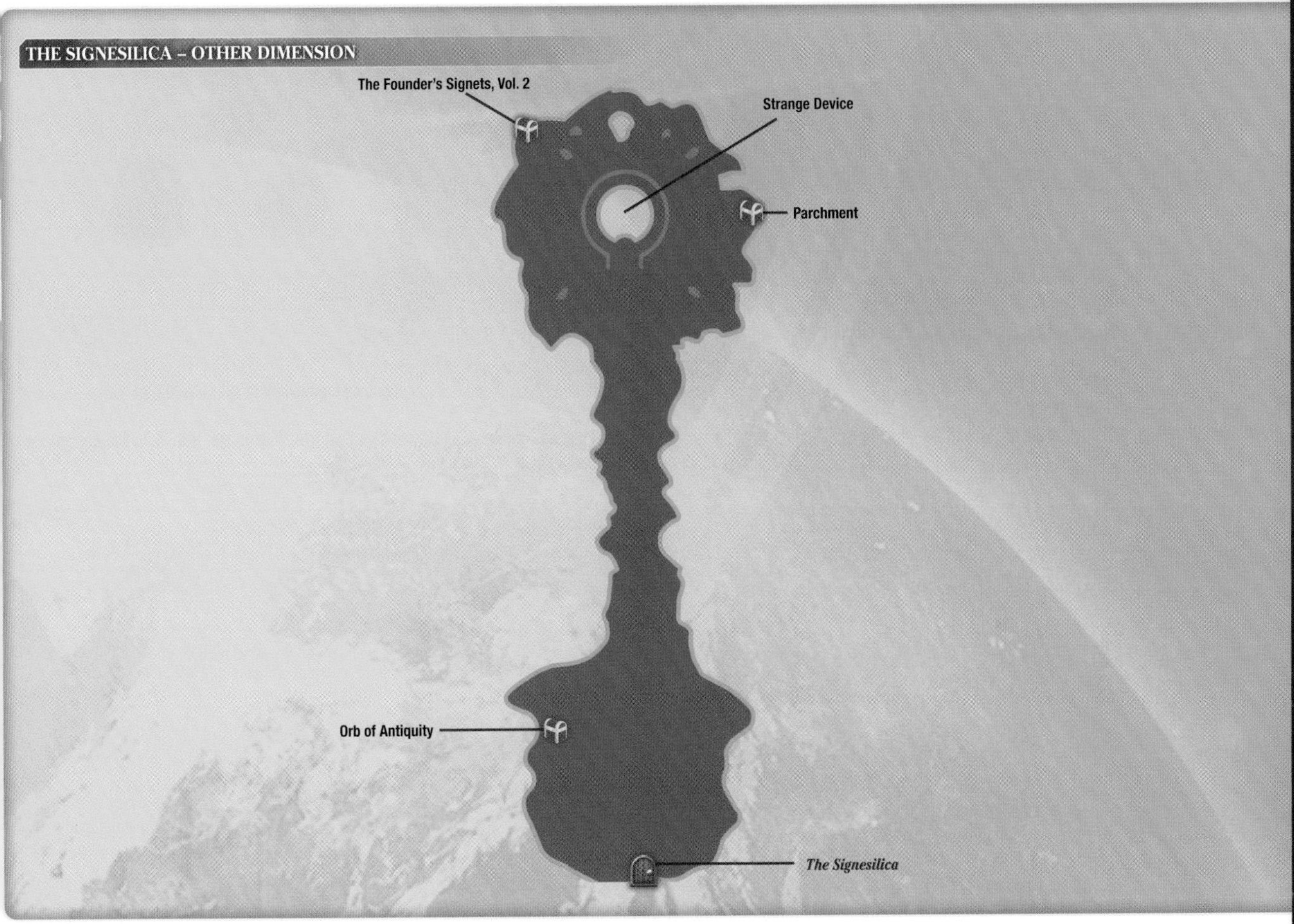
THE SIGNESILICA - OTHER DIMENSION
The Founder's Signets, Vol. 2
Strange Device
Parchment
Orb of Antiquity
The Signesilica

Relia recognizes this otherworldly area and seems to be attracted to something up ahead. Continue following her up the hill, where you'll come across a strange circular structure.

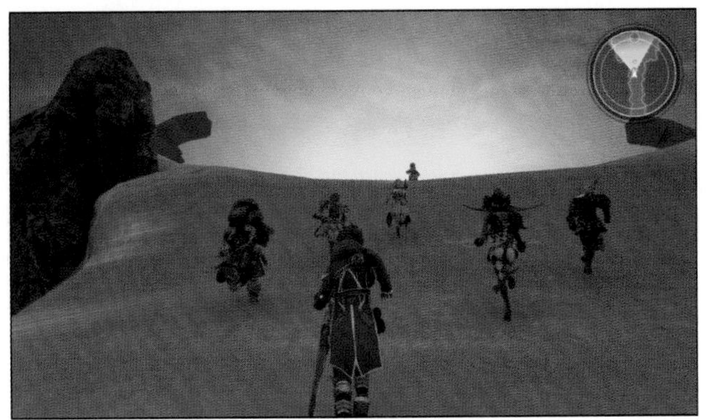

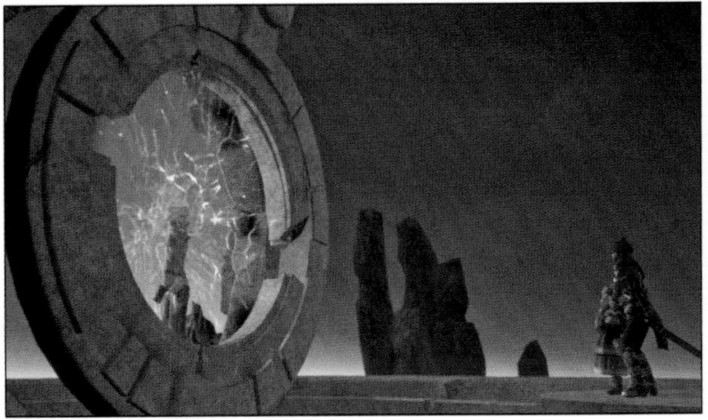

The device activates, displaying Relia's past and reminding her of her painful existence as a man-made weapon. However, Fidel assures her that she's more than that now, considering how much she's protected her new friends. After his words of encouragement, a newfound strength emerges from her.

After the cutscene, there are three chests in the area to loot. To the northwest of the extraterrestrial device is a copy of **The Founder's Signets, Vol. 2**. To the east of the platform, pick up a piece of **Parchment**. On your way out, open the chest near the exit for an **Orb of Antiquity**.

PART 03

When you re-enter the Signesilica from the otherworldly desert, Emmerson receives a call from the Charles D. Goale G. Unfortunately, the signeturgical interference prevents the use of the Communicator Model G, so the party must trek their way out of the dilapidated labyrinth by foot. The good news is you can take the short way back, so head east, then south from the save point, where the door is now open for you to leave. This path takes you to the previously barred door near the main hall of the Signesilica.

On your way out, there's a room to the south on the way east. Enter the room to pick up a copy of **Pneuma Signets, Vol. 2**. Have Miki read the book to learn the Resurrection signeturgical spell, then continue on out of the Signesilica. Once outside, you can use the Communicator Model G for a transport back to the starship. Time to check in with Delacroix regarding the Kronos transmission he received.

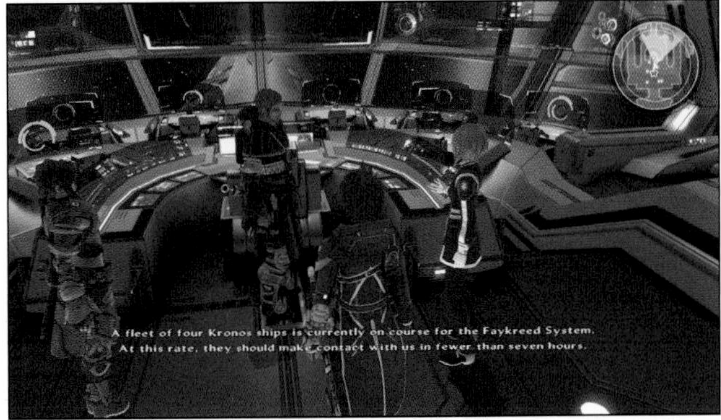

MAKE AN UNLIKELY ALLIANCE

Take the turbo lift to the Bridge. President Mutal of the Kronos government starts a communication line with Emmerson and his crew. It seems General Alma is working on his own accord, executing a coup d'état.

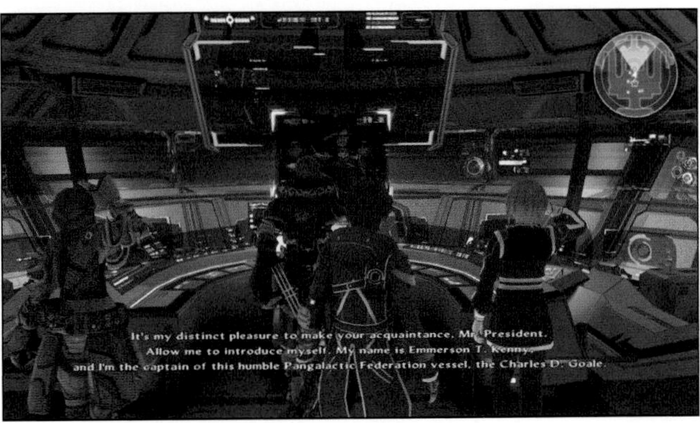

After the cutscene, you assume control of Fidel in his room aboard the starship's Private Quarters. Just outside, Victor questions Emmerson about Kronos' true intentions and whether they can be trusted.

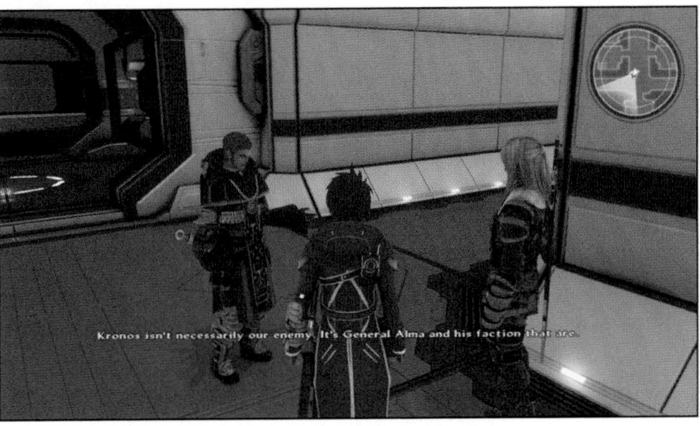

Now, return to the Bridge, and President Mutal will start another conference call (this time with Commander Dean of the Pangalactic Federation). The commander permits lending aid to the Kronos fleet and appoints Emmerson as the federation's official ambassador.

After an intermission, General Alma calls in. Emmerson attempts to negotiate a peaceful outcome to the conflict, but without any luck, as Alma threatens to destroy everyone in his way. The heroes now have no choice but to stop him forcefully.

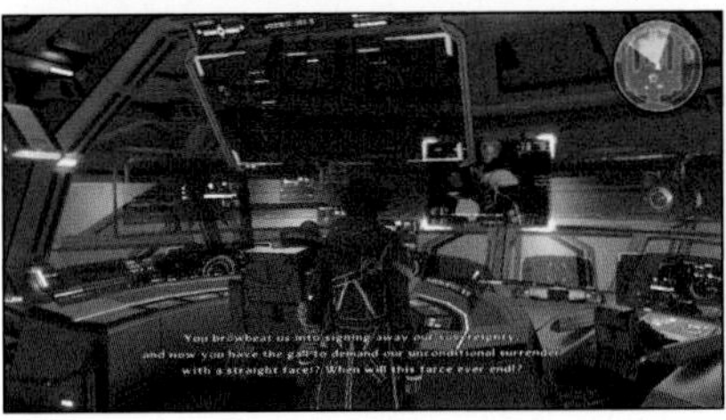

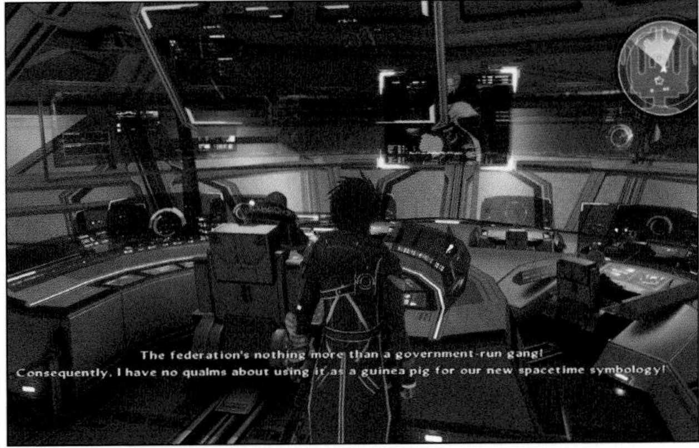

CHAPTER 12

MOMENT OF TRUTH

Alma's mind is set in stone. With a vindictive mentality, he's out to destroy what he sees to be Kronos's enemies, even its own governing body. Negotiations of peace are unsuccessful, so Fidel and his allies have no choice but to deal with the general in a final confrontation.

MISSION: INFILTRATE THE ASTEROID BASE

President Mutal, the Kronos governing leader, helps the Pangalactic Federation by relaying coordinates of the rebellion base of operations. However, simply finding the headquarters isn't enough. Emmerson's crew must find a way to get through the asteroid base's force fields if they want to rescue Feria.

Action Checklist

1. Optional: Undertake and complete remaining side quests
2. Rest in the Private Quarters on the Charles D. Goale G
3. Take the shuttle and infiltrate the enemy base, the Alcazar of the Golden Age

Mission Walkthrough

Your main objective here is to rescue Feria within the rebellion headquarters, the Alcazar of the Golden Age. There's a point of no return (albeit, a temporary one), so finish up any side quests and optional tasks before undertaking your final mission.

TAKE A BREAK

Emmerson recommends that everyone take a break before the next mission, so your next step is to rest in the Private Quarters of the Charles D. Goale G. At this point, a few new Private Actions become available, one being Anne's First Mission. Viewing it unlocks the Instructor role, which drastically increases EXP gain. This is a good spot to complete any side quests and Private Actions you may have queued up, as well. If you commit to resting, you won't be able to return to Faykreed until the mission is completed.

THE HOLY TRINITY OF SUPPORT ROLES

Before undertaking the next mission, you can obtain the Instructor role from triggering the Anne's First Mission Private Action in the Transport Room of the Charles D. Goale. At max level, Instructor increases EXP gain by 50%! This effect, combined with Altruist (EXP converted into SP) and Minstrel (bonus SP gain), speeds up SP progress drastically. To enhance it even more, you can eat EXP-boosting food such as Heavenly Pudding or Lemon Tarts. Slaying monsters with all of these buffs active can help you quickly fill out all of your SP-related skills and roles.

PRIVATE ACTIONS

CHARLES D. GOALE G
Anne's First Mission

SANTEROULE
Sorry, Sis
Reason to Fight

CENTRAL RESULIA
It's Better to Have Loved and Lost?

When you're ready, rest up in Fidel's private quarters to commence the next operation. Fidel wakes up, unable to sleep. You can find one of the other party members gazing out at the fleeting stars in the Transport Room (the ally found here depends on whoever has the most affinity with Fidel). Walk up to your friend to trigger a cutscene.

HIGHEST FIDELITY

The hidden affinity value between characters results in changes to certain events. These include the main story's ending and the person who appears the night after Fidel sleeps in the private quarters in this chapter.

You can control affinity throughout the game through Private Actions, either by ignoring them (which, of course, results in much less affinity) or triggering them. The more Private Actions you view with a certain character, the more affinity is gained between the people involved. Certain responses to Private Actions with choices will also either result in more or less affinity, depending on the character's reaction to your answer.

Additionally, there are two usable items that alter Fidel's affinity values with his friends: **Emotional Destabilizer** and **Love Potion No. 256**. You can find these throughout the game or craft them with the Compounding skill (although the love potion can be considerably difficult to find ingredients for).

So, if you want to force a certain person to appear at the starship window the night after Fidel rests before the final mission, you can apply several doses of Love Potion No. 256 on one character while having the other members drink Emotional Destabilizers. Be warned, though: this also affects which ending you'll receive.

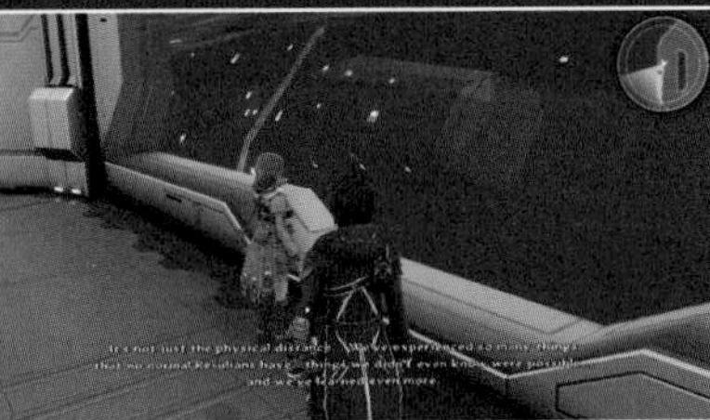

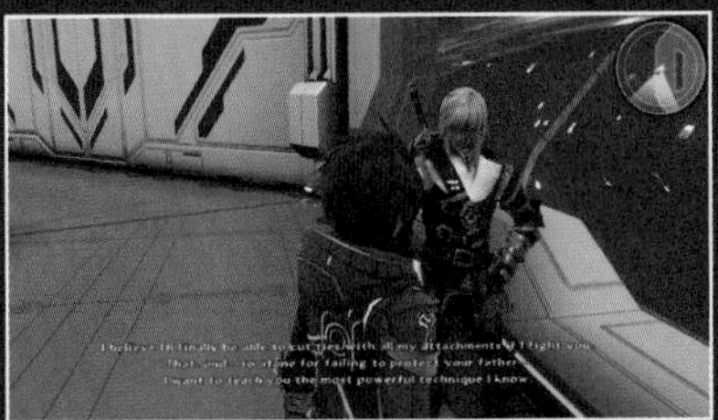

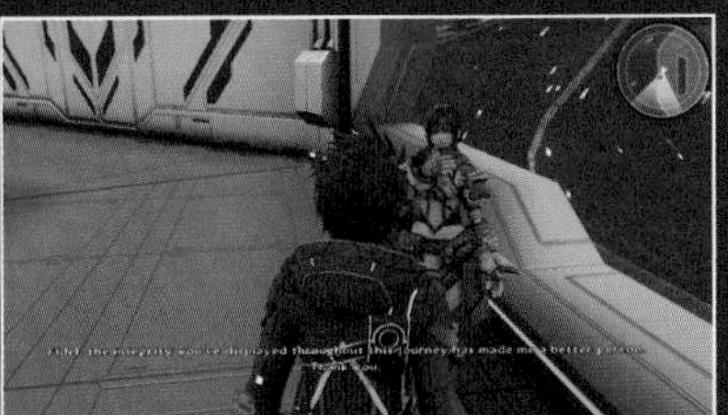

BOARD THE SHUTTLE

After their heart-to-heart colloquy, the scene transitions into a comm-link between President Mutal and General Alma. The operation to rescue Feria while putting an end to General Alma officially begins.

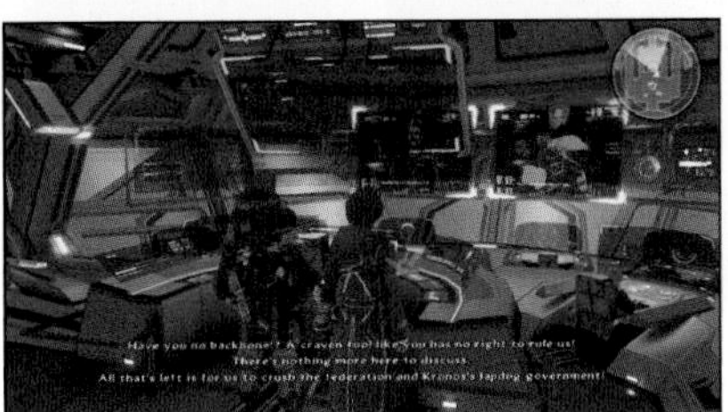

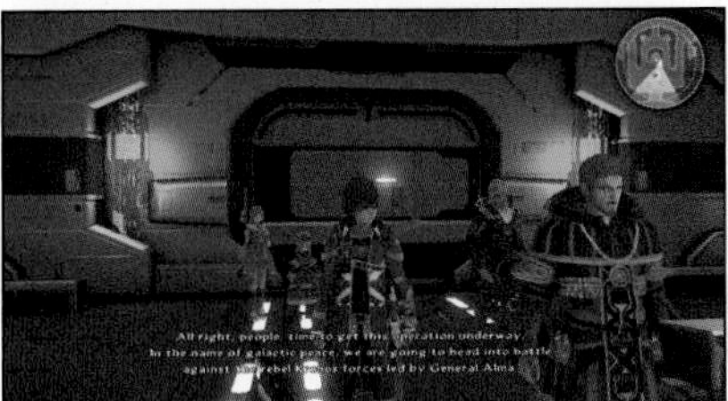

As the Charles D. Goale G takes enemy fire, Fidel suggests an attack directly on General Alma, reasoning that defeating him will put an end to the rebellion for good. Although impractical, Anne posits that it's possible by using spacetime symbology with Relia's powers to deactivate the enemy's shields, allowing a direct transport in.

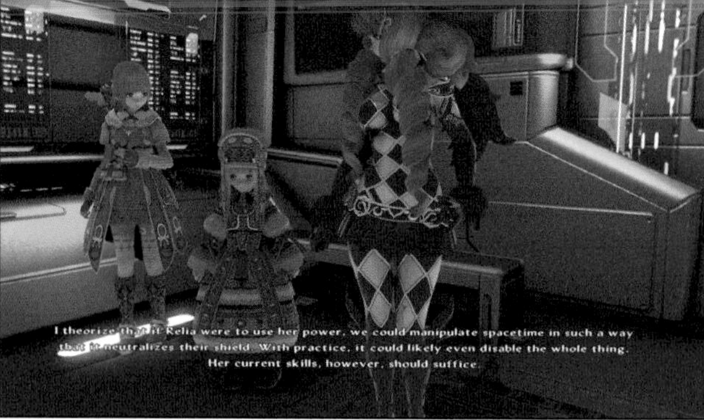

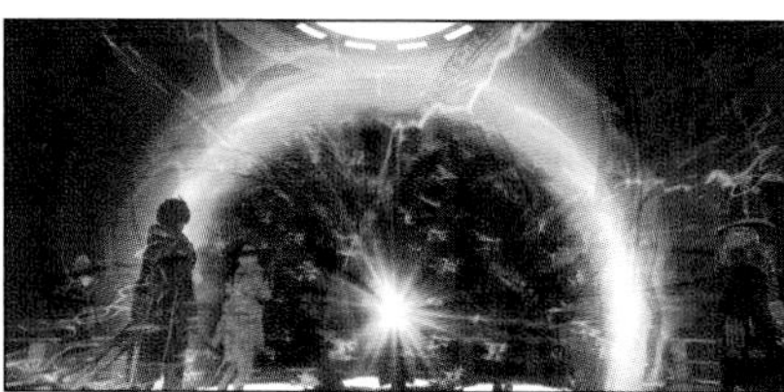

Get to the transporter to activate another cutscene. Unfortunately, Feria's powers are blocking Relia's, so the plan won't work. However, Anne and Emmerson come up with another idea involving taking the shuttle directly into the enemy base.

Take the turbo lift to the Cargo Bay, then enter the shuttle to trigger a cutscene. Emmerson and crew find the entrance to the Kronos asteroid base, the Alcazar of the Golden Age. Relia confidently fires up her signeturgical powers, disabling the shields and allowing the satellite shuttle to dock safely inside.

NO TURNING BACK

Once inside the Kronos asteroid base, there's no turning back until you finish your objective here. However, there are resources to help you survive. There's an HP and MP restore point near the entrance, as well as a shopkeeper with everything you'll need, including usable medicines and equipment upgrades.

ALCAZAR OF THE GOLDEN AGE

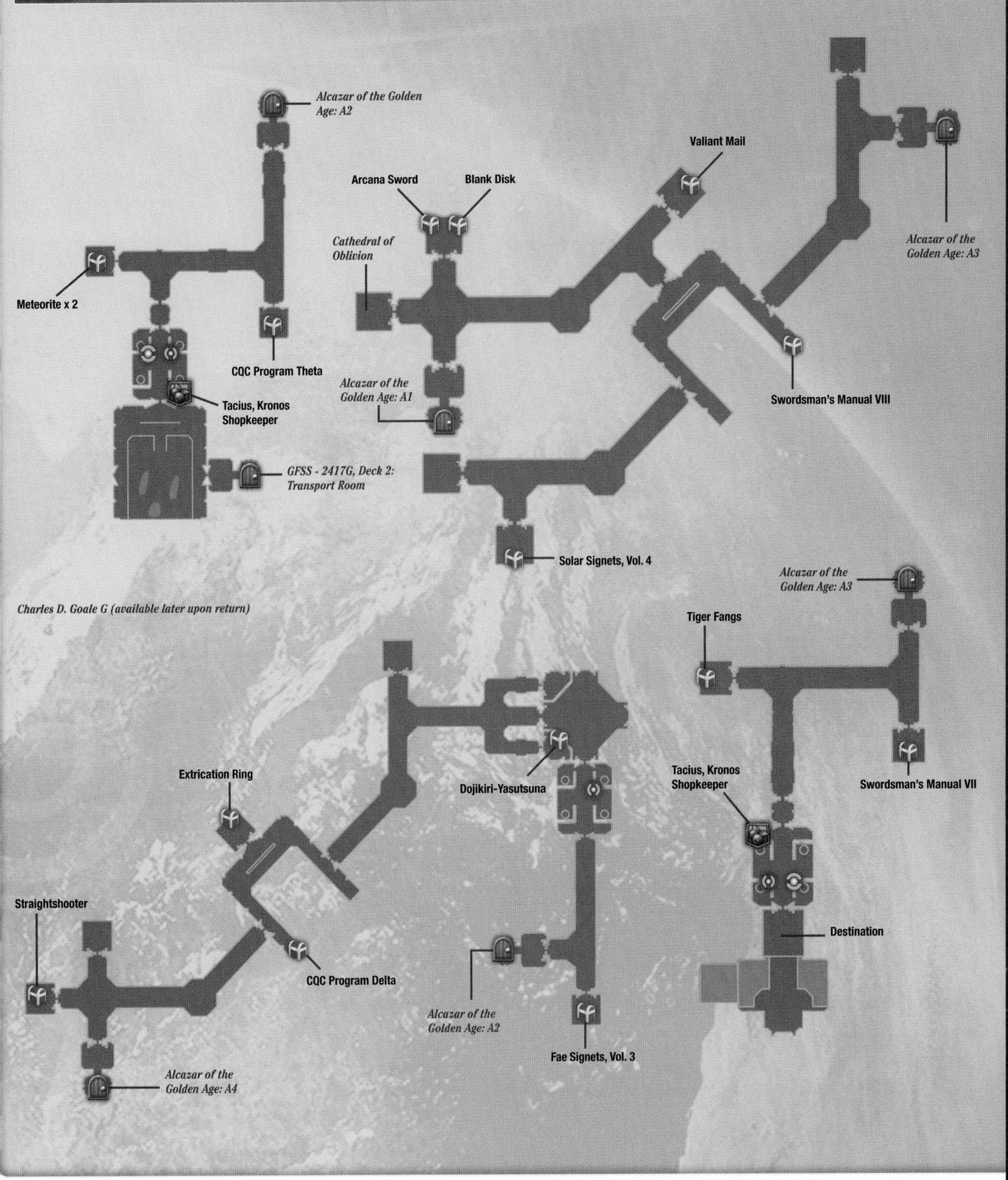

Alcazar of the Golden Age: A2

Valiant Mail

Arcana Sword

Blank Disk

Cathedral of Oblivion

Alcazar of the Golden Age: A3

Meteorite x 2

CQC Program Theta

Alcazar of the Golden Age: A1

Swordsman's Manual VIII

Tacius, Kronos Shopkeeper

GFSS - 2417G, Deck 2: Transport Room

Solar Signets, Vol. 4

Alcazar of the Golden Age: A3

Charles D. Goale G (available later upon return)

Tiger Fangs

Extrication Ring

Dojikiri-Yasutsuna

Tacius, Kronos Shopkeeper

Swordsman's Manual VII

Straightshooter

Destination

CQC Program Delta

Alcazar of the Golden Age: A2

Fae Signets, Vol. 3

Alcazar of the Golden Age: A4

KRONOS COMMANDER LVL 71

P. 290 — Heroism Potion, Wire

VALIANT CONSCRIPT LVL 73

P. 315 — Quantum Processor, Laser Oscillator

AVENGER LVL 72

P. 314 — Diffusion Device, Quantum Processor, High-Power Generator, Blank Disk

KRONOS AUTHORITY LVL 71

P. 290 — Vitalitea, Wire

KRONOS SCHOLAR LVL 71

P. 291 — Acuity Potion, Signet Card: Shadow Needles +, Signet Card: Dark Devourer +

PART 03

After the maniacal Alma taunts Fidel and friends, make your way deeper into the Kronos asteroid through the north path. On your way up, you'll encounter a Kronos Researcher shopkeeper who assists you with regards from Raffine. Several armor and weapon upgrades are available here; however, the weapons aren't as strong as the final Cathedral of Oblivion rewards if you've obtained those already. After you're done shopping, you can save your game and restore your HP and MP just up ahead.

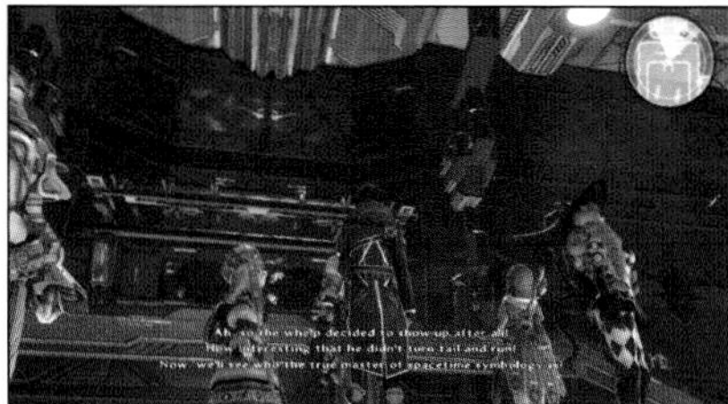

Shops

Tacius

ITEM	COST	TYPE
Acuity Bracelet	10000	Accessory
Arcane Bracelet	5000	Accessory
Attack Bracelet	10000	Accessory
Energy Bracelet	5000	Accessory
Fortitude Bracelet	10000	Accessory
Mind Bracelet	10000	Accessory
Mystic Robe	30000	Armor
Mythril Mesh	28000	Armor
Mythril Plate	34000	Armor
Basil	90	Usable
Blackberries	80	Usable
Blueberries	40	Usable
Chamomile	180	Usable
Cinnamon	300	Usable
Fresh Sage	160	Usable
Jasmine	90	Usable
Lavender	300	Usable
Mint	90	Usable
Mythril Gauntlets	36000	Weapon
Mythril Rod	32000	Weapon
Mythril Sword	40000	Weapon
Orb of Antiquity	50000	Weapon
Silvance	44000	Weapon
Sylvan Ray	42000	Weapon

When you're ready, your destination is in the northeast region of the first map. On your way there, you'll encounter several high-level Kronos military units, including deadly machinery known as Avengers. Avengers can deal a large amount of damage in a short period of time due to their heavy firepower, so equip your party members accordingly (Machine Slayer on Fidel works wonders here).

At the first divergence, make a left, going westward, into a room with a treasure sphere containing **Meteorite x 2**. Open it, then turn around and head all the way east until you come across a group of Avengers and Valiant Conscripts. Slay them, then go south into another room with a sphere holding a **CQC Program Theta** skill disk.

Turn around and head all the way north to operate the teleport pad, boosting the party to the next level of the asteroid.

From here, if you pause the game with the OPTIONS button, you can check for the final Cathedral of Oblivion instance in the westernmost room of the map. If you're up for a challenge (and it is, indeed, quite a difficult one), you can force it to spawn by exiting the area back to the A1 area and re-entering A2. You can always come back to complete it later to obtain Fidel's second-best weapon.

To the north of the initial intersection here is a room with two treasure spheres. Open them to obtain an **Arcana Sword** and a **Blank Disk**. Now, take the east path from the intersection. Keep going as it bends northeast into a room with another treasure sphere containing **Valiant Mail** armor.

Now, turn around and take the southeast path, crossing over into the second half of the map, where you'll see a Kronos spacecraft docked.

Your destination is to the northeast from here, labeled Alcazar of the Golden Age: A3 on your map. However, you can pick up some treasure if you travel to the southwest corner of the area. Fight your way to the southernmost room to pick up a copy of a **Solar Signets, Vol. 4** skill book.

Return to the docking area in the middle of the map. Before you enter the northeast path, there's a treasure sphere in the east corner with **Swordsman's Manual VIII** in it. Grab it, then continue to the transport pad located in the northeast area to get to the next area of the asteroid base.

The path in the third area is relatively linear, with a couple of chests along the way. Run east from the starting point, then south into a room to collect a copy of **Fae Signets, Vol. 3** from the treasure sphere.

Now, take the path north until you reach a multilevel room with a save point in the middle. Save your progress here, then continue your journey north for a mini-boss battle.

EXORCISE THORAS'S EXPERIMENTS

The mad Kronos scientist Thoras has a surprise experiment in store for you here. He summons a Corrupt-type Baskanian monster to test Relia's signeturgical powers. If you've fought the Eyebalone boss in the first iteration of the Cathedral of Oblivion, you'll be familiar with its attacks. Dodge its eye beams while the other party members dish out the damage.

Once you've defeated the monstrosity, take the west exit from the arena into a hallway with an intersection. Take the south path from here, winding up into a set of stairs that leads to a door back into the previous arena. You can find a treasure sphere up on this platform containing a weapon for Victor, the **Dojikiri-Yasutsuna**. This katana is an upgrade for him if you haven't obtained the Chrome Nightmare from the Cathedral of Oblivion. Otherwise, you can use it as augmentation material to upgrade your Chrome Nightmare.

Continue west and then south, fighting through Kronos military and their security robots. When you reach another docked spacecraft, there's a room up a small set of stairs to the northwest. It contains some enemies and a treasure sphere with an **Extrication Ring** inside. Defeat the Valiant Conscripts and take the ring, then return to the docking area. To the south of the docked ship around the corner, there's another sphere that holds a **CQC Program Delta** skill disk. Pick it up, then exit through the southwest door into another hallway.

At the final intersection here, there's a room to the west with a treasure sphere containing a **Straightshooter** phaser gun for Emmerson. After you grab it, take the transport pad to the final area south of the intersection.

From the starting point on A4, head directly south until you get to a room with a **Swordsman's Manual VII** in a treasure sphere. Open it, then turn around and take the west path all the way into another room with yet another treasure sphere. Grab the **Tiger Fangs**, and make your way down the south path until you reach another pair of save and restore points. Another Kronos shopkeeper can be found here, too. If you need to resupply, purchase whatever you need from him, and then use the save and restore points. Get ready for another boss battle just south of here.

When you enter the room, Thoras summons another experiment for you—Feria's Clone. This clone is empowered with strong signeturgical abilities, so take care, and heal anyone hit by her high-damage spells. Although she's a clone, she's also considered a human type, so consider equipping the Warrior Slayer role on Fidel, Victor, or Anne.

CHAPTER 12

After you defeat the clone, General Alma appears alongside Feria on a communication line. Upset with Thoras's insubordination, Alma beams down a behemoth-sized plant that merges with the mad scientist. At the same time, the entire party (including a transmogrified Thoras) is teleported to a parallel dimension known as Kronos's Sickle.

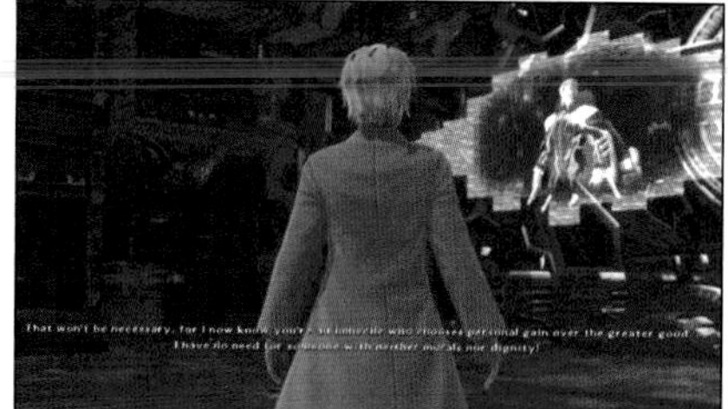

Here, you're immediately attacked by the amalgamation of plant and evil scientist, Thoras the Abomination. Although he's part human, he's mostly plant, so the Plant Slayer role works well against the abhorrent being. His main attacks are physical-based ones, so your primary concern should be moving your back line members away from him. Although he deals large amounts of melee damage, he lacks mobility, so you should be able to maneuver away accordingly. Additionally, Thoras has access to the Enhance signeturgy, boosting his ATK power. Make sure to have Fiore cast Void to dispel the effect.

After you finish slaying Thoras, General Alma shows up on a screen once again, taunting the party and alluding to a final face-off.

MISSION: FIND FERIA AND DEFEAT ALMA

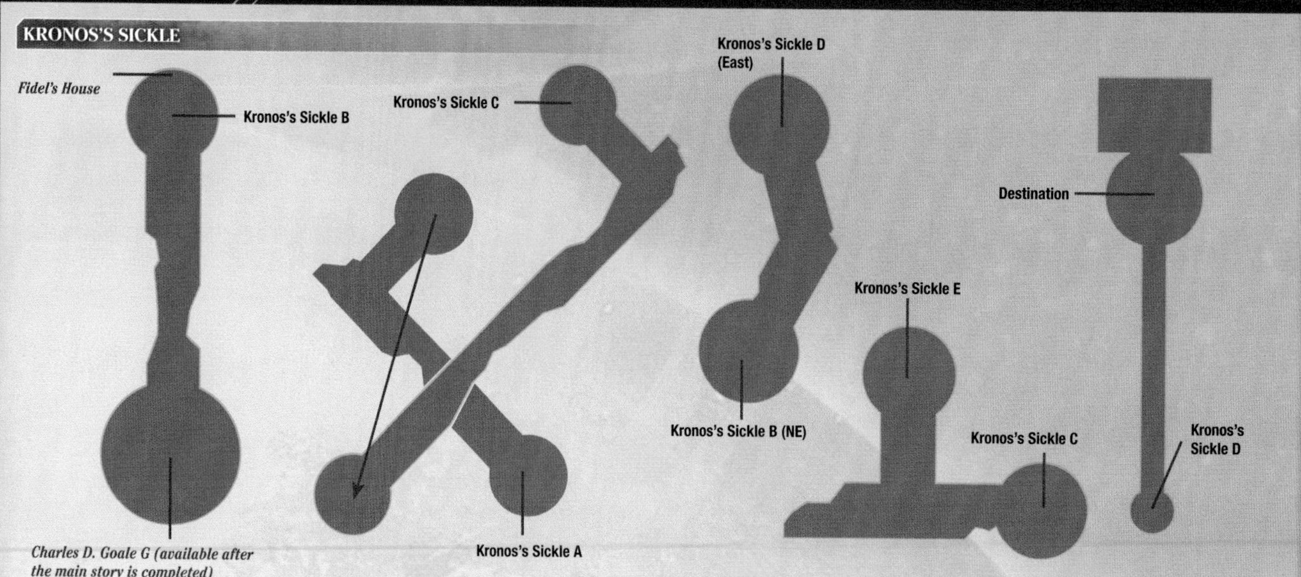

General Alma arrogantly waits for our heroes in a symbology-created dimension. Fidel, Miki, Victor, Fiore, Emmerson, Anne, and Relia set out for one final mission.

Action Checklist

1. Optional: Warp back to Faykreed to complete remaining side quests
2. Optional: Trigger outstanding Private Actions
3. Optional: Complete Cathedral of Oblivion to upgrade weapons
4. Destroy General Alma

Mission Walkthrough

With Thoras defeated, all that's left for you to do is to climb Kronos's Sickle in order to find General Alma and defeat him.

ROUT THE REBEL GENERAL

Although there's no in-game map for the area here, your path is straightforward. If you go directly north from the battle with Thoras, you'll encounter a conveniently placed physical displacement point. You can use this to travel back to Fidel's House, back on Faykreed. Of course, this is a good time to go back to complete any optional objectives like side quests and Private Actions before finishing the main story.

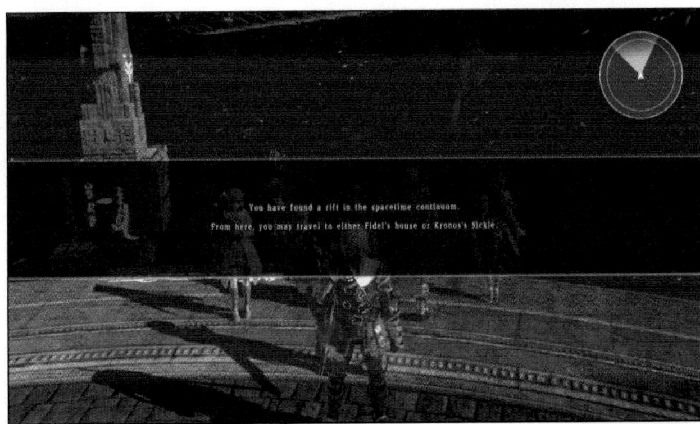

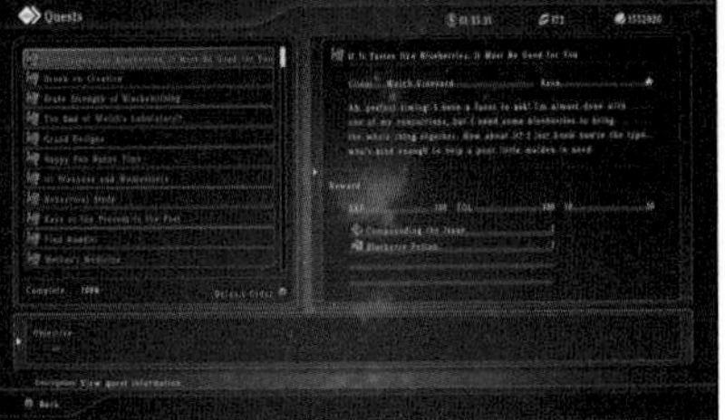

At this point in the game, the side quest log can be 100% completed. Further Private Action triggers can be unlocked, as well (if you haven't viewed them all).

When you're ready to take down Alma for good, return to Kronos's Sickle through the warp point in Fidel's House. The transport pad to the next area is directly in front of the warp point when you arrive at Kronos's Sickle. Operate it to get to the next platform in the alternate dimension.

Here, you'll see a giant beast off in the distance. This is a forced encounter (as are all of the battles here), so you'll have to defeat the Forsaken Beast to progress. This giant canine likes to initiate the fight with a luminescent beam that deals a large amount of damage to anything in its way, so avoid it as best as you can. After you slay the beast, go up the northeast ramp to get to the next area.

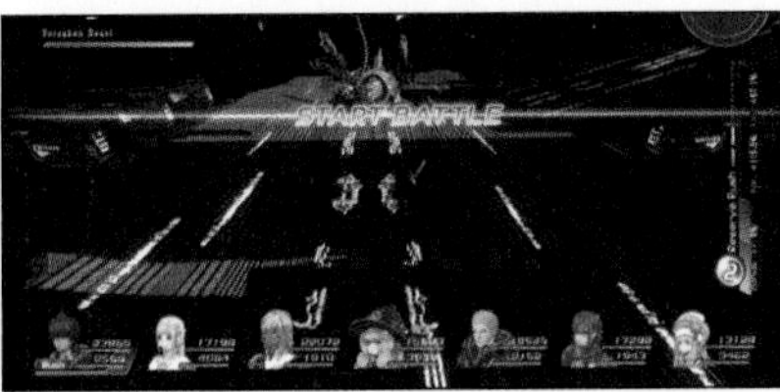

There are a few more encounters on this platform. First is a small group of Valiant Conscripts, followed by a battle with a pair of sentries, two Harbingers of the Apocalypse.

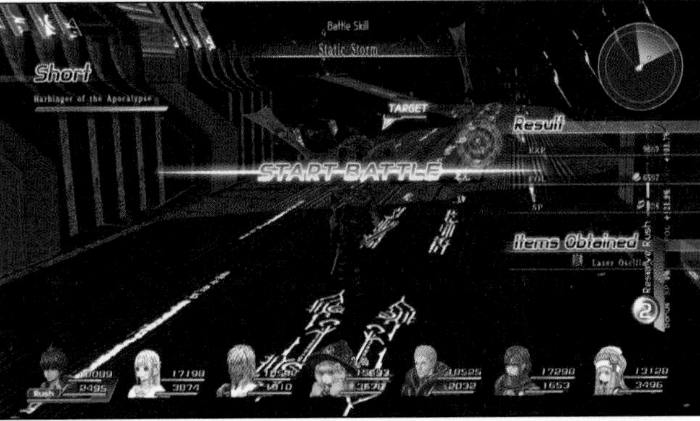

These corrupted crystal guardians cast the powerful Extinction signeturgy spell, so stay out of the spell's blast radius to minimize damage taken. Defeat them and the following Valiant Conscripts, then continue through the area up to another platform with another group of Valiant Conscript enemies. Nothing noteworthy here, so ascend another level for one more mini-boss encounter.

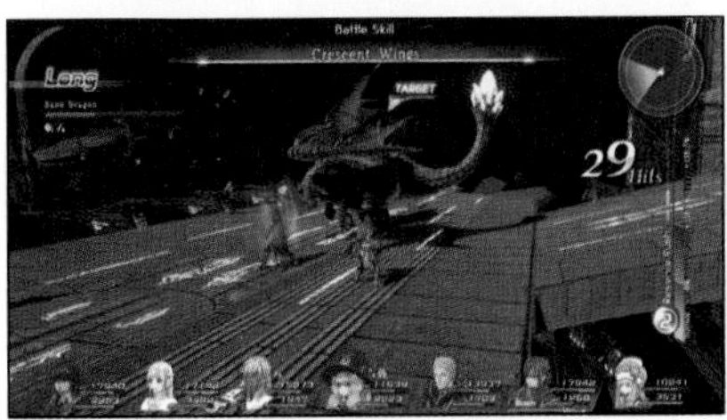

The Bane Dragon guards the remaining teleport pad up to the encounter with General Alma. It's an avian-type monster with high ATK power, as well as the Enhance ability (which should be dispelled with Fiore's Void). Slay the dragon, then make your way up the ramp and up to the final area of Kronos's Sickle.

In conventional final boss tradition, you'll have to run across a long bridge, leading up to a save point. Save your progress, heal any wounds, and get ready to confront Alma up ahead.

GENERAL ALMA

LVL 76

General Alma imbues himself with Feria's powers, then proceeds to attack the party. You won't be able to damage him at first, no matter what you do. Your goal is to simply stay alive for the meantime. Although you can't damage him, you can dispel any buffing effects he casts on himself, so make sure to cast Fiore's Void whenever you see enhancements under General Alma's status bar.

In his first form, Alma primarily deals ATK damage. He's fond of lunging across the battlefield, delivering fierce punches to your party members. After a certain period of time, a cutscene triggers, with Relia losing hope.

After Fidel's words of encouragement, Relia musters up the strength to split Alma's bond with her sister, disabling his immunity. Now's your chance to destroy him.

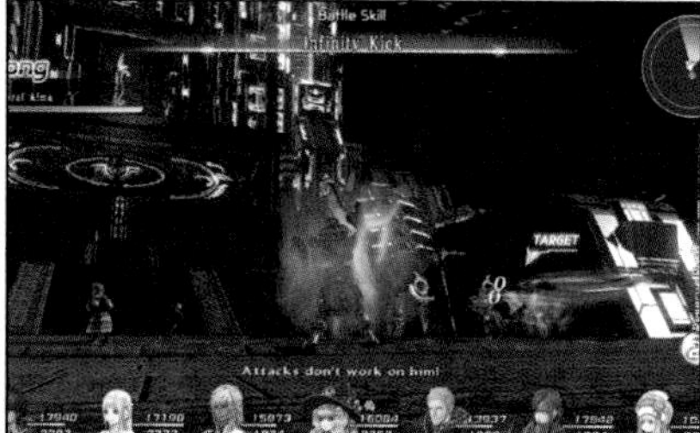

GENERAL ALMA LVL 76

P 289

NO ITEMS

Since he's only human here, the Warrior Slayer role helps greatly in depleting Alma's HP. Once he's at 50%, another cutscene triggers.

The weakened general commences phase two of his plan, imbuing signets directly onto his body. The fight becomes increasingly difficult due to his enhanced powers. He gains access to a new ability called Bosom Blow, which knocks down anyone close to him, with a chance to stun.

Take control of Miki and Fiore to keep them away from this AoE attack so they can heal your injured party members.

If Miki's roles are set up properly (with the Healer, Savior, and Sage roles), she should be able to keep all of your party members healthy while you chip away at Alma's health. Use whatever means necessary to take him down, including burning through your Reserve Rush with cancel combos.

When his life total reaches 25%, he becomes extremely desperate, forcing Feria to completely merge with him.

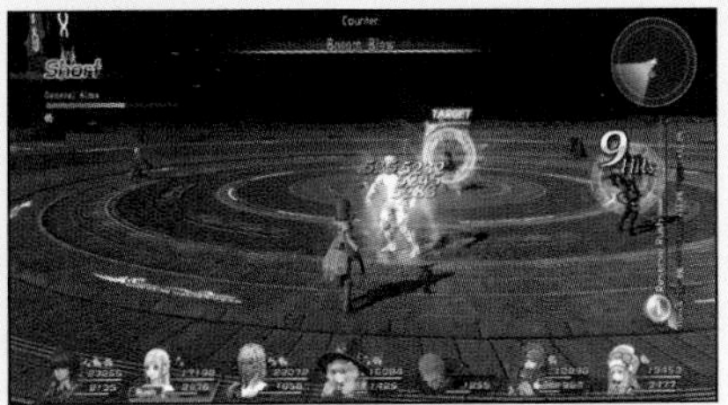

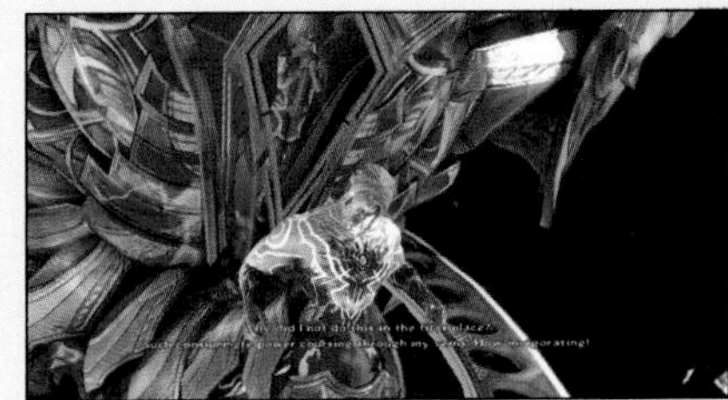

TRANSMOGRIFIED ALMA LVL 77

P.316

NO ITEMS

Like Alma's first form, you won't be able to damage him, so concentrate on evading his projectiles and attacks.

Relia is reluctant to use her powers again in fear of harming her sister.

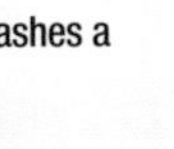

Alma recognizes her hesitation and unleashes a devastating attack called Annihilation.

This transitions into a cutscene, with everyone pleading with Relia to do what it takes to end the madness. Eventually, Feria and Relia gather their resolve to nullify Alma's invincibility.

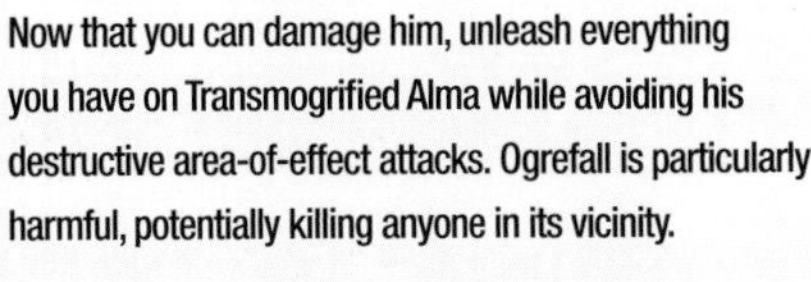
Now that you can damage him, unleash everything you have on Transmogrified Alma while avoiding his destructive area-of-effect attacks. Ogrefall is particularly harmful, potentially killing anyone in its vicinity.

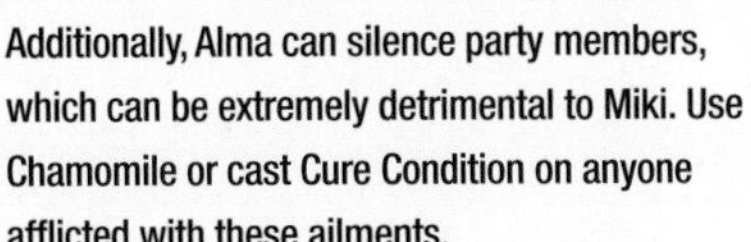
Additionally, Alma can silence party members, which can be extremely detrimental to Miki. Use Chamomile or cast Cure Condition on anyone afflicted with these ailments.

If you're fortunate enough to have unlocked the God Slayer role (Lv. 5 Mutant Slayer and Lv. 9 Warrior Slayer), you can make this encounter much more manageable, although it's not required. As long as Miki, Fiore, and Emmerson are out of harm's way, you should be able to keep most of your party members alive through Faerie Light and Resurrection. Expect to raise your close-range combatants frequently because of Alma's heavy damage output around him. If Miki goes down, spare no expense and use either Fresh Sage or Signet Card: Raise Dead to revive her as soon as possible.

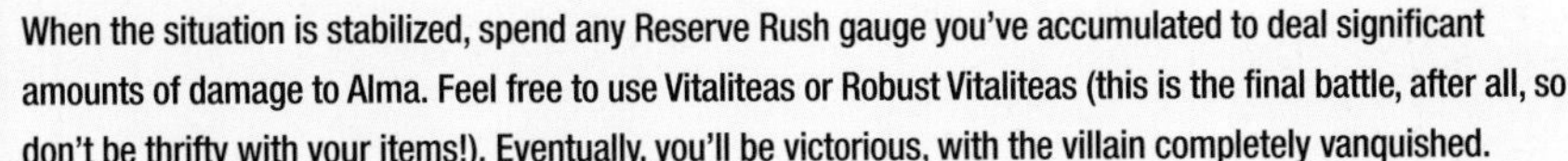
Thanks to his newfound powers, Alma can cast Angel Feather, a spell that boosts all of his stats. This requires your immediate attention and should be promptly dispelled with Fiore's Void (so it's vital to keep Fiore alive).

When the situation is stabilized, spend any Reserve Rush gauge you've accumulated to deal significant amounts of damage to Alma. Feel free to use Vitaliteas or Robust Vitaliteas (this is the final battle, after all, so don't be thrifty with your items!). Eventually, you'll be victorious, with the villain completely vanquished.

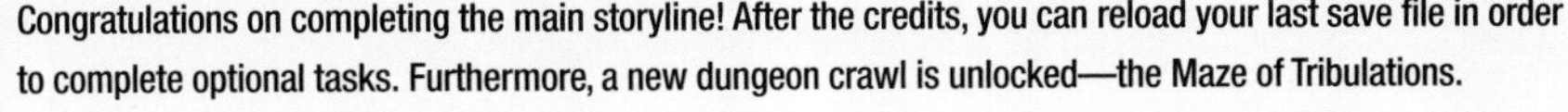
Congratulations on completing the main storyline! After the credits, you can reload your last save file in order to complete optional tasks. Furthermore, a new dungeon crawl is unlocked—the Maze of Tribulations.

MULTIPLE ENDINGS

ENDING CONDITIONS EXPLAINED

Similar to the affinity check before the final mission, an ending between Fidel and one other party member is played after Emmerson's exposition monologue and end credits.

The conditions and resulting endings are as follows:

1. Miki, Victor, Fiore, Emmerson, or Anne will appear in a cutscene with Fidel after the captain's log monologue. Out of these characters, the one with the highest affinity with Fidel is chosen.

2. If two characters tie for the highest amount of affinity with Fidel, the game will prioritize characters in the following order: Miki > Fiore > Anne > Victor > Emmerson.

3. After that cutscene is finished, it's possible for an additional cutscene involving Relia to play out. This is unlocked if Fidel's affinity with her is high enough, which can be attained by triggering most of her Private Actions (or giving her heavy doses of Love Potion No. 256).

3b. Miki will show up in Relia's additional cutscene if her cutscene was unlocked in Step 2. Otherwise, the cutscene will only involve Fidel and Relia.

AFFINITY MANIPULATION

There are a few ways to manipulate affinity. The easiest method is to craft flasks of Emotional Destabilizer or Love Potion No. 256. When used, Emotional Destabilizer decreases a character's affinity with Fidel. Therefore, if you lower a party member's affinity enough while raising another's, you can manipulate which ending is played at the end of the game.

To create Emotional Destabilizers, you'll need to have the Compounding specialty skill leveled. You can easily buy the ingredients for these potions or find them throughout the game. Lavender is a common usable item found in most consumable shops, Empty Bottles are found in most alchemy shops, and Demon's Tails are purchasable if you've unlocked Ruddle's Central Resulian shop through his quest line.

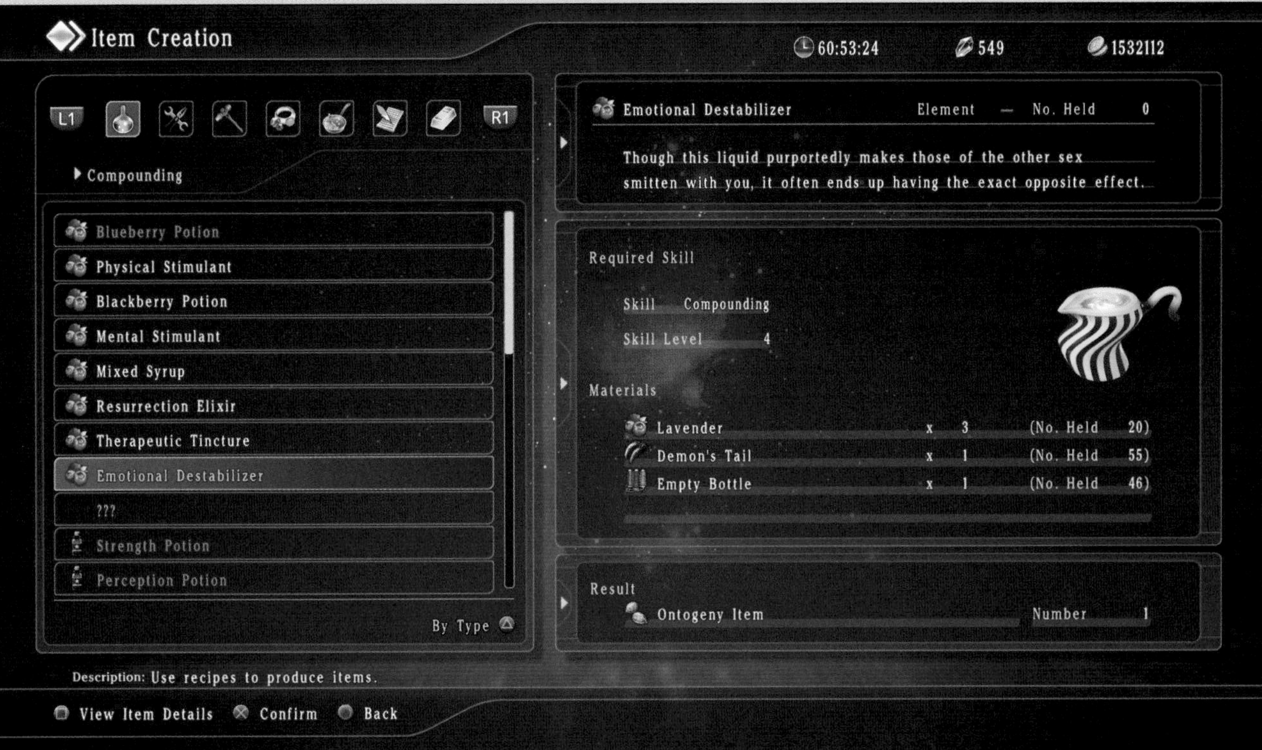

Crafting Love Potion No. 256 is a different matter and requires much more effort. To create it, you'll need Lavender, Shadow Roses, and a rare synthesis item, Lezard's Flask. Shadow Roses can be found off of Welwitschia plant enemies, and Lezard's Flask is created by synthesizing a medicine-type item with an added 50 Impurities factor. This is much more difficult than it sounds, especially since synthesis results are random. However, you can find several flasks of Love Potion No. 256 spread throughout chests in the game, so it shouldn't be too difficult to get the ending you want if you've followed this guide and opened all possible chests.

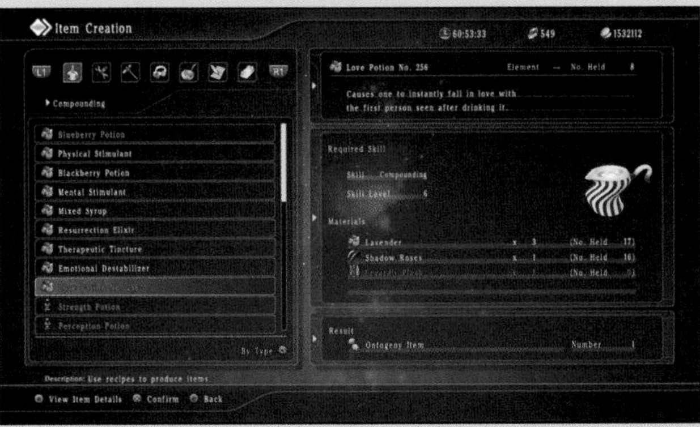

An alternative way to raise or lower affinity is by triggering Private Actions. Generally, viewing a character's Private Action raises affinity among everyone involved. Skipping certain characters' Private Actions or responding negatively when given a choice during specific Private Actions can lower Fidel's affinity with said party member. For instance, if you really want to see Fiore's ending with Fidel without having to feed your party members potions, simply view all of her Private Actions while ignoring everyone else's throughout your playthrough.

CHAPTER 13

POST-ENDGAME DUNGEON—THE MAZE OF TRIBULATIONS

PART 04

The Maze of Tribulations is a challenging dungeon crawl aimed at testing the player's mettle. The encounters within are designed to take the would-be dungeon dweller's knowledge of the game's combat and character-building mechanics to the limit. This daunting gauntlet encourages players not only to level up all of their skills, roles, and specialties to the max, but also to prepare as best as they can using the abundance of resources available by the endgame.

To unlock the maze, the main story must be completed at least once and with a file saved at the save point directly before the final encounter against General Alma. When this save file is loaded, the party then needs to travel back down to the first floor of Kronos's Sickle in order to transport back to the Charles D. Goale G by interacting with the transport pad at the beginning of the area. The Maze of Tribulations becomes a selectable travel location from the starship's transporter.

MAZE MECHANICS

The Maze of Tribulations consists of three floors: Chasm of Repose, Indra's Return, and finally, Terpsichorean Genesis. Each floor contains five bosses that must be defeated before you can proceed to the next floor. Each of the four intercardinal paths on the lobby of a floor leads to a monster-filled, multi-level area where a boss battle awaits at the top level. You must clear these four area bosses to unlock the fifth boss of the floor, located through the north path in the lobby. The first four bosses can be considered mini bosses and are generally less powerful than the final boss of the floor (except for perhaps one particular encounter…). Once the fifth boss is defeated, the center platform in the lobby transports the party to the next floor.

Each of the four subareas in the Chasm of Repose contains three levels to trek through. Indra's Return's areas consist of four, while Terpsichorean Genesis' areas have five.

Unlike all other zones in *Star Ocean: Integrity and Faithlessness*, no in-game map is provided while you explore the Maze of Tribulations. The mazes aren't too complex, but it can be confusing to navigate without a map (which can be found in the following pages of this guide). Usually, each level of an area will have one path leading to a dead end or a chest, with the other leading to the next level.

You can exit the maze any time you want using the Communicator Model G transport function. When you return, any bosses you've cleared will remain banished from the dungeon. However, they will return once you've completed the entire maze and enter its next iteration.

FAMILIARIZE YOURSELF WITH THE BUNNY

The Familiar Spirit specialty skill is a major convenience for your survival within the depths of the Maze of Tribulations. This special bunny fetches essential consumables and brings them back to you after a short period of time. You'll most likely need to refuel with restoration items like Blueberries and Blackberries as you grind through the trial. You can also buy valuable signet cards like Signet Card: Angel Feather + if you've leveled the Familiar Spirit skill high enough. If you don't have access to this skill yet, it's obtained through the **Runaround Ruddle** bulletin board quest in Santeroule.

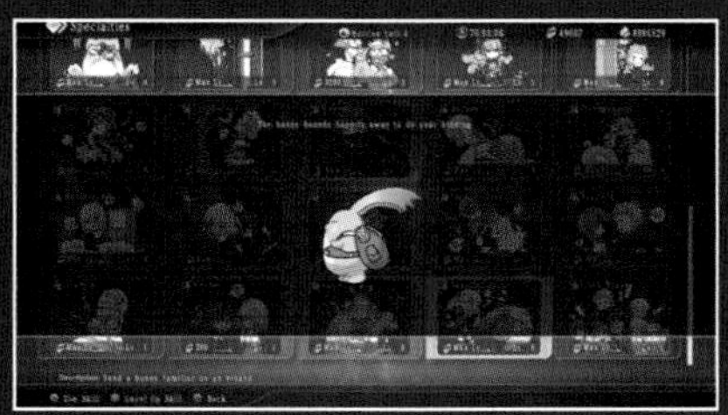

Once the three floors are completed and all 15 bosses are vanquished, the dungeon's second and third floor main bosses, Gabriel Celeste and Ethereal Queen, level up and become increasingly difficult for much more of a challenge if the player decides to return to the maze. These changes in the bosses are evident by a visual distinction. The first time these divine beings are encountered, they'll only have one pair of energy projection wings. The second time, they'll have two pairs, and the third time, three pairs. The other bosses in the labyrinth do not power up at all and can most likely be defeated without much trouble since the party will have vastly leveled up and strengthened through the powerful equipment gained in the first run. Additionally, the treasure chests in the maze do not respawn after the maze's first completion. However, all bosses still drop loot. This is useful for gathering Orichalcum and other rare materials for crafting better gear.

There's a rather peculiar merchant by the name of Santa, the Mercantilean, who resides next to the save point on each floor. Interestingly enough, he has many more items for sale than he lets on; he'll display a random set of items each time he's interacted with. He carries a variety of items, including stat-buffing accessories, crafting materials, and defense-boosting consumables such as Signet Card: Angel Feather and Signet Card: Enlighten +. After Ethereal Queen is defeated for the first time and the maze is re-entered, Santa will have new stock, conveniently containing even more types of rare crafting materials. When the maze is completed for the second time and is entered in its third iteration, he'll have the most powerful amulets in the game in stock—an incredibly excellent resource for augmenting the party's equipment.

JOLLY OLD...?

Santa, the Mercantilean is an interesting shopkeeper to say the least. His store, The Rabid Reindeer, contains useful consumables, accessories, and crafting items you may need for your journey into the depths of the maze. Since his inventory is randomly generated, make sure to talk to him several times to see what he's been hiding in his gift bag! Unfortunately, Santa's gifts aren't free. He's got to earn a living, after all.

SANTA'S GIFTS

First Maze Iteration

ITEM	COST	TYPE
Acuity Bracelet	10000	Accessory
Acuity Crest	3000	Accessory
Arcane Amulet	25000	Accessory
Fortitude Bracelet	10000	Accessory
Fortitude Crest	3000	Accessory
Mind Crest	3000	Accessory
Signet Card: Angel Feather	3200	Consumable
Signet Card: Enlighten +	1600	Consumable
Blue Roses	1200	Material
Coal	800	Material
Crystal	3000	Material
Ebony	900	Material
Gold	2000	Material
Iron	400	Material
Ruby	1400	Material
Silver	800	Material
Wooden Stick	300	Material

Second Maze Iteration

ITEM	COST	TYPE
Bee Stinger	240	Material
Blue Roses	1200	Material
Coal	800	Material
Crystal	3000	Material
Demon's Tail	200	Material
Dwarven Embroidery Thread	1800	Material
Ebony	900	Material
Fish Scales	160	Material
Gerel Secretion	200	Material
Giant Bird Feather	400	Material
Gold	2000	Material
Hand-Spun Thread	300	Material
Iron	400	Material
Lizardskin	500	Material
Peryton Droppings	3	Material
Signet Card: Angel Feather	3200	Consumable
Signet Card: Enlighten +	1600	Consumable
Silk	1200	Material
Silver	800	Material
Snakeskin	800	Material
Taffeta Ribbon	600	Material
Tortoise Shell	400	Material
Velvet Ribbon	2400	Material
Wolf Fang	320	Material
Wooden Stick	300	Material
Wool	600	Material

Third Maze Iteration

ITEM	COST	TYPE
Acuity Amulet	50000	Accessory
Arcane Amulet	25000	Accessory
Attack Amulet	50000	Accessory
Energy Amulet	25000	Accessory
Fortitude Amulet	50000	Accessory
Mind Amulet	50000	Accessory
tri-Emblum	300000	Accessory
Signet Card: Angel Feather	3200	Consumable
Signet Card: Enlighten +	1600	Consumable
Bee Stinger	240	Material
Blue Roses	1200	Material
Coal	800	Material
Crystal	3000	Material
Demon's Tail	200	Material
Dwarven Embroidery Thread	1800	Material
Ebony	900	Material
Fish Scales	160	Material
Gerel Secretion	200	Material
Giant Bird Feather	400	Material
Gold	2000	Material
Hand-Spun Thread	300	Material
Iron	400	Material
Lizardskin	500	Material
Peryton Droppings	3	Material
Ruby	1400	Material
Silk	1200	Material
Silver	800	Material
Snakeskin	800	Material
Taffeta Ribbon	600	Material
Tortoise Shell	400	Material
Velvet Ribbon	2400	Material
Wolf Fang	320	Material
Wooden Stick	300	Material
Wool	600	Material

CHASM OF REPOSE

Chasm of Repose

Corridor of Repose 4a

Headstone of Repose (S)

Corridor of Repose 3a

Indra's Return (S)

Corridor of Repose 2a

Corridor of Repose 1a

Charles D. Goale G

POLYPHAGA GAMBOGE LVL 80
P. 304
Insect Egg, Silk, Red Fruit

GUST HORNET LVL 80
P. 303
Bee Stinger, Nectar, Amber

MAIDENLY BLOSSOM LVL 80
P. 306
Nectar, Mint, Poison Hemlock, Laurel Tree

BASKANIA LVL 80
P. 308
Mati, Scalestone, Philosopher's Stone, Alchemist's Water

MELUSINE LVL 80
P. 315
Parchment, Taffeta Ribbon, Velvet Ribbon, Manacloth

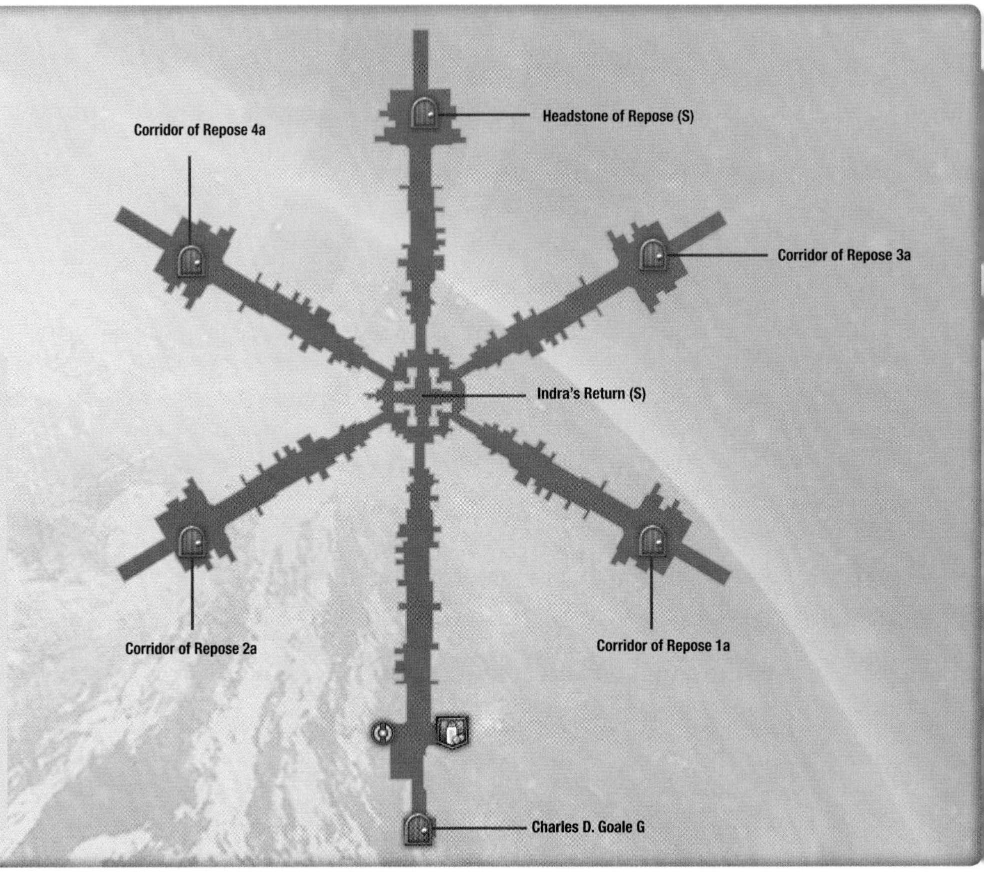

HAIL TO THE CHEF

The majority of boss battles in the maze have incredibly high stats, especially ATK and INT. To help close the stat gap, make sure to eat the right foods before engaging. If you haven't already, start investing into the Cooking specialty so you can cook up proper meals for your hungry crew. Ideal foods to eat before fighting a boss include Grilled Steak (ATK+30%), Cheese Fondue (MEN+30%), Pasta Bolognese (DEF+30%), and Crab Rice Stew (Max HP+30%). These are party-wide buffs that boost your battle capabilities immensely, although only one can be active at a time. It's important to note that most of the ingredients for these *cannot* be purchased while inside the Maze of Tribulations, so consider heading to town to do some grocery shopping before you delve into the dungeon!

MASTER CRAFTER

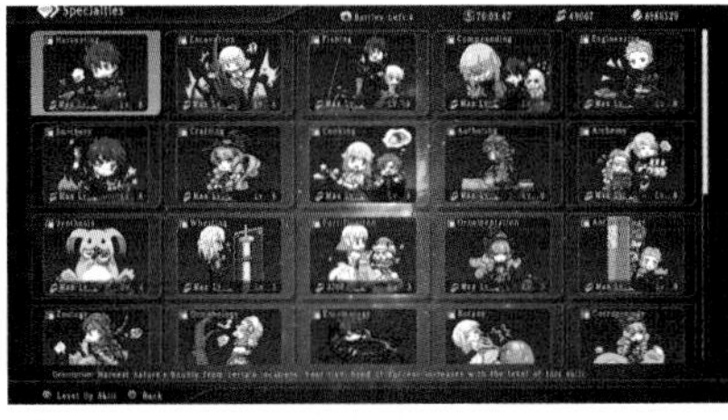

Before you start, it's recommended that you've exhausted and completed most of the bulletin board quests in town and also have most (if not all) of your Item Creation specialties unlocked and maxed. At the minimum, you'll want Crafting and Smithery maxed or close to it before you head into the maze. Take advantage of the Charles D. Goale G's transportation functionality to go around shopping at various towns to stock up on creation materials for anything you might need when you're in the Maze of Tribulations. A particularly important material you'll want to gather two of is Faerie Embroidery Thread, which is a drop from various Scumbag enemies you've come across. You can get these from Great Scumbags in the Resulian Plains if you don't have them yet.

BOUNTIFUL BOOTY

All treasure chests inside the Maze of Tribulations are locked, but at this point in the game, you should have the Lock Picking skill available. You can obtain it via the **Survive This!** Central Resulian bulletin board quest. If you want to be rewarded for your troubles, don't forget to complete this quest!

When you enter the Maze of Tribulations from your starship, you'll start in the Chasm of Repose, which serves as the lobby connecting to the five areas you'll need to complete before gaining access to the next floor. The southeast path takes you to a transporter to the Corridor of Repose I, the southwest path to the Corridor of Repose II, the northeast path to the Corridor of Repose III, and the northwest path to the Corridor of Repose IV. When you've defeated the bosses in these four rooms, the north path's transporter unlocks, allowing you to face off with the floor's gatekeeper. This pattern is consistent for the subsequent floors, and you can complete the first four areas in any order you want. The enemies you encounter in each area of the floor are generally the same, save the bosses.

LEVELING UP IN THE LABYRINTH

Be prepared to face enemies much more challenging than ones you've been dealing with. The maze's residents deal much more damage to your party than you're used to, and the battles can be chaotic in the confined spaces you're given. However, they also grant a lot more EXP and SP than the monsters you've been slaying. Take advantage of this by equipping Relia with the Instructor and Minstrel roles (which you should have if you've been diligent in unlocking Private Actions). Instructor is unlocked through the "Anne's First Mission" Private Action, while the Minstrel role is unlocked by witnessing "Miki's Grandiose Dream." You can boost EXP gain even more by baking and eating delicious Shortcake.

Corridor of Repose I

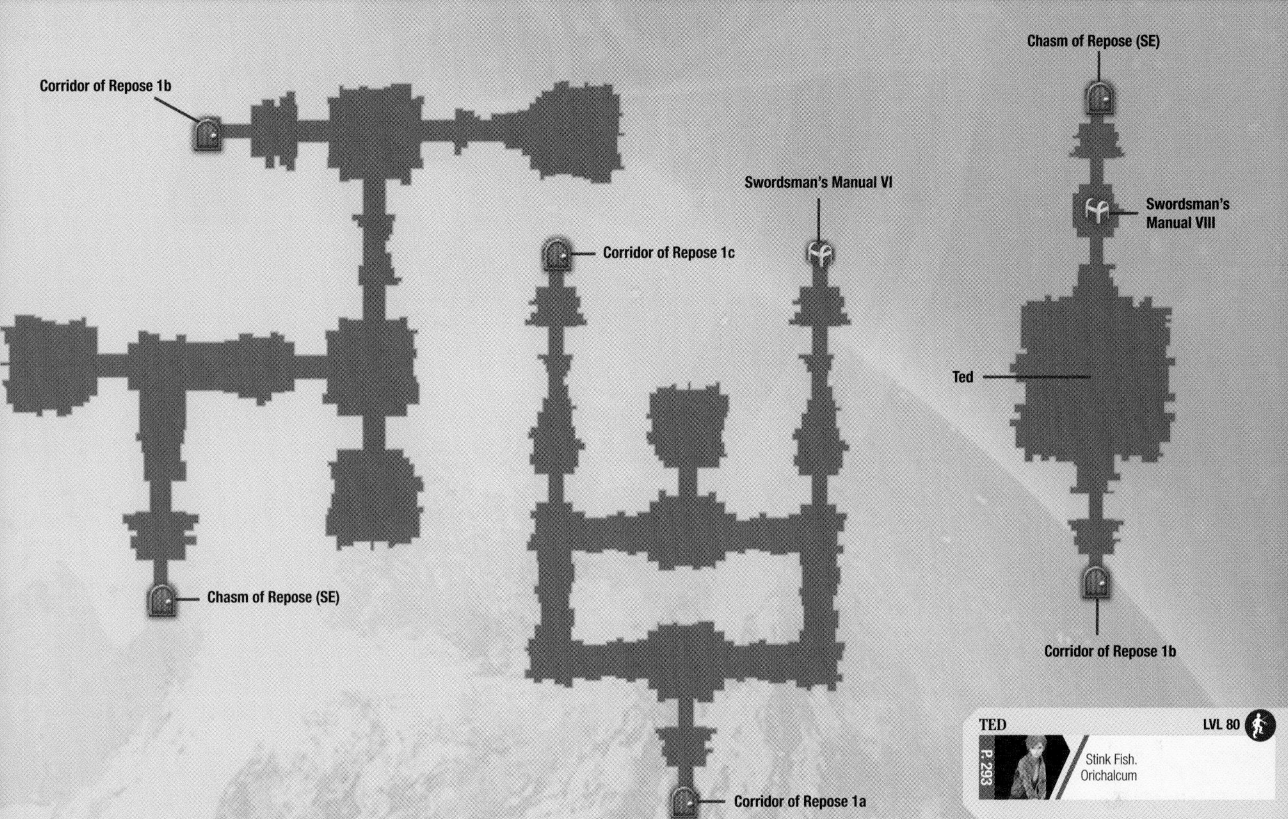

Head north and then east from your current position, and fight any enemies along the way, especially if it's your first foray into the dungeon (you're going to need all the EXP and SP you can get for the ultra-powerful bosses you'll face soon). When you reach the fork, head north, and then go west to transport to the next level. From the start of the second level, if you make a right turn and book it to the northeast part of the level, you'll find a chest containing a copy of **Swordsman's Manual VI**. Pick it up, then head back out and take a right, going west until you come across a fork. Then, take the path north to jump to the boss level. Here, you'll face off with none other than Ted. Hopefully, he's just an evil copy of Fidel's childhood buddy.

As Fidel's training partner and fellow Sthalian, Ted has access to the same attack skills Fidel does. He'll use everything ranging from Shotgun Blast to Mirror Blade, with Cyclone Blade being a particular nuisance. These are primarily melee skills, though, so Fiore and Emmerson will generally be safe from harm. Just make sure to keep your close-range fighters healed up throughout the fight. You can opt to guard and counter most of his attack skills, as well. After you total Ted, pick up the **Swordsman's Manual VIII** from a chest in the room north of the arena, then take the transporter north of the chest back to the Chasm of Repose.

THEY'RE ONLY HUMAN

All of the bosses in the Chasm of Repose are human, so hopefully you've been generously investing SP into the Warrior Slayer role. If not, you can unlock it by leveling the Raven Slayer and Beast Slayer roles up to Lv. 3. The Warrior Slayer role can be increased to a maximum of nine, which increases your damage done to humans by 50% while taking 50% less damage from them! It's an excellent role for Fidel, Victor, or Anne.

Corridor of Repose II

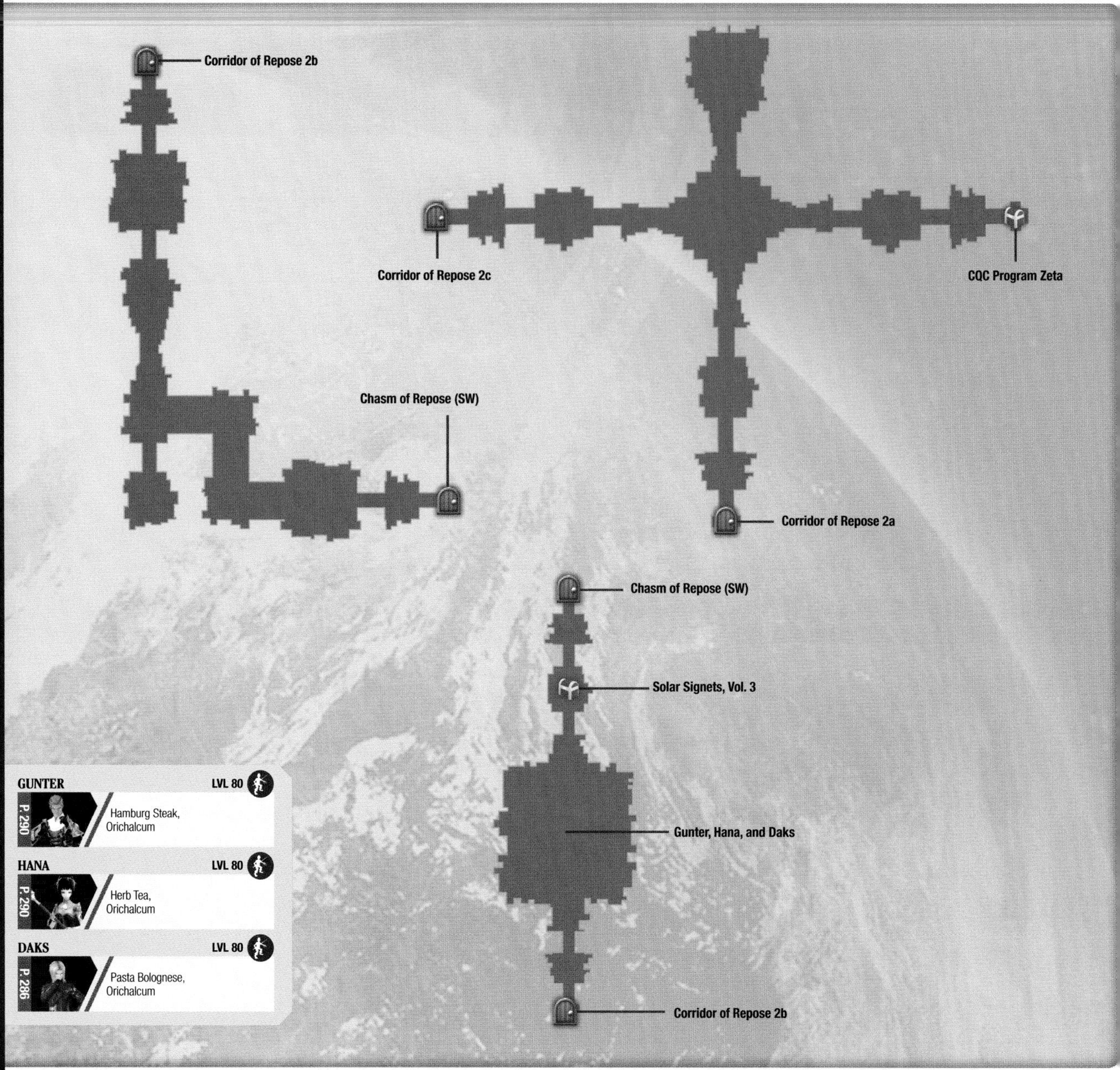

Corridor of Repose 2b
Corridor of Repose 2c
CQC Program Zeta
Chasm of Repose (SW)
Corridor of Repose 2a
Chasm of Repose (SW)
Solar Signets, Vol. 3
Gunter, Hana, and Daks
Corridor of Repose 2b

Enemy	Level	Page	Drops
GUNTER	LVL 80	P. 290	Hamburg Steak, Orichalcum
HANA	LVL 80	P. 290	Herb Tea, Orichalcum
DAKS	LVL 80	P. 286	Pasta Bolognese, Orichalcum

The first level here is relatively straightforward. Follow the path while battling monsters in your way until the path diverges. From there, make a right turn, going all the way north, where you can ascend to the next level. The second level's layout is cross-shaped. There's a chest containing a **CQC Program Zeta** disk in the easternmost room. Grab it and then turn around, heading due west to the opposite end of the level. Take the transporter to confront Victor's posse, consisting of Gunter, Hana, and Daks in the boss arena.

This trio of the King's Chosen makes a well-rounded party, with Hana being the supporting signeturge, Gunter the brawler, and Daks the crossbow-wielding sniper. Hana has the least HP out of all of them, and she can buff her allies' stats with Angel Feather, so it's wise to take her out first. If she's successful in casting Angel Feather, make sure to dispel it from her benefactor with Fiore's Void spell. Without their healer, you can take out the rest of the gang without worrying about enemy signeturgies. After you've defeated Victor's subordinates, you're rewarded with **Solar Signets, Vol. 3** in the chest in the north room. Pick it up, then take the transporter back to the lobby.

SET PHASERS TO STUN

Most of the bosses in the Maze of Tribulations can be afflicted with the stun effect, disabling them for a short time and increasing your survivability. When combined, the Stun Supporter and Interceptor roles can grant one of your members a 30% chance of stunning an enemy on a normal attack if these roles are leveled up completely. Thanks to his range and ease of landing shots, Emmerson is one of the best members to utilize this strategy, keeping your foes constantly dazed. You can obtain Interceptor by leveling Menace to Lv. 7. Stun Supporter is obtained through a battle trophy (score a 250-hit combo).

Corridor of Repose III

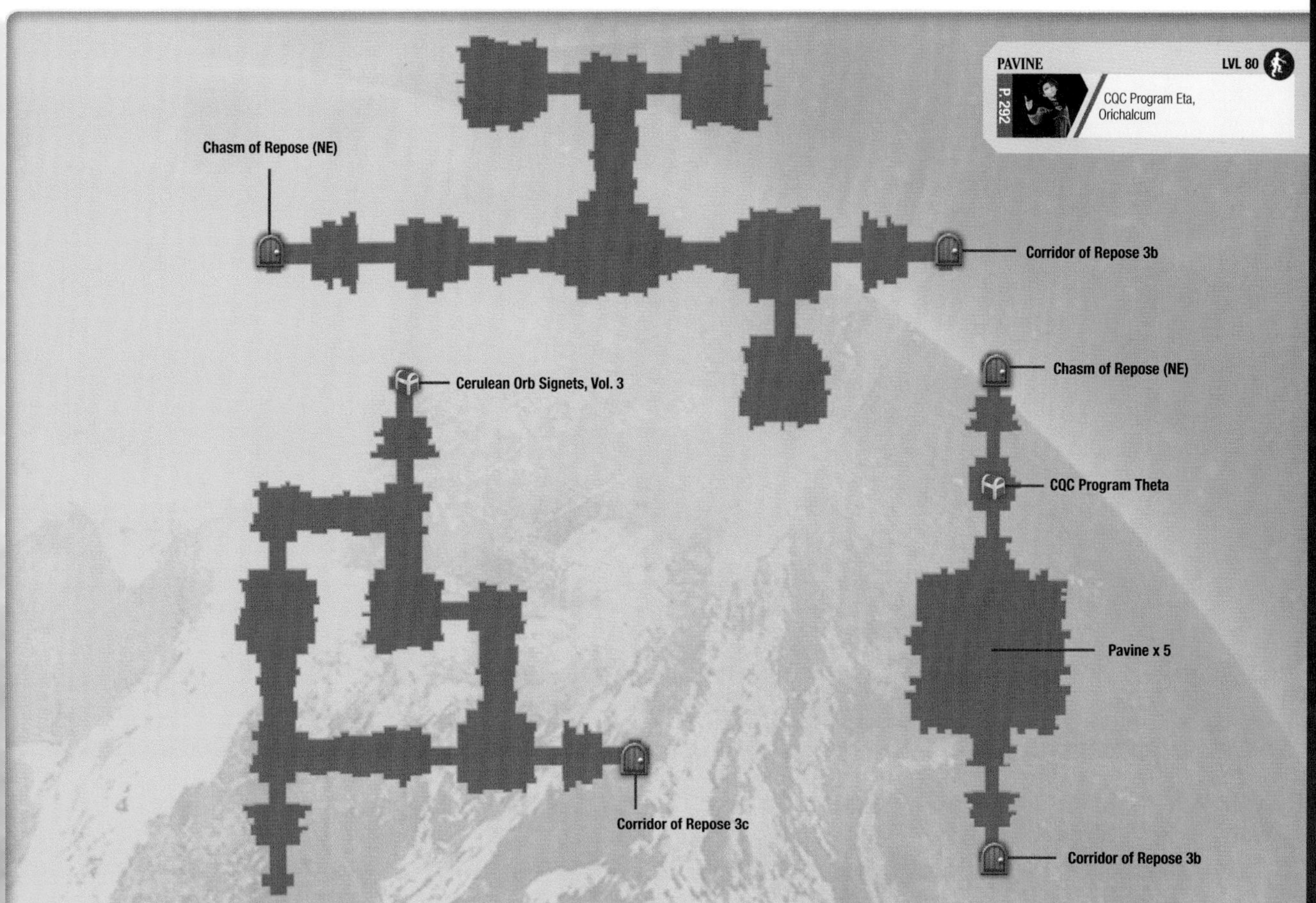

From the starting point here, you can simply go straight ahead to the room farthest east, taking you to the second level. There's no chest here, so if you want to farm some EXP and SP, you can kill the monsters hanging out in the rooms to the north. Once you're on the second level, run north until the path forces you to make a right. Keep going until you reach the fork, and then make a left to the room north, where you'll find a chest containing a **Cerulean Orb Signets, Vol. 3** book. Take the book, and then follow the path southward and around a corner. When the path splits, take a left to the transporter, bringing you to the next boss battle.

PREY ON THE WEAK

There are a couple of encounters in *Star Ocean: Integrity and Faithlessness* that require you to prioritize certain enemies to make battles more manageable. Usually, you'll want to make quick work of enemies with the lowest HP to reduce the amount of threats on the battlefield. You can accomplish this by micromanaging your troops with the LEFT and RIGHT controls on the D-Pad, which you can do even while the game is paused with the Menu button. You can set your characters' AI to the manual setting by pressing UP or DOWN on the D-Pad during battle to ensure that your party members aren't stuck in attack animations and ready to take on your next command. If you want one of your members to attack low-HP targets on their own, you can equip them with the Executioner role, gained through leveling Ace and Pulverizer to Lv. 3. Make sure to unequip the Fringe Fighter role if you're going after the weakest link, since it causes that party member to prioritize high-HP enemies.

Pavine's gunfire was annoying the first time you encountered him, but now, you have to deal with five of him. Try to keep Miki, Fiore, and Emmerson away from each other to minimize area-of-effect damage from Pavine's Ignition X and Y skills. These explosions may also inflict a fog effect, so be sure to cast Miki's Cure Condition or use a Jasmine curative on the afflicted. The Pavine foes can also cast a few signeturgical spells, like Wind Blade and Lightning Blast. Lightning Blast can inflict paralysis, so remedy it as soon you can. The fight can get hectic, with the quintuplets being able to transport around the room with their Redeployment skill while pestering your party with knockdown effects from Ignition Burst. An ideal strategy is to focus your party's fire on a single Pavine by cycling through and controlling your characters in order to issue high-damage skills. You can also have one of your automatically controlled members focus on low-HP targets using the Executioner role. Alternatively, you can use Fidel's Ethereal Blast Reserve Rush to deal a huge amount of damage to one or more of the Kronos officers.

Once you've culled the herd of Pavines, reap your reward of a **CQC Program Theta** disk in the chest north of the warzone. Then, proceed back to the Chasm of Repose.

Corridor of Repose IV

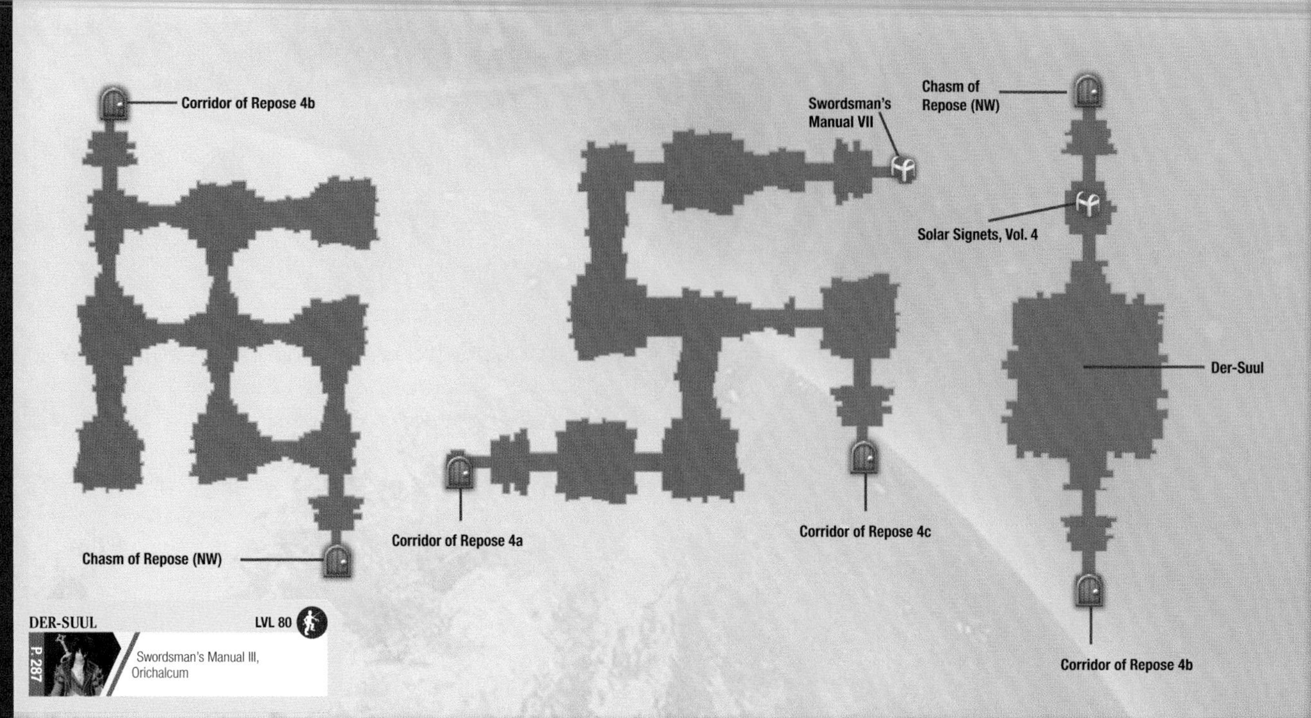

Head north, and either take the left turn or proceed straight ahead. These paths eventually converge at a crossroads. Keep going northwest from the intersection, where you'll see a room to the north with the level two transporter in it. On the second level, the initial path takes you to a divergence. Take a left here and follow the path until you get to the chest, located northeast of the level. Pick up the **Swordsman's Manual VII** book, and then make your way back to take the east path, leading you to the transporter to the fourth boss, Der-Suul.

Here, you get to avenge Fidel's father for the second time. At first, Der-Suul seems like a pushover, merely swinging at your close-range party members with normal attacks. This is just the calm before the storm. When you've whittled his health down to 50%, he has an important lesson to teach you about positioning. At this point, he'll gain access to his Spicule attack, where he super-jumps into the air and follows that up with a descending ground pound, causing a devastating inferno around him. This destructive physical attack will potentially instantly kill any nearby party members without high HP and DEF ratings. He doesn't just do this once, either: this is practically the only thing he'll do from now on. Have everyone but your most defensive melee members as far as possible before you burn his health down.

STAY OUT OF THE FIRE

Der-Suul is one of many of the maze's bosses with high-damage area of effect skills. You'll need to be vigilant about positioning your party members correctly so that you either minimize casualties or avoid damage altogether. It's particularly essential to keep Miki safe since she's your main healer and raiser. Your priority in these types of situations is to stabilize if one or more of your members go down. If Miki dies, raise her immediately with a Fresh Sage, Resurrection Elixir, or Fiore's Raise Dead spell. Once stabilized, manually control your party members while setting the appropriate long-range battle skills to keep the AI from running into melee distance. Alternatively, set your aggressive party members to the manual setting to keep them from running in and dying. Take control of your manual members, and do as much micromanaging as you can to keep your party safe.

It's recommended that you equip long-range signeturgical spells and attack skills on your damage-dealing characters. Also, make sure to manually move Miki as far as possible to raise and heal her friends when needed. Fiore can snipe at Der-Suul from virtually full battlefield distance with Wind Blade, Arctic Impact, or Thunder Flare (which helpfully lowers enemy ATK). Emmerson should have his long-range battle set assigned to Crescent Wings and Avian Rage, while Victor can make do with Dragon Roar and Flying Guillotine. Hopefully you've been putting SP into the Warrior Slayer role, which reduces damage done by humans by 50% at max level. Set this on either Fidel or Anne to help them survive the blast as they hack away at Der-Suul. Additionally, the Sharpshooter role can be equipped on Victor to encourage his AI to attack from range. After you defeat the Trei'kuran general, head north to the transporter back to the Chasm of Repose, picking up a copy of **Solar Signets, Vol. 4** along the way.

Headstone of Repose

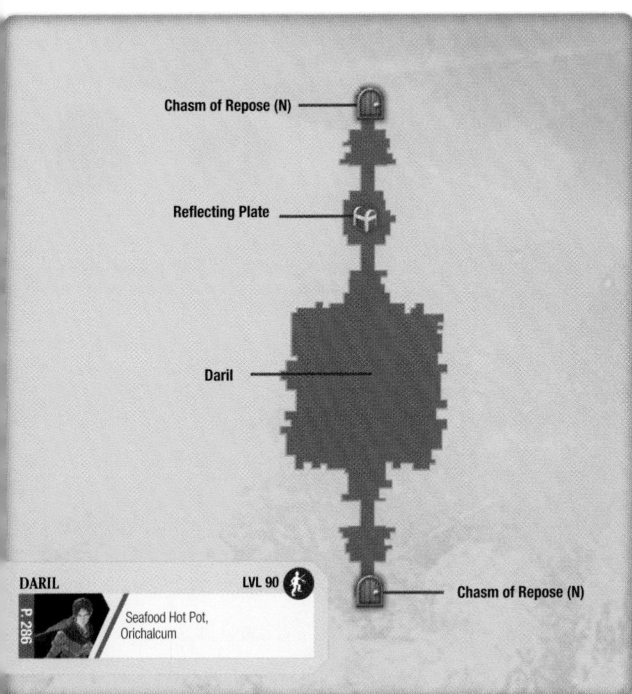

Once you've bested the four subarea bosses, you can access the north path's transporter in the Chasm of Repose lobby. If you haven't saved yet, make sure to do so now. If you're in need of supplies, use your Familiar Spirit specialty to restock with Blueberries, Blackberries, Signet Card: Angel Feather +, and Signet Card: Enshelter +. You have a tough battle ahead, so be prepared.

CAN'T KILL ME! I'M ALREADY DEAD

If you haven't unlocked the Berserker and Dead Man Walking roles, drop everything you're doing and do so now. Berserker is obtained by leveling Brawler to Lv. 5. Dead Man Walking can be unlocked by leveling Shrewd Overseer and Pulverizer to Lv. 3, then Necromancer to Lv. 3. Berserker combined with Dead Man Walking is the most efficient and effective roles combination for dealing damage and soaking it. Not only does it make that party member invincible to enemies, but it nullifies all of the negative effects of Berserker, essentially giving that character an ATK+150% boost for free when maxed out. Dead Man Walking is almost a necessity for surviving the upcoming challenges! It constantly drains a percentage of the user's maximum HP (1% per tick, fewer ticks at Lv. 3), so you'll need to make sure you're keeping up with healing them. However, that party member becomes immune to sudden deaths, which are all too common against the most powerful entities in the maze. Assigning these roles to Anne is recommended since she has the lowest base HP pool out of your close-range fighters (HP total is then inconsequential).

REUNION—DARIL

As the protagonist's father, Daril has all of the abilities you'd expect to see from Fidel. The main ability to look out for is the familial Reserve Rush, Ethereal Blast. You'll know it's coming when Daril levitates into the air, donning a pair of giant phoenix wings. This attack can wipe out your entire party at the start of the battle unless you take the proper precautions. Daril loves to do this as his opening move, particularly on Miki. Open the battle menu as soon as the fight starts, and select Miki so you can maneuver far away from the initial area-of-effect damage. Heal and revive anyone you need to. An easy way to do this is to save three Reserve Rush gauges before the fight (or craft and collect Vitalitea potions) and simply cast Miki's Lv. 3 Arcadia after Daril's Ethereal Blast.

Once you stabilize, make sure to keep your back line members as far from the fray as possible, where the fight becomes much more manageable. Like Fidel's Air Raid, Daril's version is just as deadly, potentially killing any of your non-defensive members in one blow. Be sure to have defensive capabilities on at least one of your melee characters, and be ready to heal up anyone in the vicinity. Signet Card: Enlighten+ can be purchased from Santa, the Mercantilean, and this helps your close-range members survive Daril's onslaught. As with all of the strong Maze of Tribulations bosses, having Anne or one of your swordsmen equipped with Dead Man Walking is a huge boon in this fight.

Fortunately, Daril needs to build his Reserve Rush gauge, so he won't execute back-to-back Ethereal Blasts, but expect it to come the longer the battle goes. He won't just use it on your front line characters, either: he'll occasionally make a beeline to your healer and more fragile party members before unleashing his wrath. If you see him making a dash for one of your back line heroes, open the battle menu immediately and move your characters out of harm's way. The area-of-effect coverage is massive, at about half of the entire battlefield. Standing at the opposite end of the battlefield with your ranged attackers and signeturges can't be emphasized enough. Members with high HP and high DEF can survive the secondary explosion from Ethereal Blast, but most members won't be able to survive the initial beam coupled with the follow-up, unless, of course, they have invincibility from a Heroism Potion or the Dead Man Walking role.

Daril's susceptible to status effects like stun and fog. If you have the Stun Supporter and Interceptor roles maxed out, you can have a dedicated normal attacker attempt to keep him afflicted with both of these ailments. Thanks to his range and quick normal attacks, Emmerson is ideal for this role. The preferred roles build on him for this encounter is Interceptor, Daemon, Stun Supporter, and Charlatan. Additionally, you can supplement this strategy by setting Fidel's Shotgun Blast to one of his close-range attack skills. Fog is incredibly effective against Daril; it makes him much less accurate and unable to rush your back line with Abyssal Gate and Ethereal Blast since it completely disables long-range attacks.

After you've defeated Fidel's father, proceed north, pick up the **Reflecting Plate** from the chest, and head back out to the Chasm of Repose. You can now ascend to the next challenge, Indra's Return, by interacting with the center platform of the lobby.

INDRA'S RETURN

Indra's Abyss (S)

Indra's Peregrination 4a

Indra's Peregrination 3a

Terpsichorean Genesis (S)

Indra's Peregrination 2a

Indra's Peregrination 1a

Chasm of Repose (Center)

Enemy	Level	Page	Drops
VISCOUS CLOD	LVL 100	P. 308	Gerel Secretion, Gelatinous Slime, Alchemist's Water
NETHERPHANTOM	LVL 100	P. 312	Crystal, Amber, Light Gem
ANCIENT GUARD	LVL 100	P. 314	Silver, Gold, Platinum, Meteorite
METAL SCUMBAG	LVL 100	P. 315	Silver, Platinum, Mythril, Faerie Embroidery Thread
GRIM REAPER	LVL 100	P. 311	Bloodstained Cloth, Ghost's Soul, Nereidstone

The layout of the lobby here is an exact replica of the previous floor. The primary differences are that monsters are more difficult and there are more levels per subarea. There's also a notable spike in difficulty from the previous enemies, especially when it comes to the bosses. It's highly recommended that you fight as many foes as you can with your EXP- and SP-boosting roles equipped to fill out the roles and specialty skills you need (but remember to equip better supportive ones before bosses). The average level of the foes here is around 100, so you should farm up enough EXP to match them.

THAT'S SO METAL

Indra's Return has strange-looking enemies called Metal Scumbags littered throughout its halls. If you've played previous *Star Ocean* titles, you'll be familiar with these sneaky little thieves. They have insanely high DEF and MEN ratings (9999 each), so they can be a huge pain to take down. Fortunately, there's a sword in the game specifically designed to destroy these little mechanized pilferers. If you've been killing the previous floor's Melusine enemies, you should have at least three Manacloths (if not, you can simply go back down a level using the southern transportation pad in the lobby). You can combine three Manacloths with two Faerie Embroidery Threads to craft into Mana Ribbons, which you can then smith into a Scumbag Slayer with a piece of Meteorite (dropped by Ancient Guards found here), three Wooden Sticks, and three High-Strength Adhesives (created using Alchemy).

The Scumbag Slayer allows Fidel to instantly kill Scumbag enemies in one hit, with a major reduction in DEF and MEN ratings. This is why it's imperative you farm enough SP to invest in your item creation skills! Alternatively, you can have one of your characters with a high ATK value equip Machine Slayer to deal relevant damage to them. This method isn't nearly as efficient, especially if you want to farm the Scumbags for EXP (which they grant an absurd amount of). Stick to farming EXP and SP here if you feel you need to (you probably do if it's your first run through the Maze of Tribulations). Don't forget to equip Fidel with a proper sword when you reach a boss!

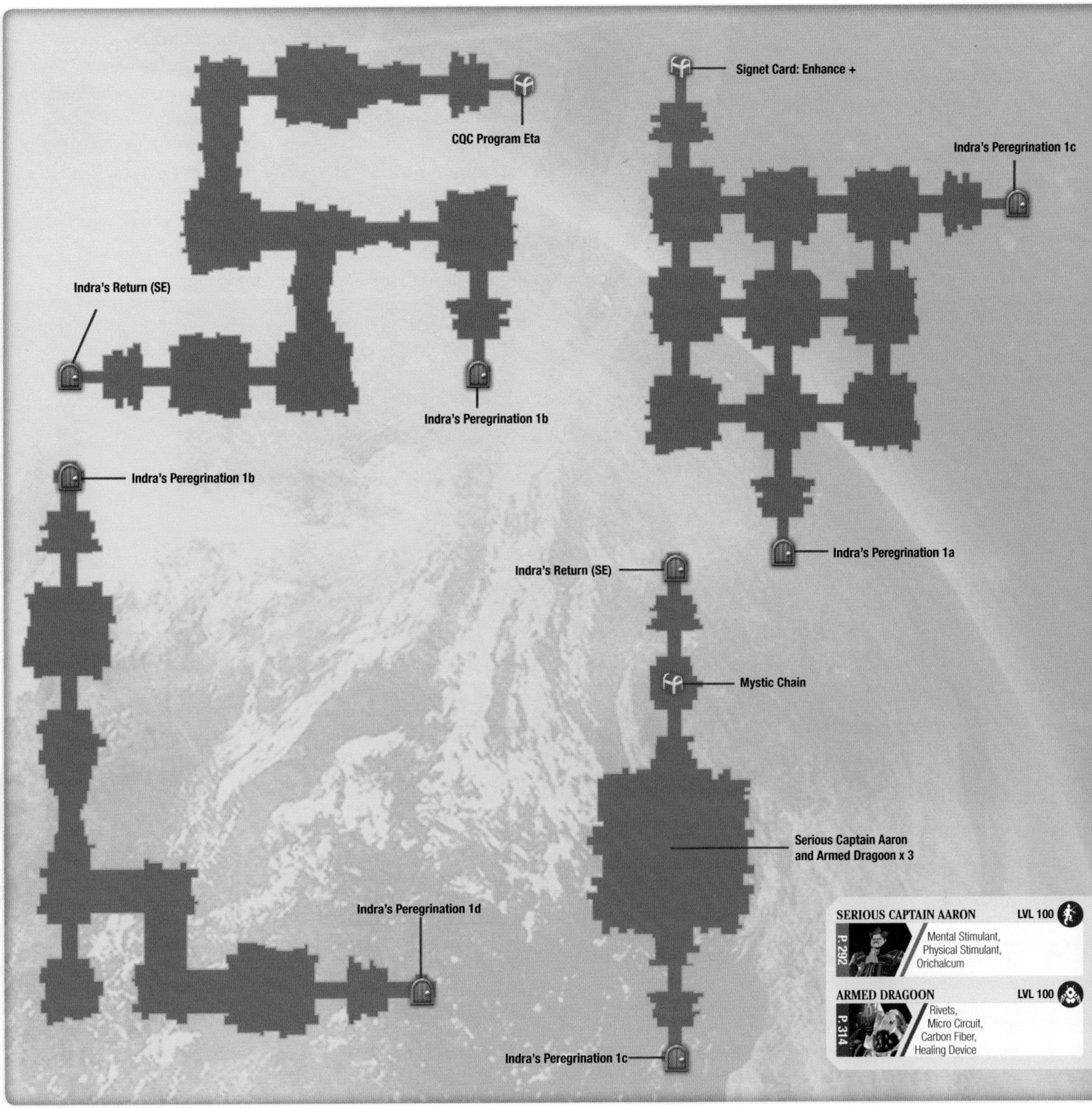

Indra's Peregrination I

CQC Program Eta

Signet Card: Enhance +

Indra's Peregrination 1c

Indra's Return (SE)

Indra's Peregrination 1b

Indra's Peregrination 1b

Indra's Return (SE)

Indra's Peregrination 1a

Mystic Chain

Serious Captain Aaron and Armed Dragoon x 3

Indra's Peregrination 1d

Indra's Peregrination 1c

SERIOUS CAPTAIN AARON LVL 100
P. 292
Mental Stimulant, Physical Stimulant, Orichalcum

ARMED DRAGOON LVL 100
P. 314
Rivets, Micro Circuit, Carbon Fiber, Healing Device

Start heading east to a path taking you north to a fork. Turning left here leads you to a chest containing a **CQC Program Eta** skill disk in the room located northeast. If your party is under Lv. 100, make sure to fight any enemies you encounter, especially if you see Metal Scumbags and you have access to the Scumbag Slayer. After you get the chest, you can backtrack to take the east path, which bends south, taking you to the transporter to the next level. The second level is a large 3x3 grid with a chest holding a **Signet Card: Enhance +** in a room in the far northwest corner. The transporter to the third level is located in the northeast corner of the grid, so head there after grabbing the signet card, and go on up. On this level, the first room you enter has three Metal Scumbags you can repeatedly slay using the Ocarina specialty. You can stay here and grind on this group of enemies to power yourself up for the upcoming bosses. It's highly recommended that you at least fill out all of your slayer roles to unlock God Slayer. You're going to need it soon.

POWER LEVELING

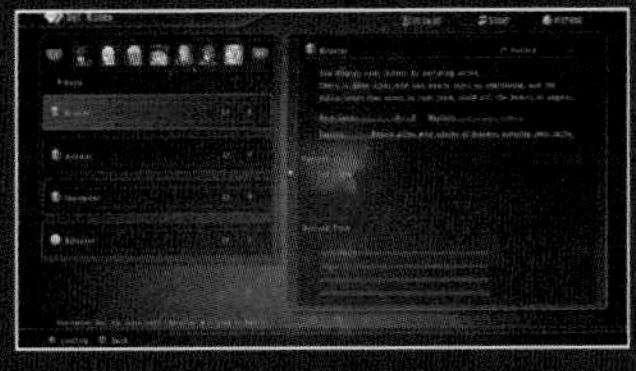

The fastest way to gain SP to max out your remaining roles and specialty skills is to equip one your members (preferably Relia) with the Minstrel, Altruist, Betrayer, and Instructor roles while eating Shortcake (+50% EXP). Lv. 9 Altruist halts any EXP gain but converts 5% of any EXP you would have received into SP, so all of the EXP gain buffs you're stacking are essentially SP buffs! Considering how much EXP Metal Scumbags reward you with, leveling the rest of your roles and specialties should be no problem in this area. Chow down on some Shortcake, destroy some Metal Scumbags, then play your Ocarina to respawn the silver suckers. Repeat until you're satisfied!

When you're done leveling up, you can backtrack to the save point in the lobby. Make your way back here, then run south and take the first left turn you see, going east. This path takes you to the first boss battle in Indra's Return.

You'll find Serious Captain Aaron here in the boss arena, and he's brought some serious artillery along with him in the form of three Armed Dragoons. These mechanical combat suits have roughly 550,000 HP each and use cannon-type ranged attacks. Initially, the battle can be frantic because of so many enemies blasting away at your party. The first thing you'll want to do is take control of Miki and maneuver her out of harm's way. Captain Aaron's goons can cause some headache with their ranged attacks and area-of-effect damage. Captain Aaron likes to cast signeturgical area of effect damage spells on your weaker members, so be careful.

Keep Miki alive as best as you can so she can cast Faerie Star to heal up any damaged party members. Once she's safe, you'll want to focus your fire to quickly reduce enemy troops. The best way to do this is to have one of your high ATK close-range attackers build up a 175% combo ratio with fast attack skills or normal attacks, and then finish off with a 200% Reserve Rush finisher. This should destroy at least one of the dragoons, especially if you get your other party members to focus fire on the same foe. For instance, have Anne use Hammer of Might => Hammer of Might => Hammer of Might => Lv. 1 Blazing Cannon, then immediately switch to Fidel and perform Air Raid => Air Raid => Air Raid => Lv. 1 Ethereal Blast on the same target.

Ideally, you'll have one of the Reserve Rush users equipped with the Machine Slayer role for an extra 50% damage to the dragoons. Keep an eye on Miki while you perform the aforementioned combo, and make sure that Captain Aaron and his armored troops aren't targeting her. A good way to keep Miki healthy is to equip her with the Skulker role, making it less likely for enemies to target her, especially if the role is leveled up completely.

FAERIE SUPERSTAR

As you've probably noticed by now, Miki is an all-star. As your primary healer, she has access to an incredible party-wide healing spell, Faerie Star, which usually heals your party's HP pools completely. She's especially invaluable in these difficult trials, and you'll want her to be able to heal your party from area-of-effect damage as fast as possible. Ideally, have her equipped with the Healer and Sage roles. Healer encourages the AI to begin healing as soon as your members take damage, while Sage reduces signeturgy casting time by up to 70% when maxed out. Other roles you might want to have her use are Skulker and Crusader, depending on what's required of her during any particular battle. In these trying boss encounters, you should turn off all of her offensive spells in her Signeturgy On list. Do so by going into the Set Battle Skills menu, then press the Set Signeturgy button (default is ◙ on the PS4). Toggle off all of her spells except important healing ones like Faerie Light, Faerie Star, Ex Healing, Cure Condition, Raise Dead, and Resurrection. This ensures that she's ready to heal whenever there's an emergency. And remember to thank your healer!

When you've thinned out the horde of robots, you can send the Kronos captain packing by switching out the Machine Slayer role with the Warrior Slayer one. His spells should be manageable now that you've singled him out. On your way out through the north path, you'll find a **Mystic Chain** in a chest. This chain mail synergizes well with characters using the Evasionist role for a combined boost of -50% Critical Hit Rate from foes.

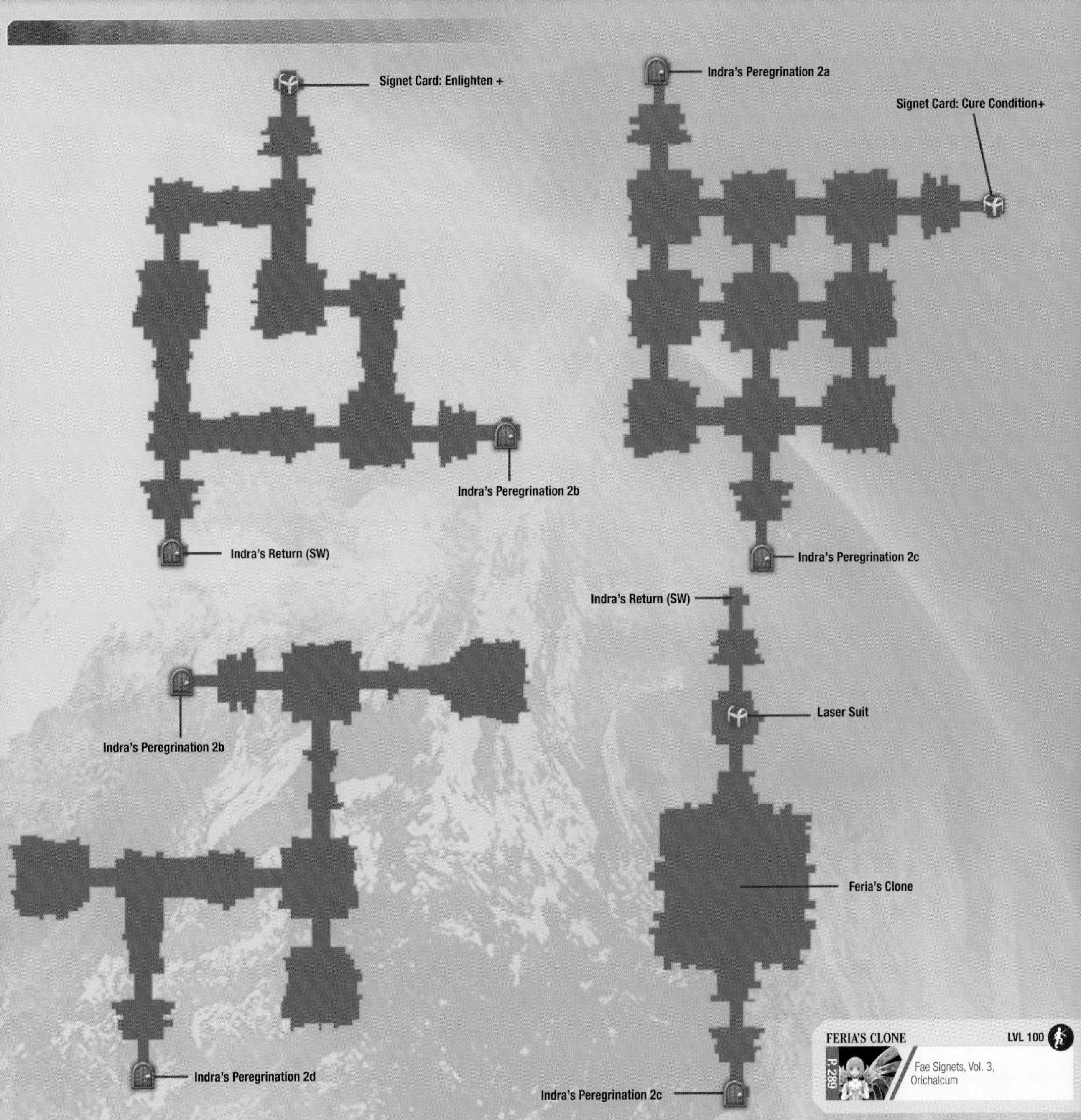

FERIA'S CLONE LVL 100

P 289

Fae Signets, Vol. 3, Orichalcum

In the first level of this area, there's a chest containing a **Signet Card: Enlighten +** in the northeast corner of the map. Get there by following the path all the way north, turning east, and then making a left into a room. After grabbing it, turn around and take the south path that eventually winds into a divergence. Make a left here, heading east to go up to the second level. There's another 3x3 grid here with a chest in the northeast corner. Get to the chest by making an immediate left outside of your starting point and heading directly east. Pick up the **Signet Card: Cure Condition +,** and head back out into the grid, making a left turn to go south. Keep going until you're forced to make a right turn west, and the transport pad to the third level will be on your left to the south. There's no chest here on the third level, so make the first right you see and head south. Make the first right, and then left, going south, to the transport room in the south part of the map. Go up to the boss arena, and get ready for a boss encounter with one of Feria's experimental clones!

PART 04

Before you greet Feria's clone, consider eating a Crab Rice Stew or Cheese Fondue to help your survivability against this spell-heavy boss. Be sure to equip Warrior Slayer on one of your damage-dealing melee members, too.

Don't be fooled by her size; this weaponized child of war packs a mean punch with high-damage signeturgical spells like Extinction and Deep Freeze. She'll also buff herself with Angel Feather, which increases all of her stats, most notably her INT. This makes her spells even more devastating, so dispel it immediately with Fiore's Void spell. Her other skills are primarily projectile orbs that have a high chance to silence targets. Revolution is a single-hit projectile that deals a large amount of damage, roughly 30000-40000 hit points. If it doesn't kill a party member, it might silence them. Oppressive Effulgence is an area-of-effect version that shoots out in all directions, but deals less damage per shot. The main mechanic in this fight is remedying silence as soon as you can, especially if Miki is afflicted. Otherwise, you'll need to heal through her spell damage while raising anyone who's annihilated from an Extinction or a Deep Freeze spell. As a spell caster, a particularly effective strategy is to keep her stunned, so equip Emmerson or one of your other aggressive members with the Stun Supporter and Interceptor roles and manually control them. Cycle between your weak and strong attacks to take advantage of quick combo-canceling so you can fire off a flurry of normal hits that each has a chance to stun. When you've defeated the Kronos experiment, head north to collect a **Laser Suit** from the chest, and then head back out to Indra's Return.

MANAGEABLE MALADIES

You'll encounter a couple of devastating status effects in the worst possible moments in some of the challenging boss fights in the maze, so keep a keen eye on your characters' status bars. Some ailments are worse than others, depending on the situation you're in. Miki can usually handle these with her Cure Condition spell, but if she's silenced or paralyzed herself, you'll have to have one of your other members use a Chamomile on her immediately since she's your primary healer. Fog can be a nuisance on ranged characters like Emmerson and Fiore since it completely disables long-range skills. It also hinders close-range fighters because they won't be able to aim their close-range attack skills properly. Occasionally, you'll find yourself in a pickle, having to decide whether to heal up your party's HP or to cure a condition. Generally, you'll want to spread out your actions in these situations and let Miki focus on healing HP, with one of your other characters dealing with status ailments. Be sure to keep plenty of restorative items in your inventory! Additionally, it's possible to cast Cure Condition or use a Therapeutic Tincture on a stunned ally, as long as you notice their dazed animation (since the status bar doesn't reflect this).

Indra's Peregrination III

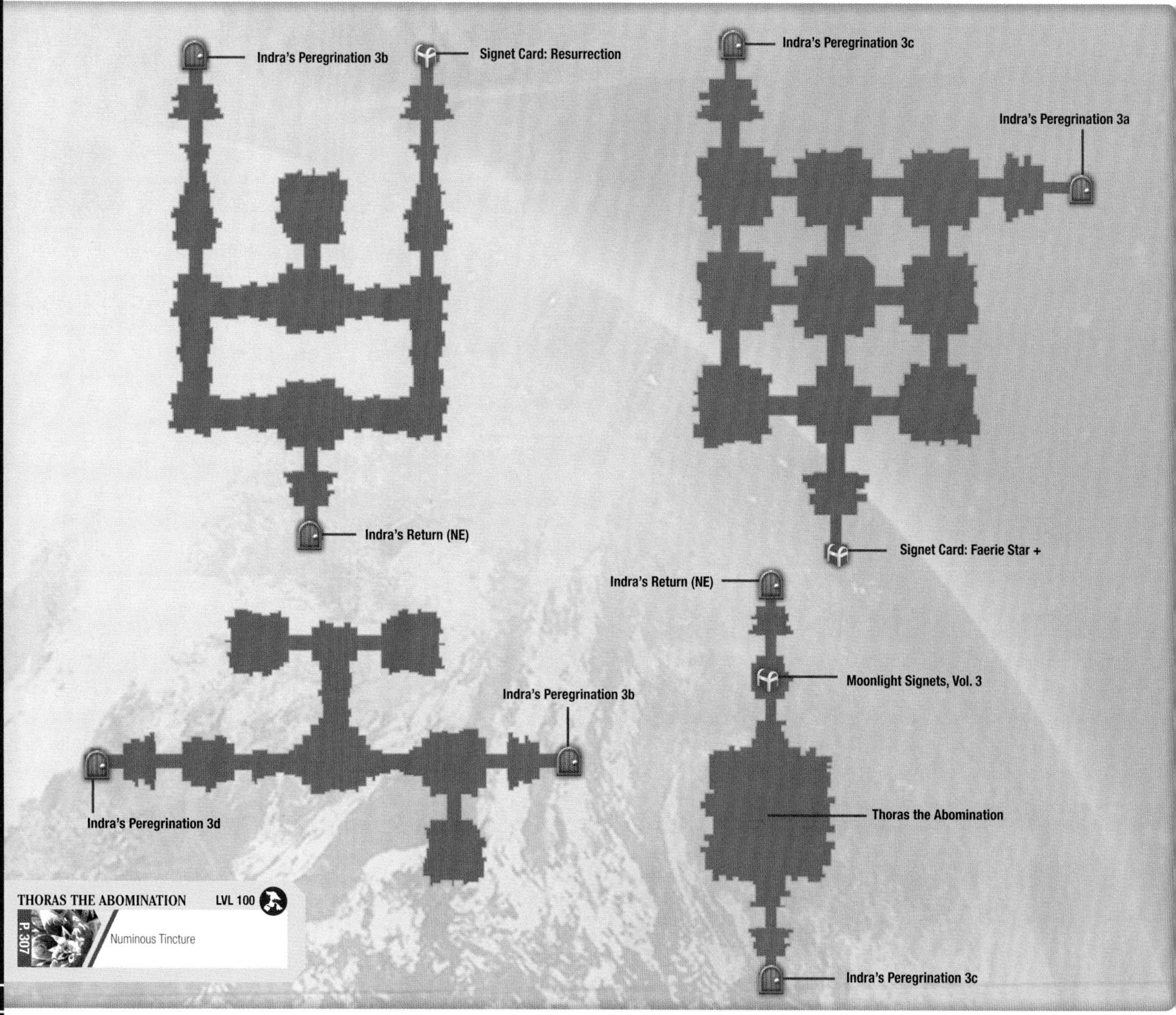

THORAS THE ABOMINATION LVL 100
P.307
Numinous Tincture

Go straight ahead, making a right turn in the first room you walk into, then head straight north until you find a chest in the far northeast corner of the map. You'll score a **Signet Card: Resurrection** in the chest here. Head back out and make your first right, going west. When you get to the farthest west point of the map, turn right again, and you'll be greeted by another transporter to the next level. Here is another 3x3 grid-based level. If you reach the center of the grid and head straight south at the intersection, you'll find a room with a chest that holds a **Signet Card: Faerie Star +**. Pick it up, and then head back out, making a left going west, then turning right, northward. The transporter to the third level is in the room to the far northwest. It's the last level before the boss arena; just run straight ahead west from your starting position to get to the transporter. After transporting up and opening the arena's door, you'll be greeted with a rematch against the corrupted plant-like creature aptly named Thoras the Abomination.

This corrupted mutant is capable of casting signeturgies like Sunflare and Dark Devourer, but he also has a few annoying physical tendril attacks. Eat some Grilled Steak to boost your offensive capabilities, or perhaps a serving of Cheese Fondue to help mitigate spell damage from the monstrosity.

His Sunflare can inflict an INT down debuff that you can't cure with Miki's Cure Condition, but it's merely a nuisance at best. Flagellant Tendril Furor is a physical frontal area-of-entry attack that breaks guard and frequently knocks down your close-range fighters. Thoras is slow, but he'll occasionally move toward your more delicate characters in an attempt to lash at them with his tendrils.

As long as you're moving your back line members out of the way, your fragile characters will be safe from his knockdown effects. Thoras also has access to an ATK buff called Enhance, which can be dispelled using Fiore's Void. When you see a ring of light-based shields surrounding him, he's about to unleash Divine Wave. This is a guardable area-of-effect spell that deals a high amount of damage, so get ready to open the battle menu, and then guard with your healer. Ultimately, this is a battle of recognizing his movements and keeping your lower HP members away from his grotesque extremities. Having Plant Slayer on one of your damage dealers and Skulker on Miki makes this fight go smoother, as well. After you put Thoras out of his misery, you can secure a copy of the **Moonlight Signets, Vol. 3** skill book in the room to the north on your way back out to the lobby.

Indra's Peregrination IV

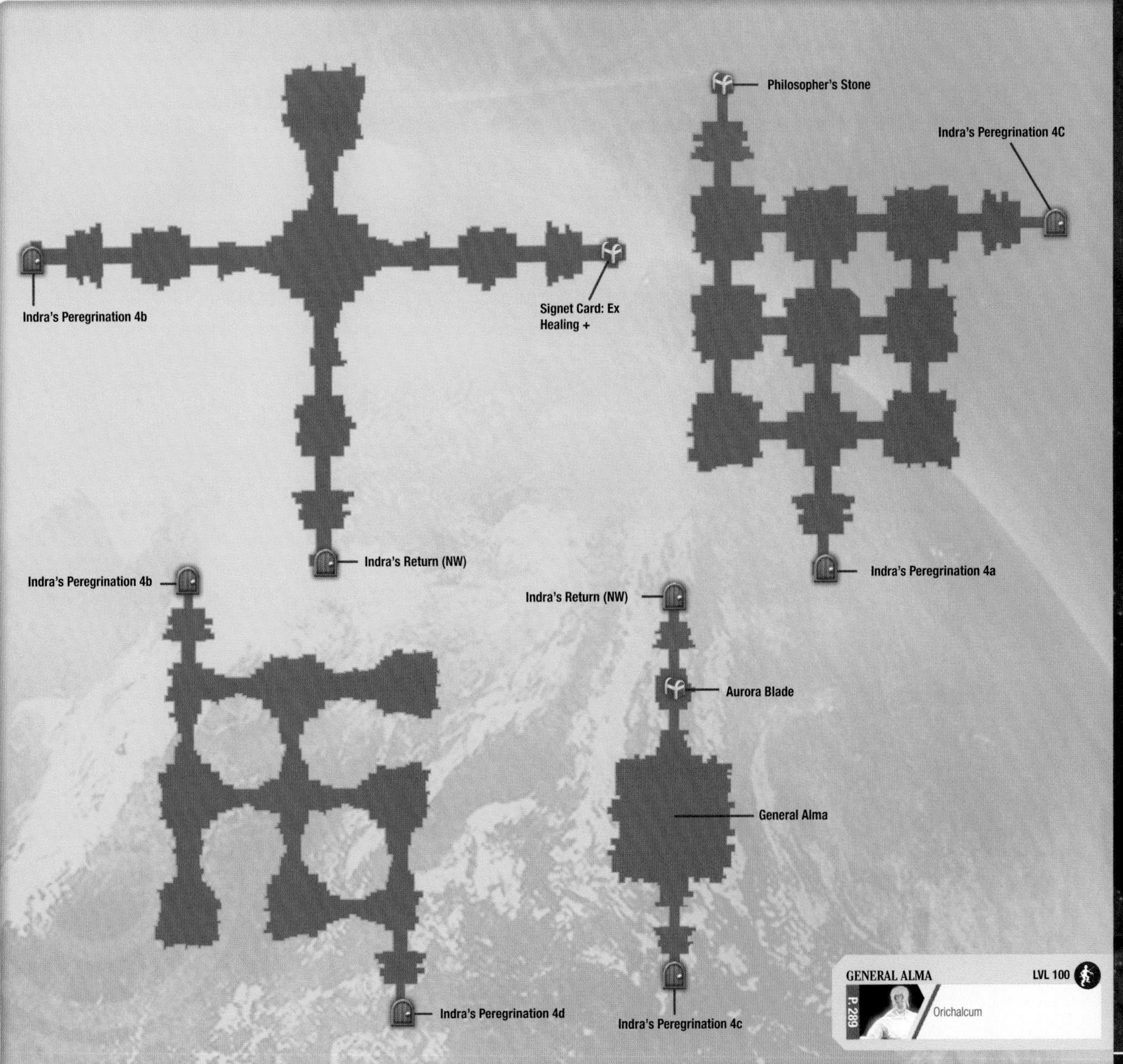

The first level here has the familiar cross layout, with a **Signet Card: Ex Healing +** located in the room farthest east. Run to the intersection and make a right, fighting through any foes you encounter. Pick up the signet card, then turn around and trek back to the intersection, where you can keep heading straight, going west, until you get to a transport pad to the next level. The second level is a set of rooms in a 3x3 layout, with a **Philosopher's Stone** in a room in the northwest part of the map. Going north from your original position, make a left, then make a right, going straight ahead until you reach the chest room. Pick it up, and re-enter the grid, where you'll make a left turn. Go all the way east until you reach the transporter to the third level. There's no chest here, so if you're itching to get to the boss, make the first left you come across, then take a right after, heading toward the farthest southeast point of the map. The transporter is in a room south from the eastern section of the area. Transport up to the boss arena, where you get to have a rematch against the Kronos rebel General Alma.

In his signeturgically fused state, General Alma is a maniacal brawler who frequently targets random allies with brutal punch attacks. His damage is primarily physical, so it's recommended that you munch on some Pasta Bolognese before entering the battlefield. Alternatively, you can go with a savory Grilled Steak for a boost in ATK power.

One of the main mechanics behind the fight is to avoid using guardable attacks. When Alma guards, he will counter with Bosom Blow, an energy-powered reversal burst that knocks down nearby heroes. This is generally difficult to avoid if you have all of your party members set to automatic AI, but it's manageable nonetheless. You can mitigate it by constantly barraging him with strong attacks (default ● button), or with attack skills like Fidel's Mirror Blade. Another powerful and potentially devastating attack is Hammergeddon, a jumping ground pound that deals a large amount of physical area-of-effect damage around him. Open the battle menu frequently, and move your nearby members out of the way accordingly. Alma also has a propensity for making a mad dash toward one of your fragile members, following it up with either Divine Bullet or Transitory Shock. Divine Bullet is a rather slow teleport chest punch, but it breaks guard and does a moderate amount of damage. You can sidestep it or move the character being targeted out of the way. Transitory Shock is a teleport into a guardable area-of-effect attack. Alma can buff himself with the Enhance signeturgy, so dispel it with Fiore's Void to limit his damage.

ERRATIC ENMITY

Some of the bosses in the Maze of Tribulations are extremely intelligent. They won't stand in place flailing at your nearby close-range combatants just so you can heal them up. These bosses will frequently target Miki, and if they're successful in killing her, this makes your life difficult as you struggle to stabilize. To counter these attacks, you'll need to micromanage and pause into the battle menu frequently to assess the situation. Identify whom your foe is after, take control of that party member, and run away! It's imperative that you try to minimize these party members' Signeturgy On skills list so that the AI isn't constantly stuck in long casting animations, as well. This affords you more liberty in moving them away from potential danger.

Other physical attacks in Alma's repertoire include Bloody Blight and Ground Wave. Bloody Blight is an unguardable uppercut, knocking down and stunning anyone in front of him, and Ground Wave is a guardable combination punch sequence.

An extremely effective strategy against the treacherous Kronos general is to equip Emmerson with the Stun Supporter and Interceptor roles. Like with other bosses, you can take control of Emmerson and execute quick normal attack combos to constantly incapacitate Alma.

As long as you're vigilantly pausing to check on the general's movements, you can avoid most of his damage while your AI-controlled members chip away at his health. After you banish your nemesis, pick up the **Aurora Blade** in the chest to the north. Aurora Blade is one of the strongest weapons in the game and is mostly like an upgrade for Fidel if it's your first run through the Maze of Tribulations. Now, exit the arena and prepare yourself for an epic confrontation with a divine being!

Indra's Abyss

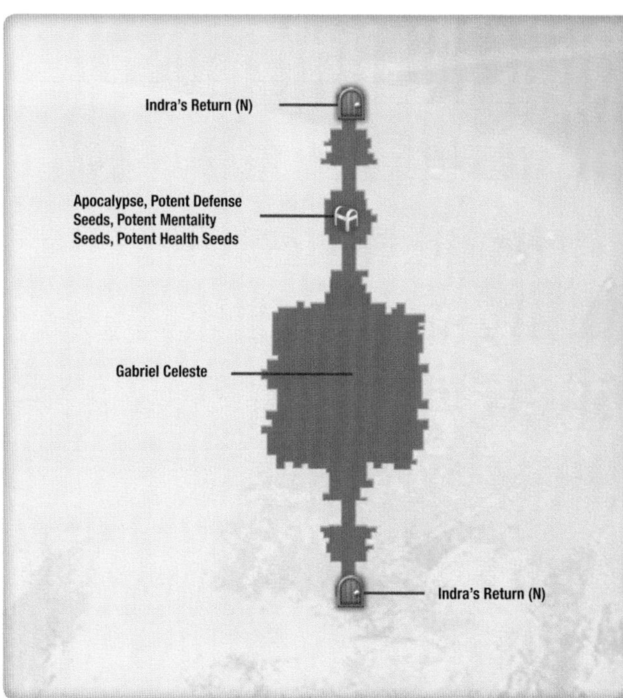

After you've beaten the four intercardinal areas' bosses, you'll gain access to the north path's transporter, which will take you to a foe much more challenging than you've ever faced up to this point. Don't forget to save your game!

PRIDE PUNISHER— GABRIEL CELESTE

Gabriel Celeste is back and stronger than ever in *Star Ocean: Integrity and Faithlessness*, and as usual, he's the penultimate super-boss in the game's optional dungeon.

DIVINE EVOLUTION

Each time you complete the Maze of Tribulations, Gabriel Celeste becomes much more powerful than before when you re-enter the dungeon. There are no new rewards for completing the maze a second time and third time, but these upgraded challenges make a great test of your skill!

STATS AND DROPS

GABRIEL CELESTE 1RST ITERATION

HP	12723000	ATK	4349	DEF	2634	FOL	60420
MP	10090000	INT	2974	MEN	1835	EXP	75525

Lv. 120

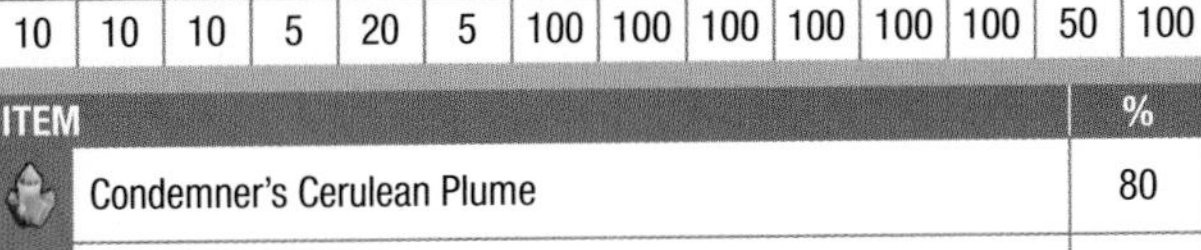

						POI	FRZ	PAR	SIL	CUR	FOG	STN	DTH
10	10	10	5	20	5	100	100	100	100	100	100	50	100

ITEM	%
Condemner's Cerulean Plume	80
Moonstone	16

GABRIEL CELESTE 2ND ITERATION

HP	23333000
MP	18017000
ATK	5517
INT	3800
DEF	3664
MEN	2527
FOL	102231
EXP	127789

Lv. 160

ITEM	%
Condemner's Cerulean Plume	90
Moonstone	18

						POI	FRZ	PAR	SIL	CUR	FOG	STN	DTH
10	10	10	5	20	5	100	100	100	100	100	100	50	100

GABRIEL CELESTE 3RD ITERATION

HP	46020000
MP	36487000
ATK	6177
INT	4266
DEF	4228
MEN	3029
FOL	151810
EXP	189763

Lv. 200

ITEM	%
Condemner's Cerulean Plume	100
Moonstone	22

						POI	FRZ	PAR	SIL	CUR	FOG	STN	DTH
10	10	10	5	20	5	100	100	100	100	100	100	50	100

GABRIEL'S ABILITIES

Abject Misery

- A single projectile cutting through the battlefield
- Moderate damage

Brutish Bolt

- Large, devastating area-of-effect storm centered on Gabriel, causing massive damage to those around him
- Hits several times and paralyzes
- Anyone in the storm will most likely die unless they're invincible from a Heroism Potion or Dead Man Walking role
- More likely to cast when his HP is low
- Keep non-invincible members as far away from him as possible, especially Miki, Fiore, and Emmerson

Celestial Fists of Fury

- A physical damage combo ending with a long-range beam
- Does massive physical damage unless the target has defensive buffs like God Slayer and DEF+ roles/items
- The beam may hit a back line member even if they're far away
- Can inflict stun

Indiscrimination

- Quickly fires several projectiles all around him, similar to Divine Wave
- Minimal damage, but can cause silence and/or fog
- Cast Cure Condition or use curative items immediately

Partizan Gravepost

- Massive area-of-effect around the divine being, causing low damage
- Extremely fast casting and causes knockdown
- Keep Miki, Fiore, and Emmerson away

Thunderstroke Spear

- Melee-range area-of-effect almost as destructive as Brutish Bolt
- Can cause paralysis; cure with Cure Condition or Basil
- Keep Miki, Fiore, and Emmerson away

RECOMMENDED POWER LEVEL & EQUIPMENT

All party members are at least Lv. 120 for the first iteration (Lv. 160 for second, and Lv. 200 for third)

All roles unlocked, with all specialties available

Restorative consumables stocked, including Blueberry Potions, Blackberry Potions, Fresh Sages, Resurrection Elixirs (requires plenty of Caterpillar Fungi), Vitaliteas, ailment curatives, Signet Card: Resurrection, and Signet Card: Angel Feather+

All Cathedral of Oblivion weapons, preferably augmented (for second and third forms, all Terpsichorean Interlude weapons obtained and unlocked)

Equip best armor available, especially ones with special abilities like Reflecting Plate (-10% damage from divine beings)

Augment your gear as best as you can with the resources you have available: preferably ATK+ and Critical Hit+ augments for Anne and Emmerson, DEF+ on Victor and Fidel, HP+ on Miki, and INT+ on Fiore

Food: Sukiyaki (50 quality food synthesis) OR Grilled Steak OR Fruit Gummies

RECOMMENDED PARTY SETUP

Roles

CHARACTER				
Fidel	Aggressor	Tri-Ace	God Slayer	Gritty Warrior
Miki	Healer	Crusader	Skulker	Sage
Victor	Evasionist	Stamina Stockpiler	Defensive Devotee	Turtle
Fiore	Lightning Strike => Intelligence Indulger	Solar Emissary	Enchanter	Master Tactician
Emmerson	Interceptor	Stun Supporter	Daemon	Item Expender AND/OR Menace
Anne	Berserker	Warmonger	Attack Advocate OR Critical Combatant	Dead Man Walking
Relia	Vivifier	Holy Mother	Pacifist	Princess

Battle Set

CHARACTER	SHORT RANGE ⊗	SHORT RANGE ◎	LONG RANGE ⊗	LONG RANGE ◎
Fidel	Air Raid	Mirror Blade	Air Slash	Air Slash
Miki	Any	Any	Sunflare	Terra Hammer
Victor	Mirror Blade	Bloodstorm Revolution	Flying Guillotine	Dragon Roar
Fiore	Any	Any	Wind Blade	Thunder Flare
Emmerson	Gravity Bullet	Heavenly Flight	Crescent Wings	Crescent Wings
Anne	Crescent Locus	Hammer of Might	Electric Fists	Hammer of Might

Signeturgy ON

CHARACTER						
Miki	Ex Healing	Faerie Light	Faerie Star	Raise Dead	Resurrection	Cure Condition
Fiore	Healing	Raise Dead	Arctic Impact OR Wind Blade	Thunder Flare	Void	—

SETUP EXPLANATIONS

FIDEL

God Slayer increases damage dealt to and damage taken from divine beings by 50%, which helps Fidel survive everything, save for Brutish Bolt and Thunderstroke Spear. Air Raid and Mirror Blade are powerful while decently quick enough to build combos reasonably, although you'll most likely not be controlling Fidel manually for the majority of the battle. Air Slash is Fidel's only ranged attack, and you might need to use it occasionally when you're moving him out of range when the battle becomes increasingly difficult. Tri-Ace and Gritty Warrior are excellent survival roles, but these may be switched out with other defensive abilities. However, guard tactics are generally not advised against Gabriel because of his many guard-crushing abilities.

MIKI

As usual, she's your primary healer and raiser. Skulker gives her more survivability, which equates to more leeway for healing allies, as Gabriel will target her less often. However, it can be switched out for Savior. Sage is crucial to cut down on signeturgy casting time, resulting in much quicker Faerie heals. Make sure to turn off all of her offensive signeturgical spells in the set battle skills menu. You can cast them on your own if you have the time.

VICTOR

Since Gabriel's main attacks are physical-based, boosting Victor's DEF and HP ratings is recommended, as well as lowering the chance of being hit critically. Turtle synergizes well with high HP and high DEF, so it's an incredibly handy role since many of the god's attacks are sure to lower Victor's HP below 10%.

FIORE

She'll be your all-out INT-based signeturgical damage dealer, so stack as much INT as you can. Start the fight using the Lightning Strike role, and then switch it out through the battle menu to Intelligence Indulger for the permanent INT+20% increase. Thunder Flare can inflict an ATK down debuff, so when you have time, you may want to manually control Fiore to combo-cast repeated Thunder Flares. Master Tactician will encourage your allies to move away to safety while increasing her INT by a large margin.

EMMERSON

Gabriel is susceptible to being stunned, so use the tried-and-true stunner build. Daemon works on every single enemy in the game and helps speed up battles immensely thanks to its powerful DEF and MEN debuffs. Menace encourages Emmerson's AI to stay actively shooting while prioritizing quick pot shots, synergizing with the two stunner roles. It's recommended that you use Crescent Wings for Emmerson's long-range skills; his other long-range skills have lengthy animations that may hinder your ability to move him out of harm's way or to heal party members with curatives. If you've been diligent in your item use, you might have the Item Expender role unlocked by now (obtained by using items 500 times in battle). Equip this role during battle if the situation becomes dire and you need potions or Fresh Sages tossed out quickly.

ANNE

This is a must-have build for the Gabriel and Ethereal Queen battles. Because of her relatively low base HP total, Anne is much too susceptible to dying without it. She doesn't have ranged attacks, and you need her to be useful, so have her be your Dead Man Walking. With Warmonger and Critical Combatant, she'll have an extra 40% chance of dealing critical damage while staying active (thanks to "Take more actions +10" factor). With the proper augments, you can potentially boost her Critical Hit figure up to 100%! Alternatively, you can use Attack Advocate in place of Critical Combatant. Controlling Anne or Fiore when your party is stabilized is ideal for optimal damage output. You can perform the following combo for massive damage: Hammer of Might => Hammer of Might => Hammer of Might => Blazing Cannon.

RELIA

A universally strong support setup when you're not farming EXP or SP. Vivifier and Holy Mother are crucial; Vivifier keeps your allies active while Holy Mother decreases the enemy's activity, which, in turn, increases your survivability.

Before you enter the fight, make sure to eat the appropriate foods. Eating Sukiyaki is highly recommended for this fight (synthesized with food quality of 50). Otherwise, you can boost your ATK or Critical Hit Rate with either Grilled Steak or Fruit Gummies. Begin the fight as you would against most of the maze bosses. Take control of Miki, Fiore, and Emmerson, and run far, far away. Your front line members shouldn't go down too quickly if you've equipped them well enough.

You can either let Miki heal on her own (which she should do well enough if your roles are set up with the suggested build earlier in this guide), or you can manually control her to ensure that your party's HP is capped. When everyone is safe from potential Brutish Bolts, you can take control of either Anne or Fiore to perform combos. Be mindful of any status effects that land on your heroes, since many of Gabriel's attack skills inflict extremely hindering ailments like paralysis, fog, silence, and stun. Stun doesn't have to be cured since it doesn't last too long.

The main mechanic to look out for here is Brutish Bolt. If you see the red combat message with Gabriel's Brutish Bolt startup animation, open the battle menu and take control of Miki so you can be ready to cast Resurrect on Fidel or Victor. Anne should be fine if she's using Dead Man Walking (as long as she's healed up enough). Occasionally, Gabriel will run at one of your ranged members. If this happens, open the battle menu immediately and move your fragile members away. He may be looking to wreak some havoc with Brutish Bolt on your back line!

Repeat until Gabriel's HP is about 35%. Things get scary here, and you'll know when it does because Gabriel will be covered in an electrical field, signaling his new power. He'll start using Brutish Bolt and Thunderstroke Spear quite often. Thunderstroke Spear is similar in damage to Brutish Bolt in that it can instantly kill anyone caught in it. If your party is healthy, you can usually out-heal and out-raise the damage output. However, if multiple members go down, you should start using Emmerson and Fiore to raise members while Miki heals Anne. If the need arises, you can set Fidel and Victor's AI to manual, while invulnerable Anne remains in the fray. Move them away to heal them up, and have them use their ranged skill attacks. When you're comfortable, you can put them back to automatic AI so they can help burn down Gabriel's HP.

If Miki ever goes down, make sure to prioritize raising her with Fiore and having one of your other members heal up Anne with a Blueberry Potion. It's important to spread out these tasks since they take up valuable time from each member. If you have the valuable Item Expender role, this task becomes much easier since it essentially removes the item cooldown timer.

If things get extremely bad, you can resort to using Miki's Lv. 3 (or higher) Arcadia Reserve Rush. If you have spare Vitaliteas (or a Robust Vitalitea), you can use those and immediately execute Arcadia for a party-wide raise and heal.

After you've committed proper deicide, head north from the arena to obtain your well-deserved reward—**Apocalypse**! Congratulations! Apocalypse should be Miki's best weapon if this is your first time through the Maze of Tribulations. Have her equip it, and head on out back to the lobby. You can now ascend to the third floor of the maze through the center platform in Indra's Return.

SUPERLATIVE SYNTHESES

You'll notice that the three celestial beings (Transmogrified Alma, Gabriel Celeste, and the Ethereal Queen) can drop ores called Moonstones. You can use Moonstones to create the best weapons and armor in the game through the Synthesis skill. To increase your chances of making an ultimate weapon or armor, raise any type of synthesis item quality to 50, and then add a Moonstone to the ingredients. For instance, you can create a Mindhealer, an Aether-in-Stasis, or a Valkyrie's Garb by creating a signeturgy-based item quality of 50 with a Moonstone added to the recipe. However, you can't control the exact outcome, so it's recommended that you save your game before going for these syntheses.

TERPSICHOREAN GENESIS

Terpsichorean Genesis

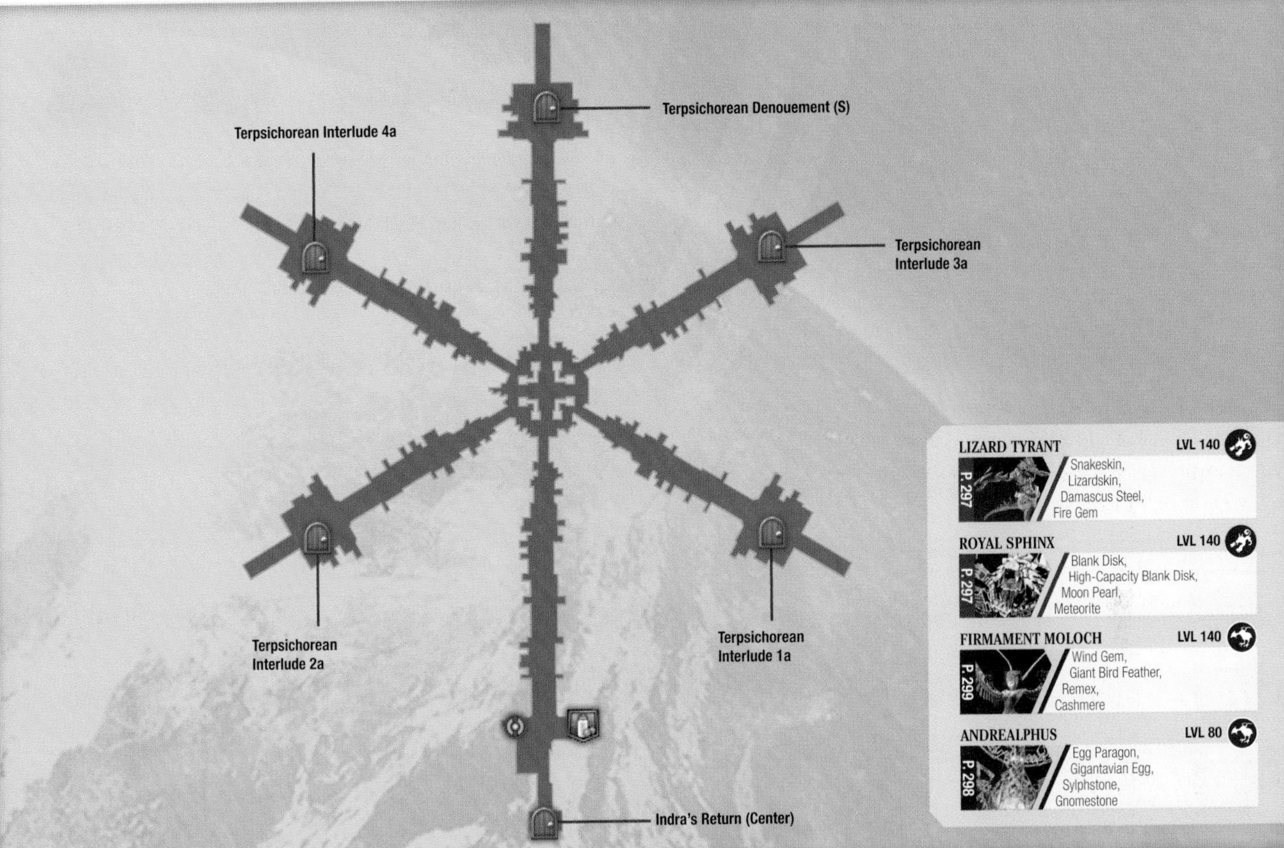

Enemy	Level	Page	Drops
LIZARD TYRANT	LVL 140	P. 297	Snakeskin, Lizardskin, Damascus Steel, Fire Gem
ROYAL SPHINX	LVL 140	P. 297	Blank Disk, High-Capacity Blank Disk, Moon Pearl, Meteorite
FIRMAMENT MOLOCH	LVL 140	P. 299	Wind Gem, Giant Bird Feather, Remex, Cashmere
ANDREALPHUS	LVL 80	P. 298	Egg Paragon, Gigantavian Egg, Sylphstone, Gnomestone

If you haven't saved your progress, go ahead and do so. There's a significant difficulty spike here, not only in the boss battles, but also with the standard enemies who are loitering the maze's hallways. Royal Sphinxes are particularly painful encounters, with their ability to wipe out multiple party members in one shot if you aren't careful.

If you need to go back to town for item creation supplies or to finish some quests, you should do so before attempting the final floor of the maze. It's also a good idea to augment all of your gear for a bit of a performance boost. When you're ready, the queen awaits!

GET ON MY LEVEL

The monsters you'll be facing in the Terpsichorean Genesis areas are much stronger than the ones in Indra's Return. These baddies have an average level of around 140, so it's highly recommended that you level your party up accordingly to boost your stats for the tough opponents ahead. You can either bash on the enemies on this floor for EXP and SP, or you can farm the Metal Scumbags in the areas of the previous floor for even more points. Either way, make sure to have your party members equip the Instructor and Betrayer roles for a nice EXP multiplier. Don't forget to bake some Shortcakes, too!

You'll notice that the layout here is exactly the same as the previous two floors. The only difference is that the subareas of the four prerequisite bosses will have five floors, whereas the previous floor's areas contained four. You can complete these four intercardinal areas in any order, but be warned: one of these sub-area bosses can be especially challenging!

Terpsichorean Interlude I

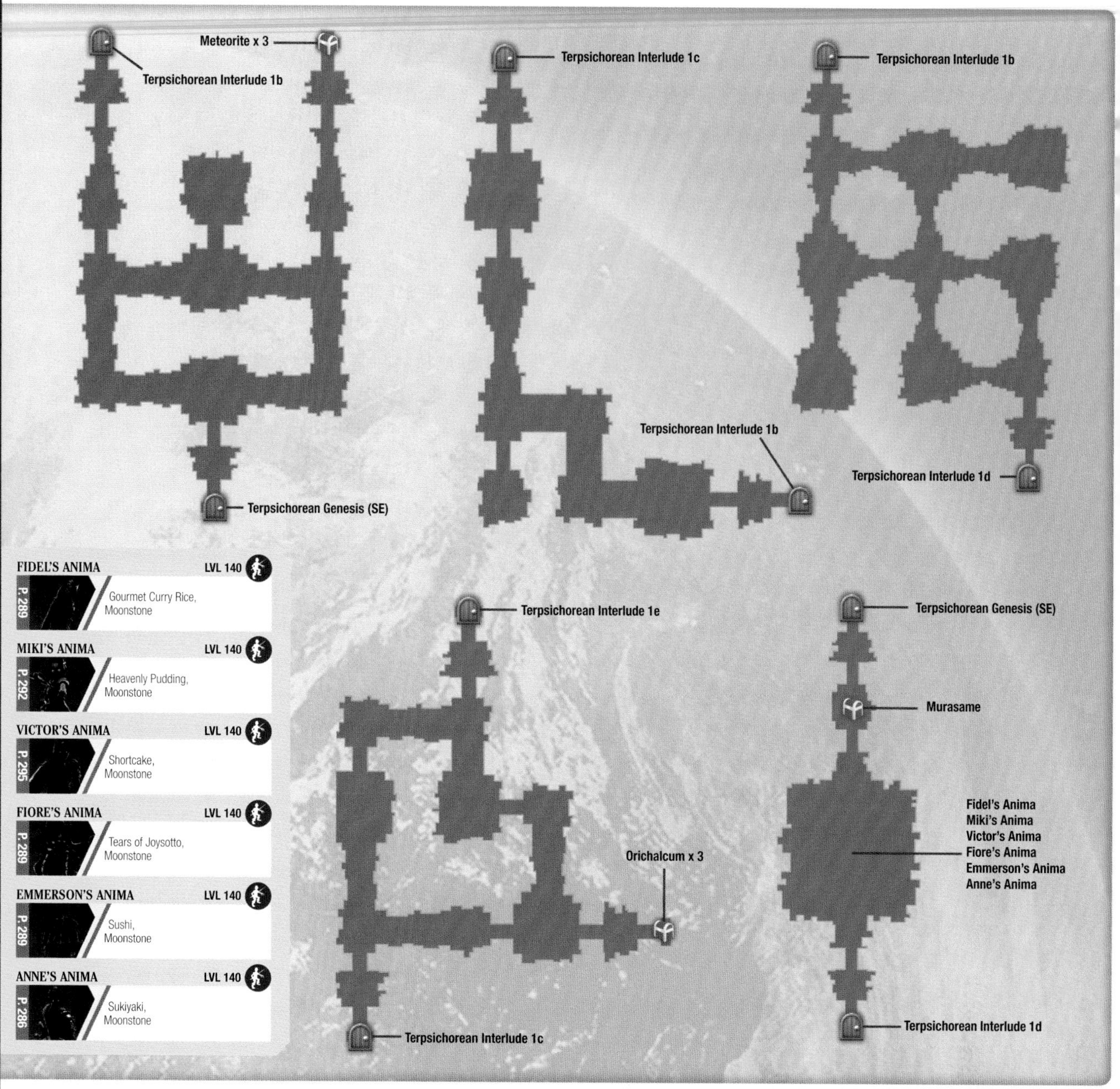

Meteorite x 3
Terpsichorean Interlude 1b
Terpsichorean Genesis (SE)
Terpsichorean Interlude 1c
Terpsichorean Interlude 1b
Terpsichorean Interlude 1b
Terpsichorean Interlude 1d
Terpsichorean Interlude 1e
Orichalcum x 3
Terpsichorean Interlude 1c
Terpsichorean Genesis (SE)
Murasame
Fidel's Anima
Miki's Anima
Victor's Anima
Fiore's Anima
Emmerson's Anima
Anne's Anima
Terpsichorean Interlude 1d

FIDEL'S ANIMA LVL 140
P. 289
Gourmet Curry Rice, Moonstone

MIKI'S ANIMA LVL 140
P. 292
Heavenly Pudding, Moonstone

VICTOR'S ANIMA LVL 140
P. 295
Shortcake, Moonstone

FIORE'S ANIMA LVL 140
P. 289
Tears of Joysotto, Moonstone

EMMERSON'S ANIMA LVL 140
P. 289
Sushi, Moonstone

ANNE'S ANIMA LVL 140
P. 286
Sukiyaki, Moonstone

This first area consists of two long hallways running parallel to each other, with three rooms protruding to the north. There's a chest in the farthest northeast room containing **Meteorite x 3**. Take the first right, then head north along the east part of the map to reach it. After you grab the meteorites, make your way back out and take your first right, heading west. At the end of the trail, make a right to head up to the second level. A straightforward path here. You'll reach a fork at the end of the initial path. Turn right here, going north, to get to the third level. Your destination here on the third level is to the southeast. Take the second left along the western path, then take the second right and keep going until you reach the southernmost room. The transport pad here takes you to the fourth level.

There's a very valuable chest here containing **Orichalcum x 3**. Get to it by heading all the way east from your starting point. Then, turn around and take the first right, northbound and around a bend. You'll see a room to the north, with a transport to the boss arena in it. Take the transport, and prepare for one of the most arduous battles you'll come across in the maze.

This is arguably the most difficult battle in the entire game if you're not prepared well in advance. This is an epitomic case of offense being the best defense, since it's nigh impossible to win through attrition against these evil doppelgangers. Not only do they have all of your abilities, but each one of them has more than one million HP. On top of their ridiculous damage output, lockdown combos, status-inflicting spells, and the overall chaotic nature of the six-on-six brawl, they also have a dedicated healer that can heal for around 50% of their max HP at a moment's notice. They're essentially as effective as your party, except with absurd amounts of health. The most effective way to deal with this is to assassinate Miki's Anima as early as possible, but even this is not an easy task thanks to the chaos the opposing team forces on you.

It's highly recommended that you come into the battle with at least three or four Reserve Gauge stocks. You'll need them to unleash as much firepower as possible within a small frame of time. Otherwise, Miki's Anima will start healing up her allies for tens of thousands of hit points, nullifying your efforts.

Before you enter, make sure everyone is healed fully and equipped with proper roles. The most important factor is the Dead Man Walking, Berserker, and Instigator roles combination. You can put these on either Fidel or Anne. Fidel has a more effective Reserve Rush that scales well with high ATK power, but Anne's Reserve Rush is strong against single targets. Have Fiore or Emmerson equipped with Executioner and any other damage-boosting roles so that they target Miki's Anima on their own. It's also important to have Miki equipped with the Skulker role so she's less likely to be targeted; it's imperative she doesn't die early on. Other roles to consider are Holy Mother and Terror Knight, preferably equipped on Relia.

Make sure to have an ATK-enhancing food active before engaging, either Sukiyaki or Grilled Steak. Now, when you enter, you'll want to (as usual) pause the game with the battle menu. Take control of Miki, and maneuver her away from danger immediately while healing up anyone who needs it. Once party-wide HP is full, open the battle menu and switch to your ATK-enhanced Dead Man Walking damage dealer. Unpause, and quickly select Miki's Anima as your target, then execute a Lv. 2 Ethereal Blast (or Blazing Cannon if you're using Anne). As soon as the animation goes off, switch to your other ATK-boosted damage dealer and deplete the rest of your Reserve Rush gauge on Miki's Anima. Open the battle menu as soon as you can to take control of Miki to stabilize and heal any damaged members. If you've done the sequence correctly, it should now be a six-on-five match, with the foes' healer dead.

RESERVE RUSHDOWN

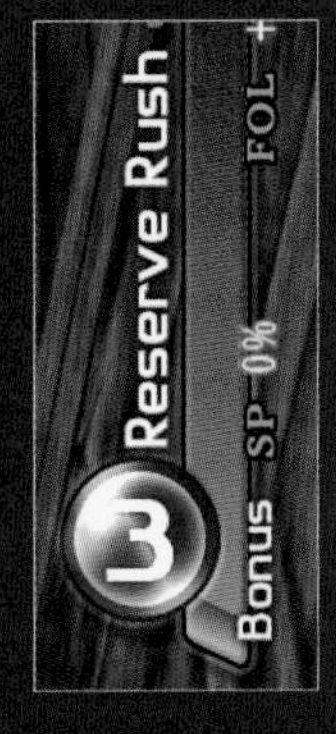

Unleashing a synchronized sequence of two Reserve Rush limit breaks is crucial for assassinating a particular threat. You can do this by limiting the amount of gauge your Reserve Rush uses. Hold the R2 button and press L2 during battle (or during the paused battle menu) to select how many gauges you'll use for your next Reserve Rush. You can make managing which character uses Reserve Rush gauge easier by going into the Settings menu (outside of battle only) and selecting Reserve Rush Scheme. The "Character You Control Activates" option can make your life easier when you're performing these double and triple Reserve Rush team combos.

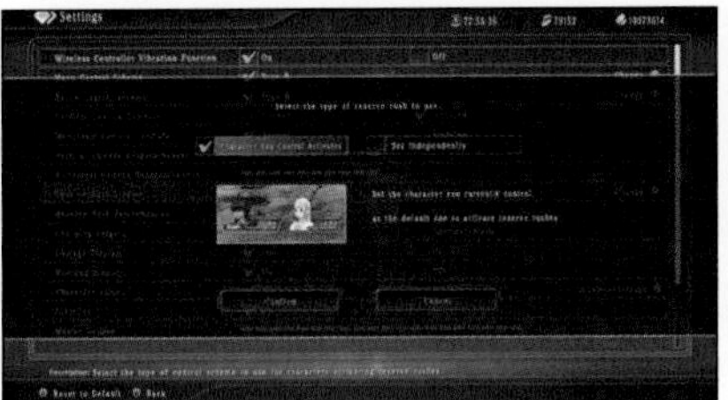

It's not over yet, though. The fight remains incredibly difficult thanks to all of the powerful abilities the enemies still can access. Fiore's Anima and Emmerson's Anima can dish out extreme punishment with their long-ranged attacks. Emmerson's Anima can use Avian Rage from a distance, locking down one of your party members and dealing insane amounts of damage. Try to target him next with Fidel and Anne if you can. If you need to, use Vitalitea or Robust Vitalitea to boost your Reserve Rush gauge so you can make quick work of a remaining threat. Once you've put down Miki's, Emmerson's, and Fiore's Animas, go after Anne's Anima next. She has a 0 DEF rating, so she should go down much easier than the others. Do this all while vigilantly keeping Miki safe and healing up members along the way.

Hopefully, you'll have all of your teammates alive against just Fidel's Anima and Victor's Anima. Send them back to where they came from, and pat yourself on the back for a well-executed strategy!

Your just reward consists of the famous **Murasame** katana, an upgrade for Victor if this is your first runthrough of the Maze of Tribulations. Equip him with it, and head back out to the lobby.

Terpsichorean Interlude II

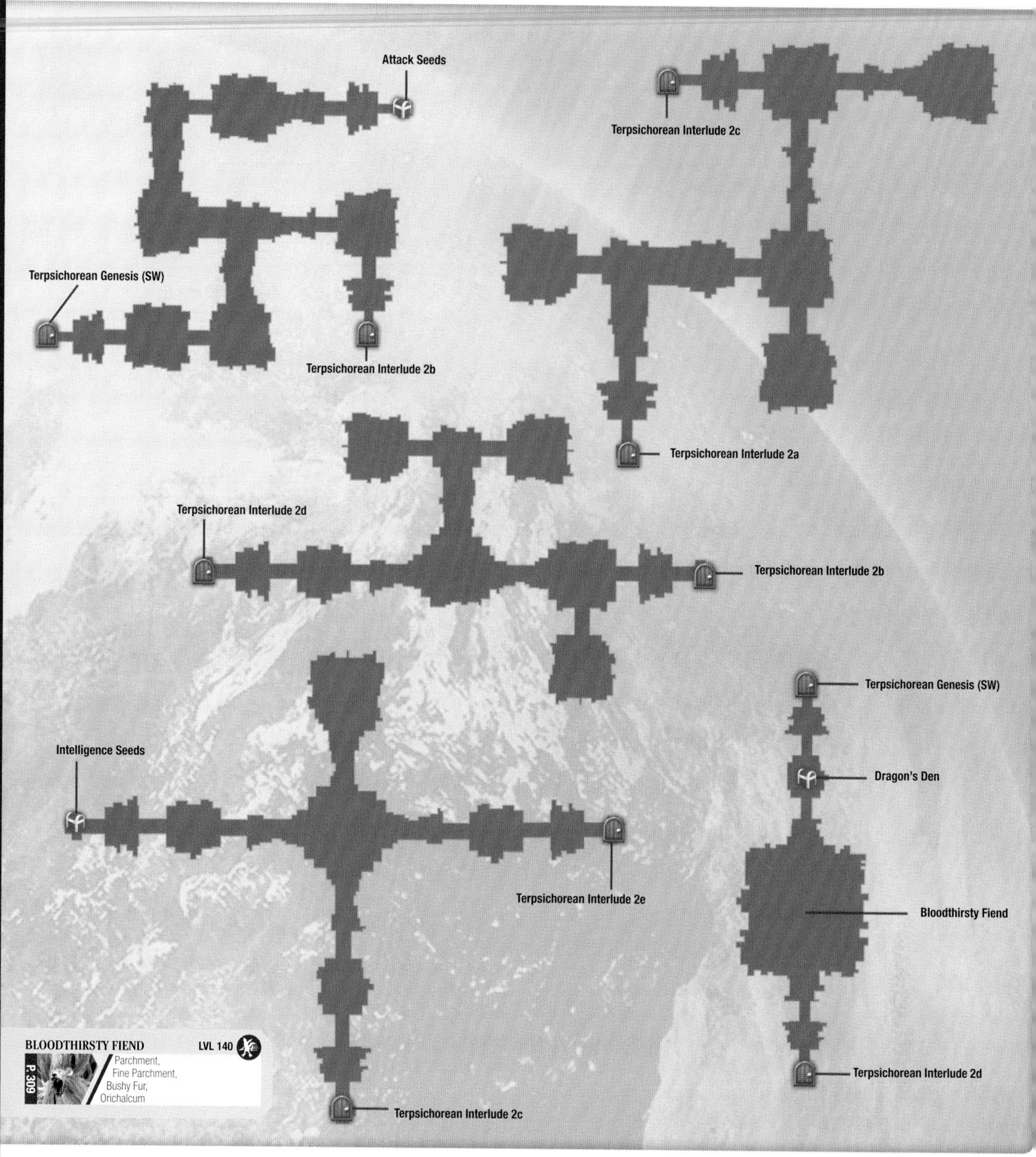

BLOODTHIRSTY FIEND LVL 140

P.309

Parchment, Fine Parchment, Bushy Fur, Orichalcum

Head east from the start, then turn left at the bend. When you reach a split, taking a left and following the path leads you to a chest holding **Attack Seeds** in the northeast room. Grab it and then backtrack, taking the other path at the split, going east. It eventually leads you south into the room to the second level. There's no chest on this floor, so if you want to get to the third level, make a right at the first fork, then take a left at the second fork, going north. At the third split, take a left to take the transport pad to the third level. There's no chest here, either, and your waypoint to the next level is directly west from the starting point. You can find enemies in the north and south paths if you want to earn some EXP and SP. The fourth level is a cross-shaped layout, with your destination in the east path of the intersection. There's a chest containing **Intelligence Seeds** in the westernmost room. Pick them up, fight any enemies along the way, and then turn around and make your way east to the boss arena.

BLOODTHIRSTY FIEND

FOL 6337 EXP 97140 Lv. 140

HP	13155800
MP	10312000
ATK	5031
INT	3430
DEF	2689
MEN	2151

ITEM	%
Parchment	20
Fine Parchment	18
Bushy Fur	26
Orichalcum	18

						POI	FRZ	PAR	SIL	CUR	FOG	STN	DTH
-20	0	6	0	0	0	100	100	100	100	100	100	100	100

The Bloodthirsty Fiend here is a particularly annoying fight, and you'll want to set up your party builds leaning toward attack power. It's recommended that you have the group snack on Grilled Steak or other ATK-enhancing food before the fight. When you're ready, go ahead and enter the arena.

At the beginning of the battle, take control of your ranged members and healer so you can move them all away from each other. The stinger-equipped Manticore will constantly use an attack skill called Seething Inferno. It randomly seeks out a party member and proceeds to drill into the ground, ending the attack skill with an explosive whirling area-of-effect that instantly kills all but the healthiest party members if they're hit by both the stinger and the explosion. This fight is all about dealing as much damage as possible while identifying the fiend's next target. If the fiend goes after one of your fragile members, open the battle menu and take control of its potential victim so you can maneuver out of the way. You'll be forced to do this frequently if you want to keep your back line members alive.

WHO'S NEXT?

In most cases, it's entirely possible to identify which target a boss wants to go after by looking at their movement. If you see a boss turn and make a beeline for Miki, Fiore, or Emmerson, you can be sure that the boss wants one of them dead. Open the battle menu frequently to give yourself time to see what the boss is going to do next, especially if Miki is a potential target. Take control of the target, and run your party member away to safety!

The Bloodthirsty Fiend can't be stunned, but it can be inflicted with the Daemon role's DEF and MEN down afflictions. Equipping one of your attackers (preferably Emmerson) with the Daemon role greatly helps burn the monstrosity down.

There are some other unconventional considerations to take during this fight. You don't want your ranged damage dealers casting or executing skills that keep them stuck in place for too long. Most of Fiore's offensive abilities come with high cast and travel times. This is terrible when you're trying to be as mobile as possible. Most spells end up missing because of the fiend's propensity for constantly traveling across the battlefield. Additionally, you don't want your party members stuck in lengthy attack animations, preventing you from evading the adversary's stinger and area-of-effect combos.

The recommended signeturgical spell to equip for Fiore is Ice Needles in both long-range battle set slots. These almost always hit and do large amounts of damage when combo-casted. Ice Needles also recovers slightly faster than her other spells. It synergizes well with the Emissary of the Blue Sphere role, so make sure to set one of her roles with it. For Emmerson, you can equip Crescent Wings in both long-range battle set slots because of its high damage and relatively fast execution time. For his roles setup, equip Daemon and other damage boosters like Attack Advocate and Critical Combatant to maximize his damage.

As for your melee fighters, have them take on more offensive roles while removing any guard-enhancing ones (most of the Manticore's attacks crush guard anyway). If you're leveled and equipped well enough, your close-range fighters should be able to withstand most attacks without suddenly dying. Anne with the Berserker plus Dead Man Walking combo is an optimal build, particular in conjunction with Hammer of Might (which should be assigned to all four battle skill slots). She'll be invincible while constantly pummeling the flying beast with Hammer of Might's superb damage and tracking effect.

Victor can be equipped with a few HP-enhancing roles and equipment to survive the inferno. Alternatively, you can play him as a ranged attacker equipped with Dragon Roar and offensive-based roles. This lets you do damage while avoiding taking any yourself, with the caveat that you're actively switching to Victor when his AI opts to engage at close range.

Since the Bloodthirsty Fiend is a Corrupt-type monster, you can equip Fidel with the Mutant Slayer role, which reduces damage from corrupted monsters by 50% while boosting damage done by 30%. However, you can make your life much easier by equipping Miki with this role. Otherwise, she'll die in one Seething Inferno combo, which disrupts much of your strategy because you'll need to raise and heal party members instead of dishing out damage. As long as she can withstand an entire Seething Inferno, an AI-controlled Miki can usually keep up with healing all damage done to the party while they hack at the flying beast. Miki should have all of her non-healing signeturgical spells turned off, as well.

The fiend has a few other attack skills up its furry sleeves, but rarely uses them. When it does, it's more of a relief since they're not as devastating as Seething Inferno. Keep at it, and the foe eventually goes down. Your reward for exorcising the monster is a **Dragon's Den** orb for Fiore, located in the chest to the north. Have her equip it if it's an upgrade, and then return to Terpsichorean Genesis through the north room's transport pad.

Terpsichorean Interlude III

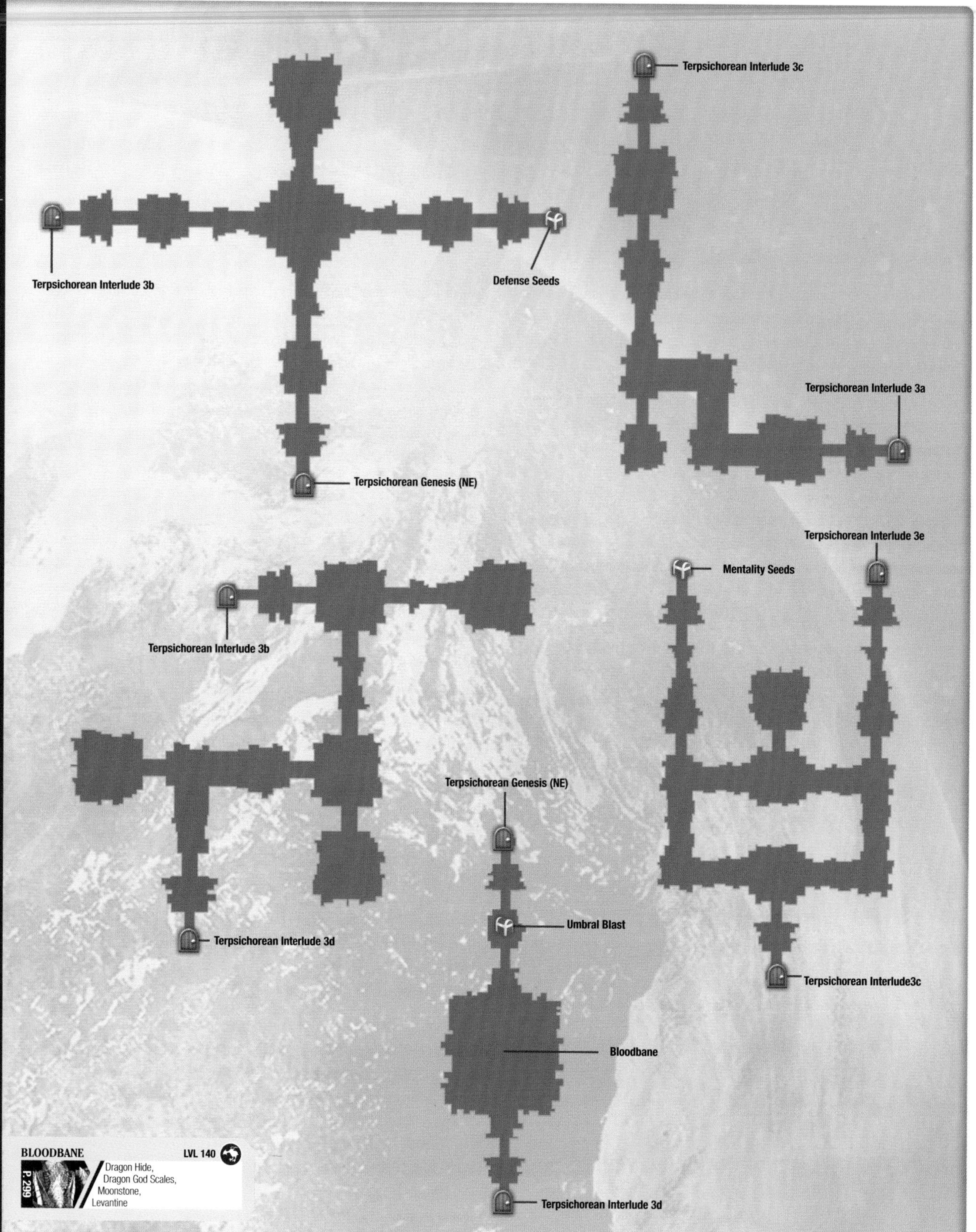

Terpsichorean Interlude 3b

Defense Seeds

Terpsichorean Genesis (NE)

Terpsichorean Interlude 3c

Terpsichorean Interlude 3a

Terpsichorean Interlude 3e

Mentality Seeds

Terpsichorean Interlude 3b

Terpsichorean Genesis (NE)

Umbral Blast

Terpsichorean Interlude 3d

Terpsichorean Interlude3c

Bloodbane

Terpsichorean Interlude 3d

BLOODBANE LVL 140

P.299

Dragon Hide,
Dragon God Scales,
Moonstone,
Levantine

Another cross-shaped level here, with **Defense Seeds** in a chest in a room at the end of the east path. Pick them up, and then head in the opposite direction to the room at the west to get to the next level. On the second level, run west and follow the bends until you get to a split. Turn right, heading north, to get to the third level. From the starting point here, make a right heading south, then take another right through a door when you can. While heading west, there will be a room to the left, heading south, with a transporter taking you to the fourth level. The fourth level is another familiar layout. There's a chest in the farthest northwest room. Make a left from the starting point, then go all the way north along the western path. Pick up the **Mentality Seeds** in a chest here, then head to the other side of the level by making a left turn out of the chest room, going east. When you can go no farther, make a left, and then take the transport pad in a room at the end of the hallway to the boss arena.

BLOODBANE

FOL 3457 | EXP 96351 | Lv. 140

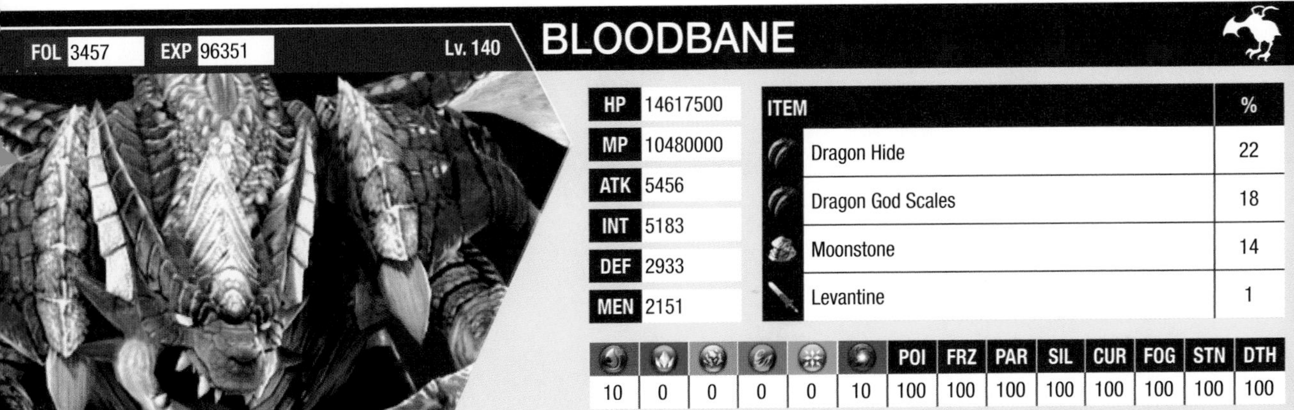

HP	14617500
MP	10480000
ATK	5456
INT	5183
DEF	2933
MEN	2151

ITEM	%
Dragon Hide	22
Dragon God Scales	18
Moonstone	14
Levantine	1

						POI	FRZ	PAR	SIL	CUR	FOG	STN	DTH
10	0	0	0	0	10	100	100	100	100	100	100	100	100

Bloodbane is an avian dark-based dragon with a tendency of casting spells like Vampiric Blade and Shadow Needles. This encounter is similar to that of the Bloodthirsty Fiend in that Bloodbane is fond of picking on random party members to attack. It will often run across the battlefield to attack one of the weaker back line members. Its main physical attack is a tail swipe that crushes guard and can knock its victim down. It's completely survivable, but it's recommended that you run your fragile party members away from it.

Most of the damage you'll be doing will come from Emmerson, Fiore, and Anne (if she's your designated Dead Man Walking). Bloodbane isn't susceptible to any status effects, save for Daemon's DEF and MEN down debuff, so have Emmerson's roles built for damage, with either Attack Advocate or Critical Combatant roles set. Fiore can do well here by combo-casting Arctic Impact and Ice Needles while equipped with the Emissary of the Blue Sphere role. You'll also want to have Fidel's and Victor's long-range battle sets include their ranged attacks since the dragon is rather mobile. Fidel or Emmerson can equip the Raven Slayer role to boost their damage significantly against the winged wyrm.

Occasionally, Bloodbane will cast Sacred Pain on one of your heroes, but this effect *cannot* be dispelled. However, Bloodbane's damage output should still be manageable since its dark-based spells generally won't kill a full-health character. Additionally, many of its attacks and spells can be guarded and countered, allowing you to build some Reserve Rush gauge. When you're not busy running from it, you can burn down its health by stacking Anne's combo ratio and unleashing a 200% Blazing Cannon combo.

HYPER MEGA ULTRA COMBOS

Like most attacks, you can boost Reserve Rush abilities with the combo cancel mechanic. You can efficiently use your Reserve Rush gauge by performing quick-cancel combos up to 175% by chaining between weak and strong normal attacks or repeated attack skills before executing your Reserve Rush. Set your Reserve Rush user to the character you're controlling (or simply change Reserve Rush Scheme settings in the Settings menu), perform a four-hit combo, then execute your Reserve Rush immediately.

If your ATK is high enough, you can potentially unleash max damage Reserve Rush skills while only using one stock of Reserve Rush gauge!

When slain, Bloodbane has a chance of dropping **Levantine**, Fidel's ultimate weapon. Unfortunately, it's only a chance at a drop, so if you're unlucky, you may have to resort to reloading your save file to try again (or complete the entire maze to enter its second iteration). Alternatively, you can try to synthesize if you have a Moonstone (50 quality metal-based synthesis). You can increase the drop chance by having the Ornithology specialty leveled up fully (you should have everything SP-related maxed at this point). The chest north of the arena contains an **Umbral Blast** phaser weapon. Equip it on Emmerson if it's better than what he's currently using, then proceed back to the lobby.

Terpsichorean Interlude IV

PART 04

Go straight north from your starting position, and then follow the bend to the right, heading east. Keep going until you hit a fork, and take a left into a room with a chest containing some **Health Seeds**. Turn around and keep running along a path heading southeast until you come across a divergence. Take a left turn here into a room with a transport pad to the second level. From here, if you run all the way east, you'll find a transporter to the third level. There are enemies in the other rooms if you need to grind out some EXP for the upcoming boss battle. On the third level, you can get to the exit by heading south, making a left, then your first right, then left, and then right again, taking you to the southeastern area of the map. Go into the room to the south to get to the fourth level. Now, head east here until the trail forces you north. At the fork, if you make a right turn, there's a chest holding **Magic Seeds** at the end of the east path. Grab it, and then go back and take the western path instead, eventually leading you to a transport pad in the northeastern section of the level. Now, get ready to face off with General Alma for the third time!

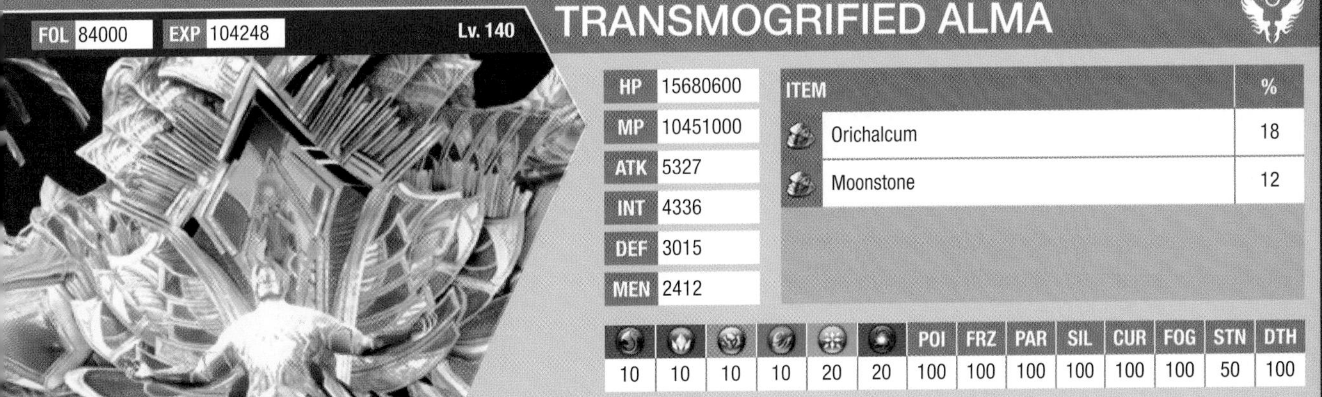

TRANSMOGRIFIED ALMA

FOL	84000	EXP	104248	Lv. 140

HP	15680600
MP	10451000
ATK	5327
INT	4336
DEF	3015
MEN	2412

ITEM	%
Orichalcum	18
Moonstone	12

(Earth)	(Fire)	(Wind)	(Water)	(Light)	(Dark)	POI	FRZ	PAR	SIL	CUR	FOG	STN	DTH
10	10	10	10	20	20	100	100	100	100	100	100	50	100

Your third encounter with the Kronos rebel is a bit different than the first two. General Alma and Feria have now been strongly fused together, resulting in a monstrous divine being. Transmogrified Alma retains a few of his human abilities, such as Bosom Blow. He has relatively high ATK and DEF ratings, so you'll want to have Grilled Steak, Sukiyaki, or Pasta Bolognese here for your choice of food.

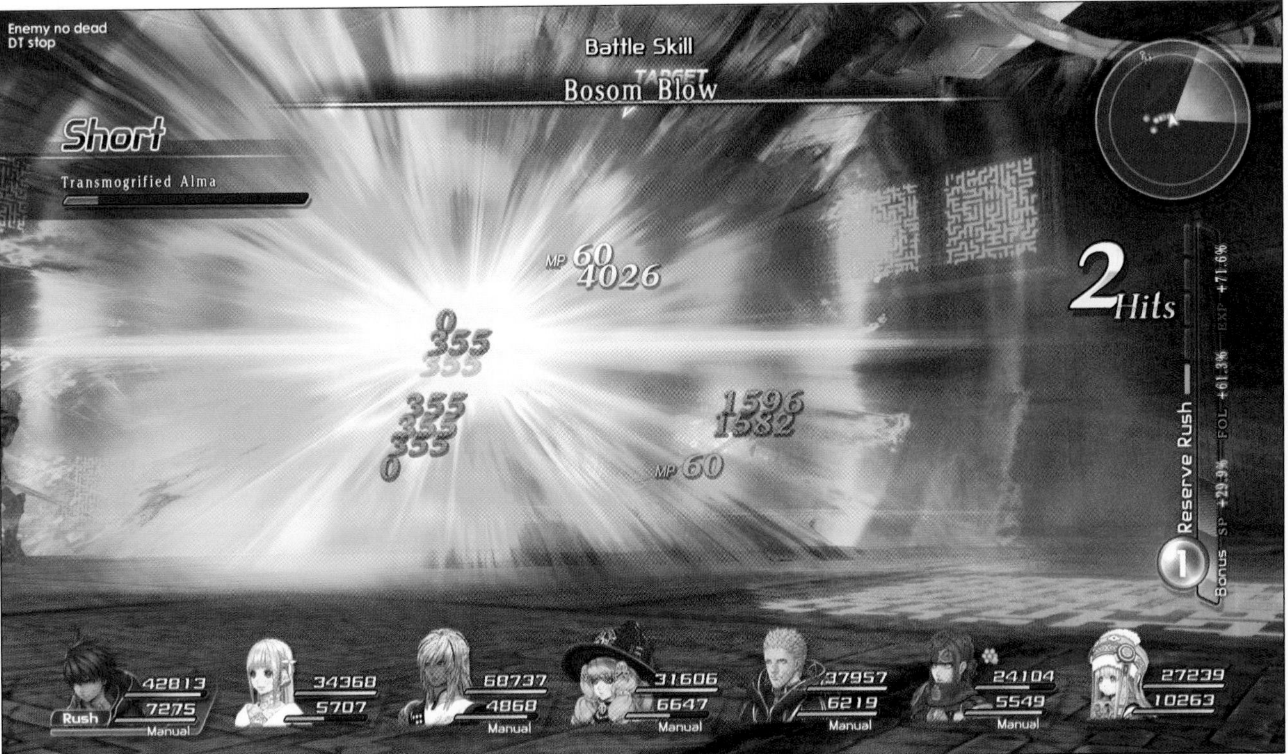

For your roles and battle skills setups, you'll want to go with tried-and-true defensive builds on both Fidel and Victor. Equip Fidel with the God Slayer role and a Reflecting Plate to drastically reduce the damage done to him. For his battle set, equip Air Raid and Mirror Blade. Alma has strong light and dark resistances, so Fiore should be built to deal either wind or ice damage. Arctic Impact and Ice Needles coupled with the Emissary of the Blue Sphere role is effective here. With the Dead Man Walking setup, Anne should be fine because taking 0 damage also nullifies any potential status effects. Emmerson can be on stunning duty, with Stun Supporter, Interceptor, and Daemon roles to effectively keep the abomination dazed and debuffed.

The general has several debilitating ailment-inflicting attacks. Seraphic Rebuke features several projectiles that shoot out and travel around the battlefield, dealing moderate damage and potentially inflicting silence on your members. Alma has access to a combination attack called Baleful Winds. He lunges forward with several lashes, inflicting high damage in a large area in front of him while potentially inflicting fog, freeze, and silence status ailments. Remedy these ailments quickly. While he'll often target non-melee characters with it, his travel speed is quite slow, making it a bit easier to escape from if you're attentive.

The general likes to use a physical drilling attack to damage your close-range fighters and break their guard. Ogrefall is a high-damage slam into the ground, followed by a spinning area-of-effect attack. You can avoid it if you move out of the way fast enough.

Feria will arm Alma with powerful signeturgical abilities, telegraphed by four symbols gradually forming in front of Alma's body. One of these abilities is called Acceleration. Similar to Relia's time freeze ability, it briefly slows down all of your party members. Another one to look out for is called Aggravation, which lowers all elemental resistances on your entire party. It's incurable, but it's manageable for the most part as long as you're able to heal up efficiently. It's possible to break these symbols through high-damage skills so that Alma can never cast these ultimate abilities.

If you don't defeat him quickly, Alma gain access to an ability called Initialization, the last of his symbol-fueled attacks. Initialization itself doesn't do anything at first except warn you of incoming disaster. After a period of time, though, he'll unleash a finishing move called Annihilation, a massively destructive area-of-effect with a radius of about half of the battlefield. It will kill any non-invincible characters within its vicinity, so you'll need to either have your vital healer outside of its detonation or destroy Alma before he can activate it. An effective strategy is to go all out on him while he's stunned by Emmerson's normal attacks, so burn your Reserve Rush gauge efficiently at the end of your combo chains before Alma can unleash Annihilation.

Other abilities he'll have access to during the battle are Angel Feather (which can be dispelled with Fiore's Void), Deflagration (moderate-damage projectiles), and Healing (heals for about 25% of his total HP).

Once you've vanquished the general for the third time, there's a pair of **Kaiser Knuckles** awaiting in the room to the north. These knuckles made of Orichalcum come with a nice ATK+5% bonus for Anne. Equip them, and head back out to the Terpsichorean Genesis lobby.

Terpsichorean Denouement

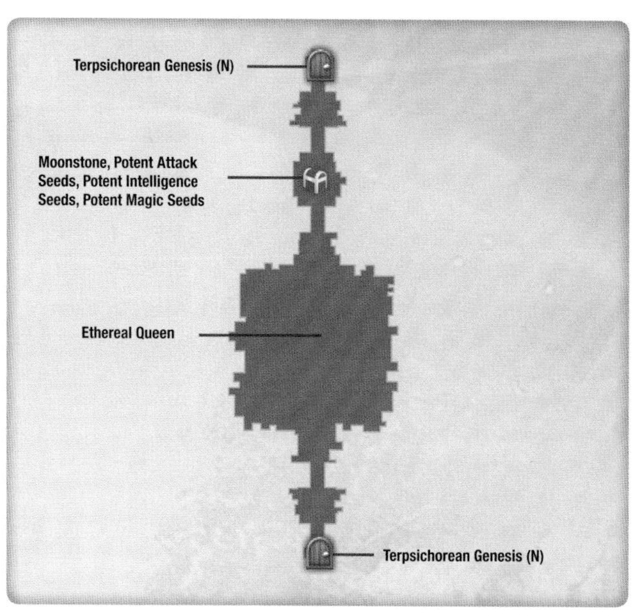

Now that you've defeated the four subarea bosses, prepare for the final challenge with the Ethereal Queen! Save your game now if you haven't done so already, and head to the north part of Terpsichorean Genesis to face the queen of the maze.

HERALD OF RUIN—
THE ETHEREAL QUEEN

The Ethereal Queen makes her return in *Star Ocean: Integrity and Faithlessness.* This iconic super-boss is the ultimate test of your combat skills and provides an extremely difficult challenge. Like Gabriel Celeste, she can be defeated up to three times. With each iteration, her level and attributes increase drastically.

STATS AND DROPS

ETHEREAL QUEEN 1RST ITERATION

HP	39732000	ATK	5529	DEF	3045	FOL	121994
MP	31237000	INT	4163	MEN	2699	EXP	152493

Lv. 180

						POI	FRZ	PAR	SIL	CUR	FOG	STN	DTH
20	5	10	10	20	5	100	100	100	100	100	100	100	100

ITEM	%
Matriarch's Resplendent Plume	80
Moonstone	20

ETHEREAL QUEEN 3RD ITERATION

HP	129600000
MP	83600000
ATK	6309
INT	4874
DEF	3758
MEN	3523
FOL	224500
EXP	305529

Lv. 255

ITEM	%
Matriarch's Resplendent Plume	100
Moonstone	26

						POI	FRZ	PAR	SIL	CUR	FOG	STN	DTH
20	5	10	10	20	5	100	100	100	100	100	100	100	100

ETHEREAL QUEEN 2ND ITERATION

HP	82008000
MP	62826000
ATK	5764
INT	4611
DEF	3529
MEN	3207
FOL	183604
EXP	229505

Lv. 220

ITEM	%
Matriarch's Resplendent Plume	90
Moonstone	24

						POI	FRZ	PAR	SIL	CUR	FOG	STN	DTH
20	5	10	10	20	5	100	100	100	100	100	100	100	100

ETHEREAL QUEEN'S ABILITIES

ANGEL FEATHER (third iteration only)

- Raises ALL stats
- Cast Void to dispel the effect
- In her third iteration, the queen will use this buff instead of Enhance and Enshelter

CELESTIAL STAR

- High-damage area-of-effect spell just outside of point-blank range
- Accessible once Ethereal Queen's HP drops below 35%
- Avoidable by staying near Ethereal Queen or at max distance
- Usually kills anyone inside its blast radius
- If it doesn't kill, can inflict a curse, paralysis, or silence status ailment

DIVINE WAVE

- Full-screen area-of-effect spell with a high startup
- Easily identifiable by a ring of blocks once she casts it
- When unleashed, Divine Wave shoots out with a "shotgun" effect

- At close range, it deals much more damage as multiple projectiles will hit, potentially killing non-tanky characters at this range
- Avoidable by staying as far as possible or standing extremely close to the queen, and also has a chance to miss if your character is standing between projectiles
- Guardable—it's recommended that you open the battle menu and then select one of your low-HP characters to guard it to conserve HP

EMPRESS MASSACRE

- Single-target physical damage skill
- Tank characters with high HP, DEF, or invincibility will usually survive if their health is capped off and her ATK isn't enhanced

ENHANCE

- Raises ATK
- Cast Void to dispel the effect

ENSHELTER

- Raises DEF
- Cast Void to dispel the effect

EXPLOSION (third iteration only)

- Like her second form's Volcanic Burst, she will more than likely target your healer, mage, or ranged attacker
- Almost always kills its target, along with anyone inside the inferno
- Keep party members separated to avoid ultiple deaths
- Miki will only survive this with high HP, high MEN, and the Marshal role equipped
- Ethereal Queen's third iteration uses this attack on your back line instead of Fire Bolt/Volcanic Burst

- A fireball spell that she favors aiming at one of your back line party members
- Not too much of an issue for most characters but can be devastating against weaker members like Miki and Fiore

REFLECTION

- Raises MEN
- Cast Void to dispel the effect

SAPPHIRE PERDITION

- A thin blue beam that travels the entire battlefield
- Deals devastating damage, usually killing even your non-invincible tanks in one shot
- Have your party members split up and away from each other to minimize casualties
- Be ready to raise one or more of your members as soon as you see it fire

SERAPHIC WINGS

- A shield of feathers that revolves around the queen, constantly damaging anyone within melee range
- Keep away from her until the feathers dissipate
- Can be guarded followed by a backdash to prevent further damage
- Sliver of Ruin

- Three-hit physical attack
- Fast, but not too threatening
- Can be guarded, and you can react to the on-screen text if you're fast enough

SUPERNOVA

- An extremely destructive area-of-effect spell centered around the queen
- Ethereal Queen gains access to this spell once her HP depletes below 35%
- Has an instant startup with a gravitational pull before erupting
- Avoid by having all of your non-invincible party members stand far away from the queen
- Be ready to raise or heal anyone caught inside the blast, prioritizing your healers
- If it doesn't kill you, it can inflict a fog or stun status ailment

VOLCANIC BURST (second iteration only)

- A long-range spell that's generally targeted at one of your back line members
- Will most likely kill your healer, so raise them immediately
- Can be avoided by moving when she starts casting it, but this can prove difficult
- Minimize destruction by separating your back line members to prevent multiple deaths
- Ethereal Queen's second iteration uses this attack on your back line instead of Fire Bolt

RECOMMENDED POWER LEVEL & EQUIPMENT

All party members are at least Lv. 180 for the first iteration (Lv. 200 for second, and Lv. 255 for the third)

All roles unlocked, with all specialties available

Restorative consumables stocked, including Blueberry Potions, Blackberry Potions, Fresh Sages, Resurrection Elixirs (requires plenty of Caterpillar Fungi), Vitaliteas, and ailment curatives, Signet Card: Resurrection, Signet Card: Angel Feather+

Augment your gear as best as you can with the resources you have available: preferably ATK+ and Critical Hit+ augments for Anne and Emmerson, DEF+ and MEN+ on Victor and Fidel, MEN+ and HP+ on Miki, and INT+ on Fiore

All Terpsichorean Genesis boss chest weapons equipped and augmented accordingly

Equip best armor available, especially ones with special abilities like Reflecting Plate (-10% damage from divine beings)

Valkyrie's Garb can be synthesized as a 50 quality signeturgical item if synthesized with a Matriarch's Resplendent Plume, and it's recommended for Miki and Fiore if you can get your hands on it

Food: Cheese Fondue OR Gourmet Curry Rice (highly recommended for the queen's third iteration). Can be obtained as a rare synthesis item: 50 quality food

RECOMMENDED PARTY SETUP

Roles

CHARACTER				
Fidel	Whirlwind => Defender	Tri-Ace	God Slayer	Gritty Warrior
Miki	Healer	Crusader	Marshal	Sage
Victor	Vainglory Omega	Stamina Stockpiler	Mentality Maven	Avenger OR Sharpshooter
Fiore	Lightning Strike => Intelligence Indulger	Solar Emissary	Enchanter	Master Tactician
Emmerson	Critical Combatant	Menace => Item Expender	Daemon	Warmonger
Anne	Dead Man Walking	Spendthrift	Attack Advocate	Berserker
Relia	Vivifier	Holy Mother	Terror Knight	War God

Battle Set

CHARACTER	SHORT RANGE ⊗	SHORT RANGE ◎	LONG RANGE ⊗	LONG RANGE ◎
Fidel	Air Raid	Mirror Blade	Air Slash	Air Slash
Miki	Any	Any	Sunflare	Terra Hammer
Victor	Mirror Blade	Bloodstorm Revolution	Flying Guillotine	Dragon Roar
Fiore	Any	Any	Arctic Impact	Thunder Flare
Emmerson	Gravity Bullet	Heavenly Flight	Crescent Wings	Crescent Wings
Anne	Crescent Locus OR Hammer of Might	Hammer of Might OR Infinity Kick	Electric Fists	Hammer of Might

Signeturgy ON

CHARACTER						
Miki	Ex Healing	Faerie Light	Faerie Star	Raise Dead	Resurrection	Cure Condition
Fiore	Healing	Raise Dead	Arctic Impact OR Wind Blade	Thunder Flare	Void	

SETUP EXPLANATIONS

FIDEL

God Slayer helps Fidel survive while dealing much more damage against divine beings like the Ethereal Queen. Air Raid and Mirror Blade are powerful while decently quick enough to build combos reasonably. Eventually, you may need to have Fidel fight from range when the Ethereal Queen gains access to Supernova and Celestial Star, so Air Slash becomes handy. You might have to resort to setting Fidel's AI to manual in the latter portions of the fight. The battle becomes extremely chaotic since being anywhere near the queen ensures death, especially against her second and third iterations.

MIKI

She's purely a healer here, and you probably won't have time to use any of her offensive spells in the latter parts of the battle. Early on, you can go for Sunflare or Terra Hammer for a chance of reducing enemy stats, provided you're not encumbered with healing or raising your allies. First Responder helps keep her alive slightly when she's inevitably hit by the queen's myriad back line projectile attacks. Sage is essential to cut down on her casting times.

VICTOR

With the highest base HP of all of your party members, Victor can utilize Stamina Stockpiler most efficiently. The Sharpshooter role encourages the AI to keep Victor outside of range, but it isn't a surefire way to prevent him from killing himself. Keep an eye on him or set him as your party leader to prevent him from committing suicide in a Supernova. You can swap one of his roles out to Sharpshooter when the queen enrages and starts using Supernova frequently. Even with his massive HP and stacked MEN+ buffs, he'll likely die in a single Supernova, especially in the second and third Ethereal Queen encounters. Additionally, Vainglory Omega fits nicely considering Victor's high HP pool, making it less likely for him to be knocked down when taking damage.

FIORE

Fiore can use a standard offense-based build because of her ability to provide damage and utility from range. Even so, she'll need to prioritize raising and healing members because of the high amount of damage that the Ethereal Queen dishes out. Otherwise, if everyone's health is capped off and you're fortunate enough to have time, you can combo-cast repeated Thunder Flares from the safety of full battlefield distance, scoring high magic damage and a chance of decreasing the queen's ATK power. Alternatively, you can go with a more dark-based damage build using the Moonlight Emissary role with the Dark Devourer signeturgy.

EMMERSON

His normal attacks are quick with the advantage of being ranged, so he's naturally fit to be your primary debuffer. He can apply an extremely powerful DEF and MEN down debuff. Since he's safe at long distances, he's usually alive to revive your knocked-out party members with Fresh Sages and Resurrection Elixirs quickly thanks to the Item Expender role, which you can switch to when the battle becomes more chaotic. This makes him an excellent situation stabilizer if multiple members of your group fall victim to the queen's nasty area-of-effect insta-kill attacks. Additionally, you don't want to equip him with his lengthy attack skills in case you need him to raise or heal someone in a pinch. It's recommended that you stick to using normal attacks and Crescent Wings since they recover much more quickly.

ANNE

With this roles setup, you can never die unless it's on your terms, so pairing Dead Man Walking with Berserker is a no-brainer. Hammer of Might will almost always do 80,000–99,999 damage if your ATK is at 9999 (which is very possible at this stage in the game). Anne's other attack skills have incredibly long animations that don't exactly make for great combo ratio stackers, so avoid them. Hammer of Might and Crescent Lotus are super fast skills for the amount of damage they inflict, allowing you to unleash a 200% Reserve Rush finisher when you're not busy healing and raising your party. Switch to Anne if the situation is stabilized so you can maximize damage output by repeatedly using Hammer of Might => Hammer of Might => Crescent Locus => Crescent Locus OR Blazing Cannon. Alternatively, you can use Hammer of Might in slot 1 and Infinity Kick in slot 2 if you want to conserve Reserve Rush gauge for Miki's healing Reserve Rush. In this instance, use Hammer of Might => Hammer of Might => Hammer of Might => Infinity Kick as your bread-and-butter combo.

RELIA

Vivifier, Holy Mother, and Terror Knight all affect the AI positively for you and negatively for the enemy, so it's ideal for Relia to equip these supporting roles.

As the final encounter in the Maze of Tribulations, the Ethereal Queen will test your knowledge of all of the game's battle mechanics you've learned up to this point. She has incredibly high stats, inflicts damage in multiple ways, and can even terrorize your party with status ailments. Her first iteration, in which she's donning only a single pair of wings, can be a difficult trial for even the most prepared parties.

It's recommended that you've leveled up to at least Lv. 180 and have all SP-related abilities unlocked. You should also have access to all of the weapons gained from completing the previous floor's bosses. If you've been trying your hand at synthesis, you might also have the Gourmet Curry Rice rare food item. If not, you can cook up some Cheese Fondue (MEN+30%) or Grilled Steak (ATK+30%). Additionally, you can refer to the recommended roles setup in the preceding data tables to help you defeat this notoriously arrogant celestial being.

When you're ready, eat up and enter the coliseum to test your might against a god's.

As always, the first thing you'll want to do is take control of Miki, Fiore, and Emmerson and position them as far from the queen as possible. With your defensive abilities set up properly on the other three members, you shouldn't have to worry about them too much.

Attacks to watch out for are Divine Wave and Seraphic Wings. Divine Wave is a high-damage signeturgical spell, blasting out from all sides of the queen. As she readies it, you'll see a circle of light-based projectiles around her before they fire off. These are guardable, so make sure to open the battle menu and select one of your members to guard it (preferably one of your close-range fighters susceptible to being hit by more than one of its projectiles). Most high HP and high MEN-rated party members will survive it if they're hit by a single shot, so heal up accordingly. You should also take control of any damaged close-range fighters to reposition them away from the queen while the AI-controlled Miki heals them.

The queen occasionally casts a spell called Seraphic Wings. It's not a conventional attack. The Ethereal Queen will surround herself with flaming feathers that act as a force field, constantly damaging anyone they make contact with. Like Divine Wave, these are also guardable. You can take control of Fidel or Victor if they're fighting in melee range in order to guard and backdash away from the feathers.

You'll rarely need to take control of Anne, but if you want to speed up the fight and all of your members are healthy, you can use her to perform high-damage combos by chaining together Hammer of Mights. If it's assigned to Anne's power attack (default Circle button) battle set, you can easily score 99999 damage with subsequent hammers. If you prefer to use the Infinity Kick combo finisher, you can use Hammer of Might x 3 into a 200% combo ratio Infinity Kick for an efficient way of dealing damage while building Reserve Rush gauge.

Alternatively, you can take control of Fiore to combo-cast back-to-back Thunder Flares. Her INT can easily reach 9999 at this point, so your spells will do amazing amounts of damage if you manage to get them off at the end of combos. You can either raw cast Thunder Flare x 4, or you can start it off with three normal attacks. For instance, weak attack => strong attack => weak attack => Thunder Flare is a quick way to fire off a 200% Thunder Flare.

While you're fighting, keep an eye on the buffs that the queen casts on herself. She'll occasionally cast Enhance, Enshelter, or Angel Feather (third iteration), so have Fiore counter these with Void when possible. These buffs can make a huge difference when it comes to whether your party members survive certain attacks like Empress Massacre, Fire Bolt, or Volcanic Burst/Explosion in the later iterations.

PUT YOURSELF IN MY SHOES

One of the many advantages of being able to pause with the battle menu is being able to switch up equipment, roles, battle sets, and signeturgical spells. This lets you squeeze out every ounce of advantage you can get in the more difficult encounters, like the Ethereal Queen. For instance, you can totally switch up a character's stats and AI behavior by completely swapping their roles out. You can even replace temporary stat-boosting roles like Lightning Strike and Whirlwind with permanent boosts after the start of a battle.

For the queen's fiery enraged form, you'll most likely want to exchange Fidel's roles, giving the God Slayer role to Victor while leaving Fidel as a ranged attacker with a role like Sharpshooter to encourage his AI to deal damage from a safe distance. Try it out, and utilize these battle menu functions according to the situation you're in!

Keep whittling her health down while keeping up with good party positioning. The queen will occasionally move toward your back line to set up for her destructive area-of-effect attacks. A notable problem you'll face is her propensity to cast fire spells on Miki, Fiore, or Emmerson. Fire Bolt can instantly kill Miki due to her lower HP pool, so be ready to heal or raise her if the need arises.

If at any time you have multiple party members down, open the battle menu and raise everyone accordingly. Remember that items have a cooldown limit (unless you have the Item Expender role equipped), so you'll want to spread out your raising actions. Fiore can cast Raise Dead while you get one item use at any given time. Your raise priority should be Miki, Anne, Fiore, then Emmerson.

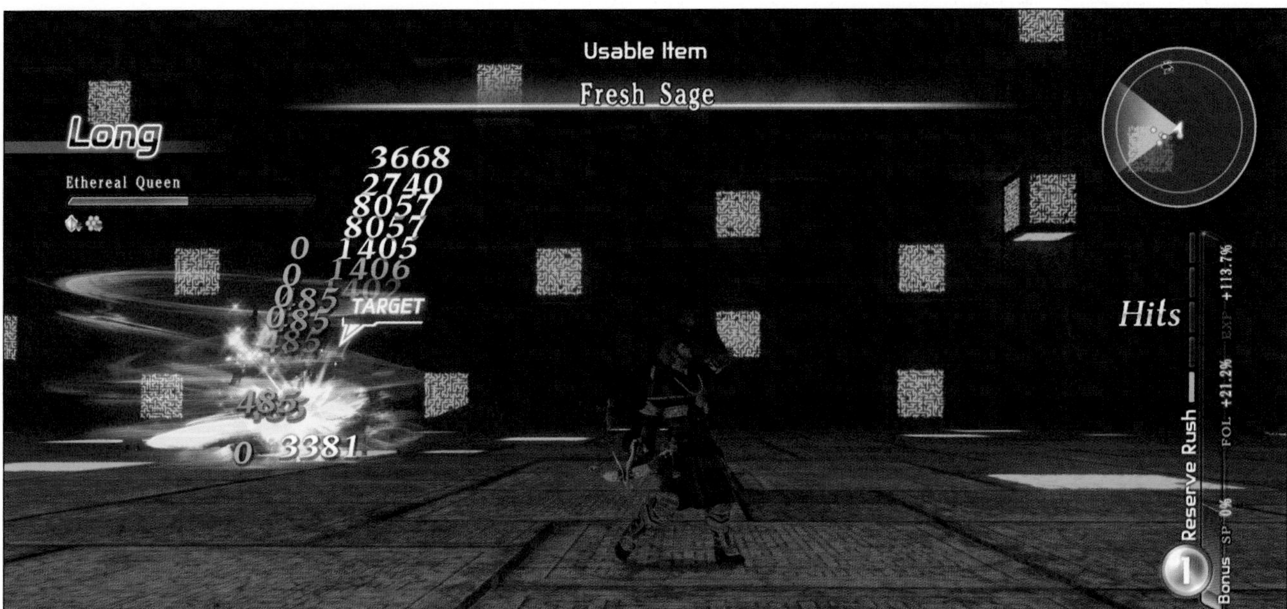

At lower health (35% of her total HP), the Ethereal Queen enrages, evident by an engulfing flame surrounding her. This signals the real challenge of the battle, where she obtains her two most destructive abilities: Celestial Star and Supernova. It's recommended here that you start to switch up your party's roles so that Fidel becomes primarily a ranged attacker and Victor becomes your God Slayer tank. This gives Victor much-needed survivability against Supernova while keeping Fidel safe and useful with his quick repeated Air Slash combos from a distance.

THIS ISN'T EVEN MY FINAL FORM!

Unlike the rest of the maze's bosses, Gabriel Celeste and the Ethereal Queen will come back stronger than before. The strategies here still apply, except these fights become less forgiving and much longer. Considering these two celestial beings enrage when they're at low health, their extremely high HP totals become a straining hurdle to get over. For instance, the third queen's enraged form still has roughly 45 million HP—almost as much as the first queen's *entire* health pool! It's a true test of your fortitude.

If you're fighting against the second and third iterations of the queen, you'll notice that Fire Bolt is replaced by Volcanic Burst and Explosion, respectively. These are devastating area-of-effect spells and will most likely kill Miki in one cast. Keep your members separated to help minimize deaths, and raise your members accordingly, especially during the last portion of the battle. If things become extremely dire and multiple members go down, you can use one Robust Vitalitea or three Vitaliteas in conjunction with Item Expender to have Miki unleash her Lv. 3 Arcadia, healing and raising all allies on the battlefield.

Keep it up, and you'll eventually be successful in humbling the queen. Your reward for defeating her in the north room is a chest containing several items: a **Moonstone**, **Potent Attack Seeds**, **Potent Intelligence Seeds**, and **Potent Magic Seeds**. Congratulations! If you'd like to challenge these deities again, you can exit the maze with the Communicator Model G and re-enter through the Charles D. Goale G's transporter.

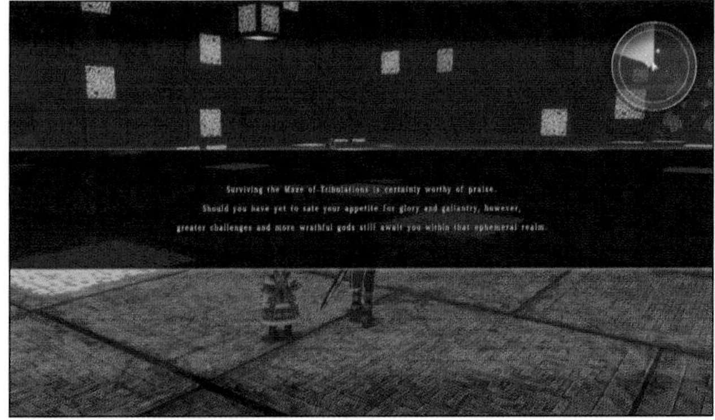

OPTIONAL TASKS

Players are introduced to optional tasks called side quests when they either visit Welch in Myiddok or interact with a bulletin board for the first time.

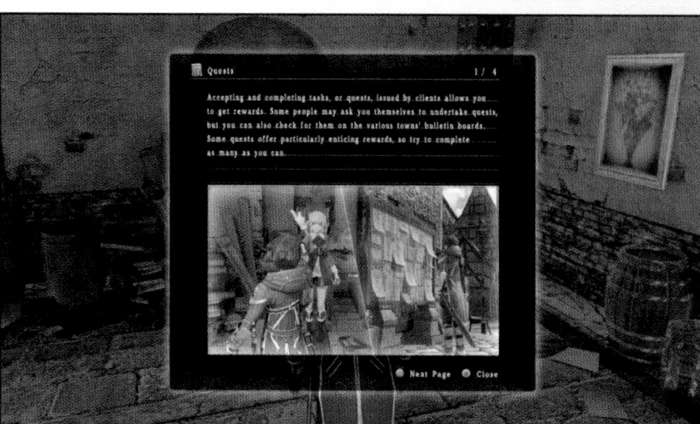

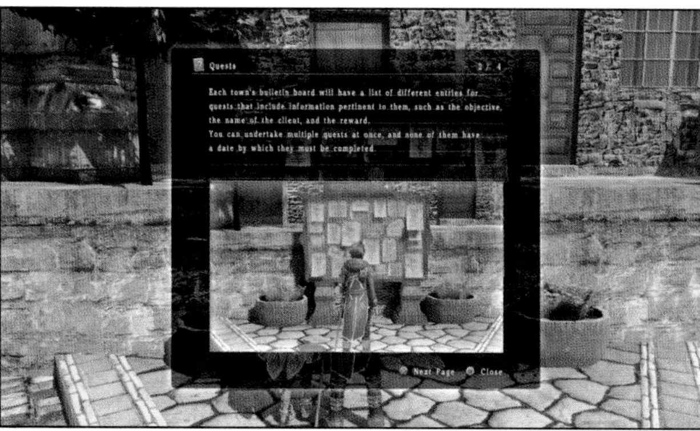

Whenever there's a new Welch quest available and the player visits Welch's Laboratory, the quest is automatically added to the quest log.

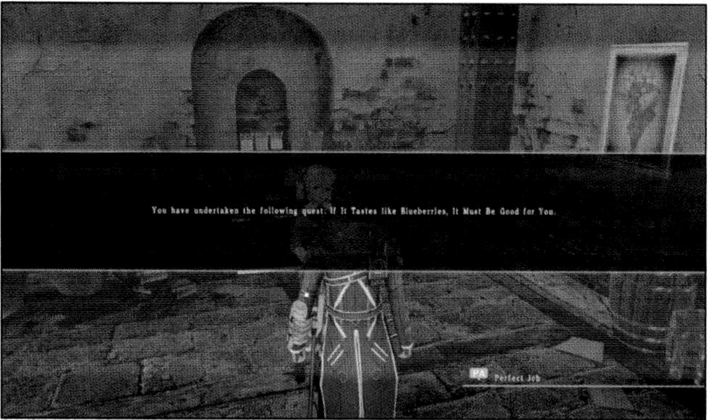

Bulletin board quests must be accepted by pressing the Confirm button (default ⊗) while browsing the bulletin board listing.

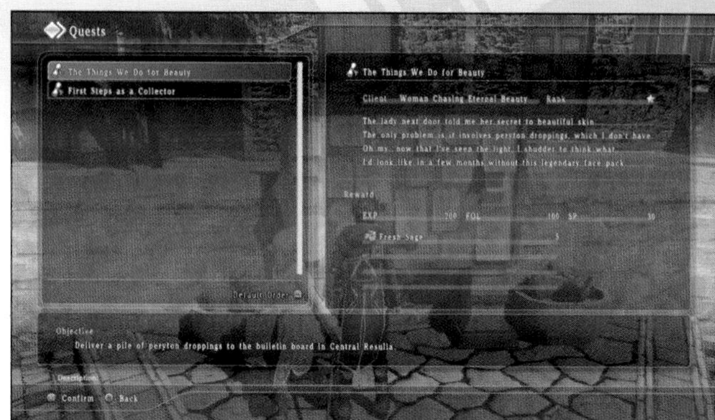

Most quests fall into one of two categories (item collection and monster hunting), with a third type of unique quest involving a manhunt. When undertaken, monster-hunting quests spawn uniquely named enemies in their respective areas. This means that regardless of how far into the story you are, you can still complete the quest.

Quests may also have prerequisites before becoming available, such as required progress through the main story. Some require completion of preceding quests before they appear on a bulletin board.

Completing quests rewards the player with valuable EXP, FOL, SP, and items. A few quests also unlock specialty skills, which can be purchased with SP in the Specialties Skills menu.

The following quest list is sorted by the in-game's default quest log order (Welch's Laboratory > Central Resulia > Santeroule > Eastern Trei'kur).

WELCH'S LABORATORY

Q001—If It Tastes like Blueberries, It Must Be Good for You

REWARD

EXP	100	SP
100	100	30
ITEMS		
Compounding the Issue (unlocks Compounding specialty), Blueberry Potion		

WALKTHROUGH

Prerequisites: None

Blueberries can be purchased at any consumables shop. You can also find them in chests littered across Faykreed or obtain them from harvesting nodes.

Q002—Drunk on Creation

REWARD

EXP	FOL	SP
300	150	75
ITEMS		
Just Enough Cooks (unlocks Cooking specialty), Fishing: An Alluring Pastime (unlocks Fishing specialty), Lemon Juice		

WALKTHROUGH

Prerequisites: Complete If It Tastes like Blueberries, It Must Be Good for You

Lemons and bottles of Spring Water can be bought from the grocer in Myiddok. You can also find Lemons in the chest near Myiddok's inn.

Q003—Brute Strength of Blacksmithing

REWARD

EXP	FOL	SP
500	400	80
ITEMS		
Smithing the Night Away (unlocks Smithery specialty), Dig Deep Within (unlocks Excavation specialty)		

WALKTHROUGH

Prerequisites: Complete Drunk on Creation

Iron can be dug up from excavation nodes. Additionally, you can find three in a chest in the Passage on the Cliffs on your way to Myiddok. Wooden Sticks can be harvested from harvesting points or bought from the material vendor in Myiddok.

Q004—The End of Welch's Laboratory!?

REWARD

EXP	FOL	SP
800	300	100
ITEMS		
We All Scream For Alchemy (unlocks Alchemy specialty), Alchemist's Water x 3		

WALKTHROUGH

Prerequisites: Complete Brute Strength of Blacksmithing, progress to at least Chapter 3

This quest requires defeating two named enemies in the Dakaav Footpath. Find Tinat of the Dawning Light on a platform in between two bridges on the east side of the area.

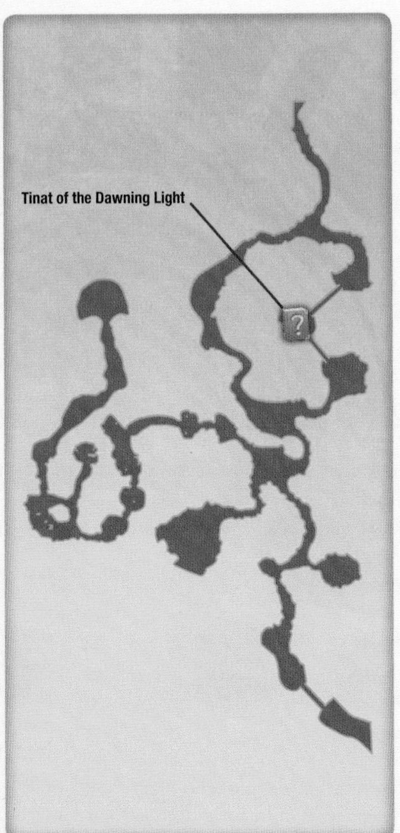

Find Uen of the Midnight Wail at the waterfall where you previously encountered Eitalon's Leader.

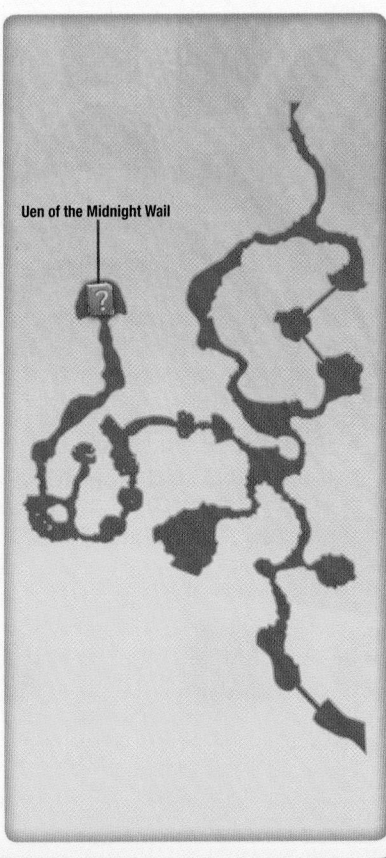

Q005—Grand Designs

REWARD

EXP	FOL	SP
1100	700	125

ITEMS
Crafty Crafting Techniques (unlocks Crafting specialty), Mind Bracelet

WALKTHROUGH

Prerequisites: Complete The End of Welch's Laboratory!?, progress to at least Chapter 4, have Fiore in the party

You can find pieces of Silver and Ruby at certain excavation points, such as from the mining nodes in West of the Eastern Eihieds. Sheets of Silk can be obtained from enemies or simply bought from the material vendor in Myiddok.

Q006—Happy Fun Bunny Time

REWARD

EXP	FOL	SP
1600	1000	150

ITEMS
Intro to Intelligent Item Design (unlocks Synthesis specialty), Vitalitea x 3, Unlocks Bunny role

WALKTHROUGH

Prerequisites: Complete Grand Designs, progress to at least Chapter 4

This quest requires the Cooking specialty leveled since you need to cook up five Bunnylicious Pies. The ingredients for the pie, Wheat Flour and Nectar, can be found at the grocer in Santeroule. Find Red Fruit and Green Fruit on enemies or obtain them from harvesting points.

Q007—Of Weapons and Womanizers

REWARD

EXP	FOL	SP
2000	1300	180

ITEMS
The Little Engineer That Could (unlocks Engineering specialty), Healing Device x 3

WALKTHROUGH

Prerequisites: Complete Happy Fun Bunny Time, progress to at least Chapter 7, have Emmerson in the party

Micro Circuits can be found as drops from various machine-type enemies, as well as purchased from Atoms R Us Provisions aboard the Charles D. Goale.

Q008—Behavioral Study

REWARD

EXP	FOL	SP
4000	2500	250

ITEMS
The Pen Is Mightier (unlocks Authoring specialty), Parchment

WALKTHROUGH

Prerequisites: Complete Of Weapons and Womanizers, progress to at least Chapter 8

The key item that Welch is looking for is dropped off a named enemy in the middle of the Trei'kuran Dunes.

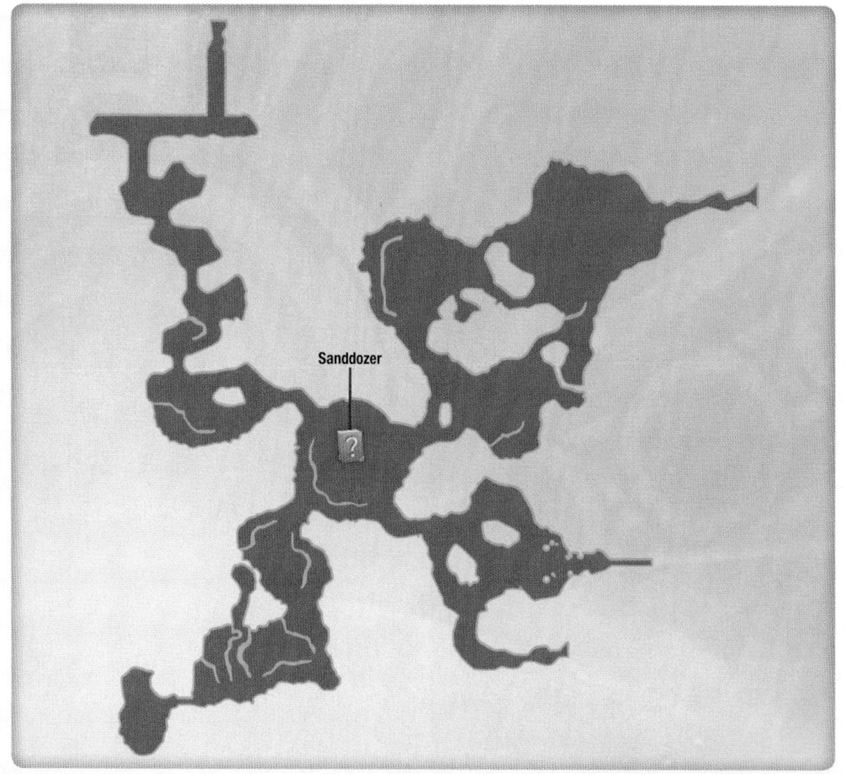

Q009—Keys to the Present in the Past

REWARD

EXP	FOL	SP
6000	5000	280

ITEMS
Equipped to Handle Anything (unlocks Whetting and Fortification specialties), Heroism Potion

WALKTHROUGH

Prerequisites: Complete Behavioral Study, progress to at least Chapter 10

The Erstwhile Ultimate Sword is obtained by defeating a group of enemies located at the west end of the Northern Territory of Sohma.

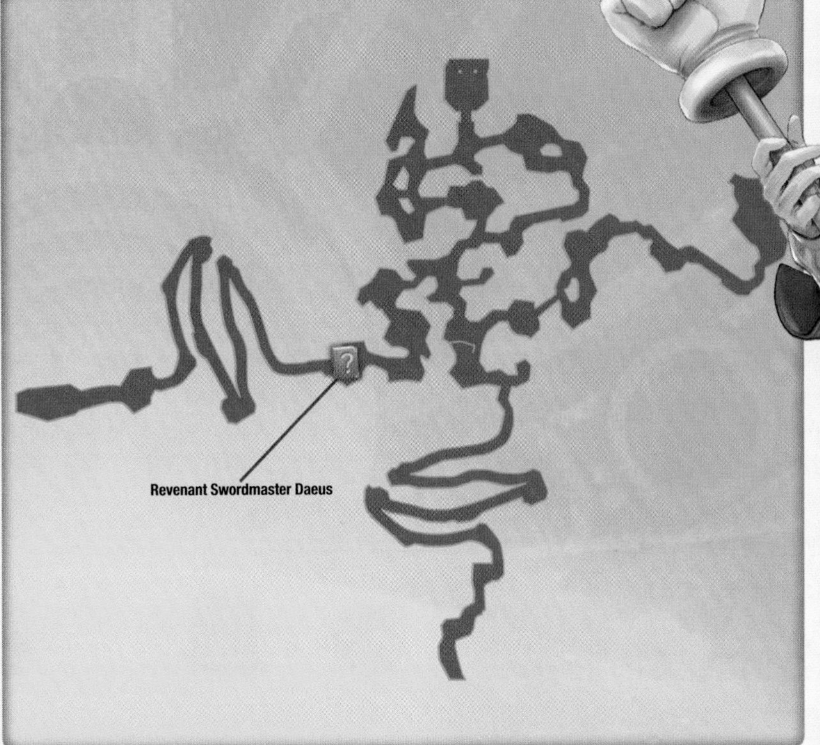

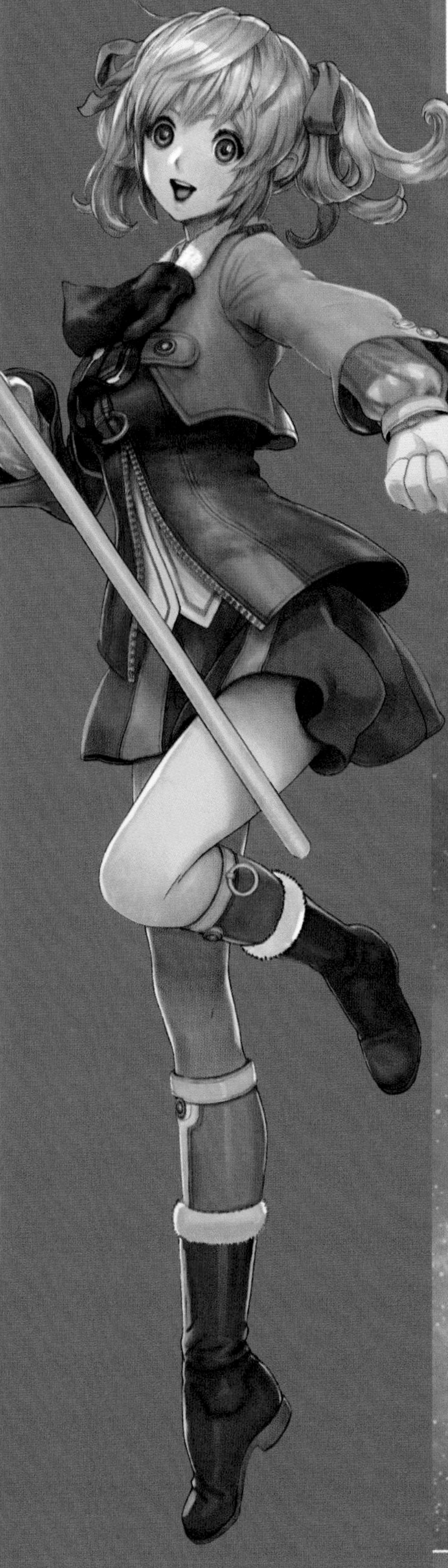

Q010—Find Ruddle!

REWARD

EXP	FOL	SP
800	400	100
ITEMS		
Earth Charm		

WALKTHROUGH

Prerequisites: Progress to at least Chapter 3

Tips on finding Ruddle are displayed on the in-game mini-map, indicated by a yellow star. First, talk to the residents of Ye Grand Ole Castle of Comfort in Central Resulia. Then, speak to the drunk man (or one of the vendors) in Myiddok. The next clue is in the Infirmary in Sthal. The last step is finding Ruddle shopping for wares in Central Resulia along the western alley.

Q011—Mother's Medicine

REWARD

EXP	FOL	SP
550	500	100
ITEMS		
Energy Amulet		

WALKTHROUGH

Prerequisites: Progress to at least Chapter 3

You can create a vial of Physical Stimulant using the Compounding specialty, or find it in a chest in the Resulian Plains.

Q012—Trauma to Go

REWARD

EXP	FOL	SP
600	600	100
ITEMS		
Solar Signets, Vol. 1, Seasonings x 2		

WALKTHROUGH

Prerequisites: Progress to at least Chapter 3

Vegetable Stir-Fry and Fried Fish can be crafted with the Cooking specialty (Lv. 3).

Q013—Birthday Boy

REWARD

EXP	FOL	SP
1000	500	125
ITEMS		
Scale Mail		

WALKTHROUGH

Prerequisites: Progress to at least Chapter 4

Hunks of Iron can be dug up at excavation points, while Wind Gems are found on certain enemies (such as Blightcaps and the Eyebalone).

Q014—The Things We Do for Beauty

REWARD

EXP	FOL	SP
200	100	30
ITEMS		
Fresh Sage x 5		

WALKTHROUGH

You can obtain Peryton Droppings from failed Synthesis recipes (similar to Bunny Droppings) or from Peryton enemies residing in the Resulian Plains.

Q015—Cat Cozy

REWARD

EXP	FOL	SP
300	250	75
ITEMS		
Fire Gem x 2		

WALKTHROUGH

Prerequisites: Progress to at least Chapter 3

Tortoise Shells drop from the Horned Tortoise in the Passage on the Cliffs.

Q016—Shiny, Shiny Scales!

REWARD

EXP	FOL	SP
700	600	100
ITEMS		
X Marks the Spot, Anti-stun Amulet		

WALKTHROUGH

Prerequisites: Progress to at least Chapter 3

Fish Scales are dropped from defeated fish-type enemies off the Coast of Minoz and the Passage on the Cliffs.

Q017—First Steps as a Collector

REWARD

EXP	FOL	SP
200	200	30
ITEMS		
Attack Crest		

WALKTHROUGH

Excavate Iron from various mining nodes, find it in chests, or collect it as a reward from The Sweet Smell of Collection. Lizard Soldiers in the Resulian Plains also drop Iron.

Q018—The Sweet Smell of Collection

REWARD

EXP	FOL	SP
350	200	75

ITEMS
Iron x 4

WALKTHROUGH

Prerequisites: Progress to at least Chapter 3

You can simply buy Nectar from the grocery vendor in Myiddok, or collect it when it drops off of slain bee-like monsters in the Resulian Plains.

Q019—Collection: The Cure for Youthful Fears

REWARD

EXP	FOL	SP
1200	550	125

ITEMS
Wind Charm

WALKTHROUGH

Prerequisites: Progress to at least Chapter 4

You can find Red Fruit from harvesting points around the world or buy it from Ruddle (if you've completed his entire quest line).

Q020—The Four Stooges

REWARD

EXP	FOL	SP
800	500	100

ITEMS
Swordsman's Manual V

WALKTHROUGH

Prerequisites: Progress to at least Chapter 3

Defeat the invaders in the Camuze Training Hall located in Sthal near the start of the game.

Q021—Subjugation Directive: Gileeghas

REWARD

EXP	FOL	SP
300	100	30

ITEMS
Insectopedia (unlocks Entomology specialty)

WALKTHROUGH

Prerequisites: Progress to at least Chapter 3

You can find Keen-Eyed Gileeghas at various points in the Passage on the Cliffs.

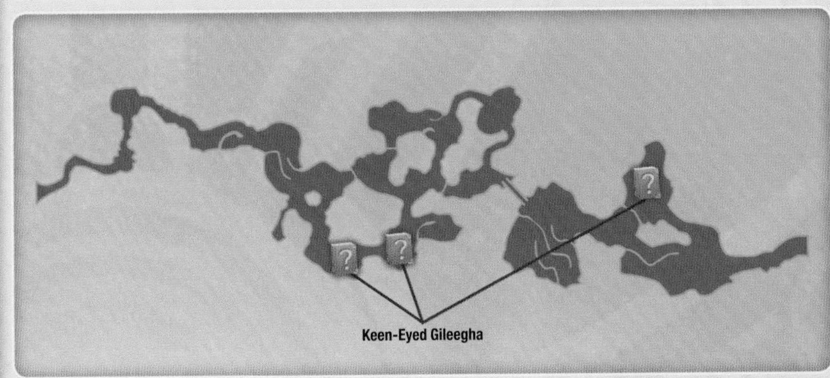

Q022—Subjugation Directive: Lnkyri

REWARD

EXP	FOL	SP
400	200	30
ITEMS		
Arcane Crest		

WALKTHROUGH

Prerequisites: Progress to at least Chapter 3

You can find Glaciating Lnkyri at various points in the Coast of Minoz.

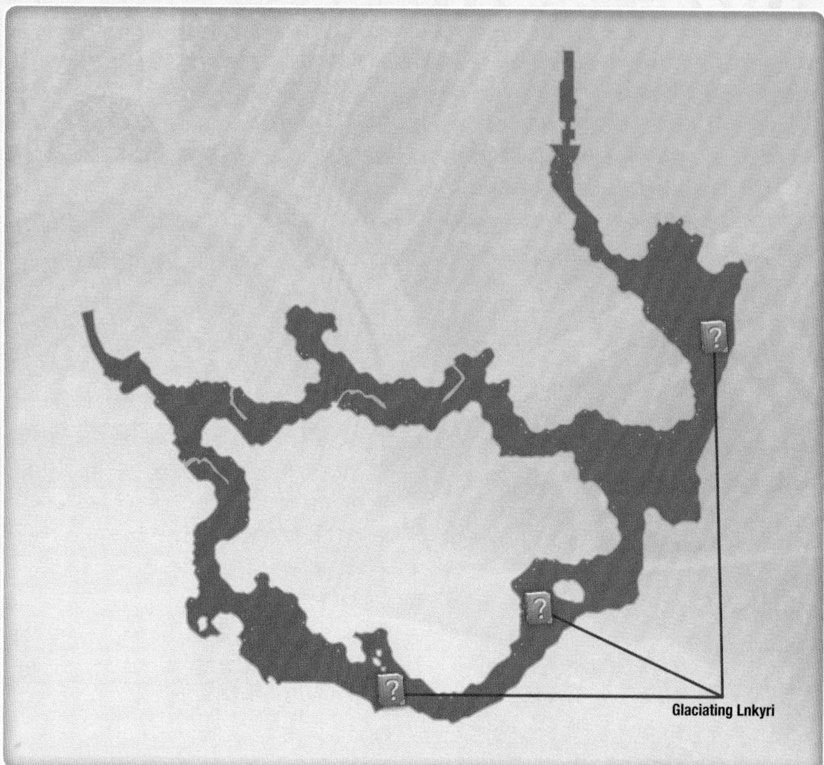

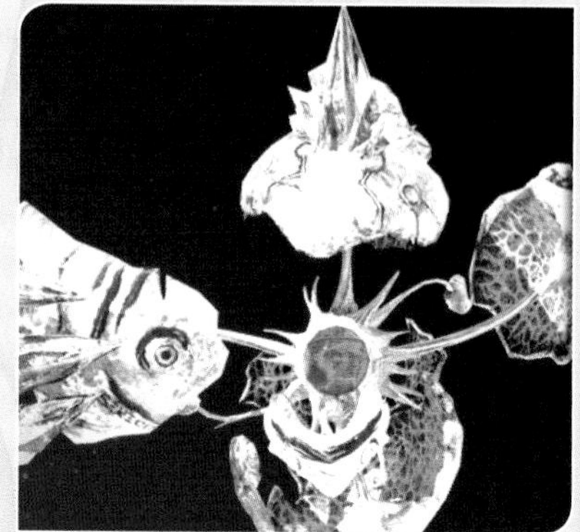

Q023—Subjugation Directive: Dek

REWARD

EXP	FOL	SP
500	250	100
ITEMS		
Broadening Your Horizons (unlocks Lookout specialty), Vegetable Stir-Fry		

WALKTHROUGH

Prerequisites: Progress to at least Chapter 3

The named Corrupt, Dek of the Boiling Blood, can be found near the center of the Resulian Plains.

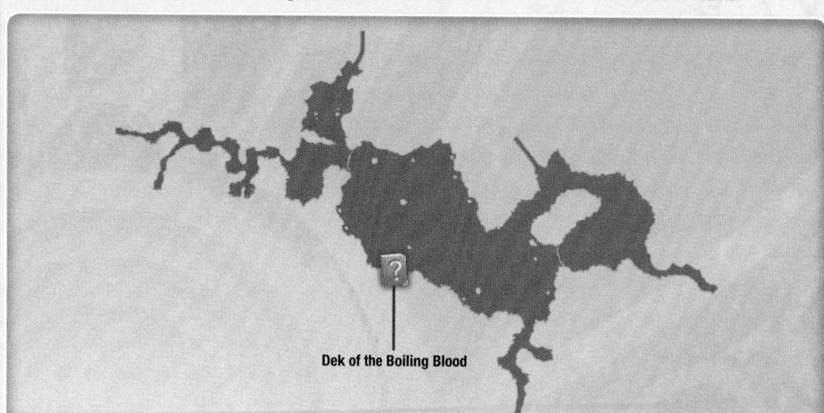

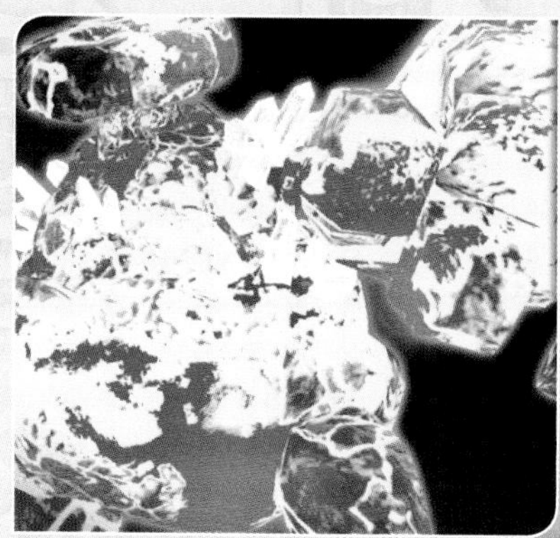

Q024—Subjugation Directive: Gargans

REWARD

EXP	FOL	SP
500	200	100
ITEMS		
The Best Bestiary, Bar None (unlocks Zoology specialty), Blueberries x 5		

WALKTHROUGH

Prerequisites: Progress to at least Chapter 4

Twin-Fanged Gargans are found in the Dakaav Footpath, near the center of the map.

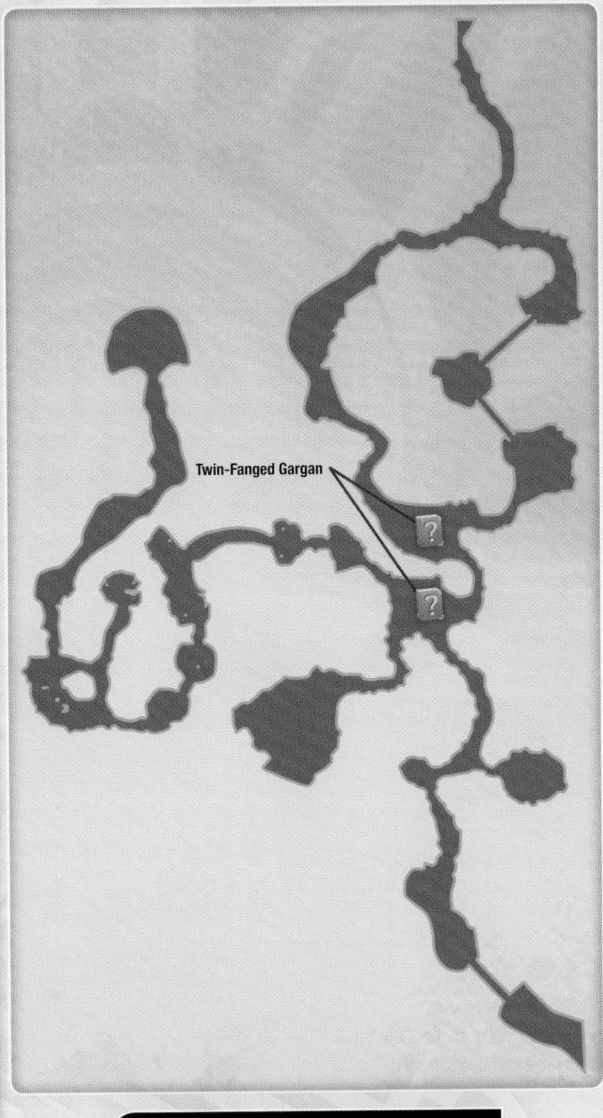

Q025—Subjugation Directive: Magvors

REWARD

EXP	FOL	SP
1000	600	125
ITEMS		
Plants & Pictures (unlocks Botany specialty), Diligence Potion		

WALKTHROUGH

Prerequisites: Progress to at least Chapter 4,
complete Subjugation Directive: Gargans

You can find Corpulent Magvors littered around the Dakaav Footpath's east paths.

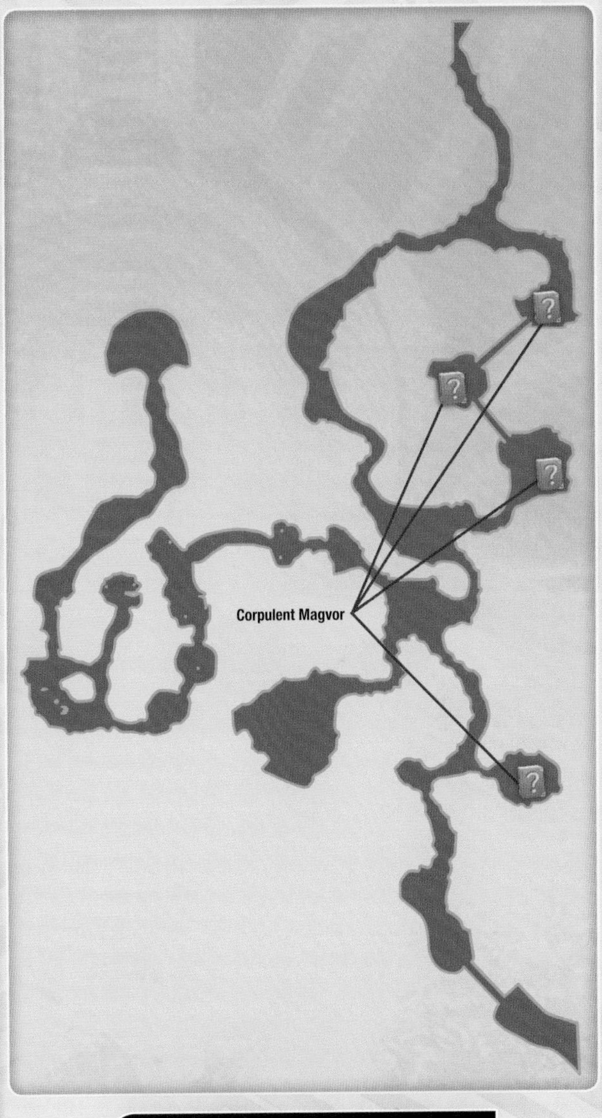

Q026—Corruption of the Land

REWARD

EXP	FOL	SP
500	150	100
ITEMS		
Purification Signets, Vol. 1		

WALKTHROUGH

Prerequisites: Progress to at least Chapter 4, complete Subjugation Directive: Dek

These two enemy types are located in the Resulian Plains. One spawn point is just outside of Central Resulia's southwest exit, while the other points are along the southern portion, near the center of the map.

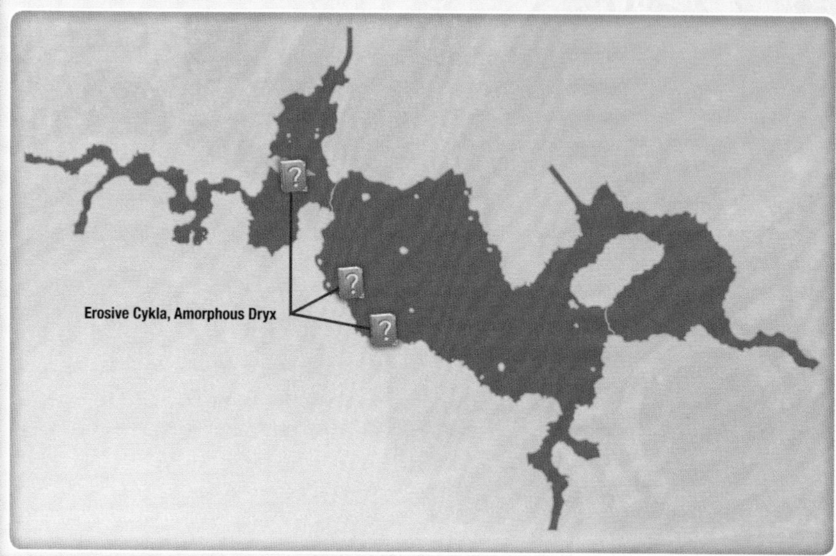

Q027—Wanted: The Skoudde Brothers

REWARD

EXP	FOL	SP
1500	600	125
ITEMS		
Darkness Gem x 2		

WALKTHROUGH

Prerequisites: Progress to at least Chapter 4, complete Corruption of the Land

You can find these lizardmen in the western half of the Resulian Plains, accessed through the southwest exit from Central Resulia.

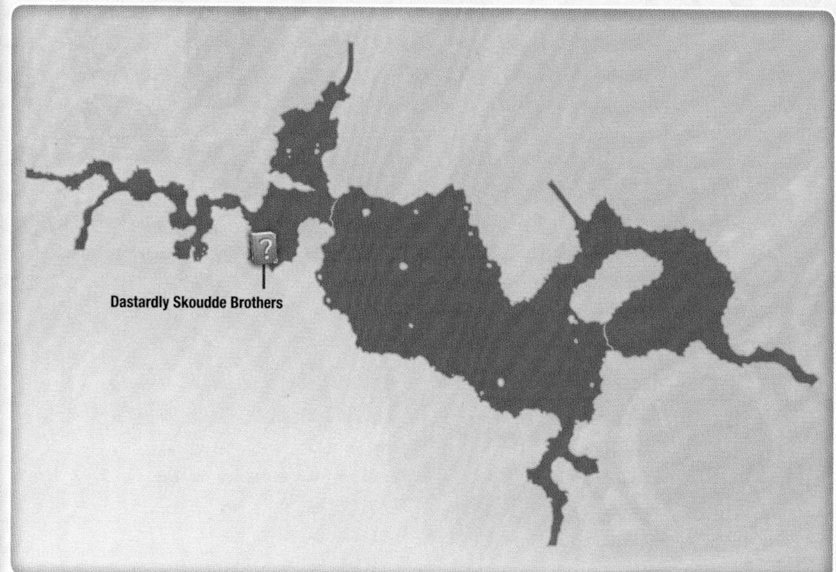

Q028—Batting 1.000 Against Luck Suckers

REWARD

EXP	FOL	SP
400	200	75

ITEMS
Kindred Spirits (unlocks Augury specialty), Fire Charm

WALKTHROUGH

Prerequisites: Progress to at least Chapter 3

These bat-like avians plague the Dakaav Footpaths caves, as well as the western path near the entrance to the Resulian Plains.

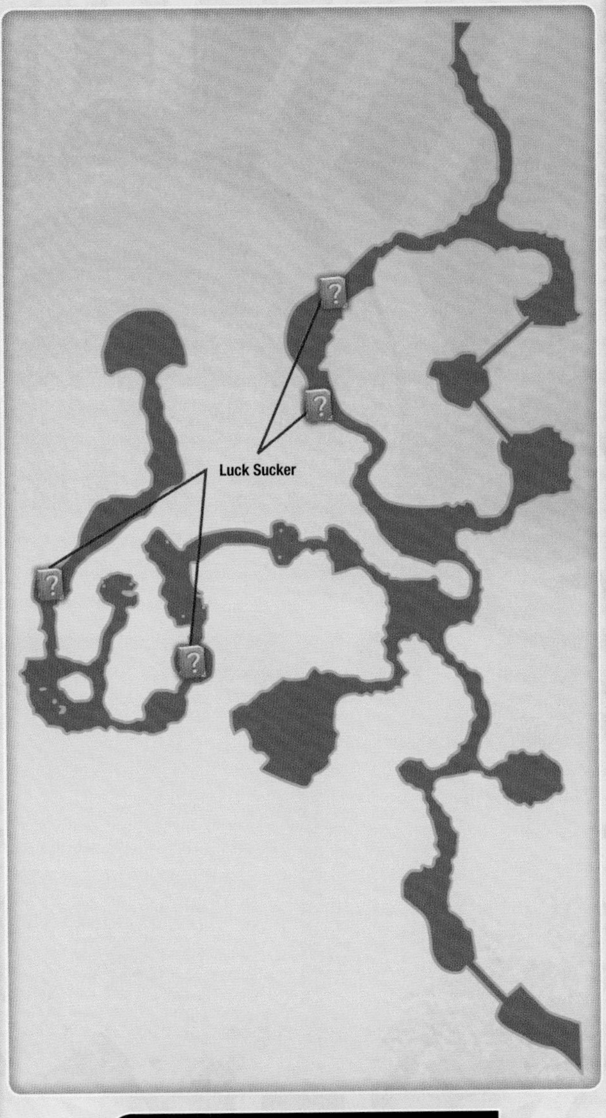

Q029—Give Back that Bonus

REWARD

EXP	FOL	SP
700	700	100

ITEMS
Anti-poison Amulet

WALKTHROUGH

Prerequisites: Progress to at least Chapter 3, complete Subjugation

Directive: Lnkyri

This interestingly named harpy creature is found along the northern path, near the entrance to the Passage on the Cliffs.

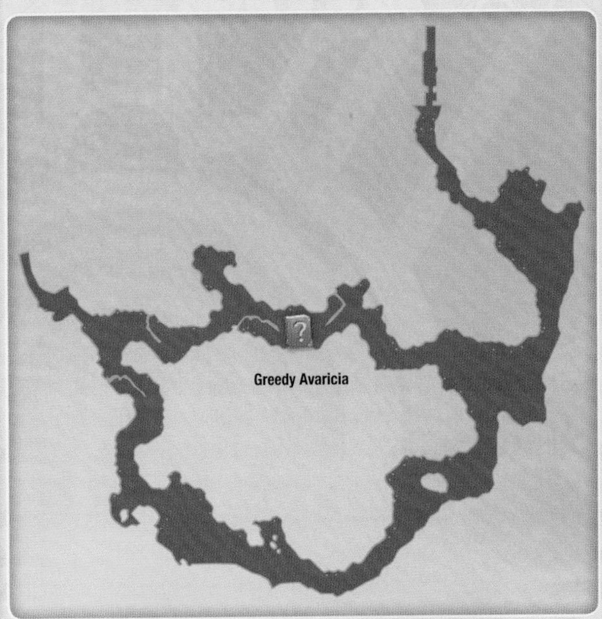

PART 05

Q030—Building Character into Your Crafts

REWARD

EXP	FOL	SP
1500	1200	150
ITEMS		
Earth Gem x 3		

WALKTHROUGH

Prerequisites: Progress to at least Chapter 5

Lizardmen in the Resulian Plains commonly drop lizardskins. Oak can be dug up from harvesting points (and is a drop from tree enemies, like the Treant). High-Strength Adhesive can be crafted with at least Alchemy upgraded to Lv. 2.

Q031—Enrollment Gift

REWARD

EXP	FOL	SP
2100	1650	180
ITEMS		
Anti-paralysis Amulet		

WALKTHROUGH

Prerequisites: Progress to at least Chapter 6

Obtain Crystals by defeating Damascus Fort enemies in the Western Dakaav Tunnel. Purchase sheets of Silk from the materials vendor in Myiddok. Thieving Scumbags in the Resulian Plains drop Dwarven Embroidery Thread.

Q032—Reconstructing an Enigma

REWARD

EXP	FOL	SP
2700	1850	200
ITEMS		
Nuts and Bolts (unlocks Mechanology specialty)		

WALKTHROUGH

Prerequisites: Progress to at least Chapter 7

Valiant Conscripts in the Kronos spaceship, Alcazar of the Golden Age, drop Laser Oscillators. One instance of this item is found in a chest on the Cavaliero.

Q033—By the Skin of His False Teeth

REWARD

EXP	FOL	SP
1100	500	125
ITEMS		
How to Express Yourself (unlocks Emoter specialty), Gold x 2		

WALKTHROUGH

Prerequisites: Progress to at least Chapter 4

Wolf Fangs are common items from the wolf-like beasts in the Resulian Plains.

Q034—Feeling Fuzzy All Over

REWARD

EXP	FOL	SP
2200	1350	180
ITEMS		
Acuity Amulet		

WALKTHROUGH

Prerequisites: Progress to at least Chapter 6

Fluffy Fur is dropped from wolves like the Unicorn Wolf in the Resulian Plains.

Q035—Emblematic of Knighthood

REWARD

EXP	FOL	SP
4000	2900	260
ITEMS		
Attack Bracelet		

WALKTHROUGH

Prerequisites: Progress to at least Chapter 9

Dragons like the Ash Dragon and Bane Dragon encountered in the latter portions of the game drop Dragon Hides.

Q036—Collecting Coal for the Fire

REWARD

EXP	FOL	SP
1700	1500	150
ITEMS		
Light Charm		

WALKTHROUGH

Prerequisites: Progress to at least Chapter 5

Coal is most easily found from mining points in the Western Dakaav Tunnel. There are a few instances of Coal in treasure chests, as well, but you'll probably need to excavate the majority of the seven pieces required.

Q037—Resulian Beauty: Collector's Edition

REWARD

EXP	FOL	SP
2300	1400	180
ITEMS		
Ice Gem x 3		

WALKTHROUGH

Prerequisites: Progress to at least Chapter 6

Zephyr Lilies are drops from plant-type monsters like the Man Trap and Welwitschia found in the second half of the main story.

Q038—Collection of Romantic Entanglements

REWARD

EXP	FOL	SP
2900	2000	200

ITEMS
Darkness Charm

WALKTHROUGH

Prerequisites: Progress to at least Chapter 7

Moon Pearls are drops from the Amber Princess in the Northern Territory of Sohma. They appear in the latter portions of the main story.

Q039—Survive This!

REWARD

EXP	FOL	SP
3000	1900	200

ITEMS
Under Lock and Keynote (unlocks Lockpicking specialty), Stink Fish

WALKTHROUGH

Prerequisites: Progress to at least Chapter 7

Eitalon Higher-Up Survivors are found in groups with other Eitalon forces in the Passage on the Cliffs.

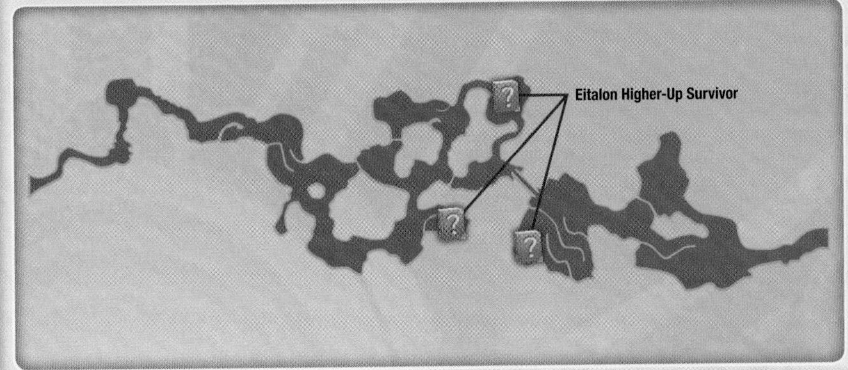

Q040—The Four Stooges Strike Again

REWARD

EXP	FOL	SP
2200	1400	180

ITEMS
People of All Stripes (unlocks Anthropology specialty)

WALKTHROUGH

Prerequisites: Progress to at least Chapter 6, complete The Four Stooges

Round two of this quest line involves the same four foes, except they've come back with a bit more training under their belts. Find them in the Camuze Training Hall, and chase them out with a beating.

Q041—Subjugation Directive: Napto

REWARD

EXP	FOL	SP
1800	1100	150
ITEMS		
Arcane Amulet, Minestrone x 2		

WALKTHROUGH

Prerequisites: Progress to at least Chapter 5, complete Give Back that Bonus

This named phantom is found haunting an alcove along the upper paths (near the entrance to the Passage on the Cliffs) in the Coast of Minoz.

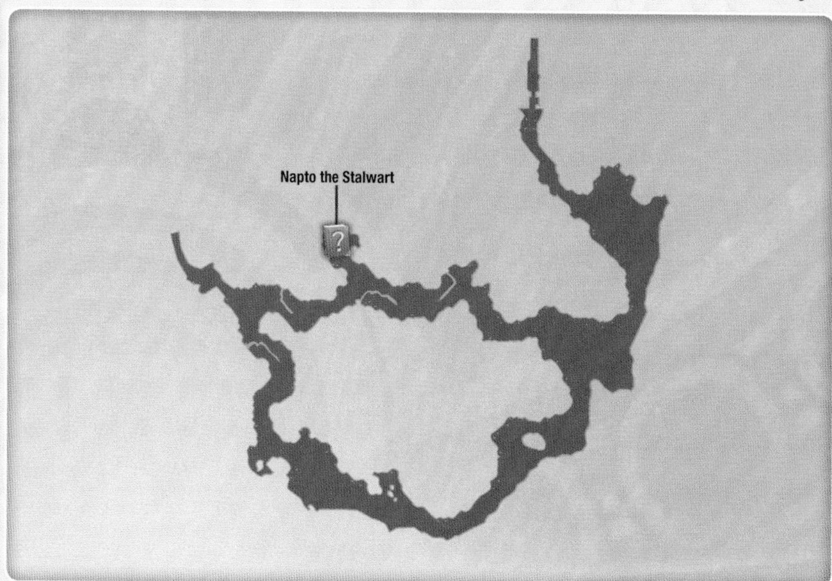

Q042—Subjugation Directive: Moogmorts

REWARD

EXP	FOL	SP
1700	1500	150
ITEMS		
Birds Illustrated (unlocks Ornithology specialty), Fried Fish x 2		

WALKTHROUGH

Prerequisites: Progress to at least Chapter 5

Find these winged creatures in flocks around the northern region of the Northern Territory of Sohma.

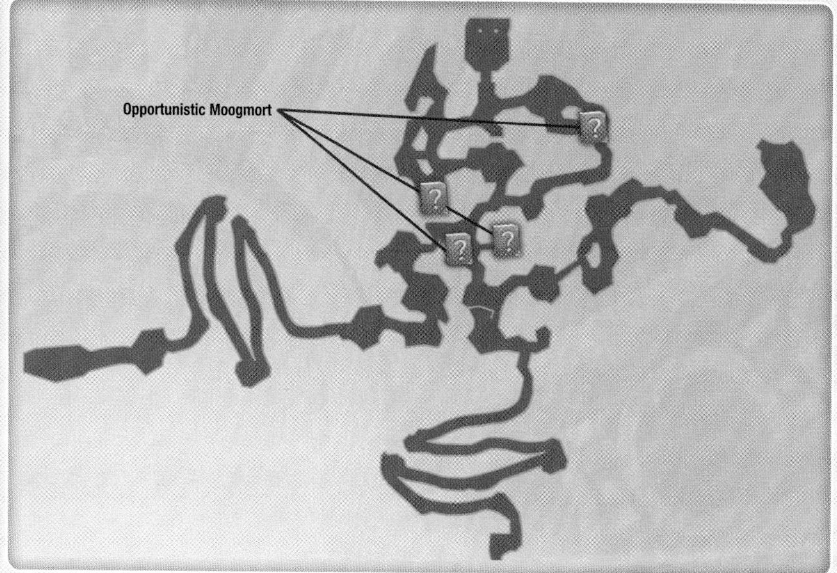

Q043—Subjugation Directive: Pargyns

REWARD

EXP	FOL	SP
2500	1400	180

ITEMS
CQC Program Gamma, Curry Rice x 2

WALKTHROUGH

Prerequisites: Progress to at least Chapter 8

Underhanded Pargyns are fledgling demons found near the center of the Western Dakaav Tunnel.

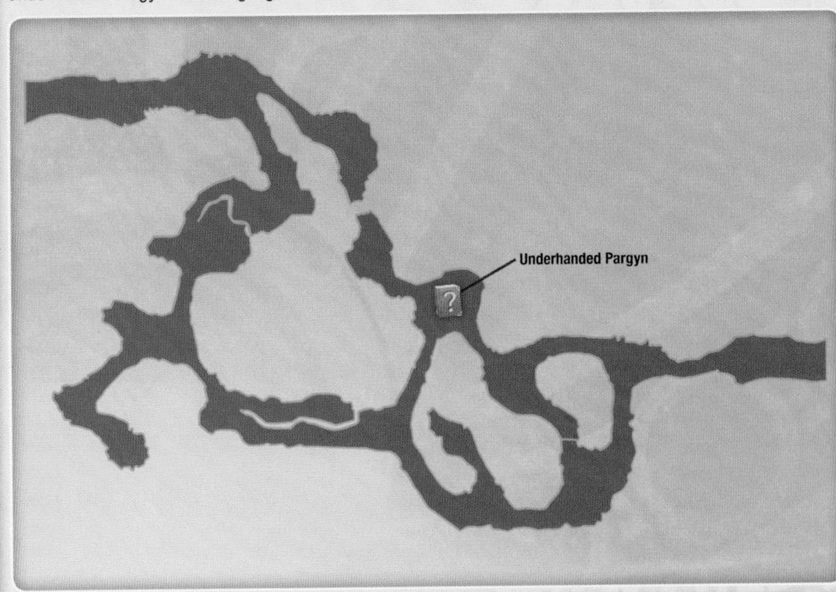

Q044—Subjugation Directive: Donadello

REWARD

EXP	FOL	SP
2800	1800	200

ITEMS
CQC Program Epsilon, Physical Stimulant x 3

WALKTHROUGH

Prerequisites: Progress to at least Chapter 8, complete Subjugation Directive: Pargyns

This not-so-ninja-like turtle resides in an alcove near the middle of the Western Dakaav Tunnel.

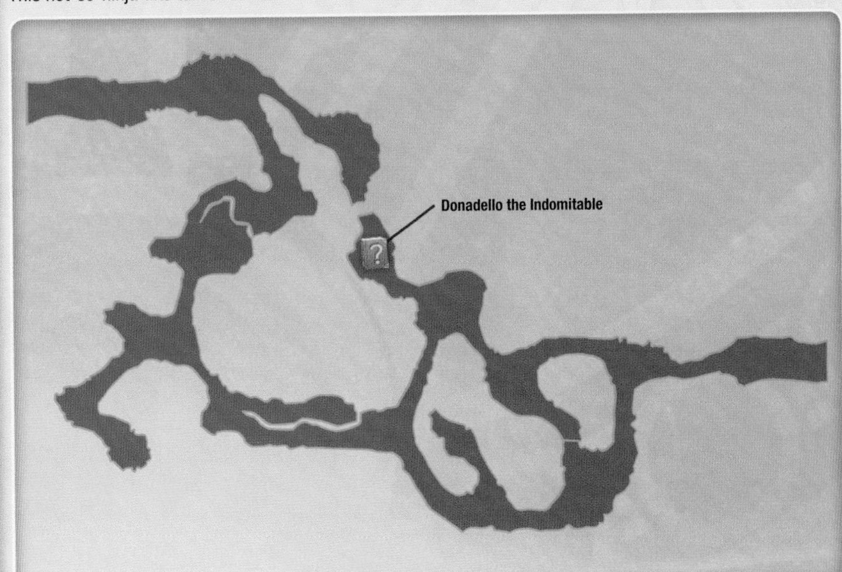

Q045—Subjugation Directive: Walking Conflagrations

REWARD

EXP	FOL	SP
1900	1300	150
ITEMS		
Swordsman's Manual IV, Golden Omelet x 2		

WALKTHROUGH

Prerequisites: Progress to at least Chapter 5

Find and destroy these pyromaniac spellcasters roaming the Passage on the Cliffs.

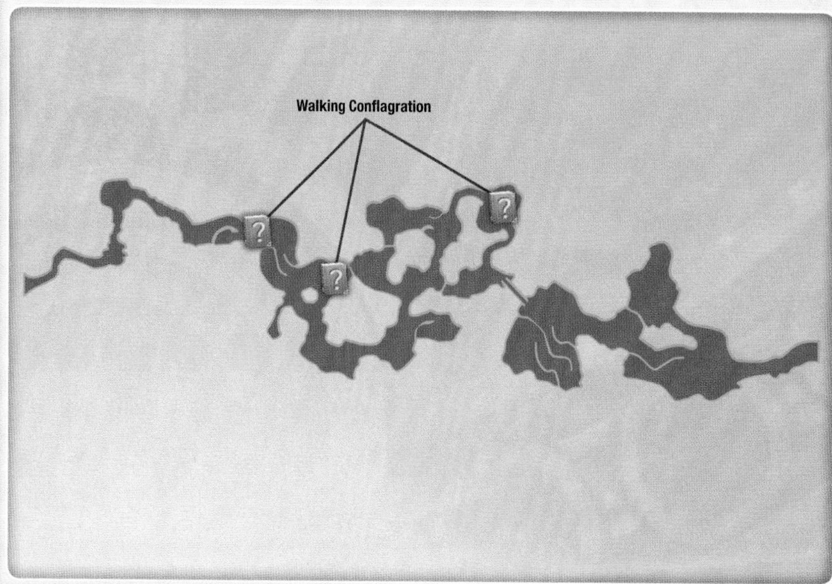

Q046—Wanted: Chaos Corpse Corporals

REWARD

EXP	FOL	SP
1300	600	125
ITEMS		
Anti-fog Amulet		

WALKTHROUGH

Prerequisites: Progress to at least Chapter 4

Find this pack of undead Kobolds in the Western Dakaav Tunnel, near the entrance to the Trei'kuran Dunes.

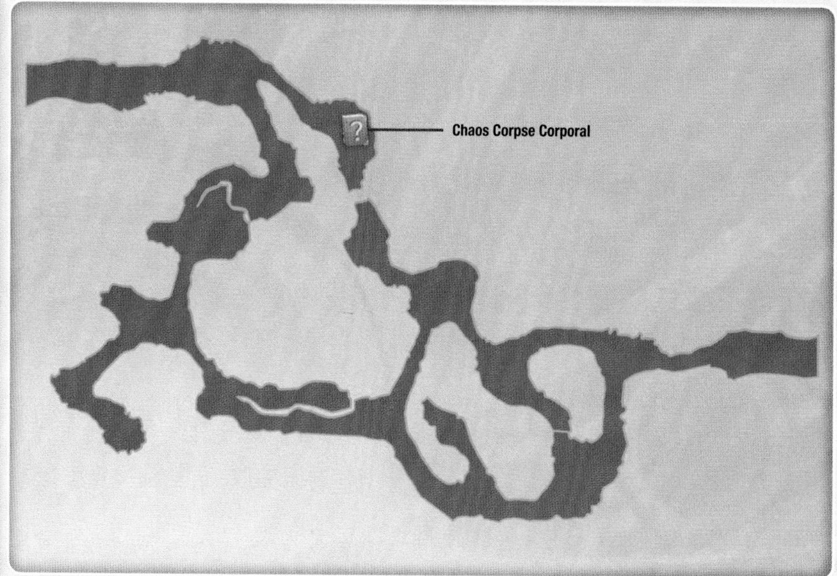

Q047—Death to the Dine-and-Dasher

REWARD

EXP	FOL	SP
1800	1000	150

ITEMS
Physical Stimulant x 3

WALKTHROUGH

Prerequisites: Progress to at least Chapter 5, complete Subjugation Directive: Moogmorts

Gula the Gluttonous is an insect-type enemy found just east from the center of the Northern Territory of Sohma.

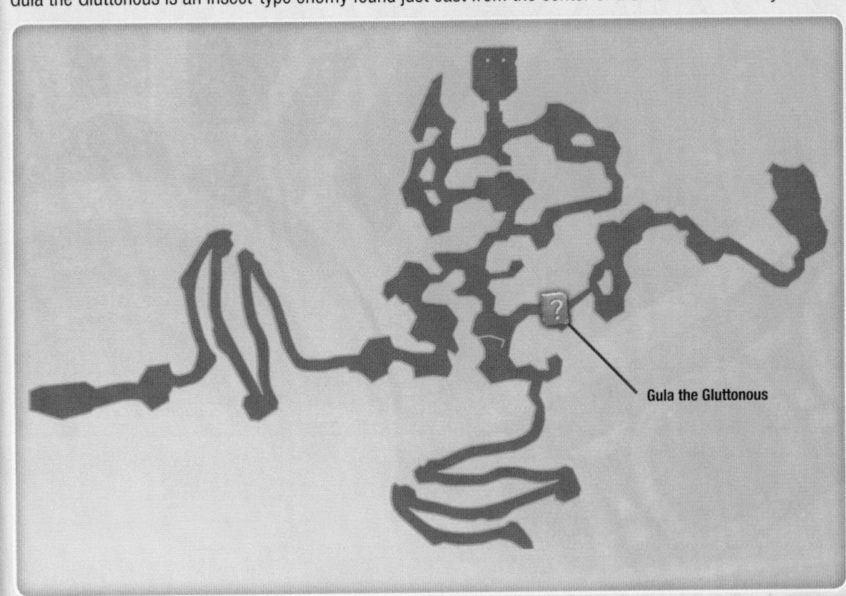

Q048—Spleen for a Spleen

REWARD

EXP	FOL	SP
3100	2800	200

ITEMS
Extrication Ring

WALKTHROUGH

Prerequisites: Progress to at least Chapter 7

This formidable duo of dragon and beast is found dead center of the Resulian Plains.

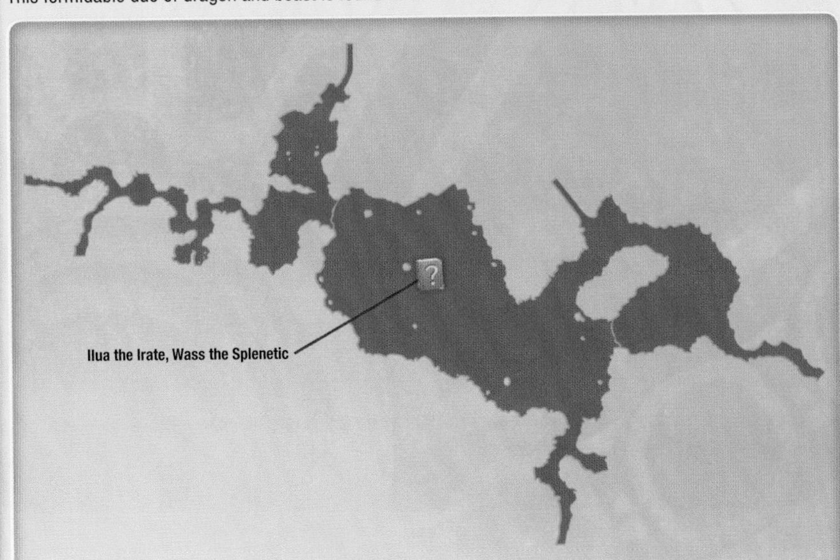

Q049—Showdown at the Training Hall

REWARD

EXP	FOL	SP
5000	3000	280

ITEMS
Swordsman's Manual VI

WALKTHROUGH

Prerequisites: Progress to at least Chapter 9, complete The Four Stooges Strike Again

This quest line ends with a final battle between the four challengers in the Camuze Training Hall. Defeat them to send them packing for good.

Q050—Always Be Prepared

REWARD

EXP	FOL	SP
5700	3900	280

ITEMS
Fortitude Amulet, Vitalitea x 3

WALKTHROUGH

Prerequisites: Progress to at least Chapter 10

Gravity Bombs can be crafted using the Engineering specialty. Alternatively, you can find them by slaying Trei'kuran Sharpshooters (in the Trei'kur Slaughtery).

Low-Frequency Bombs can be crafted with Engineering skill Lv. 5, but the materials can be rare. The Kronos weaponry enemies on the Alcazar of the Golden Age, Eliminators and Avengers, drop Quantum Processors. Micro Circuits are much more common and are purchasable from the vendor on the Charles D. Goale G.

Q051—Medal of Honor

REWARD

EXP	FOL	SP
4800	10000	280

ITEMS
Sylphide's Mail

WALKTHROUGH

Prerequisites: Progress to at least Chapter 9

Dragon Scales can be found from Armored Lizards (early on in the game) or Lesser Dragons (in the latter portion of the main story). Both enemies roam the Dakaav Footpath.

Hunks of Platinum are dropped from slain Kobold Knaves in the Trei'kuran Dunes or crafted with Alchemy (Lv. 4). It's a bit easier to obtain these from the Kobolds instead of crafting because the recipe requires two Alchemist's Waters (you can buy these from Ruddle if his store is open in Central Resulia).

Q052—Device of the Ancients

REWARD

EXP	FOL	SP
3900	2600	250

ITEMS
Lezard's Flask

WALKTHROUGH

Prerequisites: Progress to at least Chapter 8

You can obtain Primeval Fossils by defeating Hades Crabs, located in the Passage on the Cliffs. These crabs spawn at the same point in the story when this quest can be undertaken.

Q053—It Came from the North

REWARD

EXP	FOL	SP
4000	2400	250

ITEMS
Anti-curse Amulet

WALKTHROUGH

Prerequisites: Progress to at least Chapter 8

The Chaotic Cell monsters in the Signesilica commonly drop Gelatinous Slime.

Q054—Eggcellent Haul

REWARD

EXP	FOL	SP
5200	2900	280
ITEMS		
Salamanderstone x 2		

WALKTHROUGH

Prerequisites: Progress to at least Chapter 9

At earlier points in the story, you can harvest Gigantavian Eggs from harvesting nodes in the Northern Territory of Sohma (they are rare, though, even with maximum Harvesting skill).

Later on, as the enemies evolve, these eggs are commonly dropped from the Jatayu avians residing in the same area.

Q055—Heavyweight Champion of the Insect World

REWARD

EXP	FOL	SP
5800	4000	280
ITEMS		
Attack Amulet, Heavenly Pudding		

WALKTHROUGH

Prerequisites: Progress to at least Chapter 10

Most beetle-like enemies drop Insect Eggs. These are commonly found throughout the story, including in the early game (such as from Polyphagas).

Q056—Collection as Innocent as a Valkyrie

REWARD

EXP	FOL	SP
3800	2400	250
ITEMS		
Alchemist's Water x 6		

WALKTHROUGH

Prerequisites: Progress to at least Chapter 8

In the latter portion of the main story, Lava Golems (Trei'kuran Dunes) and Jade Golems (West of the Eastern Eihieds) drop hunks of Platinum. Otherwise, you can craft them with the Alchemy specialty.

Q057—Lurking in the Shadows of Collection

REWARD

EXP	FOL	SP
5400	2600	280
ITEMS		
Love Potion No. 256 x 3		

WALKTHROUGH

Prerequisites: Progress to at least Chapter 9

You can dig up Shadow Roses from harvesting nodes in the Northern Territory of Sohma. They also drop from slain Little Satan demons in the Signesilica, as well as from Welwitschia plants (one group is encountered in the main story in Symbological Facility Prime: B5F).

Q058—Collecting a Taste from the Heavens

REWARD

EXP	FOL	SP
5900	4200	280

ITEMS
Fae Signets, Vol. 2, Sushi

WALKTHROUGH

Prerequisites: Progress to at least Chapter 10

Empyreanase is a rare fish found from fishing points in the Coast of Minoz. You can also obtain them using the Synthesis specialty by combining a food product with a quality of 50.

Q059—Subjugation Directive: Arjain

REWARD

EXP	FOL	SP
3800	2500	250

ITEMS
Defense Seeds x 2

WALKTHROUGH

Prerequisites: Progress to at least Chapter 8

Arjain the Fierce is found flying about in the northern section of the Passage on the Cliffs.

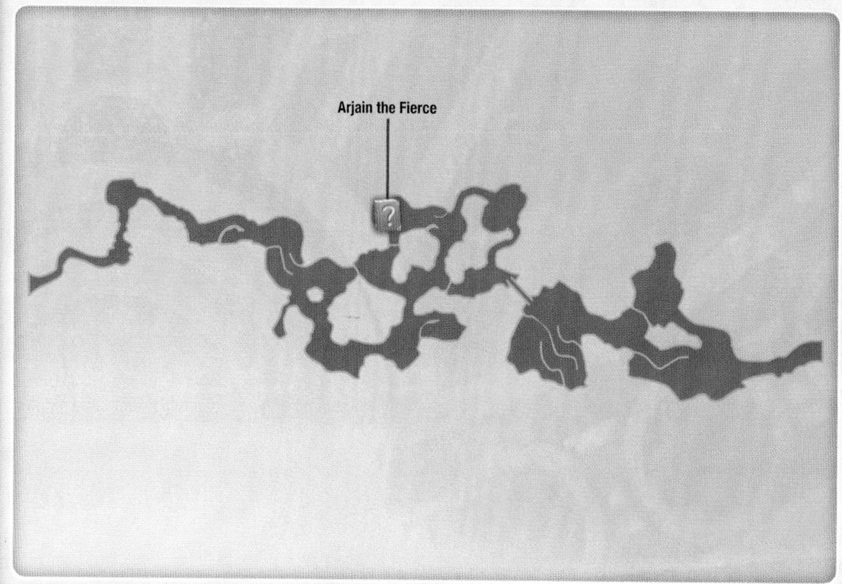

Q060—Subjugation Directive: Vejheerits

REWARD

EXP	FOL	SP
5300	2800	280

ITEMS
Solar Signets, Vol. 3

WALKTHROUGH

Prerequisites: Progress to at least Chapter 9, complete Subjugation Directive: Arjain

Stubborn Vejheerits spawn at various points in the Passage on the Cliffs.

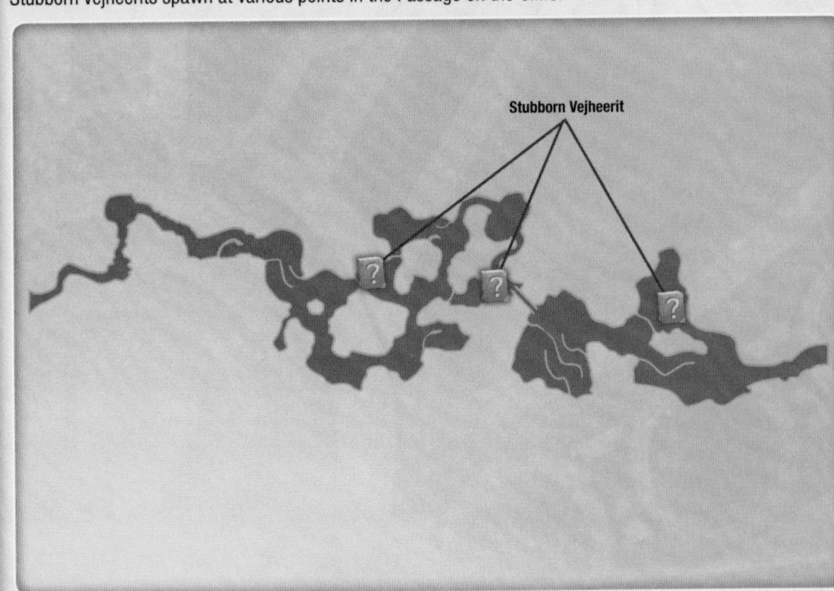

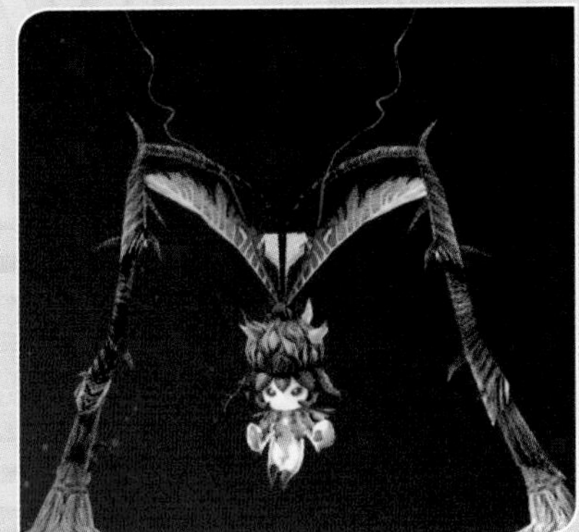

Q061—Subjugation Directive: Shelda

REWARD

EXP	FOL	SP
4300	2400	250

ITEMS
Diligence Potion x 5

WALKTHROUGH

Prerequisites: Progress to at least Chapter 8

You can find this named tortoise in the Dakaav Footpath in an alcove in the southern region of the area, close to the entrance to Sthal.

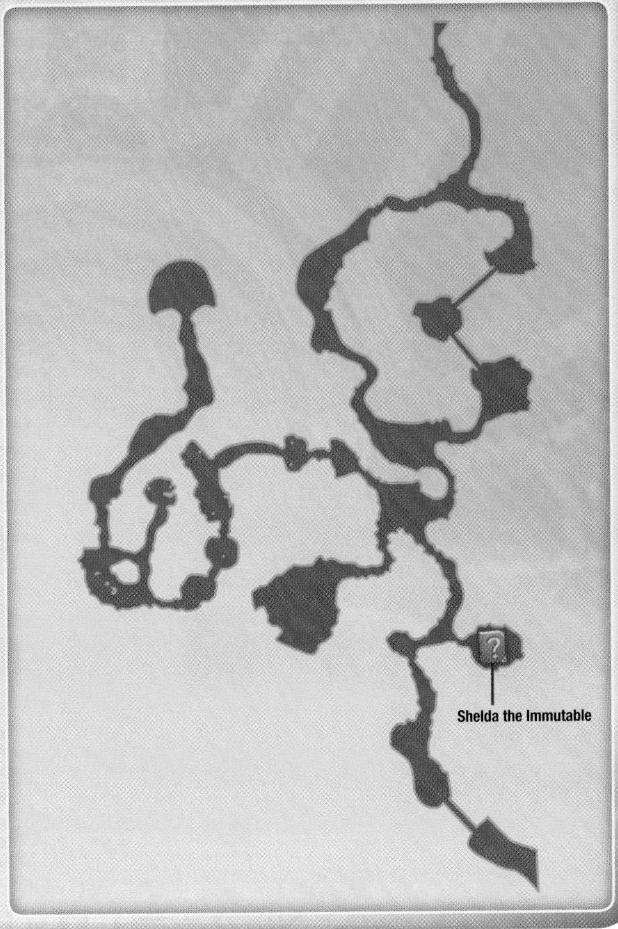

Q062—Subjugation Directive: Hoodini

REWARD

EXP	FOL	SP
5500	2500	280
ITEMS		
Health Seeds x 2		

WALKTHROUGH

Prerequisites: Progress to at least Chapter 9

Hoodini the Morose is a ghost-like named enemy residing in the Dakaav Footpath, in front of the Kronos crash point.

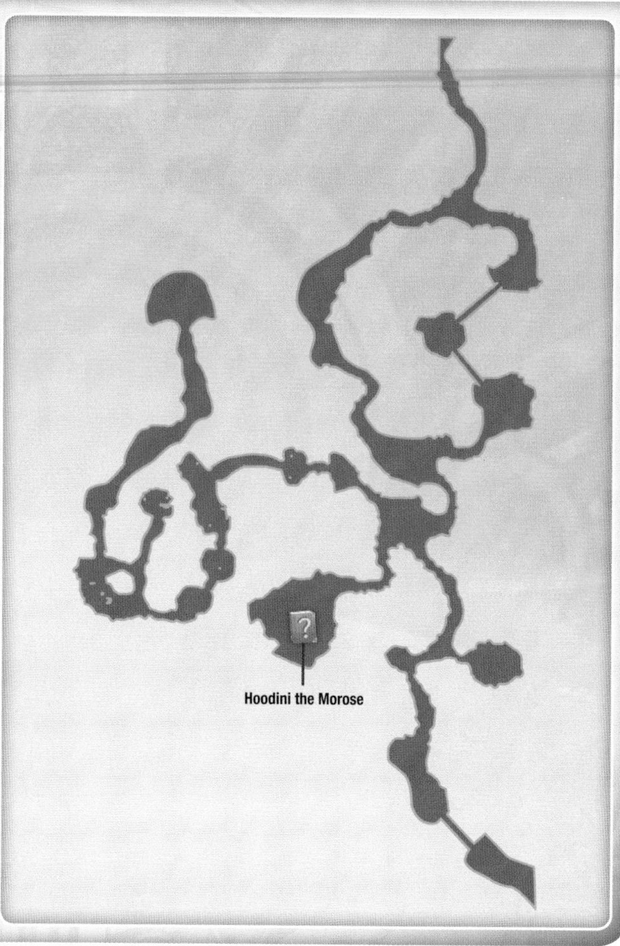

Q063—Subjugation Directive: Mojangos

REWARD

EXP	FOL	SP
6200	4800	280
ITEMS		
Fortitude Amulet, Therapeutic Tincture x 3		

WALKTHROUGH

Prerequisites: Progress to at least Chapter 10

These little demons are scattered across the Resulian Plains (central and eastern regions of the map).

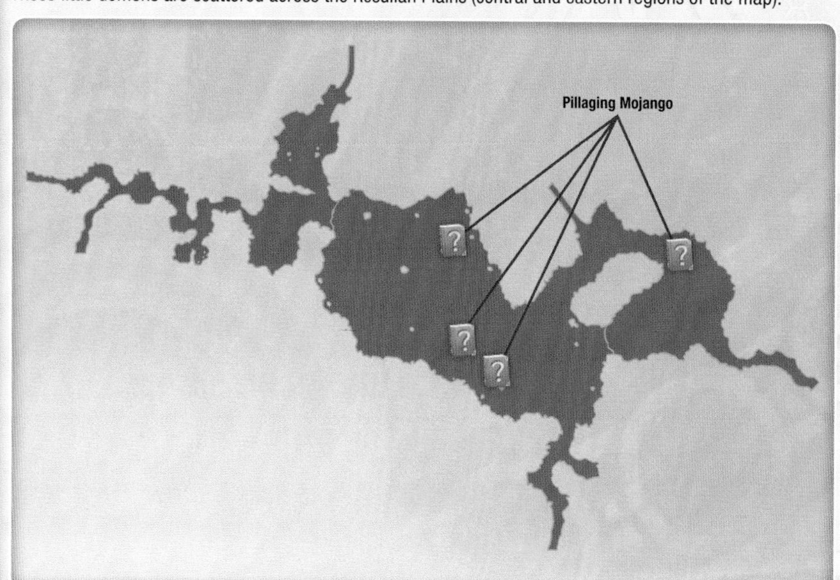

Q064—Subjugation Directive: Rihvnauts

REWARD

EXP	FOL	SP
5000	2700	280

ITEMS
CQC Program Zeta, Chai Tea

WALKTHROUGH

Prerequisites: Progress to at least Chapter 9

Hesitant Rihvnauts are wolf-like enemies that you can find wandering at various points in the Coast of Minoz.

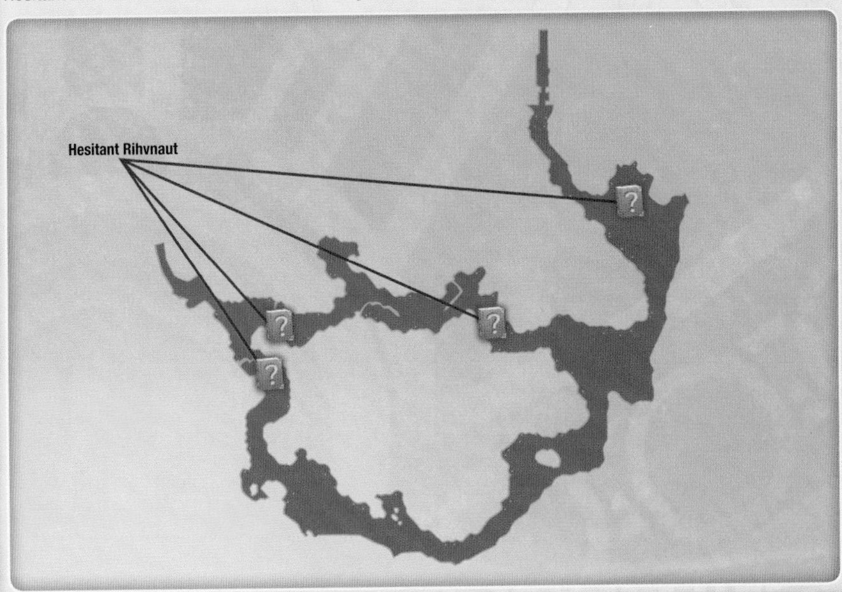

Q065—Wanted: Anonnus

REWARD

EXP	FOL	SP
4200	2700	250

ITEMS
Intelligence Seeds x 2

WALKTHROUGH

Prerequisites: Progress to at least Chapter 8, complete Spleen for a Spleen

The named wolfman, Anonnus the Disperser, is found in the alcove in the southern region of the Resulian Plains (near the entrance to the Dakaav Footpath).

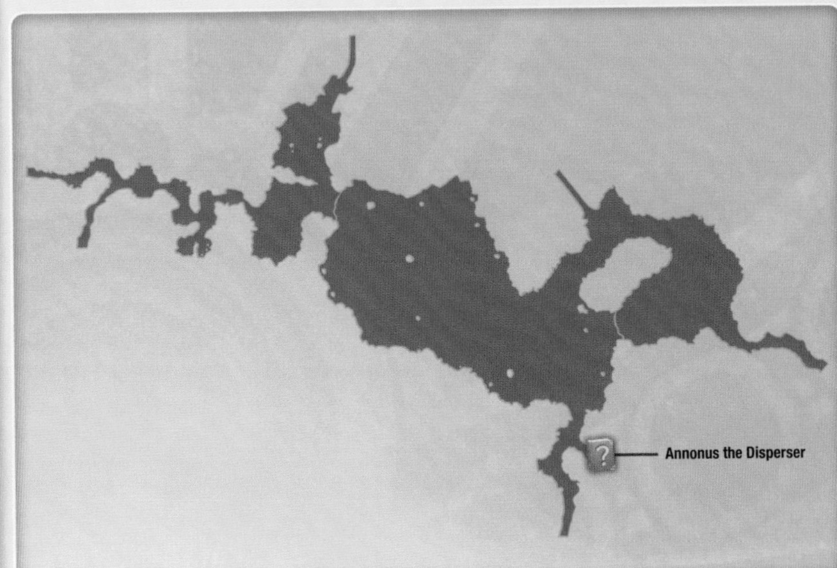

Q066—Indecent Exposure

REWARD

EXP	FOL	SP
7000	4500	300
ITEMS		
Moonlight Signets, Vol. 3, Resurrection Elixir x 2		

WALKTHROUGH

Prerequisites: Progress to at least Chapter 11, complete Wanted: Abigail

Envious Invidiads are wolves roaming almost the entirety of the Northern Territory of Sohma.

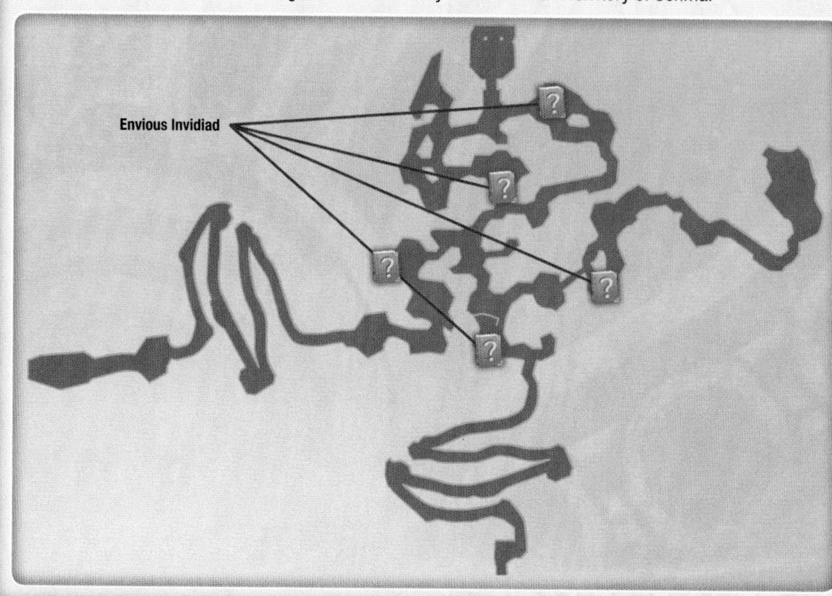

SANTEROULE—BULLETIN BOARD

Q067—Runaround Ruddle

REWARD

EXP	FOL	SP
2000	2000	180
ITEMS		
Familiarizing with Familiars (unlocks Familiar Spirit specialty), Tiramisu		

WALKTHROUGH

Prerequisites: Progress to at least Chapter 6, complete Find Ruddle!

This is the second quest in the Ruddle quest trilogy. Start by speaking to one of the guests in the Sultanic Slumber Lodging inn, then find one of the signeturges in the Royal Institute of Signetary Studies. Finally, you'll find Ruddle waiting at the shipping dock in Myiddok.

Q068—Sweet on the Outside...

REWARD

EXP	FOL	SP
2400	1300	180

ITEMS
Anti-freezing Amulet

WALKTHROUGH

Prerequisites: Progress to at least Chapter 6

You'll need to bake 10 Lemon Tarts for this quest, which requires at least Lv. 2 Cooking. Materials can be purchased from The Silver Spoon in Santeroule.

Q069—Of Vital Importance After Hours

REWARD

EXP	FOL	SP
1700	1400	150

ITEMS
Testament to Triumph

WALKTHROUGH

Prerequisites: Progress to at least Chapter 5

You can find vials of Vitalitea in treasure chests throughout the game. Additionally, you can make more using the Compounding specialty (Lv. 4). The ingredients include Physical Stimulant (another Compounding creation), Colorful Mushrooms (found by defeating fungi enemies), and Lemon Juice (a product of Cooking).

Q070—Revenge is a Dish Best Served Burnt

REWARD

EXP	FOL	SP
1200	500	125

ITEMS
The Founder's Signets, Vol. 1

WALKTHROUGH

Prerequisites: Progress to at least Chapter 4

There's only one instance of Charred Meat in the entire game, so it's imperative that you save it when you find it (don't eat it!). It's sitting in a treasure chest in the Central Resulian inn, Ye Grand Ole Castle of Comfort.

Q071—Sexy Little Devil

REWARD

EXP	FOL	SP
1600	900	150

ITEMS
Riot Potion

WALKTHROUGH

Prerequisites: Progress to at least Chapter 5

Demon's Tails are commonly dropped from the small demon enemies found in various areas, such as from Demon Imps in the West of the Eastern Eihieds area.

Q072—Steel Yourself for the Future

REWARD

EXP	FOL	SP
2000	1400	180

ITEMS
Signeturgical Book of Quietude

WALKTHROUGH

Prerequisites: Progress to at least Chapter 6

The Damascus Fort enemies in the Western Dakaav Tunnel drop hunks of Damascus Steel.

Q073—Too Little, Too Late

REWARD

EXP	FOL	SP
2800	1850	200
ITEMS		
Love Potion No. 256 x 2		

WALKTHROUGH

Prerequisites: Progress to at least Chapter 7

You can find Velvet Ribbons by defeating the succubus enemy called Ridiculers around the Eastern Eihieds areas. In the Maze of Tribulations, these also drop from Melusines.

Q074—Collecting the Metal that Plays Second Fiddle

REWARD

EXP	FOL	SP
1300	500	125
ITEMS		
Ocarina of Temptation, Light Gem x 2		

WALKTHROUGH

Prerequisites: Progress to at least Chapter 4

You can excavate hunks of Silver from mining points around the Eastern Eihieds region, although they're slightly rare. Early on in the main story, these may be difficult to find unless you do a lot of mining. Later on in the story, you can collect Silver by defeating golems, like the Metal Golem and Lava Golem.

Q075—Building a House Takes a Collective Effort

REWARD

EXP	FOL	SP
1500	1100	150
ITEMS		
Wind Gem x 3		

WALKTHROUGH

Prerequisites: Progress to at least Chapter 5

Ebony is difficult to come by at the earliest point when you can start this quest. However, after the events occur at the Symbological Research Facility, you can find Ebony by chopping down the Treant enemies named Albero di Anima.

Q076—Collecting the Fungus among Us

REWARD

EXP	FOL	SP
2200	1500	180
ITEMS		
Mental Stimulant x 3		

WALKTHROUGH

Prerequisites: Progress to at least Chapter 6

You can find Caterpillar Fungus from Myconids and Myconid Sporelings in Central Resulia.

Q077—Open Season on Ostharks

REWARD

EXP	FOL	SP
1500	500	125
ITEMS		
Swordsman's Manual I, Golden Omelet		

WALKTHROUGH

Prerequisites: Progress to at least Chapter 4

These ghoulish enemies can be found roaming the northern area of North of the Eastern Eihieds. You can complete this quest while taking Relia to the Ancient Institute.

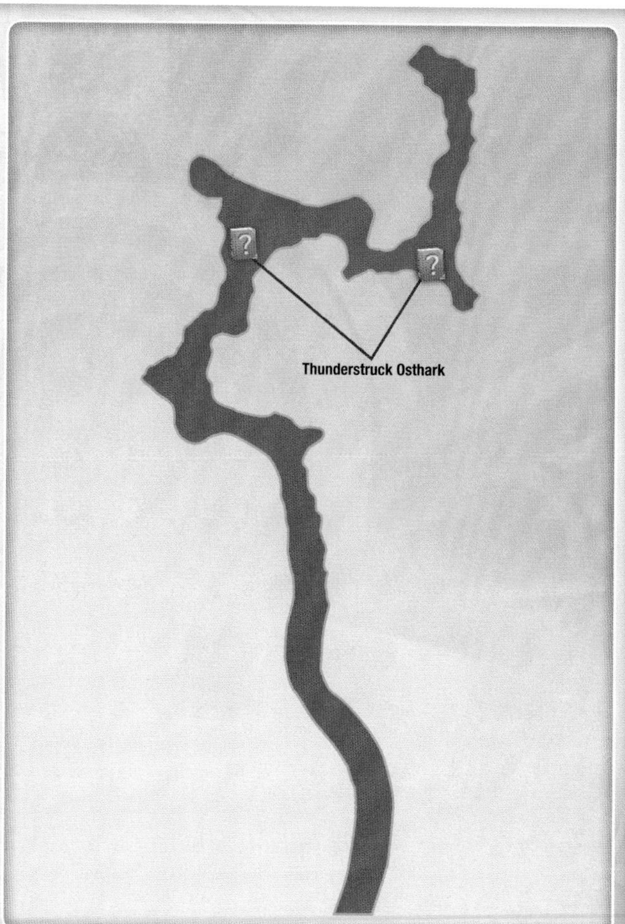

Q078—Open Season on Hados

REWARD

EXP	FOL	SP
1300	600	125

ITEMS
Ice Charm

WALKTHROUGH

Prerequisites: Progress to at least Chapter 4, complete Open Season on Fran

Lancing Hados are bees flying about in the West of the Eastern Eihieds area. There are several spawn points for them, spanning almost the entire area.

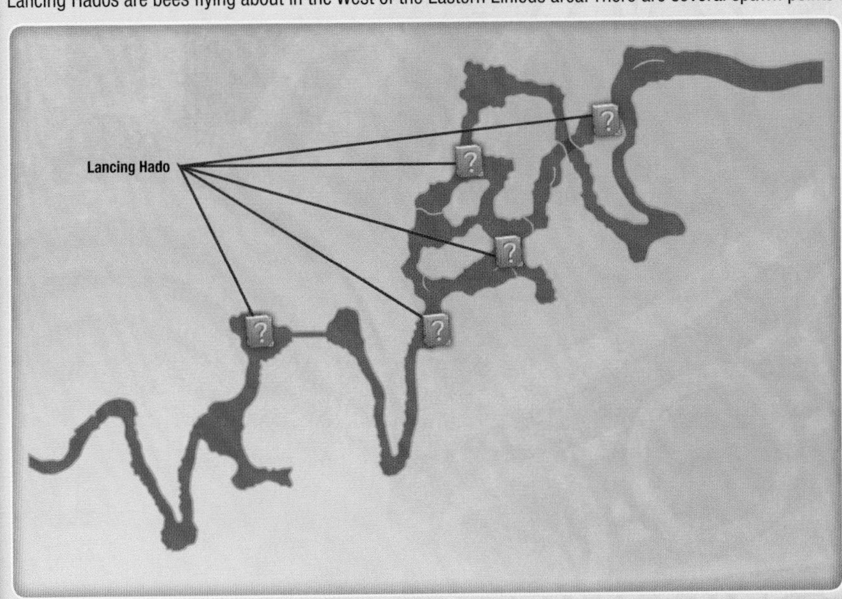

Q079—Open Season on Fran

REWARD

EXP	FOL	SP
1600	800	150

ITEMS
Fae Signets, Vol. 1, Pasta Peperoncino

WALKTHROUGH

Prerequisites: Progress to at least Chapter 5

You can find Fran of Constant Decay, a slime enemy, in a cul-de-sac southwest from the entrance to Santeroule.

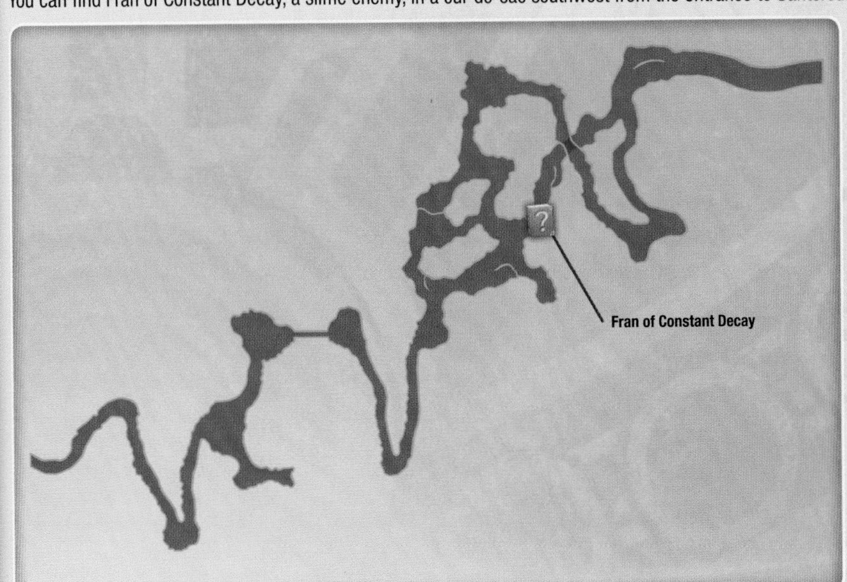

Q080—Open Season on Karacins

REWARD

EXP	FOL	SP
2300	1500	180
ITEMS		
Solar Signets, Vol. 2, Chocolate Scones		

WALKTHROUGH

Prerequisites: Progress to at least Chapter 6

These land-dwelling fish are found in the North of the Eastern Eihieds area, with three spawn points on the way to the Ancient Institute.

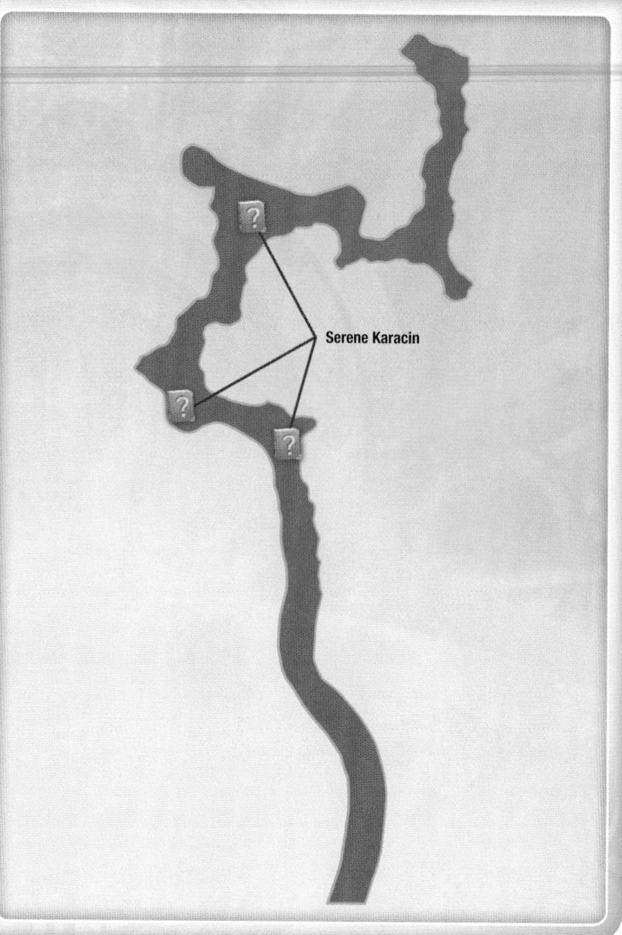

Q081—Open Season on Mujas

REWARD

EXP	FOL	SP
2800	1900	200
ITEMS		
Signeturgical Book of Quietude, Mental Stimulant x 3		

WALKTHROUGH

Prerequisites: Progress to at least Chapter 7

Verdant Mujas are bipedal plant enemies that are found lurking in the West of the Eastern Eihieds area.

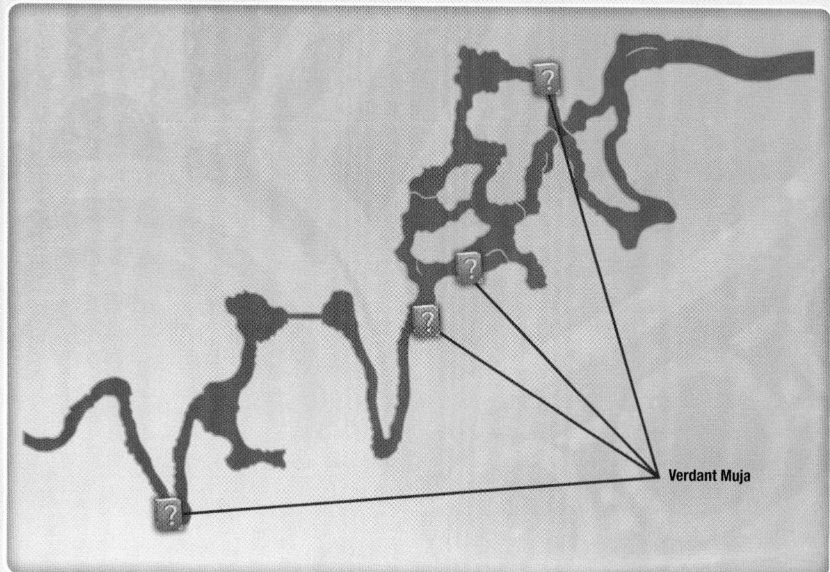

Q082—Wanted: Randaghor

REWARD

EXP	FOL	SP
2500	2100	200
ITEMS		
Pneuma Signets, Vol. 1, Mint Chocolate Ice Cream		

WALKTHROUGH

Prerequisites: Progress to at least Chapter 7, complete Open Season on Karacins

Randaghor the Render is an avian-type reptile residing near the center of the North of the Eastern Eihieds area.

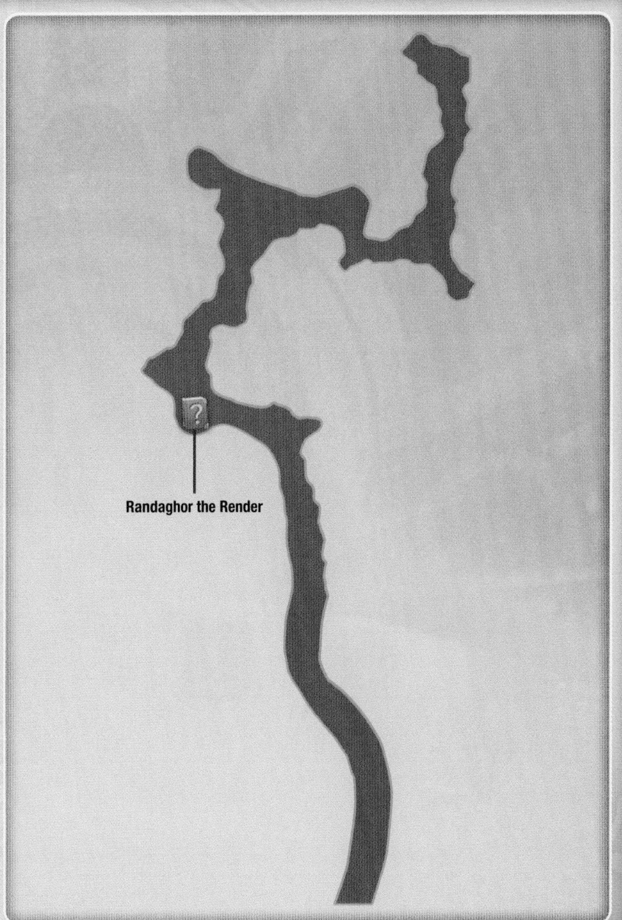

Q083—Quiet Down in There!

REWARD

EXP	FOL	SP
1800	1000	150
ITEMS		
Smooth as Silk Sales Talk (unlocks Haggling specialty), Anti-silence Amulet		

WALKTHROUGH

Prerequisites: Progress to at least Chapter 7

You can find this musical duo consisting of a harpy and a succubus in the southeast region of the Western Dakaav Tunnel. Silence them to claim your reward.

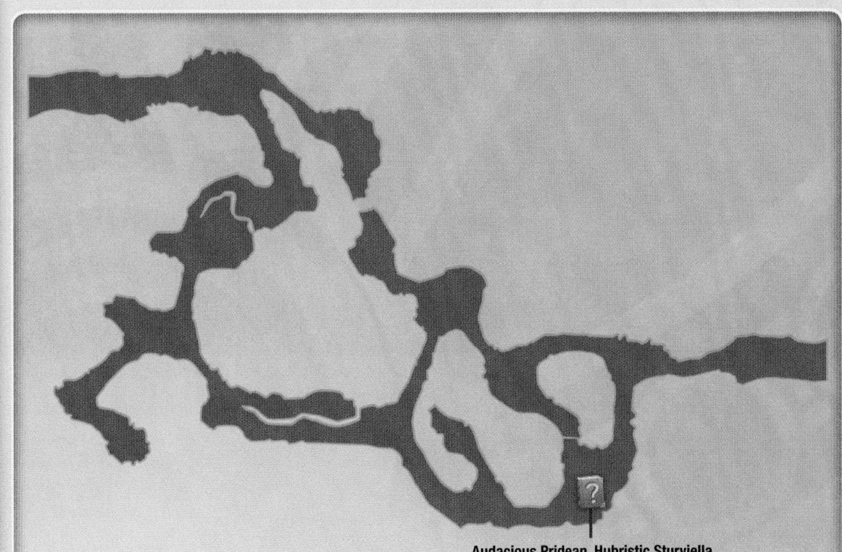

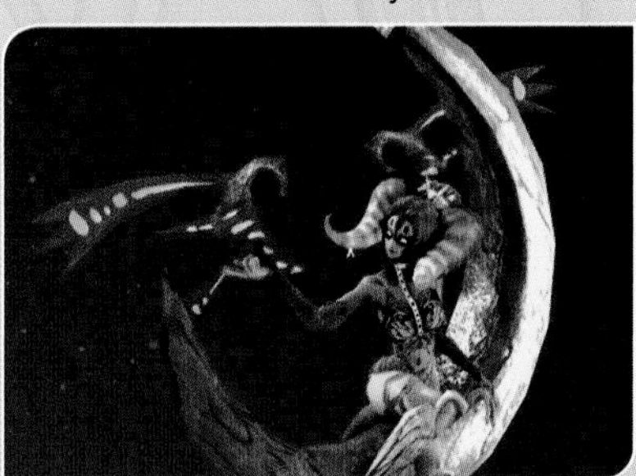

Q084—Changing History: Young Women, Power, and Pets

REWARD

EXP	FOL	SP
6000	4000	280
ITEMS		
Shadestone x 2		

WALKTHROUGH

Prerequisites: Progress to at least Chapter 10

A domesticated Gerel has gone rogue and run off. You can find it near the save point in the West of the Eastern Eihieds area. Defeat it to send it back home to its owner.

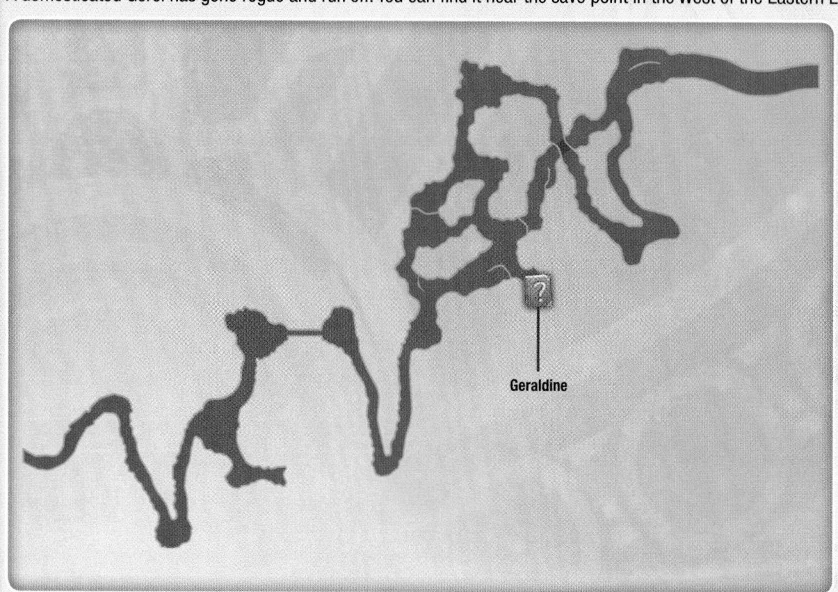

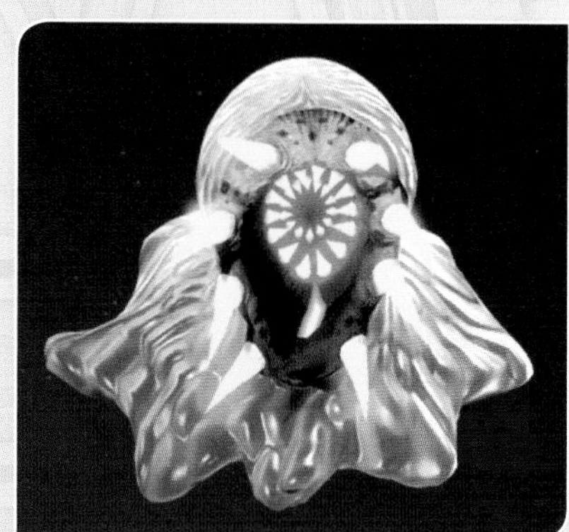

Q085—For Whom the Bell Tomes

REWARD

EXP	FOL	SP
4000	2600	250
ITEMS		
Sylphstone x 2		

WALKTHROUGH

Prerequisites: Progress to at least Chapter 8

You can find three copies of Solar Signets, Vol. 2 in treasure chests throughout the world. You can learn both Miki's Volcanic Burst and Fiore's Lightning Blast and still have one to turn in for this quest. However, if you use all of them for bonus mastery in one of those spells, you can craft the book with the Authoring specialty (Lv. 3). The recipe includes two Crystals, one piece of Parchment, three Fire Paints, and three Wind Paints.

Q086—Cloaked in Mistakes

REWARD

EXP	FOL	SP
5100	2700	280
ITEMS		
Mind Amulet, Robust Vitalitea		

WALKTHROUGH

Prerequisites: Progress to at least Chapter 9

This quest requires a significant investment in the crafting specialties, as you'll need Lv. 5 Alchemy and Lv. 5 Authoring to craft the signet cards. The recipe for Signet Card: Divine Wave is two Crystals, a Signet Card, and Nil Paint. The recipe for Signet Card: Ex Healing is three pieces of Oak, a Signet Card, and a Healing Paint. The paints are created with Alchemy, and the other items can be purchased or found on various enemies. Refer to the Item Creation section of this book for details and recipes.

Q087—An Emotional Gift Idea

REWARD

EXP	FOL	SP
6000	5300	280
ITEMS		
Heroism Potion		

WALKTHROUGH

Prerequisites: Progress to at least Chapter 10

You can craft an Emotional Destabilizer with relatively common items. Its ingredients include three Lavenders, one Demon's Tail, and one Empty Bottle. Demon's Tails drop from the small imp enemies, and the other two ingredients can be purchased from various shops around the world. You'll need the Compounding specialty leveled to at least Lv. 4.

Q088—An Inkling for Artistry

REWARD

EXP	FOL	SP
3900	2400	250

ITEMS
Greater Demon's Fetish x 3

WALKTHROUGH

Prerequisites: Progress to at least Chapter 8

Earth, Ice, Fire, and Wind Paint can all be crafted with the Alchemy specialty (at least Lv. 3). Each paint element shares two common ingredients: Spring Water (purchasable from vendors) and High-Strength Adhesive (another Alchemy creation). You'll also need to collect at least two hunks of Iron, two Blue Roses, two Red Fruits, and two Giant Bird Feathers. These are all easily accessible at this point in the game, either as drops from enemies or from resource nodes.

Q089—The Enchanted Quill

REWARD

EXP	FOL	SP
5200	2800	280

ITEMS
Cerulean Orb Signets, Vol. 3, Parchment

WALKTHROUGH

Prerequisites: Progress to at least Chapter 9

A Remex bird feather is required to complete this quest. These are commonly dropped from the Peryton family of foes, such as the Crater Peryton in the West of Eastern Eihieds area.

Q090—Sylph-Sewn Robes

REWARD

EXP	FOL	SP
6100	3300	280

ITEMS
Faerie Band

WALKTHROUGH

Prerequisites: Progress to at least Chapter 10

The many Great Scumbag enemies running around in the Resulian Plains at this point in the main story drop Faerie Embroidery Threads.

Q091—Collecting Something Blue

REWARD

EXP	FOL	SP
4000	2500	250

ITEMS
Attack Seeds x 2

WALKTHROUGH

Prerequisites: Progress to at least Chapter 8

The Ridiculer (in West of the Eastern Eihieds) or the Man Trap plant enemy (found later on in the game) both drop Blue Roses. You'll need to collect 10 of them to complete this quest.

Q092—Airing Out a Collection

REWARD

EXP	FOL	SP
5400	2900	280

ITEMS
Relaxation Device x 2

WALKTHROUGH

Prerequisites: Progress to at least Chapter 9

You can craft Sylphstones with an Alchemy skill level of Lv. 6. The recipe is three Remex feathers, two Wind Gems, and an Alchemist's Water. However, the For Whom the Bell Tomes quest rewards you with two Sylphstones, so if you've done that quest, you can simply turn in a Sylphstone to complete this one.

Q093—The Golden Rule of Collecting

REWARD

EXP	FOL	SP
5600	3200	280

ITEMS
Purification Signets, Vol. 2, Tears of Joysotto

WALKTHROUGH

Prerequisites: Progress to at least Chapter 10

You'll need a whopping 18 pieces of Gold to complete this quest. They can be mined from the excavation points in the Western Dakaav Tunnel, crafted with Alchemy Lv. 3 (with a recipe of three hunks of Silver and two bottles of Alchemist's Water), or obtained by slaying Jade Golems in West of the Eastern Eihieds.

Q094—Open Season on Orizons

REWARD

EXP	FOL	SP
3800	2500	250
ITEMS		
Cerulean Orb Signets, Vol. 2, Hamburg Steak		

WALKTHROUGH

Prerequisites: Progress to at least Chapter 8, complete Open Season on Mujas

Parched Orizons are Corrupt sword-wielding ghouls found in at three points in the West of the Eastern Eihieds area.

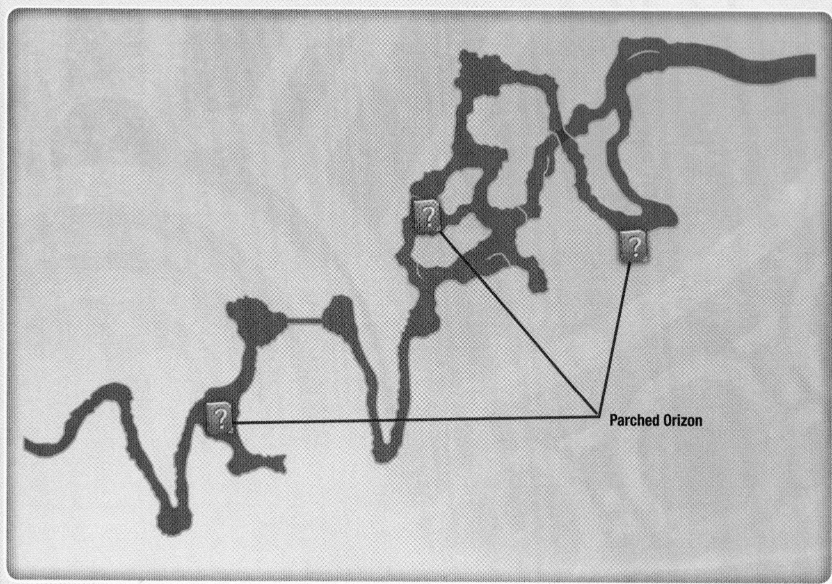

Q095—Open Season on Ouyeits

REWARD

EXP	FOL	SP
6200	3500	280
ITEMS		
Moonlight Signets, Vol. 2, Physical Stimulant x 3		

WALKTHROUGH

Prerequisites: Progress to at least Chapter 10

You'll need to travel to North of the Eastern Eihieds to perform pest control on these insect-type monsters roaming the area.

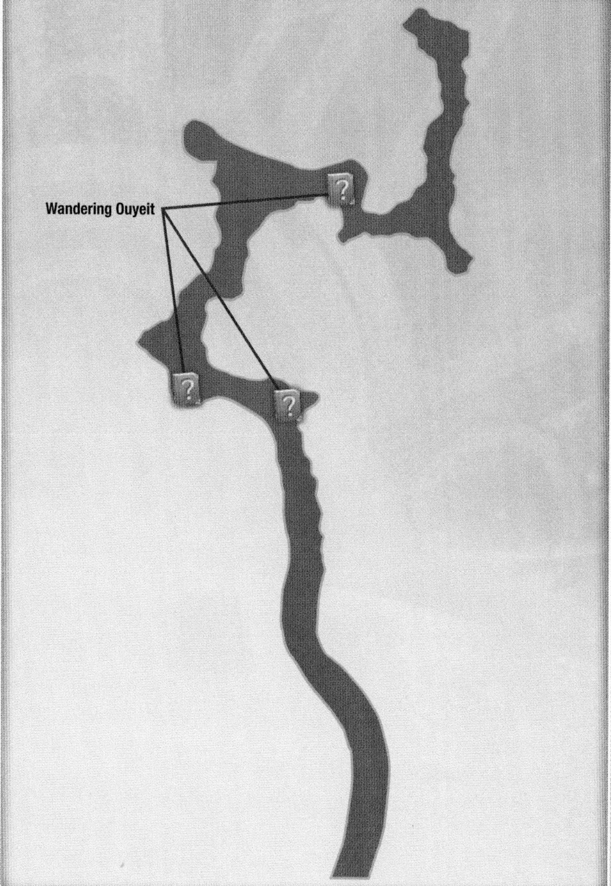

Q096—Open Season on Hourigh

REWARD

EXP	FOL	SP
5300	2800	280

ITEMS
Magic Seeds x 2

WALKTHROUGH

Prerequisites: Progress to at least Chapter 9, complete Open Season on Orizons

You can find this named flying psynard in the northern region in West of the Eastern Eihieds. From the save point, head north along the path to confront and defeat Hourigh the Intrepid.

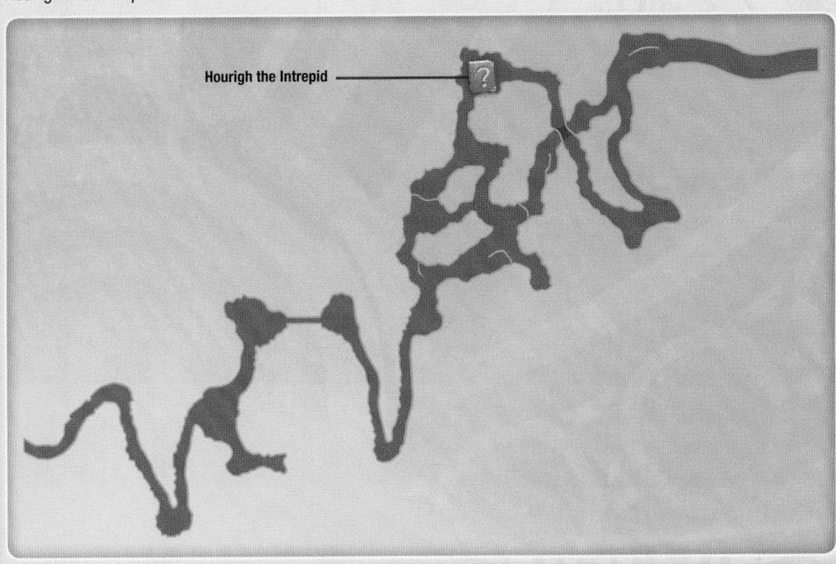

Q097—Open Season on Bordnaks

REWARD

EXP	FOL	SP
5000	2700	280

ITEMS
Angel's Cloak

WALKTHROUGH

Prerequisites: Progress to at least Chapter 11, complete Open Season on Ruphin

There are three groups of these flying fiends in the Signesilica. One group resides west of the main hall through the shortcut door, and you can find the other two groups roaming the northeastern region of the map.

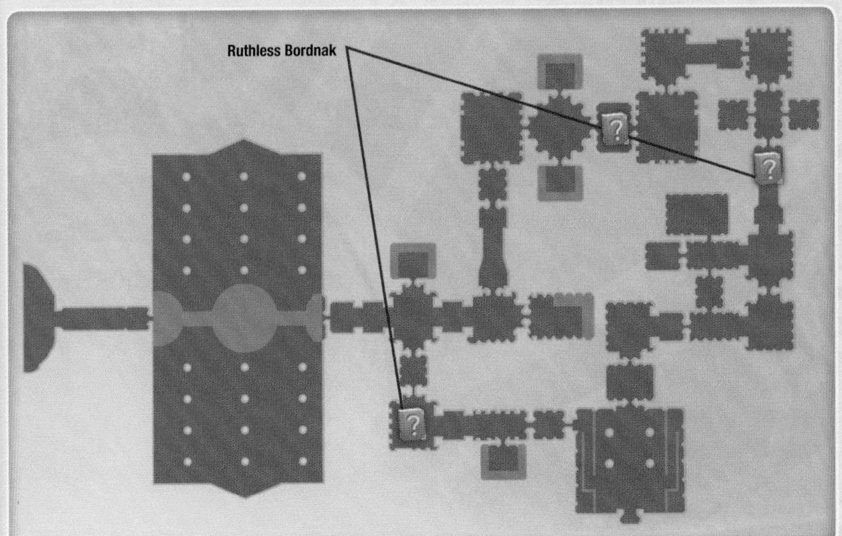

Q098—Open Season on Doraux

REWARD

EXP	FOL	SP
6100	3300	280
ITEMS		
Darkness Scarf		

WALKTHROUGH

Prerequisites: Progress to at least Chapter 11, complete Open Season on Pyekards

Douxrah of the Frozen Touch is a Corrupt golem lumbering in the southeast room in the Signesilica. From the main hall, head north and then east until you reach the corner room to find the golem.

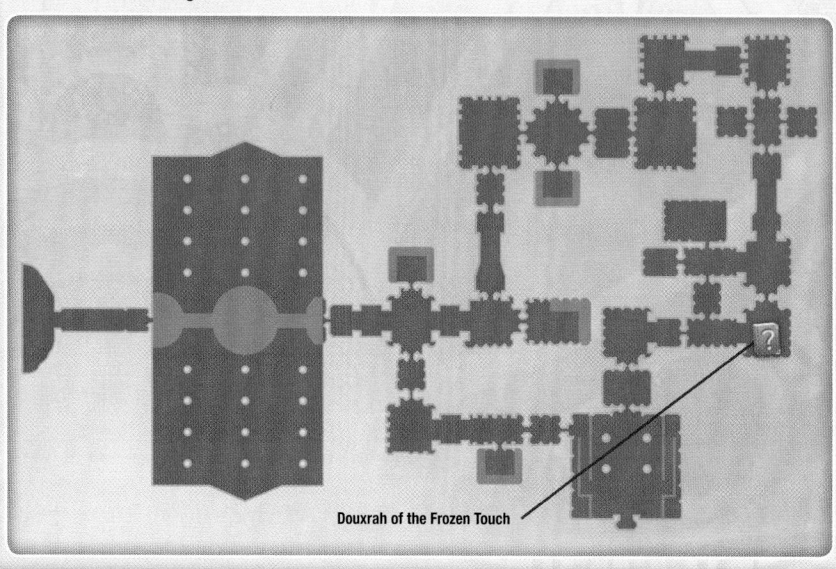

Q099—Open Season on Pyekards

REWARD

EXP	FOL	SP
5900	4200	280
ITEMS		
Solar Signets, Vol. 3, Mental Stimulant x 3		

WALKTHROUGH

Prerequisites: Progress to at least Chapter 11, complete Open Season on Bordnaks

There are four flocks of peryton enemies throughout the Signesilica. Two are near the shortcut door to the west of the main hall, and you can encounter the other two by going through the Signesilica's northeast passage.

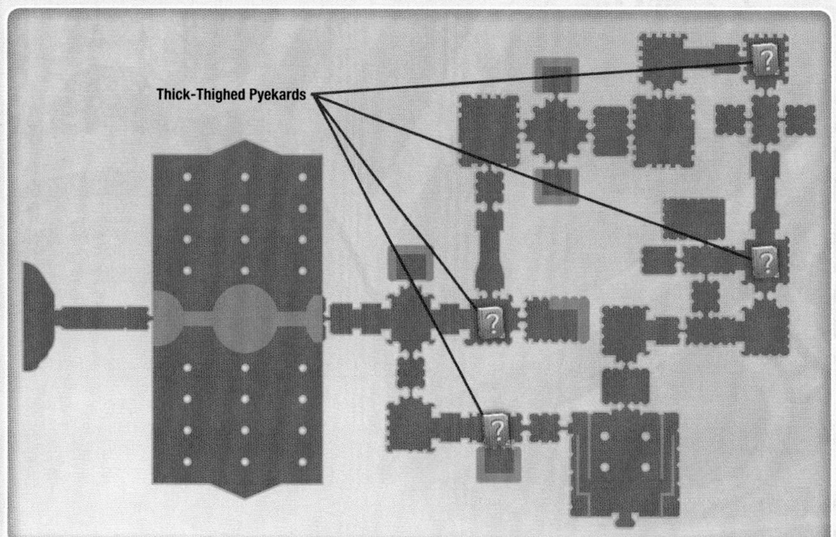

Q100—Open Season on Ruphin

REWARD

EXP	FOL	SP
3900	2600	250

ITEMS
Wondrous Tincture

WALKTHROUGH

Prerequisites: Progress to at least Chapter 11

Ruphin the Imperious is an Aquaregia dwelling in a room in the center of the Signesilica map (where the Mythril Rod treasure chest is).

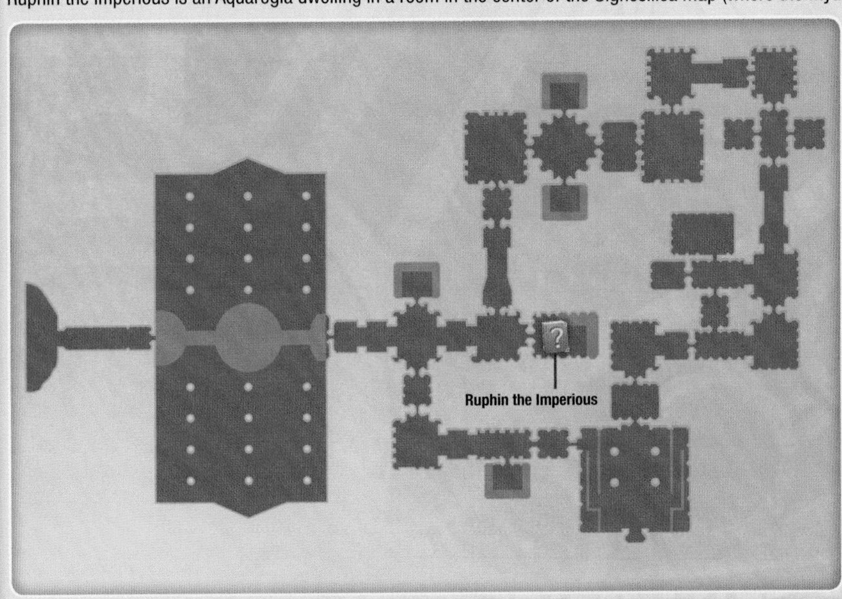

Q101—Wanted: Abigail

REWARD

EXP	FOL	SP
6000	4000	280

ITEMS
Meteorite x 3

WALKTHROUGH

Prerequisites: Progress to at least Chapter 10

You can find this human fugitive far to the north in the Northern Territory of Sohma, west of the entrance to the Signesilica.

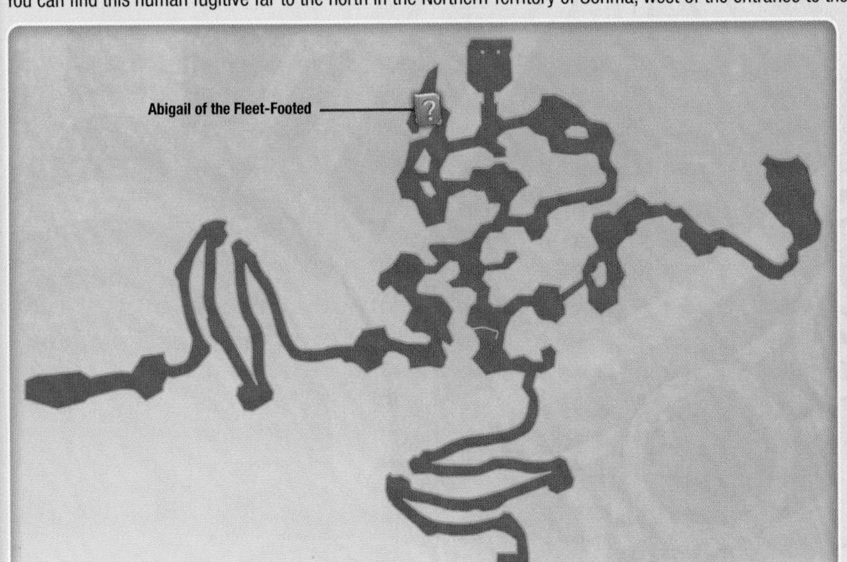

Q102—On the Trail of Eitalon Stragglers

REWARD

EXP	FOL	SP
5500	6000	280
ITEMS		
Anti-death Amulet		

WALKTHROUGH

Prerequisites: Progress to at least Chapter 10

There are groups of Eitalons scattered around the Western Dakaav Tunnel. Two groups hide in the southwest portion of the area, while another two can be found near the Resulian Plains entrance.

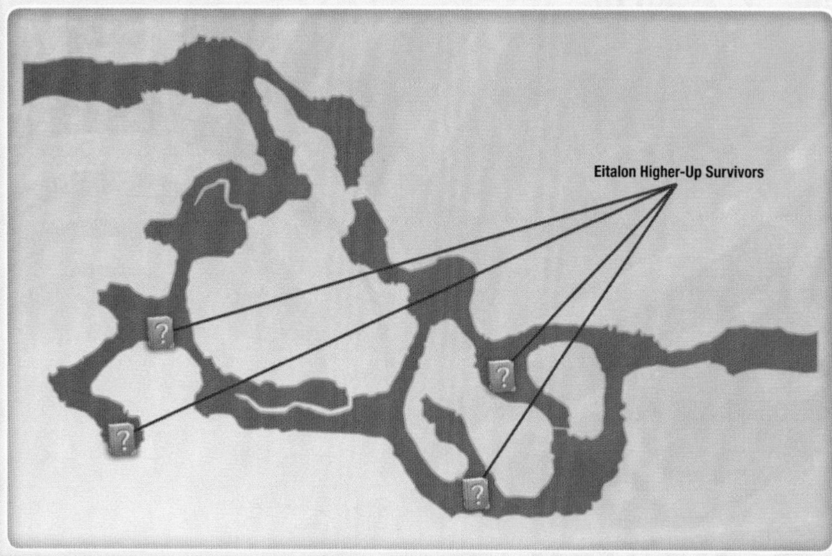

Q103—Uprooting Families

REWARD

EXP	FOL	SP
7000	3500	300
ITEMS		
Swordsman's Manual VII, Wondrous Tincture		

WALKTHROUGH

Prerequisites: Progress to at least Chapter 11, complete Changing History: Young Women, Power, and Pets

Defeat this group of plant enemies in West of the Eastern Eihieds to send them back home to their horticulturist caretaker. You can find them near the save point in the area.

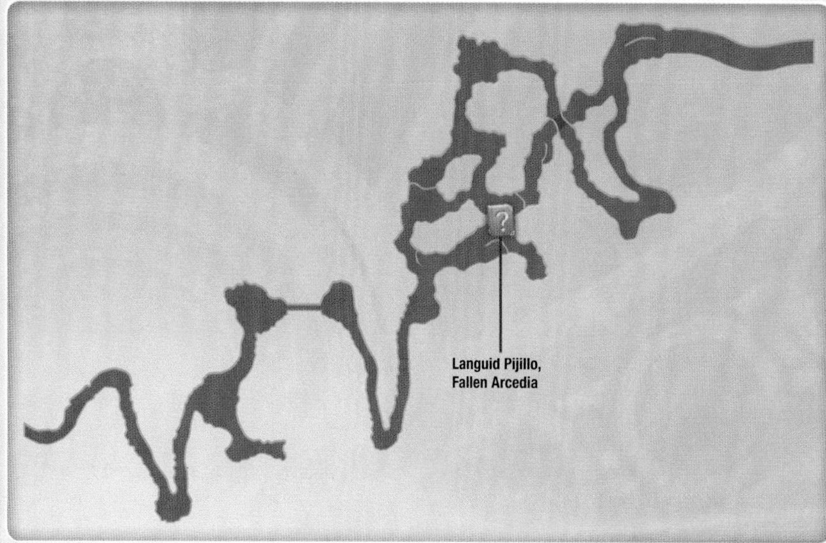

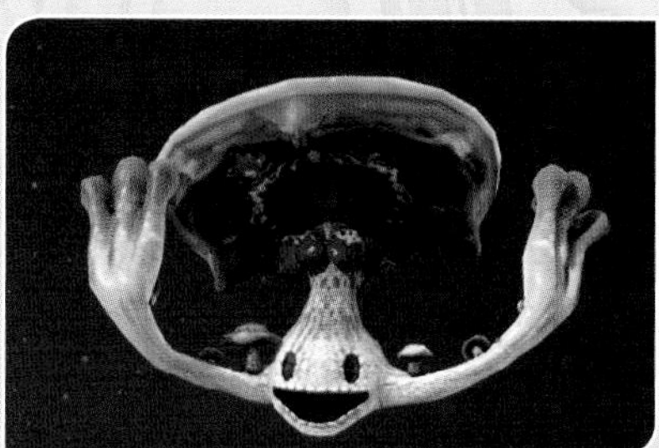

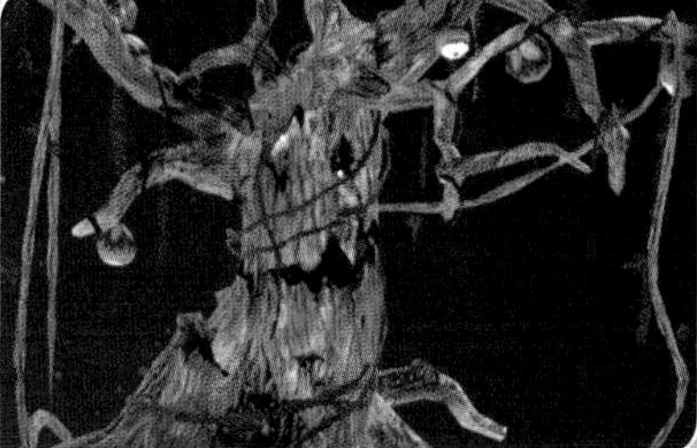

EASTERN TREI'KUR—BULLETIN BOARD

Q104—That Darn Ruddle

REWARD

EXP	FOL	SP
9000	6000	300

ITEMS
CQC Program Delta, Resurrection Mist, Unlocks Ruddle's Shop in Central Resulia

WALKTHROUGH

Prerequisites: Progress to at least Chapter 11, complete Runaround Ruddle

At this point in the game, finding Ruddle is made extra convenient thanks to the starship's teleporter functionality. The quest starts at the guard next to the bulletin board where this quest is undertaken. Next, talk to the steward of The Yawning Kobold in Myiddok for another clue. In the center of Santeroule, talk to the elderly woman there for another hint. Then, teleport to the Resulian Plains, enter Central Resulia, and make your way to the bulletin board. Talk to the cheeky young girl standing in front of the bulletin board for the final hint. Head to Sthal, and in Fidel's House, you'll find Ruddle there waiting.

When the quest is turned in, you can find Ruddle selling valuable wares in Ye Grand Ole Castle of Comfort in Central Resulia.

Q105—Medical Emergency

REWARD

EXP	FOL	SP
4100	2400	250

ITEMS
Arcane Amulet, Robust Vitalitea

WALKTHROUGH

Prerequisites: Progress to at least Chapter 7

The reward from Of Weapons and Womanizers (a Welch's Laboratory quest) consists of three Healing Devices. You can craft the other two with the Engineering specialty leveled to at least Lv. 5. The recipe includes three Physical Stimulants and one Diffusion Device. Diffusion Devices are dropped off of Toy Soldiers (on the Kronos ship, the Cavaliero) and off of Avengers (in the Alcazar of the Golden Age).

Q106—Taste of Home

REWARD

EXP	FOL	SP
5000	2500	280

ITEMS
Healing Band

WALKTHROUGH

Prerequisites: Progress to at least Chapter 9

Crab Rice Stew can be crafted with Lv. 5 Cooking. The recipe includes three Fresh Vegetables, three White Rice, three Shellfish Meat, and one Seaweed. These can all be purchased from The Upper Crust Gourmet Foods in Central Resulia.

Q107—Empty Shelves, Empty Coffers

REWARD

EXP	FOL	SP
6300	3000	280

ITEMS
Mythril Mesh

WALKTHROUGH

Prerequisites: Progress to at least Chapter 10

Hunks of Damascus Steel are dropped from Damascus Forts in the Western Dakaav Tunnel or mined at excavation nodes there. Snakeskins are dropped from Lizard Warriors and Lizard Shamans in Eastern Trei'kur. However, these enemies are no longer found there in the latter portion of the main quest, so make sure to gather at least five of these skins while you can. The alternative to finding Snakeskin is post-end game, in the Maze of Tribulations (from Lizard Tyrants). Alternatively, you can find these lizardmen in the second iteration of the Cathedral of Oblivion.

Q108—Grannie Never Rests on Her Laurels

REWARD

EXP	FOL	SP
3900	2500	250

ITEMS
Mentality Seeds x 2

WALKTHROUGH

Prerequisites: Progress to at least Chapter 7

You can obtain Laurel Trees by defeating bipedal plant enemies like the Lamia Radix commonly encountered in the eastern region of the Resulian Plains.

Q109—Processing the Possibilities

REWARD

EXP	FOL	SP
5100	2700	280

ITEMS
Cerulean Orb Signets, Vol. 3

WALKTHROUGH

Prerequisites: Progress to at least Chapter 9

Kronos machinery enemies such as Toy Soldiers, Valiant Conscripts, and Avengers drop Quantum Processors. Toy Soldiers are encountered on the Cavaliero, while the other two enemies can be found in the Alcazar of the Golden Age.

Q110—Reaping Bloody Benefits

REWARD

EXP	FOL	SP
6200	4000	280
ITEMS		
Angelstone x 2		

WALKTHROUGH

Prerequisites: Progress to at least Chapter 10

There are two Bloodstained Cloths in chests in the Trei'kuran Dunes. Additionally, most ghost-like enemies (such as the Misfortuners encountered in the Trei'kuran Dunes) drop sheets of these.

Q111—Collective Parting of the Sands

REWARD

EXP	FOL	SP
4200	2300	250
ITEMS		
Gnomestone x 2		

WALKTHROUGH

Prerequisites: Progress to at least Chapter 8

At the earliest point this quest is undertaken, you can only obtain a Sandfish from fishing spots in the Trei'kuran Dunes. The chance to fish it up is rare, however. You can reset fishing nodes by sleeping at an inn or in the starship's Private Quarters. Alternatively, you can get Sandfish from defeating Horned Turtles in the Northern Territory of Sohma between story chapters 9 and 10. When the turtles no longer appear in this area, you'll have to resort to fishing Sandfish up in the Trei'kuran Dunes.

Q112—Mouth-Watering Collection

REWARD

EXP	FOL	SP
5300	2900	280
ITEMS		
Therapeutic Tincture x 3		

WALKTHROUGH

Prerequisites: Progress to at least Chapter 9

Marbled Meat can only be procured through Synthesis, with a resulting food quality of 50.

Q113—The Collective Gift of Giving

REWARD

EXP	FOL	SP
6400	4500	280

ITEMS
Mind Amulet, Sukiyaki

WALKTHROUGH

Prerequisites: Progress to at least Chapter 10

You can craft Mythril with the Alchemy specialty skill if it's leveled to at least Lv. 5. The recipe is six hunks of Platinum and two bottles of Alchemist's Water. Otherwise, you can obtain pieces of Mythril by defeating Dark Materials in the Signesilica.

Q114—Subjugation Directive: Sandra

REWARD

EXP	FOL	SP
4400	2400	250

ITEMS
Encyclopedia Corruptionem (unlocks Corruptology specialty), Resurrection Elixir

WALKTHROUGH

Prerequisites: Progress to at least Chapter 8

Sandra the Majestic is found on the way to the Trei'kur Slaughtery in the northwest region of the Trei'kuran Dunes.

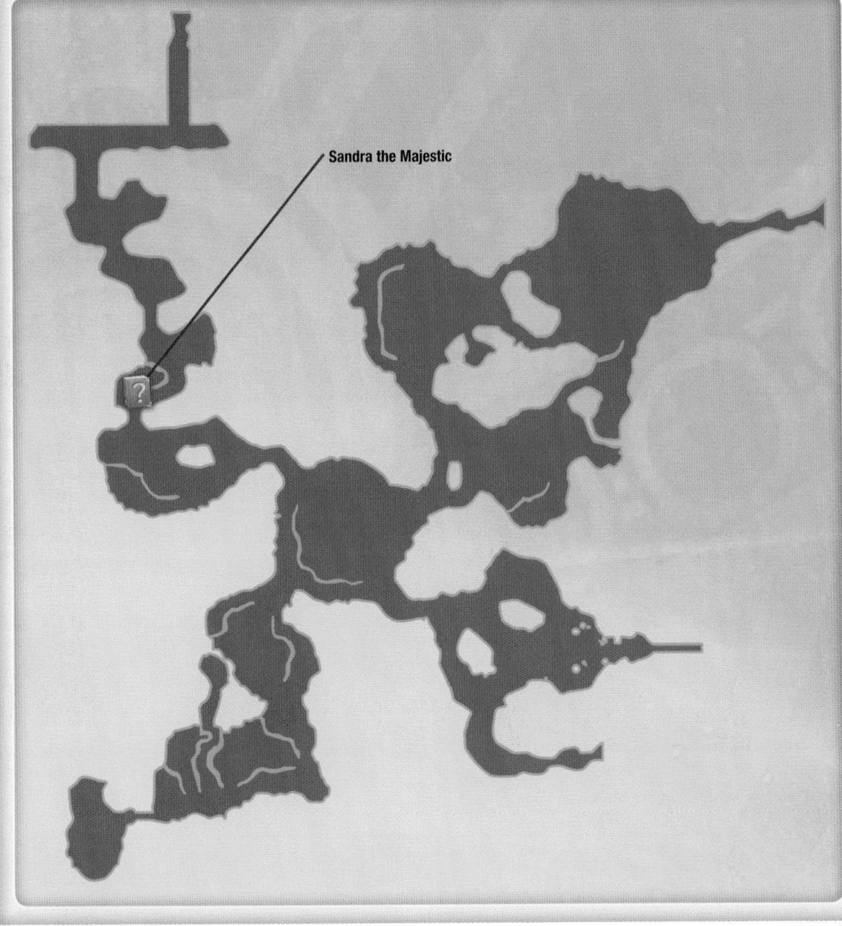

Q115—Subjugation Directive: Zurtails

REWARD

EXP	FOL	SP
4000	3000	250
ITEMS		
Swordsman's Manual III, Salmon Meuniere		

WALKTHROUGH

Prerequisites: Progress to at least Chapter 8

Cunning Zurtails are demon imps roaming the Trei'kur Slaughtery while this quest is active. You can find two groups in the northeast tower, with the other two in the northwest region of the slaughtery.

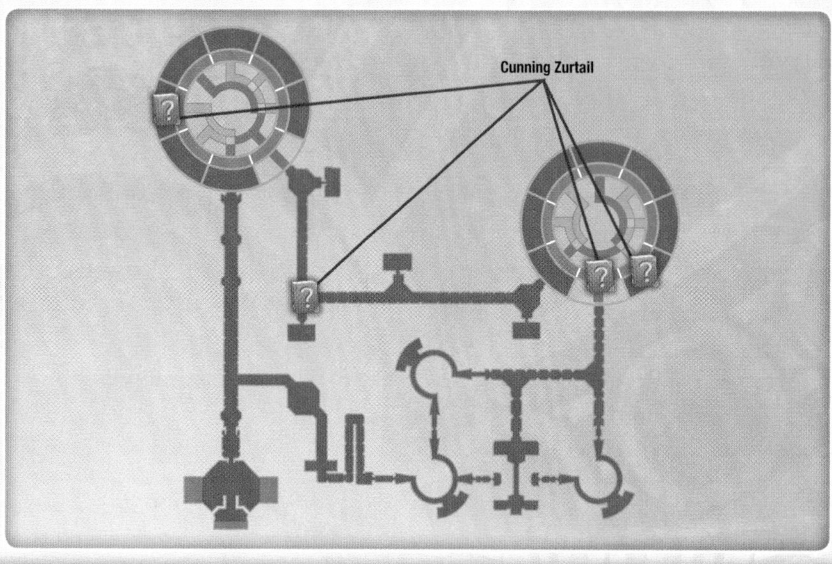

Q116—Subjugation Directive: Vlad

REWARD

EXP	FOL	SP
5500	3500	280
ITEMS		
Ifrit Mail		

WALKTHROUGH

Prerequisites: Progress to at least Chapter 9

You can find Vlad the Unsullied haunting the Western Dakaav Tunnel. His exact location is in the southwest region of the area, near the locked chest.

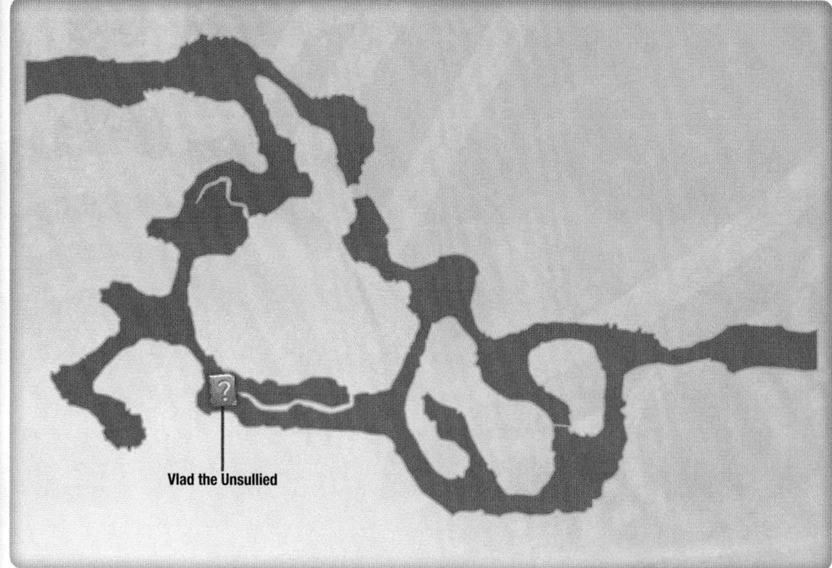

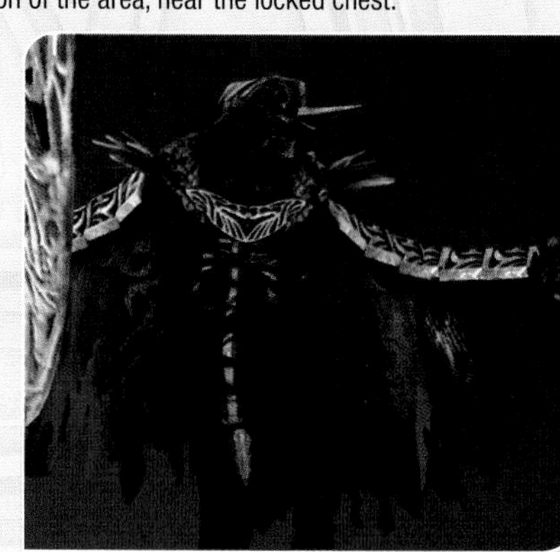

Q117—Subjugation Directive: Dante and Mateo

REWARD

EXP	FOL	SP
7200	5800	300

ITEMS
Superior Chain Mail

WALKTHROUGH

Prerequisites: Progress to at least Chapter 11

These two possessed suits of hulking armor are found near the save point in the Western Dakaav Tunnel. Like the encounter with Niflhel and Niflheim, watch out for their devastating area of effect attacks!

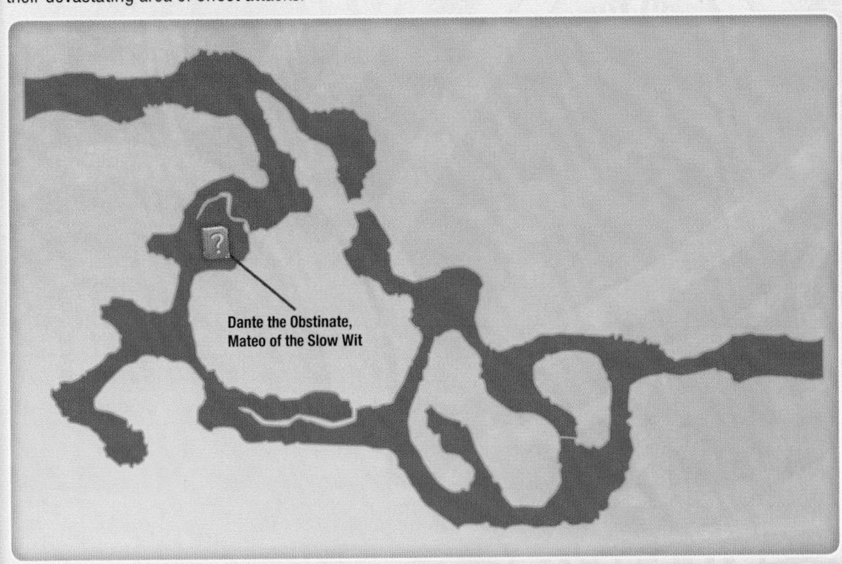

Q118—Subjugation Directive: Sythwas

REWARD

EXP	FOL	SP
6500	4800	280

ITEMS
Light Scarf

WALKTHROUGH

Prerequisites: Progress to at least Chapter 10

There are two groups of Garish Sythwas in the Trei'kur Slaughtery. One is in the northeast tower, while the other group is in the northwest tower.

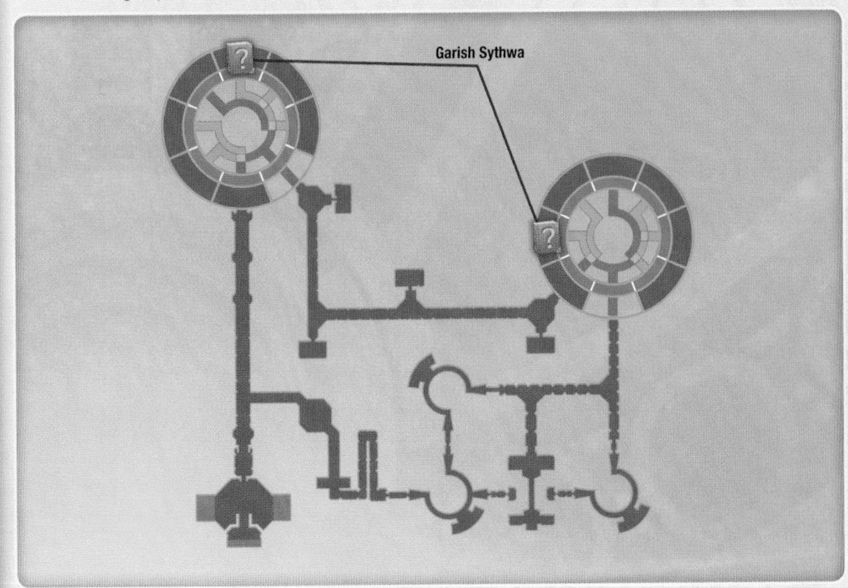

Q119—Garrote the Guerillas

REWARD

EXP	FOL	SP
6000	4500	280
ITEMS		
Energy Amulet, Riot Potion x 2		

WALKTHROUGH

Prerequisites: Progress to at least Chapter 10

Trei'kuran survivors, simply named "Guerrillas," are found littered across the Trei'kuran Dunes. Two groups dwell in the northwest region (near the Trei'kur Slaughtery), one group resides in the southwest, and one is found in the northeast portion of the area.

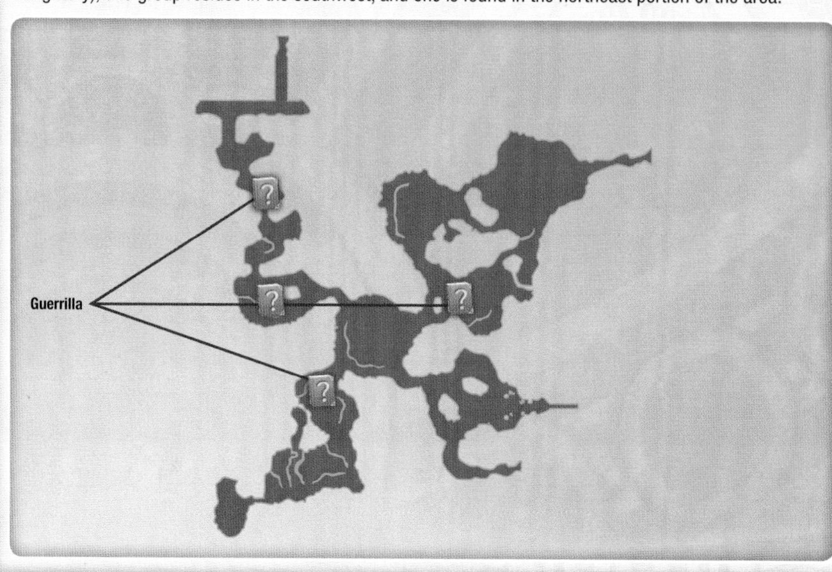

Q120—Wanted: Hannah

REWARD

EXP	FOL	SP
5400	2500	280
ITEMS		
Miraculous Device x 2		

WALKTHROUGH

Prerequisites: Progress to at least Chapter 9

Hannah the Rapturous is a humanoid-type enemy found in the Trei'kur Slaughtery. The fastest way to reach her is through the shortcut door that unlocks after you complete the main mission involving the Trei'kur Slaughtery. From the entrance of the tower, go north until you reach a divergence, then head west, leading into the southwest portion of the area.

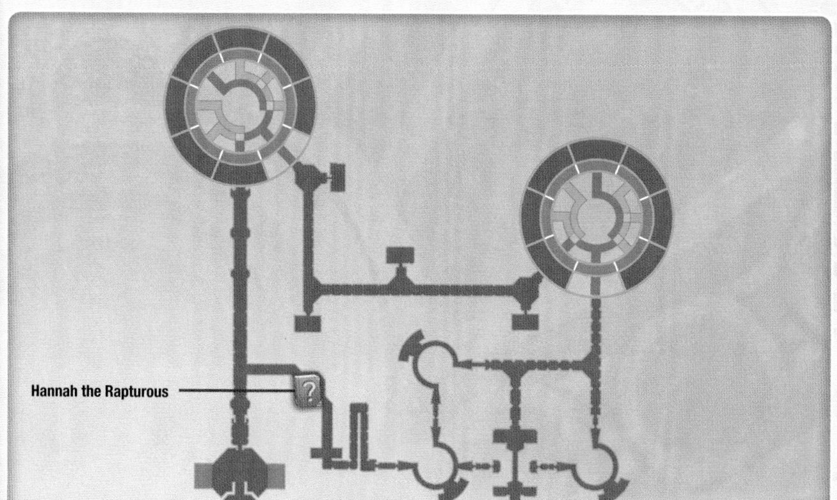

Q121—War and Peace

REWARD

EXP	FOL	SP
6900	3000	300

ITEMS
CQC Program Eta, Holy Mist

WALKTHROUGH

Prerequisites: Progress to at least Chapter 11

You can find Idealistic Insurgents in the Trei'kuran Dunes, just outside of Eastern Trei'kur. You'll need to defeat at least 10 of them, so you may have to use the Ocarina specialty to respawn them (or simply re-enter the area).

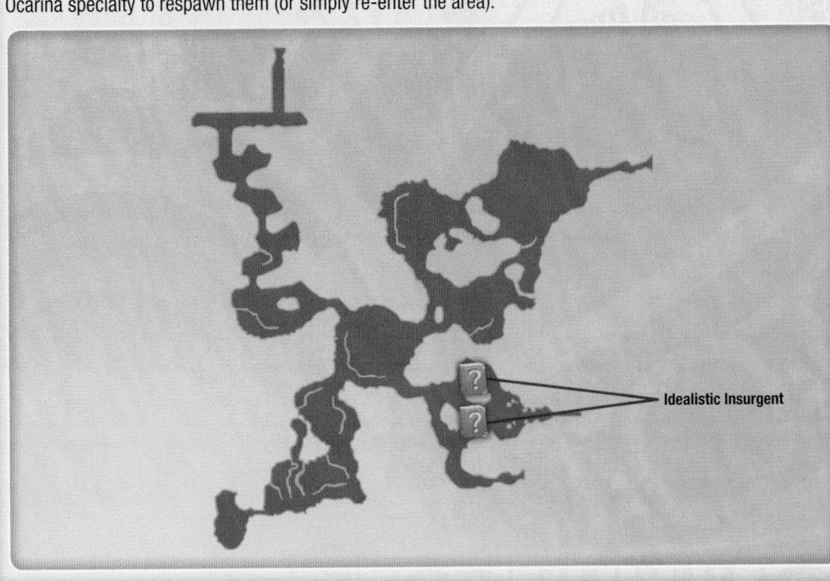

Q122—A Peeping Golem!

REWARD

EXP	FOL	SP
5500	3000	280

ITEMS
Nereidstone

WALKTHROUGH

Prerequisites: Progress to at least Chapter 9

Ivor of the Lustful Look is a Corrupt enemy in the Trei'kuran Dunes. Like other Baskanias, its eye attacks deal a constant and significant amount of damage to anyone it's focused on, so make sure to run away from its eye beams!

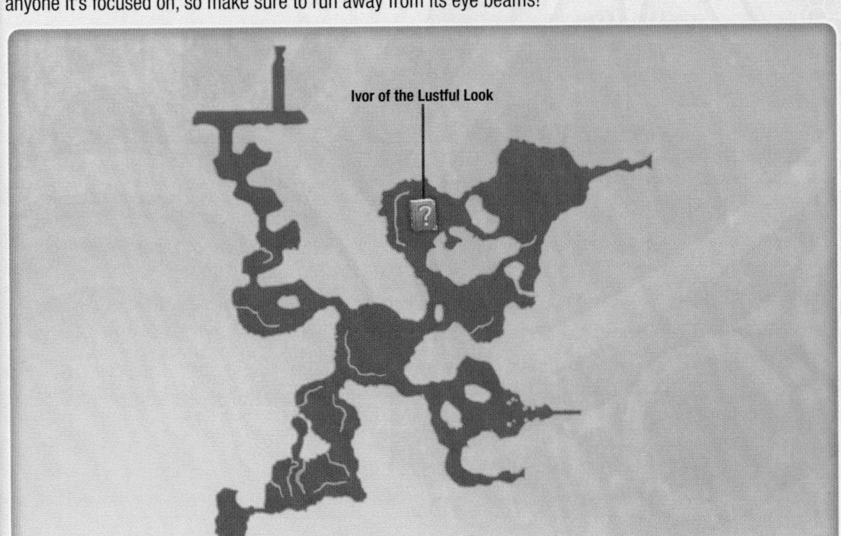

PRIVATE ACTIONS

Private Actions return in *Star Ocean: Integrity and Faithlessness*. These character-based events serve to provide personal insight into the party members' backstories. Additionally, the more Private Actions that you view increases the affinity between characters. This hidden affinity value affects certain events in the game, most notably the ending. The way you respond to multiple choice Private Actions also affects the affinity value. For instance, if you (as Fidel) respond positively to one of the other party members' inquisitions, the affinity between Fidel and said party member increases. You can further manipulate this value with potions and by other means. For details, see the **Multiple Endings** chapter in this guide following the main story walkthrough.

There are two types of Private Actions: triggered ones and random ones. Triggered Private Actions are initiated in specific spots in towns and on the Charles D. Goale. Random Private Actions are a separate series of Private Actions that are seemingly randomly generated by traveling around the world (and can also be triggered in towns when there are no normal Private Action events outstanding). Private Actions and random Private Actions are loosely connected. Some Private Actions unlock when prerequisite random Private Actions are triggered, and vice versa. For example, if you trigger the random Private Action called "Victor on Love," it unlocks a hidden normal Private Action called "Enter a Mysterious Woman" (Chapter 7).

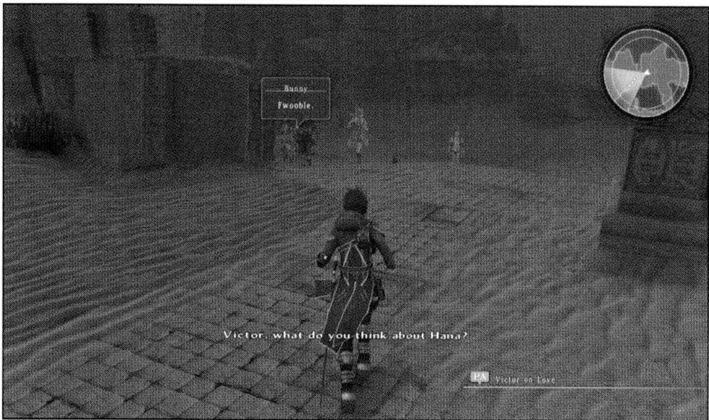

When a set of normal Private Actions is available in the current area, a whistle icon displays on the map. Stepping onto the whistle starts the Private Actions event.

A set of stars in the lower-right side of the screen appears, indicating the currently available Private Actions that can be triggered in the current area.

When all of the stars are filled out, stepping on the whistle icon again ends the Private Actions event. However, this doesn't necessarily mean that all of the current Private Actions are exhausted. More may be queued up depending on how far along into the story you are and how many you've viewed from the current area. To check for more, you can exit the area (or enter a nearby inn), then re-enter the area to check for the whistle icon on the map.

DESIGNATED PRIVATE ACTION EVENT LOCATIONS

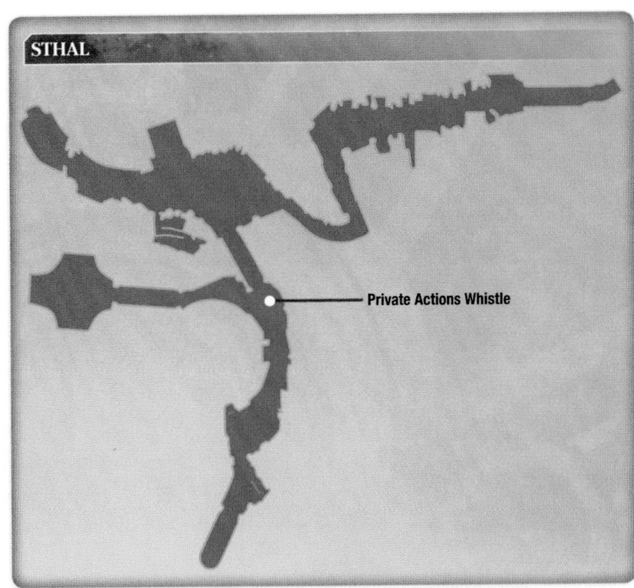

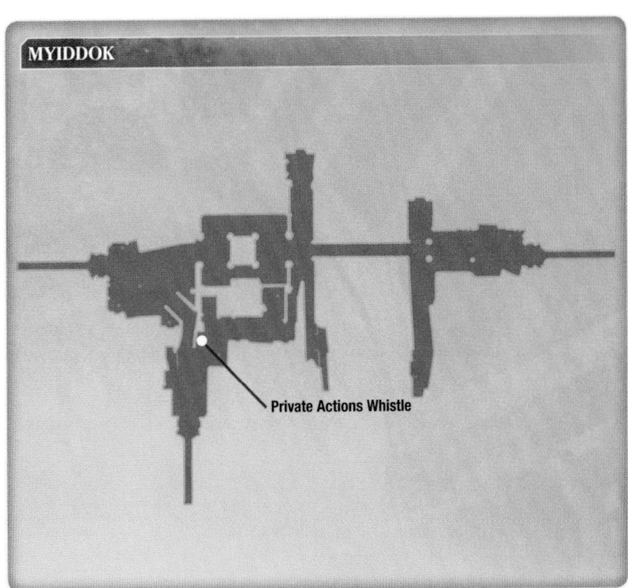

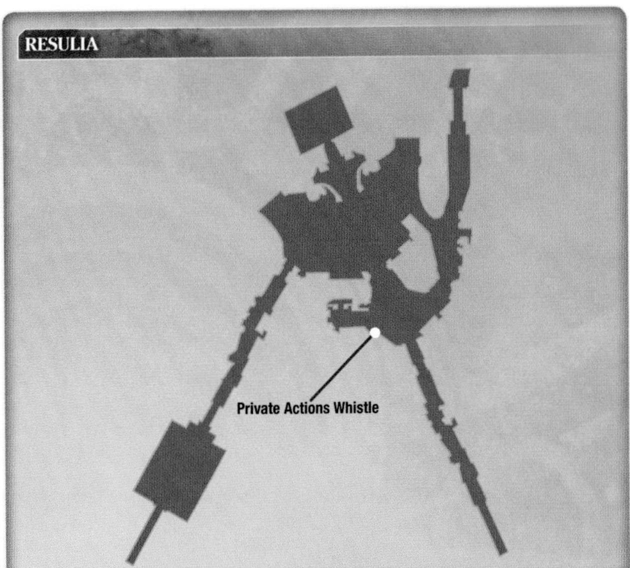

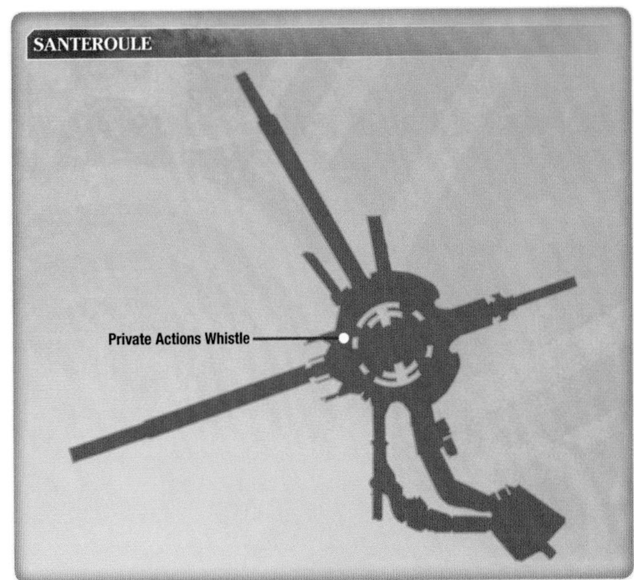

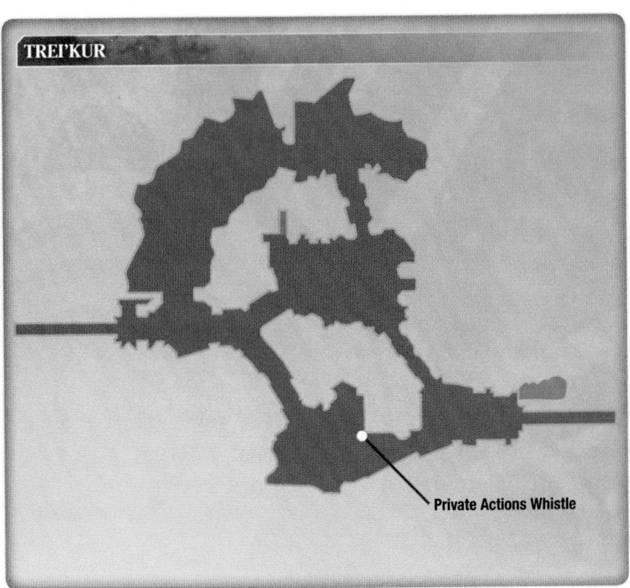

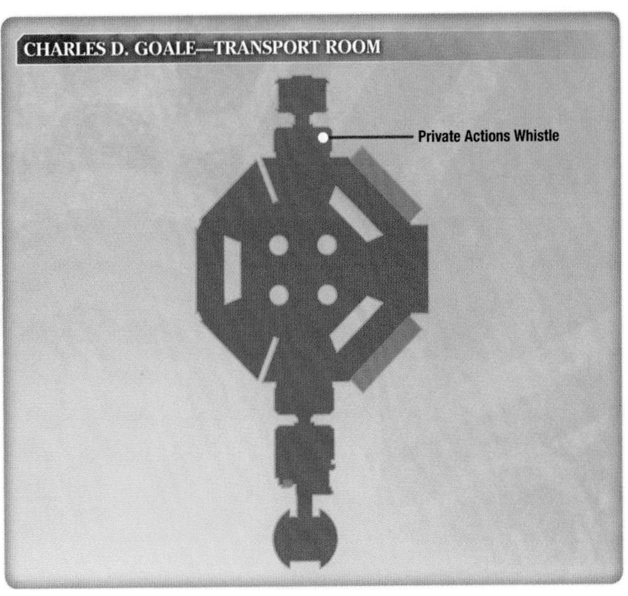

DESIGNATED RANDOM PRIVATE ACTION TRIGGER LOCATIONS

If you find yourself unable to trigger any of the normal Private Actions in the data tables at the end of this chapter, you can unlock them by viewing random Private Actions at the points designated in the following maps, or by making further progress through the main storyline.

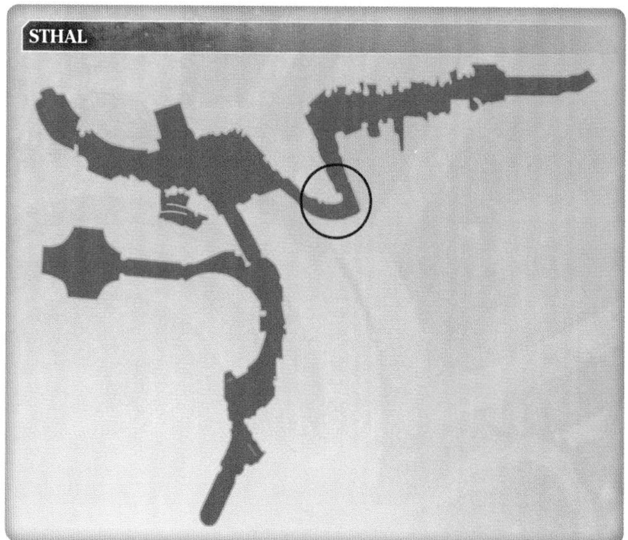

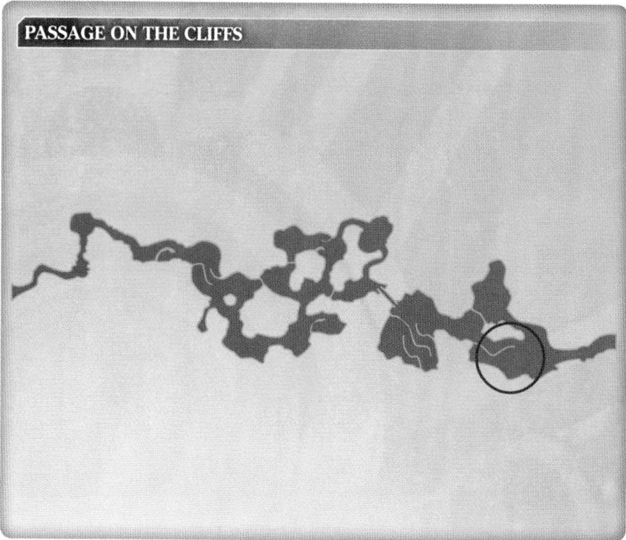

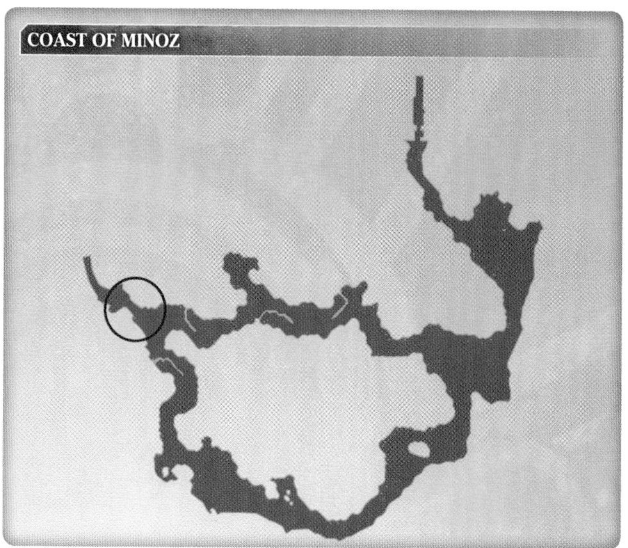

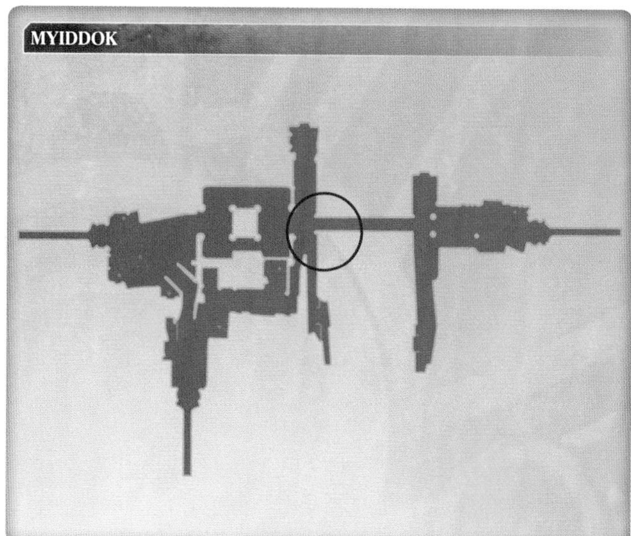

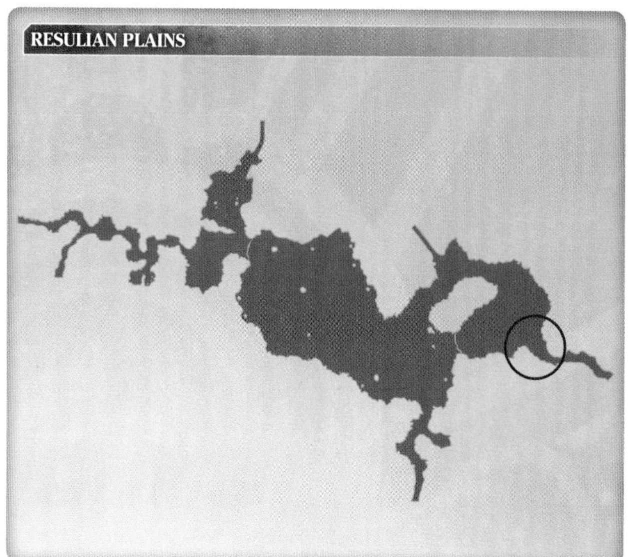

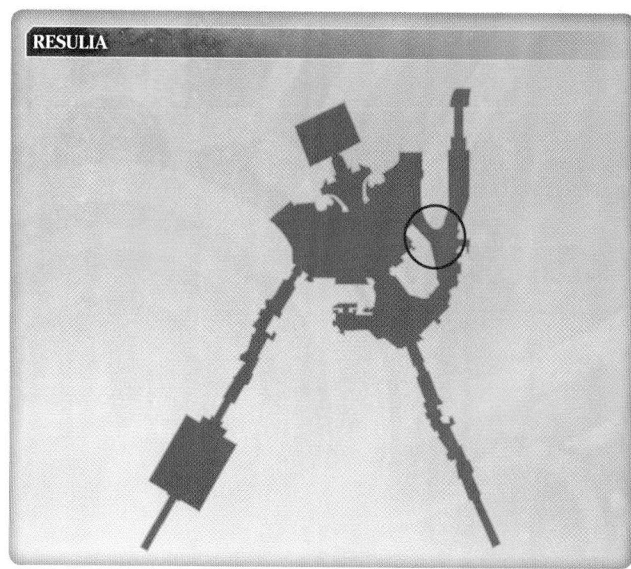

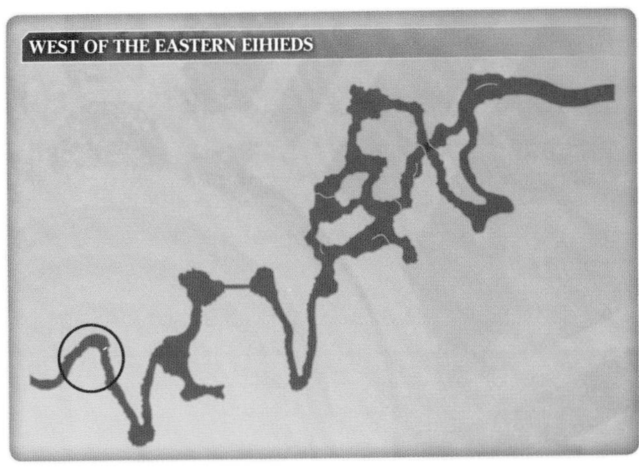
WEST OF THE EASTERN EIHIEDS

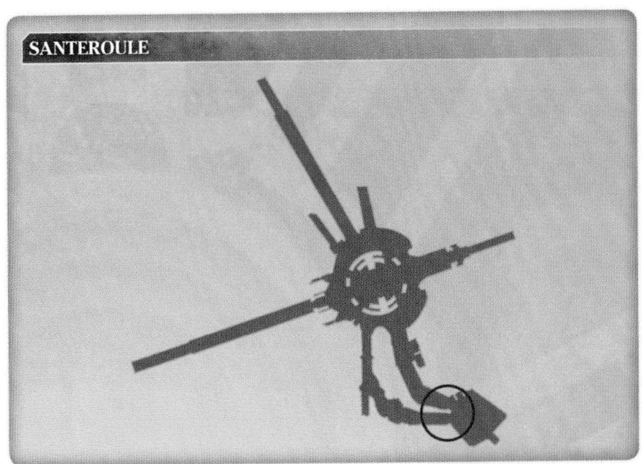
SANTEROULE

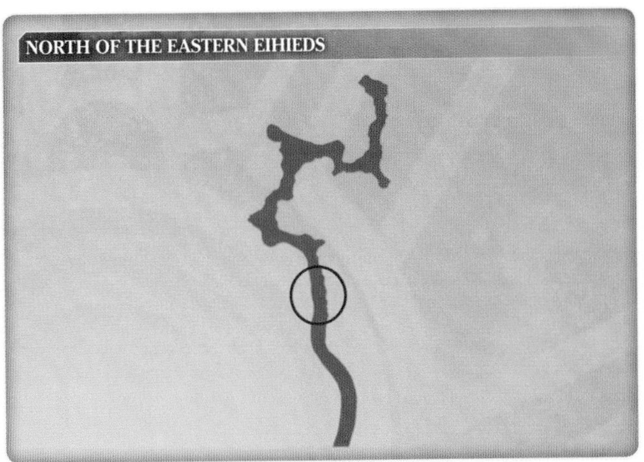
NORTH OF THE EASTERN EIHIEDS

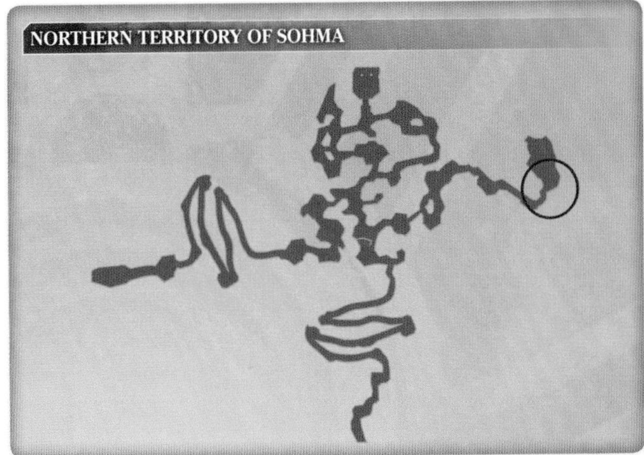
NORTHERN TERRITORY OF SOHMA

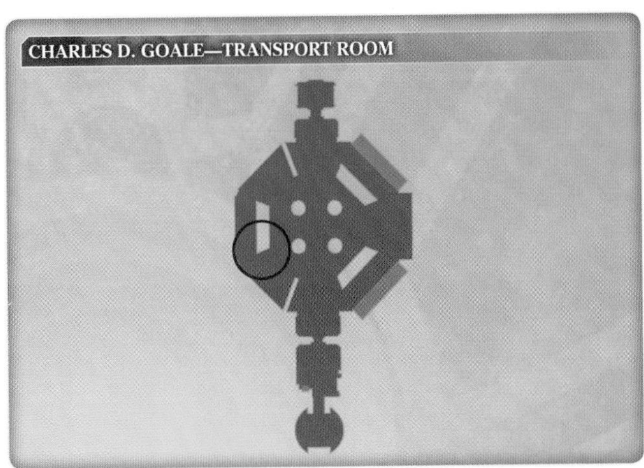
CHARLES D. GOALE—TRANSPORT ROOM

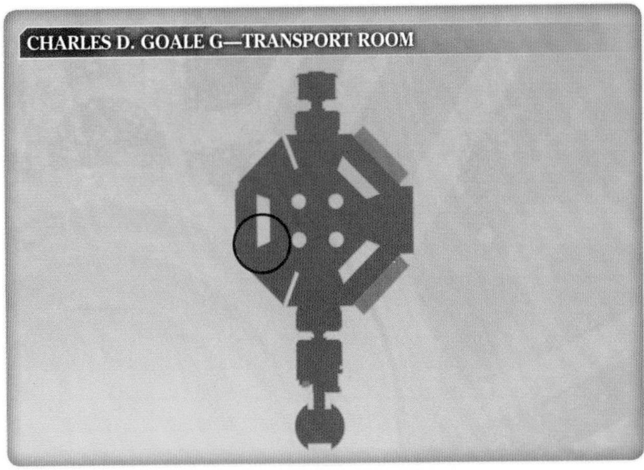
CHARLES D. GOALE G—TRANSPORT ROOM

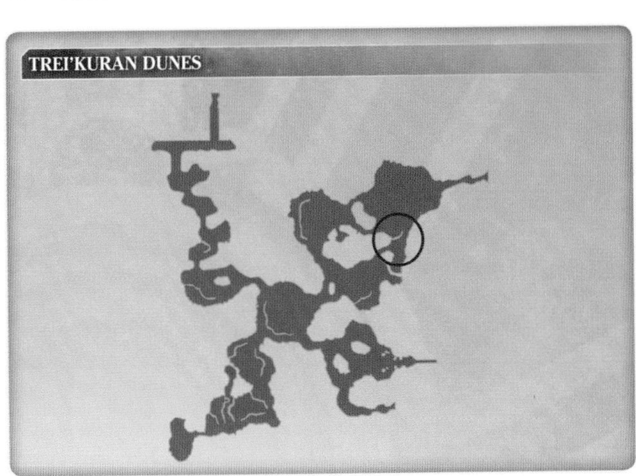
TREI'KURAN DUNES

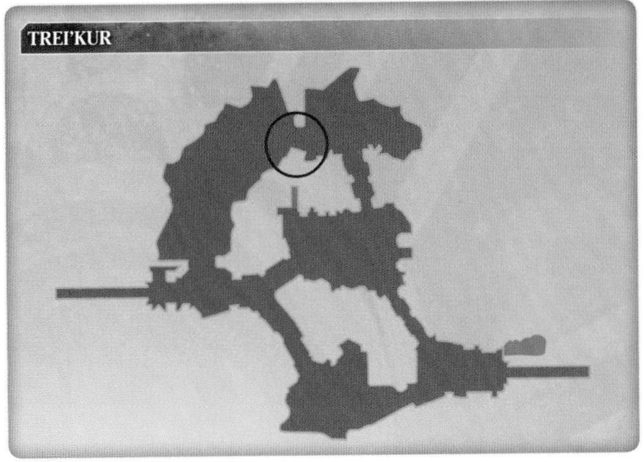
TREI'KUR

The following tables list triggered Private Actions, sorted by area.

STHAL

NAME	AVAILABLE	MISSABLE	CHARACTERS INVOLVED	NOTES
Miki's Hatred of Gambling	Chapter 1	No	Miki	—
Eat Your Vegetables	Chapter 1	No	Victor	Multiple choice response
Miki's Hatred of Frogs	Chapter 3	No	Miki/Relia	—
Into the Wild with Fidel	Chapter 3	No	Miki/Victor	—
Miki's Hatred of Surprises	Chapter 3	No	Miki	—
Unsupported Assumption	Chapter 4	No	Fiore	—
You Can Only Save One	Chapter 4	No	Emmerson	Multiple choice response
Fun with Frogs	Chapter 4	No	Relia	—
The Benefit of Being a Snake	Chapter 4	No	Relia/Emmerson	—
Fidel's Angels	Chapter 4	No	Miki	Multiple choice response
Watching Fidel	Chapter 4	No	Relia	—
Barrage of Questions	Chapter 4	No	Relia	Multiple choice response
Mom and Dad	Chapter 4	Yes	Relia	Multiple choice response, can only be triggered before meeting Relia's parents
Someone	Chapter 4	Yes	Relia	Can only be triggered before learning of Feria's existence
Emmerson's Reconnaissance Methods	Chapter 4	No	Emmerson/Anne	—
A Skirt for Fidel	Chapter 4	No	Relia/Fiore	Multiple choice response
Selfish Children	Chapter 4	No	Fiore	Multiple choice response
Mom and Dad for Fidel	Chapter 5	No	Relia	—
Climate Change	Chapter 5	No	Anne	Multiple choice response
While Fidel's Away, Ted Plays	Chapter 6	No	Miki	—
Dueling a Vicious Beast	Chapter 6	No	Miki/Victor	—
Dueling a Trained Professional	Chapter 6	No	Miki/Victor	—
Like Father, Like Son	Chapter 7	Yes	Anne	Multiple choice response; can only be viewed before Daril is killed
Space Food	Chapter 7	No	Miki/Emmerson	—
High-Stakes Gambling	Chapter 7	No	Miki/Emmerson	—
Over Fidel's Head	Chapter 7	No	Emmerson	Multiple choice response
Talking with Ted	Chapter 8	No	Miki	—
Fastidious about Food	Chapter 8	Yes	Miki/Victor/Relia (Feria)	Can only be viewed while Feria is in the party
Singing	Chapter 8	Yes	Miki/Relia (Feria)	Can only be viewed while Feria is in the party
The Apple	Chapter 8	Yes	Relia (Feria)	Can only be viewed while Feria is in the party; multiple choice response
Imitating Fidel Poorly	Chapter 8	Yes	Relia (Feria)	Can only be viewed while Feria is in the party
Warmth	Chapter 8	Yes	Relia (Feria)	Can only be viewed while Feria is in the party
Introspective Fidel	Chapter 9	No	Anne	Multiple choice response
Thoughts on the Military	Chapter 10	No	Anne	Multiple choice response
Thank You	Chapter 10	No	Relia	—
Remembering Feria	Chapter 10	No	Relia	—

MYIDDOK

NAME	AVAILABLE	MISSABLE	CHARACTERS INVOLVED	NOTES
Terrible Dining in Myiddok	Chapter 3	No	Miki	—
Fidel and Fighting Styles	Chapter 3	No	Victor	Multiple choice response
Warm Places	Chapter 4	No	Relia	—
Here, Kitty, Kitty	Chapter 4	No	Anne	—
Watching Miki	Chapter 4	No	Miki/Relia	—
It's the Thought that Counts	Chapter 4	No	Miki/Relia	—
Miki the Patissier	Chapter 4	No	Miki/Relia	—
Can't Find Kitty	Chapter 4	No	Anne	—
The Most Bitter Drink Is Life	Chapter 4	No	Relia/Emmerson	—
In the Mood for Sweets	Chapter 4	No	Miki/Relia	—
Mistaken Identity	Chapter 5	No	Anne	—
Fidel's Relationship Status	Chapter 5	No	Fiore	Multiple choice response
Survey on Singing	Chapter 5	No	Emmerson	Multiple choice response
Fidel's Type	Chapter 5	No	Fiore	Multiple choice response
Fidel's First Love	Chapter 5	No	Fiore	Multiple choice response
The Luxury of Eating	Chapter 6	No	Miki	Multiple choice response
Fidel and Outer Space	Chapter 6	Yes	Victor	Multiple choice response, can only be triggered before Victor visits the Charles D. Goale G for the first time
Enter a Mysterious Woman	Chapter 7	Yes	Victor/Mysterious woman	Requires viewing of "Victor on Love," a random Private Action. The mysterious woman can appear in Myiddok, Eastern Trei'kur, or Santeroule. Must acknowledge Fidel's acquaintance with Victor to fulfill prerequisite of next two mysterious woman Private Actions
Neverending Story of Sweets	Chapter 7	No	Miki	—

NAME	AVAILABLE	MISSABLE	CHARACTERS INVOLVED	NOTES
The Duchess of Duking It Out	Chapter 7	No	Victor/Anne	—
Fidel and Love	Chapter 7	No	Victor	Multiple choice response
Reverse Psychology	Chapter 7	No	Emmerson/Anne	—
More Cat Capers	Chapter 7	No	Anne	—
Portrait of the Creature as a Young Kitten	Chapter 7	No	Anne	—
Tipping the Scales When Tipsy	Chapter 7	No	Fiore/Emmerson	Unlocks Spendthrift role
No Hangovers, No Reason to Decline	Chapter 7	No	Fiore/Emmerson	—
Guzzle It Like Granny	Chapter 7	No	Fiore/Anne	—
Its and Her Circumstances	Chapter 8	No	Emmerson/Anne	—
Mutterings	Chapter 8	Yes	Relia (Feria)	Can only be viewed while Feria is in the party
More Mutterings	Chapter 8	Yes	Relia (Feria)	Can only be viewed while Feria is in the party
Miki's Grandiose Dream	Chapter 9	No	Miki/Emmerson	Unlocks Minstrel role
Alcohol Appreciation	Chapter 9	No	Emmerson	Multiple choice response
Brains of the Family	Chapter 9	No	Miki/Anne	—
The Consensus on Anne's Grandmother	Chapter 9	No	Miki/Victor/Fiore/ Emmerson/Anne	—

CENTRAL RESULIA

NAME	AVAILABLE	MISSABLE	CHARACTERS INVOLVED	NOTES
Practical Applications of Signeturgy	Chapter 1	No	Miki	—
The Phantom Malko	Chapter 3	No	Victor	—
Why Signeturgy?	Chapter 3	No	Miki/Victor	—
Another Chance at Life	Chapter 3	No	Victor	Multiple choice response
The ABCs of Dining in Resulia	Chapter 3	No	Miki	—
Malko Strikes Back	Chapter 3	No	Victor	—
A New Hopeless Malko	Chapter 3	No	Victor	—
Technologically Advanced Country Mouse	Chapter 4	No	Emmerson/Anne	—
Are You My Friend?	Chapter 4	No	Relia	Multiple choice response
Mundane Magic Trick	Chapter 4	No	Relia/Emmerson	—
Anne's Priorities	Chapter 4	No	Anne	—
Has Love Blossomed?	Chapter 4	No	Miki/Relia	—
Love Is in the Hair?	Chapter 4	No	Miki/Relia	—
Seemingly Unattainable	Chapter 5	No	Relia	—
Faykreedian Beauty	Chapter 5	No	Anne	—
Stuffed Full of Kindness	Chapter 5	No	Anne	Multiple choice response
Return to Sender	Chapter 5	No	Fiore	Multiple choice response
Picking Presents	Chapter 5	No	Fiore	—
Outstretched Hand	Chapter 5	No	Fiore/Relia	—
The Joy of Giving	Chapter 5	No	Fiore/Emmerson	—
Gift Guidance	Chapter 5	No	Fiore	Multiple choice response
Cheeky Spot for a Signet	Chapter 6	No	Miki/Fiore	—
The True Cause of the Corrupt	Chapter 7	No	Miki/Anne	—
Trouble Brewing Between Nations	Chapter 7	No	Victor/Emmerson	—
Anne and Canines	Chapter 7	No	Victor/Anne	—
Manly Miki	Chapter 7	No	Miki	Multiple choice response
Asking About Accessories	Chapter 7	No	Anne	Multiple choice response
Anything You Want?	Chapter 8	Yes	Emmerson/Relia (Feria)	Can only be viewed while Feria is in the party
Reason to Smile	Chapter 8	Yes	Relia (Feria)	Multiple choice response; can only be viewed while Feria is in the party
Like Brother and Sister	Chapter 9	No	Miki/Emmerson	—
Return of the Jocular Malko	Chapter 9	No	Victor	—
Hitting on Hana	Chapter 9	No	Emmerson	—
Resulia's in Good Hands	Chapter 9	No	Victor	—
When to Trust	Chapter 9	No	Victor/Anne	—
Love Is Pain?	Chapter 10	No	Relia	—
Parents and Loneliness	Chapter 10	No	Miki/Relia	—
Watching Victor	Chapter 10	No	Victor/Relia	—
Easily Understandable Animals	Chapter 10	No	Victor/Relia	—
Under My Thumb?	Chapter 11	No	Miki/Fiore/Relia	—
New Friend	Chapter 11	No	Relia	Multiple choice response
Friends for Now	Chapter 11	No	Miki/Fiore/Relia	—
It's Better to Have Loved and Lost?	Chapter 12	No	Relia	—

SANTEROULE

NAME	AVAILABLE	MISSABLE	CHARACTERS INVOLVED	NOTES
Signeturgical Tools	Chapter 4	No	Miki/Fiore	—
Caught in the Act	Chapter 4	No	Emmerson	Multiple choice response
The Daily Lives of Signeturgical Researchers	Chapter 4	No	Miki/Fiore	—
Family Ties	Chapter 4	No	Miki/Relia	—
Who's Most Popular?	Chapter 4	No	Relia/Fiore	Multiple choice response
Spicy or Sweet?	Chapter 4	No	Miki	Multiple choice response
From Prodigious to Pedestrian	Chapter 4	No	Fiore	—
One Has Smarm, the Other Charm	Chapter 4	No	Miki/Emmerson	—
Fidel as a Kid	Chapter 4	No	Relia	—
Figment of Anne's Imagination	Chapter 4	No	Anne	—
Bird Watching	Chapter 4	No	Miki/Relia	—
Different Frame of Reference	Chapter 5	No	Fiore	—
Different Perspectives	Chapter 5	No	Emmerson/Anne	—
Emotionally Distant	Chapter 5	No	Fiore/Emmerson	—
Mr. Rabbit's Change of Clothes	Chapter 5	No	Relia/Fiore	—
Aptitude for Ambiguity	Chapter 6	No	Miki/Fiore	—
Suspicions Arise over Baths	Chapter 6	No	Victor	—
Chez Miki	Chapter 6	No	Miki/Fiore	—
Suspicions Arise over the Male Form	Chapter 6	No	Victor	—
Fidel and Fish: Dining in Santeroule	Chapter 6	No	Miki	—
Enter a Mysterious Woman	Chapter 7	Yes	Victor/Mysterious woman	Requires viewing of "Victor on Love," a random Private Action. The mysterious woman can appear in Myiddok, Eastern Trei'kur, or Santeroule. Must acknowledge Fidel's acquaintance with Victor to fulfill prerequisite of next two mysterious woman Private Actions
Nothing's There	Chapter 7	No	Miki/Anne	—
Asceticism over Affections	Chapter 7	No	Victor/Emmerson	Multiple choice response
Conversational Battle of the Sexes	Chapter 7	No	Victor/Emmerson	—
Helping Hand Towel	Chapter 7	No	Fiore/Anne	—
Fixated on Fiore	Chapter 7	No	Emmerson	Multiple choice response
Out for Blood	Chapter 7	No	Victor/Fiore/Anne	—
Sneaking Suspicion	Chapter 7	No	Emmerson/Anne	—
Haunted by the Unknown	Chapter 7	No	Anne	Multiple choice response
Condolences Cut Short	Chapter 8	Yes	Emmerson/Relia (Feria)	Can only be viewed while Feria is in the party
Girls' Hair	Chapter 8	Yes	Fiore/Relia (Feria)	Can only be viewed while Feria is in the party
Mother and Child	Chapter 8	Yes	Miki/Relia (Feria)	Can only be viewed while Feria is in the party
Finding Fidel	Chapter 8	Yes	Relia (Feria)	Multiple choice response; can only be viewed while Feria is in the party
The Nut	Chapter 8	Yes	Relia (Feria)	Multiple choice response; can only be viewed while Feria is in the party
The Letter	Chapter 11	No	Miki/Fiore/Anne	—
Sorry, Sis	Chapter 12	No	Relia	—
Reason to Fight	Chapter 12	No	Relia	—

EASTERN TREI'KUR

NAME	AVAILABLE	MISSABLE	CHARACTERS INVOLVED	NOTES
No Two-Timing	Chapter 7	No	Fiore/Emmerson	—
Reminiscing with Daril	Chapter 7	Yes	Miki	Can only be viewed before Daril is killed
Position of Power	Chapter 7	No	Emmerson	—
You a Cat Person or Dog Person?	Chapter 7	No	Miki/Fiore/Anne	Multiple choice response
A Fine Young Man	Chapter 7	Yes	Victor	Can only be viewed before Daril is killed
Patch Conversion	Chapter 7	No	Miki/Fiore	Unlocks Pinchfist role
No Different	Chapter 7	No	Emmerson/Anne	—
Ask Him Yourself	Chapter 7	Yes	Victor	Can only be triggered before Daril is killed
Crossing the Line	Chapter 7	No	Fiore	Multiple choice response
Sweet and Sour Personalities	Chapter 7	No	Miki/Anne	—
Combat and Concern	Chapter 7	Yes	Victor	Can only be viewed before Daril is killed
Prepared to Take Lives	Chapter 7	No	Victor/Emmerson	—
Spirited Conversation	Chapter 7	No	Miki/Fiore/Anne	—
Overshadowed by Fear	Chapter 7	No	Miki/Fiore/Anne	—
Only So Much You Can Do	Chapter 7	No	Miki/Anne	—
Enter a Mysterious Woman	Chapter 7	Yes	Victor/Mysterious woman	Requires viewing of "Victor on Love," a random Private Action. The mysterious woman can appear in Myiddok, Eastern Trei'kur, or Santeroule. Must acknowledge Fidel's acquaintance with Victor to fulfill prerequisite of next two mysterious woman Private Actions
The Mysterious Woman's Name	Chapter 7	Yes	Victor	Requires viewing of "Enter a Mysterious Woman"; multiple choice response: correct reply is "Rebecca"

NAME	AVAILABLE	MISSABLE	CHARACTERS INVOLVED	NOTES
The Mysterious Woman's Identity Revealed	Chapter 7	Yes	Victor	Requires viewing of "The Mysterious Woman's Name"
Rendered Speechless While Dining in Trei'kur	Chapter 8	No	Miki	—
Support from His Subordinates	Chapter 8	No	Victor	—
Especially Observant	Chapter 8	No	Emmerson/Anne	—
Bathroom Breakdown	Chapter 8	No	Miki/Anne	—
Hold Hands	Chapter 8	Yes	Miki/Relia (Feria)	Can only be viewed while Feria is in the party
Time for Remembrance	Chapter 8	No	Fiore	—
Can't Wind Back the Clock	Chapter 8	No	Emmerson	—
More Mundane Magic	Chapter 8	Yes	Emmerson/Relia (Feria)	Can only be viewed while Feria is in the party
Happy Together	Chapter 8	Yes	Relia (Feria)	Unlocks the Equal Opportunist role; only available when Feria is in the party
The Path They've Tread	Chapter 9	No	Miki	Multiple choice response
The Horror of War	Chapter 9	No	Miki	—
Cleaning for Klutzes	Chapter 9	No	Miki/Anne	—
Yearning for Home	Chapter 9	No	Miki	Multiple choice response
Kronos's Namesake	Chapter 9	No	Emmerson/Anne	—
The Plague	Chapter 9	No	Miki	Unlocks Vivifier role
Work Within the System	Chapter 9	No	Emmerson/Anne	—
Miki the Matron	Chapter 10	No	Miki/Relia/Fiore/Emmerson	—
Thanks for All You Do	Chapter 10	No	Miki	Reward: Wondrous Tincture
Bye-Bye, Sanity	Chapter 10	No	Relia/Anne	—
Drawing a Blank	Chapter 10	No	Relia	—
Far from Home	Chapter 11	No	Relia	Multiple choice response
Remembering Mom and Dad	Chapter 11	No	Relia	—

CHARLES D. GOALE TRANSPORT ROOM

NAME	AVAILABLE	MISSABLE	CHARACTERS INVOLVED	NOTES
Resulian Fruit Wine	Chapter 5	No	Emmerson/Anne	—
Fiore's Mentor Waxes Inspirational	Chapter 5	No	Fiore/Anne	—
Fiore's Mentor Waxes Admonitory	Chapter 5	No	Fiore/Emmerson	—
Mechanical Marvel	Chapter 9	No	Miki/Anne	—
He's a Good Man…and Thorough	Chapter 9	No	Victor/Emmerson	—
Faykreed's Exquisite Scenery	Chapter 9	No	Anne	—
The Military Elite	Chapter 9	No	Miki/Anne	—
Clueless Cupid	Chapter 9	No	Emmerson	—
Difficulty with Directories	Chapter 9	No	Victor/Anne	—
Ghost Story	Chapter 9	No	Emmerson	—
Feelings for Emmerson	Chapter 9	No	Miki/Anne	—
No Rest for the Storyteller	Chapter 9	No	Emmerson	—
Another Peaceful Day on the Bridge	Chapter 9	No	Emmerson	—
Threat to Society	Chapter 9	No	Emmerson/Anne	—
A Gift for Anne	Chapter 9	No	Miki/Emmerson	—
Punctuality's Imperative	Chapter 9	No	Emmerson/Anne	—
Every Second Counts	Chapter 9	No	Emmerson/Anne	—
Much to Learn	Chapter 9	No	Emmerson/Anne	—
Latest in a Long Line of Heroes	Chapter 9	No	Emmerson	—
Turbo Lift Luddite	Chapter 10	No	Victor	—
Whipped	Chapter 10	No	Relia/Emmerson	—
Heart Says Yes	Chapter 10	No	Miki/Relia	—
Relia's Fate	Chapter 11	No	Emmerson/Anne	—
Anne's First Mission	Chapter 12	No	Emmerson/Anne	Unlocks Instructor role

LOCKED CHESTS

Several locked chests are found throughout the game that you can only open once you've obtained the Lock Picking specialty skill. Lock Picking is a reward from **Survive This!**, a quest from the Central Resulian bulletin board that becomes available after you visit Eastern Trei'kur for the first time in the main story (Chapter 7). See Q039—Survive This! in the **Side Quests** chapter of this book for details.

The first locked chest you may encounter is in Sthal, in the Camuze Training Hall.

As you'd expect, these chests contain valuable items, ranging from skill books to powerful equipment. The earlier that you acquire these items, the stronger your party becomes relative to your enemies. Although the skill books in these chests aren't exclusive, most of them aren't naturally obtainable in the main story until much later in the game, giving you an edge early on.

While it's recommended that you unlock Lock Picking as soon as possible, all of the locked chests in the game are **not** missable. This means you can come back to loot them at any point later on in the game.

However, note that Lock Picking is required for the Maze of Tribulations post-ending content (if you want to be rewarded for your efforts, that is!), as all of the chests in the maze are locked.

Locked Chests on Faykreed

AREA	CONTENTS	LOCATION DESCRIPTION
Sthal—Camuze Training Hall	Swordsman's Manual III (Mirror Blade)	Southwest of the area
Passage on the Cliffs	Cerulean Orb Signets, Vol. 2 (Stone Rain, Deep Freeze)	In an alcove branching south in the western portion of the area
Coast of Minoz	CQC Program Gamma (Red Rain, Crescent Locus)	Northeast corner of the beach, next to the entrance to Myiddok
Dakaav Footpath	Moonlight Signets, Vol. 1 (Radiant Lancer, Shadow Needles)	In a treasure room just northeast of the Eitalon encampment
The Resulian Plains	Solar Signets, Vol. 2 (Volcanic Burst, Lightning Blast)	Near the center of the map, next to the Cathedral of Oblivion warp point
Royal Institute of Signetary Studies	Cerulean Orb Signets, Vol. 2 (Stone Rain, Deep Freeze)	In Ceisus's office
North of the Eastern Eihieds	Pneuma Signets, Vol. 1 (Raise Dead)	In an alcove just south of the entrance to the Ancient Institute
Central Resulia—Castle Bariff	Diligence Potion	First floor, in the southeast room
Central Resulia—Castle Bariff	Love Potion No. 256	Second floor, in the northeast room
Northern Territory of Sohma	Purification Signets, Vol. 2 (Cure Condition)	In a small alcove just west of the center of the area
Western Dakaav Tunnel	Signeturgical Book of Quietude (Silence, Sacred Pain)	In the southwest region of the map
Eastern Trei'kur	Resurrection Elixir	Northeast region of the area
Trei'kuran Dunes	CQB Program Epsilon (Hunter's Moon, Shockwave)	On a platform in the southwest region of the area, next to the Cathedral of Oblivion warp point
Trei'kur Slaughtery	Alastor (Victor weapon)	In a room in the upper level, close to the northeast tower
Trei'kur Slaughtery	Heroism Potion	In a cell in the northwest tower, next to a normal chest

Locked Chests in the Maze of Tribulations

AREA	CONTENTS	LOCATION DESCRIPTION
Maze of Tribulations: Corridor of Repose I	Swordsman's Manual VI (Abyssal Gate, Diabolic Edge)	Northeast corner on the second floor
Maze of Tribulations: Corridor of Repose I	Swordsman's Manual VIII (Air Raid, Dragon Roar)	In the room north of the boss arena
Maze of Tribulations: Corridor of Repose II	CQC Program Zeta (Crescent Wings, Acrobat Locus)	Easternmost room on the second floor
Maze of Tribulations: Corridor of Repose II	Solar Signets, Vol. 3 (Sunflare, Tornado)	In the room north of the boss arena
Maze of Tribulations: Corridor of Repose III	Cerulean Orb Signets, Vol. 3 (Terra Hammer, Arctic Impact)	In a room to the north on the second floor
Maze of Tribulations: Corridor of Repose III	CQC Program Theta (Avian Rage, Fists of Fury)	In the room north of the boss arena
Maze of Tribulations: Corridor of Repose IV	Swordsman's Manual VII (Cyclone Blade, Bloodstorm Revolution)	Northeast corner of the second floor
Maze of Tribulations: Corridor of Repose IV	Solar Signets, Vol. 4 (Explosion, Thunder Flare)	In the room north of the boss arena
Maze of Tribulations: Headstone of Repose	Reflecting Plate	In the room north of the boss arena
Maze of Tribulations: Indra's Peregrination I	CQC Program Eta (Heavenly Flight, Infinity Kick)	Northeast corner of the first floor
Maze of Tribulations: Indra's Peregrination I	Signet Card: Enhance +	In the northwest corner of the second floor
Maze of Tribulations: Indra's Peregrination I	Mystic Chain	In the room north of the boss arena
Maze of Tribulations: Indra's Peregrination II	Signet Card: Enlighten +	In a room to the north on the first floor
Maze of Tribulations: Indra's Peregrination II	Signet Card: Cure Condition +	In a room to the northeast of the second floor
Maze of Tribulations: Indra's Peregrination II	Laser Suit	In the room north of the boss arena
Maze of Tribulations: Indra's Peregrination III	Signet Card: Resurrection	Northeast corner of the first floor
Maze of Tribulations: Indra's Peregrination III	Signet Card: Faerie Star +	In a room to the south of the 9x9 grid on the second floor
Maze of Tribulations: Indra's Peregrination III	Moonlight Signets, Vol. 3 (Divine Wave, Dark Devourer)	In the room north of the boss arena
Maze of Tribulations: Indra's Peregrination IV	Signet Card: Ex Healing +	Easternmost room on the first floor
Maze of Tribulations: Indra's Peregrination IV	Philosopher's Stone	Northwest corner on the second floor
Maze of Tribulations: Indra's Peregrination IV	Aurora Blade (Fidel weapon)	In the room north of the boss arena
Maze of Tribulations: Indra's Abyss	Apocalypse (Miki weapon), Potent Defense/Mentality/ Health Seeds	In the room north of the boss arena
Maze of Tribulations: Terpsichorean Interlude I	Meteorite x3	Northeast room on the first floor
Maze of Tribulations: Terpsichorean Interlude I	Orichalcum x3	Southeast room on the fourth floor
Maze of Tribulations: Terpsichorean Interlude I	Murasame (Victor weapon)	In the room north of the boss arena
Maze of Tribulations: Terpsichorean Interlude II	Attack Seeds	In the room to the northeast on the first floor
Maze of Tribulations: Terpsichorean Interlude II	Intelligence Seeds	Westernmost room on the fourth floor
Maze of Tribulations: Terpsichorean Interlude II	Dragon's Den (Fiore weapon)	In the room north of the boss arena
Maze of Tribulations: Terpsichorean Interlude III	Defense Seeds	Easternmost room on the first floor
Maze of Tribulations: Terpsichorean Interlude III	Mentality Seeds	In the room to the northwest on the fourth floor
Maze of Tribulations: Terpsichorean Interlude III	Umbral Blast (Emmerson weapon)	In the room north of the boss arena
Maze of Tribulations: Terpsichorean Interlude IV	Health Seeds	In the room to the north on the first floor
Maze of Tribulations: Terpsichorean Interlude IV	Magic Seeds	Southeast corner room on the fourth floor
Maze of Tribulations: Terpsichorean Interlude IV	Kaiser Knuckles (Anne weapon)	In the room north of the boss arena
Maze of Tribulations: Terpsichorean Denouement	Moonstone, Potent Attack/Intelligence/Magic Seeds	In the room north of the boss arena

CATHEDRAL OF OBLIVION

INTRODUCTION

The Cathedral of Oblivion is an optional set of dungeons containing incredible rewards for players who defeat the enemies within. There are a total of 14 instances of the cathedral, spread across three distinct tiers. The first tier of the cathedral consists of three instances, the second tier consists of five, and the final tier consists of six.

When the cathedral spawns in an area, you can find a distortion in the space-time continuum designated on the in-game map (OPTIONS/START button). However, the chance of spawning is a coin flip. If there's one available in the area, you can force it to spawn by continuously leaving and re-entering the area and checking the map for the warp icon.

The first time you enter the cathedral prompts a tutorial regarding the optional dungeon. Once you've committed to taking the first warp point inside at the end of the aisle, you won't be able to leave—so it's do or die. Consider saving your progress, resting at an inn, and restocking your consumables before undertaking one of these trials (especially if it's your first time).

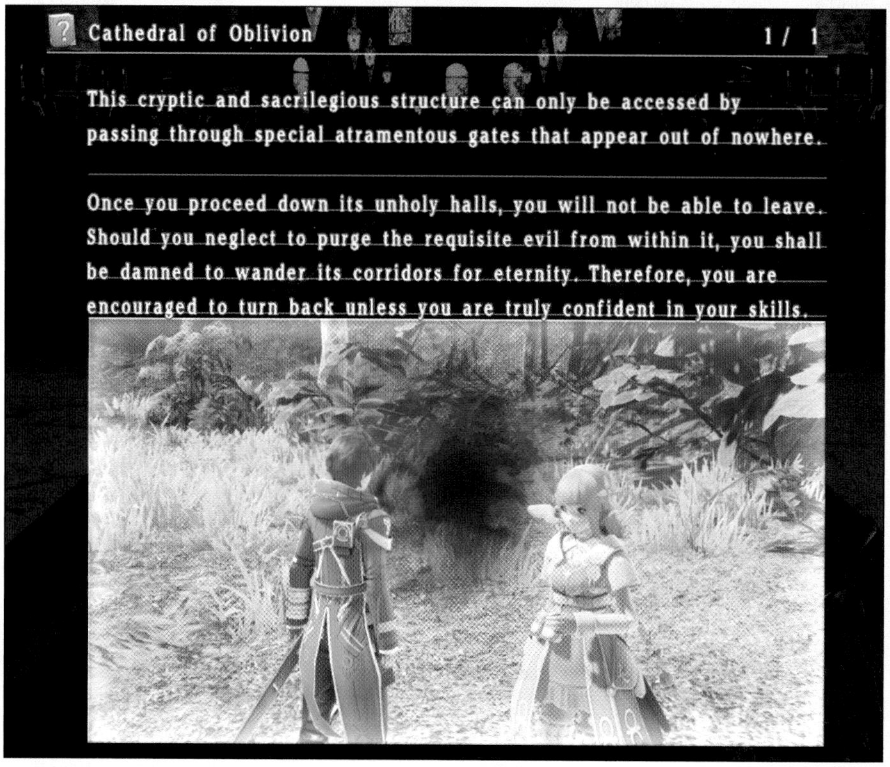

Each instance of the Cathedral of Oblivion consists of several rooms; each room prior to the final room is filled with enemies that you must defeat in order to progress to the next area. The last room contains a boss, usually one that's significantly higher in level than you (assuming that you enter at the earliest time possible).

As you progress through the story, the previous cathedral instances evolve into more difficult ones, with higher-level enemies, more rooms to traverse, more chests, and a significantly tougher boss. The first generation of the cathedral features a Corrupt-type boss called the Eyebalone, the second generation's boss is an avian called Vidofnir, and the third set's boss is the Storm Dragon.

First-generation instances of the cathedral are accessible between story chapters 3-6, with the cutoff after the siege of Eastern Trei'kur.

Second set of instances is available between chapters 7-10.

The final set of the Cathedral of Oblivion opens up in Chapter 10, after reuniting Relia with her parents.

Treasure chests found in the Cathedral of Oblivion are a constant. This means that even if you forgo completing the initial generations, you can still reap the rewards from them when you finish subsequent ones. For example, the first cathedral in the Coast of Minoz contains a final reward of a **Blue Talisman** in the third room. If you skip this first iteration and then return at a later point in the story to complete the second iteration, the Blue Talisman treasure chest will still be there in the third room (even though the boss in that room is replaced by a normal group of enemies).

The Cathedral of Oblivion trials primarily test your skills in combat, resourcefulness, preparation, and overall party level. Although it's possible to defeat the bosses within at earlier levels, it's recommended that you tackle them in order of boss levels. For instance, the power level of the Vidofnir boss in the second-generation instances of the cathedral varies depending on which area you enter from. The easiest encounter is in the Coast of Minoz, where Vidofnir is Lv. 45. At the other end of the spectrum, Vidofnir is Lv. 65 in the Northern Territory of Sohma—a staggering 20-level difference! Thus, you might want to take on the ones in the Coast of Minoz and the Resulian Plains before trying to defeat the higher-level ones. See the data tables following the Boss Battle Tips section for enemy details.

EYEBALONE

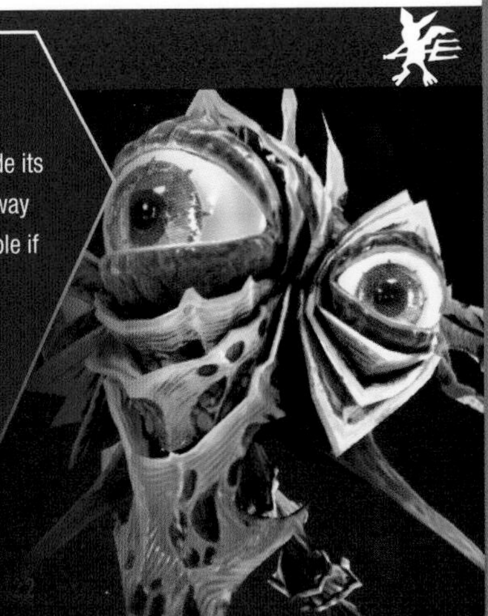

This Corrupt-type boss is found in the first iteration of the Cathedral of Oblivion. Its primary attacks are laser beams that originate from its giant eyeballs. Your main concern against the Eyebalone is to make sure that your party members evade its tracking beam attacks. Dry Eye is a three-pronged beam focused in a cone in front of Eyebalone. Keep your members away from it as best as you can. Eye of the Beholder is a tracking beam that follows a single party member. It's mostly avoidable if the character it's targeting is in your control, since you can maneuver away from it.

Eyebalone's physical damage primarily comes from a ground pound, dealing damage in an area around it with a chance of inflicting paralysis. Aside from its beams and area-of-effect attacks, it can cast a long-range signeturgical spell called Radiant Lancer. Eyebalone summons a large projectile through a portal above a target party member, dealing extensive damage. You can avoid this by moving out of the way.

Although Eyebalone is weak to the Mutant Slayer role, it's most likely too early in the game to have the role unlocked (it requires the Raven, Beast, Plant, and Insect Slayer roles maxed out).

VIDOFNIR

Vidofnir is an avian menace with a propensity for using fire- and wind-based attacks. Its main attacks to watch out for include Tornado, Volcanic Burst, and Divergent Shade.

To avoid Tornado, you'll need to be sharp. Move your back line members out of harm's way as soon as you see Vidofnir initiate the Tornado spell. This is best done by pausing into the Battle menu, then selecting and moving the endangered party member out of the way of the tornado's path. Volcanic Burst is much more difficult to avoid since it appears quickly in a large area. It's best to keep your party members away from each other (especially Miki, Fiore, and Emmerson) to mitigate the destruction done.

While battling against an avian, make sure to equip one of your damage-dealing party members like Fidel or Anne with the Raven Slayer role. This drastically reduces damage taken while increasing damage done to the flying beast.

Keep up with your defensive tactics while raising knocked-out party members as quickly as possible. Keep Miki alive to ensure that you always have healing available to the rest of your party.

STORM DRAGON

The Storm Dragon is an extremely dangerous foe and is likely the most difficult encounter you come across if you attempt the third iteration of the cathedral before you attempt the Maze of Tribulations. It's highly recommended that you take on the Cathedral of Oblivion from the Coast of Minoz first (the third generation of cathedrals opens up after the events on the fifth basement floor of the Symbological Facility Prime).

Preparation is vital here, and you should strongly consider the following precautions and measures before taking on the Storm Dragon. For healing roles, Healer, Sage, and Savior should be leveled and equipped on Miki. These help her heal up your hurt allies quickly and efficiently.

Since the Storm Dragon has a tremendous amount of physical defense, offense-based roles such as Berserker, Daemon, and Raven Slayer are highly recommended. If you fight the Storm Dragon without proper ATK ratings on your physical damage-dealers, you might not be able to do enough damage to last the entirety of the battle, so equip your party with the best weapons possible.

The Storm Dragon can cast the Enshelter spell, considerably raising its defense, so be sure to have the Void spell unlocked for Fiore (this requires the Purification Signets, Vol. 2 skill book). Learning the Cooking specialty to prepare attack-enhancing food such as Grilled Steak is a major boon for this encounter, too.

Interestingly, although its attributes don't reflect this fact, the Storm Dragon absorbs all wind-based damage. Spells like Wind Blade and Tornado are not only ineffective, but also heal the dragon of lost HP. Also, keep in mind that Emmerson's Seraphic Thunder is a wind-based attack. If you find that something is healing the dragon during the fight, check on your members' battle sets to ensure that they aren't using these types of attacks.

Like Vidofnir, the Storm Dragon can cast a devastating Tornado spell destroying anything in its way. This attack can instantly kill most party members, especially your weaker ones like Miki and Fiore, so maneuvering them away from danger is extremely important here!

Coast of Minoz

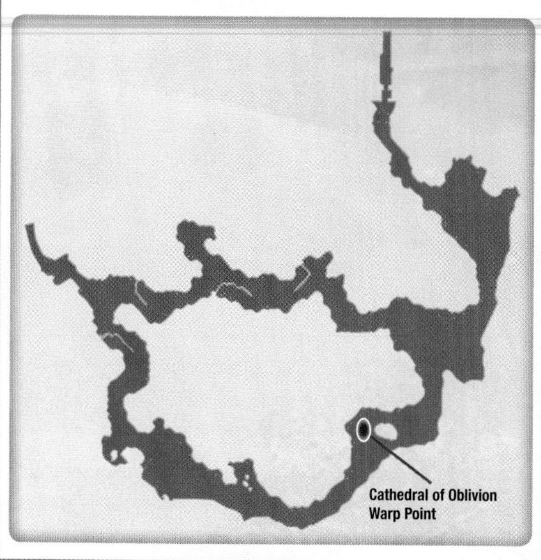

CATHEDRAL ITERATION	ROOM 1	ROOM 2	ROOM 3 BLUE TALISMAN	ROOM 4	ROOM 5 BLOOD CHAIN MAIL	ROOM 6	ROOM 7 ASCLEPIUS
First-Generation Enemies	Apprentice Scumbag x 3	Axe Beak x 2, Stone Golem	Eyebalone x1 (Lv. 25)	—	—	—	—
Second-Generation Enemies	Lizard Warrior x 3	Corpse Bat x 2, Ridiculer	Adephaga Milies x 3	Devil Child x 2, Seventh Core	Vidofnir (Lv. 45)	—	—
Third-Generation Enemies	Bone Knight x 3	Toy Soldier x 3	Lamia Radix x 2, Welwitschia	Dinosaurus x 3	Guiafairo x 2, Jatayu	Chaotic Cell x 2, Sacred Guard	Storm Dragon (Lv. 80)

Resulian Plains

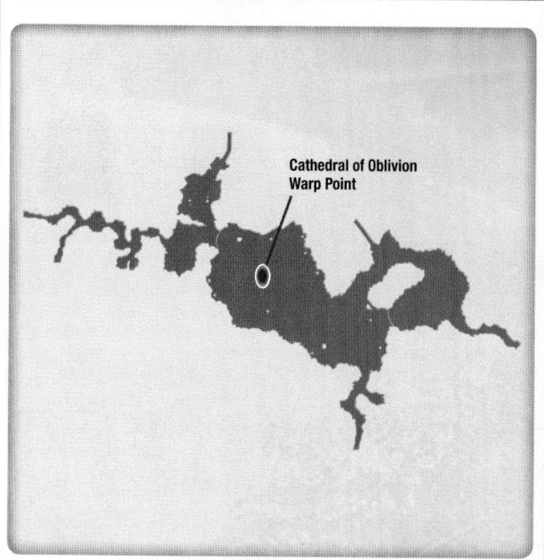

CATHEDRAL ITERATION	ROOM 1	ROOM 2	ROOM 3 GREEN TALISMAN	ROOM 4	ROOM 5 DUEL ARMOR	ROOM 6	ROOM 7 ARCADIAN SERENITY
First-Generation Enemies	Apprentice Scumbag x 3	Harpyia x 2, Carnivorous Plant	Eyebalone (Lv. 30)	—	—	—	—
Second-Generation Enemies	Lizard Warrior x 3	Corpse Bat x 2, Ridiculer	Stroper x 3	Devil Child x 2, Cursed Horror	Vidofnir (Lv. 50)	—	—
Third-Generation Enemies	Adephaga Prox x 3	Toy Soldier x 3	Lamia Radix x 2, Welwitschia	Dinosaurus x 3	Guiafairo x 2, Jatayu	Chaotic Cell x 2, Sacred Guard	Storm Dragon (Lv. 84)

West of the Eastern Eihieds

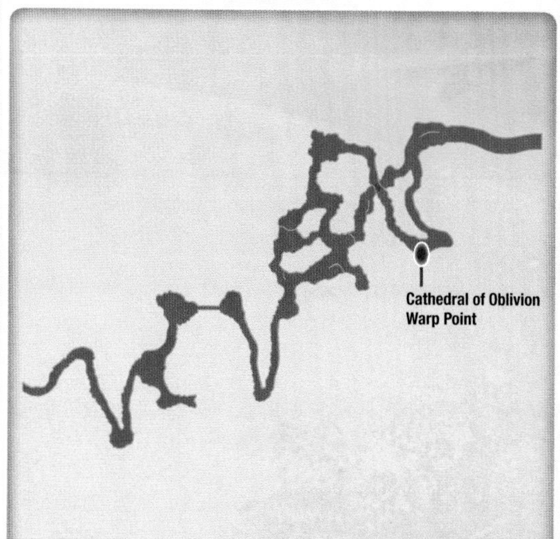

CATHEDRAL ITERATION	ROOM 1	ROOM 2	ROOM 3 RED TALISMAN	ROOM 4	ROOM 5 ATREMENTOUS USURPER	ROOM 6	ROOM 7 CARBUNCLE'S PRISON
First-Generation Enemies	Saber-Toothed Tiger x 3	Kobold Bandit x 3	Eyebalone (Lv. 35)	—	—	—	—
Second-Generation Enemies	Lizard Shaman x 3	Corpse Bat x 2, Ridiculer	Stroper x 3	Devil Child x 2, Cursed Horror	Vidofnir (Lv. 55)	—	—
Third-Generation Enemies	Great Scumbag x 3	Toy Soldier x 3	Lamia Radix x 2, Welwitschia	Dinosaurus x 3	Guiafairo x 2, Jatayu	Chaotic Cell x 2, Sacred Guard	Storm Dragon (Lv. 88)

Trei'kuran Dunes

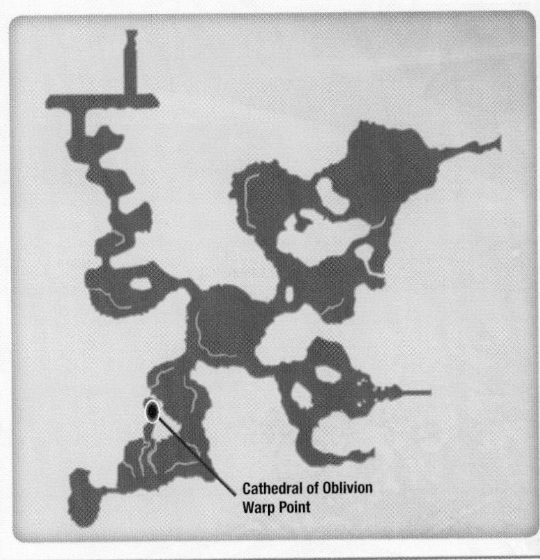

CATHEDRAL ITERATION	ROOM 1	ROOM 2	ROOM 3	ROOM 4	ROOM 5 FAERIE BAND	ROOM 6	ROOM 7 BLOODY KNUCKLES
Second-Generation Enemies	Metal Golem x 3	Vampire Bat x 2, Cursed Horror	Hades Crab x 3	Lesser Dragon x 3	Vidofnir (Lv. 60)	—	—
Third-Generation Enemies	Kobold Ranger x 3	Skeleton Soldier x 2, Doleful Lord Brahms	Amber Princess x 3	Chaotic Cell x 2, Sacred Guard	Avenger x 3	Valiant Conscript x 2, Blutgang	Storm Dragon (Lv. 92)

Northern Territory of Sohma

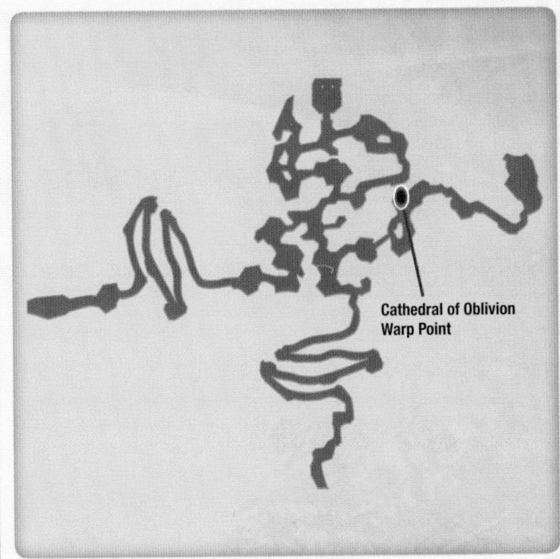

CATHEDRAL ITERATION	ROOM 1	ROOM 2	ROOM 3	ROOM 4	ROOM 5 HEALING BAND	ROOM 6	ROOM 7 CHROME NIGHTMARE
Second-Generation Enemies	Metal Golem x 3	Stroper x 2, Cursed Horror	Adephaga Prox x 3	Antlered Tortoise x 3	Vidofnir (Lv. 65)	—	—
Third-Generation Enemies	Kobold Knave x 3	Skeleton Soldier x 2, Doleful Lord Brahms	Amber Princess x 3	Chaotic Cell x 2, Sacred Guard	Avenger x 3	Valiant Conscript x 2, Blutgang	Storm Dragon (Lv. 96)

Alcazar of the Golden Age: A2

CATHEDRAL ITERATION	ROOM 1	ROOM 2	ROOM 3	ROOM 4	ROOM 5	ROOM 6	ROOM 7 FARWELL
Third-Generation Enemies	Avenger x 3	Valiant Conscript x 2, Blutgang	Bane Dragon x 3	Maidenly Blossom x 3	Gust Hornet x 2, Polyphaga Gamboge	Melusine x 3	Storm Dragon (Lv. 99)

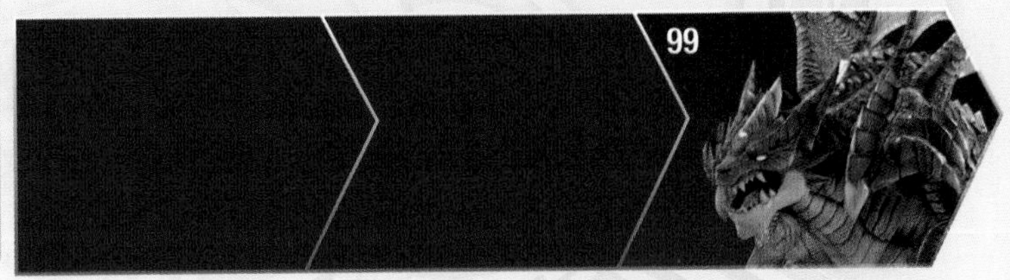

ITEMS

USABLE ITEMS

Blueberries

FACTORS:	Recover 30% HP
Value	40
Acquisition Methods	Shops

Wild berries with a perfect balance of sweetness and sourness similar to that of grapes.

Blueberry Potion

FACTORS:	Recover 70% HP
Value	(1200)
Acquisition Methods	Treasure Chests, Item Creation

Made from blueberries, this small bottle's worth of extract is nutrient-rich and concentrated enough to cure the weary.

Physical Stimulant

FACTORS:	Recover 100% HP
Value	(3200)
Acquisition Methods	Treasure Chests, Item Creation

A bottle's worth of liquid that invigorates fatigued fighters. Though not considered delectable by any means, it is still potable.

Healing Device

FACTORS:	Recover 50% HP (All)
Value	(5400)
Acquisition Methods	Enemy Drop, Treasure Chest

A small contraption that emits a pleasantly cool mist with physical stimulant properties, which in turn help recover stamina.

Blackberries

FACTORS:	Recover 30% MP
Value	80
Acquisition Methods	Shops

Wild berries with a strong, bitter taste due to their high tannin content. Known to soothe mental fatigue.

Blackberry Potion

FACTORS:	Recover 70% MP
Value	(1500)
Acquisition Methods	Treasure Chests, Item Creation

A blackberry extract contained within a small bottle. It's as effective at curing mental fatigue as it is bitter.

Mental Stimulant

FACTORS:	Recover 100% MP
Value	(3800)
Acquisition Methods	Treasure Chest, Item Creation, Synthesis

The components of this liquid invigorate the mind, but half the work is done by its decadent flavor.

Relaxation Device

FACTORS:	Recover 50% MP (All)
Value	(3600)
Acquisition Methods	Enemy Drop, Item Creation, Quest

A small apparatus that disperses mental stimulants over an area. The scent it emits is known to clear one's head.

Mixed Syrup

FACTORS:	Recover 30% HP	Recover 30% MP
Value		(600)
Acquisition Methods		Enemy Drop, Item Creation, Synthesis

A sweet syrup made from a variety of seasonal fruits. Its high sugar content is perfect for weary minds and bodies.

Miraculous Device

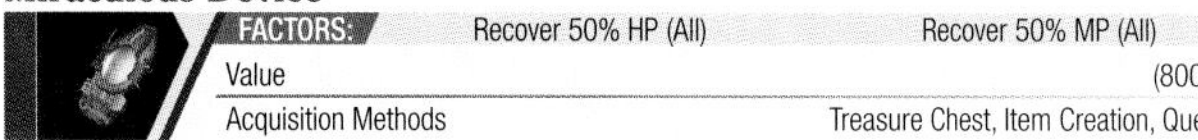

FACTORS:	Recover 50% HP (All)	Recover 50% MP (All)
Value		(8000)
Acquisition Methods		Treasure Chest, Item Creation, Quest

A small gadget that sprays a mist made of mixed syrup all around. Its fresh scent leaves one feeling jubilant.

Wondrous Tincture

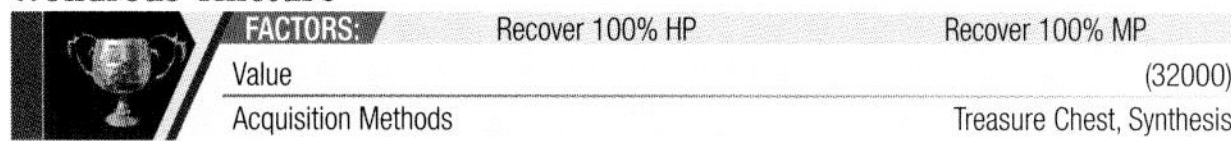

FACTORS:	Recover 100% HP	Recover 100% MP
Value		(32000)
Acquisition Methods		Treasure Chest, Synthesis

As this elusive elixir vastly enhances the recovery power of life forms, rulers throughout history have sought it out.

Numinous Tincture

FACTORS:	Recover 100% HP (All)	Recover 100% MP (All)	Cure ailments (All)
Value			(56000)
Acquisition Methods			Treasure Chest, Synthesis

A remedy that employs nanomachines to instantly mend any wound. Sadly, it also leaves behind an unforgettable aftertaste.

Aquaberries

FACTORS:	Recover 20% HP (All)	Cure poison
Value		(60)
Acquisition Methods		Enemy Drop, Treasure Chest, Item Creation

Wild berries with a fresh, minty flavor.

Fresh Sage

FACTORS:	Revive / Recover 30% HP
Value	160
Acquisition Methods	Shops

A medicinal herb that boosts the body's natural resistance. It is also perfect for masking the odor of meat dishes.

Resurrection Elixir

FACTORS:	Revive / Recover 100% HP
Value	(4800)
Acquisition Methods	Locked Chest, Item Creation, Synthesis

Holy water that heals wounded party members and gives them the strength to return to battle.

Resurrection Mist

FACTORS:	Revive / Recover 50% HP (All)
Value	(15000)
Acquisition Methods	Treasure Chest, Synthesis, Quest

A small contraption that diffuses vapor composed of resurrection elixir. The vapor's sweet scent heals allies as it wafts pleasantly about.

Mint

FACTORS:	Cure poison
Value	90
Acquisition Methods	Shops

A medicinal herb with a wintry scent, brisk flavor, and powerful antiseptic properties that neutralize bodily toxins.

Basil

FACTORS:	Cure paralysis
Value	90
Acquisition Methods	Shops

The king of aromatic herbs, basil not only goes well with all sorts of dishes, it is also known to relieve paralysis in the extremities.

Chamomile

FACTORS:	Cure silence
Value	180
Acquisition Methods	Shops

Pure-white flowers with a scent reminiscent of apples that is known to calm tense individuals.

Cinnamon

FACTORS:	Thaw
Value	300
Acquisition Methods	Shops

This edible tree bark with a distinctive aromatic scent is a popular medicine for alleviating poor circulation.

Jasmine

FACTORS:	Clear fog
Value	90
Acquisition Methods	Shops

These edible flowers exude a fragrance redolent of exotic elegance and are used mainly in beverages that rejuvenate the mind.

Lavender

FACTORS:	Remove curse
Value	300
Acquisition Methods	Shops

A purple flower that emits a floral scent and is often used in perfumes. Extremely popular among women for its ability to ward off evil.

Therapeutic Tincture
FACTORS: Cure ailments
Value: (1500)
Acquisition Methods: Treasure Chest, Item Creation, Synthesis, Quests

An essential oil with medicinal properties. Its unknown ingredients impart to it a faint smell of licorice.

Holy Mist
FACTORS: Cure ailments (All)
Value: (5400)
Acquisition Methods: Synthesis, Quest

Elusive holy water believed to be a panacea. Legends say only innocent maidens can collect it from a lake at the summit of a sacred mountain.

Emotional Destabilizer
FACTORS: Lose favor with friends
Value: (1)
Acquisition Methods: Item Creation, Synthesis

Though this liquid purportedly makes those of the other sex smitten with you, it often ends up having the exact opposite effect.

Love Potion No. 256
FACTORS: Gain favor with your friends
Value: (1)
Acquisition Methods: Treasure Chest, Locked Chest, Item Creation, Synthesis, Quests

Causes one to instantly fall in love with the first person seen after drinking it.

EM Bomb (S)
FACTORS: Deal a foe 1,000 damage
Value: (200)
Acquisition Methods: Treasure Chest, Item Creation, Synthesis

An advanced electromagnetic bomb.

EM Bomb (L)
FACTORS: Large area: 2,000 damage to foes
Value: (600)
Acquisition Methods: Treasure Chest, Item Creation, Synthesis

An electromagnetic bomb with an expanded effect radius. What it lacks in destructive power, it makes up for in ease of use.

Gravity Bomb
FACTORS: Damage foe 25% of its current HP
Value: (1600)
Acquisition Methods: Enemy Drop, Item Creation, Synthesis

A bomb that generates a localized gravitational field that supposedly strips targets' clothes off before affecting anything else.

Low-Frequency Bomb
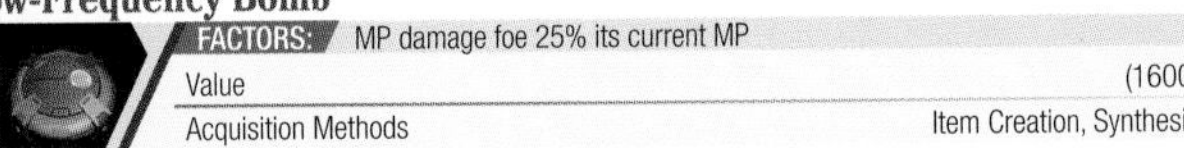
FACTORS: MP damage foe 25% its current MP
Value: (1600)
Acquisition Methods: Item Creation, Synthesis

A bomb that neutralizes enemies by generating a low-frequency sound strong enough to leave them reeling until the next day.

Ultimate Bomb
FACTORS: Vast area: 9,999 damage to foes
Value: (2664)
Acquisition Methods: Treasure Chest, Item Creation, Synthesis

Large, incredibly powerful, and created completely on accident, this bomb exemplar bears a seal depicting its inventor—Welch.

Self-Destructor 3000
FACTORS: Causes target to explode
Value: (100)
Acquisition Methods: Item Creation, Synthesis

A powerful bomb that engulfs the area around its target in flames. Remember, every life is sacred.

Poison Bomb
FACTORS: Deal a foe 500 damage — Chance to poison a foe
Value: (600)
Acquisition Methods: Enemy Drop, Item Creation, Synthesis

A bomb with the added thaumaturgical power of poison cider.

Deluxe Poison Bomb
FACTORS: Large area: 1,000 damage to foes — Chance to poison foes in area
Value: (1200)
Acquisition Methods: Item Creation, Synthesis

A poison bomb with an expanded blast radius, meaning it can afflict even more targets with its toxicity.

Stun Bomb
FACTORS: Deal a foe 500 damage — Chance to stun a foe
Value: (600)
Acquisition Methods: Enemy Drop, Treasure Chest, Item Creation, Synthesis

A bomb with the added thaumaturgical power of spark cider.

Deluxe Stun Bomb
FACTORS: Large area: 1,000 damage to foes — Chance to stun foes in area
Value: (1200)
Acquisition Methods: Item Creation, Synthesis

A stun bomb with an expanded blast radius and liquid contents that splatter far and wide to stun even more targets.

Freezing Bomb
FACTORS: Deal a foe 500 damage — Chance to freeze a foe
Value: (600)
Acquisition Methods: Item Creation, Synthesis

A bomb with the added thaumaturgical power of frozen cider.

Deluxe Freezing Bomb
FACTORS: Large area: 1,000 damage to foes — Chance to freeze foes in area
Value: (1200)
Acquisition Methods: Item Creation, Synthesis

A freezing bomb that, when it explodes, emits frigid air over an expanded blast radius to crystallize an even larger number of foes.

Smoke Bomb
FACTORS: Deal a foe 500 damage — Chance to cloud foe's vision
Value: (600)
Acquisition Methods: Enemy Drop, Item Creation, Synthesis

A bomb with the added thaumaturgical power of cloudy cider.

Deluxe Smoke Bomb
FACTORS: Large area: 1,000 damage to foes — Chance to cloud foes' vision in area
Value: (1200)
Acquisition Methods: Item Creation, Synthesis

A smoke bomb with an expanded effect radius and piceous vapors that bellow forth to obscure the sight of even more targets.

Lesser Demon's Fetish
FACTORS: Deal a foe 500 damage — Chance to curse a foe
Value: (800)
Acquisition Methods: Item Creation, Synthesis

A sheet of vellum inscribed with an occult diagram used for summoning an imp. Be not fooled by the creature's innocuous moniker.

Greater Demon's Fetish
FACTORS: Large area: 1,000 damage to foes — Chance to curse foes in area
Value: (1600)
Acquisition Methods: Treasure Chest, Item Creation, Synthesis, Quest

A piece of vellum inscribed with an occult diagram for summoning a greater demon, which can deliver crushing blows to your enemies.

Attack Breaker
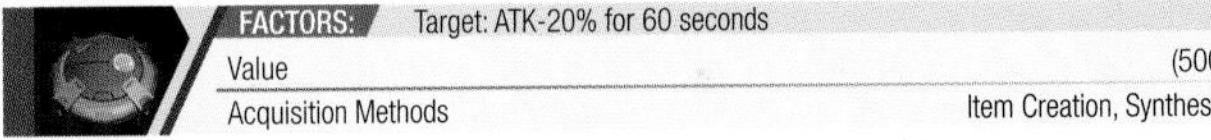
FACTORS: Target: ATK-20% for 60 seconds
Value: (500)
Acquisition Methods: Item Creation, Synthesis

A device that disperses a chemical agent for suppressing ATK.

Intelligence Breaker
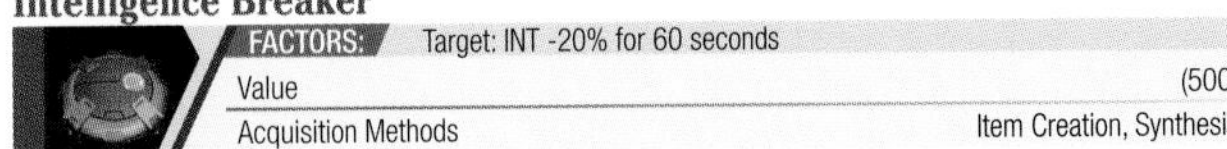
FACTORS: Target: INT -20% for 60 seconds
Value: (500)
Acquisition Methods: Item Creation, Synthesis

A device that disperses a chemical agent for suppressing INT.

Defense Breaker
FACTORS: Target: DEF -20% for 60 seconds
Value: (500)
Acquisition Methods: Item Creation, Synthesis

A device that disperses a chemical agent for suppressing DEF.

Mentality Breaker
FACTORS: Target: MEN -20% for 60 seconds
Value: (500)
Acquisition Methods: Item Creation, Synthesis

A device that disperses a chemical agent for suppressing MEN.

HP Absorber
FACTORS: Absorb a foe's HP
Value: (1400)
Acquisition Methods: Treasure Chest, Item Creation, Synthesis

A disposable apparatus that absorbs HP from enemies.

MP Absorber
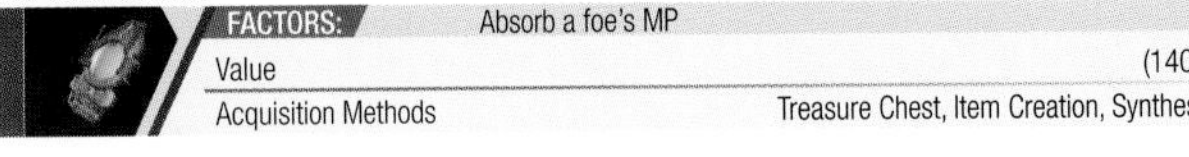
FACTORS: Absorb a foe's MP
Value: (1400)
Acquisition Methods: Treasure Chest, Item Creation, Synthesis

A disposable apparatus that absorbs MP from enemies.

Strength Potion

FACTORS: Target: ATK +20% for 60 seconds

Value	(400)
Acquisition Methods	Treasure Chest, Item Creation, Synthesis

A potion that temporarily boosts ATK.

Perception Potion

FACTORS: Target: INT +20% for 60 seconds

Value	(400)
Acquisition Methods	Treasure Chest, Item Creation, Synthesis

A potion that temporarily boosts INT.

Fortitude Potion

FACTORS: Target: DEF +20% for 60 seconds

Value	(400)
Acquisition Methods	Treasure Chest, Item Creation, Synthesis

A potion that temporarily boosts DEF.

Acuity Potion

FACTORS: Target: MEN +20% for 60 seconds

Value	(400)
Acquisition Methods	Enemy Drop, Treasure Chest, Item Creation

A potion that temporarily boosts MEN.

Diligence Potion

FACTORS: Target: crit. +30% for 60 seconds

Value	(600)
Acquisition Methods	Treasure Chest, Locked Chest, Item Creation, Synthesis, Quest

A potion that enhances the imbiber's concentration drastically.

Riot Potion

FACTORS: Target: MP cost = 0 for 60 seconds

Value	(1200)
Acquisition Methods	Treasure Chest, Item Creation

A potion that grants the imbiber unbridled occult powers.

Heroism Potion

FACTORS: Target: invincibility for 10 seconds

Value	(1600)
Acquisition Methods	Enemy Drop, Locked Chest, Item Creation

A legendary potion that grants the imbiber superhuman strength.

Vitalitea

FACTORS: Fill up reserve gauge once

Value	(500)
Acquisition Methods	Enemy Drop, Treasure Chest, Item Creation, Synthesis, Quests

A single sip of this drink causes the body to burst with energy.

Robust Vitalitea

FACTORS: Fill up reserve gauge thrice

Value	(1500)
Acquisition Methods	Item Creation, Synthesis, Quests

This powerful beverage has three times the active ingredients of regular vitalitea.

Earth Charm

FACTORS: Target: earth resistance +20 for 60 seconds

Value	(400)
Acquisition Methods	Item Creation, Synthesis, Quest

A charm imbued with the power of an earth gem.

Ice Charm

FACTORS: Target: ice resistance +20 for 60 seconds

Value	(400)
Acquisition Methods	Item Creation, Synthesis, Quest

A charm imbued with the power of an ice gem.

Fire Charm

FACTORS: Target: fire resistance +20 for 60 seconds

Value	(400)
Acquisition Methods	Treasure Chest, Item Creation, Synthesis

A charm imbued with the power of a fire gem.

Wind Charm

FACTORS: Target: wind resistance +20 for 60 seconds

Value	(400)
Acquisition Methods	Item Creation, Synthesis, Quest

A charm imbued with the power of a wind gem.

Light Charm

FACTORS: Target: light resistance +20 for 60 seconds

Value	(400)
Acquisition Methods	Treasure Chest, Item Creation, Synthesis

A charm imbued with the power of a light gem.

Darkness Charm

FACTORS: Target: darkness resistance +20 for 60 seconds

Value	(400)
Acquisition Methods	Treasure Chest, Item Creation, Quest

A charm imbued with the power of a darkness gem.

Poison Cider

FACTORS: Chance to poison target

Value	(100)
Acquisition Methods	Enemy Drop, Item Creation, Synthesis

A potent concoction that poisons anyone who drinks it.

Spark Cider

FACTORS: Chance to stun target.

Value	(100)
Acquisition Methods	Treasure Chest, Item Creation, Synthesis

A potent concoction that stuns anyone who drinks it.

Frozen Cider

FACTORS: Chance to freeze target

Value	(100)
Acquisition Methods	Item Creation, Synthesis

A potent concoction that freezes anyone who drinks it.

Cloudy Cider

FACTORS: Chance to cloud target's vision

Value	(100)
Acquisition Methods	Item Creation, Synthesis

A potent concoction that clouds the vision of anyone who drinks it.

DANGER! DO NOT DRINK!

FACTORS: Chance target's HP becomes critical

Value	(100)
Acquisition Methods	Item Creation, Synthesis

A potent concoction that puts anyone who drinks it into critical condition.

Forbidden Tonic

FACTORS: Chance to instantly kill target

Value	(1000)
Acquisition Methods	Synthesis

A potent concoction that leads to a tragic end for whoever drinks it. Due to its inhumane effects, consumption of this elixir has been banned.

Attack Seeds

FACTORS: ATK +4 (Permanent)

Value	(3000)
Acquisition Methods	Treasure Chests, Synthesis

Mysterious seeds with the power to raise ATK.

Potent Attack Seeds

FACTORS: ATK +10 (Permanent)

Value	(8000)
Acquisition Methods	Item Creation

Mysterious seeds with the power to drastically raise ATK.

Intelligence Seeds

FACTORS: INT +4 (Permanent)

Value	(3000)
Acquisition Methods	Treasure Chests, Synthesis

Mysterious seeds with the power to raise INT.

Potent Intelligence Seeds

FACTORS: INT +10 (Permanent)

Value	(8000)
Acquisition Methods	Item Creation

Mysterious seeds with the power to drastically raise INT.

Defense Seeds

FACTORS: DEF +4 (Permanent)

Value	(3000)
Acquisition Methods	Treasure Chests, Synthesis

Mysterious seeds with the power to raise DEF.

Potent Defense Seeds
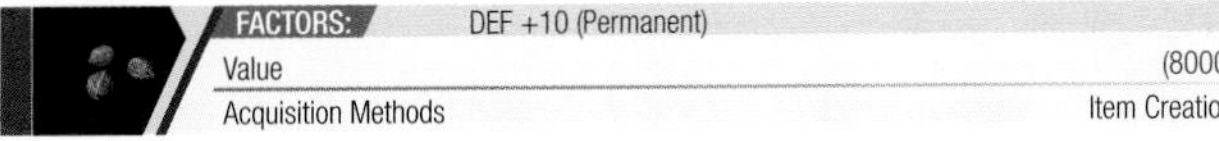

FACTORS:	DEF +10 (Permanent)
Value	(8000)
Acquisition Methods	Item Creation

Mysterious seeds with the power to drastically raise DEF.

Mentality Seeds

FACTORS:	MEN +4 (Permanent)
Value	(3000)
Acquisition Methods	Treasure Chest, Synthesis

Mysterious seeds with the power to raise MEN.

Potent Mentality Seeds

FACTORS:	MEN +10 (Permanent)
Value	(8000)
Acquisition Methods	Item Creation

Mysterious seeds with the power to drastically raise MEN.

Health Seeds

FACTORS:	Max HP +50 (Permanent)
Value	(3000)
Acquisition Methods	Treasure Chest, Synthesis, Quest

Mysterious seeds with the power to raise maximum HP.

Potent Health Seeds

FACTORS:	Max HP +200 (Permanent)
Value	(8000)
Acquisition Methods	Item Creation

Mysterious seeds with the power to drastically raise maximum HP.

Magic Seeds

FACTORS:	Max MP +30 (Permanent)
Value	(3000)
Acquisition Methods	Treasure Chest, Synthesis, Quest

Mysterious seeds with the power to raise maximum MP.

Potent Magic Seeds

FACTORS:	Max MP +100 (Permanent)
Value	(8000)
Acquisition Methods	Item Creation

Mysterious seeds with the power to drastically raise maximum MP.

Signet Card: Healing

FACTORS:	Activate Healing Lv.1
Value	400
Acquisition Methods	Shop, Treasure Chest, Item Creation

When cast into the air, this signet-imbued card allows even those who have not learned the spell Healing to invoke it.

Signet Card: Healing +

FACTORS:	Activate Healing Lv.5
Value	(1600)
Acquisition Methods	Item Creation

When cast into the air, this signet-imbued card allows even those who have not learned the spell Healing to invoke a powerful version of it.

Signet Card: Ex Healing

FACTORS:	Activate Ex Healing Lv.1
Value	(3200)
Acquisition Methods	Item Creation

When cast into the air, this signet-imbued card allows even those who have not learned the spell Ex Healing to invoke it.

Signet Card: Ex Healing +

FACTORS:	Activate Ex Healing Lv.5
Value	(6400)
Acquisition Methods	Locked Chest, Item Creation

When cast into the air, this signet-imbued card allows even those who have not learned the spell Ex Healing to invoke a powerful version of it.

Signet Card: Faerie Healing

FACTORS:	Activate Faerie Healing Lv.1
Value	1500
Acquisition Methods	Shop, Item Creation, Synthesis

When cast into the air, this signet-imbued card allows even those who have not learned the spell Faerie Healing to invoke it.

Signet Card: Faerie Healing +
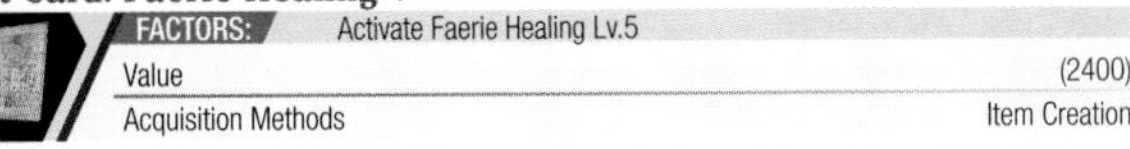

FACTORS:	Activate Faerie Healing Lv.5
Value	(2400)
Acquisition Methods	Item Creation

When cast into the air, this signet-imbued card allows even those who have not learned the spell Faerie Healing to invoke a powerful version of it.

Signet Card: Faerie Light
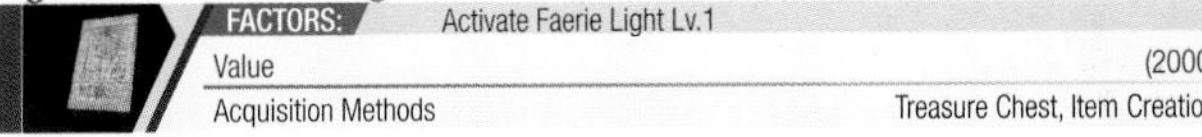

FACTORS:	Activate Faerie Light Lv.1
Value	(2000)
Acquisition Methods	Treasure Chest, Item Creation

When cast into the air, this signet-imbued card allows even those who have not learned the spell Faerie Light to invoke it.

Signet Card: Faerie Light +

FACTORS:	Activate Faerie Light Lv.5
Value	(4000)
Acquisition Methods	Item Creation

When cast into the air, this signet-imbued card allows even those who have not learned Faerie Light to invoke a powerful version of it.

Signet Card: Faerie Star

FACTORS:	Activate Faerie Star Lv.1
Value	(3200)
Acquisition Methods	Item Creation

When cast into the air, this signet-imbued card allows even those who have not learned the spell Faerie Star to invoke it.

Signet Card: Faerie Star +

FACTORS:	Activate Faerie Star Lv.5
Value	(6400)
Acquisition Methods	Locked Chest, Item Creation

When cast into the air, this signet-imbued card allows even those who have not learned Faerie Star to invoke a powerful version of it.

Signet Card: Antidote
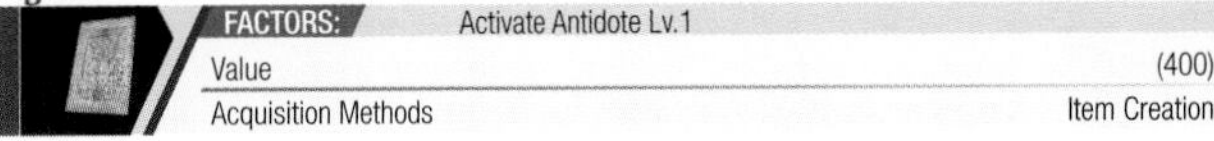

FACTORS:	Activate Antidote Lv.1
Value	(400)
Acquisition Methods	Item Creation

When cast into the air, this signet-imbued card allows even those who have not learned the spell Antidote to invoke it.

Signet Card: Antidote +
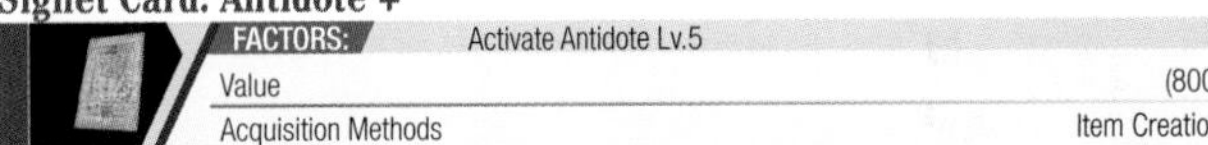

FACTORS:	Activate Antidote Lv.5
Value	(800)
Acquisition Methods	Item Creation

When cast into the air, this signet-imbued card allows even those who have not learned the spell Antidote to invoke a powerful version of it.

Signet Card: Cure Condition

FACTORS:	Activate Cure Condition Lv.1
Value	(2400)
Acquisition Methods	Enemy Drop, Item Creation

When cast into the air, this signet-imbued card allows even those who have not learned the spell Cure Condition to invoke it.

Signet Card: Cure Condition +
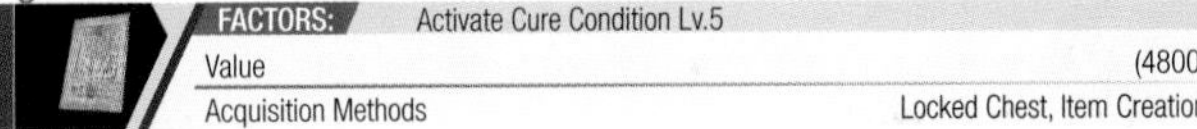

FACTORS:	Activate Cure Condition Lv.5
Value	(4800)
Acquisition Methods	Locked Chest, Item Creation

When cast into the air, this signet-imbued card allows even those who have not learned Cure Condition to invoke a powerful version of it.

Signet Card: Raise Dead

FACTORS:	Activate Raise Dead Lv.1
Value	(800)
Acquisition Methods	Treasure Chest, Item Creation

When cast into the air, this signet-imbued card allows even those who have not learned the spell Raise Dead to invoke it.

Signet Card: Raise Dead +

FACTORS:	Activate Raise Dead Lv.5
Value	(1600)
Acquisition Methods	Item Creation

When cast into the air, this signet-imbued card allows even those who have not learned the spell Raise Dead to invoke a powerful version of it.

Signet Card: Resurrection
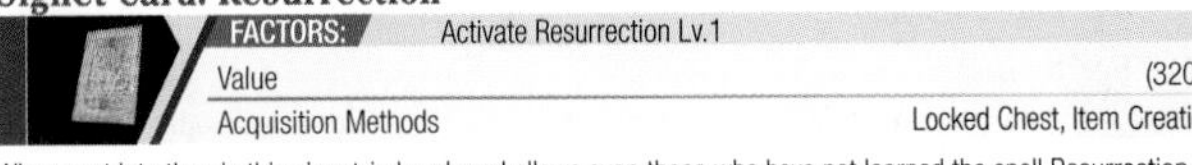

FACTORS:	Activate Resurrection Lv.1
Value	(3200)
Acquisition Methods	Locked Chest, Item Creation

When cast into the air, this signet-imbued card allows even those who have not learned the spell Resurrection to invoke it.

Signet Card: Earth Glaive

FACTORS:	Activate Earth Glaive Lv.1
Value	800
Acquisition Methods	Shop, Item Creation, Synthesis

When cast into the air, this signet-imbued card allows even those who have not learned the spell Earth Glaive to invoke it.

Signet Card: Earth Glaive +
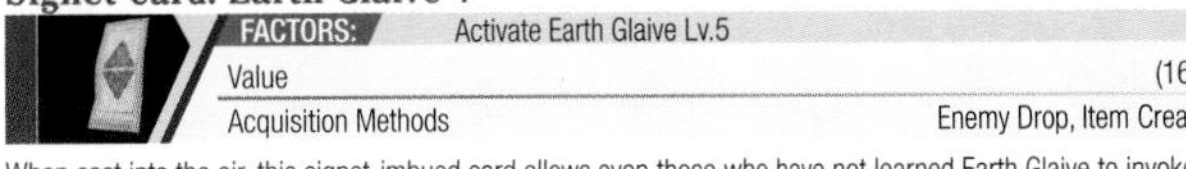

FACTORS:	Activate Earth Glaive Lv.5
Value	(1600)
Acquisition Methods	Enemy Drop, Item Creation

When cast into the air, this signet-imbued card allows even those who have not learned Earth Glaive to invoke a powerful version of it.

PART 06

Signet Card: Stone Rain

FACTORS:	Activate Stone Rain Lv.1
Value	(1600)
Acquisition Methods	Item Creation

When cast into the air, this signet-imbued card allows even those who have not learned the spell Stone Rain to invoke it.

Signet Card: Stone Rain +

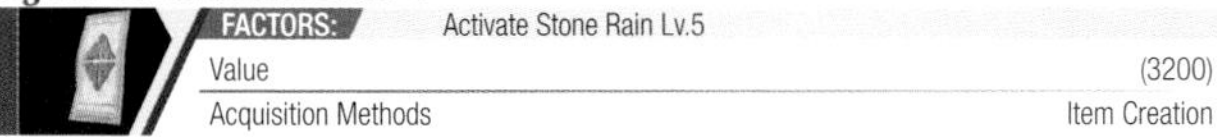

FACTORS:	Activate Stone Rain Lv.5
Value	(3200)
Acquisition Methods	Item Creation

When cast into the air, this signet-imbued card allows even those who have not learned the spell Stone Rain to invoke a powerful version of it.

Signet Card: Terra Hammer

FACTORS:	Activate Terra Hammer Lv.1
Value	(3200)
Acquisition Methods	Item Creation

When cast into the air, this signet-imbued card allows even those who have not learned the spell Terra Hammer to invoke it.

Signet Card: Terra Hammer +

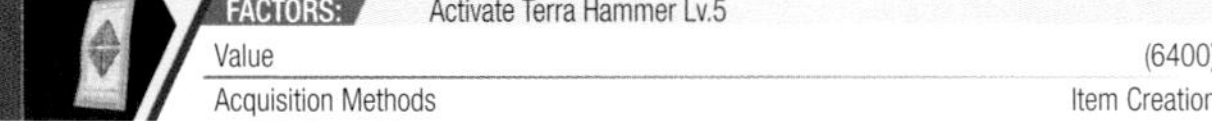

FACTORS:	Activate Terra Hammer Lv.5
Value	(6400)
Acquisition Methods	Item Creation

When cast into the air, this signet-imbued card allows even those who have not learned Terra Hammer to invoke a powerful version of it.

Signet Card: Ice Needles

FACTORS:	Activate Ice Needles Lv.1
Value	800
Acquisition Methods	Shop, Enemy Drop, Item Creation

When cast into the air, this signet-imbued card allows even those who have not learned the spell Ice Needles to invoke it.

Signet Card: Ice Needles +

FACTORS:	Activate Ice Needles Lv.5
Value	(1600)
Acquisition Methods	Item Creation

When cast into the air, this signet-imbued card allows even those who have not learned Ice Needles to invoke a powerful version of it.

Signet Card: Deep Freeze

FACTORS:	Activate Deep Freeze Lv.1
Value	(1600)
Acquisition Methods	Item Creation

When cast into the air, this signet-imbued card allows even those who have not learned the spell Deep Freeze to invoke it.

Signet Card: Deep Freeze +

FACTORS:	Activate Deep Freeze Lv.5
Value	(3200)
Acquisition Methods	Item Creation

When cast into the air, this signet-imbued card allows even those who have not learned Deep Freeze to invoke a powerful version of it.

Signet Card: Arctic Impact

FACTORS:	Activate Arctic Impact Lv.1
Value	(3200)
Acquisition Methods	Treasure Chest, Item Creation

When cast into the air, this signet-imbued card allows even those who have not learned Arctic Impact to invoke it.

Signet Card: Arctic Impact +

FACTORS:	Activate Arctic Impact Lv.5
Value	(6400)
Acquisition Methods	Item Creation

When cast into the air, this signet-imbued card allows even those who have not learned Arctic Impact to invoke a powerful version of it.

Signet Card: Fire Bolt

FACTORS:	Activate Fire Bolt Lv.1
Value	800
Acquisition Methods	Shop, Enemy Drop, Item Creation

When cast into the air, this signet-imbued card allows even those who have not learned the spell Fire Bolt to invoke it.

Signet Card: Fire Bolt +

FACTORS:	Activate Fire Bolt Lv.5
Value	(1600)
Acquisition Methods	Item Creation

When cast into the air, this signet-imbued card allows even those who have not learned Fire Bolt to invoke a powerful version of it.

Signet Card: Explosion

FACTORS:	Activate Explosion Lv.1
Value	(1600)
Acquisition Methods	Enemy Drop, Treasure Chest, Item Creation

When cast into the air, this signet-imbued card allows even those who have not learned the spell Explosion to invoke it.

Signet Card: Explosion +

FACTORS:	Activate Explosion Lv.5
Value	(3200)
Acquisition Methods	Item Creation, Synthesis

When cast into the air, this signet-imbued card allows even those who have not learned the spell Explosion to invoke a powerful version of it.

Signet Card: Volcanic Burst

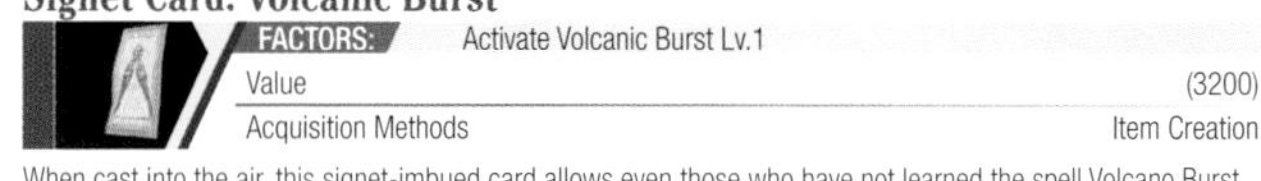

FACTORS:	Activate Volcanic Burst Lv.1
Value	(3200)
Acquisition Methods	Item Creation

When cast into the air, this signet-imbued card allows even those who have not learned the spell Volcano Burst to invoke it.

Signet Card: Volcanic Burst +

FACTORS:	Activate Volcanic Burst Lv.5
Value	(6400)
Acquisition Methods	Item Creation

When cast into the air, this signet-imbued card allows even those who have not learned Volcanic Burst to invoke a powerful version of it.

Signet Card: Wind Blade

FACTORS:	Activate Wind Blade Lv.1
Value	800
Acquisition Methods	Shop, Item Creation, Synthesis

When cast into the air, this signet-imbued card allows even those who have not learned the spell Wind Blade to invoke it.

Signet Card: Wind Blade +

FACTORS:	Activate Wind Blade Lv.5
Value	(1600)
Acquisition Methods	Item Creation

When cast into the air, this signet-imbued card allows even those who have not learned Wind Blade to invoke a powerful version of it.

Signet Card: Tornado

FACTORS:	Activate Tornado Lv.1
Value	(1600)
Acquisition Methods	Item Creation

When cast into the air, this signet-imbued card allows even those who have not learned the spell Tornado to invoke it.

Signet Card: Tornado +

FACTORS:	Activate Tornado Lv.5
Value	(3200)
Acquisition Methods	Item Creation

When cast into the air, this signet-imbued card allows even those who have not learned the spell Tornado to invoke a powerful version of it.

Signet Card: Lightning Blast

FACTORS:	Activate Lightning Blast Lv.1
Value	(800)
Acquisition Methods	Item Creation

When cast into the air, this signet-imbued card allows even those who have not learned the spell Lightning to invoke it.

Signet Card: Lightning Blast +

FACTORS:	Activate Lightning Blast Lv.5
Value	(1600)
Acquisition Methods	Item Creation

When cast into the air, this signet-imbued card allows even those who have not learned Lightning Blast to invoke a powerful version of it.

Signet Card: Thunder Flare

FACTORS:	Activate Thunder Flare Lv.1
Value	(3200)
Acquisition Methods	Treasure Chest, Item Creation

When cast into the air, this signet-imbued card allows even those who have not learned the spell Thunder Flare to invoke it.

Signet Card: Thunder Flare +

FACTORS:	Activate Thunder Flare Lv.5
Value	(6400)
Acquisition Methods	Item Creation

When cast into the air, this signet-imbued card allows even those who have not learned Thunder Flare to invoke a powerful version of it.

Signet Card: Radiant Lancer

FACTORS:	Activate Radiant Lancer Lv.1
Value	
Acquisition Methods	

When cast into the air, this signet-imbued card allows even those who have not learned the spell Radiant Lancer to invoke it.

Signet Card: Radiant Lancer +

FACTORS:	Activate Radiant Lancer Lv.5
Value	(1600)
Acquisition Methods	Enemy Drop, Item Creation

When cast into the air, this signet-imbued card allows even those who have not learned Radiant Lancer to invoke a powerful version of it.

Signet Card: Aurora Rings

FACTORS: Activate Aurora Rings Lv.1

Value	(3200)
Acquisition Methods	Item Creation

When cast into the air, this signet-imbued card allows even those who have not learned the spell Aurora Rings to invoke it.

Signet Card: Aurora Rings +

FACTORS: Activate Aurora Rings Lv.5

Value	(6400)
Acquisition Methods	Item Creation

When cast into the air, this signet-imbued card allows even those who have not learned Aurora Rings to invoke a powerful version of it.

Signet Card: Sunflare

FACTORS: Activate Sunflare Lv.1

Value	(1600)
Acquisition Methods	Item Creation

When cast into the air, this signet-imbued card allows even those who have not learned the spell Sunflare to invoke it.

Signet Card: Sunflare +

FACTORS: Activate Sunflare Lv.5

Value	(3200)
Acquisition Methods	Item Creation

When cast into the air, this signet-imbued card allows even those who have not learned Sunflare to invoke a powerful version of it.

Signet Card: Shadow Needles

FACTORS: Activate Shadow Needles Lv.1

Value	(800)
Acquisition Methods	Item Creation

When cast into the air, this signet-imbued card allows even those who have not learned the spell Shadow Needles to invoke it.

Signet Card: Shadow Needles +

FACTORS: Activate Shadow Needles Lv.5

Value	(1600)
Acquisition Methods	Enemy Drop, Item Creation

When cast into the air, this signet-imbued card allows even those who have not learned Shadow Needles to invoke a powerful version of it.

Signet Card: Dark Devourer

FACTORS: Activate Dark Devourer Lv.1

Value	(3200)
Acquisition Methods	Item Creation

When cast into the air, this signet-imbued card allows even those who have not learned the spell Dark Devourer to invoke it.

Signet Card: Dark Devourer +

FACTORS: Activate Dark Devourer Lv.5

Value	(6400)
Acquisition Methods	Enemy Drop, Item Creation, Synthesis

When cast into the air, this signet-imbued card allows even those who have not learned Dark Devourer to invoke a powerful version of it.

Signet Card: Vampiric Blade

FACTORS: Activate Vampiric Blade Lv.1

Value	(2400)
Acquisition Methods	Item Creation

When cast into the air, this signet-imbued card allows even those who have not learned the spell Vampiric Blade to invoke it.

Signet Card: Vampiric Blade +

FACTORS: Activate Vampiric Blade Lv.5

Value	(4800)
Acquisition Methods	Item Creation

When cast into the air, this signet-imbued card allows even those who have not learned Vampiric Blade to invoke a powerful version of it.

Signet Card: Divine Wave

FACTORS: Activate Divine Wave Lv.1

Value	(3200)
Acquisition Methods	Treasure Chest, Item Creation

When cast into the air, this signet-imbued card allows even those who have not learned the spell Divine Wave to invoke it.

Signet Card: Divine Wave +

FACTORS: Activate Divine Wave Lv.5

Value	(6400)
Acquisition Methods	Item Creation

When cast into the air, this signet-imbued card allows even those who have not learned Divine Wave to invoke a powerful version of it.

Signet Card: Extinction

FACTORS: Activate Extinction Lv.1

Value	(3200)
Acquisition Methods	Item Creation

When cast into the air, this signet-imbued card allows even those who have not learned the spell Extinction to invoke it.

Signet Card: Extinction +

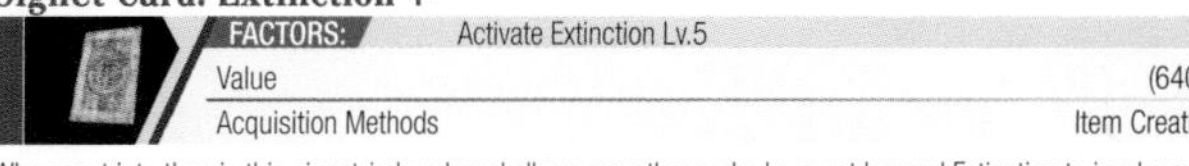

FACTORS: Activate Extinction Lv.5

Value	(6400)
Acquisition Methods	Item Creation

When cast into the air, this signet-imbued card allows even those who have not learned Extinction to invoke a powerful version of it.

Signet Card: Reaping Spark

FACTORS: Activate Reaping Spark Lv.1

Value	(1600)
Acquisition Methods	Item Creation

When cast into the air, this signet-imbued card allows even those who have not learned the spell Reaping Spark to invoke it.

Signet Card: Reaping Spark +

FACTORS: Activate Reaping Spark Lv.5

Value	(3200)
Acquisition Methods	Item Creation

When cast into the air, this signet-imbued card allows even those who have not learned Reaping Spark to invoke a powerful version of it.

Signet Card: Enhance

FACTORS: Activate Enhance Lv.1

Value	800
Acquisition Methods	Shop, Enemy Drop, Synthesis

When cast into the air, this signet-imbued card allows its bearer to increase the ATK of an ally.

Signet Card: Enhance +

FACTORS: Activate Enhance Lv.5

Value	(1600)
Acquisition Methods	Locked Chest, Synthesis

When cast into the air, this signet-imbued card allows its bearer to greatly increase the ATK of an ally.

Signet Card: Enlighten

FACTORS: Activate Enlighten Lv.1

Value	800
Acquisition Methods	Shop

When cast into the air, this signet-imbued card allows its bearer to increase the INT of an ally.

Signet Card: Enlighten +

FACTORS: Activate Enlighten Lv.5

Value	1600
Acquisition Methods	Shop, Locked Chest

When cast into the air, this signet-imbued card allows its bearer to greatly increase the INT of an ally.

Signet Card: Enshelter

FACTORS: Activate Enshelter Lv.1

Value	800
Acquisition Methods	Shop

When cast into the air, this signet-imbued card allows its bearer to increase the DEF of an ally.

Signet Card: Enshelter +

FACTORS: Activate Enshelter Lv.5

Value	1600
Acquisition Methods	Shop

When cast into the air, this signet-imbued card allows its bearer to greatly increase the DEF of an ally.

Signet Card: Angel Feather

FACTORS: Activate Angel Feather Lv.1

Value	3200
Acquisition Methods	Shop, Treasure Chest

When cast into the air, this signet-imbued card allows its bearer to increase all of an ally's attributes.

Signet Card: Angel Feather +

FACTORS: Activate Angel Feather Lv.5

Value	6400
Acquisition Methods	Shop

When cast into the air, this signet-imbued card allows its bearer to greatly increase all of an ally's attributes.

Signet Card: Reflection

FACTORS: Activate Reflection Lv.1

Value	800
Acquisition Methods	Shop

When cast into the air, this signet-imbued card allows its bearer to increase the MEN of an ally.

Signet Card: Reflection +

FACTORS: Activate Reflection Lv.5

Value	1600
Acquisition Methods	Shop

When cast into the air, this signet-imbued card allows its bearer to greatly increase the MEN of an ally.

Signet Card: Sacred Pain
FACTORS: Activate Sacred Pain Lv.1

Value	800
Acquisition Methods	Shop, Item Creation

When cast into the air, this signet-imbued card allows even those who have not learned the spell Sacred Pain to invoke it.

Signet Card: Sacred Pain +
FACTORS: Activate Sacred Pain Lv.5

Value	(1600)
Acquisition Methods	Enemy Drops, Item Creation

When cast into the air, this signet-imbued card allows even those who have not learned Sacred Pain to invoke a powerful version of it.

Signet Card: Silence
FACTORS: Activate Silence Lv.1

Value	(800)
Acquisition Methods	Enemy Drop, Item Creation, Synthesis

When cast into the air, this signet-imbued card allows even those who have not learned the spell Silence to invoke it.

Signet Card: Silence +
FACTORS: Activate Silence Lv.5

Value	(1600)
Acquisition Methods	Item Creation

When cast into the air, this signet-imbued card allows even those who have not learned Silence to invoke a powerful version of it.

Signet Card: Void
FACTORS: Activate Void Lv.1

Value	(2400)
Acquisition Methods	Item Creation

When cast into the air, this signet-imbued card allows even those who have not learned the spell Void to invoke it.

Signet Card: Void +
FACTORS: Activate Void Lv.5

Value	(4800)
Acquisition Methods	Item Creation

When cast into the air, this signet-imbued card allows even those who have not learned Void to invoke a powerful version of it.

Signet Card: Arcane Weapon
FACTORS: Activate Arcane Weapon Lv.1

Value	(2400)
Acquisition Methods	Item Creation

When cast into the air, this signet-imbued card allows even those who have not learned the spell Arcane Weapon to invoke it.

Signet Card: Arcade Weapon +
FACTORS: Activate Arcane Weapon Lv.5

Value	(4800)
Acquisition Methods	Item Creation

When cast into the air, this signet-imbued card allows even those who have not learned Arcane Weapon to invoke a powerful version of it.

SKILL BOOKS

Swordsman's Manual I
INFLUENCES: Fidel and Victor's Air Slash skill

Value	(4800)
Acquisition Methods	Treasure Chests, Item Creation, Quest

A tome describing the tenets and techniques of Resulian swordsmanship. This volume outlines only some basic principles of the art.

Swordsman's Manual II
INFLUENCES: Fidel and Victor's Double Slash skill

Value	(4800)
Acquisition Methods	Item Creation

A tome describing the tenets and techniques of Resulian swordsmanship. This volume delves deeper into more practical skills.

Swordsman's Manual III
INFLUENCES: Fidel and Victor's Mirror Blade skill

Value	(6000)
Acquisition Methods	Enemy Drop, Locked Chest, Item Creation, Quest

A tome describing the tenets and techniques of Resulian swordsmanship. Only mature practitioners can complete the advanced lessons within.

Swordsman's Manual IV
INFLUENCES: Fidel's Shotgun Blast skill — Victor's Nether Strike skill

Value	(6000)
Acquisition Methods	Treasure Chest, Item Creation, Quest

A tome describing the tenets and techniques of Resulian swordsmanship. It imparts rare information coveted by swordsmen far and wide.

Swordsman's Manual V
INFLUENCES: Fidel's Death Palm skill — Victor's Flying Guillotine skill

Value	(6000)
Acquisition Methods	Treasure Chest, Item Creation, Quest

A tome describing the tenets and techniques of Resulian swordsmanship. It teaches adept warriors how to sense foes with one's eyes closed.

Swordsman's Manual VI
INFLUENCES: Fidel's Abyssal Gate skill — Victor's Diabolic Edge skill

Value	(8000)
Acquisition Methods	Treasure Chest, Locked Chest, Item Creation, Quest

A tome describing Resulian swordsmanship techniques. Its contents are rather disconcerting, but one must know darkness to know the light.

Swordsman's Manual VII
INFLUENCES: Fidel's Cyclone Blade skill — Victor's Bloodstorm Revolution skill

Value	(8000)
Acquisition Methods	Treasure Chests, Item Creation, Quest

A tome describing Resulian swordsmanship techniques. Reading this volume is imperative for all who seek to master the sword.

Swordsman's Manual VIII
INFLUENCES: Fidel's Air Raid skill — Victor's Dragon Roar skill

Value	(12000)
Acquisition Methods	Treasure Chest, Locked Chest, Item Creation

A tome describing the techniques of the famous swordsman Daril Camuze. Fathers always seem to cast a long shadow.

CQC Program Alpha
INFLUENCES: Emmerson's Sound Spike skill — Anne's Electric Fists skill

Value	(4800)
Acquisition Methods	Treasure Chest, Item Creation

An electronic manual on close quarters combat that was developed using actual combat data. The label reads "CQC for Dummies!"

CQC Program Beta
INFLUENCES: Emmerson's Seraphic Thunder skill — Anne's Hammer of Might skill

Value	(4800)
Acquisition Methods	Enemy Drop, Item Creation

An electronic manual on close quarters combat that was compiled using actual combat data. The label claims, "Easy enough to do in your sleep!"

CQC Program Gamma
INFLUENCES: Emmerson's Red Rain skill — Anne's Crescent Locus skill

Value	(6000)
Acquisition Methods	Enemy Drop, Treasure Chest, Item Creation, Quest

An electronic manual on close quarters combat that was compiled using actual combat data. The label claims, "Don't knock it until you try it!"

CQC Program Delta
INFLUENCES: Emmerson's Gravity Bullet skill — Anne's Triple Kick skill

Value	(6000)
Acquisition Methods	Treasure Chest, Item Creation, Quest

An electronic manual on close quarters combat that was compiled using actual combat data. The label says, "Don't give up now!"

CQC Program Epsilon
INFLUENCES: Emmerson's Hunter's Moon skill — Anne's Shockwave skill

Value	(6000)
Acquisition Methods	Treasure Chest, Item Creation, Quest

An electronic manual on close quarters combat that was compiled using actual combat data. The label claims, "You've got a long road ahead!"

CQC Program Zeta
INFLUENCES: Emmerson's Crescent Wings skill — Anne's Acrobat Locus skill

Value	(8000)
Acquisition Methods	Enemy Drop, Treasure Chest, Item Creation

An electronic manual on close quarters combat that was compiled using actual combat data. The label says, "If you can master this, great!"

CQC Program Eta
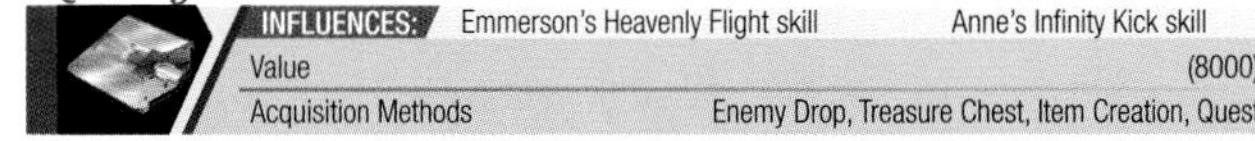

INFLUENCES: Emmerson's Heavenly Flight skill — Anne's Infinity Kick skill

Value	(8000)
Acquisition Methods	Enemy Drop, Treasure Chest, Item Creation, Quest

An electronic manual on close quarters combat that was compiled using actual combat data. The label claims, "There's an off chance you can do this!"

CQC Program Theta
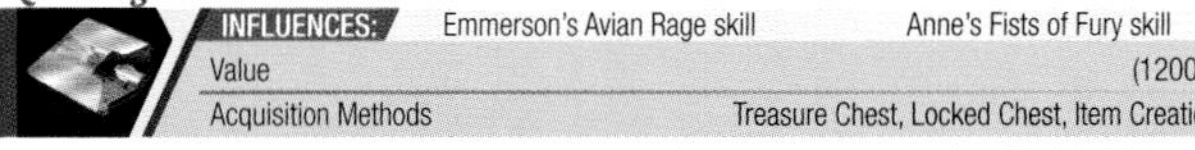

INFLUENCES: Emmerson's Avian Rage skill — Anne's Fists of Fury skill

Value	(12000)
Acquisition Methods	Treasure Chest, Locked Chest, Item Creation

An electronic manual on close quarters combat that was compiled using actual combat data. The label claims, "For the best in the business only!"

Cerulean Orb Signets, Vol.1

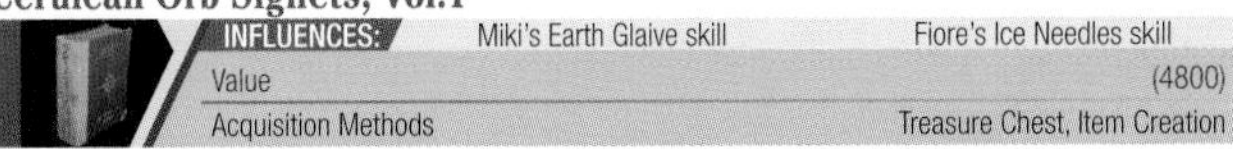

INFLUENCES:	Miki's Earth Glaive skill	Fiore's Ice Needles skill
Value		(4800)
Acquisition Methods		Treasure Chest, Item Creation

The first book in a trilogy on ice and earth signeturgy, it describes how to draw power from frozen water and to lend an ear to the earth.

Cerulean Orb Signets, Vol.2

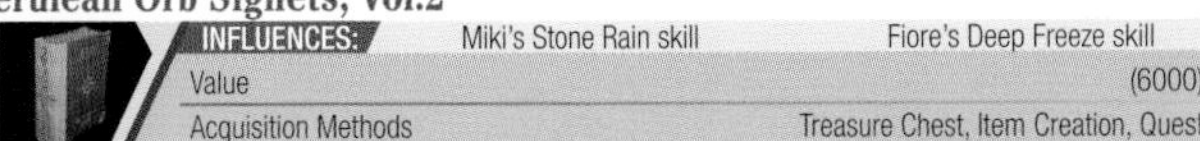

INFLUENCES:	Miki's Stone Rain skill	Fiore's Deep Freeze skill
Value		(6000)
Acquisition Methods		Treasure Chest, Item Creation, Quest

The second book in a trilogy on ice and earth signeturgy, it describes how to draw power from frozen water and to lend an ear to the earth.

Cerulean Orb Signets, Vol.3

INFLUENCES:	Miki's Terra Hammer skill	Fiore's Arctic Impact skill
Value		(8000)
Acquisition Methods		Treasure Chest, Item Creation, Quest

The third book in a trilogy on ice and earth signeturgy, it describes how to draw power from frozen water and to lend an ear to the earth.

Solar Signets, Vol.1

INFLUENCES:	Miki's Fire Bolt skill	Fiore's Wind Blade skill
Value		(4800)
Acquisition Methods		Treasure Chest, Item Creation, Quest

The first book in a tetralogy on fire and wind signeturgy, it describes how to manipulate flickering flames and capture tempestuous roars.

Solar Signets, Vol.2

INFLUENCES:	Miki's Volcanic Burst skill	Fiore's Lightning Blast skill
Value		(6000)
Acquisition Methods		Treasure Chest, Item Creation, Quest

The second book in a tetralogy on fire and wind signeturgy, it describes how to manipulate flickering flames and capture tempestuous roars.

Solar Signets, Vol.3

INFLUENCES:	Miki's Sunflare skill	Fiore's Tornado skill
Value		(8000)
Acquisition Methods		Treasure Chest, Item Creation, Quest

Slated to be the third book in a tetralogy on fire and wind signeturgy, due to a transcription error, it discusses light signeturgy instead of fire.

Solar Signets, Vol.4

INFLUENCES:	Miki's Explosion skill	Fiore's Thunder Flare skill
Value		(12000)
Acquisition Methods		Treasure Chest, Locked Chest, Item Creation

The undeniably definitive book on fire and wind signeturgy, it describes how to manipulate flickering flames and capture tempestuous roars.

Moonlight Signets, Vol.1

INFLUENCES:	Miki's Radiant Lancer skill	Fiore's Shadow Needles skill
Value		(4800)
Acquisition Methods		Treasure Chest, Locked Chest, Item Creation

The first book in a trilogy on light and dark signeturgy, it describes how to efficiently control astral radiance and bear somber gloom.

Moonlight Signets, Vol.2

INFLUENCES:	Miki's Arcane Weapon skill	Fiore's Vampiric Blade skill
Value		(6000)
Acquisition Methods		Treasure Chests, Item Creation, Quest

The second book in a trilogy on light and dark signeturgy, it describes how to efficiently control astral radiance and bear somber gloom.

Moonlight Signets, Vol.3

INFLUENCES:	Miki's Divine Wave skill	Fiore's Dark Devourer skill
Value		(8000)
Acquisition Methods		Enemy Drop, Locked Chest, Item Creation, Quest

Slated to be the third book in a trilogy on light and dark signeturgy, due to a transcription error, it discusses non-elemental facets, not light.

The Founder's Signets, Vol.1

INFLUENCES:	Miki's Aurora Rings skill	Fiore's Reaping Spark skill
Value		(4800)
Acquisition Methods		Treasure Chest, Item Creation, Quest

A book written by the founder of signeturgy, it is the first of its kind to systematize the effusion of life that sprung from chaos.

The Founder's Signets, Vol.2

INFLUENCES:	Fiore's Extinction skill	
Value		(12000)
Acquisition Methods		Treasure Chest, Item Creation

The definitive book written by the founder of signeturgy on systematizing the effusion of life that sprung from chaos.

Restorative Signets, Vol.1

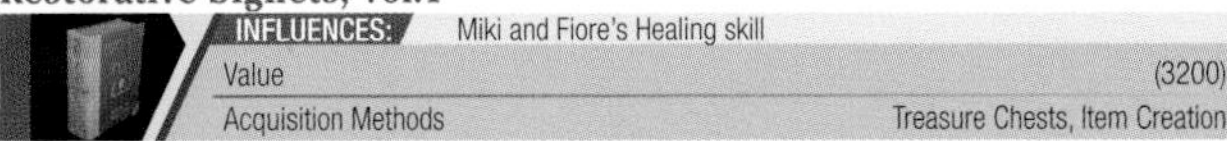

INFLUENCES:	Miki and Fiore's Healing skill	
Value		(3200)
Acquisition Methods		Treasure Chests, Item Creation

The first in a pair of books on restorative signeturgy, it describes how to gather the light of spirits for the sake of healing wounds.

Restorative Signets, Vol.2

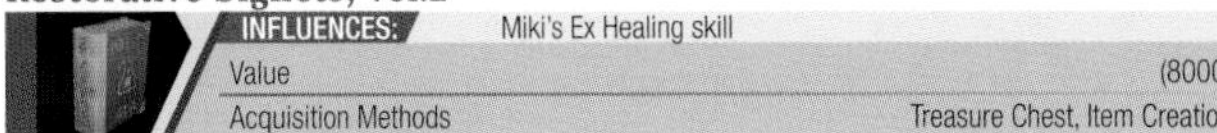

INFLUENCES:	Miki's Ex Healing skill	
Value		(8000)
Acquisition Methods		Treasure Chest, Item Creation

The second in a pair of books on restorative signeturgy, it describes how to gather the light of spirits for the sake of healing wounds.

Fae Signets, Vol.1

INFLUENCES:	Miki's Faerie Healing skill	
Value		(3200)
Acquisition Methods		Treasure Chest, Item Creation, Quest

The first book in a trilogy on fae signeturgy, it describes the art of conversing with capricious nymphs and sprites.

Fae Signets, Vol.2

INFLUENCES:	Miki's Faerie Light skill	
Value		(6000)
Acquisition Methods		Treasure Chest, Item Creation, Quest

The second book in a trilogy on fae signeturgy, it describes the art of conversing with capricious nymphs and sprites.

Fae Signets, Vol.3

INFLUENCES:	Miki's Faerie Star skill	
Value		(8000)
Acquisition Methods		Enemy Drop, Treasure Chest, Item Creation

The third book in a trilogy on fae signeturgy, it describes the art of conversing with capricious nymphs and sprites.

Purification Signets, Vol.1

INFLUENCES:	Miki and Fiore's Antidote skill	
Value		(3200)
Acquisition Methods		Treasure Chest, Item Creation, Quest

The first in a pair of books on purification signeturgy, it describes how to cleanse bodily impurities and instill virtue in people.

Purification Signets, Vol.2

INFLUENCES:	Miki's Cure Condition skill	Fiore's Void skill
Value		(8000)
Acquisition Methods		Treasure Chest, Item Creation, Quest

The second in a pair of books on purification signeturgy, it describes how to cleanse bodily impurities and instill virtue in people.

Pnuema Signets, Vol.1

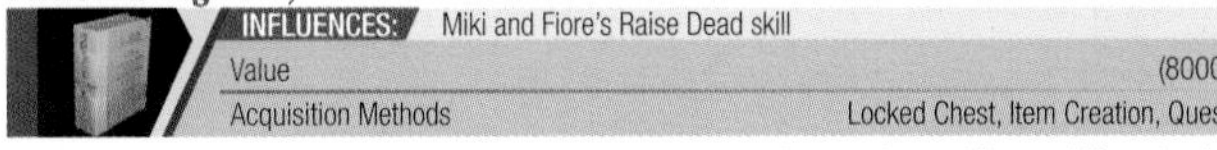

INFLUENCES:	Miki and Fiore's Raise Dead skill	
Value		(8000)
Acquisition Methods		Locked Chest, Item Creation, Quest

The first in a pair of books on revival signeturgy, it describes how to stoke the ephemeral flames of life and revive the fallen.

Pnuema Signets, Vol.2

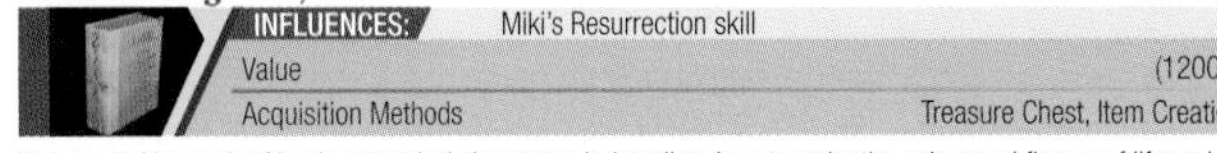

INFLUENCES:	Miki's Resurrection skill	
Value		(12000)
Acquisition Methods		Treasure Chest, Item Creation

The second in a pair of books on revival signeturgy, it describes how to stoke the ephemeral flames of life and revive the fallen.

Signeturgical Book of Quietude

INFLUENCES:	Miki's Silence skill	Fiore's Sacred Pain skill
Value		(6000)
Acquisition Methods		Locked Chest, Item Creation, Quests

This book on quietude signeturgy describes the art of creating a pervasive silence around subjects by isolating them from all sound.

FOOD

Prehistoric Meat

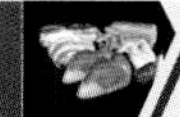

FACTORS:	Recover 10% HP	Chance target is poisoned
Value		180
Acquisition Methods		Shops, Enemy Drop, Synthesis

Children the world over have oft dreamed of sinking their teeth into this flesh like starving cavemen, but it sadly cannot be eaten as is.

Raw Fish

FACTORS:	Recover 10% HP
Value	240
Acquisition Methods	Shops, Harvesting, Enemy Drop

Fish so fresh it can be eaten off the line without a second thought. It goes splendidly with a drink, meaning juice for those not yet of age.

Common Eggs

FACTORS:	Recover 5% HP
Value	90
Acquisition Methods	Shops, Enemy Drops

Standard, nondescript eggs that can be used in all kinds of dishes.

Roe

FACTORS:	Recover 5% HP
Value	(300)
Acquisition Methods	Harvesting, Enemy Drops

The delicacy of salted fish eggs is meant to be savored one at a time.

Fresh Vegetables

FACTORS:	Recover 5% MP
Value	180
Acquisition Methods	Shops, Harvesting, Enemy Drop

An assorted bounty of nature's candy.

Tomato

FACTORS:	Recover 10% MP
Value	240
Acquisition Methods	Shop, Harvesting, Enemy Drop, Treasure Chest

A piece of fruit that is red, ripe, and bursting with juicy goodness. It almost seems to be begging for someone to grab it and take a bite.

Lemon

FACTORS:	Recover 5% MP
Value	90
Acquisition Methods	Shops, Harvesting, Enemy Drop

A piece of notably sour fruit with a bright yellow skin.

Tasty Mushrooms

FACTORS:	Recover 20% HP
Value	240
Acquisition Methods	Shops, Harvesting, Enemy Drops

Delicious fungi that hardly need any preparing to be served. They also retain their freshness for extended periods of time.

Colorful Mushrooms

FACTORS:	Recover 20% MP	Chance target is poisoned
Value		(120)
Acquisition Methods		Harvesting, Enemy Drops

Fungi with foreboding coloration that both fascinates and repels all who see them. They may be edible, but no one wants to be the first to try.

Seaweed

FACTORS:	Recover 5% MP
Value	90
Acquisition Methods	Shops, Harvesting, Enemy Drop

Kelp that has been dried for long-term storage. When reconstituted, it expands far beyond the size that one might expect.

Whole Milk

FACTORS:	Recover 20% MP
Value	360
Acquisition Methods	Shops, Synthesis

Milk with barely any of the fat skimmed off. A glass of it before bed is the perfect prescription for a good night's sleep.

Well-Aged Cheese

FACTORS:	Recover 20% HP
Value	360
Acquisition Methods	Shop, Enemy Drop, Synthesis

Flavorful cheese that has been aged for quite some time. Under its bloomy rind hides a creamy goodness that melts in your mouth.

Nectar

FACTORS:	Recover 5% HP
Value	120
Acquisition Methods	Shops, Enemy Drops

A hearty serving of the sweet, sugar-rich liquid harvested from flowers.

Spring Water

FACTORS:	Recover 10% MP
Value	240
Acquisition Methods	Shops, Harvesting

Crystal clear water drawn from deep underground.

Caterpillar Fungus

FACTORS:	Recover 10% MP
Value	(2400)
Acquisition Methods	Harvesting, Enemy Drop

A parasitic fungus that feeds off insect larvae. When dried, it can be used for either medicinal or culinary purposes.

Poison Hemlock

FACTORS:	Chance target is poisoned
Value	(1800)
Acquisition Methods	Harvesting, Enemy Drops

A nocuous plant in the parsley family that is used as a medicinal herb. From its roots and leaves emanates a nearly unbearable, putrid stench.

Marbled Meat

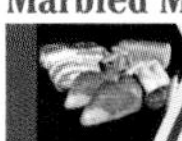

FACTORS:	Recover 20% HP
Value	(3600)
Acquisition Methods	Synthesis

Premium meat with vividly red flesh and mouth-wateringly white marbling. Its succulent flavor is guaranteed to send one into ecstasy.

Empyreanase

FACTORS:	Recover 20% HP
Value	(3000)
Acquisition Methods	Harvesting, Synthesis

An uncanny fish said to have long ago inhabited a celestial sea, its aroma and flavor are said to be embodiments of the ocean itself.

Egg Paragon

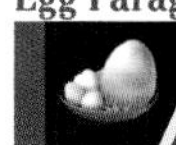

FACTORS:	Recover 20% MP
Value	(2500)
Acquisition Methods	Enemy Drops, Synthesis

The finest of eggs, with whites as clear as melted snow and yolks as bright as the midday sun.

Roe Rice

FACTORS:	Max HP +10% for 3 battles	Recover 10% HP (All)
Value		(600)
Acquisition Methods		Item Creation, Synthesis

The product of a fateful meeting between fish eggs and white rice. It is an exceedingly simple, yet undeniably popular dish.

Curry Rice

FACTORS:	Max HP +20% for 5 battles	Recover 20% HP (All)
Value		(960)
Acquisition Methods		Item Synthesis, Synthesis, Quest

A dish consisting of various sautéed ingredients mixed with spices and slowly simmered. Its piquant aroma is hard for anyone to resist.

Tears of Joysotto

FACTORS:	Max HP +20% for 5 battles Max MP +20% for 5 battles	Recover 20% HP (All) Recover 20% MP (All)
Value		(2400)
Acquisition Methods		Enemy Drop, Item Creation, Synthesis, Quest

A masterpiece of risotto so delicious that it could make even the most thick-skinned of warriors bawl from bliss.

Crab Rice Stew

FACTORS:	Max HP +30% for 3 battles	Recover 30% HP (All)
Value		(1680)
Acquisition Methods		Item Creation

A dish made by simmering white rice, shredded crab meat, mushrooms, and wild vegetables in a lightly flavored stock.

Grilled Steak

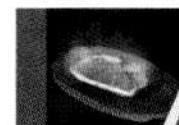

FACTORS:	ATK +30% for 3 battles	Recover 5% HP (All)
Value		(960)
Acquisition Methods		Item Creation, Synthesis

A thick-cut slab of beef grilled to perfection. Each juicy bite is guaranteed to leave you wanting another.

Hamburg Steak

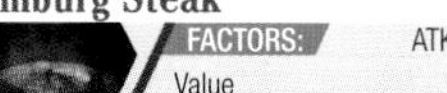

FACTORS:	ATK +20% for 5 battles	Recover 5% HP (All)
Value		(1440)
Acquisition Methods		Enemy Drop, Item Creation, Synthesis, Quest

Ground meat delicately mixed with onions, eggs, and breadcrumbs, and then grilled to retain just the right amount of juices.

Golden Omelet

FACTORS:	ATK +10% for 3 battles	Recover 5% HP (All)
Value		(720)
Acquisition Methods		Item Creation, Synthesis, Quests

This meal of sautéed ground beef wrapped in a blanket of fluffy, golden eggs is so aesthetically pleasing, few dare to pierce it with utensils.

Grilled Fish

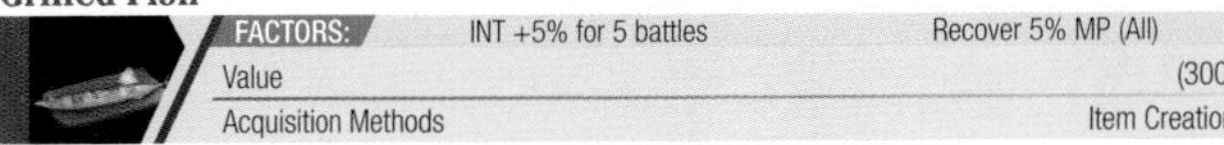

FACTORS:	INT +5% for 5 battles	Recover 5% MP (All)
Value		(300)
Acquisition Methods		Item Creation

Fish generously salted, cooked over an open flame, and served with grated radish.

Fried Fish

FACTORS:	INT +10% for 3 battles	Recover 5% MP (All)
Value		(720)
Acquisition Methods		Item Creation, Synthesis, Quest

A simple dish of white fish dipped in batter and fried to a golden crisp, a texture that perfectly complements fried potatoes.

Sushi

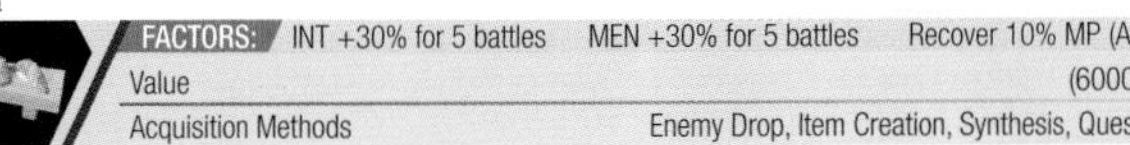

FACTORS:	INT +30% for 5 battles	MEN +30% for 5 battles	Recover 10% MP (All)
Value			(6000)
Acquisition Methods			Enemy Drop, Item Creation, Synthesis, Quest

Hand-pressed, vinegar-splashed rice topped with expertly cut slices of fish. Though this food may seem easy to prepare, it is not.

Salmon Meuniere

FACTORS:	INT +20% for 5 battles	Recover 5% MP (All)
Value		(900)
Acquisition Methods		Item Creation, Quest

A well-seasoned salmon fillet sautéed on both sides and topped with a squeeze of fresh lemon.

Stink Fish

FACTORS:	INT +50% for 5 battles	EXP -50% for 5 battles
Value		(1080)
Acquisition Methods		Enemy Drop, Item Creation, Synthesis, Quest

Fish fillet pickled in brine and then sun dried to give it a distinctive aroma. An overlooked food, it is neither loved nor hated by anyone.

Cream Stew

FACTORS:	MEN +20% for 5 battles.	Recover 5% MP (All)
Value		(1680)
Acquisition Methods		Item Creation, Synthesis

A stew of meat and vegetables simmered in a creamy white sauce. Simmering long enough for the veggies to dissolve can give it character.

Minestrone

FACTORS:	MEN +10% for 3 battles	Recover 5% MP (All)
Value		(1000)
Acquisition Methods		Item Creation, Synthesis, Quest

A chunky soup made with a tomato-based broth and piles of vegetables. Its faint notes of sourness serve to whet the appetite.

Cheese Fondue

FACTORS:	MEN +30% for 3 battles	Recover 5% MP (All)
Value		(1500)
Acquisition Methods		Item Creation, Synthesis

Bread and vegetables dipped in melted cheese. Even the cheese that sticks to the bottom of the pot is irresistibly delicious.

Vegetable Stir-Fry

FACTORS:	MP cost -10% for 3 battles	
Value		(600)
Acquisition Methods		Treasure Chest, Item Creation, Synthesis, Quest

A small amount of meat sautéed with a cornucopia of vegetables.

Caesar Salad

FACTORS:	MP cost -10% for 5 battles	
Value		(960)
Acquisition Methods		Item Creation, Synthesis

Lettuce topped with parmesan cheese, croutons, and a special buttermilk dressing.

Seaweed Salad

FACTORS:	MP cost -20% for 3 battles	
Value		(780)
Acquisition Methods		Item Creation

A salad made with lettuce, myriad seaweed types, and a soy sauce-based dressing. It is both delicious and nutritious.

Caprese Salad

FACTORS:	MP cost -20% for 5 battles	
Value		(1200)
Acquisition Methods		Item Creation, Synthesis

A salad combining sliced tomatoes and fresh cheese, with basil and olive oil drizzled on top for added flavor.

Pasta Peperoncino

FACTORS:	DEF +10% for 3 battles	Recover 5% HP (All)
Value		(960)
Acquisition Methods		Item Creation, Synthesis, Quest

Spaghetti in a light sauce made with garlic, pepperoncini, and olive oil. Of all the pasta dishes, this is purportedly the most rudimentary.

Pasta Bolognese

FACTORS:	DEF +30% for 3 battles	Recover 5% HP (All)
Value		(1800)
Acquisition Methods		Enemy Drop, Item Creation, Synthesis

Spaghetti with a slow-simmered sauce of tomatoes, ground meat, and spices. It is delectable enough to make one forget how much it splatters.

Spaghetti with Roe

FACTORS:	DEF +20% for 5 battles	Recover 5% HP (All)
Value		(1560)
Acquisition Methods		Item Creation, Synthesis

Spaghetti sautéed with roe, butter, salt, and pepper. Many chefs and household cooks alike rave about its divine medley of flavors.

Sukiyaki

FACTORS:	ATK +30% for 5 battles	DEF +30% for 5 battles	Recover 10% HP (All)
Value			(9600)
Acquisition Methods			Enemy Drop, Item Creation, Synthesis, Quest

This dish of beef, vegetables, and tofu simmered in a salty-sweet soy sauce broth is so beguiling, families fight over each piece.

Seafood Hot Pot

FACTORS:	INT +30% for 3 battles	Recover 5% MP (All)
Value		(1620)
Acquisition Methods		Enemy Drop, Item Creation, Synthesis

A hot pot dish packed with a plethora of ocean delicacies. The sheer assortment of shellfish used is so extravagant, it could be criminal!

Shortcake

FACTORS:	EXP +50% for 3 battles	
Value		(1980)
Acquisition Methods		Enemy Drop, Item Creation, Synthesis

An airy sponge cake topped with whipped cream and fruit. The epitome of confections, it is adored by sweet-toothed children everywhere.

Lemon Tart

FACTORS:	EXP +20% for 3 battles	
Value		(1380)
Acquisition Methods		Item Creation, Synthesis

A crispy pastry crust topped with lemon-flavored cream. Its invigorating, fruity sourness makes it a quintessential early summer snack.

White Bread

FACTORS:	Max MP +10% for 3 battles	Recover 10% MP (All)
Value		(600)
Acquisition Methods		Item Creation, Synthesis

Fluffy bread made from bleached wheat flour.

Chocolate Scones

FACTORS:	Max MP +20% for 5 battles	Recover 20% MP (All)
Value		(1080)
Acquisition Methods		Item Creation, Synthesis, Quest

This tasty variation on a tried-and-true pastry recipe goes wonderfully with tea, thanks in part to its rich chocolate chips.

Melon Bun

FACTORS:	Max MP +30% for 3 battles	Recover 30% MP (All)
Value		(600)
Acquisition Methods		Item Creation, Synthesis

A sweet roll made from white bread covered in cookie dough. Despite its name, no melons whatsoever were used in its creation.

Heavenly Pudding

FACTORS:	EXP +50% for 3 battles	Fol +50% for 3 battles
Value		(7800)
Acquisition Methods		Enemy Drop, Item Creation, Synthesis, Quest

It is said that eating this irresistible pudding gives one the feeling of ascending to the heavens, bite after irresistible bite.

Tiramisu

FACTORS:	EXP +20% for 3 battles	Fol +20% for 3 battles
Value		(1200)
Acquisition Methods		Item Creation, Synthesis, Quest

A sophisticated dessert consisting of a coffee-flavored sponge cake that is topped with cream cheese.

Vanilla Ice Cream

FACTORS:	Fol +20% for 3 battles	
Value		(1000)
Acquisition Methods		Item Creation, Synthesis

The real deal for connoisseurs of vanilla, this frozen dessert is made with vanilla beans, cream, and sugar.

Mint Chocolate Chip Ice Cream

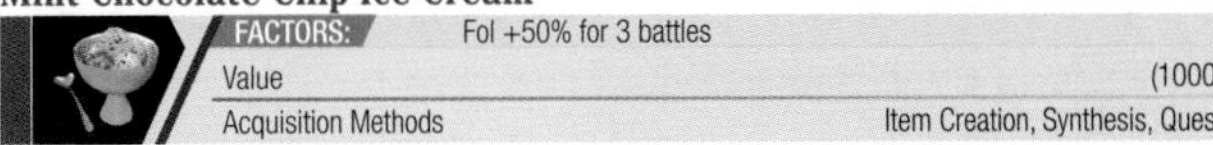

FACTORS:	Fol +50% for 3 battles	
Value		(1000)
Acquisition Methods		Item Creation, Synthesis, Quest

The cooling flavor of this frozen treat is accented by the rich chocolate chips that bespeckle its vivid green surface.

Fruit Gummies

FACTORS: Critical +15% for 3 battles | Recover 10% HP (All) | Recover 10% MP (All)
Value: (540)
Acquisition Methods: Item Creation, Synthesis

This chewy candy, of which kids can never get enough, comes in five spectacular flavors.

Hot Chocolate

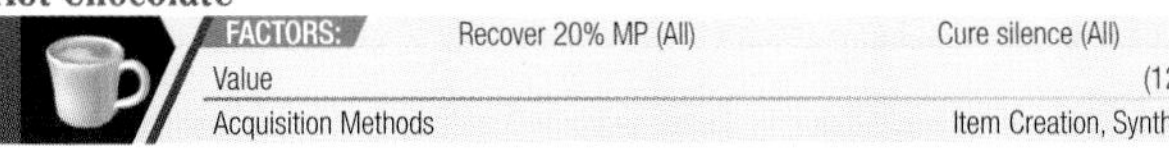

FACTORS: Recover 20% MP (All) | Cure silence (All)
Value: (1200)
Acquisition Methods: Item Creation, Synthesis

A comforting drink made from warm milk mixed with cocoa powder and sugar. Some adults add a touch of brandy to make it a soporific.

Lemon Juice

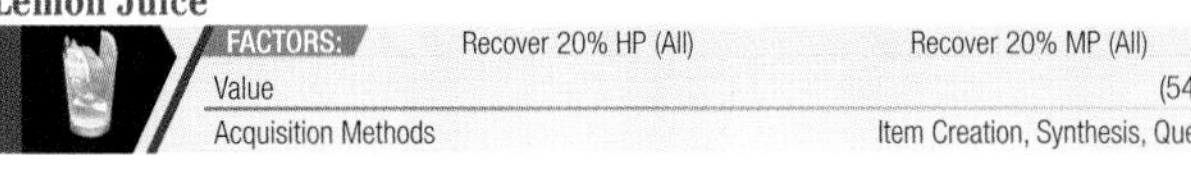

FACTORS: Recover 20% HP (All) | Recover 20% MP (All)
Value: (540)
Acquisition Methods: Item Creation, Synthesis, Quest

Juice made from freshly squeezed lemons. Though normally thought to be sour, it is rather easy on the palate.

Herb Tea

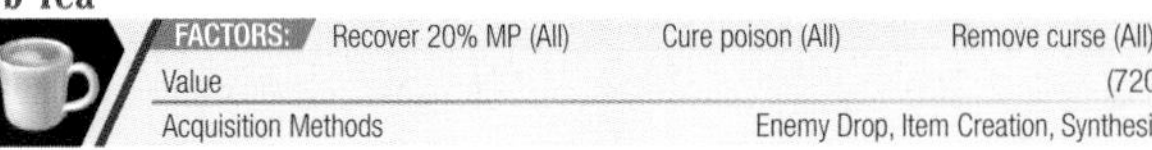

FACTORS: Recover 20% MP (All) | Cure poison (All) | Remove curse (All)
Value: (720)
Acquisition Methods: Enemy Drop, Item Creation, Synthesis

A tea with floral notes that arise from a blend of herbs packed with medicinal properties.

Chai Tea

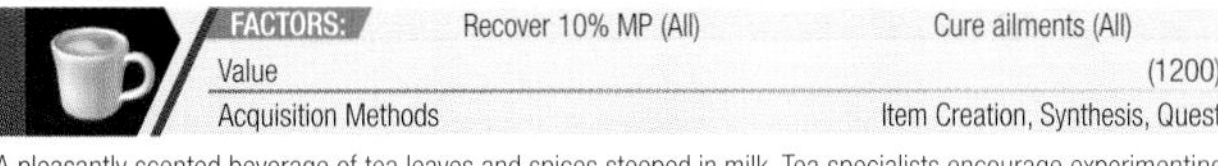

FACTORS: Recover 10% MP (All) | Cure ailments (All)
Value: (1200)
Acquisition Methods: Item Creation, Synthesis, Quest

A pleasantly scented beverage of tea leaves and spices steeped in milk. Tea specialists encourage experimenting with the spices used.

Gourmet Curry Rice

FACTORS: ATK +30% for 5 battles | DEF +30% for 5 battles | INT +30% for 5 battles | Men +30% for 5 battles
Value: (18000)
Acquisition Methods: Enemy Drop, Synthesis

The apotheosis of curry and rice, this dish has an exquisite balance of phenomenal ingredients. Normal curry will never taste the same.

Umai-bo Candy

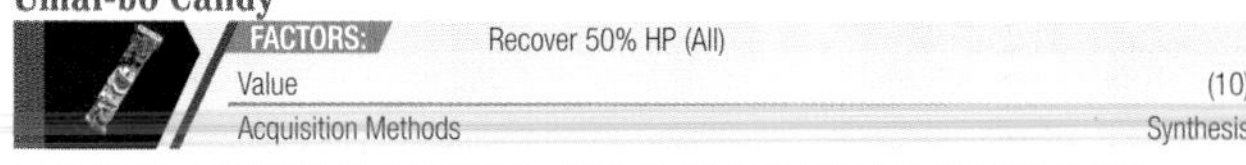

FACTORS: Recover 50% HP (All)
Value: (10)
Acquisition Methods: Synthesis

A puffed corn snack with fish roe flavoring in the shape of a cylinder. It carries the president of Yaokin's seal of approval.

Bunnylicious Pie

FACTORS: Recover 10% HP (All)
Value: (600)
Acquisition Methods: Item Creation, Synthesis

A pie made solely from ingredients that spoiled, epicurean bunnies love.

Charred Meat

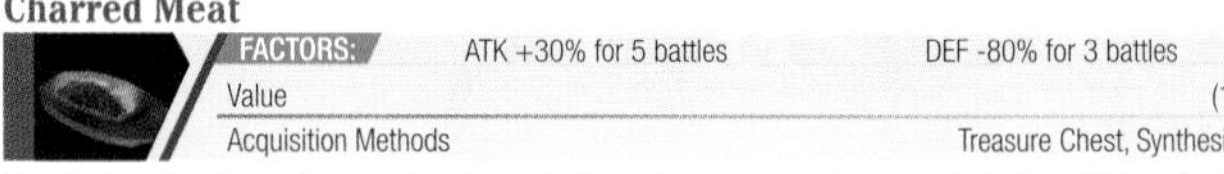

FACTORS: ATK +30% for 5 battles | DEF -80% for 3 battles
Value: (1)
Acquisition Methods: Treasure Chest, Synthesis

Meat that was burnt to a crisp under too strong of a flame. It serves as a poignant reminder that all things should be done in moderation.

Poisonous Hot Pot

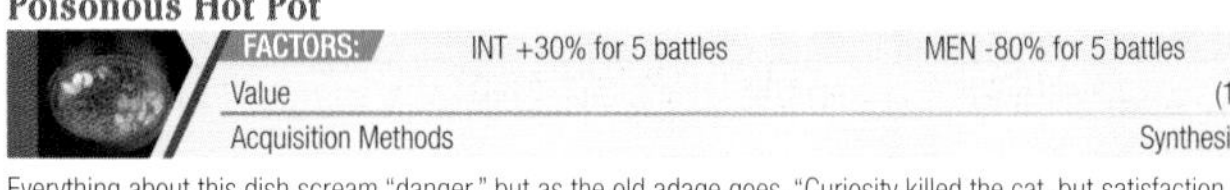

FACTORS: INT +30% for 5 battles | MEN -80% for 5 battles
Value: (1)
Acquisition Methods: Synthesis

Everything about this dish scream "danger," but as the old adage goes, "Curiosity killed the cat, but satisfaction brought it back."

Cake-like Substance

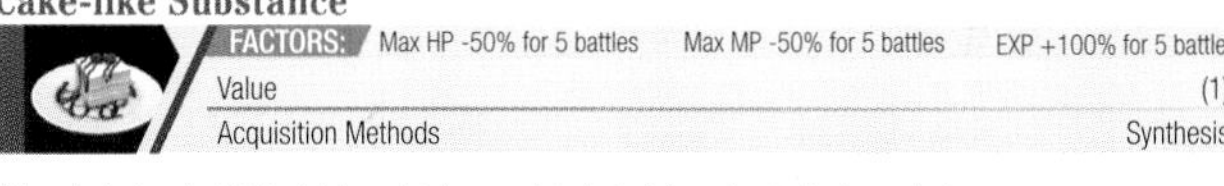

FACTORS: Max HP -50% for 5 battles | Max MP -50% for 5 battles | EXP +100% for 5 battles
Value: (1)
Acquisition Methods: Synthesis

This cake looks absolutely delicious, but its complete lack of flavor is utterly disappointing.

Dish Formerly Known as Food

FACTORS: MP cost -50% for 10 battles | Almost no EXP for 10 battles
Value: (1)
Acquisition Methods: Synthesis

A dish so complex, the general public cannot hope to understand it. It was seasoned not with love, but with self-satisfaction.

WEAPONS

FIDEL

Longsword

FACTORS: —
Value: 200
Acquisition Methods: Shops, Synthesis

ELEMENT	ATK	INT	DEF	AUGMENT
—	20	—	—	3

A particularly well-balanced longsword that can easily be wielded by novices and hardened veterans alike.

Broadsword

FACTORS: —
Value: 600
Acquisition Methods: Shops, Synthesis

ELEMENT	ATK	INT	DEF	AUGMENT
—	50	—	—	6

A simple, run-of-the-mill, one-handed sword designed to cleave foes by generating power with its heavy weight.

Falchion

FACTORS: Damage to plants +20%
Value: 1000
Acquisition Methods: Shops, Enemy Drop, Synthesis

ELEMENT	ATK	INT	DEF	AUGMENT
—	100	—	—	6

A small curved sword suited for cutting enemies to shreds. It is also used in religious rituals.

Storm Blade

FACTORS: —
Value: (1250)
Acquisition Methods: Item Creation

ELEMENT	ATK	INT	DEF	AUGMENT
	120	10	—	4

A longsword with a wind signet engraved upon it. It is far lighter than it appears, possibly due to the signet's power.

Blessed Sword

FACTORS: —
Value: 1500
Acquisition Methods: Shop, Enemy Drop

ELEMENT	ATK	INT	DEF	AUGMENT
	150	20	—	6

Forged from consecrated materials, this sword is tremendously effective at disposing of evil entities.

Bastard Sword

FACTORS: ATK +10
Value: 2500
Acquisition Methods: Shops, Synthesis

ELEMENT	ATK	INT	DEF	AUGMENT
—	180	—	—	7

A longsword with an extra-long hilt that allows for wielding with one or both hands. It is intended only for use by expert swordsmen.

Ceramic Sword

FACTORS: —
Value: 3500
Acquisition Methods: Shop, Synthesis

ELEMENT	ATK	INT	DEF	AUGMENT
—	200	—	—	6

A sword of ceramic material fashioned into a form optimal for dismembering foes. The blade's glint speaks to its razor sharpness.

Venom Sword

FACTORS: Normal attack poison chance +5%
Value: (6000)
Acquisition Methods: Item Creation

ELEMENT	ATK	INT	DEF	AUGMENT
—	250	40	—	4

A one-handed sword forged from venom-stepped steel. Merely touching the blade's point opens a venous-purple wound.

Moonfalx

FACTORS: —
Value: 7000
Acquisition Methods: Shops, Enemy Drop, Synthesis

ELEMENT	ATK	INT	DEF	AUGMENT
—	300	—	—	6

A modest greatsword with a blade that curves like a crescent moon and glows brilliantly when exposed to moonlight.

Insignivon

FACTORS: Fill reserve gauge by +7 units
Value: (15000)
Acquisition Methods: Synthesis

ELEMENT	ATK	INT	DEF	AUGMENT
—	400	—	—	12

An ancient sword traditionally bestowed upon the commander of Resulia's army. Upon its hilt is emblazoned the kingdom's coat of arms.

Icicle Sword

FACTORS: Ice-based damage +30%
Value: (30000)
Acquisition Methods: Item Creation, Synthesis

ELEMENT	ATK	INT	DEF	AUGMENT
	450	80	—	5

A demonic weapon that emits frigid, jet-black gales from the signet engraved upon its blade. All it touches is encased in ice.

Mythril Sword

FACTORS: —
Value: 40000
Acquisition Methods: Shop, Item Creation

ELEMENT	ATK	INT	DEF	AUGMENT
—	600	—	—	8

Forged from the cryptic metal called mythril, this longsword possesses an extraordinarily strong affinity with signets.

Arcana Sword

FACTORS: MP cost -5%
Value: (50000)
Acquisition Methods: Treasure Chest, Item Creation

ELEMENT	ATK	INT	DEF	AUGMENT
—	800	—	—	6

A mystical sword that harbors the power of the moon and soothes the mind of its wielder.

Veinslay

FACTORS: DEF +5%
Value: (60000)
Acquisition Methods: Synthesis

ELEMENT	ATK	INT	DEF	AUGMENT
—	900	—	—	6

Once brandished by a legendary swordsman, this blade is said to hew away emotions such as resentment and loathing.

Farwell

FACTORS: —
Value: (80000)
Acquisition Methods: Treasure Chest, Synthesis

ELEMENT	ATK	INT	DEF	AUGMENT
	1400	120	—	4

This sacred sword rains divine judgment down upon the forces of evil with the conviction of an immortal wronged.

Aurora Blade

FACTORS: Max HP +7%
Value: (90000)
Acquisition Methods: Locked Chest, Item Creation, Synthesis

ELEMENT	ATK	INT	DEF	AUGMENT
—	2000	200	—	8

The resplendent gleam that traverses the length of the blade is a manifestation of the life-giving force contained within it.

Levantine

FACTORS: ATK +10%
Value: (100000)
Acquisition Methods: Enemy Drop, Synthesis

ELEMENT	ATK	INT	DEF	AUGMENT
—	2400	400	—	7

This legendary demon sword has been tempered by heating it in an apocalyptic conflagration, then dipping it in the blood of the dead.

Metal Pipe

FACTORS: —
Value: (100)
Acquisition Methods: Synthesis

ELEMENT	ATK	INT	DEF	AUGMENT
—	10	—	—	16

A section of metal piping that can serve as a makeshift weapon.

Scumbag Slayer

FACTORS: Deal 99,999 damage to scumbags / DEF -100% / MEN -100%
Value: (1000)
Acquisition Methods: Item Creation, Synthesis

ELEMENT	ATK	INT	DEF	AUGMENT
—	5	5	—	3

According to some, using this weapon would besmirch the name of one's house, but it does send scumbags to their graves in one strike.

Laser Weapon

FACTORS: —
Value: (70000)
Acquisition Methods: Synthesis

ELEMENT	ATK	INT	DEF	AUGMENT
—	1000	1000	—	5

A close-quarters weapon utilizing a high-power laser that takes on alternate forms according to the wielder's need.

Walloon Sword

FACTORS: —
Value: 5000
Acquisition Methods: Shops, Synthesis

ELEMENT	ATK	INT	DEF	AUGMENT
—	240	—	—	7

A type of long sword. Though often confused for a broadsword, it does not possess the double-edge blade that would classify it as such.

Flamberge

FACTORS: —
Value: 9000
Acquisition Methods: Shops, Synthesis

ELEMENT	ATK	INT	DEF	AUGMENT
—	380	—	—	7

A one-handed sword with a unique blade shaped like the flames of a funeral pyre, licking at their victim before fully consuming him.

Titan's Nail

FACTORS: —
Value: 20000
Acquisition Methods: Shop

ELEMENT	ATK	INT	DEF	AUGMENT
—	440	—	—	7

Composed of a miraculous metal, this sword is as light as vellum, is as well-balanced as the horizon, and never succumbs to rust.

MIKI

Petaline Wand

FACTORS: Curative spell potency +5%

Value: 160

Acquisition Methods: Shops, Synthesis

ELEMENT	ATK	INT	DEF	AUGMENT
—	10	15	—	3

A cute wand with an even cuter petal design. The signet inscribed upon its shaft assists with spell casting.

Rod of Jewels

FACTORS: —

Value: 400

Acquisition Methods: Shops, Synthesis

ELEMENT	ATK	INT	DEF	AUGMENT
—	20	40	—	6

The most popular type of rod used by signeturges. A small orb is affixed to its tip.

Crescent Rod

FACTORS: —

Value: 800

Acquisition Methods: Shops, Synthesis

ELEMENT	ATK	INT	DEF	AUGMENT
—	50	90	—	6

A rod with an image of the moon carved into it. Swinging it about causes a clarion note to reverberate.

Ruby Wand

FACTORS: Fire-based damage +10%

Value: (1000)

Acquisition Methods: Item Creation

ELEMENT	ATK	INT	DEF	AUGMENT
	60	110	—	4

A wand inlaid with bright red gems and graven with a fire signet.

Magus Staff

FACTORS: INT +10

Value: 1200

Acquisition Methods: Shop

ELEMENT	ATK	INT	DEF	AUGMENT
—	75	140	—	6

A staff nearly impossible to use correctly without having the knowledge of a high-ranking signeturge.

Cordon Scepter

FACTORS: —

Value: 2000

Acquisition Methods: Shops

ELEMENT	ATK	INT	DEF	AUGMENT
—	90	170	—	6

A scepter adorned with interlocking rings at its end. The intertwined design symbolizes the circle of transmigration.

Floral Brume Wand

FACTORS: Normal attack fog chance +5%

Value: (4800)

Acquisition Methods: Item Creation

ELEMENT	ATK	INT	DEF	AUGMENT
	140	270	—	4

A wand designed to look like scattering blossoms. Vestiges of light constantly stream forth from its apex.

Sacred Scepter

FACTORS: —

Value: 5600

Acquisition Methods: Shops

ELEMENT	ATK	INT	DEF	AUGMENT
—	160	300	—	6

A replica of the sacred scepters once used by ancient signeturges. Despite being a mere imitation, it possesses incredible power.

Amber Mace

FACTORS: Earth-based damage +30%

Value: (24000)

Acquisition Methods: Item Creation, Synthesis

ELEMENT	ATK	INT	DEF	AUGMENT
	210	440	—	5

A flail inlaid with an earth crystal. It responds to earth-based signeturgy and heightens the power of the hose who wield it.

Mythril Rod

FACTORS: —

Value: 32000

Acquisition Methods: Shop, Treasure Chest, Item Creation

ELEMENT	ATK	INT	DEF	AUGMENT
—	300	560	—	8

A rod made from the cryptic substance mythril. It is well-suited for use with almost any type of signet.

Adept's Staff

FACTORS: —

Value: (40000)

Acquisition Methods: Item Creation

ELEMENT	ATK	INT	DEF	AUGMENT
—	400	740	—	6

A staff of great prestige and a tradition that spans multiple ages. Only the most accomplished of signeturges are permitted to carry it.

Calamity Staff

FACTORS: MP cost -10%

Value: (48000)

Acquisition Methods: Synthesis

ELEMENT	ATK	INT	DEF	AUGMENT
—	450	880	—	6

A staff graven with a crystal fashioned into a skull. The occult power it exudes is potent enough to induce natural disasters.

Asclepius

FACTORS: Curative spell potency +20%

Value: (64000)

Acquisition Methods: Treasure Chest, Synthesis

ELEMENT	ATK	INT	DEF	AUGMENT
—	500	1250	—	4

A staff once borne by a healer deemed to be a god. The alabaster serpent composing its design symbolizes the concept of regeneration.

Apocalypse

FACTORS: —

Value: (72000)

Acquisition Methods: Locked Chest, Item Creation

ELEMENT	ATK	INT	DEF	AUGMENT
—	600	1800	—	8

A staff chiseled into the form of gigantic and sinister snakes. The power it harbors is capable of sending the entire world into ruin.

Mindhealer

FACTORS: Max MP +15%

Value: (80000)

Acquisition Methods: Synthesis

ELEMENT	ATK	INT	DEF	AUGMENT
	700	2400	—	7

A staff said to grant its bearer omniscience and thaumaturgical prowess. Those it deems unworthy, though, are devoured by the power it bestows.

Welch's Handy Stick

FACTORS: —

Value: (100)

Acquisition Methods: Synthesis

ELEMENT	ATK	INT	DEF	AUGMENT
—	—	10	—	16

The trademark gadget Welch uses to point at things. Its fingers, though delightfully charming, do not actually move.

Booster Wand

FACTORS: —

Value: 2800

Acquisition Methods: Shop

ELEMENT	ATK	INT	DEF	AUGMENT
—	110	210	—	6

A wand that represents the culmination of symbometric research over countless years, it amplifies the potency of the bearer's spells.

Rune Wand

FACTORS: —

Value: 4000

Acquisition Methods: Shops

ELEMENT	ATK	INT	DEF	AUGMENT
—	130	250	—	7

This wand adds some extra vim and vigor to its bearer's signeturgy.

Crystal Wand

FACTORS: —

Value: 7200

Acquisition Methods: Shops

ELEMENT	ATK	INT	DEF	AUGMENT
—	190	380	—	7

A wand that features a glimmering crystal atop its shaft. It overflows with so much power that only experienced mages dare lay a hand on it.

Resonance Scepter

FACTORS: —

Value: 16000

Acquisition Methods: Shop

ELEMENT	ATK	INT	DEF	AUGMENT
—	220	440	—	7

This staff was manufactured using the latest in symbometric technology. It attunes the frequency of multiple symbols to magnify spell power.

VICTOR

Knight's Saber

FACTORS: MEN +5
Value: 600
Acquisition Methods: Shops, Synthesis

ELEMENT	ATK	INT	DEF	AUGMENT
—	55	—	—	3

A saber supplied to Resulia's commissioned officers. It is lightweight and not cumbersome in the least.

Pallasch

FACTORS: —
Value: 1100
Acquisition Methods: Shops, Synthesis

ELEMENT	ATK	INT	DEF	AUGMENT
—	110	—	—	6

A knight's sword with an especially sharp point. To adapt it for use in mounted combat, it features a slightly longer blade than most.

Rune Blade

FACTORS: MEN +10
Value: (6600)
Acquisition Methods: Item Creation, Synthesis

ELEMENT	ATK	INT	DEF	AUGMENT
—	290	50	—	6

This longsword's blade is engraved with a signet of ineffable power, which gives off a brilliant incandescence each time the sword is swung.

Alastor

FACTORS: Normal attack instakill chance +1%
Value: (15950)
Acquisition Methods: Locked Chest, Synthesis

ELEMENT	ATK	INT	DEF	AUGMENT
—	410	100	—	4

An infernal sword bearing the name of a chthonic executioner. Its grotesquely spinescent edges are designed to leave macabre gashes.

Searing Sword

FACTORS: Fire-based damage +30%
Value: (33000)
Acquisition Methods: Item Creation, Synthesis

ELEMENT	ATK	INT	DEF	AUGMENT
	460	150	—	4

This blade of suspect origin is a veritable prison for a certain fiend. The beast's fury causes the steel to burn a scalding red hue.

Silvance

FACTORS: —
Value: 44000
Acquisition Methods: Shop, Item Creation

ELEMENT	ATK	INT	DEF	AUGMENT
—	620	—	—	8

A gleaming silver sword forged from mythril ore.

Dojikiri-Yasutsuna

FACTORS: Damage to humanoids +20%
Value: (55000)
Acquisition Methods: Treasure Chest, Item Creation

ELEMENT	ATK	INT	DEF	AUGMENT
—	840	—	—	6

A fabled sword said to have slain a wicked ogre that plagued the land.

Crimson Scourge

FACTORS: —
Value: (66000)
Acquisition Methods: Synthesis

ELEMENT	ATK	INT	DEF	AUGMENT
—	950	—	—	6

An otherworldly sword that was supposedly bestowed upon humanity by a seraph as part of a set long, long ago.

Chrome Nightmare

FACTORS: Normal attacks absorb 1% MP
Value: (88000)
Acquisition Methods: Treasure Chest, Synthesis

ELEMENT	ATK	INT	DEF	AUGMENT
	1450	—	—	4

Created by channeling rancor into a physical form, this weapon reaps the souls of all those it pierces.

Murasame

FACTORS: Critical hit rate +15%
Value: (99000)
Acquisition Methods: Locked Chest, Item Creation

ELEMENT	ATK	INT	DEF	AUGMENT
	2100	—	—	8

A legendary blade that is constantly enshrouded in an icy brume. Its true potential can only be realized by a determined individual.

Ama-no-Murakumo

FACTORS: MEN +10%
Value: (110000)
Acquisition Methods: Synthesis

ELEMENT	ATK	INT	DEF	AUGMENT
—	2500	—	—	7

A sturdy sword blessed by the gods during the age of creation. Legend states it was born from the tail of a mountainous dragon.

Wooden Sword

FACTORS: EXP +20%
Value: (100)
Acquisition Methods: Synthesis

ELEMENT	ATK	INT	DEF	AUGMENT
—	10	—	—	16

A shoddy wooden sword of the kind found discarded on training hall floors. The acrid stench of sweat is thoroughly ingrained in its hilt.

Sinclair

FACTORS: —
Value: 2750
Acquisition Methods: Shops, Synthesis

ELEMENT	ATK	INT	DEF	AUGMENT
—	200	—	—	7

This saber is unremarkable in every way except for how straight its blade runs.

Deadly Edge

FACTORS: —
Value: 5500
Acquisition Methods: Shops, Synthesis

ELEMENT	ATK	INT	DEF	AUGMENT
—	270	—	—	7

A sword with an edge so acutely whetted that simply laying one's finger upon it can cause blood to gush forth.

Farcutter

FACTORS: —
Value: 7700
Acquisition Methods: Shops

ELEMENT	ATK	INT	DEF	AUGMENT
—	330	—	—	6

A sword forged with an exceedingly long blade to increase its reach, thereby allowing its bearer to sunder opponents from great distances.

Oriental Blade

FACTORS: —
Value: 9900
Acquisition Methods: Shops, Synthesis

ELEMENT	ATK	INT	DEF	AUGMENT
—	390	—	—	7

This curved blade was tempered via a process known only to those of the clan who craft it, and is ideal for easily severing flesh and bone.

Amalgametal Blade

FACTORS: —
Value: 22000
Acquisition Methods: Shop

ELEMENT	ATK	INT	DEF	AUGMENT
—	450	—	—	7

A longsword born of a revolution in the smelting process. Its weight makes it difficult to wield, but also more intimidating.

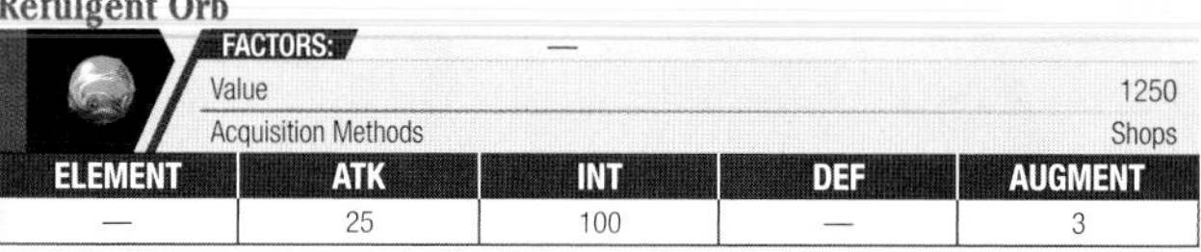

FIORE

Refulgent Orb

FACTORS:	—
Value	1250
Acquisition Methods	Shops

ELEMENT	ATK	INT	DEF	AUGMENT
—	25	100	—	3

A signet can be seen carved upon the interior of this arcane sphere, which shines with a warm light when laid bare before the sun.

Gelid Orb

FACTORS:	Ice-based damage +10%
Value	1850
Acquisition Methods	Shop

ELEMENT	ATK	INT	DEF	AUGMENT
	50	150	—	5

Before being quarried and chiseled into its current shape, this sphere was originally a piece of permafrost in a land of eternal winter.

Conflagrant Soul

FACTORS:	—
Value	3200
Acquisition Methods	Shops, Item Creation

ELEMENT	ATK	INT	DEF	AUGMENT
	60	180	—	5

A crystal that seals away a fire elemental. The flames that roil inside are so hot that they warp and bend in unimaginable ways.

Star Flail

FACTORS:	Normal attack stun chance +5%
Value	(7500)
Acquisition Methods	Item Creation, Synthesis

ELEMENT	ATK	INT	DEF	AUGMENT
—	120	280	—	4

The head of a mace hammered into the shape of a shooting star. It causes stars to appear when it hits somewhere particularly painful.

Corvine Orb

FACTORS:	Damage to insects +20%
Value	8750
Acquisition Methods	Shops, Synthesis

ELEMENT	ATK	INT	DEF	AUGMENT
—	150	320	—	5

A crystal designed to resemble the infamous black bird of death. Those exposed to its piercing gaze are said to eftsoons perish.

Vatic Looking Glass

FACTORS:	Normal attack silence chance +1%
Value	(18200)
Acquisition Methods	Item Creation, Synthesis

ELEMENT	ATK	INT	DEF	AUGMENT
—	180	400	—	6

A crystal within which burns the soul of a righteous sinner. The ephemeral flames that consume him illuminate the future of its bearer.

Orb of Antiquity

FACTORS:	—
Value	(37500)
Acquisition Methods	Item Creation, Synthesis

ELEMENT	ATK	INT	DEF	AUGMENT
—	250	600	—	8

A layer of sediment excavated from deep within the earth, triturated, and molded into an orb. The remains of myriad creatures shift inside it.

Infernal Gaze

FACTORS:	Darkness-based damage +30%
Value	50000
Acquisition Methods	Shop, Treasure Chest, Item Creation

ELEMENT	ATK	INT	DEF	AUGMENT
	200	450	—	6

A crystal embedded with what is believed to be the eye of a demon. It unleashes untold power by feeding off the life force of its bearer.

Armillary Sphere

FACTORS:	Max MP +100
Value	(62500)
Acquisition Methods	Item Creation

ELEMENT	ATK	INT	DEF	AUGMENT
—	300	800	—	6

A model for mapping the movements of celestial objects. Amongst the academic community, it is seen as a symbol of knowledge and wisdom.

Sacrosanct Orb

FACTORS:	—
Value	(75000)
Acquisition Methods	Synthesis

ELEMENT	ATK	INT	DEF	AUGMENT
	350	900	—	6

An orb of crystal hallowed by the gods themselves. The names of the three creator deities are etched upon it in a bygone script.

Carbuncle's Prison

FACTORS:	Fol +50%
Value	(100000)
Acquisition Methods	Treasure Chest, Synthesis

ELEMENT	ATK	INT	DEF	AUGMENT
—	400	1300	—	4

A gem so vividly crimson that it bewitches all who lay eyes upon it. Within dwells a sprite that brings good fortune to the orb's bearer.

Dragon's Den

FACTORS:	Max MP +7%
Value	(112500)
Acquisition Methods	Locked Chest, Item Creation

ELEMENT	ATK	INT	DEF	AUGMENT
	500	1900	—	8

An orbicular crystal in which writhes the soul of a savage dragon. Only a consummate signeturge would be able to harness its power.

Aether-in-Stasis

FACTORS:	INT +10%
Value	(125000)
Acquisition Methods	Synthesis

ELEMENT	ATK	INT	DEF	AUGMENT
—	600	2500	—	7

Purportedly manifested by a goddess, this fabled artifact is imbued with such power as to make all who disobey it fall prostrate.

Terrestrial Globe

FACTORS:	—
Value	(100)
Acquisition Methods	Synthesis

ELEMENT	ATK	INT	DEF	AUGMENT
—	—	10	—	16

Despite being so detailed that anyone can instantly grasp the geography of the planet it represents, it is useless to most Faykreedians.

Mekhanesphere

FACTORS:	—
Value	4400
Acquisition Methods	Shop

ELEMENT	ATK	INT	DEF	AUGMENT
—	90	220	—	7

An orb containing a machine of unknown origins that is remarkably small, intricately detailed, and seemingly enhances signeturgical powers.

Sunsylph Orb

FACTORS:	—
Value	6250
Acquisition Methods	Shops

ELEMENT	ATK	INT	DEF	AUGMENT
—	100	260	—	7

An orb said to have been legated by mystical worshipers of the sun. Whenever daylight falls upon it, the sphere turns brilliantly coruscant.

Marmoreal Sphere

FACTORS:	—
Value	11250
Acquisition Methods	Shops

ELEMENT	ATK	INT	DEF	AUGMENT
—	170	380	—	7

An orb of crystallized lime that was imbued with occult powers. It is revered by many due to its gently-flowing, naturally-formed signet.

Sybilline Orb

FACTORS:	—
Value	25000
Acquisition Methods	Shop

ELEMENT	ATK	INT	DEF	AUGMENT
—	190	420	—	7

From whence it came and what god deigned to infuse it with power is a mystery, but this orb strikes fear into all who foolishly gaze upon it.

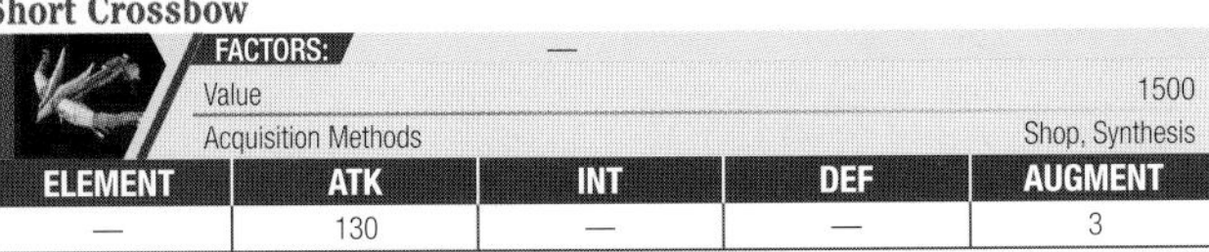

EMMERSON

Short Crossbow

FACTORS: —

Value: 1500

Acquisition Methods: Shop, Synthesis

ELEMENT	ATK	INT	DEF	AUGMENT
—	130	—	—	3

A bow for hunting small animals. It lacks in killing power, but is quite portable.

Hunting Bow

FACTORS: Damage to avians +20%

Value: 2700

Acquisition Methods: Shops, Synthesis

ELEMENT	ATK	INT	DEF	AUGMENT
—	160	—	—	6

Made specifically for hunting, this bow is carefully designed to take down one's prey with a single arrow.

Microblaster

FACTORS: —

Value: 3700

Acquisition Methods: Shop

ELEMENT	ATK	INT	DEF	AUGMENT
—	200	—	—	6

A small phaser with exceptional accuracy. Faykreedians cannot fathom how it works.

Williwaw Bow

FACTORS: Damage to machines +20%

Value: (6300)

Acquisition Methods: Treasure Chest, Item Creation, Synthesis

ELEMENT	ATK	INT	DEF	AUGMENT
	250	30	—	4

A crossbow imbued with a signet of wind. The entire weapon becomes scintillant after nocking an arrow and drawing the bowstring.

Composite Bow

FACTORS: ATK +5

Value: 7350

Acquisition Methods: Shops, Synthesis

ELEMENT	ATK	INT	DEF	AUGMENT
—	290	—	—	6

A bow made from sundry materials designed to make it even more lethal.

Atrementous Usurper

FACTORS: —

Value: (15250)

Acquisition Methods: Treasure Chest, Item Creation, Synthesis

ELEMENT	ATK	INT	DEF	AUGMENT
	370	60	—	4

A crossbow imbued with the power of darkness. The arrows it looses are said to siphon the virtue from any saintly souls in which they land.

Saint's Bow

FACTORS: Light-based damage +30%

Value: (31500)

Acquisition Methods: Item Creation

ELEMENT	ATK	INT	DEF	AUGMENT
	420	80	—	4

A crossbow created for the sole purpose of exorcising the wicked.

Sylvan Ray

FACTORS: —

Value: 42000

Acquisition Methods: Shop, Item Creation

ELEMENT	ATK	INT	DEF	AUGMENT
—	550	—	—	8

A phaser produced with the uncanny metal known as mythril and imbued with Faykreedian signeturgy.

Straightshooter

FACTORS: —

Value: (52500)

Acquisition Methods: Treasure Chest, Item Creation

ELEMENT	ATK	INT	DEF	AUGMENT
—	750	—	—	6

A phaser of such incredible precision is only produced once every million units.

Failnaught

FACTORS: Critical hit rate +10%

Value: (63000)

Acquisition Methods: Synthesis

ELEMENT	ATK	INT	DEF	AUGMENT
—	850	—	—	6

A bow thought to only have existed in folklore. It is rumored to fire arrows that never miss their mark.

Arcadian Serenity

FACTORS: —

Value: (84000)

Acquisition Methods: Treasure Chest, Synthesis

ELEMENT	ATK	INT	DEF	AUGMENT
—	1300	150	—	4

A sacred bow passed down through generations of woodland spirits.

Umbral Blast

FACTORS: —

Value: (94500)

Acquisition Methods: Locked Chest, Item Creation

ELEMENT	ATK	INT	DEF	AUGMENT
	1750	200	—	8

Every single specification of this phaser has been calibrated so exactly as if to suggest it was manufactured in a higher dimension.

Dragon's Bellow

FACTORS: MP cost -20%

Value: (105000)

Acquisition Methods: Synthesis

ELEMENT	ATK	INT	DEF	AUGMENT
—	2100	—	—	7

A phaser redolent of a dragon's jaw. The sound it makes when fired is as low and massive as the roar of a colossal wyrm.

Squirt Gun

FACTORS: —

Value: (100)

Acquisition Methods: Synthesis

ELEMENT	ATK	INT	DEF	AUGMENT
	10	—	—	16

A nostalgic gun that brings back summer memories of blue skies, puffy white clouds, and the laughter of childhood friends.

Wild Arc

FACTORS: —

Value: 5250

Acquisition Methods: Shops

ELEMENT	ATK	INT	DEF	AUGMENT
—	230	—	—	7

A bow impishly imbued with a signet that amplifies recoil.

Homing Arc

FACTORS: —

Value: 9450

Acquisition Methods: Shops, Synthesis

ELEMENT	ATK	INT	DEF	AUGMENT
—	350	—	—	7

This bow has been enhanced with signeturgy, allowing it to fire arrows with laudable accuracy, even if its wielder is a terrible shot.

Photonic Blaster

FACTORS: —

Value: 21000

Acquisition Methods: Shop, Treasure Chest, Synthesis

ELEMENT	ATK	INT	DEF	AUGMENT
—	400	—	—	7

A phaser that was built with no other thought in mind than to optimize its destructive capabilities—a goal which it fulfills admirably.

ANNE

Metal Knuckles

FACTORS: —
Value: 1350
Acquisition Methods: Shop, Synthesis

ELEMENT	ATK	INT	DEF	AUGMENT
—	140	—	—	3

A metal weapon gripped in one's fist and designed to deal powerful blows. Though it is small, it is not to be underestimated.

Gauntlets

FACTORS: DEF +5
Value: 2250
Acquisition Methods: Shops

ELEMENT	ATK	INT	DEF	AUGMENT
—	170	—	3	6

Gloves made of steel used to protect one's hands. They were originally conceived as pieces of armor, but also serve as exceptional weapons.

Mechanical Fists

FACTORS: Critical hit rate +5%
Value: 3150
Acquisition Methods: Shop

ELEMENT	ATK	INT	DEF	AUGMENT
—	210	—	—	6

Gauntlets fitted with several gears that promote fluid movement of the arms.

Damask Knuckles

FACTORS: —
Value: (5400)
Acquisition Methods: Item Creation, Synthesis

ELEMENT	ATK	INT	DEF	AUGMENT
	260	—	—	6

Knuckles made of tough Damascus steel and inlaid with a most beautiful design.

Fragmenters

FACTORS: DEF +10
Value: 6300
Acquisition Methods: Shops

ELEMENT	ATK	INT	DEF	AUGMENT
—	300	—	8	6

Gauntlets with expanded articulation for improved offensive capabilities. They generate a small shockwave upon impact.

Vermilion Claws

FACTORS: —
Value: (13050)
Acquisition Methods: Item Creation

ELEMENT	ATK	INT	DEF	AUGMENT
—	380	—	—	6

Knuckle-like weapons with bright red talons extending from their hand coverings. They were made with leather and claws from a Corrupt.

Hurricane Claws

FACTORS: Wind-based damage +30%
Value: (27000)
Acquisition Methods: Item Creation

ELEMENT	ATK	INT	DEF	AUGMENT
	430	20	—	4

A claw weapon with three long, thin, curved blades apiece. They slice and dice foes with the speed of a hurricane.

Mythril Gauntlets

FACTORS: —
Value: 36000
Acquisition Methods: Shop, Item Creation

ELEMENT	ATK	INT	DEF	AUGMENT
—	580	—	15	8

Mythril gauntlets that serve as wonderful examples of both offensive and defensive pieces of equipment.

Tiger Fangs

FACTORS: Damage to beasts +20%
Value: (45000)
Acquisition Methods: Treasure Chest, Item Creation

ELEMENT	ATK	INT	DEF	AUGMENT
—	770	—	—	6

Knuckles patterned after the fearsome tiger whose power they house. Everything they strike is rent to ribbons.

Feral Claws

FACTORS: —
Value: (54000)
Acquisition Methods: Synthesis

ELEMENT	ATK	INT	DEF	AUGMENT
—	880	—	—	6

Wild-but-beautiful claws that effortlessly cleave all with which they come into contact, making the battlefield run red with blood.

Bloody Knuckles

FACTORS: Normal attacks absorb 3% HP
Value: (72000)
Acquisition Methods: Treasure Chest, Synthesis

ELEMENT	ATK	INT	DEF	AUGMENT
	1350	50	—	4

Knuckle-dusters that were favored by the King of the Undead. They were once a more congenial color, but now glow a nefarious oxblood red.

Kaiser Knuckles

FACTORS: ATK +5%
Value: (81000)
Acquisition Methods: Locked Chest, Item Creation

ELEMENT	ATK	INT	DEF	AUGMENT
—	1800	—	—	8

Knuckles made from the legendary metal orichalcum. Their name is more than fitting, seeing the amount of destruction they can wreak.

Immolating Fangs

FACTORS: Critical hit rate +30%
Value: (90000)
Acquisition Methods: Synthesis

ELEMENT	ATK	INT	DEF	AUGMENT
—	2200	200	—	7

Knuckles made from the teeth of a fearless beast whose massive pelt blazed as red as a bonfire.

Paws

FACTORS: —
Value: (100)
Acquisition Methods: Synthesis

ELEMENT	ATK	INT	DEF	AUGMENT
—	10	—	—	16

Gloves resembling the soft and springy paws of a domesticated animal. With mitts this cute, your sweetheart will simply have to fall for you.

Slasher Claws

FACTORS: —
Value: 4500
Acquisition Methods: Shops

ELEMENT	ATK	INT	DEF	AUGMENT
—	240	—	—	7

Claws of utmost endurance whetted on a stone of the finest grit, their blades cut through challengers better than many swords do.

Cesti of Torment

FACTORS: —
Value: 8100
Acquisition Methods: Shops, Synthesis

ELEMENT	ATK	INT	DEF	AUGMENT
—	360	—	—	7

Powerful knuckles that have been outfitted with needles to puncture opponents' skin and force them to writhe in pain with every punch.

Gatling Gauntlets

FACTORS: —
Value: 18000
Acquisition Methods: Shop, Synthesis

ELEMENT	ATK	INT	DEF	AUGMENT
—	410	—	—	7

Gauntlets designed to have their wearer unleash weighty blow after weighty blow with nary a pause in between.

ARMOR

HEAVY ARMOR—FIDEL AND VICTOR

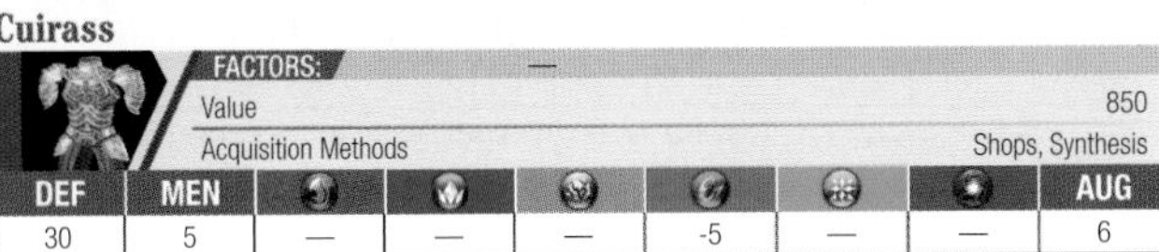

Cuirass

FACTORS: —

Value: 850

Acquisition Methods: Shops, Synthesis

DEF	MEN							AUG
30	5	—	—	—	-5	—	—	6

Armor made from metal plates that are held together by leather. It is designed to primarily protect the torso.

Shell Armor

FACTORS: Successful guard: Damage taken -5%

Value: (1000)

Acquisition Methods: Item Creation

DEF	MEN							AUG
45	10	-5	10	—	—	—	—	6

Armor made from sturdy carapace and reinforced with iron plates. It is surprisingly light for the amount of protection it provides.

Plate Armor

FACTORS: —

Value: 2150

Acquisition Methods: Shops, Synthesis

DEF	MEN							AUG
60	—	-10	—	—	-10	—	—	6

A suit of armor consisting of many metal plates. It is exactly as heavy as one would expect.

Damask Plate

FACTORS: DEF +10

Value: (5100)

Acquisition Methods: Item Creation

DEF	MEN							AUG
90	45	—	—	10	—	—	—	6

Plate armor made of sturdy Damascus steel.

Silver Cuirass

FACTORS: —

Value: 5950

Acquisition Methods: Shops, Synthesis

DEF	MEN							AUG
120	60	—	—	—	-5	15	—	6

Armor made from silvery steel plates connected by leather.

Duel Armor

FACTORS: Foe critical hit rate -10%

Value: (12350)

Acquisition Methods: Treasure Chest, Item Creation, Synthesis

DEF	MEN							AUG
150	50	10	10	10	10	—	-30	6

This homemade suit of armor was given to a warrior by his family before a battle. It is graven with their prayers for his safe return.

Ifrit Mail

FACTORS: 3% chance to absorb 10% fire damage

Value: (25500)

Acquisition Methods: Item Creation, Quest

DEF	MEN							AUG
200	75	40	40	—	—	-5	-5	4

Armor that bears the name of a djinn who manipulates fire. It has the power to both absorb heat and repel cold.

Mythril Plate

FACTORS: —

Value: 34000

Acquisition Methods: Shop, Item Creation, Synthesis

DEF	MEN							AUG
240	100	—	—	—	—	10	10	8

Plate armor made of the mysterious substance mythril.

Valiant Mail

FACTORS: Successful guard: Damage taken -10%

Value: (42500)

Acquisition Methods: Treasure Chest, Item Creation

DEF	MEN							AUG
280	90	—	—	—	—	—	—	6

Armor worn by a warrior renowned for his valiance. As his ghost lives on inside, wearing this piece summons torrents of fighting spirit.

Astral Armor

FACTORS: MEN +5%

Value: (51000)

Acquisition Methods: Synthesis

DEF	MEN							AUG
320	100	—	—	15	—	—	—	8

Those searching for armor to protect both the body and the mind need look no further.

Reflecting Plate

FACTORS: Damage from divinities -10%

Value: (68000)

Acquisition Methods: Locked Chest, Item Creation

DEF	MEN							AUG
400	200	10	10	10	10	30	30	6

Gleaming plate armor that has been polished to the extreme using a secret technique.

Universal Armor

FACTORS: DEF +10%

Value: (76500)

Acquisition Methods: Synthesis

DEF	MEN							AUG
500	250	—	—	—	—	40	-20	10

If this suit of armor's intensely lustrous sheen is not proof enough of its preeminence, the degree to which it absorbs impacts will be.

Superior Armor Plate

FACTORS: —

Value: 4250

Acquisition Methods: Shops

DEF	MEN							AUG
80	40	—	—	—	—	—	—	7

Thanks to this plate armor's brilliant patina, it boasts outstanding pliancy and is one of the most durable suits for its weight.

Ogre's Armor

FACTORS: —

Value: 7650

Acquisition Methods: Shops, Synthesis

DEF	MEN							AUG
140	50	—	—	—	—	—	—	7

A suit of heavy armor that provides the same protection as if its wearer had draped himself in one of those stocky behemoths' hides.

Bronto Armor

FACTORS: —

Value: 17000

Acquisition Methods: Shop, Synthesis

DEF	MEN							AUG
180	75	—	—	—	—	—	—	7

This suit's filigree is not simply for show, as it channels lightning away from the wearer to disperse harmlessly in the ground.

LIGHT ARMOR—FIDEL, VICTOR, EMMERSON, AND ANNE

Rudimentary Protector

FACTORS:	—
Value	140
Acquisition Methods	Shop, Item Creation, Synthesis

DEF	MEN							AUG
10	—	—	—	10	—	—	—	3

A tunic made from the simplest of materials. It is much too light to provide satisfactory protection.

Leather Armor

FACTORS:	Max HP +50
Value	350
Acquisition Methods	Shops, Synthesis

DEF	MEN							AUG
15	—	—	—	—	—	—	—	8

Lightweight armor made from cured leather that has been stitched together over a layer of wood.

Chainmail

FACTORS:	—
Value	700
Acquisition Methods	Shops

DEF	MEN							AUG
25	10	—	—	—	—	—	—	6

A simple habergeon consisting of small, interlocking iron rings.

Crest Mail

FACTORS:	—
Value	1050
Acquisition Methods	Shops, Enemy Drop

DEF	MEN							AUG
45	30	—	—	—	—	15	-5	6

Lightweight armor engraved with a signeturgical crest of sunbeams.

Scale Mail

FACTORS:	—
Value	(550)
Acquisition Methods	Item Creation, Synthesis, Quest

DEF	MEN							AUG
20	5	—	—	—	—	—	—	6

Armor made of durable fish scales stitched together with metal wire.

Riot Gear

FACTORS:	—
Value	2450
Acquisition Methods	Shop, Synthesis

DEF	MEN							AUG
60	45	—	—	—	—	—	—	8

Made of a nearly impervious material, this protective gear is issued by the Pangalactic Federation for use in quelling riots.

Superior Leather

FACTORS:	Max HP +200
Value	(4200)
Acquisition Methods	Item Creation

DEF	MEN							AUG
80	65	—	—	—	—	—	—	6

Leather armor brushed with an esoteric coating. Its distinctive stygian luster makes it stand out in any crowd.

Silver Mesh

FACTORS:	—
Value	4900
Acquisition Methods	Shops, Synthesis

DEF	MEN							AUG
100	85	—	—	—	—	15	—	6

Lightweight armor made from a steel mesh with a silver glint.

Blood Chain Mail

FACTORS:	5% chance to nullify darkness damage
Value	(10150)
Acquisition Methods	Treasure Chest, Item Creation, Synthesis

DEF	MEN							AUG
130	115	—	—	—	—	-30	30	6

Chain mail stained dark red with the blood of demons and imbued with infernal powers.

Sylphide's Mail

FACTORS:	3% chance to absorb 10% wind damage
Value	(14000)
Acquisition Methods	Item Creation, Quest

DEF	MEN							AUG
180	165	—	—	40	40	-5	-5	4

Lightweight armor over which a guardian wind spirit watches. Donning it allows one to control life energy and endure earth-based attacks.

Mythril Mesh

FACTORS:	—
Value	28000
Acquisition Methods	Shop, Item Creation, Quest

DEF	MEN							AUG
220	200	10	10	10	10	10	10	8

Lightweight armor made from a bewilderingly fine mythril mesh that gleams like a freshly polished silver chalice.

Superior Chain Mail

FACTORS:	—
Value	(35000)
Acquisition Methods	Item Creation, Quest

DEF	MEN							AUG
250	220	—	—	—	—	—	—	6

A fine suit of chain mail that glistens with the power of light. Despite the use of metal plates, it is not the least bit cumbersome.

Elemental Leather

FACTORS:	Damage from Corrupt -10%
Value	(42000)
Acquisition Methods	Synthesis

DEF	MEN							AUG
300	250	40	40	40	40	—	—	4

This sublime piece of armor has been consecrated by all four elemental spirits.

Mystic Chain

FACTORS:	Foe critical hit rate -20%
Value	(56000)
Acquisition Methods	Locked Chest, Item Creation

DEF	MEN							AUG
380	300	—	—	—	—	—	—	6

Chain mail that employs the fabled metal orichalcum. Vestiges of the metal's original color peek out from behind occasional cracks in the dye.

Dragon Leather

FACTORS:	Max HP +15%
Value	(63000)
Acquisition Methods	Synthesis

DEF	MEN							AUG
450	350	50	-20	—	—	—	—	10

Making the most of the dragon hide brought to him, a smith scaled it and fashioned this piece of armor in the monster's image.

Banded Mail

FACTORS:	—
Value	1400
Acquisition Methods	Shops

DEF	MEN							AUG
45	20	—	—	—	—	-5	15	6

Metal armor reinforced with leather and engraved with a crest meant to ward off evil.

Streaked Chainmail

FACTORS:	—
Value	3500
Acquisition Methods	Shops, Synthesis

DEF	MEN							AUG
70	55	—	—	—	—	—	—	7

Chain mail woven with special links that mitigates conduction.

Superior Mesh

FACTORS:	—
Value	6300
Acquisition Methods	Shops

DEF	MEN							AUG
120	100	—	—	—	—	—	—	7

Not even the durable plates interwoven into this chain mail can diminish its ability to enhance the wearer's litheness.

Solid Protector

FACTORS:	—
Value	14000
Acquisition Methods	Shop, Treasure Chest, Synthesis

DEF	MEN							AUG
150	140	—	—	—	—	—	—	7

A protector coated in an exceptionally dense resin, which imparts the ability to repel most physical attacks.

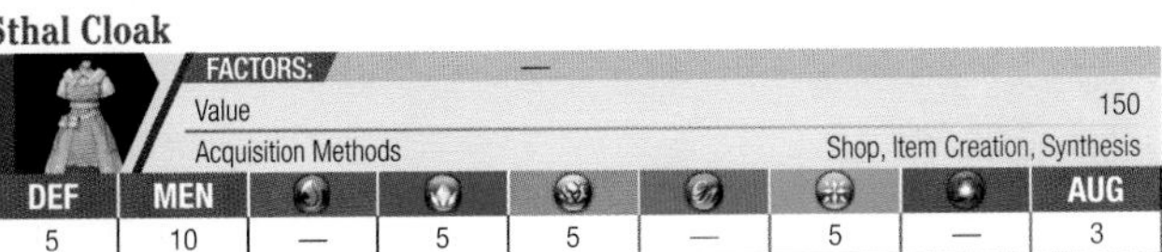

CLOTH ARMOR—MIKI, FIORE, ANNE, AND RELIA

Sthal Cloak

FACTORS: —

Value: 150

Acquisition Methods: Shop, Item Creation, Synthesis

DEF	MEN							AUG
5	10	—	5	5	—	5	—	3

A cloak commonly worn in Sthal. The local weaving technique used allows just the right amount of air to flow through the fabric.

Signeturge's Garb

FACTORS: —

Value: 400

Acquisition Methods: Shops

DEF	MEN							AUG
10	20	10	—	—	10	—	—	8

The standard signeturge outfit, it is cut from a distinctive cloth and covers the body without hiding any signets one might want to display.

Traveler's Cloak

FACTORS: —

Value: 750

Acquisition Methods: Shops, Item Creation

DEF	MEN							AUG
20	40	—	15	—	—	—	—	6

A breathable mantle made well enough to last on long journeys.

Crest Robe

FACTORS: —

Value: 1150

Acquisition Methods: Shops

DEF	MEN							AUG
25	50	—	—	—	—	15	-5	6

A silk robe embroidered with a signeturgical crest of light.

Flare Coat

FACTORS: —

Value: (1900)

Acquisition Methods: Item Creation

DEF	MEN							AUG
30	60	25	25	—	—	—	—	4

A long coat made for people who frequent cold regions. The first signet imbued upon it keeps its wearer warm.

Resistance Suit

FACTORS: MEN +10

Value: 2650

Acquisition Methods: Shop, Synthesis

DEF	MEN							AUG
35	70	10	10	10	10	—	—	8

A body suit developed by the Pangalactic Federation so its soldiers could easily withstand various extreme climates.

Crystal Robe

FACTORS: 5% chance to nullify light damage

Value: (4500)

Acquisition Methods: Item Creation

DEF	MEN							AUG
45	90	—	—	—	—	10	-10	6

A robe coated with a sorcerous patina that makes it sparkle like crystal.

Silver Cloak

FACTORS: —

Value: 5250

Acquisition Methods: Shops, Synthesis

DEF	MEN							AUG
60	120	—	—	—	—	15	—	6

A cloak woven with steel thread that gives off a cinereal luminescence.

Mirage Robe

FACTORS: 20% chance: damage taken -20%

Value: (11000)

Acquisition Methods: Treasure Chest, Synthesis

DEF	MEN							AUG
70	130	—	—	—	—	—	—	8

An enchanted robe that makes it seem as if more than one of the wearer exists.

Angel's Cloak

FACTORS: 3% chance to absorb 10% light damage

Value: (22500)

Acquisition Methods: Item Creation, Quest

DEF	MEN							AUG
100	200	-5	-5	-5	-5	40	40	4

A chaste mantle similar to the ones angels are depicted wearing. It emits a righteous light that dispels darkness.

Mystic Robe

FACTORS: —

Value: 30000

Acquisition Methods: Shop, Item Creation

DEF	MEN							AUG
120	240	10	10	10	10	10	10	8

A robe covered with so many signets that no one can tell what the color of its fabric is.

Wizard's Robe

FACTORS: INT +5%

Value: (37500)

Acquisition Methods: Item Creation, Synthesis

DEF	MEN							AUG
140	280	—	—	—	—	—	—	6

A majestic robe that imparts gravitas befitting a philosopher. An extraordinarily large hood dangles down the back.

Seraphic Garb

FACTORS: —

Value: (45000)

Acquisition Methods: Synthesis

DEF	MEN							AUG
160	320	—	—	—	20	20	-10	8

A sacred vestment into which the gods wove the azure radiance of the sky.

Laser Suit

FACTORS: —

Value: (60000)

Acquisition Methods: Locked Chest, Item Creation, Synthesis

DEF	MEN							AUG
200	400	—	—	—	—	—	—	5

A body suit armed with a high-power laser mechanism that acts as a force field when needed.

Valkyrie's Garb

FACTORS: 20% chance: damage taken -30%

Value: (250000)

Acquisition Methods: Synthesis

DEF	MEN							AUG
777	777	—	—	—	—	—	—	4

A sacred robe said to have been worn by a Valkyrie as she selected who would die in battle. It is enveloped in a blinding aura.

Amber Robe

FACTORS: —

Value: 3750

Acquisition Methods: Shops, Synthesis

DEF	MEN							AUG
40	80	—	—	—	—	—	—	7

A flowing and loose-fitting garment decorated with a seemingly infinite number of small amber gemstones.

Alchemist's Cloak

FACTORS: —

Value: 6750

Acquisition Methods: Shops, Synthesis

DEF	MEN							AUG
70	140	—	—	—	—	—	—	7

An exquisite cloak tailored specifically for use by signeturges. Woven of a fabric so fine, it puts standard issue signeturge garb to shame.

Cloak of the Stars

FACTORS: —

Value: 15000

Acquisition Methods: Shop, Treasure Chest

DEF	MEN							AUG
80	150	—	—	—	—	—	—	7

A numinous piece of armor that occasionally twinkles in patterns redolent of asterisms.

ACCESSORIES

Anti-poison Amulet

FACTORS:	25% chance to nullify poison			
Value				(3500)
Acquisition Methods				Treasure Chest, Item Creation, Synthesis, Quest
ATK	**INT**	**DEF**	**MEN**	**AUGMENT**
—	—	—	3	4

An amulet that protects against poison. It features a glittering green gem and the crest of a bird soaring through the sky.

Anti-paralysis Amulet

FACTORS:	25% chance to nullify paralysis			
Value				(3500)
Acquisition Methods				Treasure Chest, Item Creation, Synthesis, Quest
ATK	**INT**	**DEF**	**MEN**	**AUGMENT**
—	—	—	3	4

An amulet that protects against paralysis. It features a glittering yellow gem and the crest of a bird soaring through the sky.

Anti-silence Amulet

FACTORS:	25% chance to nullify silence			
Value				(3500)
Acquisition Methods				Treasure Chest, Item Creation, Synthesis, Quest
ATK	**INT**	**DEF**	**MEN**	**AUGMENT**
—	—	—	3	4

An amulet that protects against silence. It features a glittering white gem and the crest of a bird soaring through the sky.

Anti-stun Amulet

FACTORS:	25% chance to nullify stun			
Value				(2800)
Acquisition Methods				Item Creation, Synthesis, Quest
ATK	**INT**	**DEF**	**MEN**	**AUGMENT**
—	—	—	5	4

An amulet that protects against being stunned. It features a glittering red gem and the crest of a bird soaring through the sky.

Anti-freezing Amulet

FACTORS:	25% chance to nullify freeze			
Value				(3500)
Acquisition Methods				Treasure Chest, Item Creation, Synthesis
ATK	**INT**	**DEF**	**MEN**	**AUGMENT**
—	—	—	3	4

An amulet that protects against being frozen. It features a glittering blue gem and the crest of a bird soaring through the sky.

Anti-fog Amulet

FACTORS:	25% chance to nullify fog			
Value				(3500)
Acquisition Methods				Treasure Chest, Item Creation, Synthesis, Quest
ATK	**INT**	**DEF**	**MEN**	**AUGMENT**
—	—	—	3	4

An amulet that protects against fog. It features a glittering marine gem and the crest of a bird soaring through the sky.

Anti-curse Amulet

FACTORS:	25% chance to nullify curses			
Value				(3500)
Acquisition Methods				Treasure Chest, Item Creation, Synthesis, Quest
ATK	**INT**	**DEF**	**MEN**	**AUGMENT**
—	—	—	3	4

An amulet that protects against curses. It features a glittering purple gem and the crest of a bird soaring through the sky.

Anti-death Amulet

FACTORS:	25% chance to nullify instant death			
Value				(4000)
Acquisition Methods				Treasure Chest, Item Creation, Synthesis, Quest
ATK	**INT**	**DEF**	**MEN**	**AUGMENT**
—	—	—	5	4

An amulet that protects against instant death. It features a glittering orange gem and the crest of a bird soaring through the sky.

Earth Armlet

FACTORS:	5% chance to nullify earth damage			
Value				(1500)
Acquisition Methods				Item Creation
ATK	**INT**	**DEF**	**MEN**	**AUGMENT**
—	—	2	—	4

An armlet imbued with the power of earth.

Ice Armlet

FACTORS:	5% chance to nullify ice damage			
Value				(1500)
Acquisition Methods				Item Creation
ATK	**INT**	**DEF**	**MEN**	**AUGMENT**
—	—	2	—	4

An armlet imbued with the power of ice.

Fire Armlet

FACTORS:	5% chance to nullify fire damage			
Value				(1500)
Acquisition Methods				Item Creation
ATK	**INT**	**DEF**	**MEN**	**AUGMENT**
—	—	2	—	4

An armlet imbued with the power of fire.

Wind Armlet

FACTORS:	5% chance to nullify wind damage			
Value				(1500)
Acquisition Methods				Treasure Chest, Item Creation
ATK	**INT**	**DEF**	**MEN**	**AUGMENT**
—	—	2	—	4

An armlet imbued with the power of wind.

Light Scarf

FACTORS:	Turn 1% lightning damage taken to MP			
Value				(2500)
Acquisition Methods				Item Creation, Synthesis, Quest
ATK	**INT**	**DEF**	**MEN**	**AUGMENT**
—	—	—	5	4

A scarf imbued with the power of light by means of a unique dyeing process.

Darkness Scarf

FACTORS:	Turn 1% dark damage taken to MP			
Value				(2500)
Acquisition Methods				Item Creation, Quest
ATK	**INT**	**DEF**	**MEN**	**AUGMENT**
—	—	—	5	4

A scarf imbued with the power of darkness by means of a unique dyeing process.

Energy Crest

FACTORS:	Max HP +50			
Value				1500
Acquisition Methods				Shops, Synthesis
ATK	**INT**	**DEF**	**MEN**	**AUGMENT**
—	—	—	—	8

A heraldic emblem imbued with a signet that promotes the health of whoever bears it.

Energy Amulet

FACTORS:	Max HP +500			
Value				25000
Acquisition Methods				Shops, Synthesis
ATK	**INT**	**DEF**	**MEN**	**AUGMENT**
—	—	—	—	8

An amulet imbued with a signet that promotes the health of whoever wears it.

Arcane Crest

FACTORS:	Max MP +50			
Value				1500
Acquisition Methods				Shops, Synthesis, Quest
ATK	**INT**	**DEF**	**MEN**	**AUGMENT**
—	—	—	—	8

A heraldic emblem imbued with a signet that enhances the occult powers of whoever bears it.

Arcane Amulet

FACTORS:	Max MP +200			
Value				25000
Acquisition Methods				Shops, Synthesis, Quest
ATK	**INT**	**DEF**	**MEN**	**AUGMENT**
—	—	—	—	8

An amulet imbued with a signet that enhances the occult powers of whoever wears it.

Energy Bracelet

FACTORS:	Max HP +3%
Value	5000
Acquisition Methods	Shops, Item Creation

ATK	INT	DEF	MEN	AUGMENT
—	—	—	—	4

A bracelet that promotes the health of its wearer.

Arcane Bracelet

FACTORS:	Max MP +3%
Value	5000
Acquisition Methods	Shops, Treasure Chest, Item Creation

ATK	INT	DEF	MEN	AUGMENT
—	—	—	—	4

A bangle that amplifies the magic power of its wearer.

Attack Bracelet

FACTORS:	ATK +3%
Value	10000
Acquisition Methods	Shop, Treasure Chest, Item Creation

ATK	INT	DEF	MEN	AUGMENT
5	—	—	—	4

A bangle graven with a signet of destruction.

Mind Bracelet

FACTORS:	INT +3%
Value	10000
Acquisition Methods	Shop, Treasure Chest, Item Creation

ATK	INT	DEF	MEN	AUGMENT
—	5	—	—	4

A bangle graven with a signet of wisdom.

Fortitude Bracelet

FACTORS:	DEF +3%
Value	10000
Acquisition Methods	Shops, Item Creation

ATK	INT	DEF	MEN	AUGMENT
—	—	5	—	4

A bangle graven with a protective signet.

Acuity Bracelet

FACTORS:	MEN +3%
Value	10000
Acquisition Methods	Shops, Item Creation

ATK	INT	DEF	MEN	AUGMENT
—	—	—	5	4

A bangle graven with a signet that enhances bravery.

Extrication Ring

FACTORS:	Fill reserve gauge by +1 unit
Value	(3000)
Acquisition Methods	Treasure Chest, Item Creation, Quest

ATK	INT	DEF	MEN	AUGMENT
—	—	—	—	3

A bangle that gets any fighter ready and raring to go by simply donning it.

Healing Band

FACTORS:	Battle: Periodically receive 3% HP
Value	(3600)
Acquisition Methods	Treasure Chest, Item Creation, Synthesis

ATK	INT	DEF	MEN	AUGMENT
—	—	—	—	3

A cloth band blessed with the power of healing.

Faerie Band

FACTORS:	Battle: Periodically receive 1% MP
Value	(3600)
Acquisition Methods	Treasure Chest, Item Creation, Synthesis

ATK	INT	DEF	MEN	AUGMENT
—	—	—	—	3

A cloth band blessed by a fairy.

Testament to Triumph

FACTORS:	Gain SP, not EXP, at 1%
Value	(400)
Acquisition Methods	Item Creation, Quest

ATK	INT	DEF	MEN	AUGMENT
—	—	—	—	3

This memento signifies that its bearer has fought through numerous painful events and overcome all manner of obstacles with nary a gripe.

Attack Crest

FACTORS:	ATK +5%
Value	3000
Acquisition Methods	Shops

ATK	INT	DEF	MEN	AUGMENT
—	—	—	—	6

A heraldic emblem imbued with a signet of destruction.

Attack Amulet

FACTORS:	ATK +150
Value	50000
Acquisition Methods	Shop, Synthesis, Quest

ATK	INT	DEF	MEN	AUGMENT
—	—	—	—	8

An amulet emblem imbued with a signet of destruction.

Mind Crest

FACTORS:	INT +5
Value	3000
Acquisition Methods	Shops

ATK	INT	DEF	MEN	AUGMENT
—	—	—	—	6

A heraldic emblem imbued with a signet of knowledge.

Mind Amulet

FACTORS:	INT +150
Value	50000
Acquisition Methods	Shop, Synthesis, Quests

ATK	INT	DEF	MEN	AUGMENT
—	—	—	—	8

An amulet imbued with a signet of knowledge.

Star Guard

FACTORS:	Send shockwave on successful guard
Value	(16000)
Acquisition Methods	Item Creation, Synthesis

ATK	INT	DEF	MEN	AUGMENT
—	—	20	20	3

Blessed by a star, this bangle repels evil power.

Fortitude Crest

FACTORS:	DEF +5
Value	3000
Acquisition Methods	Shops

ATK	INT	DEF	MEN	AUGMENT
—	—	—	—	6

A heraldic emblem imbued with a tutelary signet.

Fortitude Amulet

FACTORS:	DEF +50
Value	50000
Acquisition Methods	Shop, Synthesis, Quests

ATK	INT	DEF	MEN	AUGMENT
—	—	—	—	8

An amulet imbued with a tutelary signet.

Acuity Crest

FACTORS:	MEN +5
Value	3000
Acquisition Methods	Quests

ATK	INT	DEF	MEN	AUGMENT
—	—	—	—	6

A heraldic emblem imbued with a signet of gallantry.

Acuity Amulet

FACTORS:	MEN +50
Value	50000
Acquisition Methods	Shop, Synthesis, Quest

ATK	INT	DEF	MEN	AUGMENT
—	—	—	—	8

An amulet imbued with a signet of gallantry.

Green Talisman

FACTORS:	5% chance to avoid dying
Value	(4800)
Acquisition Methods	Treasure Chest, Item Creation, Synthesis

ATK	INT	DEF	MEN	AUGMENT
—	—	—	5	3

A charm adorned with a green jewel.

Blue Talisman

FACTORS:	No flinch when incoming physical/ATK attack inflicts less than 5% max HP
Value	(4800)
Acquisition Methods	Treasure Chest, Item Creation, Synthesis

ATK	INT	DEF	MEN	AUGMENT
10	—	20	—	3

A charm adorned with a blue jewel.

Red Talisman

FACTORS:	No flinch when incoming signeturgical/INT attack inflicts less than 5% max HP
Value	(4800)
Acquisition Methods	Treasure Chest, Item Creation, Synthesis

ATK	INT	DEF	MEN	AUGMENT
—	10	—	20	3

A charm adorned with a red jewel.

tri-Emblum

FACTORS:	—
Value	300000
Acquisition Methods	Shop

ATK	INT	DEF	MEN	AUGMENT
—	—	—	5	8

A cheap imitation of a certain goddess's crest.

tri-Emblem

FACTORS:	MP cost -25%
Value	(100000)
Acquisition Methods	Item Creation

ATK	INT	DEF	MEN	AUGMENT
200	200	100	100	8

The crest of a certain goddess that contains the power to bring worlds to life as well as utterly annihilate them.

MATERIALS

Shellfish Meat

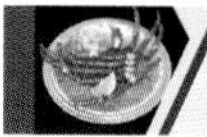

Value	240
Acquisition Methods	Shops, Harvesting, Enemy Drops, Synthesis

Plump and succulent, this marine delight tastes great alone or when used in a broth. The only downside is how hard it is to extract.

Red Fruit

Value	300
Acquisition Methods	Shops, Harvesting, Enemy Drops, Synthesis

Fruit of a deep red hue that exudes a slightly tart aroma. Its own sweetness can barely be contained within its pulp.

Green Fruit

Value	360
Acquisition Methods	Shops, Harvesting, Enemy Drops, Synthesis

A pale green fruit with an invigorating scent and a crunchy texture. A cool, refreshing sensation washes over one's body with every bite.

White Rice

Value	180
Acquisition Methods	Shops, Harvesting, Synthesis

A staple food made by removing the seeds of a rice plant from its husk and polishing the grain that results.

Wheat Flour

Value	240
Acquisition Methods	Shops, Harvesting, Synthesis

Powder made by grinding wheat into a fine consistency.

Vinegar

Value	120
Acquisition Methods	Shops

A pungent and biting liquid seasoning.

Seasonings

Value	60
Acquisition Methods	Shops, Harvesting, Treasure Chest, Synthesis, Quest

A mystic blend of herbs and spices that completely changes the flavor of any dish with just one pinch.

Olive Oil

Value	240
Acquisition Methods	Shops, Enemy Drops, Treasure Chest, Synthesis

Vegetable oil extracted from the fruit of an olive tree.

Soy Sauce

Value	90
Acquisition Methods	Shops, Synthesis

A liquid seasoning made by fermenting certain beans. Some countries have long debated whether or not it is the height of sauces.

Cocoa Powder

Value	240
Acquisition Methods	Shop, Harvesting

Made by processing cocoa beans via a special method. Its irresistible smell has tempted people throughout the ages.

Vanilla Beans

Value	360
Acquisition Methods	Shop, Harvesting, Enemy Drop, Synthesis

The dried seeds of a particular type of orchid. They lightly tickle the nostrils with a gently sweet scent.

Iron

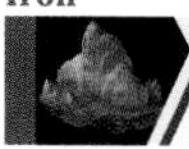

Value	400
Acquisition Methods	Shop, Harvesting, Enemy Drops, Treasure Chests, Synthesis, Quest

One of the transition metals. It is abundant in the planet's crust, and is used in all manner of products.

Silver

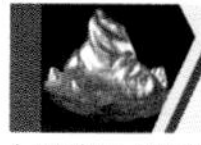

Value	800
Acquisition Methods	Shop, Harvesting, Enemy Drops, Item Creation, Synthesis

A precious metal that glistens a grayish white. It has long been used in tableware and other items by nobles, as it reacts to poisons.

Gold

Value	2000
Acquisition Methods	Shop, Harvesting, Enemy Drops, Item Creation, Synthesis, Quest

A precious metal prized by jewelers for its malleability. It has been seen as a symbol of power and captured people's hearts for ages.

Damascus Steel

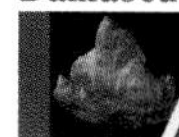

Value	(2600)
Acquisition Methods	Harvesting, Enemy Drops, Item Creation, Synthesis

A unique metal that can be manipulated to produce wave patterns on its surface. It exhibits exceptional strength and rigidity.

Mercury

Value	600
Acquisition Methods	Shop, Harvesting, Enemy Drops, Synthesis

One of few metals that does not harden at normal temperatures. Only seasoned craftsmen use it, for it is highly toxic and difficult to mold.

Platinum

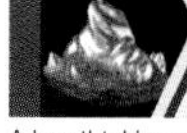

Value	(2800)
Acquisition Methods	Shop, Enemy Drops, Item Creation, Synthesis

A breathtaking precious metal with an almost transparent gleam. It is extremely rare, which is why it often adorns expensive jewelry.

Mythril

Value	(4000)
Acquisition Methods	Harvesting, Enemy Drops, Item Creation, Synthesis

Widely believed to be the crystallization of ethereal power, equipment made from this metal is guaranteed to be a masterpiece.

Meteorite

Value	(5000)
Acquisition Methods	Enemy Drops, Treasure Chest, Locked Chest, Item Creation, Synthesis, Quest

A solid chunk of meteor that possesses a strange sheen and texture.

Orichalcum

Value	(6500)
Acquisition Methods	Enemy Drops, Locked Chest

An astonishing metal that legends say can allay the effects of gravity. It is purported to be as light as a feather and incapable of rusting.

Moonstone

Value	(8000)
Acquisition Methods	Enemy Drops, Locked Chest, Synthesis

A stone imbued with intense thaumaturgical power. Despite evoking the moon in its name, its actual origins are unclear.

Coal

Value	800
Acquisition Methods	Shop, Harvesting, Enemy Drops, Treasure Chest, Synthesis

Organic matter carbonized by high subterranean temperatures and pressure. Fanning it while it burns produces an enthralling glow.

Ruby

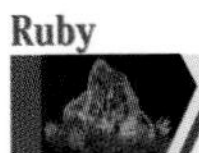

Value	1400
Acquisition Methods	Shop, Harvesting, Enemy Drops, Treasure Chests, Synthesis

A type of corundum that appears red due to the minute traces of chromium interspersed throughout it.

Crystal

Value	3000
Acquisition Methods	Shop, Harvesting, Enemy Drops, Synthesis

A quartz crystal. Though normally pellucid, impurities can cause it to appear yellow or purple.

Amber

Value	(2400)
Acquisition Methods	Enemy Drops, Synthesis

Plant sap that has crystallized over countless ages. Pieces that contain plants and insects are rare and highly valuable.

Moon Pearl

Value	Harvesting, Enemy Drops, Synthesis
Acquisition Methods	(4600)

A pearl that accrued fantastical powers after being bathed in moonlight for a millennium. Its bleak luster elicits feelings of eternal solitude.

Primeval Fossil

Value	(2000)
Acquisition Methods	Enemy Drops, Synthesis

A fossil that contains records of an era long since past. Gazing upon it gives one a glimpse as to what the beasts of antiquity were like.

Philosopher's Stone

Value	(15000)
Acquisition Methods	Enemy Drops, Locked Chest, Item Creation, Synthesis

This legendary treasure and epitome of alchemical ingenuity is said to impart the knowledge of all things upon whoever possesses it.

Earth Gem

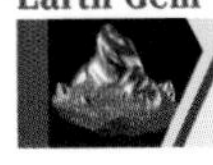

Value	(800)
Acquisition Methods	Harvesting, Enemy Drops, Treasure Chest, Synthesis, Quest

A crystallized form of the element "earth."

Ice Gem

Value	(800)
Acquisition Methods	Harvesting, Enemy Drops, Synthesis, Quest

A crystallized form of the element "ice."

Fire Gem

Value	(800)
Acquisition Methods	Harvesting, Enemy Drops, Treasure Chest, Synthesis, Quest

A crystallized form of the element "fire."

Wind Gem

Value	(800)
Acquisition Methods	Harvesting, Enemy Drops, Synthesis, Quest

A crystallized form of the element "wind."

Light Gem

Value	(800)
Acquisition Methods	Harvesting, Enemy Drops, Synthesis, Quest

A crystallized form of the element "light."

Darkness Gem

Value	(800)
Acquisition Methods	Harvesting, Enemy Drops, Treasure Chest, Synthesis, Quest

A crystallized form of the element "darkness."

Gnomestone

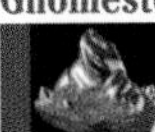

Value	(4000)
Acquisition Methods	Enemy Drop, Item Creation, Synthesis, Quest

A stone infused with the unique powers inherent in the element "earth."

Nereidstone

Value	(4000)
Acquisition Methods	Enemy Drops, Item Creation, Synthesis, Quest

A stone infused with the unique powers inherent in the element "ice."

Salamanderstone

Value	(4000)
Acquisition Methods	Enemy Drops, Item Creation, Synthesis, Quest

A stone infused with the unique powers inherent in the element "fire."

Sylphstone

Value	(4000)
Acquisition Methods	Enemy Drops, Item Creation, Synthesis, Quest

A stone infused with the unique powers inherent in the element "wind."

Angelstone

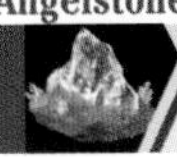

Value	(4000)
Acquisition Methods	Enemy Drops, Item Creation, Synthesis, Quest

A stone infused with the unique powers inherent in the element "light."

Shadestone

Value	(4000)
Acquisition Methods	Enemy Drops, Treasure Chest, Item Creation, Synthesis, Quest

A stone infused with the unique powers inherent in the element "darkness."

Earth Paint

Value	(600)
Acquisition Methods	Item Creation, Synthesis

Paint infused with earth-elemental powers.

Ice Paint

Value	(600)
Acquisition Methods	Item Creation, Synthesis

Paint infused with ice-elemental powers.

Fire Paint

Value	(600)
Acquisition Methods	Item Creation, Synthesis

Paint infused with fire-elemental powers.

Wind Paint

Value	(600)
Acquisition Methods	Item Creation, Synthesis

Paint infused with wind-elemental powers.

Light Paint

Value	(960)
Acquisition Methods	Item Creation, Synthesis

Paint infused with light-elemental powers.

Dark Paint

Value	(960)
Acquisition Methods	Item Creation, Synthesis

Paint infused with darkness-elemental powers.

PART 06

Nil Paint

Value (1200)
Acquisition Methods Item Creation, Synthesis

Paint infused with non-elemental powers.

Healing Paint

Value (480)
Acquisition Methods Item Creation, Synthesis

Paint infused with healing powers.

Mysterious Paint

Value (600)
Acquisition Methods Item Creation, Synthesis

Paint infused with support powers.

High-Grade Ink

Value 1200
Acquisition Methods Shop, Item Creation

Exceptional black ink that is unlikely to run. It makes writing such a pleasurable experience, those who use it will never return to normal ink.

Wooden Stick

Value 300
Acquisition Methods Shops, Enemy Drops, Treasure Chest, Synthesis

An ordinary wooden stick one might find lying around anywhere.

Ebony

Value 900
Acquisition Methods Shop, Enemy Drops, Treasure Chest, Synthesis

Beautiful black wood that is dense and heavy enough to survive even the stress placed on bows when in battle.

Oak

Value (1500)
Acquisition Methods Enemy Drops, Synthesis

Wood cut from a huge tree with a thick trunk. It has numerous uses thanks to its extreme callosity and excellent durability.

Ash

Value (2400)
Acquisition Methods Enemy Drops, Synthesis

Wood with a pliability and elasticity perfect for use in bows. It is said to come from the same type of tree as the legendary Yggdrasil.

Blue Roses

Value 1200
Acquisition Methods Shops, Harvesting, Enemy Drops, Synthesis

It was previously assumed that these vivid blue roses—the product of numerous rounds of crossbreeding—would never be able to exist.

Shadow Roses

Value (3600)
Acquisition Methods Harvesting, Enemy Drops, Synthesis

Roses that quietly grow in dark places. Their unassuming perseverance in the face of a harsh habitat is inspiring.

Wool

Value 600
Acquisition Methods Shops, Enemy Drops, Synthesis

A soft, flocculent, and warm fabric that is shorn from sheep.

Silk

Value 1200
Acquisition Methods Shops, Enemy Drops, Synthesis

A fabric woven from the fiber extracted from silkworm cocoons. So smooth is it that one cannot resist rubbing one's cheek against it.

Cashmere

Value 2800
Acquisition Methods Shop, Enemy Drops, Synthesis

A luxurious fabric woven from the wool of a special type of goat. It does a superb job of retaining heat and moisture.

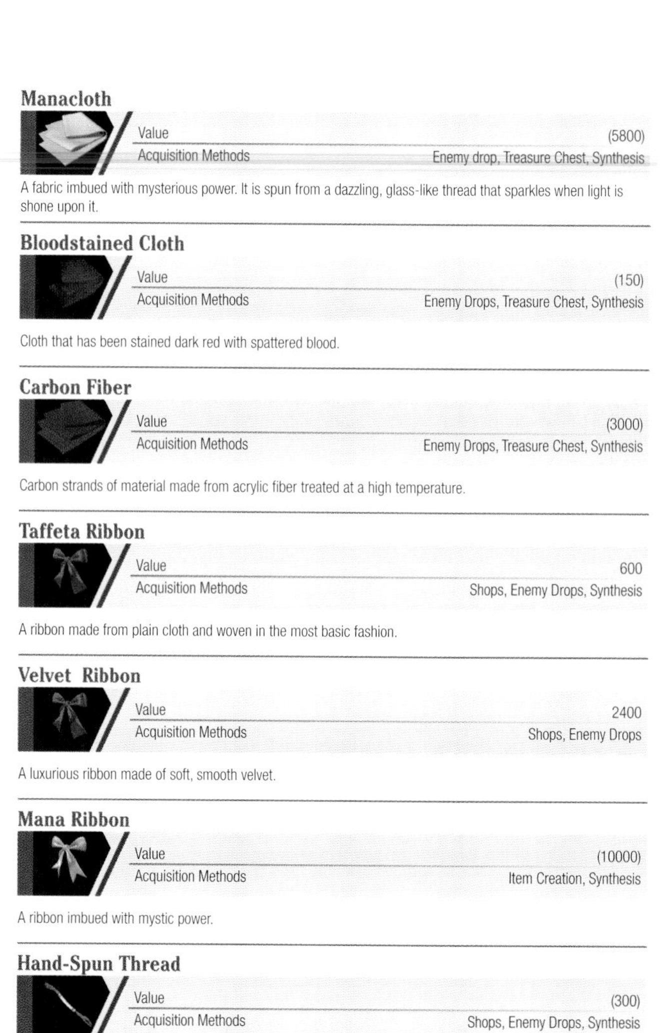

Manacloth

Value (5800)
Acquisition Methods Enemy drop, Treasure Chest, Synthesis

A fabric imbued with mysterious power. It is spun from a dazzling, glass-like thread that sparkles when light is shone upon it.

Bloodstained Cloth

Value (150)
Acquisition Methods Enemy Drops, Treasure Chest, Synthesis

Cloth that has been stained dark red with spattered blood.

Carbon Fiber

Value (3000)
Acquisition Methods Enemy Drops, Treasure Chest, Synthesis

Carbon strands of material made from acrylic fiber treated at a high temperature.

Taffeta Ribbon

Value 600
Acquisition Methods Shops, Enemy Drops, Synthesis

A ribbon made from plain cloth and woven in the most basic fashion.

Velvet Ribbon

Value 2400
Acquisition Methods Shops, Enemy Drops

A luxurious ribbon made of soft, smooth velvet.

Mana Ribbon

Value (10000)
Acquisition Methods Item Creation, Synthesis

A ribbon imbued with mystic power.

Hand-Spun Thread

Value (300)
Acquisition Methods Shops, Enemy Drops, Synthesis

Strong silk sewing thread that has been painstakingly spun.

Dwarven Embroidery Thread

Value 1800
Acquisition Methods Shops, Enemy Drops, Synthesis

Thread used by dwarves when embroidering their clothing.

Faerie Embroidery Thread

Value (5000)
Acquisition Methods Enemy Drops, Synthesis

Thread used by faeries when embroidering their clothing.

Gunpowder

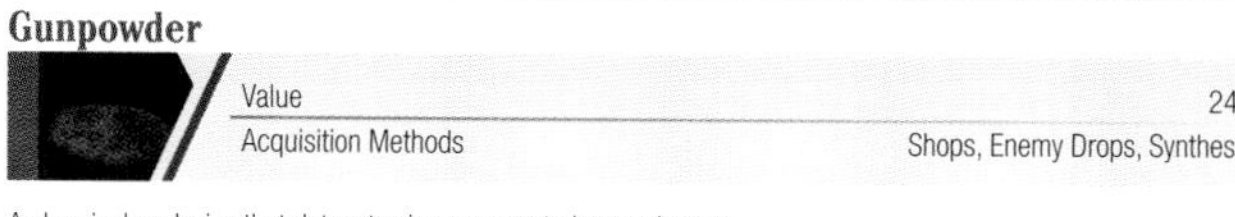

Value 240
Acquisition Methods Shops, Enemy Drops, Synthesis

A chemical explosive that detonates in response to heat or impact.

Reinforced Gunpowder

Value (900)
Acquisition Methods Enemy Drops, Treasure Chests, Item Creation, Synthesis

Bestowing thaumaturgical faculties upon this chemical explosive has increased its destructive capabilities over normal gunpowder.

Parchment

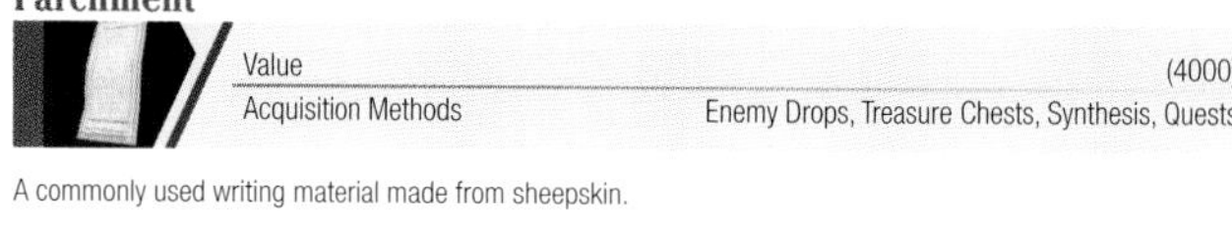

Value (4000)
Acquisition Methods Enemy Drops, Treasure Chests, Synthesis, Quests

A commonly used writing material made from sheepskin.

Fine Parchment

Value (8000)
Acquisition Methods Enemy Drop, Synthesis

High-quality parchment painstakingly made from carefully selected sheepskin.

Empty Bottle

Value	120
Acquisition Methods	Shops, Synthesis

A glass bottle for storing liquids. Care is required when handling, as it will easily break if dropped.

Lezard's Flask

Value	(48000)
Acquisition Methods	Synthesis, Quest

An uncanny flask used specifically for alchemical procedures. It is strong enough to withstand even the most abhorrent experiments.

Fermentation Pot

Value	2400
Acquisition Methods	Shop, Enemy Drops, Synthesis

A container used in the fermentation of various foods. One must take care not to inadvertently unseal it before the process is complete.

Signet Card

Value	300
Acquisition Methods	Shops, Enemy Drops, Synthesis

Special card that can be imbued with signets. Even those who have not learned a spell can invoke it by inscribing its signet on this card.

Signet Card +

Value	(1200)
Acquisition Methods	Enemy Drops, Synthesis

Special card able to contain powerful signets. Even those who have not learned a spell can invoke it by inscribing its signet on this card.

Holy Water

Value	(600)
Acquisition Methods	Enemy Drops, Treasure Chests, Item Creation, Synthesis

Water that has been blessed by means of a sacred ritual.

Alchemist's Water

Value	3600
Acquisition Methods	Shop, Enemy Drops, Treasure Chest, Synthesis, Quests

A fluid created by mixing together several acids. It is capable of dissolving any metal in existence.

High-Strength Adhesive

Value	1200
Acquisition Methods	Shop, Enemy Drops, Item Creation, Synthesis

A quick-drying adhesive that can bond any materials together. Utmost caution must be exercised when using it.

Rivets

Value	360
Acquisition Methods	Shops, Enemy Drops, Synthesis

Bolts used to affix overlapping metal plates.

Wire

Value	900
Acquisition Methods	Shops, Enemy Drops, Synthesis

Wire fortified by intertwining thin strands of iron.

Laser Oscillator

Value	(6000)
Acquisition Methods	Enemy Drops, Treasure Chest, Synthesis

A device that concentrates energy within a short period of time to emit a laser beam of any wavelength, power, and pulse width desired.

Hadron Collider

Value	(12800)
Acquisition Methods	Enemy Drop, Synthesis

A machine that propels charged particles at super-high speeds until they collide and produce a reaction.

Micro Circuit

Value	1200
Acquisition Methods	Shop, Enemy Drops, Treasure Chest, Synthesis

A small, general-purpose electronic circuit that is built into many types of equipment.

Quantum Processor

Value	(4800)
Acquisition Methods	Enemy Drops, Synthesis

A processor for implementing quantum computing functions. It enables parallel processing via the use of qubits and quantum logic gates.

High-Power Generator

Value	(8400)
Acquisition Methods	Enemy Drops, Synthesis

A miniaturized generator that maintains the same output levels as the original device.

Diffusion Device

Value	1080
Acquisition Methods	Shops, Enemy Drops, Treasure Chest, Synthesis

A device for dispersing liquid medicine over a wide area.

Blank Disk

Value	(12000)
Acquisition Methods	Enemy Drops, Treasure Chest, Synthesis

A disc that does not contain any data.

High-Capacity Blank Disk

Value	(24000)
Acquisition Methods	Enemy Drop, Synthesis

A blank disk that can store an enormous amount of data.

Scrap

Value	(1)
Acquisition Methods	Harvesting, Enemy Drop, Synthesis

Junk that might be useful for something somewhere sometime.

Peryton Droppings

Value	3
Acquisition Methods	Shop, Enemy Drops, Synthesis

Viscid animal droppings that are still slightly moist.

Gerel Secretion

Value	200
Acquisition Methods	Shop, Enemy Drop, Synthesis

A mucus-like secretion extracted from the body of a gerel. Although it looks horrid, it is apparently edible.

Gelatinous Slime

Value	(900)
Acquisition Methods	Enemy Drops

A strange substance extracted from the body of a gerel. It feels pleasurably cool in one's hand.

Wolf Fang

Value	320
Acquisition Methods	Shop, Enemy Drops, Synthesis

A sharp canine tooth from a wolf. It can be used to fashion a weapon.

Bee Stinger

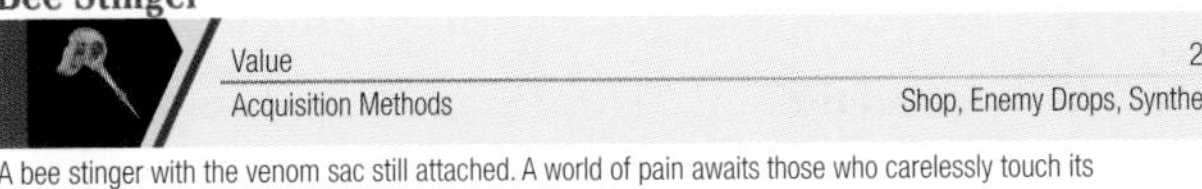

Value	240
Acquisition Methods	Shop, Enemy Drops, Synthesis

A bee stinger with the venom sac still attached. A world of pain awaits those who carelessly touch its razor-sharp point.

Tortoise Shell

Value	400
Acquisition Methods	Shop, Enemy Drop, Synthesis

A strong shell that once housed a tortoise. In ancient times, such shells were thrown in fires, with the resultant cracks used to tell one's fate.

Lizardskin

Value	500
Acquisition Methods	Shop, Enemy Drop, Synthesis

A piece of a lizard's hide.

Snakeskin

Value: 800
Acquisition Methods: Shop, Enemy Drops, Synthesis

A piece of a snake's skin.

Dragon Hide

Value: (3000)
Acquisition Methods: Enemy Drops, Synthesis

A piece of a dragon's skin.

Giant Bird Feather

Value: 400
Acquisition Methods: Shops, Enemy Drops, Synthesis

A large feather from a monstrous bird. It can be used for a quill pen, among other things.

Remex

Value: (2400)
Acquisition Methods: Enemy Drops, Synthesis

A bird feather imbued with the power of wind for increased buoyancy, making even the strongest headwind seem a gentle zephyr during flight.

Fish Scales

Value: 160
Acquisition Methods: Shops, Enemy Drops, Treasure Chests, Synthesis

Resplendent fish scales that change color depending on the angle at which they are illuminated.

Scalestone

Value: (2400)
Acquisition Methods: Enemy Drop, Synthesis

Fish scales that have been crystallized by ice-elemental powers, making it quite resilient.

Dragon Scales

Value: (2400)
Acquisition Methods: Enemy Drops, Synthesis

Dragon scales that gleam brightly. They are unbelievably hard.

Dragon God Scales

Value: (8000)
Acquisition Methods: Enemy Drop

Scales from a great dragon that lived for eons before becoming a god. They make spectacular equipment once they undergo a specific process.

Demon's Tail

Value: 200
Acquisition Methods: Shops, Enemy Drops, Synthesis

This charming appendage was clipped from a demon's backside.

Lesser Fiend's Tail

Value: (800)
Acquisition Methods: Enemy Drops

An august tail from a young fiend's backside. It is said the demon instantly turned to ash when its subordinate accidentally stepped on it.

Mati

Value: (1600)
Acquisition Methods: Enemy Drops, Synthesis

A giant eye that emits an evil aura. All who are pierced by its gaze are immediately rendered immobile.

Ghost's Soul

Value: (2400)
Acquisition Methods: Enemy Drops, Synthesis

The soul of a man who died with attachments to this world. Valkyries often take valiant souls to Valhalla, but not those beyond reconciling.

Laurel Tree

Value: (2400)
Acquisition Methods: Enemy Drops, Synthesis

A potted and verdant tree of laurel that is regarded as a sacred symbol of immortality, victory, and glory.

Insect Egg

Value: (400)
Acquisition Methods: Enemy Drops, Synthesis

The large, oval egg of a giant insect. It is packed with nutrients, but who would want to eat it?

Gigantavian Egg

Value: (2100)
Acquisition Methods: Enemy Drops

The egg of a towering avian creature. It requires a very specific technique to make it hatch.

Bushy Fur

Value: (600)
Acquisition Methods: Enemy Drops, Synthesis

A sheet of fur that is irresistibly soft and fluffy. One touch is all it will take to become obsessed with its texture.

Sandfish

Value: (800)
Acquisition Methods: Harvesting, Enemy Drop

A rare fish that lives in desert oases and is able to burrow into the sand.

Zephyr Lily

Value: (700)
Acquisition Methods: Harvesting, Enemy Drop, Synthesis

A species of lily with a refined and simple appearance. It is also known as a "rain lily" for the way it blooms after rain falls on parched lands.

Grumpy Homunculus

Value: (3000)
Acquisition Methods: Item Creation, Synthesis

An alchemical life form with great offensive capabilities. It manifests an extraordinary power when harbored within equipment.

Astute Homunculus

Value: (3000)
Acquisition Methods: Item Creation, Synthesis

An alchemical life form of great intelligence. It manifests an extraordinary power when harbored within equipment.

Protective Homunculus

Value: (3000)
Acquisition Methods: Item Creation, Synthesis

An alchemical life form with great defensive capabilities. It manifests an extraordinary power when harbored within equipment.

Poised Homunculus

Value: (3000)
Acquisition Methods: Item Creation, Synthesis

An alchemical life form with great mental fortitude. It manifests an extraordinary power when harbored within equipment.

Bunny Droppings

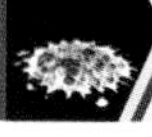

Value: (1)
Acquisition Methods: Synthesis

Dung that a bunny left behind after digesting a meal. It contains nutrients integral to preserving the ecosystem.

Condemner's Cerulean Plume

Value: (30000)
Acquisition Methods: Enemy Drop

A feather plucked from Gabriel Celeste's wings. Even on its own, it seems filled with immeasurable power.

Matriarch's Resplendent Plume

Value: (40000)
Acquisition Methods: Enemy Drop

A feather plucked from the Ethereal Queen's wings. Even on its own, it seems filled with immeasurable power.

VALUABLES

Communicator

Acquisition Methods — Chapter 5

A device for sending transmissions to and receiving them from the Charles D. Goale.

Two-Headed Corrupt's Ashes

Acquisition Methods — Enemy Drop, Quest

The ashes of a two-headed Corrupt's incinerated skulls. Academics are chomping at the bit to get their hands on this biological anomaly.

Discard Silver Spoon

Acquisition Methods — Enemy Drop, Quest

A spoon of wondrous metal that does not degrade, even after millennia. Countless scholars have tried but failed to unravel its mysteries.

Enemy Report

Acquisition Methods — Enemy Drop, Quest

A report by Welch on the ecology of the beasts she is studying. It is frighteningly detailed, accurate, and voluminous.

Erstwhile Ultimate Sword

Acquisition Methods — Enemy Drop, Quest

A martial relic previously wielded by the world's most accomplished swordsman, it stands as a reminder that weapons alone hold no power.

Communicator Model G

Acquisition Methods — Chapter 9

A device for sending transmissions to and receiving them from the Charles D. Goale G.

Dig Deep Within

Acquisition Methods — Quest

A guidebook that imparts upon its reader the basics of the Excavation specialty.

Fishing: An Alluring Pastime

Acquisition Methods — Quest

A guidebook that imparts upon its reader the basics of the Fishing specialty.

Compounding the Issue

Acquisition Methods — Quest

The most informative primer on the Compounding specialty ever, authored by the self-proclaimed omniscient inventor Welch Vineyard.

The Little Engineer That Could

Acquisition Methods — Quest

The most informative primer on the Engineering specialty ever, authored by the self-proclaimed talented tinkerer Welch Vineyard.

Smithing the Night Away
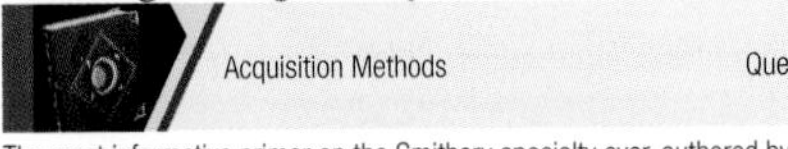
Acquisition Methods — Quest

The most informative primer on the Smithery specialty ever, authored by the self-proclaimed legendary smithy Welch Vineyard.

Crafty Crafting Techniques
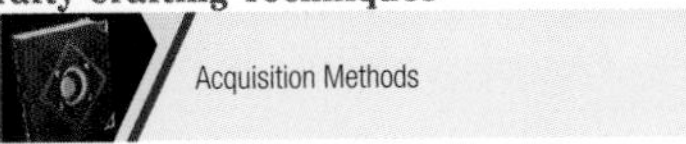
Acquisition Methods — Quest

The most informative primer on Crafting and Ornamentation ever, authored by the self-styled costumier extraordinaire Welch Vineyard.

Just Enough Cooks

Acquisition Methods — Quest

The most informative primer on the Cooking specialty ever, authored by the self-proclaimed master chef Welch Vineyard.

The Pen Is Mightier
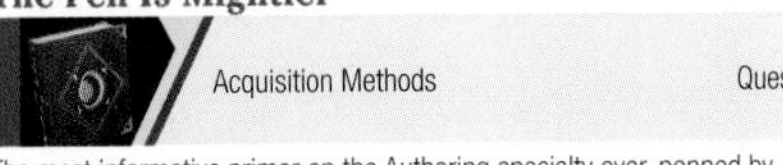
Acquisition Methods — Quest

The most informative primer on the Authoring specialty ever, penned by the self-proclaimed poet laureate Welch Vineyard.

We All Scream For Alchemy

Acquisition Methods — Quest

The most informative primer on the Alchemy specialty ever, authored by the self-proclaimed transmutacular sage Welch Vineyard.

Intro to Intelligent Item Design

Acquisition Methods — Quest

The most informative primer on the Synthesis specialty ever, authored by the self-proclaimed fusion pioneer Welch Vineyard.

Equipped to Handle Anything
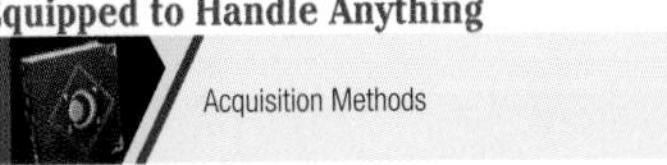
Acquisition Methods — Quest

The most informative primer on Whetting and Fortification ever, authored by the self-proclaimed armsmancer Welch Vineyard.

People of All Stripes

Acquisition Methods — Quest

A pictorial compendium on the myriad types of people in the world. Reading it helps with learning the Anthropology specialty.

The Best Bestiary, Bar None

Acquisition Methods — Quest

A pictorial compendium on the myriad types of beasts in the world. Reading it helps with learning the Zoology specialty.

Birds Illustrated

Acquisition Methods — Quest

A pictorial compendium on the myriad types of avians in the world. Reading it helps with learning the Ornithology specialty.

Insectopedia

Acquisition Methods — Quest

A pictorial compendium on the myriad types of bugs in the world. Reading it helps with learning the Entomolgy specialty.

Plants & Pictures

Acquisition Methods — Quest

A pictorial compendium on the myriad types of plants in the world. Reading it helps with learning the Botany specialty.

Encyclopedia Corruptionem

Acquisition Methods — Quest

A pictorial compendium on the myriad types of Corrupt in the world. Reading it helps with learning the Corruptology specialty.

Nuts and Bolts

Acquisition Methods — Quest

A pictorial compendium on the myriad types of machines in the world. Reading it helps with learning the Mechanology specialty.

Broadening Your Horizons

Acquisition Methods — Quest

A guidebook that imparts upon its reader the basics of the Lookout specialty.

X Marks the Spot
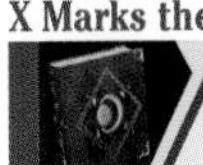
Acquisition Methods — Quest

A guidebook that imparts upon its reader the basics of the Treasure Sense specialty.

Under Lock and Keynote

Acquisition Methods — Quest

A guidebook that imparts upon its reader the basics of the Lock Picking specialty.

Smooth as Silk Sales Talk

Acquisition Methods — Quest

A guidebook that imparts upon its reader the basics of the Haggling specialty.

Ocarina of Temptation

Acquisition Methods — Quest

A guidebook that imparts upon its reader the basics of the Ocarina specialty.

How to Express Yourself

Acquisition Methods — Quest

A guidebook that imparts upon its reader the basics of the Emoter specialty.

Kindred Spirits

Acquisition Methods — Quest

A unique periodical that imparts upon its reader the basics of the Augury specialty.

Familiarizing with Familiars

Acquisition Methods — Quest

A unique periodical that imparts upon its reader the basics of the Familiar Spirit specialty.

CREATION

ITEM CREATION

You can produce just about anything with the right expertise and raw materials. With the requisite item creation specialty unlocked and sufficiently leveled up with SP, all that's needed is to gather whatever items a recipe requires. Before a recipe has actually been produced hands-on, the result will be hidden, but this chapter contains a complete list of item creation recipes. When in doubt comparing this guide to the game's Item Creation menu, confirm that the ingredients list matches up exactly.

Compounding

Unlocked through Quest 001, If It Tastes like Blueberries, It Must Be Good for You

Compounding Skill Level 1

RESULT	MATERIAL REQUIRED	QTY	MATERIAL REQUIRED	QTY	MATERIAL REQUIRED	QTY	MATERIAL REQUIRED	QTY
Blackberry Potion	Blackberries	3	Nectar	2	—	—	—	—
Mixed Syrup	Red Fruit	1	Green Fruit	1	—	—	—	—
Poison Cider	Spring Water	3	Nectar	2	Bee Stinger	3	Empty Bottle	1
Spark Cider	Spring Water	3	Nectar	2	Gerel Secretion	3	Empty Bottle	1
Frozen Cider	Spring Water	3	Nectar	2	Fish Scales	3	Empty Bottle	1
Cloudy Cider	Spring Water	3	Nectar	2	Peryton Droppings	3	Empty Bottle	1

Compounding Skill Level 2

RESULT	MATERIAL REQUIRED	QTY	MATERIAL REQUIRED	QTY	MATERIAL REQUIRED	QTY	MATERIAL REQUIRED	QTY
Blueberry Potion	Blueberries	3	Nectar	2	—	—	—	—
Fortitude Potion	Earth Gem	3	Holy Water	3	Empty Bottle	1	—	—
Acuity Potion	Wind Gem	3	Holy Water	3	Empty Bottle	1	—	—

Compounding Skill Level 3

RESULT	MATERIAL REQUIRED	QTY	MATERIAL REQUIRED	QTY	MATERIAL REQUIRED	QTY	MATERIAL REQUIRED	QTY
Strength Potion	Fire Gem	3	Holy Water	3	Empty Bottle	1	—	—
Perception Potion	Ice Gem	3	Holy Water	3	Empty Bottle	1	—	—

Compounding Skill Level 4

RESULT	MATERIAL REQUIRED	QTY	MATERIAL REQUIRED	QTY	MATERIAL REQUIRED	QTY	MATERIAL REQUIRED	QTY
Physical Stimulant	Blueberries	3	Red Fruit	1	Caterpillar Fungus	1	—	—
Emotional Destabilizer	Lavender	3	Demon's Tail	1	Empty Bottle	1	—	—
Diligence Potion	Holy Water	3	Empty Bottle	1	Seasonings	3		—
Vitalitea	Physical Stimulant	1	Colorful Mushrooms	3	Lemon Juice	1	—	—

Compounding Skill Level 5

RESULT	MATERIAL REQUIRED	QTY	MATERIAL REQUIRED	QTY	MATERIAL REQUIRED	QTY	MATERIAL REQUIRED	QTY
Mental Stimulant	Blackberries	3	Green Fruit	1	Caterpillar Fungus	1	—	—
DANGER! DO NOT DRINK!	Spring Water	3	Nectar	2	Poison Hemlock	3	Empty Bottle	1

Compounding Skill Level 6

RESULT	MATERIAL REQUIRED	QTY	MATERIAL REQUIRED	QTY	MATERIAL REQUIRED	QTY	MATERIAL REQUIRED	QTY
Therapeutic Tincture	Mint	3	Basil	2	Olive Oil	1	—	—
Love Potion No. 256	Lavender	3	Shadow Roses	1	Lezard's Flask	1	—	—
Riot Potion	Lezard's Flask	1	Vanilla Beans	2	Nectar	3	—	—
Robust Vitalitea	Vitalitea	1	Poison Hemlock	3	Caterpillar Fungus	1	—	—

Compounding Skill Level 7

RESULT	MATERIAL REQUIRED	QTY	MATERIAL REQUIRED	QTY	MATERIAL REQUIRED	QTY	MATERIAL REQUIRED	QTY
Resurrection Elixir	Fresh Sage	3	Caterpillar Fungus	1	Empty Bottle	1	—	—
Heroism Potion	Resurrection Elixir	1	DANGER! DO NOT DRINK!	1	Philosopher's Stone	2	Lezard's Flask	1

Compounding Skill Level 8

RESULT	MATERIAL REQUIRED	QTY	MATERIAL REQUIRED	QTY	MATERIAL REQUIRED	QTY	MATERIAL REQUIRED	QTY
Potent Attack Seeds	Alchemist's Water	1	Attack Seeds	2	Fermentation Pot	1	—	—
Potent Intelligence Seeds	Alchemist's Water	1	Intelligence Seeds	2	Fermentation Pot	1	—	—
Potent Defense Seeds	Alchemist's Water	1	Defense Seeds	2	Fermentation Pot	1	—	—
Potent Mentality Seeds	Alchemist's Water	1	Mentality Seeds	2	Fermentation Pot	1	—	—
Potent Health Seeds	Alchemist's Water	1	Health Seeds	2	Fermentation Pot	1	—	—
Potent Magic Seeds	Alchemist's Water	1	Magic Seeds	2	Fermentation Pot	1	—	—
Resurrection Elixir	Fresh Sage	3	Caterpillar Fungus	1	Empty Bottle	1	—	—

Engineering

Unlocked through Quest 007, Of Weapons and Womanizers

Engineering Skill Level 1

RESULT	MATERIAL REQUIRED	QTY	MATERIAL REQUIRED	QTY	MATERIAL REQUIRED	QTY	MATERIAL REQUIRED	QTY
EM Bomb (S)	Fire Gem	1	Gunpowder	3	Micro Circuit	1	—	—
Attack Breaker	EM Bomb (S)	1	Strength Potion	1	—	—	—	—
Intelligence Breaker	EM Bomb (S)	1	Perception Potion	1	—	—	—	—

Engineering Skill Level 2

RESULT	MATERIAL REQUIRED	QTY	MATERIAL REQUIRED	QTY	MATERIAL REQUIRED	QTY	MATERIAL REQUIRED	QTY
Poison Bomb	EM Bomb (S)	1	Poison Cider	1	—	—	—	—
Smoke Bomb	EM Bomb (S)	1	Cloudy Cider	1	—	—	—	—
Defense Breaker	EM Bomb (S)	1	Fortitude Potion	3	—	—	—	—
Mentality Breaker	EM Bomb (S)	1	Acuity Potion	3	—	—	—	—
CQC Program Alpha	Iron	3	Blank Disk	1	—	—	—	—
CQC Program Beta	Silver	3	Blank Disk	1	—	—	—	—

Engineering Skill Level 3

RESULT	MATERIAL REQUIRED	QTY	MATERIAL REQUIRED	QTY	MATERIAL REQUIRED	QTY	MATERIAL REQUIRED	QTY
Stun Bomb	EM Bomb (S)	1	Spark Cider	1	—	—	—	—
Freezing Bomb	EM Bomb (S)	1	Frozen Cider	1	—	—	—	—
CQC Program Gamma	Gold	5	Blank Disk	1	—	—	—	—
CQC Program Delta	Damascus Steel	1	Blank Disk	1	—	—	—	—

Engineering Skill Level 4

RESULT	MATERIAL REQUIRED	QTY	MATERIAL REQUIRED	QTY	MATERIAL REQUIRED	QTY	MATERIAL REQUIRED	QTY
Gravity Bomb	Gnomestone	1	Reinforced Gunpowder	2	Micro Circuit	1	—	—
Self-Destructor 3000	DANGER! DO NOT DRINK!	1	Gunpowder	2	Wire	1	—	—
Deluxe Poison Bomb	EM Bomb (L)	1	Poison Cider	1	—	—	—	—
Deluxe Smoke Bomb	EM Bomb (L)	1	Cloudy Cider	1	—	—	—	—
CQC Program Epsilon	Gold	5	Blank Disk	1	—	—	—	—
CQC Program Zeta	Platinum	3	High-Capacity Blank Disk	1	—	—	—	—

Engineering Skill Level 5

RESULT	MATERIAL REQUIRED	QTY	MATERIAL REQUIRED	QTY	MATERIAL REQUIRED	QTY	MATERIAL REQUIRED	QTY
Healing Device	Physical Stimulant	3	Diffusion Device	1	—	—	—	—
EM Bomb (L)	Fire Gem	1	Reinforced Gunpowder	3	Rivets	1	Micro Circuit	2
Low-Frequency Bomb	Sylphstone	1	Reinforced Gunpowder	2	Quantum Processor	1	—	—
CQC Program Eta	Platinum	4	High-Capacity Blank Disk	1	—		—	—
Sylvan Ray	Mythril	3	Laser Oscillator	1	Rivets	3	—	—

Engineering Skill Level 6

RESULT	MATERIAL REQUIRED	QTY	MATERIAL REQUIRED	QTY	MATERIAL REQUIRED	QTY	MATERIAL REQUIRED	QTY
Relaxation Device	Mental Stimulant	3	Diffusion Device	1	—	—	—	—
Deluxe Stun Bomb	EM Bomb (L)	1	Spark Cider	1	—	—	—	—
Deluxe Freezing Bomb	EM Bomb (L)	1	Frozen Cider	1	—	—	—	—
CQC Program Theta	Orichalcum	5	High-Capacity Blank Disk	1	—	—	—	—
Straightshooter	Meteorite	1	Rivets	4	Carbon Fiber	1	—	—

Engineering Skill Level 7

RESULT	MATERIAL REQUIRED	QTY	MATERIAL REQUIRED	QTY	MATERIAL REQUIRED	QTY	MATERIAL REQUIRED	QTY
Miraculous Device	Mixed Syrup	4	Caterpillar Fungus	1	Diffusion Device	1	—	—
Ultimate Bomb	Meteorite	1	Hadron Collider	1	Quantum Processor	1	—	—
HP Absorber	Ghost's Soul	1	Diffusion Device	1	Quantum Processor	1	—	—
MP Absorber	Mati	1	Diffusion Device	1	Quantum Processor	1	—	—

Engineering Skill Level 8

RESULT	MATERIAL REQUIRED	QTY	MATERIAL REQUIRED	QTY	MATERIAL REQUIRED	QTY	MATERIAL REQUIRED	QTY
Umbral Blast	Gravity Bomb	3	Orichalcum	3	Hadron Collider	1	Rivets	3
Laser Suit	Moonstone	1	Laser Oscillator	4	Carbon Fiber	2	High-Power Generator	1

Smithery

Unlocked through Quest 003, Brute Strength of Blacksmithing

Smithery Skill Level 1

RESULT	MATERIAL REQUIRED	QTY	MATERIAL REQUIRED	QTY	MATERIAL REQUIRED	QTY	MATERIAL REQUIRED	QTY
Storm Blade	Wind Gem	3	Iron	2	—	—	—	—
Ruby Wand	Ruby	1	Wooden Stick	3	—	—	—	—
Shell Armor	Iron	2	Tortoise Shell	1	Lizardskin	1	—	—
Rudimentary Protector	Iron	1	Hand-Spun Thread	2	—	—	—	—
Scale Mail	Fish Scale	5	Wire	2	—	—	—	—

Smithery Skill Level 2

RESULT	MATERIAL REQUIRED	QTY	MATERIAL REQUIRED	QTY	MATERIAL REQUIRED	QTY	MATERIAL REQUIRED	QTY
Earth Armlet	Earth Gem	1	Silver	4	—	—	—	—
Ice Armlet	Ice Gem	1	Silver	4	—	—	—	—
Fire Armlet	Fire Gem	1	Silver	4	—	—	—	—
Wind Armlet	Wind Gem	1	Silver	4	—	—	—	—
Damascus Steel	Iron	3	Coal	2	—	—	—	—

Smithery Skill Level 3

RESULT	MATERIAL REQUIRED	QTY	MATERIAL REQUIRED	QTY	MATERIAL REQUIRED	QTY	MATERIAL REQUIRED	QTY
Venom Sword	Poison Cider	4	Damascus Steel	2	Bee Stinger	2	—	—
Rune Blade	Crystal	1	Light Gem	1	Damascus Steel	2	—	—
Star Flail	Spark Cider	2	Damascus Steel	1	Platinum	1	—	—
Williwaw Bow	Light Gem	2	Damascus Steel	2	Wire	1	—	—
Damask Knuckles	Strength Potion	1	Earth Gem	2	Damascus Steel	4	—	—
Damask Plate	Damascus Steel	3	Rivets	5	Earth Gem	2	—	—

Smithery Skill Level 4

RESULT	MATERIAL REQUIRED	QTY	MATERIAL REQUIRED	QTY	MATERIAL REQUIRED	QTY	MATERIAL REQUIRED	QTY
Atrementous Usurper	Darkness Gem	3	Platinum	2	Wire	1	—	—
Vermilion Claws	Platinum	1	Wolf Fang	2	Snakeskin	2	Salamanderstone	1
Duel Armor	Fortitude Potion	1	Platinum	1	Tortoise Shell	2	—	—
Blood Chain Mail	Darkness Charm	4	Platinum	2	Bloodstained Cloth	1	—	—

Smithery Skill Level 5

RESULT	MATERIAL REQUIRED	QTY	MATERIAL REQUIRED	QTY	MATERIAL REQUIRED	QTY	MATERIAL REQUIRED	QTY
Icicle Sword	Nereidstone	4	Frozen Cider	8	Ash	1	—	—
Searing Sword	Salamanderstone	3	Dragon Scales	1	Dragon Hide	1	—	—
Saint's Bow	Angelstone	3	Gold	2	Oak	3	Wire	2
Hurricane Claws	Sylphstone	3	Giant Bird Feather	4	Faerie Embroidery Thread	3	—	—
Ifrit Mail	Salamanderstone	3	Gnomestone	2	Carbon Fiber	3	—	—
Sylphide's Mail	Sylphstone	3	Nereidstone	2	Carbon Fiber	3	—	—

Smithery Skill Level 6

RESULT	MATERIAL REQUIRED	QTY	MATERIAL REQUIRED	QTY	MATERIAL REQUIRED	QTY	MATERIAL REQUIRED	QTY
Mythril Sword	Mythril	4	Damascus Steel	2	Dragon Hide	1	—	—
Scumbag Slayer	Meteorite	1	Wooden Stick	3	Mana Ribbon	1	High-Strength Adhesive	3
Mythril Rod	Mythril	4	Laurel Tree	1	Shadow Roses	1	Ash	2
Silvance	Alchemist's Water	1	Mythril	2	Silver	3	—	—
Mythril Gauntlets	Fortitude Potion	3	Mythril	3	Rivets	6	—	—
Mythril Plate	Mythril	3	Tortoise Shell	2	Rivets	6	—	—
Mythril Mesh	Mythril	2	Gold	2	Silk	3	—	—

Smithery Skill Level 7

RESULT	MATERIAL REQUIRED	QTY	MATERIAL REQUIRED	QTY	MATERIAL REQUIRED	QTY	MATERIAL REQUIRED	QTY
Arcana Sword	Meteorite	1	Platinum	3	Carbon Fiber	3	—	—
Dojikiri-Yasutsuna	Meteorite	3	Coal	4	Bloodstained Cloth	2	—	—
Tiger Fangs	Meteorite	3	Wolf Fang	8	Primeval Fossil	3	—	—
Valiant Mail	Vitalitea	2	Meteorite	3	Dragon Hide	3	Rivets	12
Superior Chain Mail	Holy Water	3	Meteorite	3	Silver	6	Cashmere	3
Star Guard	Moon Pearl	1	Orichalcum	3	Meteorite	1	—	—

Smithery Skill Level 8

RESULT	MATERIAL REQUIRED	QTY	MATERIAL REQUIRED	QTY	MATERIAL REQUIRED	QTY	MATERIAL REQUIRED	QTY
Aurora Blade	Orichalcum	3	Laser Oscillator	1	High-Power Generator	1	—	—
Murasame	Diligence Potion	4	Orichalcum	3	Scalestone	2	—	—
Kaiser Knuckles	Strength Potion	5	Orichalcum	3	Gold	4	Dragon Hide	3
Reflecting Plate	Angelstone	3	Orichalcum	3	Philosopher's Stone	1	—	—
Mystic Chain	Orichalcum	3	Platinum	4	Manacloth	3	—	—

Crafting

Unlocked through Quest 005, Grand Designs

Crafting Skill Level 1

RESULT	MATERIAL REQUIRED	QTY	MATERIAL REQUIRED	QTY	MATERIAL REQUIRED	QTY	MATERIAL REQUIRED	QTY
Sthal Cloak	Wool	3	Hand-Spun Thread	1	—	—	—	—
Traveler's Cloak	Lizardskin	3	Wool	4	Hand-Spun Thread	3	—	—

Crafting Skill Level 2

RESULT	MATERIAL REQUIRED	QTY	MATERIAL REQUIRED	QTY	MATERIAL REQUIRED	QTY	MATERIAL REQUIRED	QTY
Flare Coat	Ruby	1	Silk	2	Taffeta Ribbon	1	Hand-Spun Thread	1
Energy Bracelet	Lizardskin	3	Oak	2	High-Strength Adhesive	1	—	—
Arcane Bracelet	Silver	1	Snakeskin	3	High-Strength Adhesive	1	—	—

Crafting Skill Level 3

RESULT	MATERIAL REQUIRED	QTY	MATERIAL REQUIRED	QTY	MATERIAL REQUIRED	QTY	MATERIAL REQUIRED	QTY
Floral Brume Wand	Blue Roses	3	Ebony	1	Taffeta Ribbon	1	—	—
Superior Leather	Damascus Steel	3	Snakeskin	4	High-Strength Adhesive	3	—	—
Crystal Robe	Crystal	1	Velvet Ribbon	3	Dwarven Embroidery Thread	3	—	—
Fortitude Bracelet	Fortitude Potion	3	Crystal	1	Gold	3	—	—
Acuity Bracelet	Acuity Potion	3	Crystal	1	Gold	3	—	—

Crafting Skill Level 4

RESULT	MATERIAL REQUIRED	QTY	MATERIAL REQUIRED	QTY	MATERIAL REQUIRED	QTY	MATERIAL REQUIRED	QTY
Amber Mace	Amber	1	Gnomestone	4	Iron	4	Velvet Ribbon	2
Angel's Cloak	Angelstone	1	Cashmere	2	Dwarven Embroidery Thread	3	Laurel Tree	1
Anti-silence Amulet	Chamomile	8	Salamanderstone	1	Ebony	3	—	—
Anti-fog Amulet	Jasmine	8	Angelstone	1	Ebony	3	—	—
Light Scarf	Light Charm	3	Angelstone	1	Cashmere	1	—	—
Darkness Scarf	Darkness Charm	3	Shadestone	1	Cashmere	1	—	—
Attack Bracelet	Strength Potion	3	Crystal	1	Platinum	3	—	—
Mind Bracelet	Perception Potion	3	Crystal	1	Platinum	3	—	—

Crafting Skill Level 5

RESULT	MATERIAL REQUIRED	QTY	MATERIAL REQUIRED	QTY	MATERIAL REQUIRED	QTY	MATERIAL REQUIRED	QTY
Mystic Robe	Shadow Roses	1	Cashmere	3	Velvet Ribbon	3	—	—
Anti-poison Amulet	Mint	8	Gnomestone	1	Ebony	3	—	—
Anti-stun Amulet	Crystal	1	Vinegar	8	Ebony	3	—	—
Anti-curse Amulet	Lavender	8	Shadestone	1	Ebony	3	—	—
Extrication Ring	Robust Vitalitea	3	Amber	1	Sylphstone	1	—	—

Crafting Skill Level 6

RESULT	MATERIAL REQUIRED	QTY	MATERIAL REQUIRED	QTY	MATERIAL REQUIRED	QTY	MATERIAL REQUIRED	QTY
Adept's Staff	Meteorite	1	Moon Pearl	1	Oak	3	Velvet Ribbon	2
Armillary Sphere	Meteorite	3	Primeval Fossil	1	—	—	—	—
Wizard's Robe	Manacloth	3	Mana Ribbon	1	Faerie Embroidery Thread	3	—	—
Anti-paralysis Amulet	Basil	8	Sylphstone	1	Oak	3	—	—
Anti-freezing Amulet	Cinnamon	8	Nereidstone	1	Oak	3	—	—
Green Talisman	Sylphstone	2	Gnomestone	3	Meteorite	1	—	—
Blue Talisman	Nereidstone	2	Angelstone	3	Meteorite	1	—	—
Red Talisman	Salamanderstone	2	Shadestone	3	Meteorite	1	—	—

Crafting Skill Level 7

RESULT	MATERIAL REQUIRED	QTY	MATERIAL REQUIRED	QTY	MATERIAL REQUIRED	QTY	MATERIAL REQUIRED	QTY
Anti-death Amulet	Resurrection Elixir	8	Philosopher's Stone	1	Ash	3	—	—
Healing Band	Red Fruit	20	Ash	1	Mana Ribbon	1	High-Strength Adhesive	3
Faerie Band	Green Fruit	20	Remex	1	Mana Ribbon	1	Dwarven Embroidery Thread	3
Testament to Triumph	Laurel Tree	1	Bloodstained Cloth	3	Gold	3	—	—
Mana Ribbon	Manacloth	3	Faerie Embroidery Thread	2	—	—	—	—

Crafting Skill Level 8

RESULT	MATERIAL REQUIRED	QTY	MATERIAL REQUIRED	QTY	MATERIAL REQUIRED	QTY	MATERIAL REQUIRED	QTY
Apocalypse	Orichalcum	3	Ash	2	Lesser Fiend's Tail	3	Mana Ribbon	1
tri-Emblem	Condemner's Cerulean Plume	3	Matriarch's Resplendent Plume	1	Moonstone	1	—	—

Cooking

Unlocked through Quest 002, Drunk on Creation

Cooking Skill Level 1

RESULT	MATERIAL REQUIRED	QTY	MATERIAL REQUIRED	QTY	MATERIAL REQUIRED	QTY	MATERIAL REQUIRED	QTY
Roe Rice	White Rice	3	Roe	3	—	—	—	—
Grilled Fish	Lemon	1	Raw Fish	1	—	—	—	—
Lemon Juice	Lemon	1	Spring Water	2	Nectar	3	—	—
Bunnylicious Pie	Wheat Flour	1	Red Fruit	1	Green Fruit	1	Nectar	2

Cooking Skill Level 2

RESULT	MATERIAL REQUIRED	QTY	MATERIAL REQUIRED	QTY	MATERIAL REQUIRED	QTY	MATERIAL REQUIRED	QTY
Minestrone	Tomato	3	Fresh Vegetables	2	Spring Water	1	—	—
Lemon Tart	Wheat Flour	3	Lemon	3	Whole Milk	1	—	—
White Bread	Wheat Flour	3	Spring Water	2	—	—	—	—

Cooking Skill Level 3

RESULT	MATERIAL REQUIRED	QTY	MATERIAL REQUIRED	QTY	MATERIAL REQUIRED	QTY	MATERIAL REQUIRED	QTY
Golden Omelet	Prehistoric Meat	1	Common Eggs	3	Tomato	1	—	—
Fried Fish	Wheat Flour	2	Raw Fish	3	Olive Oil	1	—	—
Vegetable Stir-Fry	Fresh Vegetables	3	Prehistoric Meat	1	Seasonings	1	—	—
Pasta Peperoncino	Wheat Flour	3	Seasonings	2	Olive Oil	1	—	—
Vanilla Ice Cream	Whole Milk	3	Vanilla Beans	1	—	—	—	—
Hot Chocolate	Cocoa Powder	3	Whole Milk	1	—	—	—	—

Cooking Skill Level 4

RESULT	MATERIAL REQUIRED	QTY	MATERIAL REQUIRED	QTY	MATERIAL REQUIRED	QTY	MATERIAL REQUIRED	QTY
Curry Rice	White Rice	3	Fresh Vegetables	3	Prehistoric Meat	2	Seasonings	2
Cream Stew	Wheat Flour	3	Fresh Vegetables	3	Tasty Mushrooms	2	Whole Milk	1
Caesar Salad	Fresh Vegetables	3	Lemon	1	Olive Oil	1	—	—
Spaghetti with Roe	Wheat Flour	3	Roe	2	Seaweed	1	Soy Sauce	2
Chocolate Scones	Wheat Flour	3	Common Eggs	2	Cocoa Powder	3	—	—
Tiramisu	Well-Aged Cheese	3	Whole Milk	1	Common Eggs	2	Cocoa Powder	2
Fruit Gummies	Spring Water	3	Nectar	4	Gerel Secretion	3	—	—

Cooking Skill Level 5

RESULT	MATERIAL REQUIRED	QTY	MATERIAL REQUIRED	QTY	MATERIAL REQUIRED	QTY	MATERIAL REQUIRED	QTY
Crab Rice Stew	Fresh Vegetables	3	White Rice	3	Shellfish Meat	3	Seaweed	1
Hamburg Steak	Fresh Sage	2	Prehistoric Meat	3	Fresh Vegetables	1	Common Eggs	1
Salmon Meuniere	Lemon	2	Raw Fish	3	Olive Oil	1	Basil	1
Shortcake	Wheat Flour	3	Red Fruit	1	Common Eggs	3	Whole Milk	3
Herb Tea	Mint	3	Chamomile	1	Jasmine	1	Spring Water	2

Cooking Skill Level 6

RESULT	MATERIAL REQUIRED	QTY	MATERIAL REQUIRED	QTY	MATERIAL REQUIRED	QTY	MATERIAL REQUIRED	QTY
Cheese Fondue	White Bread	3	Fresh Vegetables	1	Well-Aged Cheese	3	—	—
Seaweed Salad	Fresh Vegetables	3	Seaweed	2	Soy Sauce	1	—	—
Pasta Bolognese	Wheat Flour	3	Tomato	3	Prehistoric Meat	1	Well-Aged Cheese	1
Melon Bun	White Bread	3	Common Eggs	2	Whole Milk	1	Nectar	3
Mint Chocolate Chip Ice Cream	Mint	2	Whole Milk	3	Cocoa Powder	3	—	—
Chai Tea	Mint	3	Cinnamon	2	Seasonings	1	Whole Milk	2

Cooking Skill Level 7

RESULT	MATERIAL REQUIRED	QTY	MATERIAL REQUIRED	QTY	MATERIAL REQUIRED	QTY	MATERIAL REQUIRED	QTY
Grilled Steak	Prehistoric Meat	5	Olive Oil	1	Seasonings	1	—	—
Stink Fish	Raw Fish	3	Soy Sauce	2	Gerel Secretion	1	Fermentation Pot	2
Caprese Salad	Basil	1	Tomato	3	Well-Aged Cheese	2	Olive Oil	2
Seafood Hot Pot	Empyreanase	1	Raw Fish	3	Shellfish Meat	3	Seaweed	2

Cooking Skill Level 8

RESULT	MATERIAL REQUIRED	QTY	MATERIAL REQUIRED	QTY	MATERIAL REQUIRED	QTY	MATERIAL REQUIRED	QTY
Tears of Joysotto	Tasty Mushrooms	3	White Rice	3	Colorful Mushrooms	3	Well-Aged Cheese	2
Sushi	White Rice	4	Empyreanase	3	Vinegar	3	—	—
Sukiyaki	Fresh Vegetables	3	Marbled Meat	3	Common Eggs	1	Soy Sauce	2
Heavenly Pudding	Egg Paragon	3	Whole Milk	2	Nectar	1	Vanilla Beans	2

Authoring

Unlocked through Quest 008, Behavioral Study

Authoring Skill Level 1

RESULT	MATERIAL REQUIRED	QTY	MATERIAL REQUIRED	QTY	MATERIAL REQUIRED	QTY	MATERIAL REQUIRED	QTY
Lesser Demon's Fetish	Signet Card	1	Dark Paint	1	—	—	—	—
Earth Charm	Earth Gem	2	Signet Card	1	—	—	—	—
Ice Charm	Ice Gem	2	Signet Card	1	—	—	—	—
Fire Charm	Fire Gem	2	Signet Card	1	—	—	—	—
Wind Charm	Wind Gem	2	Signet Card	1	—	—	—	—
Signet Card: Healing	Signet Card	1	Healing Paint	1	—	—	—	—
Signet Card: Antidote	Signet Card	1	Healing Paint	1	—	—	—	—
Signet Card: Earth Glaive	Earth Gem	1	Signet Card	1	Earth Paint	1	—	—
Signet Card: Ice Needles	Ice Gem	1	Signet Card	1	Ice Paint	1	—	—
Signet Card: Fire Bolt	Fire Gem	1	Signet Card	1	Fire Paint	1	—	—
Signet Card: Wind Blade	Wind Gem	1	Signet Card	1	Wind Paint	1	—	—
Swordsman's Manual I	Giant Bird Feather	1	Parchment	1	High-Grade Ink	3	—	—
Swordsman's Manual II	Bee Stinger	1	Parchment	1	High-Grade Ink	3	—	—

RESULT	MATERIAL REQUIRED	QTY	MATERIAL REQUIRED	QTY	MATERIAL REQUIRED	QTY	MATERIAL REQUIRED	QTY
Cerulean Orb Signets, Vol. 1	Parchment	1	Earth Paint	2	Ice Paint	2	—	—
Solar Signets, Vol. 1	Parchment	1	Fire Paint	2	Wind Paint	2	—	—
Restorative Signets, Vol. 1	Oak	5	Parchment	1	Healing Paint	2	—	—
Fae Signets, Vol. 1	Parchment	1	Healing Paint	2	Dwarven Embroidery Thread	3	—	—
Purification Signets, Vol. 1	Zephyr Lily	3	Parchment	1	Healing Paint	2	—	—

Authoring Skill Level 2

RESULT	MATERIAL REQUIRED	QTY	MATERIAL REQUIRED	QTY	MATERIAL REQUIRED	QTY	MATERIAL REQUIRED	QTY
Greater Demon's Fetish	Signet Card +	1	Dark Paint	2	—	—	—	—
Light Charm	Light Gem	2	Signet Card	1	—	—	—	—
Darkness Charm	Darkness Gem	2	Signet Card	1	—	—	—	—
Signet Card: Faerie Healing	Holy Water	3	Signet Card	1	Healing Paint	1	—	—
Signet Card: Raise Dead	Ruby	3	Signet Card	1	Healing Paint	2	—	—
Signet Card: Radiant Lancer	Light Gem	1	Signet Card	1	Light Paint	1	—	—
Signet Card: Shadow Needles	Darkness Gem	1	Signet Card	1	Dark Paint	1	—	—
Signet Card: Sacred Pain	Silver	1	Signet Card	1	Mysterious Paint	1	—	—
Signet Card: Silence	Silver	1	Signet Card	1	Mysterious Paint	1	—	—
Swordsman's Manual III	Primeval Fossil	2	Parchment	1	High-Grade Ink	4	—	—
Swordsman's Manual IV	Parchment	1	Dwarven Embroidery Thread	2	High-Grade Ink	4	—	—
Moonlight Signets, Vol. 1	Parchment	1	Light Paint	2	Dark Paint	3	Velvet Ribbon	2
Pneuma Signets, Vol. 1	Ghost's Soul	3	Parchment	1	Healing Paint	4	—	—
Signeturgical Book of Quietude	Parchment	1	Mysterious Paint	4	High-Strength Adhesive	4	—	—

Authoring Skill Level 3

RESULT	MATERIAL REQUIRED	QTY	MATERIAL REQUIRED	QTY	MATERIAL REQUIRED	QTY	MATERIAL REQUIRED	QTY
Signet Card: Ex Healing	Oak	3	Signet Card	1	Healing Paint	1	—	—
Signet Card: Faerie Light	Ash	3	Signet Card	1	Healing Paint	1	—	—
Signet Card: Stone Rain	Earth Gem	2	Signet Card	1	Earth Paint	1	—	—
Signet Card: Deep Freeze	Ice Gem	2	Signet Card	1	Ice Paint	1	—	—
Signet Card: Explosion	Fire Gem	2	Signet Card	1	Fire Paint	1	—	—
Signet Card: Lightning Blast	Wind Gem	2	Signet Card	1	Wind Paint	1	—	—
Signet Card: Aurora Rings	Light Gem	2	Signet Card	1	Light Paint	1	—	—
Signet Card: Dark Devourer	Darkness Gem	2	Signet Card	1	Dark Paint	1	—	—
Signet Card: Reaping Spark	Crystal	2	Signet Card	1	Nil Paint	1	—	—
Swordsman's Manual V	Parchment	1	Bloodstained Cloth	2	High-Grade Ink	4	—	—
Swordsman's Manual VI	Ghost's Soul	1	Fine Parchment	1	High-Grade Ink	6	—	—
Cerulean Orb Signets, Vol. 2	Crystal	2	Parchment	1	Earth Paint	3	Ice Paint	3
Solar Signets, Vol. 2	Crystal	2	Parchment	1	Fire Paint	3	Wind Paint	3
Moonlight Signets, Vol. 2	Moon Pearl	2	Parchment	1	Light Paint	3	Dark Paint	3
The Founder's Signets, Vol. 1	Primeval Fossil	1	Fine Parchment	1	Nil Paint	3	—	—
Restorative Signets, Vol. 2	Ash	5	Fine Parchment	1	Healing Paint	3	—	—
Fae Signets, Vol. 2	Parchment	1	Healing Paint	2	Faerie Embroidery Thread	3	—	—

Authoring Skill Level 4

RESULT	MATERIAL REQUIRED	QTY	MATERIAL REQUIRED	QTY	MATERIAL REQUIRED	QTY	MATERIAL REQUIRED	QTY
Signet Card: Healing +	Remex	3	Signet Card +	1	Healing Paint	1	—	—
Signet Card: Faerie Healing +	Signet Card +	1	Healing Paint	1	Dwarven Embroidery Thread	2	—	—
Signet Card: Faerie Star	Signet Card	1	Healing Paint	1	Faerie Embroidery Thread	3	—	—
Signet Card: Antidote +	Therapeutic Tincture	3	Signet Card +	1	Healing Paint	1	—	—
Signet Card: Cure Condition	Crystal	3	Signet Card	1	Healing Paint	1	—	—
Signet Card: Earth Glaive +	Earth Gem	2	Signet Card +	1	Earth Paint	1	—	—
Signet Card: Terra Hammer	Earth Gem	2	Signet Card	1	Earth Paint	1	—	—
Signet Card: Ice Needles +	Ice Gem	2	Signet Card +	1	Ice Paint	1	—	—
Signet Card: Arctic Impact	Ice Gem	2	Signet Card	1	Ice Paint	1	—	—
Signet Card: Fire Bolt +	Fire Gem	2	Signet Card +	1	Fire Paint	1	—	—
Signet Card: Volcanic Burst	Fire Gem	2	Signet Card	1	Fire Paint	1	—	—
Signet Card: Wind Blade +	Wind Gem	2	Signet Card +	1	Wind Paint	1	—	—
Signet Card: Thunder Flare	Wind Gem	2	Signet Card	1	Wind Paint	1	—	—
Signet Card: Vampiric Blade	Darkness Gem	2	Signet Card	1	Dark Paint	1	—	—

RESULT	MATERIAL REQUIRED	QTY	MATERIAL REQUIRED	QTY	MATERIAL REQUIRED	QTY	MATERIAL REQUIRED	QTY
Signet Card: Void	Silver	2	Signet Card	1	Mysterious Paint	1	—	—
Signet Card: Arcane Weapon	Silver	2	Signet Card	1	Mysterious Paint	1	—	—
Swordsman's Manual VII	Remex	1	Fine Parchment	1	High-Grade Ink	6	—	—
Cerulean Orb Signets, Vol. 3	Gnomestone	3	Nereidstone	3	Fine Parchment	1	—	—
Solar Signets, Vol. 3	Fine Parchment	1	Fire Paint	3	Wind Paint	3	—	—
Moonlight Signets, Vol. 3	Angelstone	3	Shadestone	3	Fine Parchment	1	—	—
Fae Signets, Vol. 3	Sylphstone	3	Fine Parchment	1	Healing Paint	2	—	—
Purification Signets, Vol. 2	Scalestone	3	Fine Parchment	1	Healing Paint	2	—	—

Authoring Skill Level 5

RESULT	MATERIAL REQUIRED	QTY	MATERIAL REQUIRED	QTY	MATERIAL REQUIRED	QTY	MATERIAL REQUIRED	QTY
Signet Card: Raise Dead +	Signet Card +	1	Healing Paint	2	—	—	—	—
Signet Card: Resurrection	Blue Roses	3	Signet Card	1	Healing Paint	2	—	—
Signet Card: Tornado	Wind Gem	2	Signet Card	1	Wind Paint	1	—	—
Signet Card: Radiant Lancer +	Light Gem	2	Signet Card +	1	Light Paint	1	—	—
Signet Card: Sunflare	Light Gem	2	Signet Card	1	Light Paint	1	—	—
Signet Card: Shadow Needles +	Darkness Gem	2	Signet Card +	1	Dark Paint	1	—	—
Signet Card: Divine Wave	Crystal	2	Signet Card	1	Nil Paint	1	—	—
Signet Card: Extinction	Crystal	2	Signet Card	1	Nil Paint	1	—	—
Signet Card: Sacred Pain +	Silver	2	Signet Card +	1	Mysterious Paint	1	—	—
Signet Card: Silence +	Silver	2	Signet Card +	1	Mysterious Paint	1	—	—
Swordsman's Manual VIII	Laurel Tree	1	Fine Parchment	1	High-Grade Ink	6	—	—
Solar Signets, Vol. 4	Salamanderstone	3	Sylphstone	3	Fine Parchment	1	—	—
The Founder's Signets, Vol. 2	Philosopher's Stone	1	Fine Parchment	1	Nil Paint	3	—	—
Pneuma Signets, Vol. 2	Numinous Tincture	3	Fine Parchment	1	Healing Paint	4	—	—

Authoring Skill Level 6

RESULT	MATERIAL REQUIRED	QTY	MATERIAL REQUIRED	QTY	MATERIAL REQUIRED	QTY	MATERIAL REQUIRED	QTY
Signet Card: Ex Healing +	Signet Card +	1	Healing Paint	1	—	—	—	—
Signet Card: Faerie Light +	Signet Card +	1	Healing Paint	1	—	—	—	—
Signet Card: Stone Rain +	Earth Gem	2	Signet Card +	1	Earth Paint	2	—	—
Signet Card: Deep Freeze +	Ice Gem	2	Signet Card +	1	Ice Paint	2	—	—
Signet Card: Explosion +	Fire Gem	2	Signet Card +	1	Fire Paint	2	—	—
Signet Card: Lightning Blast +	Wind Gem	2	Signet Card +	1	Wind Paint	2	—	—
Signet Card: Aurora Rings +	Light Gem	2	Signet Card +	1	Light Paint	2	—	—
Signet Card: Dark Devourer +	Darkness Gem	2	Signet Card +	1	Dark Paint	2	—	—
Signet Card: Reaping Spark +	Crystal	2	Signet Card +	1	Nil Paint	2	—	—

Authoring Skill Level 7

RESULT	MATERIAL REQUIRED	QTY	MATERIAL REQUIRED	QTY	MATERIAL REQUIRED	QTY	MATERIAL REQUIRED	QTY
Signet Card: Faerie Star +	Primeval Fossil	3	Signet Card +	1	Healing Paint	1	—	—
Signet Card: Cure Condition +	Amber	3	Signet Card +	1	Healing Paint	1	—	—
Signet Card: Terra Hammer +	Earth Gem	3	Signet Card +	1	Earth Paint	3	—	—
Signet Card: Arctic Impact +	Ice Gem	3	Signet Card +	1	Ice Paint	2	—	—
Signet Card: Volcanic Burst +	Fire Gem	3	Signet Card +	1	Fire Paint	2	—	—
Signet Card: Thunder Flare +	Wind Gem	3	Signet Card +	1	Wind Paint	2	—	—
Signet Card: Vampiric Blade +	Darkness Gem	3	Signet Card +	1	Dark Paint	2	—	—
Signet Card: Void +	Silver	3	Signet Card +	1	Mysterious Paint	2	—	—
Signet Card: Arcane Weapon +	Silver	3	Signet Card +	1	Mysterious Paint	2	—	—

Authoring Skill Level 8

RESULT	MATERIAL REQUIRED	QTY	MATERIAL REQUIRED	QTY	MATERIAL REQUIRED	QTY	MATERIAL REQUIRED	QTY
Signet Card: Tornado +	Wind Gem	3	Signet Card +	1	Wind Paint	2	—	—
Signet Card: Sunflare +	Light Gem	3	Signet Card +	1	Light Paint	2	—	—
Signet Card: Divine Wave +	Crystal	3	Signet Card +	1	Nil Paint	3	—	—
Signet Card: Extinction +	Crystal	3	Signet Card +	1	Nil Paint	3	—	—

Alchemy

Unlocked through Quest 004, The End of Welch's Laboratory!?

Alchemy Skill Level 1

RESULT	MATERIAL REQUIRED	QTY	MATERIAL REQUIRED	QTY	MATERIAL REQUIRED	QTY	MATERIAL REQUIRED	QTY
Aquaberries	Blueberries	1	Mint	1	—	—	—	—
Healing Paint	Mixed Syrup	2	Spring Water	1	High-Strength Adhesive	1	—	—

Alchemy Skill Level 2

RESULT	MATERIAL REQUIRED	QTY	MATERIAL REQUIRED	QTY	MATERIAL REQUIRED	QTY	MATERIAL REQUIRED	QTY
Silver	Mercury	3	Holy Water	2	—	—	—	—
Earth Paint	Iron	2	Spring Water	1	High-Strength Adhesive	1	—	—
Ice Paint	Blue Roses	2	Spring Water	1	High-Strength Adhesive	1	—	—
High-Grade Ink	Spring Water	1	Coal	3	—	—	—	—
Holy Water	Spring Water	3	Zephyr Lily	1	—	—	—	—
High-Strength Adhesive	Gerel Secretion	1	Peryton Droppings	1	—	—	—	—

Alchemy Skill Level 3

RESULT	MATERIAL REQUIRED	QTY	MATERIAL REQUIRED	QTY	MATERIAL REQUIRED	QTY	MATERIAL REQUIRED	QTY
Conflagrant Soul	Fire Gem	3	Zephyr Lily	2	—	—	—	—
Vatic Looking Glass	Crystal	1	Darkness Gem	2	Platinum	1	Reinforced Gunpowder	2
Gold	Silver	3	Alchemist's Water	2	—	—	—	—
Fire Paint	Red Fruit	2	Spring Water	1	High-Strength Adhesive	1	—	—
Wind Paint	Giant Bird Feather	2	Spring Water	1	High-Strength Adhesive	1	—	—
Mysterious Paint	Strength Potion	2	Spring Water	1	High-Strength Adhesive	1	—	—

Alchemy Skill Level 4

RESULT	MATERIAL REQUIRED	QTY	MATERIAL REQUIRED	QTY	MATERIAL REQUIRED	QTY	MATERIAL REQUIRED	QTY
Infernal Gaze	Shadestone	4	Mati	1	Demon's Tail	3	—	—
Platinum	Gold	3	Silver	2	Alchemist's Water	2	—	—
Light Paint	Mercury	2	Spring Water	1	High-Strength Adhesive	1	—	—
Dark Paint	Demon's Tail	2	Spring Water	1	High-Strength Adhesive	1	—	—
Reinforced Gunpowder	Gunpowder	3	Coal	2	—	—	—	—

Alchemy Skill Level 5

RESULT	MATERIAL REQUIRED	QTY	MATERIAL REQUIRED	QTY	MATERIAL REQUIRED	QTY	MATERIAL REQUIRED	QTY
Orb of Antiquity	Amber	1	Mythril	3	Primeval Fossil	2	—	—
Mythril	Platinum	6	Alchemist's Water	2	—	—	—	—
Gnomestone	Amber	3	Earth Gem	2	Alchemist's Water	1	—	—
Nereidstone	Scalestone	3	Ice Gem	2	Alchemist's Water	1	—	—
Nil Paint	Moon Pearl	2	Spring Water	1	High-Strength Adhesive	1	—	—

Alchemy Skill Level 6

RESULT	MATERIAL REQUIRED	QTY	MATERIAL REQUIRED	QTY	MATERIAL REQUIRED	QTY	MATERIAL REQUIRED	QTY
Meteorite	Primeval Fossil	4	Mythril	3	Alchemist's Water	2	—	—
Salamanderstone	Dragon Scales	3	Fire Gem	2	Alchemist's Water	1	—	—
Sylphstone	Remex	3	Wind Gem	2	Alchemist's Water	1	—	—

Alchemy Skill Level 7

RESULT	MATERIAL REQUIRED	QTY	MATERIAL REQUIRED	QTY	MATERIAL REQUIRED	QTY	MATERIAL REQUIRED	QTY
Philosopher's Stone	Mercury	8	Meteorite	1	Gunpowder	4	Lezard's Flask	2
Angelstone	Laurel Tree	3	Light Gem	2	Alchemist's Water	1	—	—
Shadestone	Ghost's Soul	3	Darkness Gem	2	Alchemist's Water	1	—	—

Alchemy Skill Level 8

RESULT	MATERIAL REQUIRED	QTY	MATERIAL REQUIRED	QTY	MATERIAL REQUIRED	QTY	MATERIAL REQUIRED	QTY
Dragon's Den	Salamanderstone	3	Orichalcum	3	Dragon God Scales	1	—	—
Grumpy Homunculus	Attack Seeds	1	Philosopher's Stone	1	Lezard's Flask	1	—	—
Astute Homunculus	Intelligence Seeds	1	Philosopher's Stone	1	Lezard's Flask	1	—	—
Protective Homunculus	Defense Seeds	1	Philosopher's Stone	1	Lezard's Flask	1	—	—
Poised Homunculus	Mentality Seeds	1	Philosopher's Stone	1	Lezard's Flask	1	—	—

SYNTHESIS

The Synthesis specialty, unlocked through the early Happy Fun Bunny Time quest, allows a different kind of item creation. In standard item creation, a recipe's result is only unknown the first time it's attempted. After that, the same ingredients will always produce the same predictable result. Synthesis doesn't work like that. When items are synthesized, between two and six items are fused into one, with somewhat unpredictable results.

When you're arranging a synthesis, each fusion slot can be manually selected, or all slots can be automatically filled out with the Automatic Selection function. In either case, once several items are laid out for potential synthesis, a few pieces of information will help guide the decision to go through with it.

Under Result, the synthesis result's broad type is listed: medicine, food, metal, natural material, signeturgy, or machine. Two other parameters here help guide the decision: quality and impurities. These are arbitrary measures of how well the selected combo of ingredients works out together, and they are the main factors beyond the Result category in determining the synthesis product. A final consideration is made for certain synthesis results that can only occur when particular items are included in the fusion.

Type: The item family of the result. Toggle between different items when preparing a synthesis to affect the type of the eventual product.

Quality: The overall level of value of the product, maxing out at 50. Quality will vary depending on the value of the items assembled for the synthesis.

Impurities: A measure of the amount of imperfections holding the result back from legendary status. Like quality, it also maxes out at 50. Like type and quality, impurities will vary depending on the items selected. When targeting particular item types and quality levels, be creative and patient exploring different item combinations.

Quality and impurity ratings determine *the top of a reward's possible range.* A projected quality/impurities rating of 50, for example, does not guarantee a 50-value result. The table here illustrates the actual ranges for rewards from quality/impurity ratings.

Quality/Impurity Result Ranges

SYNTHESIS RATING	POTENTIAL RANGE
0	0-0
1	0-1
2	0-2
3	0-3
4	0-4
5	0-5
6	0-6
7	0-7
8	0-8
9	0-9
10	0-10
11	0-11
12	0-12
13	2-13
14	3-14
15	3-15
16	3-16
17	3-17
18	3-18
19	4-19
20	4-20
21	4-21
22	4-22
23	5-23
24	5-24
25	10-25

SYNTHESIS RATING	POTENTIAL RANGE
26	10-26
27	10-27
28	12-28
29	12-29
30	12-30
31	12-31
32	12-32
33	14-33
34	14-34
35	14-35
36	14-36
37	24-37
38	24-38
39	24-39
40	24-40
41	24-41
42	27-42
43	27-43
44	27-44
45	27-45
46	30-46
47	30-47
48	30-48
49	40-49
50	40-50

In other words, whenever a synthesis is undertaken, the potential reward is pulled from a pool of items along the metrics of both quality and impurity. A synthesis of quality 50 and impurities 12 can result in a quality result ranging from 40 to 50, while at the same time, it could be an "impure" result of 0-12; in this case, an impurity 0 reward from a quality 50 synth attempt is possible.

The "ultimate" synths of each type thus require a maxed Synthesis Specialty level, some item juggling when deciding the fusion (ensuring a quality/impurity rating of 50, so the top end of the scale is as high as possible), including prerequisite items (if any), and crossing fingers. There's simply some luck involved in shooting for high-level synthesis results.

The tables here show what results are possible when shooting for maxed 50-quality or 50-impurity spoils. These include many of the adventure's most powerful and exclusive weapons, armor, and items.

LESS RANDOMNESS THROUGH RELOADING

If this is frustrating when crucial synthesis materials are limited in supply, feel free to save your game progress just before attempting high-level synthesis. If you disagree with the results, reload the last save and try again. While some games have measures to ensure that you get the same result every time when you try reloading like this, *Star Ocean V* does not, so save and reload to your heart's content. If unexpected results still occur continually when saving and reloading, check to make sure that a prerequisite for some undesired result isn't included in the batch.

Top-End *Medicine*, Quality-derived

QUALITY LEVEL	RESULT	REQUIRED INGREDIENT
40	Healing Device	Physical Stimulant
41	Healing Device	—
42	Holy Mist	Therapeutic Tincture
43	Holy Mist	—
44	Miraculous Device	Mixed Syrup
45	Miraculous Device	—
46	Resurrection Mist	—
47	Resurrection Mist	—
48	Wondrous Tincture	—
49	Wondrous Tincture	—
50	Numinous Tincture	Wondrous Tincture

Top-End *Medicine*, Impurities-derived

IMPURITY LEVEL	RESULT	REQUIRED INGREDIENT
40	High-Strength Adhesive	Gerel Secretion
41	High-Strength Adhesive	—
42	Love Potion No. 256	—
43	Love Potion No. 256	—
44	Fermentation Pot	—
45	Fermentation Pot	—
46	Alchemist's Water	—
47	Alchemist's Water	—
48	Lezard's Flask	—
49	Lezard's Flask	—
50	Forbidden Tonic	—

Top-end *Food*, Quality-derived

QUALITY LEVEL	RESULT	REQUIRED INGREDIENT
40	Umai-bo Candy	—
41	Shortcake	—
42	Tears of Joysotto	—
43	Cheese Fondue	Well-Aged Cheese
44	Pasta Bolognese	—
45	Egg Paragon	—
46	Empyreanase	—
47	Heavenly Pudding	Egg Paragon
48	Marbled Meat	—
49	Sukiyaki	Marbled Meat
50	Gourmet Curry Rice	—

Top-end *Food*, Impurities-derived

IMPURITY LEVEL	RESULT	REQUIRED INGREDIENT
40	Seafood Hot Pot	—
41	Mint Chocolate Chip Ice Cream	—
42	Charred Meat	Prehistoric Meat
43	Charred Meat	—
44	Poison Hemlock	—
45	Poison Hemlock	—
46	Poisonous Hot Pot	—
47	Sushi	Empyreanase
48	Sushi	Empyreanase
49	Cake-like Substance	—
50	Dish Formerly Known as Food	—

Top-end *Metal*, Quality-derived

QUALITY LEVEL	RESULT	REQUIRED INGREDIENT
40	Elemental Leather	—
41	Astral Armor	Meteorite
42	Farwell	Orichalcum
43	Farwell	Orichalcum
44	Moonstone	Orichalcum
45	Moonstone	Orichalcum
46	Star Guard	Orichalcum
47	Star Guard	—
48	Universal Armor	Moonstone
49	Ama-no-Murakumo	Moonstone
50	Levantine	Moonstone

Top-end *Metal*, Impurities-derived

IMPURITY LEVEL	RESULT	REQUIRED INGREDIENT
40	Crimson Scourge	Meteorite
41	Chrome Nightmare	Orichalcum
42	Chrome Nightmare	Orichalcum
43	Meteorite	—
44	Meteorite	—
45	Moonstone	Orichalcum
46	Moonstone	Orichalcum
47	Bloody Knuckles	Moonstone
48	Bloody Knuckles	Moonstone
49	Wooden Sword	—
50	Metal Pipe	—

Top-end *Natural Materials*, Quality-derived

QUALITY LEVEL	RESULT	REQUIRED INGREDIENT
40	Failnaught	Meteorite
41	Failnaught	Meteorite
42	Defense Seeds	Orichalcum
43	Mentality Seeds	Orichalcum
44	Attack Seeds	Orichalcum
45	Intelligence Seeds	Orichalcum
46	Health Seeds	Orichalcum
47	Magic Seeds	Orichalcum
48	Mana Ribbon	—
49	Dragon Leather	Moonstone
50	Immolating Fangs	Moonstone

Top-end *Natural Materials*, Impurities-derived

IMPURITY LEVEL	RESULT	REQUIRED INGREDIENT
40	Nereidstone	—
41	Salamanderstone	Dragon Scales
42	Salamanderstone	—
43	Philosopher's Stone	—
44	Mentality Seeds	Orichalcum
45	Defense Seeds	Orichalcum
46	Intelligence Seeds	Orichalcum
47	Attack Seeds	Orichalcum
48	Magic Seeds	Orichalcum
49	Health Seeds	Orichalcum
50	Paws	—

Top-end *Signeturgy*, Quality-derived

QUALITY LEVEL	RESULT	REQUIRED INGREDIENT
40	Energy Amulet	—
41	Mirage Robe	—
42	Silver Cloak	—
43	Alchemist's Cloak	—
44	Corvine Orb	—
45	Seraphic Garb	Orichalcum
46	Asclepius	Orichalcum
47	Carbuncle's Prison	Orichalcum
48	Valkyrie's Garb	Matriarch's Resplendent Plume
49	Mindhealer	Moonstone
50	Aether-in-Stasis	Moonstone

Top-end *Signeturgy*, Impurities-derived

IMPURITY LEVEL	RESULT	REQUIRED INGREDIENT
40	Anti-poison Amulet	—
41	Amber Mace	Amber
42	Amber Mace	—
43	Anti-silence Amulet	—
44	Anti-fog Amulet	—
45	Anti-curse Amulet	—
46	Signet Card: Dark Devourer +	—
47	Calamity Staff	Meteorite
48	Calamity Staff	Meteorite
49	Terrestrial Globe	—
50	Welch's Handy Stick	—

Top-end *Machines*, Quality-derived

QUALITY LEVEL	RESULT	REQUIRED INGREDIENT
40	High-Capacity Blank Disk	—
41	High-Capacity Blank Disk	—
42	Composite Bow	—
43	Composite Bow	—
44	Arcadian Serenity	Orichalcum
45	Arcadian Serenity	Orichalcum
46	Hadron Collider	Meteorite
47	Hadron Collider	Meteorite
48	Laser Weapon	Hadron Collider
49	Laser Weapon	Hadron Collider
50	Dragon's Bellow	Moonstone

Top-end *Machines*, Impurities-derived

IMPURITY LEVEL	RESULT	REQUIRED INGREDIENT
40	Arcane Bracelet	Snakeskin
41	Energy Bracelet	—
42	Energy Bracelet	Lizardskin
43	Laser Suit	—
44	Laser Suit	—
45	High-Power Generator	—
46	High-Power Generator	—
47	Photonic Blaster	—
48	Photonic Blaster	—
49	Homing Arc	—
50	Squirt Gun	—

BESTIARY

There are many hostile forces roaming Sthal and beyond, and their information is recorded here in this Bestiary. Threats are separated by creature family and organized alphabetically within each group. This allows for ease of use of this Bestiary as a reference.

The game's in-game encyclopedia has the monsters organized differently, and that order is also presented here, in case you need it as a cross-reference.

Each adversary's entry contains a lot of information. Their level and base stats are detailed. Their location is also listed, whether a certain time or place, or during a particular Quest. Elemental and status effect resistances are also listed. A 0 figure here indicates the enemy in question has no innate resistance or weakness one way or another. A 100 indicates the enemy is immune to the listed effect, and a negative figure indicates a weakness—using that element against the target will result in bonus damage.

1. Enemy Name
2. Enemy Health Points
3. Enemy Magic Points
4. Attack Power
5. Enemy Intelligence
6. Enemy Defense
7. Enemy Magic Defense
8. Fol Reward
9. Experience Reward
10. Enemy Description
11. Fire Resistance
12. Ice Resistance
13. Earth Resistance
14. Wind Resistance
15. Light Resistance

(1) ABIGAIL OF THE FLEET FEET Lv. 64 (25)

(2) HP 167500
(3) MP 128500
(4) ATK 1207
(5) INT 926
(6) DEF 610
(7) MEN 503
(8) FOL 1080
(9) EXP 2020

49 (28) 29

LOC (26) ...st: Wanted: Abigail, Chapter 10+

ITEM	%
(27) ...emist's Water	14
Fermentation Pot	16
High-Strength Adhesive	18
Faerie Embroidery Thread	14

(Fire)	(Ice)	(Earth)	(Wind)	(Light)	(Dark)	POI	FRZ	PAR	SIL	CUR	FOG	STN	DTH
11	12	13	14	15	16	17	18	19	20	21	22	23	24

(10) As this thief has successfully evaded authorities for mothhs, she has likely mastered the art of survival more than the art of stealing.

16. Dark Resistance
17. Poison Resistance
18. Freeze Resistance
19. Paralysis Resistance
20. Silence Resistance
21. Curse Resistance
22. Fog Resistance
23. Stun Resistance
24. Death Resistance
25. Enemy Level
26. Location(s) where enemy can be found
27. Enemy Item Drops with % Chance of dropping the item
28. Enemy Number
29. Enemy Type

HUMANOIDS

NAME	TYPE/#
Succubus	Humanoids 1
Ridiculer	Humanoids 2
Apprentice Scumbag	Humanoids 3
Thieving Scumbag	Humanoids 4
Great Scumbag	Humanoids 5
General Alma	Humanoids 6
General Alma	Humanoids 7
General Alma	Humanoids 8
Fidel's Anima	Humanoids 9
Miki's Anima	Humanoids 10
Victor's Anima	Humanoids 11
Fiore's Anima	Humanoids 12
Emmerson's Anima	Humanoids 13
Anne's Anima	Humanoids 14
Der-Suul	Humanoids 15
Der-Suul	Humanoids 16
Der-Suul	Humanoids 17
Pavine	Humanoids 18
Pavine	Humanoids 19
Serious Captain Aaron	Humanoids 20
Feria's Clone	Humanoids 21
Feria's Clone	Humanoids 22
Eitalon Higher-Up	Humanoids 23
Eitalon Higher-Up	Humanoids 24
Eitalon's Leader	Humanoids 25
Ted	Humanoids 26
Daril	Humanoids 27
Gunter	Humanoids 28
Hana	Humanoids 29
Daks	Humanoids 30
Tyresod	Humanoids 31

NAME	TYPE/#
Ochva	Humanoids 32
Eban	Humanoids 33
Arze	Humanoids 34
Eitalon Higher-Up Survivor	Humanoids 35
Eitalon Survivor	Humanoids 36
Eitalon Survivor	Humanoids 37
Tyresod	Humanoids 38
Ochva	Humanoids 39
Eban	Humanoids 40
Arze	Humanoids 41
Walking Conflagration	Humanoids 42
Tyresod	Humanoids 43
Ochva	Humanoids 44
Eban	Humanoids 45
Arze	Humanoids 46
Thunderstruck Osthark	Humanoids 47
Audacious Pridean	Humanoids 48
Abigail of the Fleet Feet	Humanoids 49
Eitalon Higher-Up Survivor	Humanoids 50
Eitalon Survivor	Humanoids 51
Guerrilla	Humanoids 52
Hannah the Rapturous	Humanoids 53
Idealistic Insurgent	Humanoids 54
Eitalon Swordsman	Humanoids 55
Eitalon Swindler	Humanoids 56
Eitalon Archer	Humanoids 57
Eitalon Swindler	Humanoids 58
Eitalon Swordsman	Humanoids 59
Eitalon Archer	Humanoids 60
Eitalon Spellslinger	Humanoids 61
Trei'kuran Knight	Humanoids 62

NAME	TYPE/#
Trei'kuran Armored Bowman	Humanoids 63
Trei'kuran Arquebusier	Humanoids 64
Kronos Soldier	Humanoids 65
Kronos Ranger	Humanoids 66
Trei'kuran Knight	Humanoids 67
Trei'kuran Signeturge	Humanoids 68
Trei'kuran Armored Bowman	Humanoids 69
Trei'kuran Soldier	Humanoids 70
Trei'kuran Signeturge	Humanoids 71
Trei'kuran Sharpshooter	Humanoids 72
Kronos Soldier	Humanoids 73
Kronos Rifleman	Humanoids 74
Kronos Ranger	Humanoids 75
Kronos Scholar	Humanoids 76
Kronos Gunner	Humanoids 77
Trei'kuran Knight	Humanoids 78
Trei'kuran Signeturge	Humanoids 79
Trei'kuran Armored Bowman	Humanoids 80
Trei'kuran Signeturge	Humanoids 81
Trei'kuran Sharpshooter	Humanoids 82
Kronos Soldier	Humanoids 83
Kronos Soldier	Humanoids 84
Kronos Ranger	Humanoids 85
Kronos Gunner	Humanoids 86
Kronos Scholar	Humanoids 87
Kronos Commander	Humanoids 88
Kronos Authority	Humanoids 89
Kronos Commander	Humanoids 90
Kronos Authority	Humanoids 91
Kronos Scholar	Humanoids 92

BEASTS

NAME	TYPE/#
Saber-Toothed Tiger	Beasts 1
Unicorn Wolf	Beasts 2
Leonblade	Beasts 3
Lizard Soldier	Beasts 4
Wise Lizardman	Beasts 5
Lizard Commander	Beasts 6
Lizard Warrior	Beasts 7
Lizard Shaman	Beasts 8
Lizard Tyrant	Beasts 9
Kobold	Beasts 10
Kobold Bandit	Beasts 11
Kobold Ranger	Beasts 12
Kobold Knave	Beasts 13
Guardian Beast	Beasts 14
Forsaken Beast	Beasts 15
Royal Sphinx	Beasts 16
Horned Turtle	Beasts 17
Horned Tortoise	Beasts 18
Antlered Tortoise	Beasts 19
Land Turtle	Beasts 20
Marine Reaper	Beasts 21
Landswimmer	Beasts 22
Deep One	Beasts 23
Uen of the Midnight Wail	Beasts 24
Twin-Fanged Gargan	Beasts 25
Dastardly Skoudde Brother	Beasts 26
Donadello the Indomitable	Beasts 27
Chaos Corpse Corporal	Beasts 28
Wass the Splenetic	Beasts 29
Shelda the Immutable	Beasts 30
Hesitant Rihvnaut	Beasts 31
Anonnus the Disperser	Beasts 32
Envious Invidiad	Beasts 33
Serene Karacin	Beasts 34

AVIANS

NAME	TYPE/#
Bane Dragon	Avians 1
Ash Dragon	Avians 2
Bloodbane	Avians 3
Peryton	Avians 4
Axe Beak	Avians 5
Crater Peryton	Avians 6
Ancient Peryton	Avians 7
Harpyia	Avians 8
Terarin	Avians 9
Winged Nightmare	Avians 10
Firmament Moloch	Avians 11
Ravenne	Avians 12
Andrealphus	Avians 13
Jatayu	Avians 14
Giant Bat	Avians 15
Corpse Bat	Avians 16
Vampire Bat	Avians 17
Guiafairo	Avians 18
Armored Lizard	Avians 19
Lesser Dragon	Avians 20
Dinosaurus	Avians 21
Vidofnir	Avians 22
Vidofnir	Avians 23
Vidofnir	Avians 24
Vidofnir	Avians 25
Vidofnir	Avians 26
Storm Dragon	Avians 27
Storm Dragon	Avians 28
Storm Dragon	Avians 29
Storm Dragon	Avians 30
Storm Dragon	Avians 31
Storm Dragon	Avians 32
Luck Sucker	Avians 33
Greedy Avaricia	Avians 34
Opportunistic Moogmort	Avians 35
Ilua the Irate	Avians 36
Arjain the Fierce	Avians 37
Randaghor the Render	Avians 38
Hubristic Sturviella	Avians 39
Hourigh the Intrepid	Avians 40
Ruthless Bordnak	Avians 41
Thick-Thighed Pyekard	Avians 42

INSECTS

NAME	TYPE/#
Adephaga	Insects 1
Adephaga Drus	Insects 2
Adephaga Venom	Insects 3
Adephaga Milies	Insects 4
Adephaga Prox	Insects 5
Polyphaga	Insects 6
Polyphaga Drus	Insects 7
Polyphaga Gamboge	Insects 8
Killer Wasp	Insects 9
Honeybee	Insects 10
Stinger	Insects 11
Gust Hornet	Insects 12
Killer Chelae	Insects 13
Waving Pincers	Insects 14
Hades Crab	Insects 15
Sandeater	Insects 16
Sanddozer	Insects 17
Keen-Eyed Gileegha	Insects 18
Gula the Gluttonous	Insects 19
Lancing Hado	Insects 20
Wandering Ouyeits	Insects 21
Garish Sythwa	Insects 22

PLANTS

NAME	TYPE/#
Gerel	Plants 1
Vomiting Gel	Plants 2
Stroper	Plants 3
Chaotic Cell	Plants 4
Viscous Clod	Plants 5
Discord Gerel	Plants 6
Dryad	Plants 7
Mandragora	Plants 8
Lamia Radix	Plants 9
Maidenly Blossom	Plants 10
Man-Eating Tree	Plants 11
Albero di Anima	Plants 12
Treant	Plants 13
Elder Treant	Plants 14
Mist Grave	Plants 15
Giant Fungus	Plants 16
Myconid	Plants 17
Blightcap	Plants 18
Pygmy Glaive	Plants 19
Diminutive Fungus	Plants 20
Myconid Sporeling	Plants 21
Tinycap	Plants 22
Carnivorous Plant	Plants 23
Man Trap	Plants 24
Welwitschia	Plants 25
Thoras the Abomination	Plants 26
Thoras the Abomination	Plants 27
Corpulent Magvor	Plants 28
Fecund Magvorling	Plants 29
Erosive Cykla	Plants 30
Stubborn Vejheerit	Plants 31
Fran of Constant Decay	Plants 32
Verdant Muja	Plants 33
Geraldine	Plants 34
Languid Pijillo	Plants 35
Fallen Arcedia	Plants 36

CORRUPT

NAME	TYPE/#
Cursed Horror	Corrupt 1
Misfortuner	Corrupt 2
Grim Reaper	Corrupt 3
Stone Golem	Corrupt 4
Metal Golem	Corrupt 5
Lava Golem	Corrupt 6
Jade Golem	Corrupt 7
Rock Hermit	Corrupt 8
Dark Material	Corrupt 9
Flying Ice	Corrupt 10
Damascus Fort	Corrupt 11
Skeleton Soldier	Corrupt 12
Skeleton Armor	Corrupt 13
Bone Knight	Corrupt 14
Doleful Lord Brahms	Corrupt 15
Demon Imp	Corrupt 16
Devil Child	Corrupt 17
Demon Servant	Corrupt 18
Little Satan	Corrupt 19
Niflhel, the Armor that Walks	Corrupt 20
Cabrakan	Corrupt 21
Niflheim, the Armor that Roams	Corrupt 22
Grendelian Knight-Errant	Corrupt 23
Snow Mermaid	Corrupt 24
Aquaregia	Corrupt 25
Amber Princess	Corrupt 26
Baskania	Corrupt 27
Shrouded Gaze	Corrupt 28
Polyhedron	Corrupt 29
Seventh Core	Corrupt 30
Pandora's Cube	Corrupt 31
Illustrious Manticore	Corrupt 32
Bloodthirsty Fiend	Corrupt 33
Crystal Guardian	Corrupt 34
Harbinger of the Apocalypse	Corrupt 35
Netherphantom	Corrupt 36
Eyebalone	Corrupt 37
Eyebalone	Corrupt 38
Eyebalone	Corrupt 39
Tinat of the Dawning Light	Corrupt 40
Revenant Swordmaster Daeus	Corrupt 41
Malice Coalesced	Corrupt 42
Glaciating Lnkyri	Corrupt 43
Dek of the Boiling Blood	Corrupt 44
Amorphous Dryx	Corrupt 45
Napto the Stalwart	Corrupt 46
Underhanded Pargyn	Corrupt 47
Hoodini the Morose	Corrupt 48
Pillaging Mojango	Corrupt 49
Parched Orizon	Corrupt 50
Douxrah of the Frozen Touch	Corrupt 51
Ruphin the Imperious	Corrupt 52
Sandra the Majestic	Corrupt 53
Cunning Zurtail	Corrupt 54
Vlad the Unsullied	Corrupt 55
Dante the Obstinate	Corrupt 56
Mateo of the Slow Wit	Corrupt 57
Ivor of the Lustful Look	Corrupt 58

MACHINES

NAME	TYPE/#
Ancient Guard	Machines 1
Sacred Guard	Machines 2
Armed Dragoon	Machines 3
Phantom Dragoon	Machines 4
Blutgang	Machines 5
Valiant Conscript	Machines 6
Melusine	Machines 7
Metal Scumbag	Machines 8
Toy Soldier	Machines 9
Sentinel	Machines 10
Eliminator	Machines 11
Avenger	Machines 12
Robo Gunner	Machines 13
Destroyer	Machines 14
Fafnir	Machines 15

DIVINITIES

The Divinities family is small, so it isn't resorted alphabetically in the Bestiary.

HUMANOIDS

ABIGAIL OF THE FLEET FEET
Lv. 64

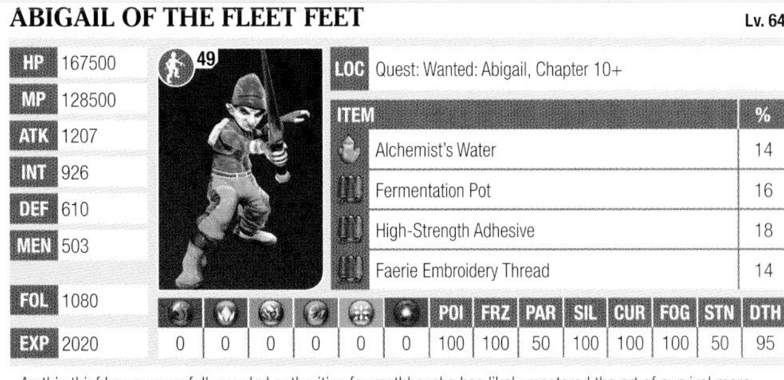

HP	MP	ATK	INT	DEF	MEN	FOL	EXP
167500	128500	1207	926	610	503	1080	2020

LOC: Quest: Wanted: Abigail, Chapter 10+

ITEM	%
Alchemist's Water	14
Fermentation Pot	16
High-Strength Adhesive	18
Faerie Embroidery Thread	14

						POI	FRZ	PAR	SIL	CUR	FOG	STN	DTH
0	0	0	0	0	0	100	100	50	100	100	100	50	95

As this thief has successfully evaded authorities for mothhs, she has likely mastered the art of survival more than the art of stealing.

ARZE
Lv. 58

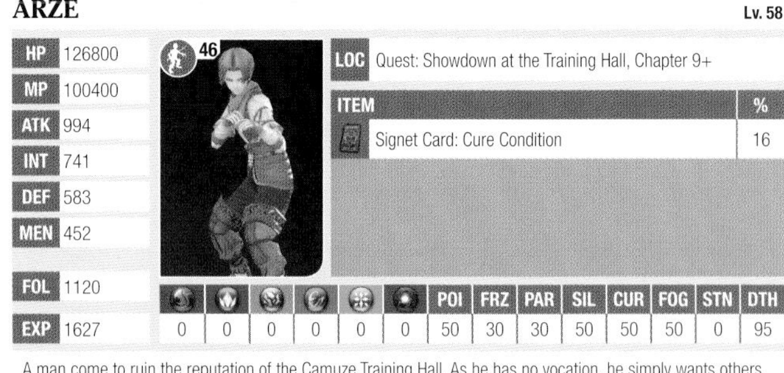

HP	MP	ATK	INT	DEF	MEN	FOL	EXP
126800	100400	994	741	583	452	1120	1627

LOC: Quest: Showdown at the Training Hall, Chapter 9+

ITEM	%
Signet Card: Cure Condition	16

						POI	FRZ	PAR	SIL	CUR	FOG	STN	DTH
0	0	0	0	0	0	50	30	30	50	50	50	0	95

A man come to ruin the reputation of the Camuze Training Hall. As he has no vocation, he simply wants others to share in his misery.

ANNE'S ANIMA
Lv. 140

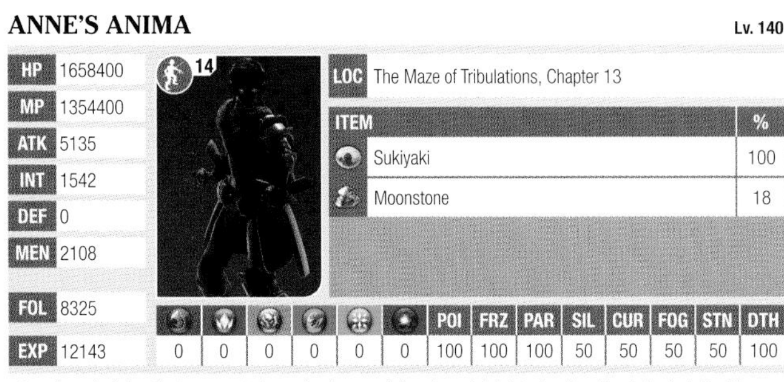

HP	MP	ATK	INT	DEF	MEN	FOL	EXP
1658400	1354400	5135	1542	0	2108	8325	12143

LOC: The Maze of Tribulations, Chapter 13

ITEM	%
Sukiyaki	100
Moonstone	18

						POI	FRZ	PAR	SIL	CUR	FOG	STN	DTH
0	0	0	0	0	0	100	100	100	50	50	50	50	100

An enigmatic being that appears to be a simulacrum of Anne's soul. It is blacker than the darkest night with eyes redder than blood worms.

AUDACIOUS PRIDEAN
Lv. 34

HP	MP	ATK	INT	DEF	MEN	FOL	EXP
38900	32400	306	288	243	209	299	633

LOC: Quest: Quiet Down in There!, Chapter 6+

ITEM	%
Signet Card	20
Taffeta Ribbon	18
Signet Card: Silence	16

						POI	FRZ	PAR	SIL	CUR	FOG	STN	DTH
0	0	0	0	-15	20	0	50	80	100	100	100	50	95

There is nothing tempting about this enchantress when she opens her mouth. Her laughter both sounds and pierces like rifle fire.

APPRENTICE SCUMBAG
Lv. 19

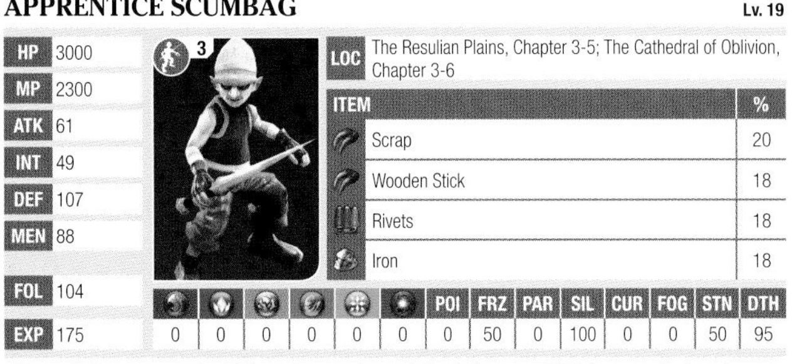

HP	MP	ATK	INT	DEF	MEN	FOL	EXP
3000	2300	61	49	107	88	104	175

LOC: The Resulian Plains, Chapter 3-5; The Cathedral of Oblivion, Chapter 3-6

ITEM	%
Scrap	20
Wooden Stick	18
Rivets	18
Iron	18

						POI	FRZ	PAR	SIL	CUR	FOG	STN	DTH
0	0	0	0	0	0	0	50	0	100	0	0	50	95

Time waits for no man, and certainly not for one who must steal hefty sums of Fol to be recognized as a true bandit. Travelers beware.

DAKS
Lv. 80

HP	MP	ATK	INT	DEF	MEN	FOL	EXP
1514800	1116800	1425	1128	1465	1136	8550	8235

LOC: The Maze of Tribulations, Chapter 13

ITEM	%
Pasta Bolognese	100
Orichalcum	20

						POI	FRZ	PAR	SIL	CUR	FOG	STN	DTH
0	0	0	0	0	0	100	100	50	100	50	50	50	100

A soldier from the same town as Victor. Though he may be older than his boss, he never lets it get in the way of his reconnaissance duties.

ARZE
Lv. 19

HP	MP	ATK	INT	DEF	MEN	FOL	EXP
3100	2400	65	48	110	85	129	179

LOC: Quest: The Four Stooges, Chapter 3+

ITEM	%
Signet Card: Healing	18

						POI	FRZ	PAR	SIL	CUR	FOG	STN	DTH
0	0	0	0	0	0	50	30	30	50	50	50	0	95

A man come to ruin the reputation of the Camuze Training Hall. As he has no vocation, he simply wants others to share in his misery.

DARIL
Lv. 90

HP	MP	ATK	INT	DEF	MEN	FOL	EXP
7223600	4856200	1775	1323	1795	1220	8550	34236

LOC: The Maze of Tribulations, Chapter 13

ITEM	%
Seafood Hot Pot	100
Orichalcum	20

						POI	FRZ	PAR	SIL	CUR	FOG	STN	DTH
0	0	0	0	0	0	100	100	100	100	50	50	50	100

Fidel's father, who is a soldier of great renown throughout Resulia. He is so busy advising the Central Resulian Army that he is hardly home.

ARZE
Lv. 38

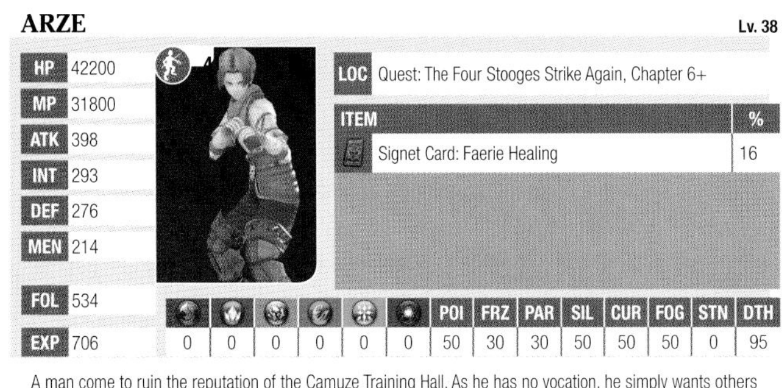

HP	MP	ATK	INT	DEF	MEN	FOL	EXP
42200	31800	398	293	276	214	534	706

LOC: Quest: The Four Stooges Strike Again, Chapter 6+

ITEM	%
Signet Card: Faerie Healing	16

						POI	FRZ	PAR	SIL	CUR	FOG	STN	DTH
0	0	0	0	0	0	50	30	30	50	50	50	0	95

A man come to ruin the reputation of the Camuze Training Hall. As he has no vocation, he simply wants others to share in his misery.

DER-SUUL
Lv. 42

HP	MP	ATK	INT	DEF	MEN	FOL	EXP
144400	119600	552	380	306	247	0	0

LOC: Chapter 6

ITEM	%

						POI	FRZ	PAR	SIL	CUR	FOG	STN	DTH
0	-10	0	0	0	0	100	100	80	100	100	100	100	100

The merciless general of the Imperial Trei'kuran Military. He is infamous for both his unquestionable cruelty and Machiavellian tactics.

DER-SUUL

Lv. 53

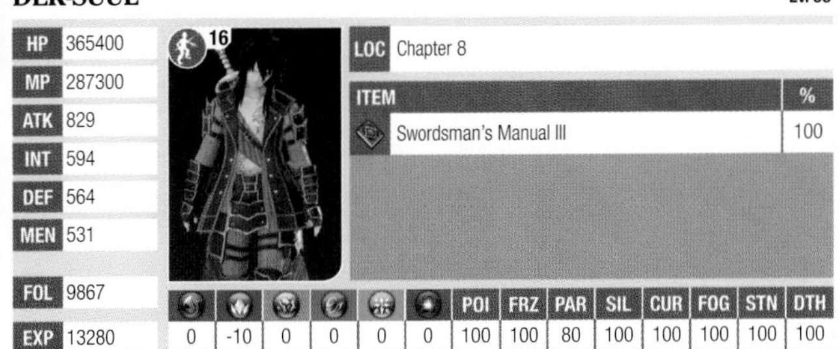

HP	365400
MP	287300
ATK	829
INT	594
DEF	564
MEN	531
FOL	9867
EXP	13280

16

LOC Chapter 8

ITEM	%
Swordsman's Manual III	100

						POI	FRZ	PAR	SIL	CUR	FOG	STN	DTH
0	-10	0	0	0	0	100	100	80	100	100	100	100	100

The merciless general of the Imperial Trei'kuran Military. He is infamous for both his unquestionable cruelty and Machiavellian tactics.

DER-SUUL

Lv. 80

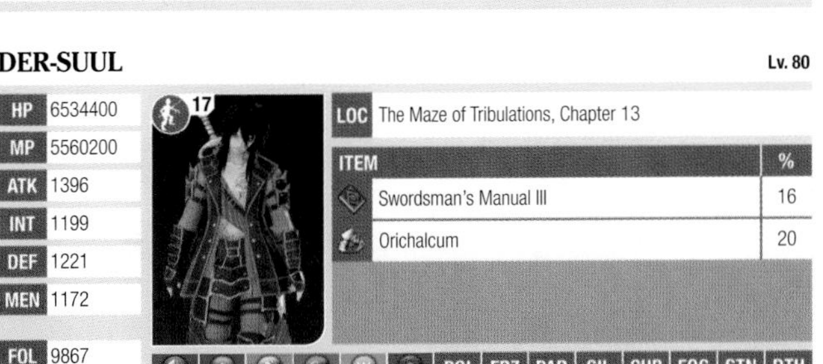

HP	6534400
MP	5560200
ATK	1396
INT	1199
DEF	1221
MEN	1172
FOL	9867
EXP	32939

17

LOC The Maze of Tribulations, Chapter 13

ITEM	%
Swordsman's Manual III	16
Orichalcum	20

						POI	FRZ	PAR	SIL	CUR	FOG	STN	DTH
0	-10	0	0	0	0	100	100	80	100	100	100	100	100

The merciless general of the Imperial Trei'kuran Military. He is infamous for both his unquestionable cruelty and Machiavellian tactics.

EBAN

Lv. 19

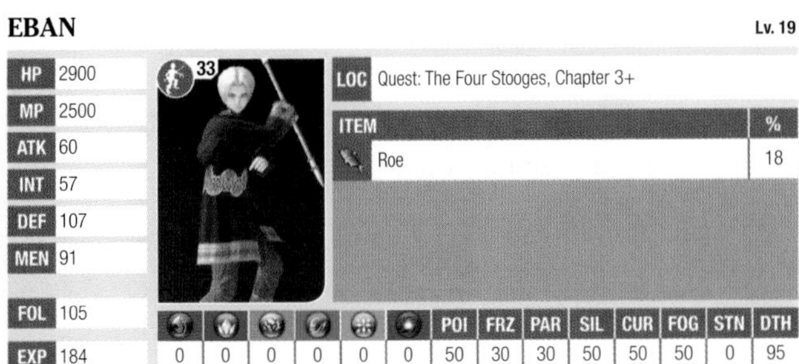

HP	2900
MP	2500
ATK	60
INT	57
DEF	107
MEN	91
FOL	105
EXP	184

33

LOC Quest: The Four Stooges, Chapter 3+

ITEM	%
Roe	18

						POI	FRZ	PAR	SIL	CUR	FOG	STN	DTH
0	0	0	0	0	0	50	30	30	50	50	50	0	95

A man come to ruin the Camuze Training Hall's reputation. As an overstressed cook, he often lambastes those under him without thinking.

EBAN

Lv. 38

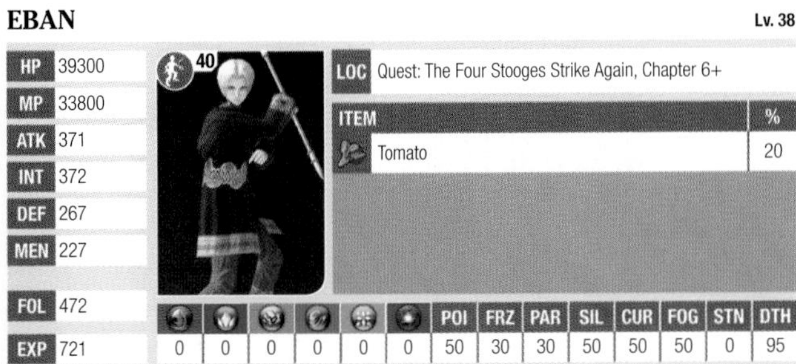

HP	39300
MP	33800
ATK	371
INT	372
DEF	267
MEN	227
FOL	472
EXP	721

40

LOC Quest: The Four Stooges Strike Again, Chapter 6+

ITEM	%
Tomato	20

						POI	FRZ	PAR	SIL	CUR	FOG	STN	DTH
0	0	0	0	0	0	50	30	30	50	50	50	0	95

A man come to ruin the Camuze Training Hall's reputation. As an overstressed cook, he often lambastes those under him without thinking.

EBAN

Lv. 58

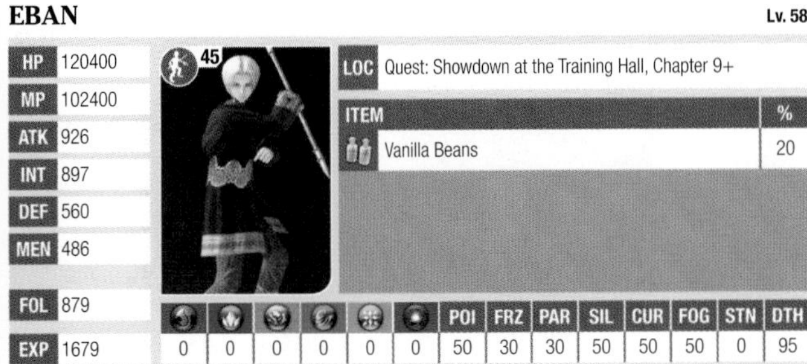

HP	120400
MP	102400
ATK	926
INT	897
DEF	560
MEN	486
FOL	879
EXP	1679

45

LOC Quest: Showdown at the Training Hall, Chapter 9+

ITEM	%
Vanilla Beans	20

						POI	FRZ	PAR	SIL	CUR	FOG	STN	DTH
0	0	0	0	0	0	50	30	30	50	50	50	0	95

A man come to ruin the Camuze Training Hall's reputation. As an overstressed cook, he often lambastes those under him without thinking.

EITALON ARCHER

Lv. 1

HP	300
MP	230
ATK	10
INT	8
DEF	39
MEN	33
FOL	107
EXP	3

57

LOC Chapter 1

ITEM	%
Blueberries	20
Blackberries	20

						POI	FRZ	PAR	SIL	CUR	FOG	STN	DTH
0	0	0	0	0	0	50	30	30	50	50	50	0	95

One of those notorious Resulian brigands and an expert archer. These bandits can loose fire arrows from far away with deadly accuracy.

EITALON ARCHER

Lv. 14

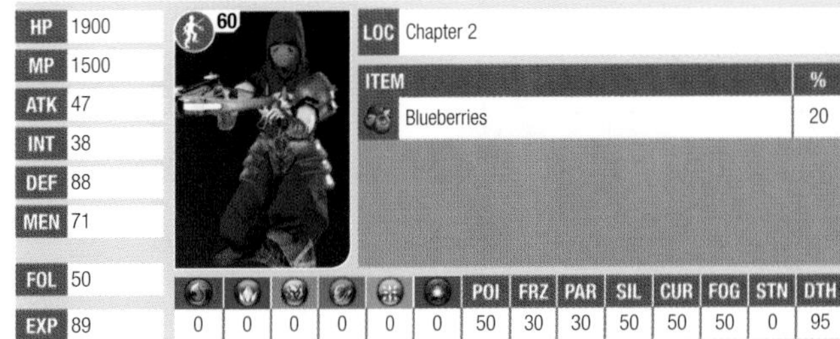

HP	1900
MP	1500
ATK	47
INT	38
DEF	88
MEN	71
FOL	50
EXP	89

60

LOC Chapter 2

ITEM	%
Blueberries	20

						POI	FRZ	PAR	SIL	CUR	FOG	STN	DTH
0	0	0	0	0	0	50	30	30	50	50	50	0	95

One of those notorious Resulian brigands and an expert archer. These bandits can loose fire arrows from far away with deadly accuracy.

EITALON HIGHER-UP

Lv. 1

HP	400
MP	220
ATK	14
INT	9
DEF	44
MEN	37
FOL	87
EXP	3

23

LOC Chapter 1

ITEM	%
Fresh Sage	100

						POI	FRZ	PAR	SIL	CUR	FOG	STN	DTH
0	0	0	0	0	0	50	30	30	50	50	50	0	95

One of the top brass in Eitalon, a group off the most degenerate bandits in all of Resulia. In reality, the brass just follow what the leader says.

EITALON HIGHER-UP

Lv. 15

HP	1900
MP	1400
ATK	49
INT	37
DEF	93
MEN	71
FOL	56
EXP	124

24

LOC Chapter 2

ITEM	%
Aquaberries	100

						POI	FRZ	PAR	SIL	CUR	FOG	STN	DTH
0	0	0	0	0	0	50	30	30	50	50	50	0	95

One of the top brass in Eitalon, a group off the most degenerate bandits in all of Resulia. In reality, the brass just follow what the leader says.

EITALON HIGHER-UP SURVIVOR

Lv. 43

HP	64400
MP	50500
ATK	571
INT	418
DEF	337
MEN	251
FOL	676
EXP	976

35

LOC Quest: Survive This!, Chapter 7+

ITEM	%
Therapeutic Tincture	16

						POI	FRZ	PAR	SIL	CUR	FOG	STN	DTH
0	0	0	0	0	0	50	50	30	50	50	50	0	95

Staunchly determined to keep Eitalon intact, this vestigial member of the ruined bandit group continues to drum up support for its old leader.

EITALON HIGHER-UP SURVIVOR
Lv. 64

HP	MP	ATK	INT	DEF	MEN	FOL	EXP
199300	153200	1342	955	674	518	1184	2124

LOC Quest: On the Trail of Eitalion Stragglers, Chapter 10+

ITEM	%
Therapeutic Tincture	18

						POI	FRZ	PAR	SIL	CUR	FOG	STN	DTH
0	0	0	0	0	0	50	30	30	50	50	50	0	95

Staunchly Determined to keep Eitalon intact, this vestigial member of the ruined bandit group continues to drum up support for its old leader.

EITALON SWINDLER
Lv. 1

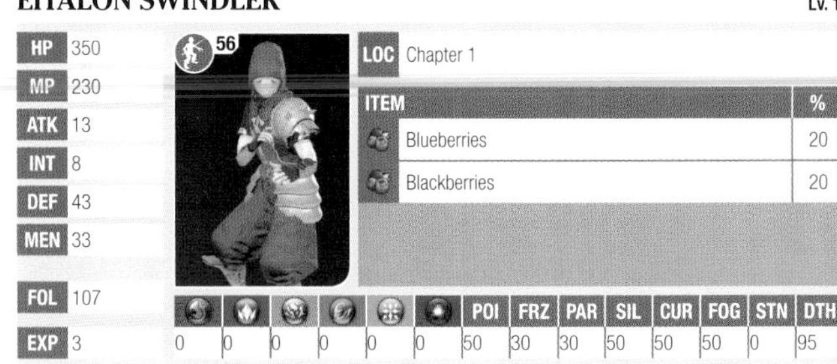

HP	MP	ATK	INT	DEF	MEN	FOL	EXP
350	230	13	8	43	33	107	3

LOC Chapter 1

ITEM	%
Blueberries	20
Blackberries	20

						POI	FRZ	PAR	SIL	CUR	FOG	STN	DTH
0	0	0	0	0	0	50	30	30	50	50	50	0	95

A group of Eitalon brigands who brawl with their bare hands. Swindlers have incredible reflexes that make it easy for them to befuddle foes.

EITALON SPELLSLINGER
Lv. 14

HP	MP	ATK	INT	DEF	MEN	FOL	EXP
1800	1500	46	42	86	86	46	94

LOC Chapter 2

ITEM	%
Signet Card: Earth Glaive	16

						POI	FRZ	PAR	SIL	CUR	FOG	STN	DTH
0	0	0	0	0	0	50	30	30	50	50	50	0	95

A class of fighter in Resulia's outlaw group who never stands on the front lines, opting to hang back and help out using signeturgy.

EITALON SWINDLER
Lv. 14

HP	MP	ATK	INT	DEF	MEN	FOL	EXP
1900	1500	49	36	89	69	54	89

LOC Chapter 2

ITEM	%
Fresh Sage	20

						POI	FRZ	PAR	SIL	CUR	FOG	STN	DTH
0	0	0	0	0	0	50	30	30	50	50	50	0	95

A group of Eitalon brigands who brawl with their bare hands. Swindlers have incredible reflexes that make it easy for them to befuddle foes.

EITALON SURVIVOR
Lv. 43

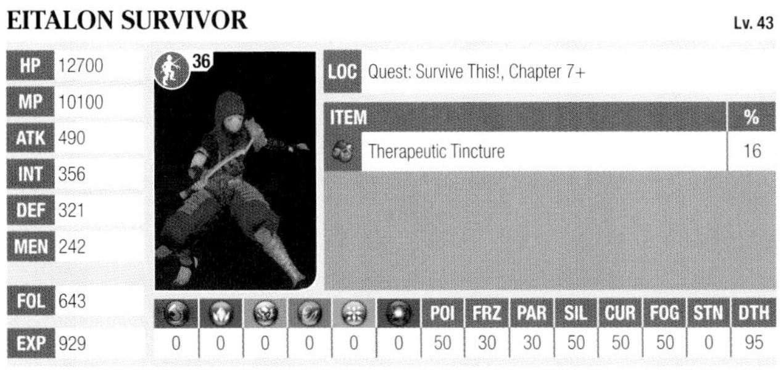

HP	MP	ATK	INT	DEF	MEN	FOL	EXP
12700	10100	490	356	321	242	643	929

LOC Quest: Survive This!, Chapter 7+

ITEM	%
Therapeutic Tincture	16

						POI	FRZ	PAR	SIL	CUR	FOG	STN	DTH
0	0	0	0	0	0	50	30	30	50	50	50	0	95

Having first joined Eitalon because they refused to make an honest living, these peons have no desire to turn over a new leaf now.

EITALON SWORDSMAN
Lv. 1

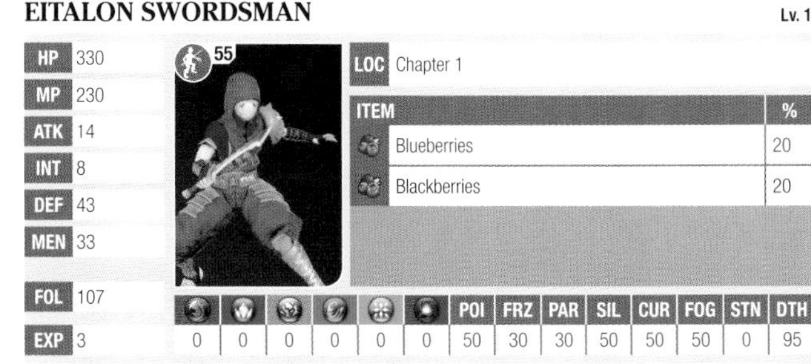

HP	MP	ATK	INT	DEF	MEN	FOL	EXP
330	230	14	8	43	33	107	3

LOC Chapter 1

ITEM	%
Blueberries	20
Blackberries	20

						POI	FRZ	PAR	SIL	CUR	FOG	STN	DTH
0	0	0	0	0	0	50	30	30	50	50	50	0	95

A type of fighter in Resulia's most violent bandit group who prefers to fight with a sword, albeit extremely poorly.

EITALON SURVIVOR
Lv. 43

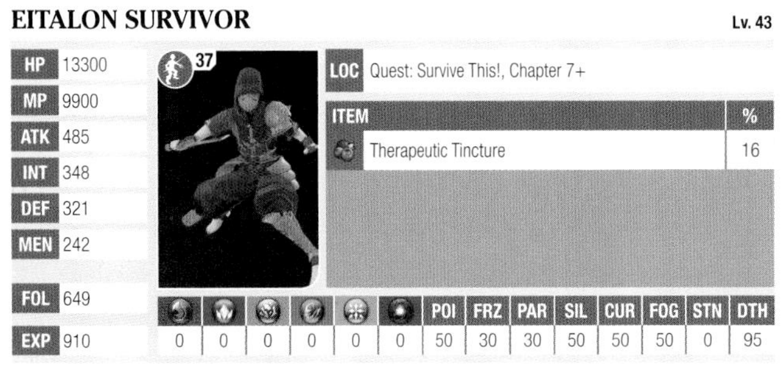

HP	MP	ATK	INT	DEF	MEN	FOL	EXP
13300	9900	485	348	321	242	649	910

LOC Quest: Survive This!, Chapter 7+

ITEM	%
Therapeutic Tincture	16

						POI	FRZ	PAR	SIL	CUR	FOG	STN	DTH
0	0	0	0	0	0	50	30	30	50	50	50	0	95

Having first joined Eitalon because they refused to make an honest living, these peons have no desire to turn over a new leaf now.

EITALON SWORDSMAN
Lv. 13

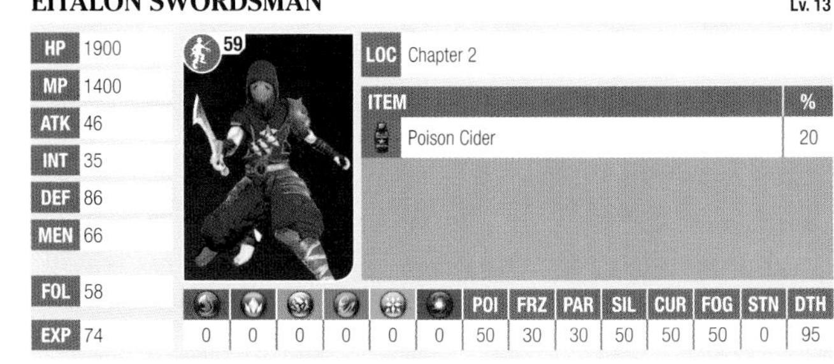

HP	MP	ATK	INT	DEF	MEN	FOL	EXP
1900	1400	46	35	86	66	58	74

LOC Chapter 2

ITEM	%
Poison Cider	20

						POI	FRZ	PAR	SIL	CUR	FOG	STN	DTH
0	0	0	0	0	0	50	30	30	50	50	50	0	95

A type of fighter in Resulia's most violent bandit group who prefers to fight with a sword, albeit extremely poorly.

EITALON SURVIVOR
Lv. 64

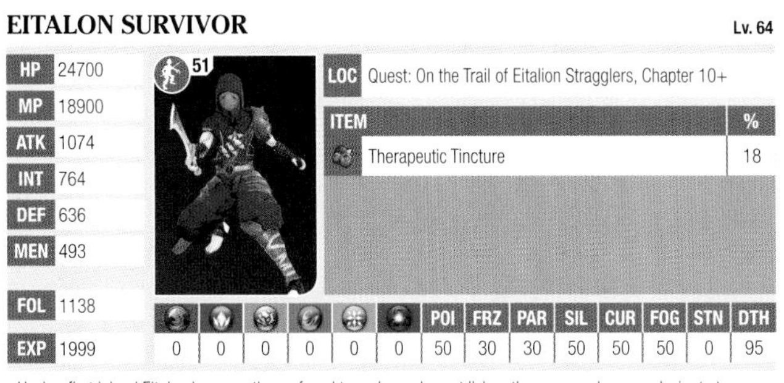

HP	MP	ATK	INT	DEF	MEN	FOL	EXP
24700	18900	1074	764	636	493	1138	1999

LOC Quest: On the Trail of Eitalion Stragglers, Chapter 10+

ITEM	%
Therapeutic Tincture	18

						POI	FRZ	PAR	SIL	CUR	FOG	STN	DTH
0	0	0	0	0	0	50	30	30	50	50	50	0	95

Having first joined Eitalon because they refused to make an honest living, these peons have no desire to turn over a new leaf now.

EITALON'S LEADER
Lv. 16

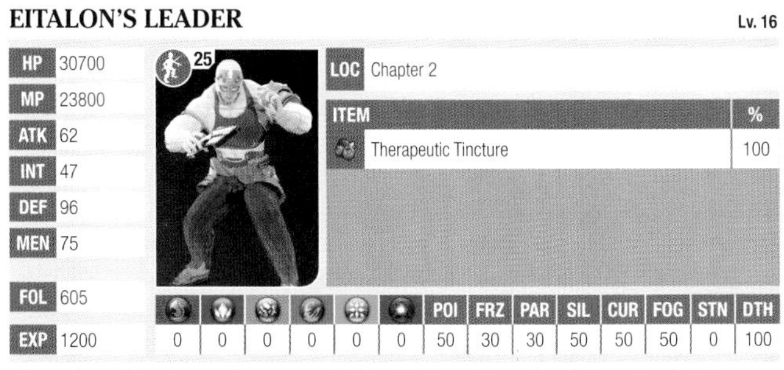

HP	MP	ATK	INT	DEF	MEN	FOL	EXP
30700	23800	62	47	96	75	605	1200

LOC Chapter 2

ITEM	%
Therapeutic Tincture	100

						POI	FRZ	PAR	SIL	CUR	FOG	STN	DTH
0	0	0	0	0	0	50	30	30	50	50	50	0	100

The most powerful and persuasive personage in Eitalon. He silences his unruly underlings with unbridled violence, but also has a silver tongue.

EMMERSON'S ANIMA
Lv. 140

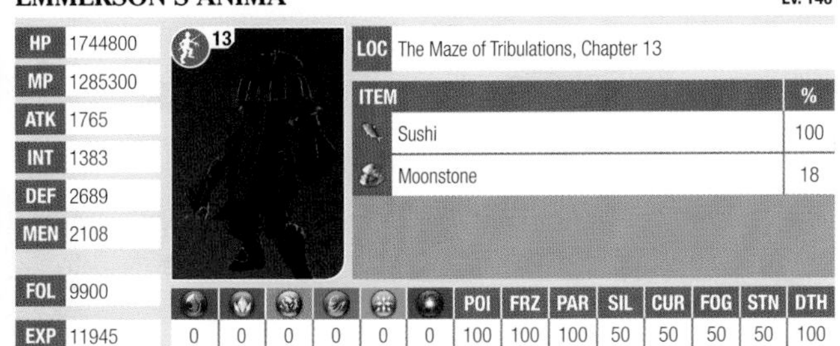

HP	1744800
MP	1285300
ATK	1765
INT	1383
DEF	2689
MEN	2108
FOL	9900
EXP	11945

13

LOC: The Maze of Tribulations, Chapter 13

ITEM	%
Sushi	100
Moonstone	18

						POI	FRZ	PAR	SIL	CUR	FOG	STN	DTH
0	0	0	0	0	0	100	100	100	50	50	50	50	100

An enigmatic being that appears to be a simulacrum of Emmerson's soul. It is blacker than the darkest night with eyes redder than blood worms.

FERIA'S CLONE
Lv. 74

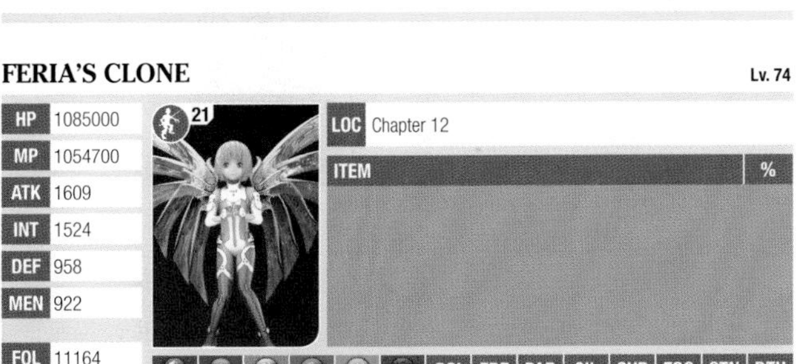

HP	1085000
MP	1054700
ATK	1609
INT	1524
DEF	958
MEN	922
FOL	11164
EXP	23943

21

LOC: Chapter 12

ITEM	%

						POI	FRZ	PAR	SIL	CUR	FOG	STN	DTH
0	0	0	0	0	0	100	100	100	100	100	100	80	100

An identical replication of Relia and Feria, except for the wings that protrude from its back and its utter lack of personality.

FERIA'S CLONE
Lv. 100

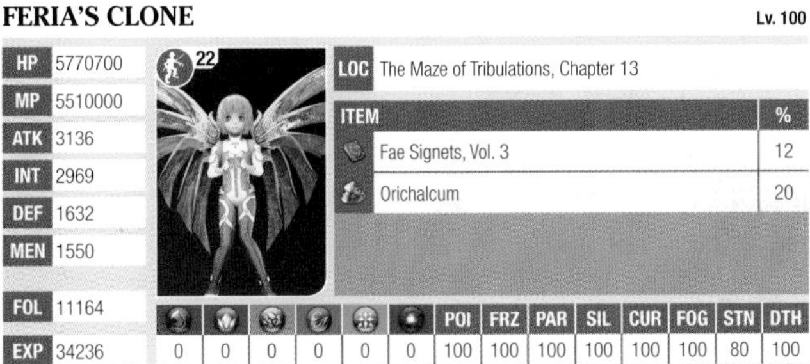

HP	5770700
MP	5510000
ATK	3136
INT	2969
DEF	1632
MEN	1550
FOL	11164
EXP	34236

22

LOC: The Maze of Tribulations, Chapter 13

ITEM	%
Fae Signets, Vol. 3	12
Orichalcum	20

						POI	FRZ	PAR	SIL	CUR	FOG	STN	DTH
0	0	0	0	0	0	100	100	100	100	100	100	80	100

An identical replication of Relia and Feria, except for the wings that protrude from its back and its utter lack of personality.

FIDEL'S ANIMA
Lv. 140

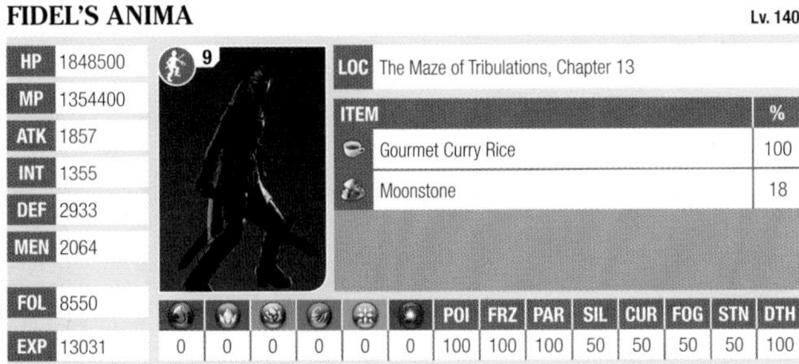

HP	1848500
MP	1354400
ATK	1857
INT	1355
DEF	2933
MEN	2064
FOL	8550
EXP	13031

9

LOC: The Maze of Tribulations, Chapter 13

ITEM	%
Gourmet Curry Rice	100
Moonstone	18

						POI	FRZ	PAR	SIL	CUR	FOG	STN	DTH
0	0	0	0	0	0	100	100	100	50	50	50	50	100

An enigmatic being that appears to be a simulacrum of Fidel's soul. It is blacker than the darkest night with eyes redder than blood worms.

FIORE'S ANIMA
Lv. 140

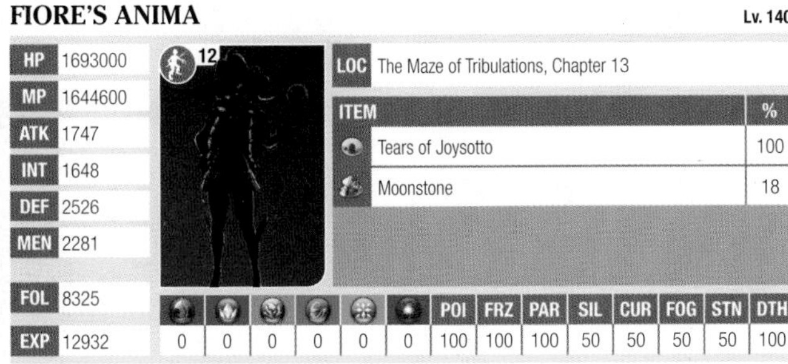

HP	1693000
MP	1644600
ATK	1747
INT	1648
DEF	2526
MEN	2281
FOL	8325
EXP	12932

12

LOC: The Maze of Tribulations, Chapter 13

ITEM	%
Tears of Joysotto	100
Moonstone	18

						POI	FRZ	PAR	SIL	CUR	FOG	STN	DTH
0	0	0	0	0	0	100	100	100	50	50	50	50	100

An enigmatic being that appears to be a simulacrum of Fiore's soul. It is blacker than the darkest night with eyes redder than blood worms.

GENERAL ALMA
Lv. 76

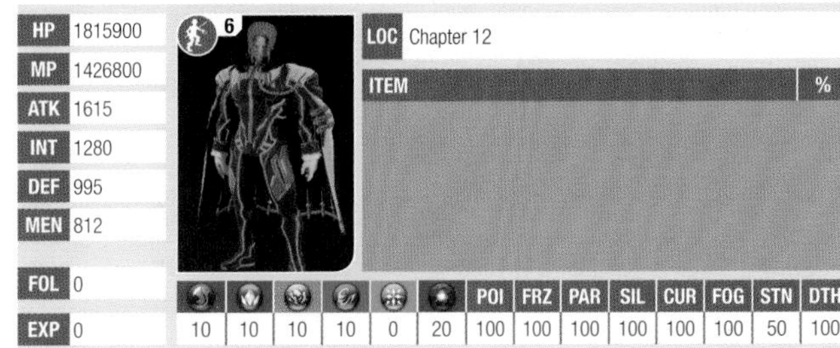

HP	1815900
MP	1426800
ATK	1615
INT	1280
DEF	995
MEN	812
FOL	0
EXP	0

6

LOC: Chapter 12

ITEM	%

						POI	FRZ	PAR	SIL	CUR	FOG	STN	DTH
10	10	10	10	0	20	100	100	100	100	100	100	50	100

The leader of the faction that seceded from Kronos's military. He plans to destroy the federation by using Relia and Feria's symbology.

GENERAL ALMA
Lv. 76

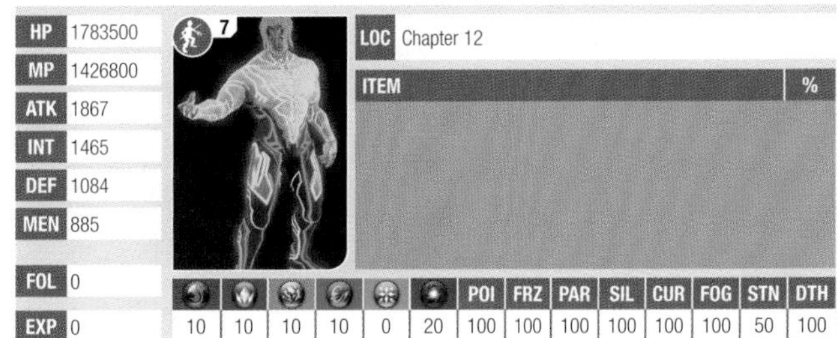

HP	1783500
MP	1426800
ATK	1867
INT	1465
DEF	1084
MEN	885
FOL	0
EXP	0

7

LOC: Chapter 12

ITEM	%

						POI	FRZ	PAR	SIL	CUR	FOG	STN	DTH
10	10	10	10	0	20	100	100	100	100	100	100	50	100

The leader of the faction that seceded from Kronos's military. He plans to destroy the federation by using Relia and Feria's symbology.

GENERAL ALMA
Lv. 100

HP	7321900
MP	5857500
ATK	2966
INT	2350
DEF	1734
MEN	1387
FOL	28000
EXP	34236

8

LOC: The Maze of Tribulations, Chapter 13

ITEM	%
Orichalcum	14

						POI	FRZ	PAR	SIL	CUR	FOG	STN	DTH
10	10	10	10	0	20	100	100	100	100	100	100	50	100

The leader of the faction that seceded from Kronos's military. He plans to destroy the federation by using Relia and Feria's symbology.

GREAT SCUMBAG
Lv. 53

HP	19800
MP	15400
ATK	707
INT	548
DEF	531
MEN	434
FOL	830
EXP	1297

5

LOC: The Resulian Plains, Chapter 9+; The Cathedral of Oblivion, Chapter 11+

ITEM	%
Alchemist's Water	14
Fermentation Pot	16
High-Strength Adhesive	18
Faerie Embroidery Thread	12

						POI	FRZ	PAR	SIL	CUR	FOG	STN	DTH
0	0	0	0	0	0	100	100	50	100	100	100	50	95

The scummiest of scum, he would betray himself if only he could. By scumbag standards, he is more than worthy of the title "great."

GUERRILLA
Lv. 64

HP	25200
MP	19300
ATK	1280
INT	955
DEF	636
MEN	493
FOL	1115
EXP	2144

52

LOC: Quest: Garrote the Guerrillas, Chapter 10+

ITEM	%
Gold	16

						POI	FRZ	PAR	SIL	CUR	FOG	STN	DTH
0	0	0	0	0	0	50	30	30	50	50	50	0	95

A survivor of the conflict with Resulia who refuses to admit Trei'kur's defeat, and has vowed to restore the desert nation to glory.

GUNTER

Lv. 80

HP	1455400
MP	1152400
ATK	1719
INT	1269
DEF	1420
MEN	1160
FOL	8550
EXP	8364

28

LOC: The Maze of Tribulations, Chapter 13

ITEM	%
Hamburg Steak	100
Orichalcum	20

						POI	FRZ	PAR	SIL	CUR	FOG	STN	DTH
0	0	0	0	0	0	100	100	50	100	50	50	50	100

A ranger under Victor's command in the King's Chosen. His role in the unit is to charge in and do as much damage as possible.

HANA

Lv. 80

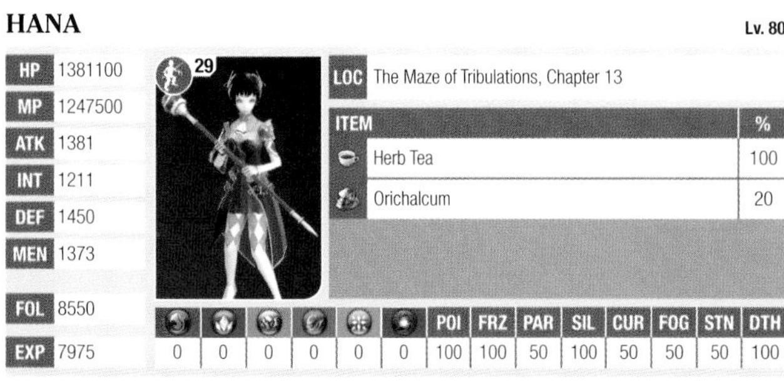

HP	1381100
MP	1247500
ATK	1381
INT	1211
DEF	1450
MEN	1373
FOL	8550
EXP	7975

29

LOC: The Maze of Tribulations, Chapter 13

ITEM	%
Herb Tea	100
Orichalcum	20

						POI	FRZ	PAR	SIL	CUR	FOG	STN	DTH
0	0	0	0	0	0	100	100	50	100	50	50	50	100

A relatively young subordinate of Victor's in the King's Chosen. At 22, she is charged with supporting the group with signeturgy.

HANNAH THE RAPTUROUS

Lv. 60

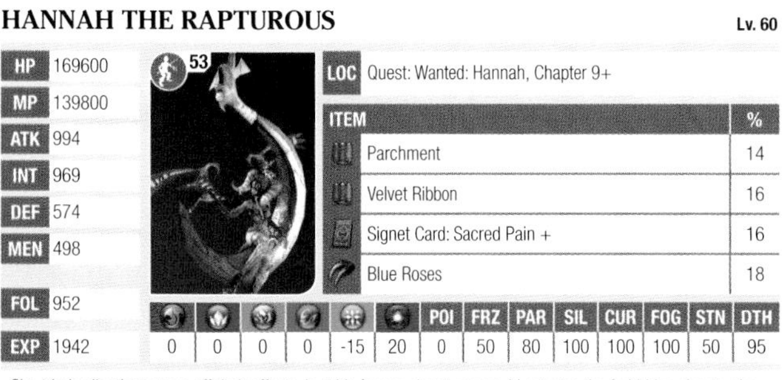

HP	169600
MP	139800
ATK	994
INT	969
DEF	574
MEN	498
FOL	952
EXP	1942

53

LOC: Quest: Wanted: Hannah, Chapter 9+

ITEM	%
Parchment	14
Velvet Ribbon	16
Signet Card: Sacred Pain +	16
Blue Roses	18

						POI	FRZ	PAR	SIL	CUR	FOG	STN	DTH
0	0	0	0	-15	20	0	50	80	100	100	100	50	95

She tried valiantly to stave off their effects, but this former signeturge could not stop the forbidden signets she imbued from transforming her.

IDEALISTIC INSURGENT

Lv. 67

HP	28600
MP	22400
ATK	1299
INT	932
DEF	680
MEN	523
FOL	1434
EXP	2234

54

LOC: Quest: War and Peace, Chapter 11+

ITEM	%
Mythril	14

						POI	FRZ	PAR	SIL	CUR	FOG	STN	DTH
0	0	0	0	0	0	50	30	30	50	50	50	0	95

This vocal anti-war activist has snapped and resorted to violence after the king ignored yet another plea to end the war peacefully.

KRONOS AUTHORITY

Lv. 63

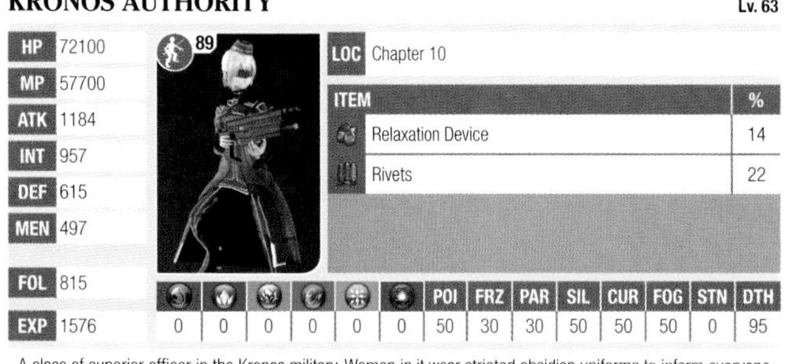

HP	72100
MP	57700
ATK	1184
INT	957
DEF	615
MEN	497
FOL	815
EXP	1576

89

LOC: Chapter 10

ITEM	%
Relaxation Device	14
Rivets	22

						POI	FRZ	PAR	SIL	CUR	FOG	STN	DTH
0	0	0	0	0	0	50	30	30	50	50	50	0	95

A class of superior officer in the Kronos military. Women in it wear striated obsidian uniforms to inform everyone of their high rank.

KRONOS AUTHORITY

Lv. 71

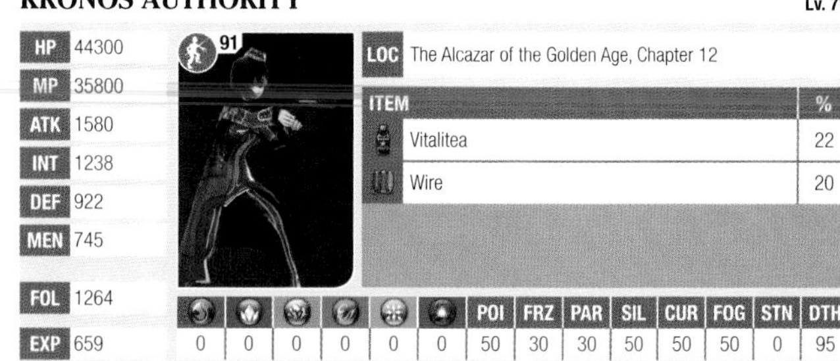

HP	44300
MP	35800
ATK	1580
INT	1238
DEF	922
MEN	745
FOL	1264
EXP	659

91

LOC: The Alcazar of the Golden Age, Chapter 12

ITEM	%
Vitalitea	22
Wire	20

						POI	FRZ	PAR	SIL	CUR	FOG	STN	DTH
0	0	0	0	0	0	50	30	30	50	50	50	0	95

A class of superior officer in the Kronos military. Women in it wear striated obsidian uniforms to inform everyone of their high rank.

KRONOS COMMANDER

Lv. 64

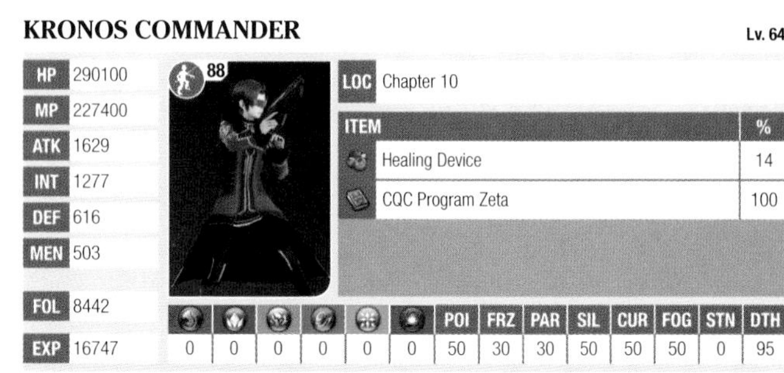

HP	290100
MP	227400
ATK	1629
INT	1277
DEF	616
MEN	503
FOL	8442
EXP	16747

88

LOC: Chapter 10

ITEM	%
Healing Device	14
CQC Program Zeta	100

						POI	FRZ	PAR	SIL	CUR	FOG	STN	DTH
0	0	0	0	0	0	50	30	30	50	50	50	0	95

An elite officer in Kronos's military. People of this station wear long, black coats as evidence of their superiority.

KRONOS COMMANDER

Lv. 71

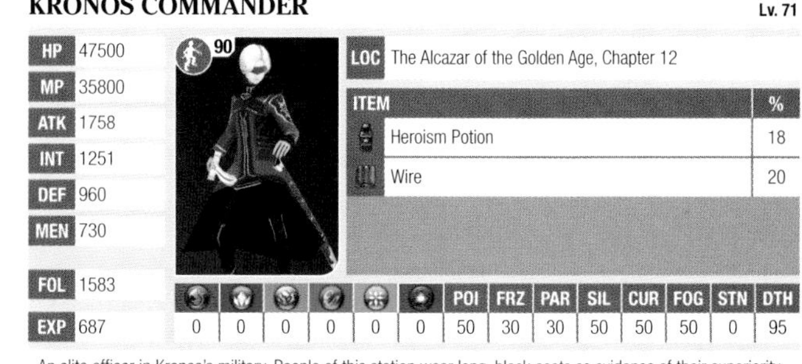

HP	47500
MP	35800
ATK	1758
INT	1251
DEF	960
MEN	730
FOL	1583
EXP	687

90

LOC: The Alcazar of the Golden Age, Chapter 12

ITEM	%
Heroism Potion	18
Wire	20

						POI	FRZ	PAR	SIL	CUR	FOG	STN	DTH
0	0	0	0	0	0	50	30	30	50	50	50	0	95

An elite officer in Kronos's military. People of this station wear long, black coats as evidence of their superiority.

KRONOS GUNNER

Lv. 44

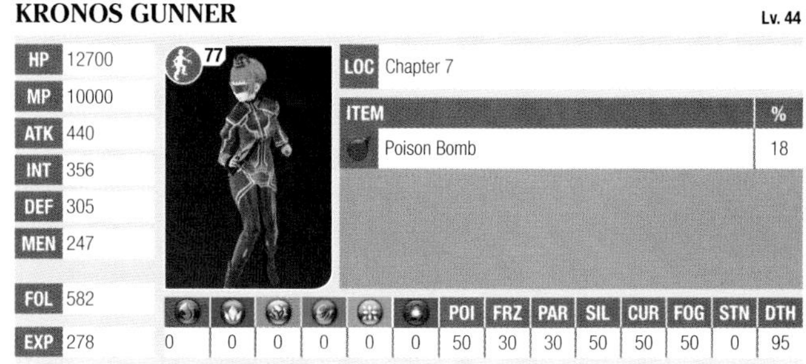

HP	12700
MP	10000
ATK	440
INT	356
DEF	305
MEN	247
FOL	582
EXP	278

77

LOC: Chapter 7

ITEM	%
Poison Bomb	18

						POI	FRZ	PAR	SIL	CUR	FOG	STN	DTH
0	0	0	0	0	0	50	30	30	50	50	50	0	95

Female rifleman in the Kronos military. During close-range combat, they adeptly employ their rock-hard fists—never giving foes any quarter.

KRONOS GUNNER

Lv. 62

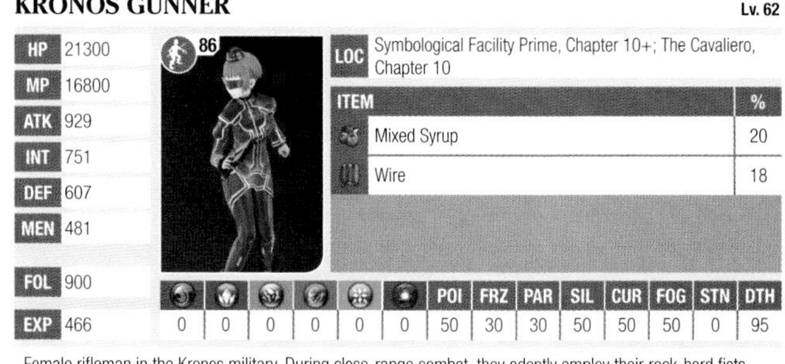

HP	21300
MP	16800
ATK	929
INT	751
DEF	607
MEN	481
FOL	900
EXP	466

86

LOC: Symbological Facility Prime, Chapter 10+; The Cavaliero, Chapter 10

ITEM	%
Mixed Syrup	20
Wire	18

						POI	FRZ	PAR	SIL	CUR	FOG	STN	DTH
0	0	0	0	0	0	50	30	30	50	50	50	0	95

Female rifleman in the Kronos military. During close-range combat, they adeptly employ their rock-hard fists—never giving foes any quarter.

KRONOS RANGER

Lv. 32

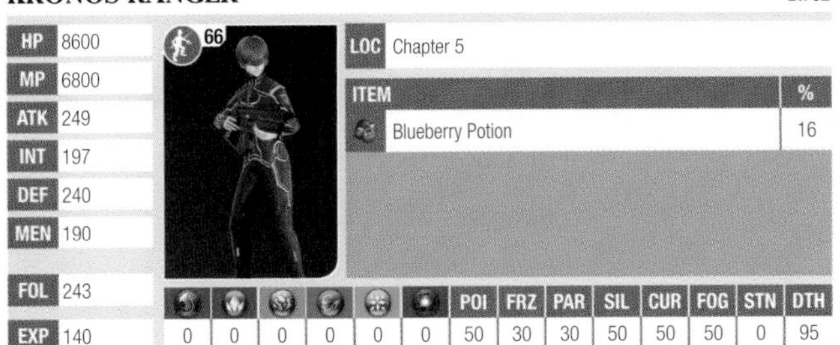

Stat	Value
HP	8600
MP	6800
ATK	249
INT	197
DEF	240
MEN	190
FOL	243
EXP	140

66

LOC: Chapter 5

ITEM	%
Blueberry Potion	16

						POI	FRZ	PAR	SIL	CUR	FOG	STN	DTH
0	0	0	0	0	0	50	30	30	50	50	50	0	95

Like riflemen, rangers employ those strange weapons that project light. They never fight in close, though, always shooting from a distance.

KRONOS RANGER

Lv. 44

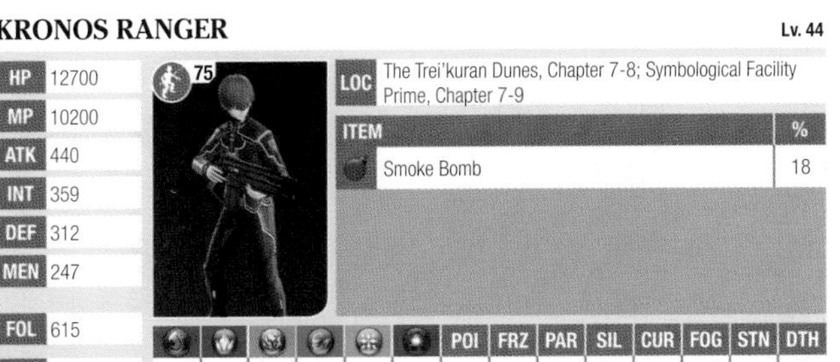

Stat	Value
HP	12700
MP	10200
ATK	440
INT	359
DEF	312
MEN	247
FOL	615
EXP	300

75

LOC: The Trei'kuran Dunes, Chapter 7-8; Symbological Facility Prime, Chapter 7-9

ITEM	%
Smoke Bomb	18

						POI	FRZ	PAR	SIL	CUR	FOG	STN	DTH
0	0	0	0	0	0	50	30	30	50	50	50	0	95

Like riflemen, rangers employ those strange weapons that project light. They never fight in close, though, always shooting from a distance.

KRONOS RANGER

Lv. 63

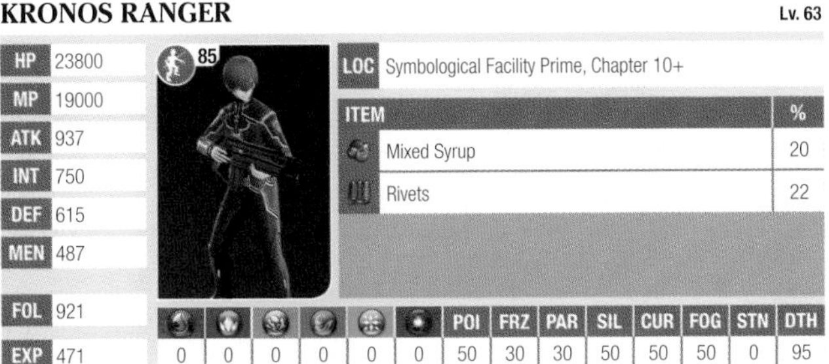

Stat	Value
HP	23800
MP	19000
ATK	937
INT	750
DEF	615
MEN	487
FOL	921
EXP	471

85

LOC: Symbological Facility Prime, Chapter 10+

ITEM	%
Mixed Syrup	20
Rivets	22

						POI	FRZ	PAR	SIL	CUR	FOG	STN	DTH
0	0	0	0	0	0	50	30	30	50	50	50	0	95

Like riflemen, rangers employ those strange weapons that project light. They never fight in close, though, always shooting from a distance.

KRONOS RIFLEMAN

Lv. 44

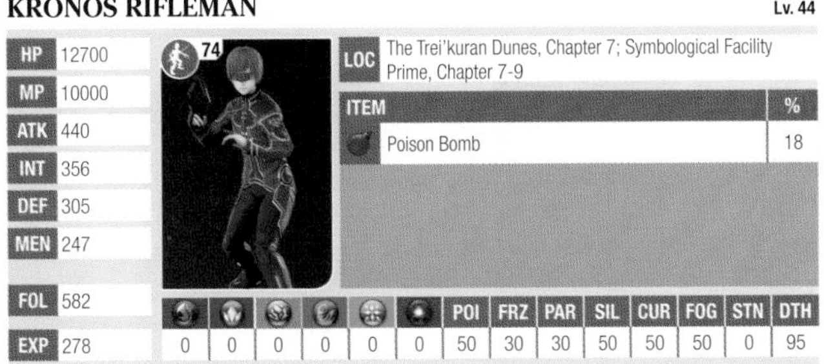

Stat	Value
HP	12700
MP	10000
ATK	440
INT	356
DEF	305
MEN	247
FOL	582
EXP	278

74

LOC: The Trei'kuran Dunes, Chapter 7; Symbological Facility Prime, Chapter 7-9

ITEM	%
Poison Bomb	18

						POI	FRZ	PAR	SIL	CUR	FOG	STN	DTH
0	0	0	0	0	0	50	30	30	50	50	50	0	95

These operatives in the Kronos army mostly rely on enigmatic light-emitting firearms, but use their bare hands in melee fights.

KRONOS SCHOLAR

Lv. 44

Stat	Value
HP	12300
MP	10700
ATK	436
INT	392
DEF	296
MEN	285
FOL	521
EXP	291

76

LOC: The Trei'kuran Dunes, Chapter 7-8

ITEM	%
Damascus Steel	14
Signet Card: Shadow Needles +	16

						POI	FRZ	PAR	SIL	CUR	FOG	STN	DTH
0	0	0	0	0	0	50	30	30	50	50	50	0	95

A Kronos military academic who performed ability-enhancing experiments that left her in constant pain and her heart on the brink of failure.

KRONOS SCHOLAR

Lv. 63

Stat	Value
HP	23000
MP	19600
ATK	928
INT	812
DEF	596
MEN	563
FOL	847
EXP	519

87

LOC: Symbological Facility Prime, Chapter 10+; The Cavaliero, Chapter 10

ITEM	%
Blackberry Potion	18
Signet Card: Shadow Needles +	18
Signet Card: Radiant Lancer +	18

						POI	FRZ	PAR	SIL	CUR	FOG	STN	DTH
0	0	0	0	0	0	50	30	30	50	50	50	0	95

A Kronos military academic who performed ability-enhancing experiments that left her in constant pain and her heart on the brink of failure.

KRONOS SCHOLAR

Lv. 71

Stat	Value
HP	43800
MP	36500
ATK	1532
INT	1380
DEF	903
MEN	837
FOL	1162
EXP	631

92

LOC: The Alcazar of the Golden Age, Chapter 12

ITEM	%
Acuity Potion	22
Signet Card: Shadow Needles +	18
Signet Card: Dark Devourer +	12

						POI	FRZ	PAR	SIL	CUR	FOG	STN	DTH
0	0	0	0	0	0	50	30	30	50	50	50	0	95

A Kronos military academic who performed ability-enhancing experiments that left her in constant pain and her heart on the brink of failure.

KRONOS SOLDIER

Lv. 32

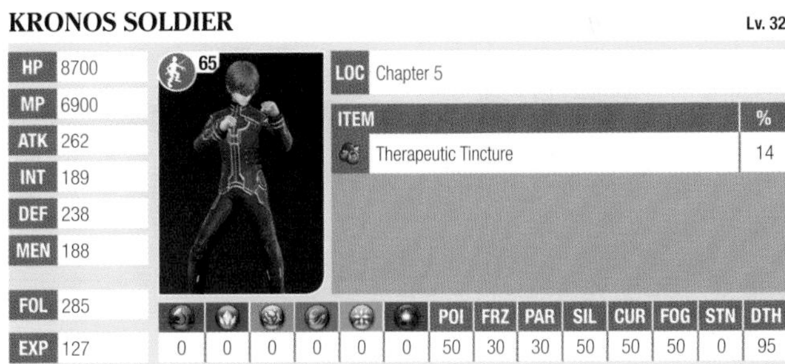

Stat	Value
HP	8700
MP	6900
ATK	262
INT	189
DEF	238
MEN	188
FOL	285
EXP	127

65

LOC: Chapter 5

ITEM	%
Therapeutic Tincture	14

						POI	FRZ	PAR	SIL	CUR	FOG	STN	DTH
0	0	0	0	0	0	50	30	30	50	50	50	0	95

Infantrymen in the Kronos military are barely human in the sense that they are trained to concentrate solely on eliminating their targets.

KRONOS SOLDIER

Lv. 44

Stat	Value
HP	12800
MP	10000
ATK	477
INT	356
DEF	315
MEN	244
FOL	717
EXP	322

73

LOC: The Trei'kuran Dunes, Chapter 7-8; Symbological Facility Prime, Chapter 7-9

ITEM	%
Damascus Steel	14

						POI	FRZ	PAR	SIL	CUR	FOG	STN	DTH
0	0	0	0	0	0	50	30	30	50	50	50	0	95

Infantrymen in the Kronos military are barely human in the sense that they are trained to concentrate solely on eliminating their targets.

KRONOS SOLDIER

Lv. 62

Stat	Value
HP	22600
MP	17000
ATK	968
INT	720
DEF	607
MEN	471
FOL	1046
EXP	448

83

LOC: The Cavaliero, Chapter 10

ITEM	%
Blueberry Potion	18
Rivets	20

						POI	FRZ	PAR	SIL	CUR	FOG	STN	DTH
0	0	0	0	0	0	50	30	30	50	50	50	0	95

Infantrymen in the Kronos military are barely human in the sense that they are trained to concentrate solely on eliminating their targets.

KRONOS SOLDIER

Lv. 62

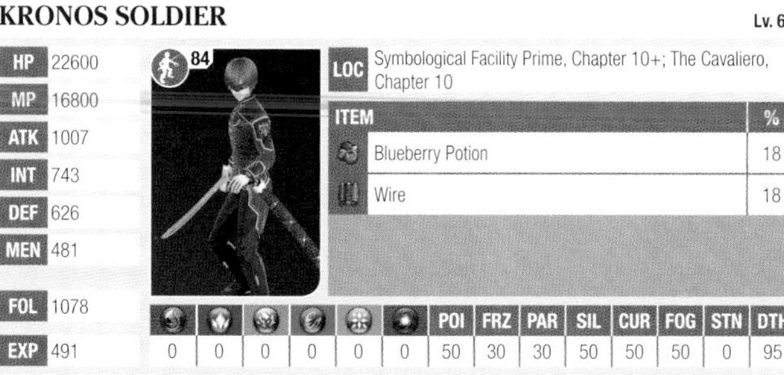

Stat	Value
HP	22600
MP	16800
ATK	1007
INT	743
DEF	626
MEN	481
FOL	1078
EXP	491

84

LOC Symbological Facility Prime, Chapter 10+; The Cavaliero, Chapter 10

ITEM	%
Blueberry Potion	18
Wire	18

						POI	FRZ	PAR	SIL	CUR	FOG	STN	DTH
0	0	0	0	0	0	50	30	30	50	50	50	0	95

Infantrymen in the Kronos military are barely human in the sense that they are trained to concentrate solely on eliminating their targets.

PAVINE

Lv. 33

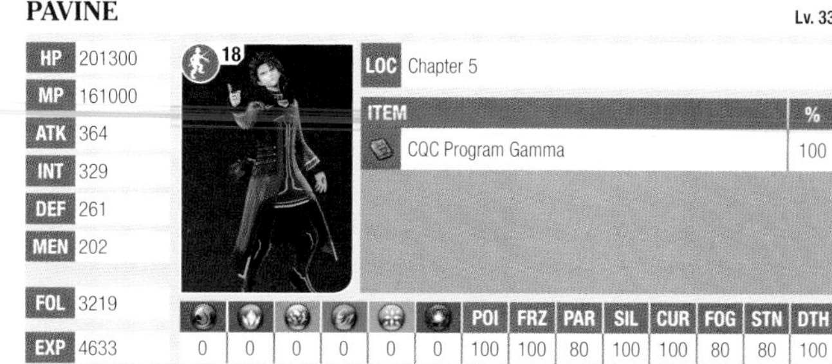

Stat	Value
HP	201300
MP	161000
ATK	364
INT	329
DEF	261
MEN	202
FOL	3219
EXP	4633

18

LOC Chapter 5

ITEM	%
CQC Program Gamma	100

						POI	FRZ	PAR	SIL	CUR	FOG	STN	DTH
0	0	0	0	0	0	100	100	80	100	100	80	80	100

A high-ranking offier in Kronos's military. He has been ordered to take Relia away from Fidel's group.

MIKI'S ANIMA

Lv. 140

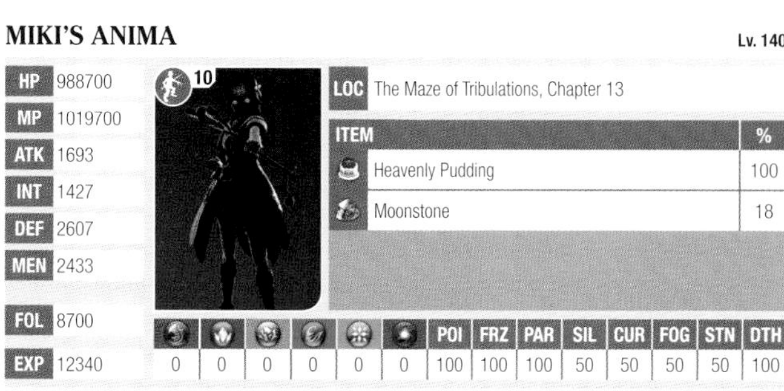

Stat	Value
HP	988700
MP	1019700
ATK	1693
INT	1427
DEF	2607
MEN	2433
FOL	8700
EXP	12340

10

LOC The Maze of Tribulations, Chapter 13

ITEM	%
Heavenly Pudding	100
Moonstone	18

						POI	FRZ	PAR	SIL	CUR	FOG	STN	DTH
0	0	0	0	0	0	100	100	100	50	50	50	50	100

An enigmatic being that appears to be a simulacrum of Miki's soul. It is blacker than the darkest night with eyes redder than blood worms.

PAVINE

Lv. 80

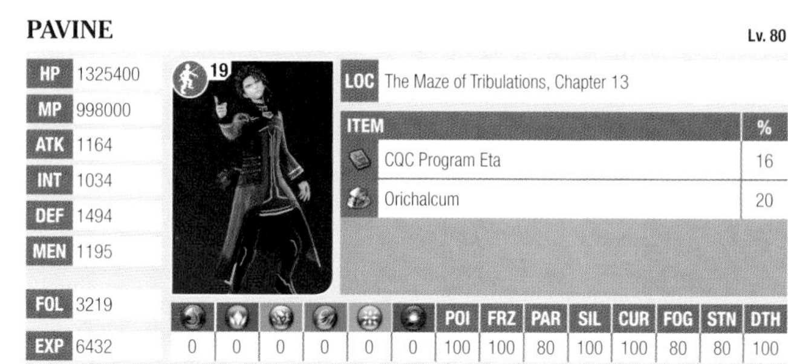

Stat	Value
HP	1325400
MP	998000
ATK	1164
INT	1034
DEF	1494
MEN	1195
FOL	3219
EXP	6432

19

LOC The Maze of Tribulations, Chapter 13

ITEM	%
CQC Program Eta	16
Orichalcum	20

						POI	FRZ	PAR	SIL	CUR	FOG	STN	DTH
0	0	0	0	0	0	100	100	80	100	100	80	80	100

A high-ranking offier in Kronos's military. He has been ordered to take Relia away from Fidel's group.

OCHVA

Lv. 19

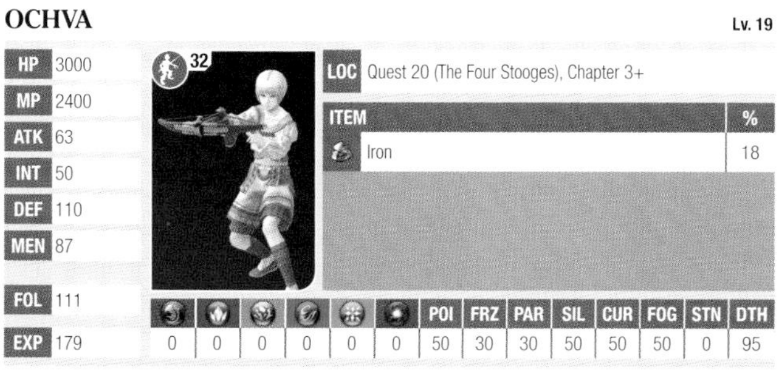

Stat	Value
HP	3000
MP	2400
ATK	63
INT	50
DEF	110
MEN	87
FOL	111
EXP	179

32

LOC Quest 20 (The Four Stooges), Chapter 3+

ITEM	%
Iron	18

						POI	FRZ	PAR	SIL	CUR	FOG	STN	DTH
0	0	0	0	0	0	50	30	30	50	50	50	0	95

A man come to ruin the Camuze Training Hall's reputation. A barber by trade, he has a penchant for fixing his bangs when they go astray.

RIDICULER

Lv. 39

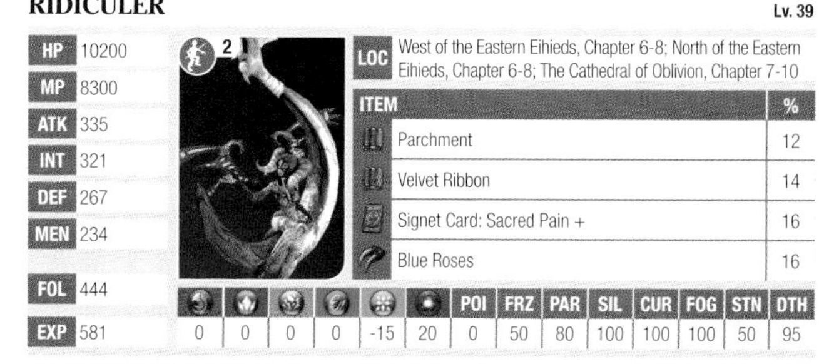

Stat	Value
HP	10200
MP	8300
ATK	335
INT	321
DEF	267
MEN	234
FOL	444
EXP	581

2

LOC West of the Eastern Eihieds, Chapter 6-8; North of the Eastern Eihieds, Chapter 6-8; The Cathedral of Oblivion, Chapter 7-10

ITEM	%
Parchment	12
Velvet Ribbon	14
Signet Card: Sacred Pain +	16
Blue Roses	16

						POI	FRZ	PAR	SIL	CUR	FOG	STN	DTH
0	0	0	0	-15	20	0	50	80	100	100	100	50	95

A seductive lesser demon that appears on moonlit nights. Once it lays eyes on a man, his fate is sealed; he will not live to see the sun rise.

OCHVA

Lv. 38

Stat	Value
HP	39800
MP	32500
ATK	383
INT	303
DEF	276
MEN	218
FOL	517
EXP	706

39

LOC Quest: The Four Stooges Strike Again, Chapter 6+

ITEM	%
Silver	18

						POI	FRZ	PAR	SIL	CUR	FOG	STN	DTH
0	0	0	0	0	0	50	30	30	50	50	50	0	95

A man come to ruin the Camuze Training Hall's reputation. A barber by trade, he has a penchant for fixing his bangs when they go astray.

SERIOUS CAPTAIN AARON

Lv. 100

Stat	Value
HP	3102500
MP	2457200
ATK	2529
INT	2110
DEF	1666
MEN	1360
FOL	100000
EXP	32939

20

LOC The Maze of Tribulations, Chapter 13

ITEM	%
Mental Stimulant	50
Physical Stimulant	50
Orichalcum	20

						POI	FRZ	PAR	SIL	CUR	FOG	STN	DTH
0	0	0	0	0	0	80	100	50	100	100	80	50	100

The captain of the Kronos vessel Darivolos. He cannot abide the fact that Emmerson comes from the most famous family in the federation.

OCHVA

Lv. 58

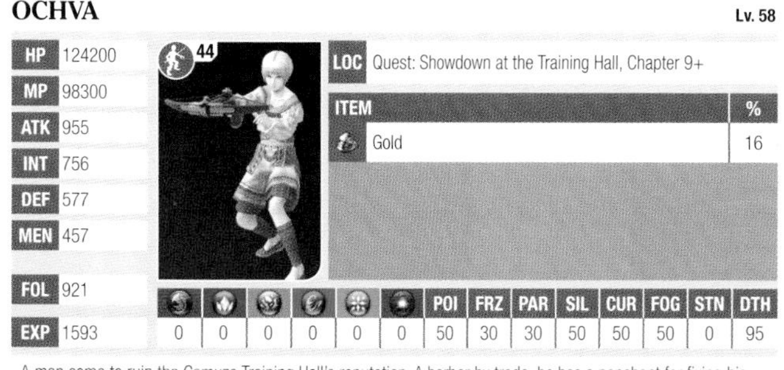

Stat	Value
HP	124200
MP	98300
ATK	955
INT	756
DEF	577
MEN	457
FOL	921
EXP	1593

44

LOC Quest: Showdown at the Training Hall, Chapter 9+

ITEM	%
Gold	16

						POI	FRZ	PAR	SIL	CUR	FOG	STN	DTH
0	0	0	0	0	0	50	30	30	50	50	50	0	95

A man come to ruin the Camuze Training Hall's reputation. A barber by trade, he has a penchant for fixing his bangs when they go astray.

SUCCUBUS

Lv. 25

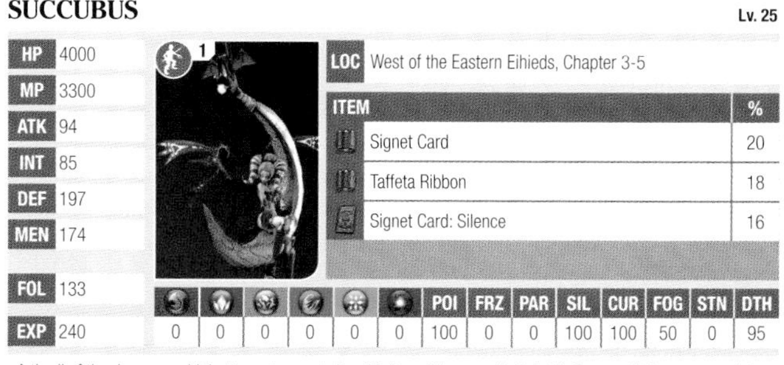

Stat	Value
HP	4000
MP	3300
ATK	94
INT	85
DEF	197
MEN	174
FOL	133
EXP	240

1

LOC West of the Eastern Eihieds, Chapter 3-5

ITEM	%
Signet Card	20
Taffeta Ribbon	18
Signet Card: Silence	16

						POI	FRZ	PAR	SIL	CUR	FOG	STN	DTH
0	0	0	0	0	0	100	0	0	100	100	50	0	95

A thrall of the demon world that tempts men to lie with it, and then quaffs their life force until they are naught but withered sacks of skin.

TED

Lv. 80

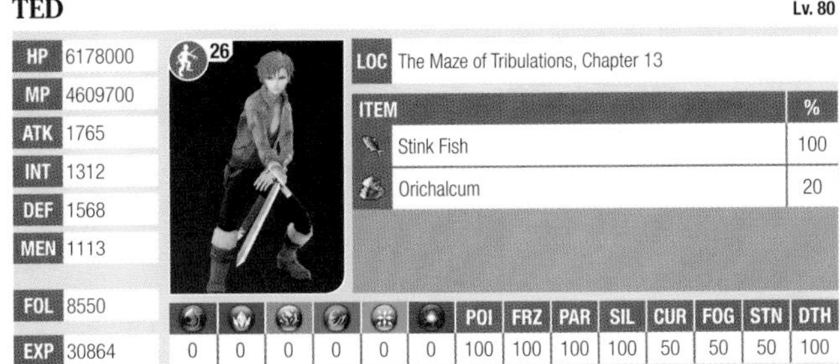

HP	MP	ATK	INT	DEF	MEN	FOL	EXP
6178000	4609700	1765	1312	1568	1113	8550	30864

LOC The Maze of Tribulations, Chapter 13

ITEM	%
Stink Fish	100
Orichalcum	20

						POI	FRZ	PAR	SIL	CUR	FOG	STN	DTH
0	0	0	0	0	0	100	100	100	100	50	50	50	100

Ted grew up with Fidel in Sthal and has practiced the way of the sword under Daril for as long as his childhood friend.

THIEVING SCUMBAG

Lv. 36

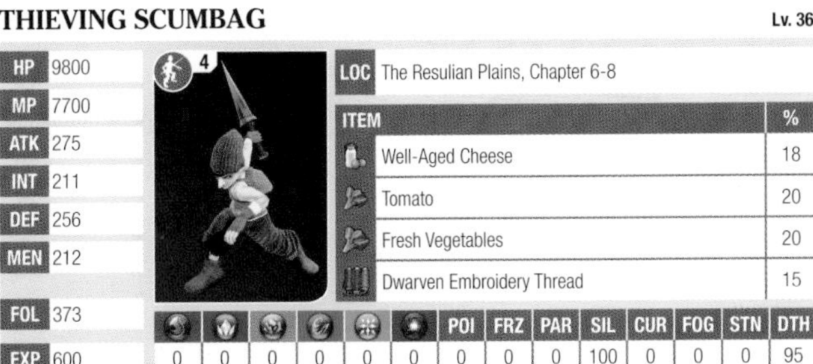

HP	MP	ATK	INT	DEF	MEN	FOL	EXP
9800	7700	275	211	256	212	373	600

LOC The Resulian Plains, Chapter 6-8

ITEM	%
Well-Aged Cheese	18
Tomato	20
Fresh Vegetables	20
Dwarven Embroidery Thread	15

						POI	FRZ	PAR	SIL	CUR	FOG	STN	DTH
0	0	0	0	0	0	0	0	0	100	0	0	0	95

Having been admitted to the clan as a bandit proper, this tiny reprobate's next mission is to prove himself more vile than his peers.

THUNDERSTRUCK OSTHARK

Lv. 28

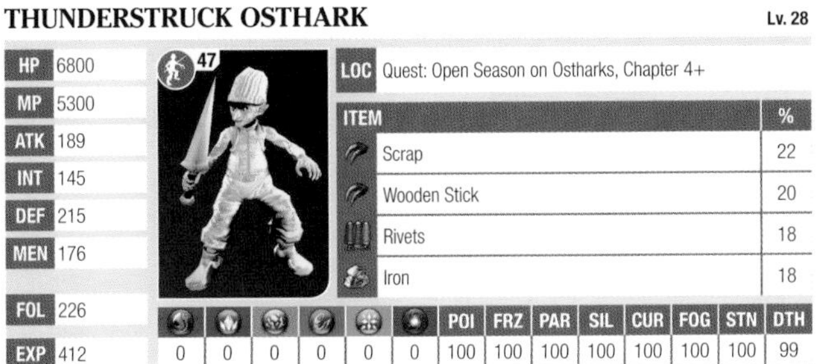

HP	MP	ATK	INT	DEF	MEN	FOL	EXP
6800	5300	189	145	215	176	226	412

LOC Quest: Open Season on Ostharks, Chapter 4+

ITEM	%
Scrap	22
Wooden Stick	20
Rivets	18
Iron	18

						POI	FRZ	PAR	SIL	CUR	FOG	STN	DTH
0	0	0	0	0	0	100	100	100	100	100	100	100	99

A subspecies of ghoul consisting of vagabonds struck by lightning. They do not even realize they are dead, making them rather unpredictable.

TREI'KURAN ARMORED BOWMAN

Lv. 22

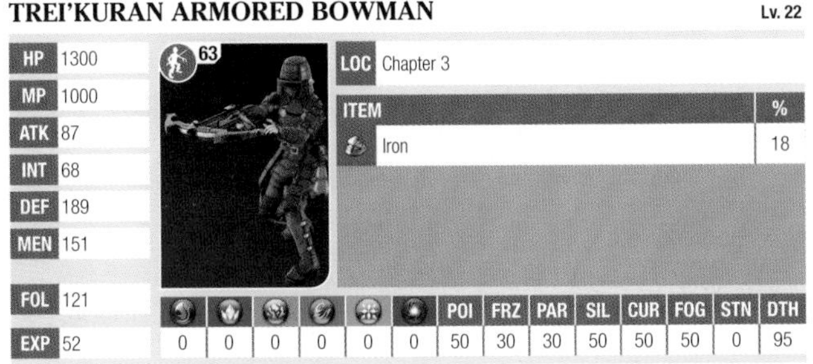

HP	MP	ATK	INT	DEF	MEN	FOL	EXP
1300	1000	87	68	189	151	121	52

LOC Chapter 3

ITEM	%
Iron	18

						POI	FRZ	PAR	SIL	CUR	FOG	STN	DTH
0	0	0	0	0	0	50	30	30	50	50	50	0	95

A marksman so adept with a bow that he can still display stunning accuracy and move with the utmost agility while wearing armor.

TREI'KURAN ARMORED BOWMAN

Lv. 41

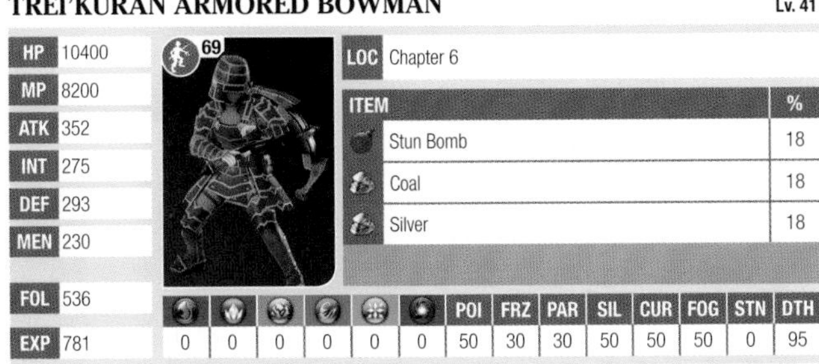

HP	MP	ATK	INT	DEF	MEN	FOL	EXP
10400	8200	352	275	293	230	536	781

LOC Chapter 6

ITEM	%
Stun Bomb	18
Coal	18
Silver	18

						POI	FRZ	PAR	SIL	CUR	FOG	STN	DTH
0	0	0	0	0	0	50	30	30	50	50	50	0	95

A marksman so adept with a bow that he can still display stunning accuracy and move with the utmost agility while wearing armor.

TREI'KURAN ARMORED BOWMAN

Lv. 49

80

HP	MP	ATK	INT	DEF	MEN	FOL	EXP
5300	4300	608	481	340	272	650	315

LOC Trei'kuran Dunes, Chapter 7-8

ITEM	%
Gravity Bomb	16

						POI	FRZ	PAR	SIL	CUR	FOG	STN	DTH
0	0	0	0	0	0	50	30	30	50	50	50	0	95

A marksman so adept with a bow that he can still display stunning accuracy and move with the utmost agility while wearing armor.

TREI'KURAN ARQUEBUSIER

Lv. 30

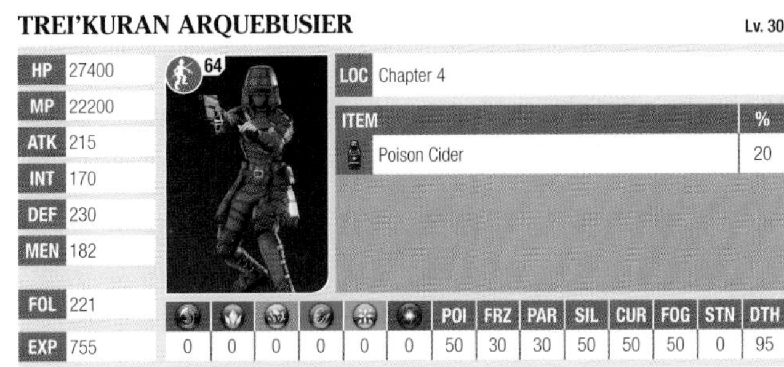

HP	MP	ATK	INT	DEF	MEN	FOL	EXP
27400	22200	215	170	230	182	221	755

LOC Chapter 4

ITEM	%
Poison Cider	20

						POI	FRZ	PAR	SIL	CUR	FOG	STN	DTH
0	0	0	0	0	0	50	30	30	50	50	50	0	95

A class of Trei'kuran soldier who is accomplished with firearms. Despite the country's abject poverty, the guns they brandish are well-crafted.

TREI'KURAN KNIGHT

Lv. 22

HP	MP	ATK	INT	DEF	MEN	FOL	EXP
1400	1000	97	68	199	155	133	58

LOC Chapter 3

ITEM	%
Iron	18

						POI	FRZ	PAR	SIL	CUR	FOG	STN	DTH
0	0	0	0	0	0	50	30	30	50	50	50	0	95

A high-ranking class of warrior in Trei'kur's military who wear suits of armor that show it. They are envied by the rest of the army

TREI'KURAN KNIGHT

Lv. 41

HP	MP	ATK	INT	DEF	MEN	FOL	EXP
10800	8300	384	281	299	235	531	855

LOC Chapter 6

ITEM	%
Iron	20
Silver	18

						POI	FRZ	PAR	SIL	CUR	FOG	STN	DTH
0	0	0	0	0	0	50	30	30	50	50	50	0	95

A high-ranking class of warrior in Trei'kur's military who wear suits of armor that show it. They are envied by the rest of the army.

TREI'KURAN KNIGHT

Lv. 48

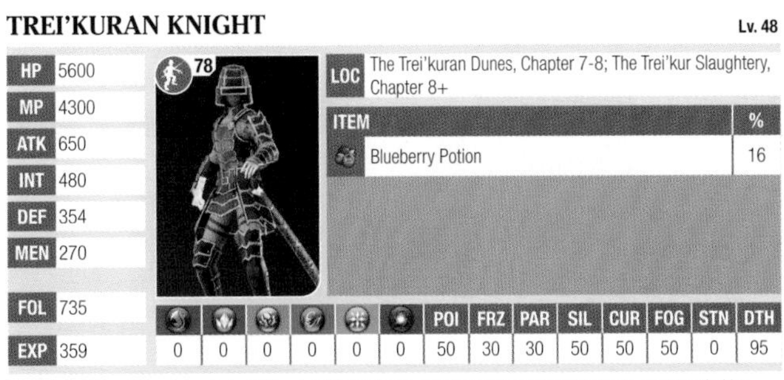

HP	MP	ATK	INT	DEF	MEN	FOL	EXP
5600	4300	650	480	354	270	735	359

LOC The Trei'kuran Dunes, Chapter 7-8; The Trei'kur Slaughtery, Chapter 8+

ITEM	%
Blueberry Potion	16

						POI	FRZ	PAR	SIL	CUR	FOG	STN	DTH
0	0	0	0	0	0	50	30	30	50	50	50	0	95

A high-ranking class of warrior in Trei'kur's military who wear suits of armor that show it. They are envied by the rest of the army.

TREI'KURAN SHARPSHOOTER
Lv. 41

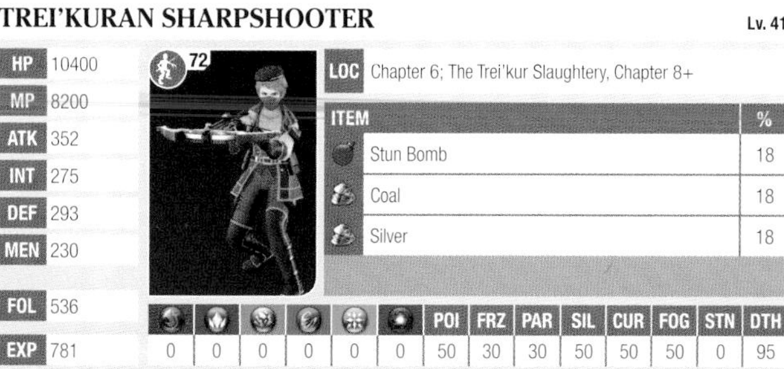

HP	MP	ATK	INT	DEF	MEN	FOL	EXP
10400	8200	352	275	293	230	536	781

LOC Chapter 6; The Trei'kur Slaughtery, Chapter 8+

ITEM	%
Stun Bomb	18
Coal	18
Silver	18

						POI	FRZ	PAR	SIL	CUR	FOG	STN	DTH
0	0	0	0	0	0	50	30	30	50	50	50	0	95

An archer in a certain desert nation's army. Most of these bow wielders' abilities are byproducts of having hunted birds to feed their families.

TREI'KURAN SIGNETURGE
Lv. 50

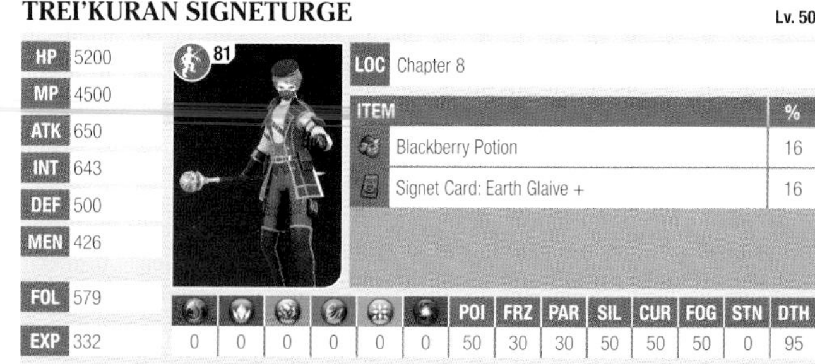

HP	MP	ATK	INT	DEF	MEN	FOL	EXP
5200	4500	650	643	500	426	579	332

LOC Chapter 8

ITEM	%
Blackberry Potion	16
Signet Card: Earth Glaive +	16

						POI	FRZ	PAR	SIL	CUR	FOG	STN	DTH
0	0	0	0	0	0	50	30	30	50	50	50	0	95

A signeturge in the Trei'kuran military. Highly trained, these soldiers can use their arcane powers to either aid others or overpower enemies.

TREI'KURAN SHARPSHOOTER
Lv. 49

HP	MP	ATK	INT	DEF	MEN	FOL	EXP
5300	4300	608	481	340	272	650	315

LOC Chapter 8

ITEM	%
Gravity Bomb	16

						POI	FRZ	PAR	SIL	CUR	FOG	STN	DTH
0	0	0	0	0	0	50	30	30	50	50	50	0	95

An archer in a certain desert nation's army. Most of these bow wielders' abilities are byproducts of having hunted birds to feed their families.

TREI'KURAN SOLDIER
Lv. 41

HP	MP	ATK	INT	DEF	MEN	FOL	EXP
10900	8200	355	267	287	228	572	806

LOC Chapter 6

ITEM	%
Coal	18
Silver	18

						POI	FRZ	PAR	SIL	CUR	FOG	STN	DTH
0	0	0	0	0	0	50	30	30	50	50	50	0	95

A member of Trei'kur's army who will do anything to win. Like general, like subordinate—these soldiers have no qualms about fighting dirty.

TREI'KURAN SIGNETURGE
Lv. 41

HP	MP	ATK	INT	DEF	MEN	FOL	EXP
10100	8500	337	321	281	239	472	822

LOC Chapter 6

ITEM	%
Iron	20
Silver	18

						POI	FRZ	PAR	SIL	CUR	FOG	STN	DTH
0	0	0	0	0	0	50	30	30	50	50	50	0	95

A signeturge in the Trei'kuran military. Highly trained, these soldiers can use their arcane powers to either aid others or overpower enemies.

TYRESOD
Lv. 19

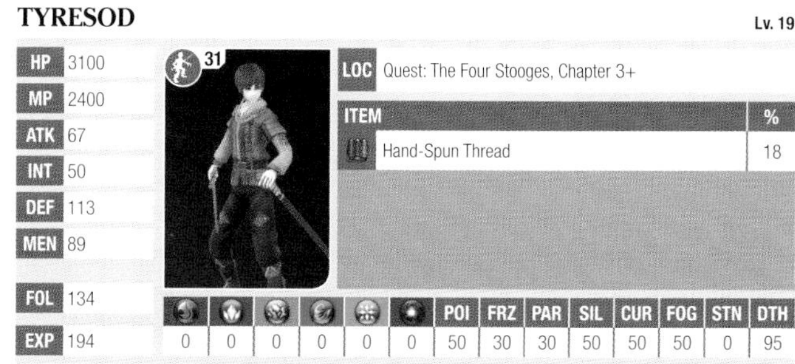

HP	MP	ATK	INT	DEF	MEN	FOL	EXP
3100	2400	67	50	113	89	134	194

LOC Quest: The Four Stooges, Chapter 3+

ITEM	%
Hand-Spun Thread	18

						POI	FRZ	PAR	SIL	CUR	FOG	STN	DTH
0	0	0	0	0	0	50	30	30	50	50	50	0	95

A man come to ruin the reputation of the Camuze Training Hall. So vain is this tailor that no brawl will keep him from flaunting his fashion.

TREI'KURAN SIGNETURGE
Lv. 41

HP	MP	ATK	INT	DEF	MEN	FOL	EXP
10100	8500	337	321	281	239	472	822

LOC The Trei'kur Slaughtery, Chapter 8+

ITEM	%
Iron	20
Silver	18

						POI	FRZ	PAR	SIL	CUR	FOG	STN	DTH
0	0	0	0	0	0	50	30	30	50	50	50	0	95

A signeturge in the Trei'kuran military. Highly trained, these soldiers can use their arcane powers to either aid others or overpower enemies.

TYRESOD
Lv. 38

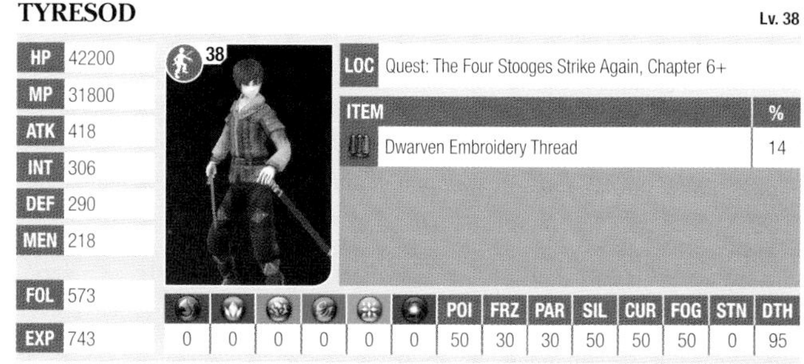

HP	MP	ATK	INT	DEF	MEN	FOL	EXP
42200	31800	418	306	290	218	573	743

LOC Quest: The Four Stooges Strike Again, Chapter 6+

ITEM	%
Dwarven Embroidery Thread	14

						POI	FRZ	PAR	SIL	CUR	FOG	STN	DTH
0	0	0	0	0	0	50	30	30	50	50	50	0	95

A man come to ruin the reputation of the Camuze Training Hall. So vain is this tailor that no brawl will keep him from flaunting his fashion.

TREI'KURAN SIGNETURGE
Lv. 50

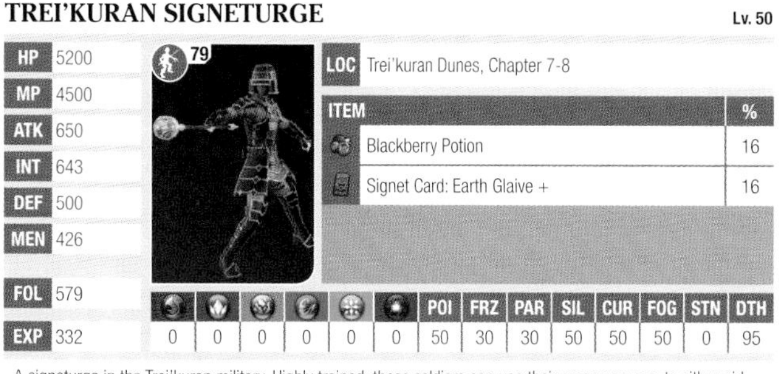

HP	MP	ATK	INT	DEF	MEN	FOL	EXP
5200	4500	650	643	500	426	579	332

LOC Trei'kuran Dunes, Chapter 7-8

ITEM	%
Blackberry Potion	16
Signet Card: Earth Glaive +	16

						POI	FRZ	PAR	SIL	CUR	FOG	STN	DTH
0	0	0	0	0	0	50	30	30	50	50	50	0	95

A signeturge in the Trei'kuran military. Highly trained, these soldiers can use their arcane powers to either aid others or overpower enemies.

TYRESOD
Lv. 58

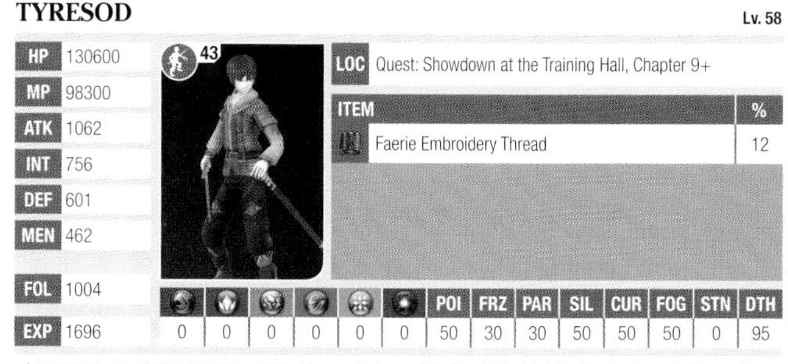

HP	MP	ATK	INT	DEF	MEN	FOL	EXP
130600	98300	1062	756	601	462	1004	1696

LOC Quest: Showdown at the Training Hall, Chapter 9+

ITEM	%
Faerie Embroidery Thread	12

						POI	FRZ	PAR	SIL	CUR	FOG	STN	DTH
0	0	0	0	0	0	50	30	30	50	50	50	0	95

A man come to ruin the reputation of the Camuze Training Hall. So vain is this tailor that no brawl will keep him from flaunting his fashion.

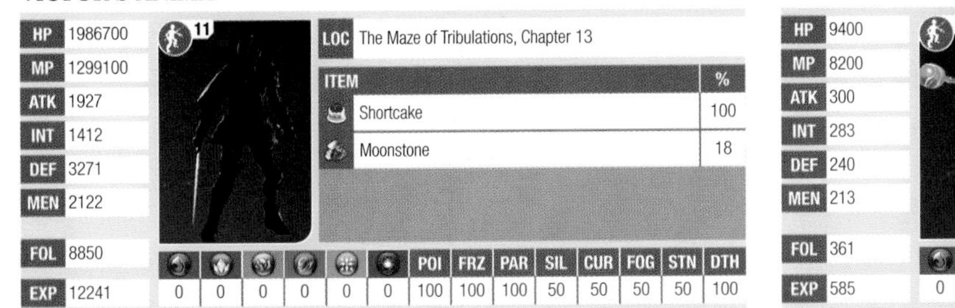

VICTOR'S ANIMA
Lv. 140

HP	MP	ATK	INT	DEF	MEN	FOL	EXP
1986700	1299100	1927	1412	3271	2122	8850	12241

11

LOC: The Maze of Tribulations, Chapter 13

ITEM	%
Shortcake	100
Moonstone	18

						POI	FRZ	PAR	SIL	CUR	FOG	STN	DTH
0	0	0	0	0	0	100	100	100	50	50	50	50	100

An enigmatic being that appears to be a simulacrum of Victor's soul. It is blacker than the darkest night with eyes redder than blood worms.

WALKING CONFLAGRATION
Lv. 34

HP	MP	ATK	INT	DEF	MEN	FOL	EXP
9400	8200	300	283	240	213	361	585

42

LOC: Quest: Subjugation Directive: Walking Conflagrations, Chapter 5+

ITEM	%
Signet Card: Explosion	14

						POI	FRZ	PAR	SIL	CUR	FOG	STN	DTH
0	0	0	0	0	0	50	30	30	50	50	50	0	95

These beasts were originally a rogue band of signeturgical pyromaniacs who eventually lost their souls after committing numerous crimes.

BEASTS

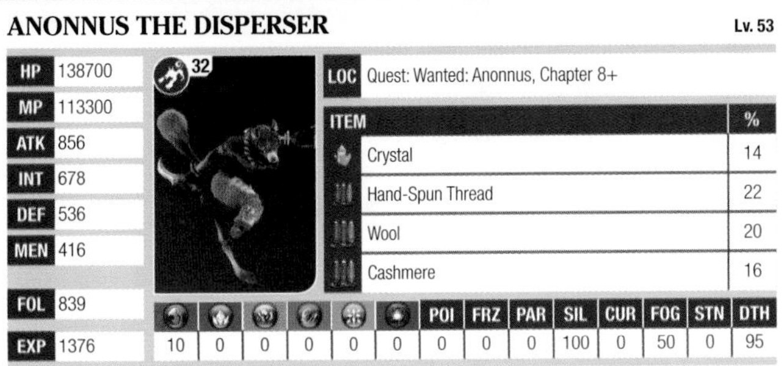

ANONNUS THE DISPERSER
Lv. 53

HP	MP	ATK	INT	DEF	MEN	FOL	EXP
138700	113300	856	678	536	416	839	1376

32

LOC: Quest: Wanted: Anonnus, Chapter 8+

ITEM	%
Crystal	14
Hand-Spun Thread	22
Wool	20
Cashmere	16

						POI	FRZ	PAR	SIL	CUR	FOG	STN	DTH
10	0	0	0	0	0	0	0	0	100	0	50	0	95

A member of an organization promoting a new world order. As all its agents mimic the same Corrupt, no one can tell who their leader is.

ANTLERED TORTOISE
Lv. 60

HP	MP	ATK	INT	DEF	MEN	FOL	EXP
21000	17000	853	629	690	469	803	1366

19

LOC: The Passage on the Cliffs, Chapter 9+; The Court of Minoz, Chapter 9+; The Cathedral of Oblivion

ITEM	%
Tortoise Shell	20
Ice Gem	18
Platinum	16

						POI	FRZ	PAR	SIL	CUR	FOG	STN	DTH
10	-20	10	10	10	10	100	0	100	100	100	100	95	95

This type of testudinate behemoth was previously thought to have gone extinct after generations of having been poaached for its shell.

CHAOS CORPSE CORPORAL
Lv. 28

HP	MP	ATK	INT	DEF	MEN	FOL	EXP
6900	5400	182	147	217	170	196	400

28

LOC: Quest: Wanted: Chaos Corpse Corporals, Chapter 4+

ITEM	%
Ruby	14
Hand-Spun Thread	20
Wool	18
Wolf Fang	20

						POI	FRZ	PAR	SIL	CUR	FOG	STN	DTH
0	10	0	0	0	0	0	50	0	100	0	100	0	95

A member of an undead kobold pack that has only become more cruel in its afterlife. It makes up for its weak eyesight with a sensitive nose.

DASTARDLY SKOUDDE BROTHER
Lv. 28

HP	MP	ATK	INT	DEF	MEN	FOL	EXP
21400	15800	193	147	222	170	231	424

26

LOC: Quest: Wanted: The Skoudde Brothers, Chapter 4+

ITEM	%
Snakeskin	16
Lizardskin	18

						POI	FRZ	PAR	SIL	CUR	FOG	STN	DTH
0	10	0	0	0	0	0	50	0	100	0	0	0	95

A trio of the baddest reptiles ever to bask in the Faykreedian sun. Their intelligence rivals that of pudding, but their strength is unmatched.

DEEP ONE
Lv. 39

HP	MP	ATK	INT	DEF	MEN	FOL	EXP
10100	8100	335	262	276	218	349	485

23

LOC: The Passage on the Cliff, Chapter 6-8; The Coast of Minoz, Chapter 6-8

ITEM	%
Fish Scales	22
Raw Fish	20
Roe	20
Holy Water	18

						POI	FRZ	PAR	SIL	CUR	FOG	STN	DTH
-10	0	0	-10	0	0	50	100	50	50	100	50	0	95

A species of divine fish that can breed with any marine life. Its offspring always lose the traits of the other parent in due time.

DONADELLO THE INDOMITABLE
Lv. 43

HP	MP	ATK	INT	DEF	MEN	FOL	EXP
62400	50500	544	405	365	244	615	1024

27

LOC: Quest: Subjugation Directive: Donadello, Chapter 7+

ITEM	%
Tortoise Shell	20
Shellfish Meat	20
Raw Fish	20

						POI	FRZ	PAR	SIL	CUR	FOG	STN	DTH
0	-20	0	0	0	0	50	0	50	0	0	0	50	95

A tortoise rumored to be as old as time itself and worshiped for centuries as a tutelary deity; in actuality it just eats farmers' crops.

ENVIOUS INVIDIAD
Lv. 68

HP	MP	ATK	INT	DEF	MEN	FOL	EXP
27900	22100	1598	1179	888	688	1188	2184

33

LOC: Quest: Indecent Exposure, Chapter 11+

ITEM	%
Wolf Fang	22
Bushy Fur	20
Prehistoric Meat	22
Fire Gem	20

						POI	FRZ	PAR	SIL	CUR	FOG	STN	DTH
-15	15	0	-10	0	0	0	100	0	0	0	0	0	95

There is arguably no creature that is fluffier or cuter than this fuzz ball. So prized are they that tame ones fetch exhorbitant prices.

FORSAKEN BEAST
Lv. 74

HP	MP	ATK	INT	DEF	MEN	FOL	EXP
313600	221800	1874	1576	948	782	2615	2512

15

LOC: Kronos's Sickle, Chapter 12

ITEM	%
Blank Disk	10
Darkness Gem	20
Shadestone	14

						POI	FRZ	PAR	SIL	CUR	FOG	STN	DTH
0	0	0	0	-15	20	100	100	100	100	100	50	50	95

A luminous canine that guards the parallel dimension Feria created. Its strong jaws, sharp claws, and searing powers annihilate trespassers.

PART 06

GUARDIAN BEAST
Lv. 63

HP	MP	ATK	INT	DEF	MEN	FOL	EXP
138500	99000	1196	986	615	523	1570	1837

LOC Chapter 10

ITEM	%
Blank Disk	10
Light Gem	20
Angelstone	14

						POI	FRZ	PAR	SIL	CUR	FOG	STN	DTH
-10	-10	0	0	10	-10	100	100	100	100	100	50	50	95

A life form created by Kronos to protect its starships. The beast reflects, refracts, and amplifies light to generate powerful laser beams.

HESITANT RIHVNAUT
Lv. 58

HP	MP	ATK	INT	DEF	MEN	FOL	EXP
20900	16000	984	733	572	452	900	1627

LOC Quest: Subjugation Directive: Rihvnauts, Chapter 9+

ITEM	%
Wolf Fang	22

						POI	FRZ	PAR	SIL	CUR	FOG	STN	DTH
0	0	0	0	0	0	100	80	50	50	80	0	50	95

This mousy tiger is fearul of anything that approaches. Thus, its first response in most situations is to sink its fangs into the nearest person.

HORNED TORTOISE
Lv. 21

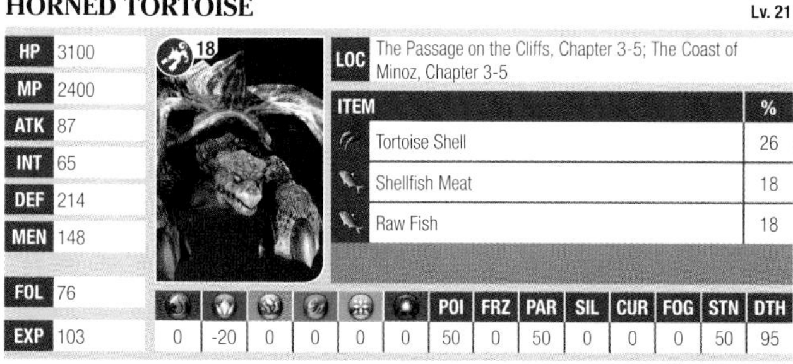

HP	MP	ATK	INT	DEF	MEN	FOL	EXP
3100	2400	87	65	214	148	76	103

LOC The Passage on the Cliffs, Chapter 3-5; The Coast of Minoz, Chapter 3-5

ITEM	%
Tortoise Shell	26
Shellfish Meat	18
Raw Fish	18

						POI	FRZ	PAR	SIL	CUR	FOG	STN	DTH
0	-20	0	0	0	0	50	0	50	0	0	0	50	95

Although most vertebrates were hunted to extinction by insectoids, this species of tortoise survived thanks to its impenetrable shell.

HORNED TURTLE
Lv. 60

HP	MP	ATK	INT	DEF	MEN	FOL	EXP
21000	16800	845	629	684	474	885	1588

LOC Northern Territory of Sohma, Chapter 9-10

ITEM	%
Tortoise Shell	24
Sandfish	18

						POI	FRZ	PAR	SIL	CUR	FOG	STN	DTH
-20	10	0	0	0	0	0	100	50	0	0	0	50	95

A reptile that closely resembles a turtle and thrives on Faykreed. Ponderous horns jut from its shell, into which it retreats when startled.

KOBOLD
Lv. 6

HP	MP	ATK	INT	DEF	MEN	FOL	EXP
350	280	22	18	58	45	31	7

LOC The Coast of Minoz, Chapter 1-2

ITEM	%
Raw Fish	18
Hand-Spun Thread	18
Wolf Fang	18

						POI	FRZ	PAR	SIL	CUR	FOG	STN	DTH
0	10	0	0	0	0	0	50	0	100	0	100	0	95

Kobolds congregate in large groups that seem nigh on endless, but they are also quick to flee when losing. They love shiny things, too.

KOBOLD BANDIT
Lv. 30

HP	MP	ATK	INT	DEF	MEN	FOL	EXP
6900	5500	210	166	230	176	275	453

LOC The Trei'kuran Dunes, Chapter 5; The Cathedral of Oblivion, Chapter 3-6

ITEM	%
Ruby	14
Hand-Spun Thread	20
Wool	18
Wolf Fang	20

						POI	FRZ	PAR	SIL	CUR	FOG	STN	DTH
10	0	0	0	0	0	0	0	0	100	0	50	0	95

An anthropomorphic lupine thief that stalks the desert around Eastern Trei'kur, waiting to pounce upon merchant caravans and lone travelers.

KOBOLD KNAVE
Lv. 59

HP	MP	ATK	INT	DEF	MEN	FOL	EXP
21100	16700	763	617	579	449	908	1357

LOC The Trei'kuran Dunes, Chapter 9+; The Cathedral of Oblivion, Chapter 11+

ITEM	%
Platinum	16
Hand-Spun Thread	22
Wool	20
Cashmere	16

						POI	FRZ	PAR	SIL	CUR	FOG	STN	DTH
0	0	0	10	-10	10	100	100	100	100	100	100	100	95

A particularly foul-mannered thief that resembles a person and a dog. It is nocturnal, preferring to ambush in large packs at night.

KOBOLD RANGER
Lv. 59

HP	MP	ATK	INT	DEF	MEN	FOL	EXP
20800	16500	772	624	579	453	856	1309

LOC Northern Territory of Sohma, Chapter 9-10; The Cathedral of Oblivion, Chapter 11+

ITEM	%
Crystal	14
Hand-Spun Thread	22
Wool	20
Cashmere	16

						POI	FRZ	PAR	SIL	CUR	FOG	STN	DTH
0	0	0	0	0	0	80	80	80	100	100	100	80	95

An upright lupine thief that makes its home in Resulia. It uses its powerful nose to sniff out any treasures adventurers might be carrying.

LAND TURTLE
Lv. 5

HP	MP	ATK	INT	DEF	MEN	FOL	EXP
330	270	22	16	64	44	27	13

LOC The Coast of Minoz, Chapter 1-2

ITEM	%
Tortoise Shell	16
Shellfish Meat	18
Raw Fish	18

						POI	FRZ	PAR	SIL	CUR	FOG	STN	DTH
0	0	10	0	0	0	0	0	0	0	0	0	0	95

A turtle-like reptile that lives near Sthal. Nature's crepehanger, it assumes anything that comes near is hostile and immediately attacks.

LANDSWIMMER
Lv. 20

HP	MP	ATK	INT	DEF	MEN	FOL	EXP
3000	2500	64	50	114	88	76	97

LOC The Passage on the Cliff, Chapter 3-5; The Coast of Minoz, Chapter 3-5

ITEM	%
Fish Scales	18
Raw Fish	18
Roe	18
Holy Water	16

						POI	FRZ	PAR	SIL	CUR	FOG	STN	DTH
-10	0	0	-20	0	0	50	100	0	0	50	50	0	95

This levitating fish thrives near Sthal. Researchers believe it can hover in the air due to its scales possessing anti-gravitational properties.

LEONBLADE

Lv. 54

HP	19900
MP	15600
ATK	734
INT	547
DEF	549
MEN	421
FOL	812
EXP	1214

LOC The Resulian Plains, Chapter 9+

ITEM	%
Wolf Fang	22
Bushy Fur	20
Prehistoric Meat	22
Fire Gem	18

						POI	FRZ	PAR	SIL	CUR	FOG	STN	DTH
0	0	0	0	0	0	100	80	50	50	80	0	50	95

A carnivorous cat that thrived in almost every clime on Faykreed. That is, before it purportedly went extinct centuries ago.

LIZARD COMMANDER

Lv. 20

HP	3200
MP	2400
ATK	66
INT	50
DEF	114
MEN	90
FOL	92
EXP	150

LOC The Resulian Plains, Chapter 3-5

ITEM	%
Lizardskin	18
Longsword	18
Blueberries	20

						POI	FRZ	PAR	SIL	CUR	FOG	STN	DTH
-10	0	0	0	0	0	0	0	0	100	0	0	0	95

As this Resulian bipedal lizard was born and bred for combat, it is a splendid fighter, but also completely ignorant of other facets of life.

LIZARD SHAMAN

Lv. 41

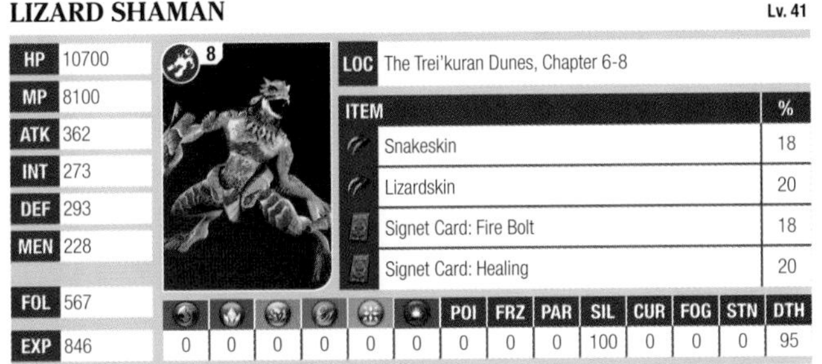

HP	10700
MP	8100
ATK	362
INT	273
DEF	293
MEN	228
FOL	567
EXP	846

LOC The Trei'kuran Dunes, Chapter 6-8

ITEM	%
Snakeskin	18
Lizardskin	20
Signet Card: Fire Bolt	18
Signet Card: Healing	20

						POI	FRZ	PAR	SIL	CUR	FOG	STN	DTH
0	0	0	0	0	0	0	0	0	100	0	0	0	95

This kind of lizardman lives around the outpost of Eastern Trei'kur. It prefers to stand away from the front line, aiding the vanguard.

LIZARD SOLDIER

Lv. 10

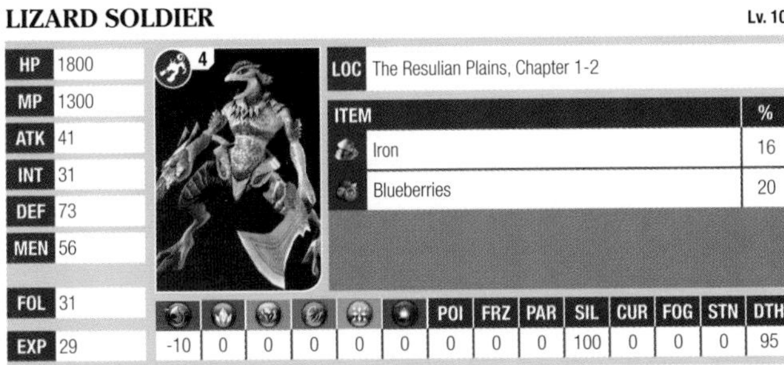

HP	1800
MP	1300
ATK	41
INT	31
DEF	73
MEN	56
FOL	31
EXP	29

LOC The Resulian Plains, Chapter 1-2

ITEM	%
Iron	16
Blueberries	20

						POI	FRZ	PAR	SIL	CUR	FOG	STN	DTH
-10	0	0	0	0	0	0	0	0	100	0	0	0	95

A human-like lizard that inhabits Resulia. Though it clads itself in armor and wields weapons, it is not intelligent enough to communicate.

LIZARD TYRANT

Lv. 140

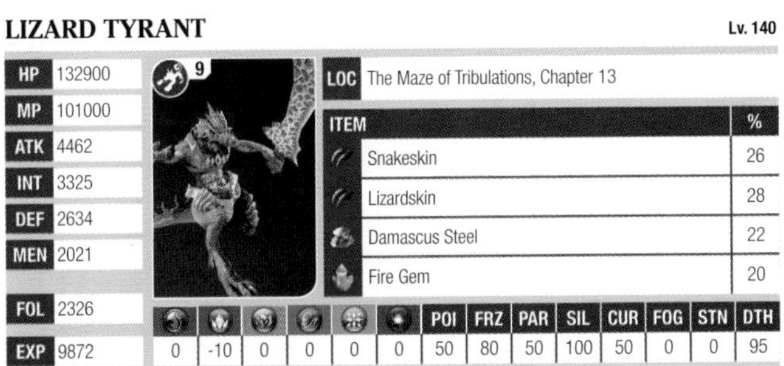

HP	132900
MP	101000
ATK	4462
INT	3325
DEF	2634
MEN	2021
FOL	2326
EXP	9872

LOC The Maze of Tribulations, Chapter 13

ITEM	%
Snakeskin	26
Lizardskin	28
Damascus Steel	22
Fire Gem	20

						POI	FRZ	PAR	SIL	CUR	FOG	STN	DTH
0	-10	0	0	0	0	50	80	50	100	50	0	0	95

Although its cold-blooded nature renders it innocuous when the sun is low, once it heats up, this lizardman more than earns its title of tyrant.

LIZARD WARRIOR

Lv. 40

HP	10400
MP	7900
ATK	350
INT	269
DEF	282
MEN	223
FOL	567
EXP	773

LOC The Trei'kuran Dunes, Chapter 6-8; The Cathedral of Oblivion, Chapter 7-10

ITEM	%
Snakeskin	18
Lizardskin	20
Damascus Steel	14

						POI	FRZ	PAR	SIL	CUR	FOG	STN	DTH
0	10	0	0	0	0	0	50	0	100	0	0	0	95

A lizardman that inhabits the arid wasteland near Eastern Trei'kur. So agile are its legs that it appears to dance as it slays.

MARINE REAPER

Lv. 3

HP	310
MP	250
ATK	19
INT	15
DEF	49
MEN	38
FOL	47
EXP	8

LOC The Passage on the Cliff, Chapter 1-2; The Coast of Minoz, Chapter 1-2

ITEM	%
Fish Scales	18
Raw Fish	18

						POI	FRZ	PAR	SIL	CUR	FOG	STN	DTH
-10	0	0	-20	0	0	50	50	0	0	0	0	0	95

A rare sight to behold, this fish that swims the coast of Sthal is actually amphibious. Land provides no haven for its prey.

ROYAL SPHINX

Lv. 140

HP	152800
MP	107400
ATK	4287
INT	3605
DEF	2607
MEN	2216
FOL	10584
EXP	9872

LOC The Maze of Tribulations, Chapter 13

ITEM	%
Blank Disk	16
High-Capacity Blank Disk	16
Moon Pearl	20
Meteorite	20

						POI	FRZ	PAR	SIL	CUR	FOG	STN	DTH
0	0	10	10	20	-10	100	100	100	100	100	100	100	95

A tutelar beast with numinous gold markings, dominon over light, and a roar that unundates foes with a deluge of crystal shards.

SABER-TOOTHED TIGER

Lv. 30

HP	6900
MP	5400
ATK	226
INT	166
DEF	230
MEN	178
FOL	240
EXP	402

LOC Northern Territory of Sohma, Chapter 5-8

ITEM	%
Wolf Fang	20

						POI	FRZ	PAR	SIL	CUR	FOG	STN	DTH
-15	15	0	-10	0	0	0	100	0	0	0	0	0	95

Despite its ferocious name, which comes from the sword-like incisors it bears, this pygmy feline is as cute as a button.

SERENE KARACIN

Lv. 38

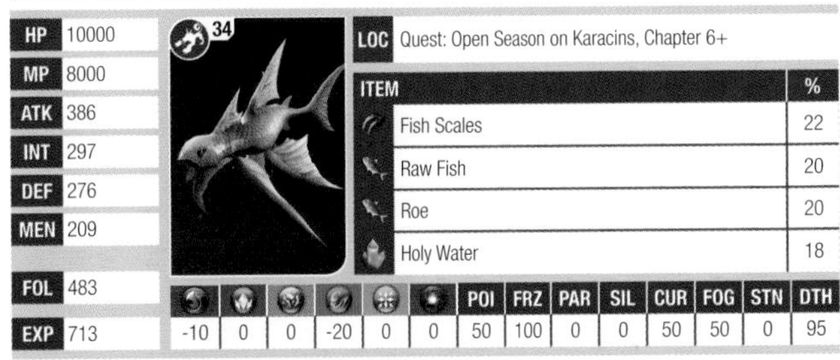

HP	10000
MP	8000
ATK	386
INT	297
DEF	276
MEN	209
FOL	483
EXP	713

LOC Quest: Open Season on Karacins, Chapter 6+

ITEM	%
Fish Scales	22
Raw Fish	20
Roe	20
Holy Water	18

						POI	FRZ	PAR	SIL	CUR	FOG	STN	DTH
-10	0	0	-20	0	0	50	100	0	0	50	50	0	95

Born on another continent, this flying fish has no natural predators. Thus, it is free to disrupt Vestiel's ecology with its insatiable appeteite.

SHELDA THE IMMUTABLE
Lv. 53

HP	MP	ATK	INT	DEF	MEN	FOL	EXP
141600	111000	910	678	648	429	821	1447

30

LOC Quest: Subjugation Directive: Shelda, Chapter 8+

ITEM	%
Tortoise Shell	20
Ice Gem	18
Mythril	14

						POI	FRZ	PAR	SIL	CUR	FOG	STN	DTH
10	-20	10	10	10	10	100	0	100	100	100	100	100	95

A tortoise with a shell stronger than some fortresses. While it is gentle by nature, it will attack anything that gets between it and its young.

UNICORN WOLF
Lv. 37

HP	MP	ATK	INT	DEF	MEN	FOL	EXP
9900	7600	338	252	267	209	369	701

2

LOC The Resulian Plains, Chapter 6-8

ITEM	%
Wolf Fang	20
Bushy Fur	18
Fire Gem	16

						POI	FRZ	PAR	SIL	CUR	FOG	STN	DTH
10	-10	0	0	0	0	0	0	0	0	0	0	0	95

This fearless carnivore hunts in packs so that it can surround and take down prey many times its size.

TWIN-FANGED GARGAN
Lv. 20

HP	MP	ATK	INT	DEF	MEN	FOL	EXP
3100	2400	71	52	114	90	111	197

25

LOC Quest: Subjugation Directive: Gargans Chapter 4+

ITEM	%
Wolf Fang	18

						POI	FRZ	PAR	SIL	CUR	FOG	STN	DTH
10	-10	0	0	0	0	0	50	0	0	0	0	0	95

A species of creature that once resided atop the monster food chain, but has since devolved into mindless brutes that live only to kill.

WASS THE SPLENETIC
Lv. 45

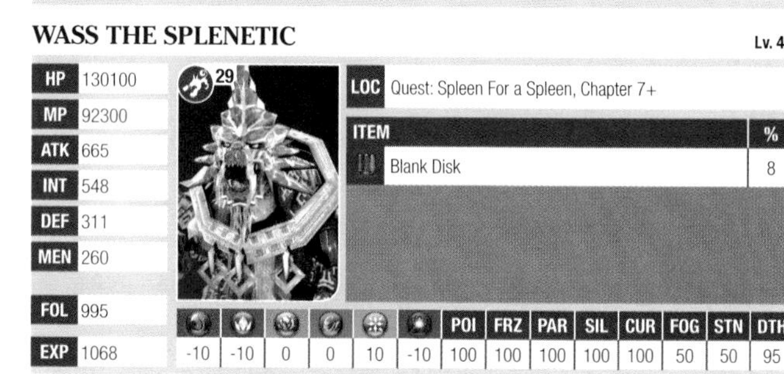

HP	MP	ATK	INT	DEF	MEN	FOL	EXP
130100	92300	665	548	311	260	995	1068

29

LOC Quest: Spleen For a Spleen, Chapter 7+

ITEM	%
Blank Disk	8

						POI	FRZ	PAR	SIL	CUR	FOG	STN	DTH
-10	-10	0	0	10	-10	100	100	100	100	100	50	50	95

Little is known of this atrocity except for its inorganic origins and that it has deprived multiple villages of their able-bodied men.

UEN OF THE MIDNIGHT WAIL
Lv. 22

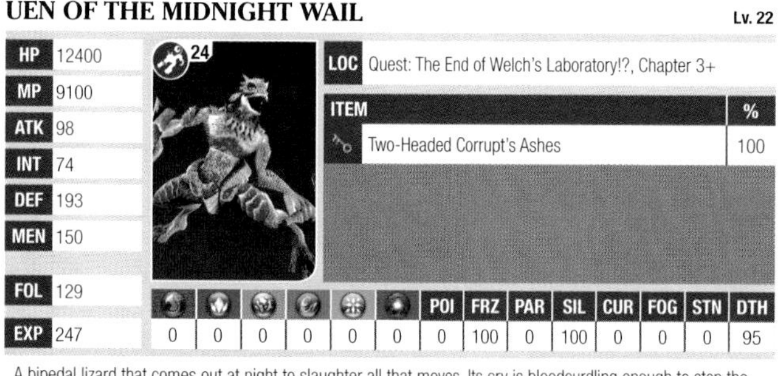

HP	MP	ATK	INT	DEF	MEN	FOL	EXP
12400	9100	98	74	193	150	129	247

24

LOC Quest: The End of Welch's Laboratory!?, Chapter 3+

ITEM	%
Two-Headed Corrupt's Ashes	100

						POI	FRZ	PAR	SIL	CUR	FOG	STN	DTH
0	0	0	0	0	0	0	100	0	100	0	0	0	95

A bipedal lizard that comes out at night to slaughter all that moves. Its cry is bloodcurdling enough to stop the hearts of those who hear it.

WISE LIZARDMAN
Lv. 21

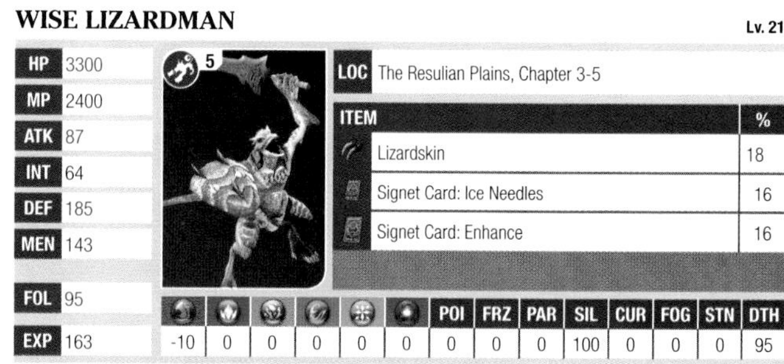

HP	MP	ATK	INT	DEF	MEN	FOL	EXP
3300	2400	87	64	185	143	95	163

5

LOC The Resulian Plains, Chapter 3-5

ITEM	%
Lizardskin	18
Signet Card: Ice Needles	16
Signet Card: Enhance	16

						POI	FRZ	PAR	SIL	CUR	FOG	STN	DTH
-10	0	0	0	0	0	0	0	0	100	0	0	0	95

As this particular type of Resulian lizardman can cast spells, scholars consider it to be moderately more intelligent than others of its species.

AVIANS

ANCIENT PERYTON
Lv. 55

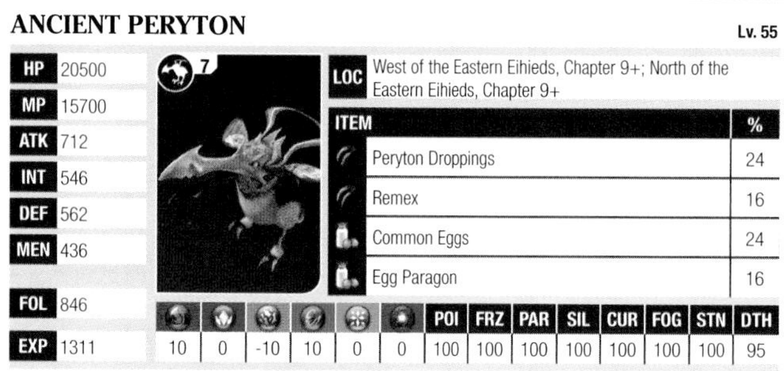

HP	MP	ATK	INT	DEF	MEN	FOL	EXP
20500	15700	712	546	562	436	846	1311

7

LOC West of the Eastern Eihieds, Chapter 9+; North of the Eastern Eihieds, Chapter 9+

ITEM	%
Peryton Droppings	24
Remex	16
Common Eggs	24
Egg Paragon	16

						POI	FRZ	PAR	SIL	CUR	FOG	STN	DTH
10	0	-10	10	0	0	100	100	100	100	100	100	100	95

This ancestor to perytons all over Faykreed eventually ceased to evolve physically and instead began to develop a higher intellect.

ARJAIN THE FIERCE
Lv. 50

HP	MP	ATK	INT	DEF	MEN	FOL	EXP
96100	78500	831	624	511	426	1218	1239

37

LOC Quest: Subjugation Directive: Arjain, Chapter 8+

ITEM	%
Wind Gem	18
Giant Bird Feather	20
Remex	16
Cashmere	16

						POI	FRZ	PAR	SIL	CUR	FOG	STN	DTH
-10	0	0	10	0	0	0	100	100	100	50	100	0	95

This harpyia constantly covets what others own. Even long after she has stolen an object and tired of it, she will refuse to relinquish it.

ANDREALPHUS
Lv. 80

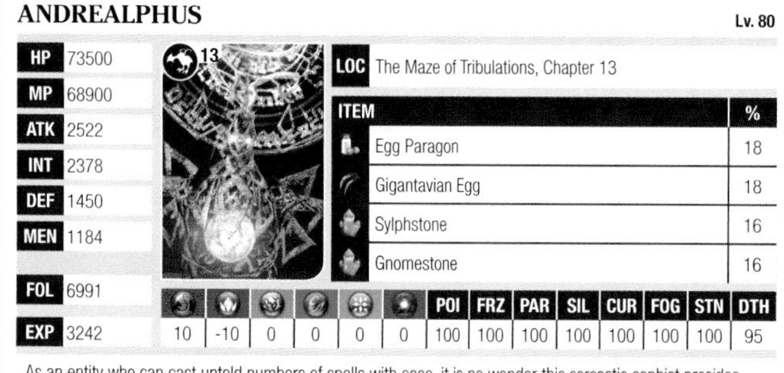

HP	MP	ATK	INT	DEF	MEN	FOL	EXP
73500	68900	2522	2378	1450	1184	6991	3242

13

LOC The Maze of Tribulations, Chapter 13

ITEM	%
Egg Paragon	18
Gigantavian Egg	18
Sylphstone	16
Gnomestone	16

						POI	FRZ	PAR	SIL	CUR	FOG	STN	DTH
10	-10	0	0	0	0	100	100	100	100	100	100	100	95

As an entity who can cast untold numbers of spells with ease, it is no wonder this sarcastic sophist presides over hordes of Corrupt.

ARMORED LIZARD
Lv. 13

HP	MP	ATK	INT	DEF	MEN	FOL	EXP
1800	1400	46	35	89	69	37	71

19

LOC Dakaav Footpath, Chapter 2-5

ITEM	%
Dragon Scales	12

						POI	FRZ	PAR	SIL	CUR	FOG	STN	DTH
0	0	0	0	0	0	100	0	100	0	0	0	0	95

A theropod with adamantine scales for armor. It developed powerful legs at the expense of its front limbs, and has remigial feathers on its back.

ASH DRAGON
Lv. 70

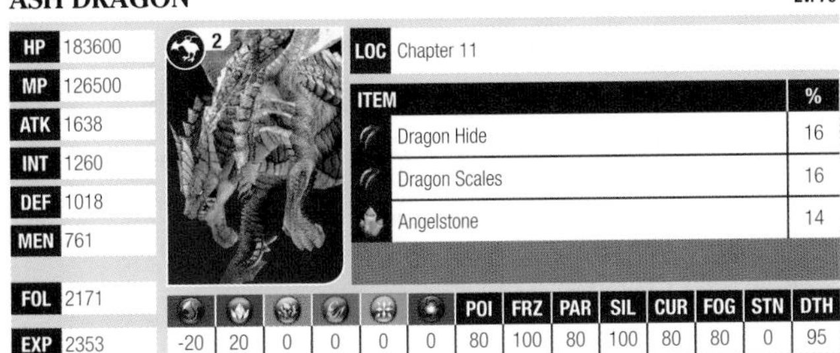

2

HP	183600
MP	126500
ATK	1638
INT	1260
DEF	1018
MEN	761
FOL	2171
EXP	2353

LOC: Chapter 11

ITEM	%
Dragon Hide	16
Dragon Scales	16
Angelstone	14

						POI	FRZ	PAR	SIL	CUR	FOG	STN	DTH
-20	20	0	0	0	0	80	100	80	100	80	80	0	95

With scales tougher than quartz and a figure as horrifying as any from tales of yore, this primordial dragon needs never worry about his spoils.

AXE BEAK
Lv. 24

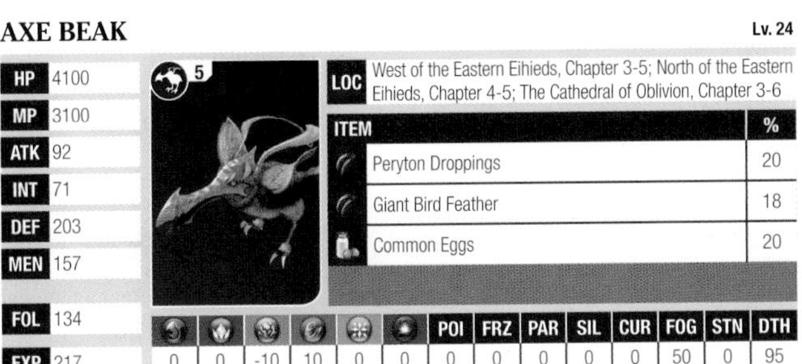

5

HP	4100
MP	3100
ATK	92
INT	71
DEF	203
MEN	157
FOL	134
EXP	217

LOC: West of the Eastern Eihieds, Chapter 3-5; North of the Eastern Eihieds, Chapter 4-5; The Cathedral of Oblivion, Chapter 3-6

ITEM	%
Peryton Droppings	20
Giant Bird Feather	18
Common Eggs	20

						POI	FRZ	PAR	SIL	CUR	FOG	STN	DTH
0	0	-10	10	0	0	0	0	0	0	0	50	0	95

A humongous bird whose beak has also evolved to such an astonishing size that the creature's territorial markings seem to be hewn with axes.

BANE DRAGON
Lv. 70

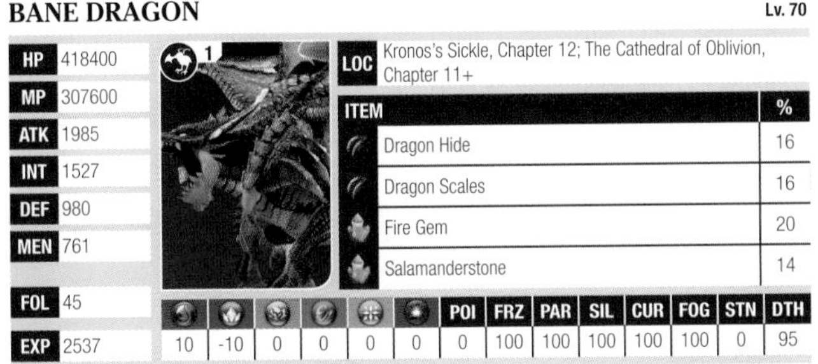

1

HP	418400
MP	307600
ATK	1985
INT	1527
DEF	980
MEN	761
FOL	45
EXP	2537

LOC: Kronos's Sickle, Chapter 12; The Cathedral of Oblivion, Chapter 11+

ITEM	%
Dragon Hide	16
Dragon Scales	16
Fire Gem	20
Salamanderstone	14

						POI	FRZ	PAR	SIL	CUR	FOG	STN	DTH
10	-10	0	0	0	0	0	100	100	100	100	100	0	95

A dragon with a temper as short as its years are long. So violent is its rage that its eyes flush a scarlet red the moment it is angered.

BLOODBANE
Lv. 140

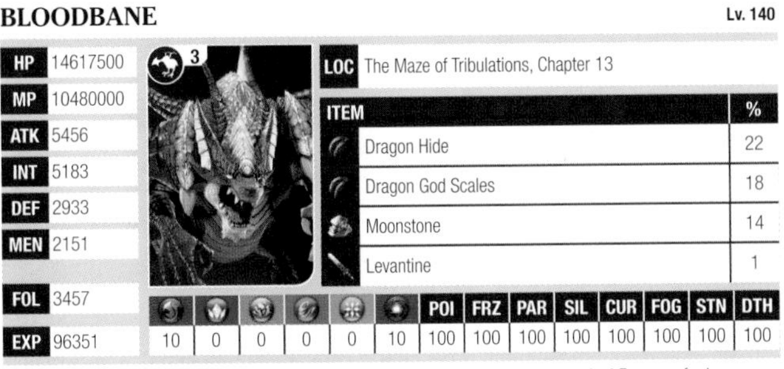

3

HP	14617500
MP	10480000
ATK	5456
INT	5183
DEF	2933
MEN	2151
FOL	3457
EXP	96351

LOC: The Maze of Tribulations, Chapter 13

ITEM	%
Dragon Hide	22
Dragon God Scales	18
Moonstone	14
Levantine	1

						POI	FRZ	PAR	SIL	CUR	FOG	STN	DTH
10	0	0	0	0	10	100	100	100	100	100	100	100	100

"These hands rend gods atwain, and this stomach sheathes the demon sword Levantine! Fear me, for I am Bloodbane: ruination incarnate!"

CORPSE BAT
Lv. 37

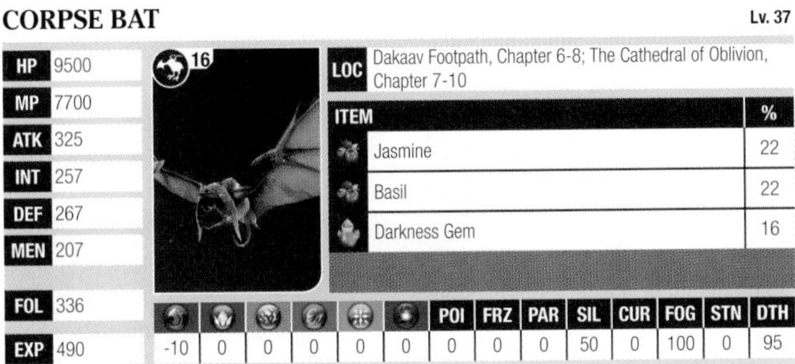

16

HP	9500
MP	7700
ATK	325
INT	257
DEF	267
MEN	207
FOL	336
EXP	490

LOC: Dakaav Footpath, Chapter 6-8; The Cathedral of Oblivion, Chapter 7-10

ITEM	%
Jasmine	22
Basil	22
Darkness Gem	16

						POI	FRZ	PAR	SIL	CUR	FOG	STN	DTH
-10	0	0	0	0	0	0	0	0	50	0	100	0	95

Though it roosts along the Dakaav Footpath, this type of chiroptera has been known to fly to the desert at night to find its next feast.

CRATER PERYTON
Lv. 38

6

HP	9900
MP	7700
ATK	329
INT	258
DEF	270
MEN	209
FOL	425
EXP	502

LOC: West of the Eastern Eihieds, Chapter 6-8; North of the Eastern Eihieds, Chapter 6-8

ITEM	%
Peryton Droppings	22
Remex	14
Common Eggs	22

						POI	FRZ	PAR	SIL	CUR	FOG	STN	DTH
0	0	-20	15	0	0	50	80	80	50	80	0	0	95

This subspecies of peryton nests underground. Its females are easily agitated during child rearing, and try to intimidate all who come near.

DINOSAURUS
Lv. 75

21

HP	52800
MP	40100
ATK	1748
INT	1370
DEF	986
MEN	773
FOL	1438
EXP	1779

LOC: Northern Territory of Sohma, Chapter 11+; The Cathedral of Oblivion, Chapter 11+

ITEM	%
Dragon Scales	18
Dragon Hide	16
Meteorite	14

						POI	FRZ	PAR	SIL	CUR	FOG	STN	DTH
0	0	0	0	0	0	100	50	100	0	80	50	50	95

This dragon's azure hue and solitary horn make it a symbol of luck, but anyone who encounters this ruthless creature would be lucky to survive.

FIRMAMENT MOLOCH
Lv. 140

11

HP	127600
MP	104200
ATK	4506
INT	3255
DEF	2553
MEN	2238
FOL	5553
EXP	9872

LOC: The Maze of Tribulations, Chapter 13

ITEM	%
Wind Gem	26
Giant Bird Feather	28
Remex	22
Cashmere	22

						POI	FRZ	PAR	SIL	CUR	FOG	STN	DTH
-10	0	0	10	0	0	0	100	100	100	50	100	0	95

This queen of the harpyia never spares the rod—or in her case, the talon—on either her prey or those in her own retinue.

GIANT BAT
Lv. 11

15

HP	1700
MP	1400
ATK	42
INT	32
DEF	76
MEN	60
FOL	32
EXP	52

LOC: Dakaav Footpath, Chapter 2-5

ITEM	%
Jasmine	20
Mint	20

						POI	FRZ	PAR	SIL	CUR	FOG	STN	DTH
0	0	0	0	0	0	50	50	50	50	50	0	0	95

A giant bat with a six-and-a-half-foot wingspan. It retreats to the comforting darkness of caves during the day and looks for prey at night.

GREEDY AVARICIA
Lv. 22

34

HP	11800
MP	9300
ATK	97
INT	74
DEF	187
MEN	159
FOL	115
EXP	250

LOC: Quest: Give Back That Bonus, Chapter 3+

ITEM	%
Wind Gem	16
Ruby	14
Giant Bird Feather	18

						POI	FRZ	PAR	SIL	CUR	FOG	STN	DTH
-20	0	0	10	0	0	0	50	80	50	0	0	0	95

There is no more egregious a hoarder than this harpyia. It has so many shiny objects that its nest gleams like another moon at night.

GUIAFAIRO

Lv. 58

HP	MP	ATK	INT	DEF	MEN	FOL	EXP
19800	16200	788	611	583	443	739	1413

18

LOC Northern Territory of Sohma, Chapter 9-10; The Cathedral of Oblivion, Chapter 11+

ITEM	%
Jasmine	24
Lavender	22
Platinum	16
Darkness Gem	18

						POI	FRZ	PAR	SIL	CUR	FOG	STN	DTH
0	0	0	0	0	0	50	80	50	80	50	100	0	95

This subspecies of corpse bat has lighter pigmentation that prevents it from blending into the night sky, meaning it must attack prey headlong.

HARPYIA

Lv. 24

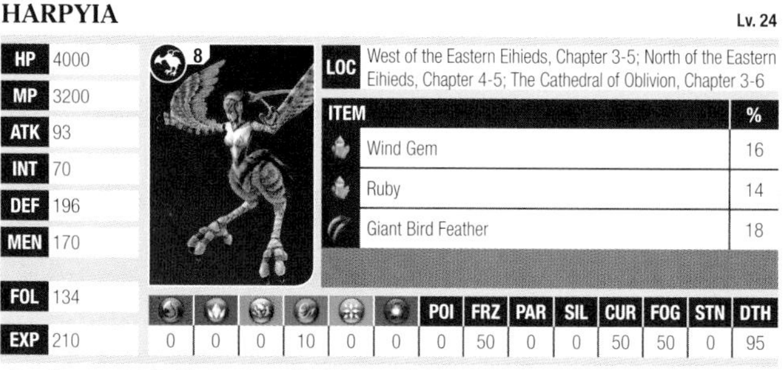

HP	MP	ATK	INT	DEF	MEN	FOL	EXP
4000	3200	93	70	196	170	134	210

8

LOC West of the Eastern Eihieds, Chapter 3-5; North of the Eastern Eihieds, Chapter 4-5; The Cathedral of Oblivion, Chapter 3-6

ITEM	%
Wind Gem	16
Ruby	14
Giant Bird Feather	18

						POI	FRZ	PAR	SIL	CUR	FOG	STN	DTH
0	0	0	10	0	0	0	50	0	0	50	50	0	95

An anthropomorphic fowl that roosts on cliffs. It sings people into a trance to abduct them, but it can also be distracted with shiny objects.

HOURIGH THE INTREPID

Lv. 59

HP	MP	ATK	INT	DEF	MEN	FOL	EXP
154900	137200	1057	903	585	492	1025	1914

40

LOC Quest: Open Season On Hourigh, Chapter 9+

ITEM	%
Egg Paragon	16
Gigantavian Egg	16

						POI	FRZ	PAR	SIL	CUR	FOG	STN	DTH
10	-10	0	0	0	0	100	100	100	100	100	100	100	95

A Corrupt psynard as old as any extant historical records. People were once able to ride the skies with him, but now, none can quell his furor.

HUBRISTIC STURVIELLA

Lv. 34

HP	MP	ATK	INT	DEF	MEN	FOL	EXP
39300	31400	316	238	246	211	295	609

39

LOC Quest: Quiet Down In There!, Chapter 6+

ITEM	%
Wind Gem	16
Giant Bird Feather	18

						POI	FRZ	PAR	SIL	CUR	FOG	STN	DTH
0	0	0	10	0	0	0	50	0	0	50	50	0	95

This minor annoyance sings in a loud alto, much to the dismay of all around. If left alone, the only thing it will hurt is one's hearing.

ILUA THE IRATE

Lv. 45

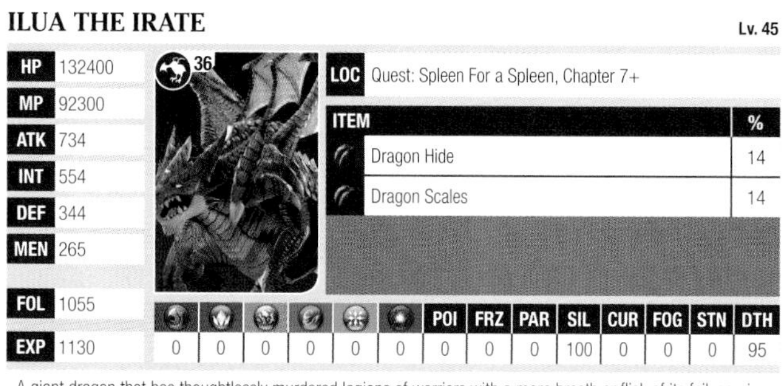

HP	MP	ATK	INT	DEF	MEN	FOL	EXP
132400	92300	734	554	344	265	1055	1130

36

LOC Quest: Spleen For a Spleen, Chapter 7+

ITEM	%
Dragon Hide	14
Dragon Scales	14

						POI	FRZ	PAR	SIL	CUR	FOG	STN	DTH
0	0	0	0	0	0	0	0	0	100	0	0	0	95

A giant dragon that has thoughtlessly murdered legions of warriors with a mere breath or flick of its fail, earning it the ire of whole countries.

JATAYU

Lv. 67

HP	MP	ATK	INT	DEF	MEN	FOL	EXP
28900	25700	1002	939	647	544	1191	2240

14

LOC Northern Territory of Sohma, Chapter 11+; The Cathedral of Oblivion, Chapter 11+

ITEM	%
Egg Paragon	16
Gigantavian Egg	16
Angelstone	14
Nereidstone	14

						POI	FRZ	PAR	SIL	CUR	FOG	STN	DTH
-10	0	0	0	0	0	100	100	100	100	100	100	100	95

A tyrant who demands undying fealty and an avian menace that delights in sinking its talons into those foolish enough to turn their backs on it.

LESSER DRAGON

Lv. 60

HP	MP	ATK	INT	DEF	MEN	FOL	EXP
21200	16300	812	623	617	479	848	1283

20

LOC Dakaav Footpath, Chapter 9+; The Cathedral of Oblivion, Chapter 7-10

ITEM	%
Dragon Scales	16
Dragon Hide	14

						POI	FRZ	PAR	SIL	CUR	FOG	STN	DTH
0	0	0	0	0	0	100	50	100	0	50	50	0	95

A subspecies of dragon that nests on the Dakaav Footpath. It is termed "lesser" as its adult form is smaller than that of other dragons'.

LUCK SUCKER

Lv. 14

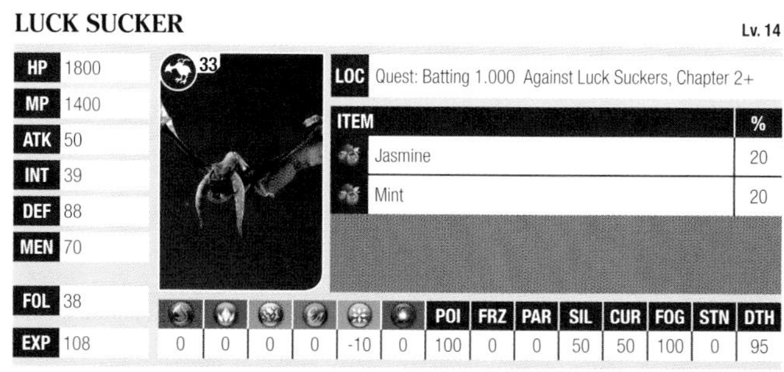

HP	MP	ATK	INT	DEF	MEN	FOL	EXP
1800	1400	50	39	88	70	38	108

33

LOC Quest: Batting 1.000 Against Luck Suckers, Chapter 2+

ITEM	%
Jasmine	20
Mint	20

						POI	FRZ	PAR	SIL	CUR	FOG	STN	DTH
0	0	0	0	-10	0	100	0	0	50	50	100	0	95

Rumor has it that these bats can suck out bad luck when they bite, but such claims have never been proven.

OPPORTUNISTIC MOOGMORT

Lv. 34

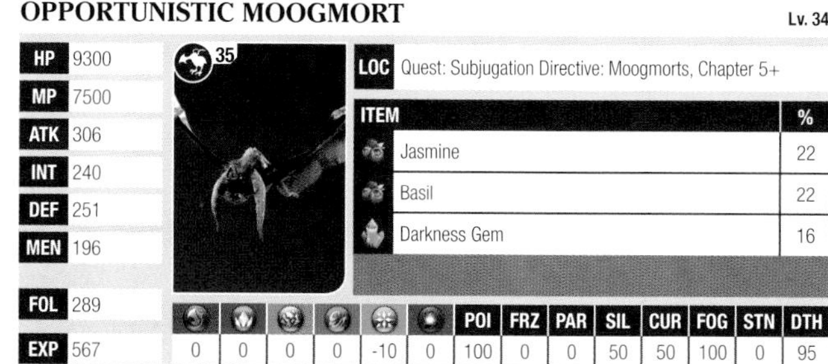

HP	MP	ATK	INT	DEF	MEN	FOL	EXP
9300	7500	306	240	251	196	289	567

35

LOC Quest: Subjugation Directive: Moogmorts, Chapter 5+

ITEM	%
Jasmine	22
Basil	22
Darkness Gem	16

						POI	FRZ	PAR	SIL	CUR	FOG	STN	DTH
0	0	0	0	-10	0	100	0	0	50	50	100	0	95

The veritable drama queen of the monster world, this species starts fights between others and sides with the group it assumes will win.

PERYTON

Lv. 9

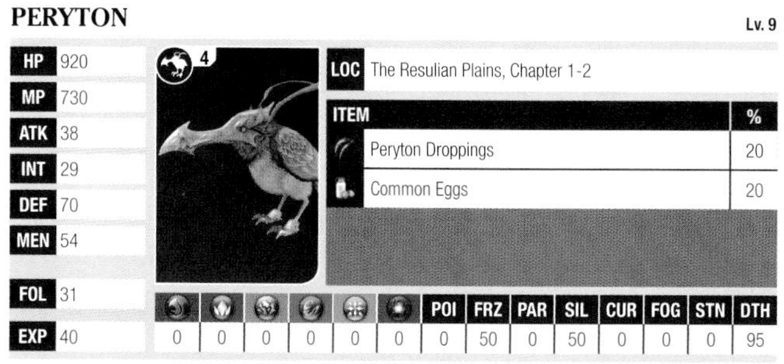

HP	MP	ATK	INT	DEF	MEN	FOL	EXP
920	730	38	29	70	54	31	40

4

LOC The Resulian Plains, Chapter 1-2

ITEM	%
Peryton Droppings	20
Common Eggs	20

						POI	FRZ	PAR	SIL	CUR	FOG	STN	DTH
0	0	0	0	0	0	0	50	0	50	0	0	0	95

An over-sized avian that, while it has an endearing appearance and gait, can grind even bedrock to powder with its durable, honed beak.

RANDAGHOR THE RENDER

Lv. 43

HP	61800
MP	48400
ATK	533
INT	414
DEF	318
MEN	244
FOL	582
EXP	976

LOC Quest: Wanted: Randaghor, Chapter 7+

ITEM	%
Dragon Scales	14

						POI	FRZ	PAR	SIL	CUR	FOG	STN	DTH
0	0	0	0	0	0	100	50	100	0	50	50	0	95

Once its food source mysteriously vanished, this towering reptile terror was forced to descend from its mountaintop domain and plunder villages.

RAVENNE

Lv. 70

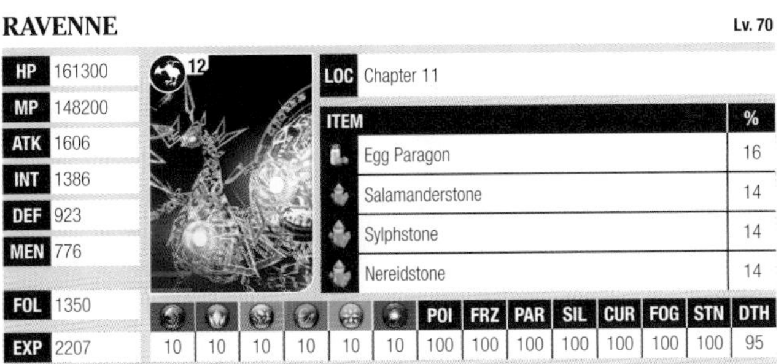

HP	161300
MP	148200
ATK	1606
INT	1386
DEF	923
MEN	776
FOL	1350
EXP	2207

LOC Chapter 11

ITEM	%
Egg Paragon	16
Salamanderstone	14
Sylphstone	14
Nereidstone	14

						POI	FRZ	PAR	SIL	CUR	FOG	STN	DTH
10	10	10	10	10	10	100	100	100	100	100	100	100	95

An avian menace that stalks the halls of the Signesilica. In its center rests a geometrically shaped core that controls its signeturgical power.

RUTHLESS BORDNAK

Lv. 58

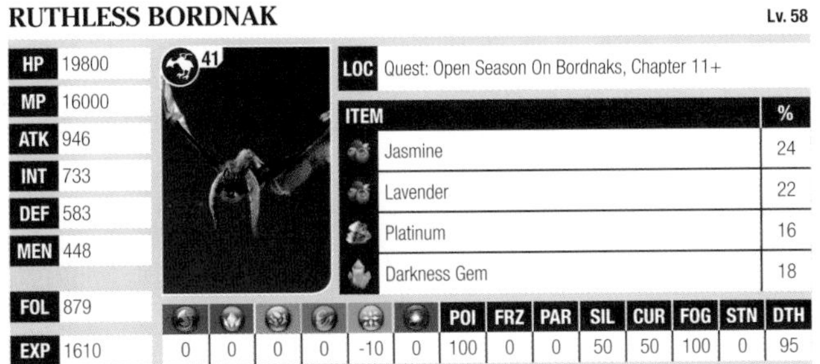

HP	19800
MP	16000
ATK	946
INT	733
DEF	583
MEN	448
FOL	879
EXP	1610

LOC Quest: Open Season On Bordnaks, Chapter 11+

ITEM	%
Jasmine	24
Lavender	22
Platinum	16
Darkness Gem	18

						POI	FRZ	PAR	SIL	CUR	FOG	STN	DTH
0	0	0	0	-10	0	100	0	0	50	50	100	0	95

A cunning species of fiend, it attacks only the weakest people it comes across. It then stores its spoils in ruins likely to attract others.

STORM DRAGON

Lv. 80

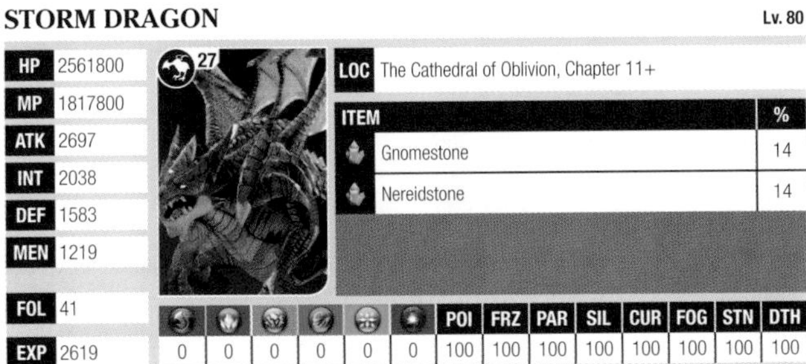

HP	2561800
MP	1817800
ATK	2697
INT	2038
DEF	1583
MEN	1219
FOL	41
EXP	2619

LOC The Cathedral of Oblivion, Chapter 11+

ITEM	%
Gnomestone	14
Nereidstone	14

						POI	FRZ	PAR	SIL	CUR	FOG	STN	DTH
0	0	0	0	0	0	100	100	100	100	100	100	100	100

An ancient beast with wings strong enough to manipulate the wind and a glare so appalling it leaves even skilled knights with chattering teeth.

STORM DRAGON

Lv. 84

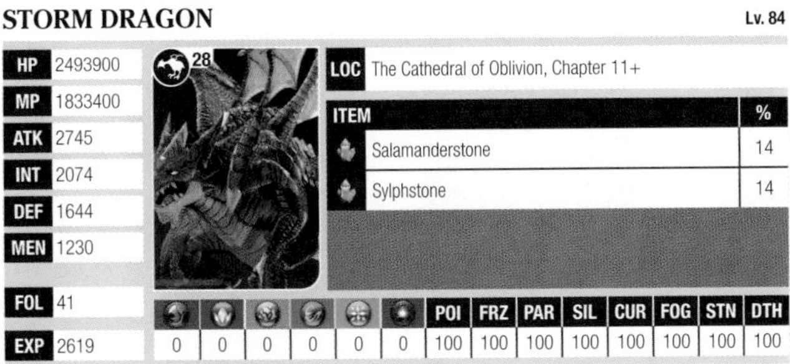

HP	2493900
MP	1833400
ATK	2745
INT	2074
DEF	1644
MEN	1230
FOL	41
EXP	2619

LOC The Cathedral of Oblivion, Chapter 11+

ITEM	%
Salamanderstone	14
Sylphstone	14

						POI	FRZ	PAR	SIL	CUR	FOG	STN	DTH
0	0	0	0	0	0	100	100	100	100	100	100	100	100

An ancient beast with wings strong enough to manipulate the wind and a glare so appalling it leaves even skilled knights with chattering teeth.

STORM DRAGON

Lv. 88

HP	2515700
MP	1849400
ATK	2818
INT	2130
DEF	1676
MEN	1265
FOL	41
EXP	2619

LOC The Cathedral of Oblivion, Chapter 11+

ITEM	%
Angelstone	16
Shadestone	16

						POI	FRZ	PAR	SIL	CUR	FOG	STN	DTH
0	0	0	0	0	0	100	100	100	100	100	100	100	100

An ancient beast with wings strong enough to manipulate the wind and a glare so appalling it leaves even skilled knights with chattering teeth.

STORM DRAGON

Lv. 92

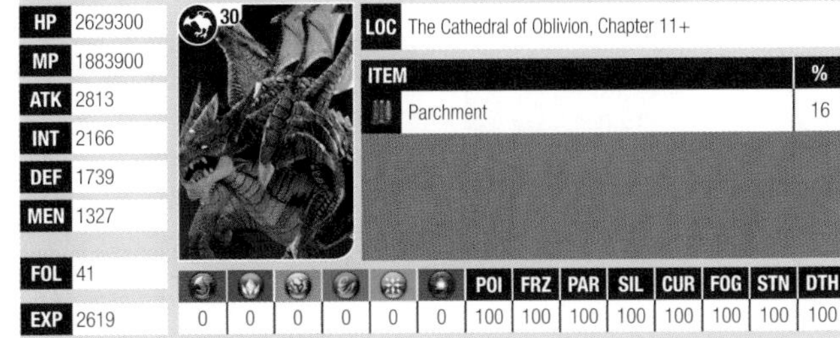

HP	2629300
MP	1883900
ATK	2813
INT	2166
DEF	1739
MEN	1327
FOL	41
EXP	2619

LOC The Cathedral of Oblivion, Chapter 11+

ITEM	%
Parchment	16

						POI	FRZ	PAR	SIL	CUR	FOG	STN	DTH
0	0	0	0	0	0	100	100	100	100	100	100	100	100

An ancient beast with wings strong enough to manipulate the wind and a glare so appalling it leaves even skilled knights with chattering teeth.

STORM DRAGON

Lv. 96

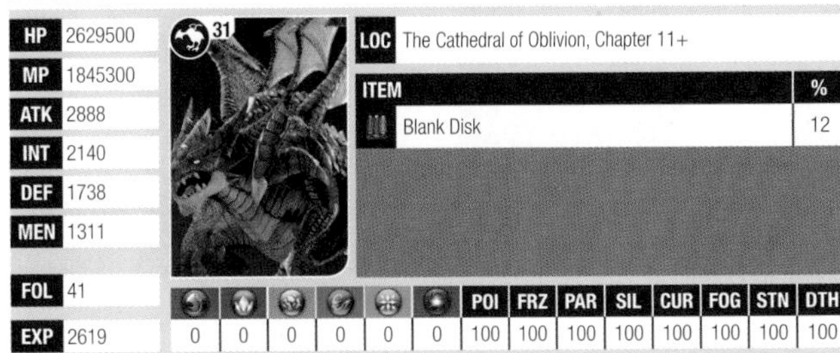

HP	2629500
MP	1845300
ATK	2888
INT	2140
DEF	1738
MEN	1311
FOL	41
EXP	2619

LOC The Cathedral of Oblivion, Chapter 11+

ITEM	%
Blank Disk	12

						POI	FRZ	PAR	SIL	CUR	FOG	STN	DTH
0	0	0	0	0	0	100	100	100	100	100	100	100	100

An ancient beast with wings strong enough to manipulate the wind and a glare so appalling it leaves even skilled knights with chattering teeth.

STORM DRAGON

Lv. 99

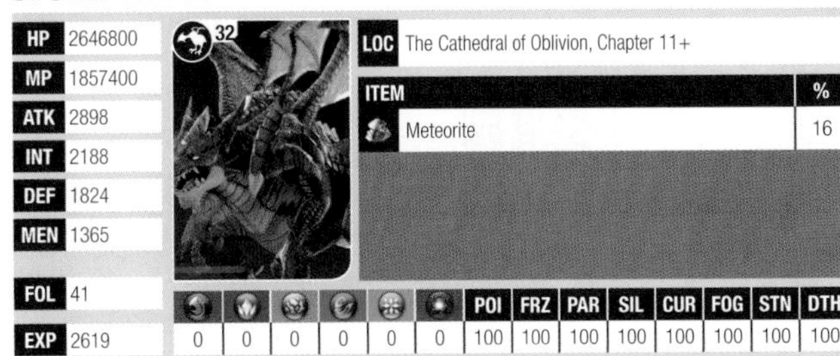

HP	2646800
MP	1857400
ATK	2898
INT	2188
DEF	1824
MEN	1365
FOL	41
EXP	2619

LOC The Cathedral of Oblivion, Chapter 11+

ITEM	%
Meteorite	16

						POI	FRZ	PAR	SIL	CUR	FOG	STN	DTH
0	0	0	0	0	0	100	100	100	100	100	100	100	100

An ancient beast with wings strong enough to manipulate the wind and a glare so appalling it leaves even skilled knights with chattering teeth.

TERARIN

Lv. 32

HP	8600
MP	6900
ATK	252
INT	193
DEF	235
MEN	198
FOL	284
EXP	572

LOC The Trei'kuran Dunes, Chapter 5

ITEM	%
Wind Gem	16
Giant Bird Feather	18

						POI	FRZ	PAR	SIL	CUR	FOG	STN	DTH
0	0	0	10	0	0	0	50	0	50	0	100	0	95

A harpyia with an enchanting, clarion voice. It also has vividly bright feathers that may only be plucked by those who pique its interest.

THICK-THIGHED PYEKARD
Lv. 63

HP	24000
MP	18600
ATK	1125
INT	891
DEF	609
MEN	477
FOL	1057
EXP	1978

LOC: Quest: Open Season On Pyekards, Chapter 11+

ITEM	%
Peryton Droppings	24
Remex	16
Common Eggs	24
Egg Paragon	16

						POI	FRZ	PAR	SIL	CUR	FOG	STN	DTH
0	0	0	0	0	0	0	50	0	50	0	0	0	95

A species of escaped peryton so insular, it evolved separately from its kin. To calm its wracked nerves, it pecks at walls until they collapse.

VIDOFNIR
Lv. 55

HP	414200
MP	398300
ATK	796
INT	718
DEF	556
MEN	454
FOL	1019
EXP	1224

LOC: The Cathedral of Oblivion, Chapter 7-10

ITEM	%
Earth Gem	18
Darkness Gem	18

						POI	FRZ	PAR	SIL	CUR	FOG	STN	DTH
0	-20	0	0	0	0	100	100	100	100	100	100	100	100

An avian menace that soars just outside the Cathedral of Oblivion. As a fire signet gave it life, it can conjure flames with a flap of its wings.

VAMPIRE BAT
Lv. 46

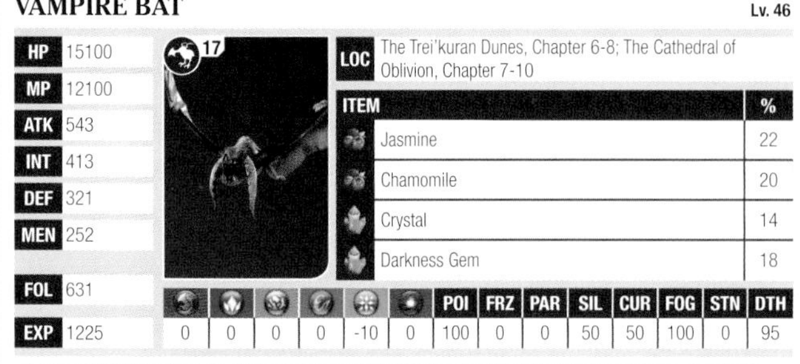

HP	15100
MP	12100
ATK	543
INT	413
DEF	321
MEN	252
FOL	631
EXP	1225

LOC: The Trei'kuran Dunes, Chapter 6-8; The Cathedral of Oblivion, Chapter 7-10

ITEM	%
Jasmine	22
Chamomile	20
Crystal	14
Darkness Gem	18

						POI	FRZ	PAR	SIL	CUR	FOG	STN	DTH
0	0	0	0	-10	0	100	0	0	50	50	100	0	95

A colossal bat that patrols the skies around Eastern Trei'kur. Unable to sate its voracious appetite, it sucks its prey dry, down to the marrow.

VIDOFNIR
Lv. 60

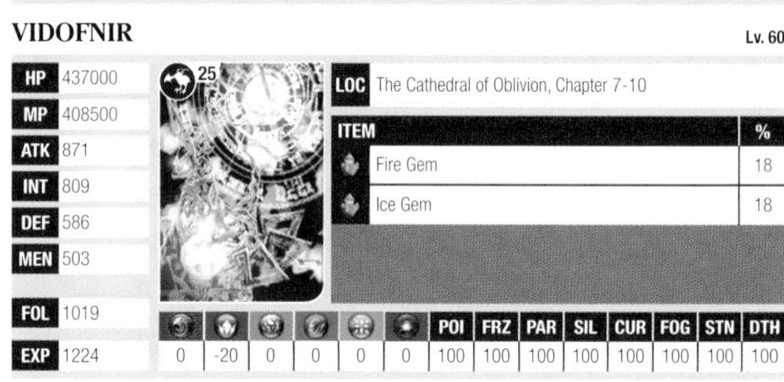

HP	437000
MP	408500
ATK	871
INT	809
DEF	586
MEN	503
FOL	1019
EXP	1224

LOC: The Cathedral of Oblivion, Chapter 7-10

ITEM	%
Fire Gem	18
Ice Gem	18

						POI	FRZ	PAR	SIL	CUR	FOG	STN	DTH
0	-20	0	0	0	0	100	100	100	100	100	100	100	100

An avian menace that soars just outside the Cathedral of Oblivion. As a fire signet gave it life, it can conjure flames with a flap of its wings.

VIDOFNIR
Lv. 45

HP	326500
MP	302600
ATK	589
INT	531
DEF	311
MEN	260
FOL	1019
EXP	1224

LOC: The Cathedral of Oblivion, Chapter 7-10

ITEM	%
Earth Gem	18
Ice Gem	18
Light Gem	18

						POI	FRZ	PAR	SIL	CUR	FOG	STN	DTH
0	-20	0	0	0	0	100	100	100	100	100	100	100	100

An avian menace that soars just outside the Cathedral of Oblivion. As a fire signet gave it life, it can conjure flames with a flap of its wings.

VIDOFNIR
Lv. 65

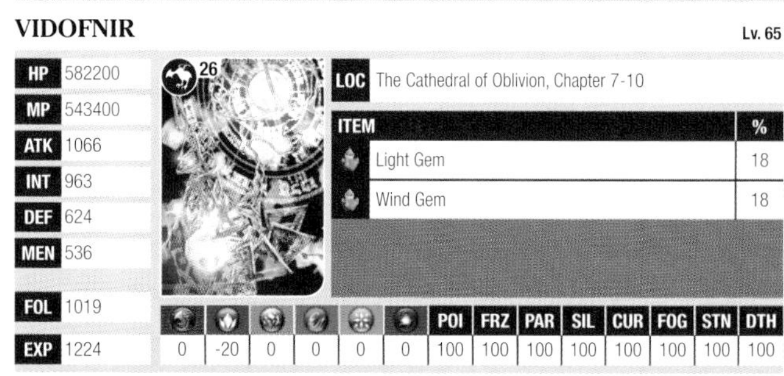

HP	582200
MP	543400
ATK	1066
INT	963
DEF	624
MEN	536
FOL	1019
EXP	1224

LOC: The Cathedral of Oblivion, Chapter 7-10

ITEM	%
Light Gem	18
Wind Gem	18

						POI	FRZ	PAR	SIL	CUR	FOG	STN	DTH
0	-20	0	0	0	0	100	100	100	100	100	100	100	100

An avian menace that soars just outside the Cathedral of Oblivion. As a fire signet gave it life, it can conjure flames with a flap of its wings.

VIDOFNIR
Lv. 50

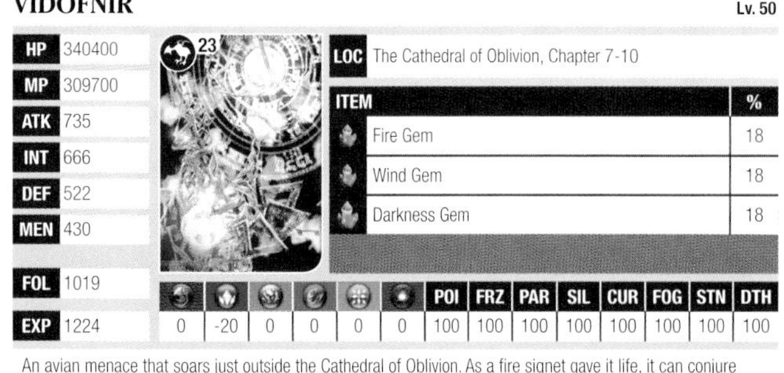

HP	340400
MP	309700
ATK	735
INT	666
DEF	522
MEN	430
FOL	1019
EXP	1224

LOC: The Cathedral of Oblivion, Chapter 7-10

ITEM	%
Fire Gem	18
Wind Gem	18
Darkness Gem	18

						POI	FRZ	PAR	SIL	CUR	FOG	STN	DTH
0	-20	0	0	0	0	100	100	100	100	100	100	100	100

An avian menace that soars just outside the Cathedral of Oblivion. As a fire signet gave it life, it can conjure flames with a flap of its wings.

WINGED NIGHTMARE
Lv. 55

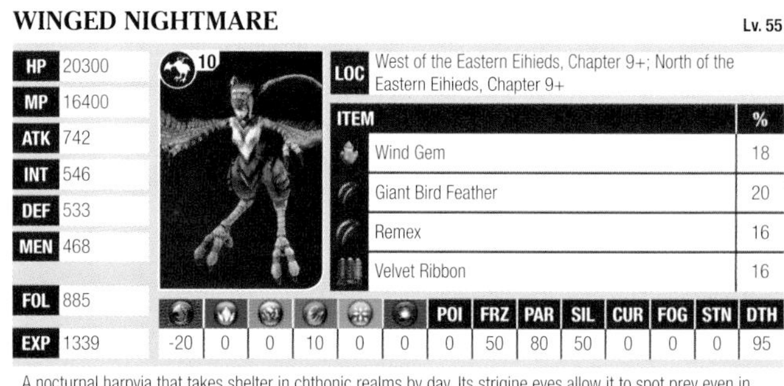

HP	20300
MP	16400
ATK	742
INT	546
DEF	533
MEN	468
FOL	885
EXP	1339

LOC: West of the Eastern Eihieds, Chapter 9+; North of the Eastern Eihieds, Chapter 9+

ITEM	%
Wind Gem	18
Giant Bird Feather	20
Remex	16
Velvet Ribbon	16

						POI	FRZ	PAR	SIL	CUR	FOG	STN	DTH
-20	0	0	10	0	0	0	50	80	50	0	0	0	95

A nocturnal harpyia that takes shelter in chthonic realms by day. Its strigine eyes allow it to spot prey even in consummate darkness.

INSECTS

ADEPHAGA
Lv. 12

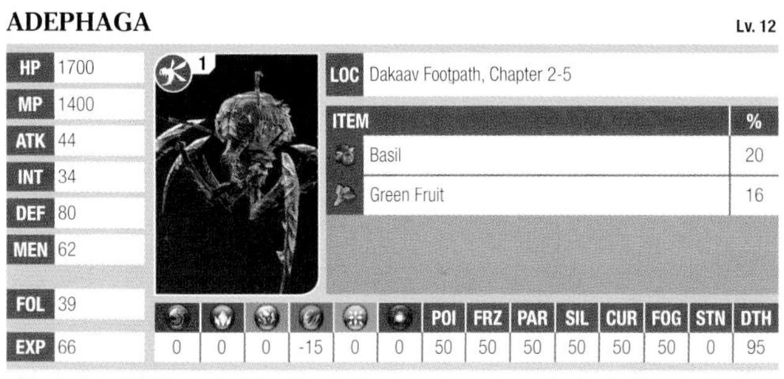

HP	1700
MP	1400
ATK	44
INT	34
DEF	80
MEN	62
FOL	39
EXP	66

LOC: Dakaav Footpath, Chapter 2-5

ITEM	%
Basil	20
Green Fruit	16

						POI	FRZ	PAR	SIL	CUR	FOG	STN	DTH
0	0	0	-15	0	0	50	50	50	50	50	50	0	95

A beetle that mainly inhabits the Dakaav Footpath. It preys on any creature smaller than itself, and lives in a colony ruled by a queen.

ADEPHAGA DRUS
Lv. 38

HP	9800
MP	7800
ATK	329
INT	258
DEF	270
MEN	214
FOL	341
EXP	475

LOC: The Passage on the Cliffs, Chapter 6-8; The Coast of Minoz, Chapter 6-8; Dakaav Footpath, Chapter 6-8

ITEM	%
Basil	22
Green Fruit	20

						POI	FRZ	PAR	SIL	CUR	FOG	STN	DTH
0	0	0	-14	0	0	50	50	50	50	50	50	0	95

Larger and more adept at fighting than a normal adephaga would be. This subspecies sprays highly acidic and viscid gastric fluid on its foes.

ADEPHAGA MILIES

Lv. 42

4

HP	MP	ATK	INT	DEF	MEN	FOL	EXP
12000	9500	439	337	293	232	433	740

LOC: The Trei'kuran Dunes, Chapter 6-8; The Cathedral of Oblivion, Chapter 7-10

ITEM	%
Insect Egg	20
Basil	22
Green Fruit	20

						POI	FRZ	PAR	SIL	CUR	FOG	STN	DTH
0	-5	0	-15	0	0	50	0	0	0	0	0	0	95

An exalted adephaga with an extremely tough shell. It is tasked with transporting eggs and caring for larvae in the nest.

ADEPHAGA PROX

Lv. 57

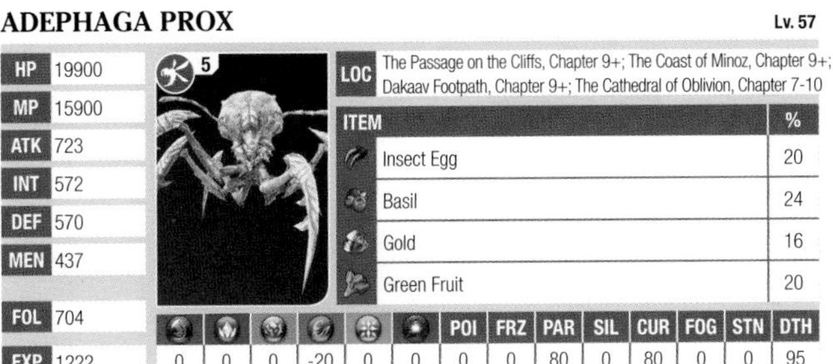

5

HP	MP	ATK	INT	DEF	MEN	FOL	EXP
19900	15900	723	572	570	437	704	1222

LOC: The Passage on the Cliffs, Chapter 9+; The Coast of Minoz, Chapter 9+; Dakaav Footpath, Chapter 9+; The Cathedral of Oblivion, Chapter 7-10

ITEM	%
Insect Egg	20
Basil	24
Gold	16
Green Fruit	20

						POI	FRZ	PAR	SIL	CUR	FOG	STN	DTH
0	0	0	-20	0	0	0	0	80	0	80	0	0	95

A unique subspecies of adephaga that evolved a white shell due to spending long periods of time living in the shadows.

ADEPHAGA VENOM

Lv. 39

3

HP	MP	ATK	INT	DEF	MEN	FOL	EXP
9900	7900	335	260	282	218	345	540

LOC: The Passage on the Cliff, Chapter 6-8; The Coast of Minoz, Chapter 6-8; Dakaav Footpath, Chapter 6-8

ITEM	%
Insect Egg	20
Basil	22
Green Fruit	20

						POI	FRZ	PAR	SIL	CUR	FOG	STN	DTH
0	-5	0	-14	0	0	100	0	100	0	0	0	50	95

This type of adephaga defends itself with a potent, venomous mucus that it secretes from cracks in its shell and sprays from its mouth.

GARISH SYTHWA

Lv. 64

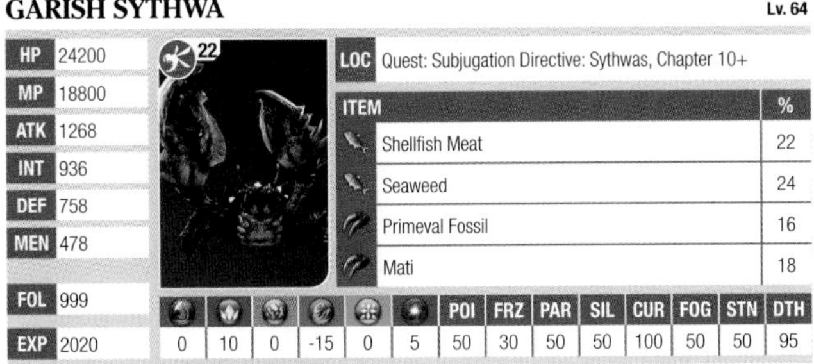

22

HP	MP	ATK	INT	DEF	MEN	FOL	EXP
24200	18800	1268	936	758	478	999	2020

LOC: Quest: Subjugation Directive: Sythwas, Chapter 10+

ITEM	%
Shellfish Meat	22
Seaweed	24
Primeval Fossil	16
Mati	18

						POI	FRZ	PAR	SIL	CUR	FOG	STN	DTH
0	10	0	-15	0	5	50	30	50	50	100	50	50	95

If only this humongous crab were a little more intelligent, it would realize that affixing the items it steals to its fetid shell devalues them.

GULA THE GLUTTONOUS

Lv. 34

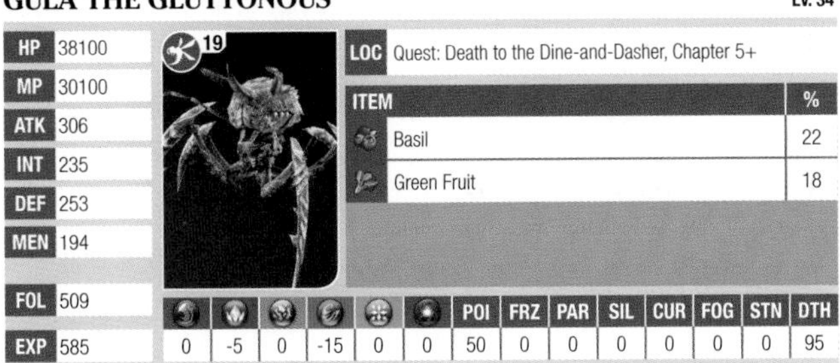

19

HP	MP	ATK	INT	DEF	MEN	FOL	EXP
38100	30100	306	235	253	194	509	585

LOC: Quest: Death to the Dine-and-Dasher, Chapter 5+

ITEM	%
Basil	22
Green Fruit	18

						POI	FRZ	PAR	SIL	CUR	FOG	STN	DTH
0	-5	0	-15	0	0	50	0	0	0	0	0	0	95

A shape-shifting beetle that transforms into a human when hungry. Once it has stolen and gorged on enough food, it reverts to its true form.

GUST HORNET

Lv. 80

12

HP	MP	ATK	INT	DEF	MEN	FOL	EXP
70500	58200	2522	1858	1420	1101	4900	3015

LOC: The Cathedral of Oblivion, Chapter 11+; The Maze of Tribulations, Chapter 13

ITEM	%
Bee Stinger	24
Nectar	24
Amber	18

						POI	FRZ	PAR	SIL	CUR	FOG	STN	DTH
0	0	-20	0	0	0	100	80	80	0	80	50	50	95

A massive wasp that lives on Faykreed. It hunts alone, but cooperates with others to defend its hive from invaders when necessary.

HADES CRAB

Lv. 58

15

HP	MP	ATK	INT	DEF	MEN	FOL	EXP
20700	16200	820	617	697	443	794	1325

LOC: The Passage on the Cliffs, Chapter 9+; The Coast of Minoz, Chapter 9+; The Cathedral of Oblivion, Chapter 7-10

ITEM	%
Shellfish Meat	22
Seaweed	24
Primeval Fossil	16
Mati	16

						POI	FRZ	PAR	SIL	CUR	FOG	STN	DTH
0	10	0	-15	0	5	50	30	50	50	100	50	50	95

This titanic scavenger drags remains of adventurers to a subterranean grotto to feed, but it will kill when no corpses can be found.

HONEYBEE

Lv. 36

10

HP	MP	ATK	INT	DEF	MEN	FOL	EXP
9700	8000	287	211	262	203	336	594

LOC: The Resulian Plains, Chapter 6-8

ITEM	%
Bee Stinger	20
Nectar	20

						POI	FRZ	PAR	SIL	CUR	FOG	STN	DTH
0	0	-11	0	0	0	0	0	0	50	0	50	0	95

A large bee-like beetle mainly found on the Resulian Plains. It mostly drinks nectar, but is known to attack small animals as a protein source.

KEEN-EYED GILEEGHA

Lv. 12

18

HP	MP	ATK	INT	DEF	MEN	FOL	EXP
1700	1400	43	34	80	63	22	78

LOC: Quest: Subjugation Directive: Gileeghas, Chapter 3+

ITEM	%
Basil	20
Green Fruit	16

						POI	FRZ	PAR	SIL	CUR	FOG	STN	DTH
0	0	0	-14	0	0	50	50	50	50	50	50	0	95

A species of over-sized beetles that feeds off livestock. They are sensitive to humans' presence, however, and thus are rarely ever seen.

KILLER CHELAE

Lv. 2

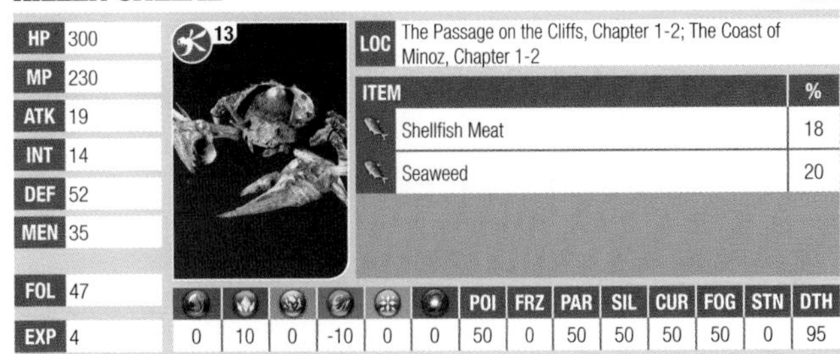

13

HP	MP	ATK	INT	DEF	MEN	FOL	EXP
300	230	19	14	52	35	47	4

LOC: The Passage on the Cliffs, Chapter 1-2; The Coast of Minoz, Chapter 1-2

ITEM	%
Shellfish Meat	18
Seaweed	20

						POI	FRZ	PAR	SIL	CUR	FOG	STN	DTH
0	10	0	-10	0	0	50	0	50	50	50	50	0	95

An enormous crustacean that bears a striking resemblance to a crab. Its tremendous pincers would feel nothing if they snipped a man in half.

KILLER WASP
Lv. 8

9

HP	MP	ATK	INT	DEF	MEN	FOL	EXP
880	730	38	28	65	52	21	22

LOC: The Resulian Plains, Chapter 1-2

ITEM	%
Bee Stinger	18

						POI	FRZ	PAR	SIL	CUR	FOG	STN	DTH
0	0	-10	0	0	0	100	50	50	50	50	50	0	95

This large beetle that resembles a wasp is often found on the Resulian Plains. It is highly territorial and instantly attacks all intruders.

SANDDOZER
Lv. 50

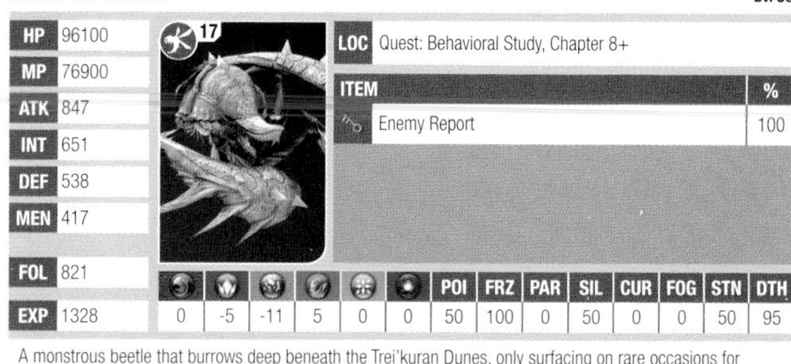

17

HP	MP	ATK	INT	DEF	MEN	FOL	EXP
96100	76900	847	651	538	417	821	1328

LOC: Quest: Behavioral Study, Chapter 8+

ITEM	%
Enemy Report	100

						POI	FRZ	PAR	SIL	CUR	FOG	STN	DTH
0	-5	-11	5	0	0	50	100	0	50	0	0	50	95

A monstrous beetle that burrows deep beneath the Trei'kuran Dunes, only surfacing on rare occasions for reasons yet to be understood.

LANCING HADO
Lv. 28

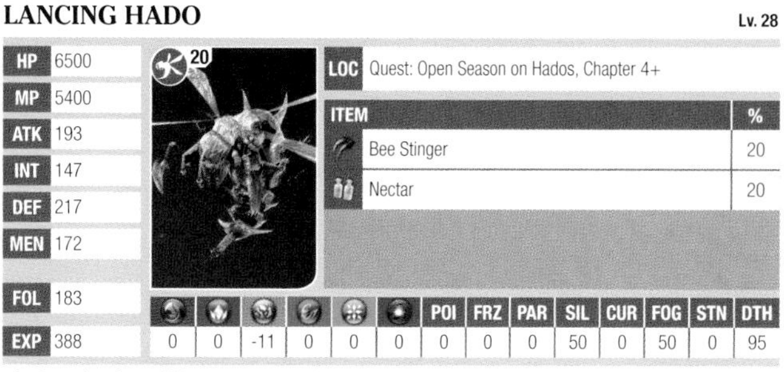

20

HP	MP	ATK	INT	DEF	MEN	FOL	EXP
6500	5400	193	147	217	172	183	388

LOC: Quest: Open Season on Hados, Chapter 4+

ITEM	%
Bee Stinger	20
Nectar	20

						POI	FRZ	PAR	SIL	CUR	FOG	STN	DTH
0	0	-11	0	0	0	0	0	0	50	0	50	0	95

A subspecies of monolithic wasp long thought to have disappeared from its hunting grounds to the north of Langdauq.

SANDEATER
Lv. 30

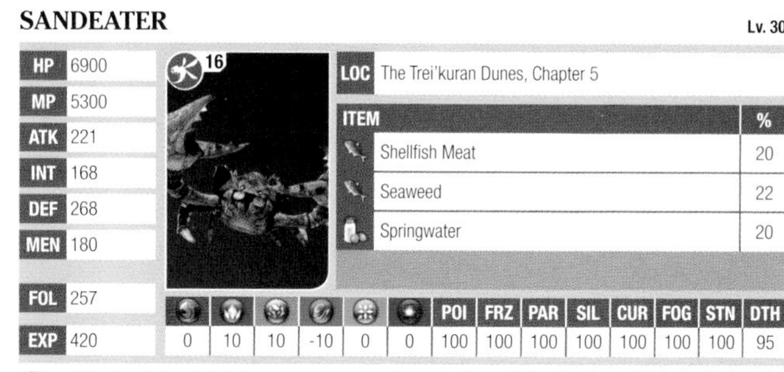

16

HP	MP	ATK	INT	DEF	MEN	FOL	EXP
6900	5300	221	168	268	180	257	420

LOC: The Trei'kuran Dunes, Chapter 5

ITEM	%
Shellfish Meat	20
Seaweed	22
Springwater	20

						POI	FRZ	PAR	SIL	CUR	FOG	STN	DTH
0	10	10	-10	0	0	100	100	100	100	100	100	100	95

This subspecies of desert-dwelling crab possesses a shell many times thicker than that of its marine brethren to cope with the searing heat.

POLYPHAGA
Lv. 18

6

HP	MP	ATK	INT	DEF	MEN	FOL	EXP
2900	2300	62	47	110	85	73	133

LOC: Dakaav Footpath, Chapter 3-5

ITEM	%
Insect Egg	18
Red Fruit	18

						POI	FRZ	PAR	SIL	CUR	FOG	STN	DTH
0	0	-10	0	0	0	50	50	50	50	50	50	0	95

An intimidating beetle with a tough carapace and sharp horns. It usually plods along the Dakaav Footpath, but can also fly.

STINGER
Lv. 53

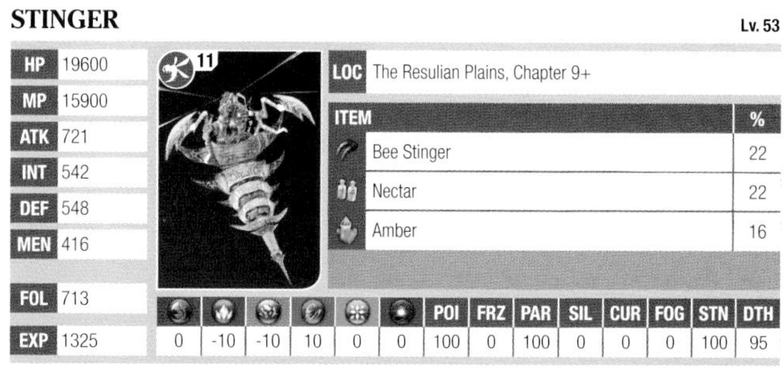

11

HP	MP	ATK	INT	DEF	MEN	FOL	EXP
19600	15900	721	542	548	416	713	1325

LOC: The Resulian Plains, Chapter 9+

ITEM	%
Bee Stinger	22
Nectar	22
Amber	16

						POI	FRZ	PAR	SIL	CUR	FOG	STN	DTH
0	-10	-10	10	0	0	100	0	100	0	0	0	100	95

A vicious and carnivorous wasp beetle that prowls the Resulian Plains. It hunts in swarms, weakening prey before carrying it back to the hive.

POLYPHAGA DRUS
Lv. 59

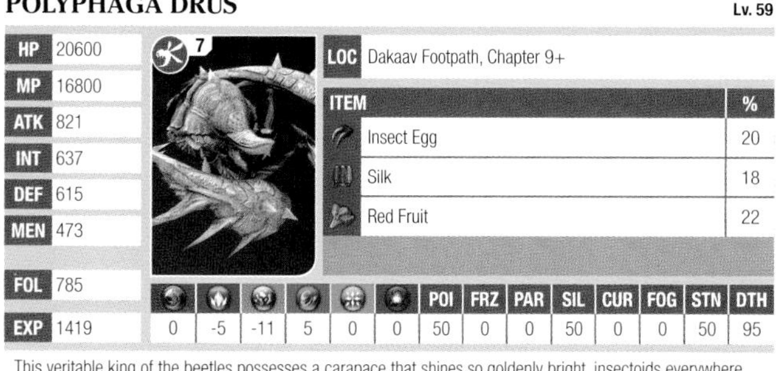

7

HP	MP	ATK	INT	DEF	MEN	FOL	EXP
20600	16800	821	637	615	473	785	1419

LOC: Dakaav Footpath, Chapter 9+

ITEM	%
Insect Egg	20
Silk	18
Red Fruit	22

						POI	FRZ	PAR	SIL	CUR	FOG	STN	DTH
0	-5	-11	5	0	0	50	0	0	50	0	0	50	95

This veritable king of the beetles possesses a carapace that shines so goldenly bright, insectoids everywhere are in awe of it.

WANDERING OUYEITS
Lv. 64

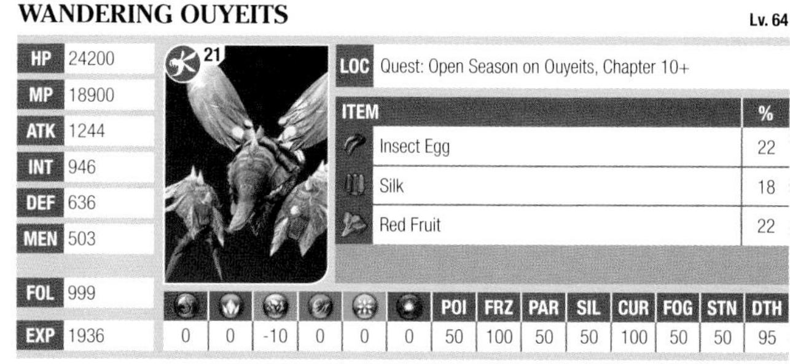

21

HP	MP	ATK	INT	DEF	MEN	FOL	EXP
24200	18900	1244	946	636	503	999	1936

LOC: Quest: Open Season on Ouyeits, Chapter 10+

ITEM	%
Insect Egg	22
Silk	18
Red Fruit	22

						POI	FRZ	PAR	SIL	CUR	FOG	STN	DTH
0	0	-10	0	0	0	50	100	50	50	100	50	50	95

This ambulant garrison of a coleoptera spears monsters and men alike, devours them whole , and then greedily licks its mandibles clean.

POLYPHAGA GAMBOGE
Lv. 80

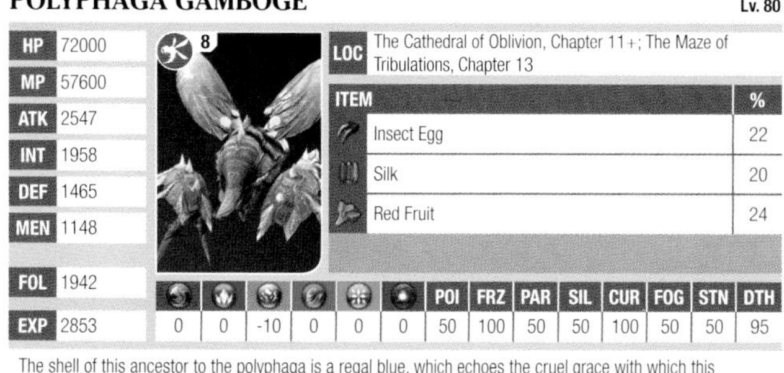

8

HP	MP	ATK	INT	DEF	MEN	FOL	EXP
72000	57600	2547	1958	1465	1148	1942	2853

LOC: The Cathedral of Oblivion, Chapter 11+; The Maze of Tribulations, Chapter 13

ITEM	%
Insect Egg	22
Silk	20
Red Fruit	24

						POI	FRZ	PAR	SIL	CUR	FOG	STN	DTH
0	0	-10	0	0	0	50	100	50	50	100	50	50	95

The shell of this ancestor to the polyphaga is a regal blue, which echoes the cruel grace with which this antiquity culls its prey.

WAVING PINCERS
Lv. 18

14

HP	MP	ATK	INT	DEF	MEN	FOL	EXP
3000	2200	62	47	124	82	72	91

LOC: The Passage on the Cliffs, Chapter 3-5; The Coast of Minoz, Chapter 3-5

ITEM	%
Shellfish Meat	18
Seaweed	20
Green Fruit	18

						POI	FRZ	PAR	SIL	CUR	FOG	STN	DTH
0	10	0	-10	0	0	0	0	0	0	0	50	0	95

This gigantic crustacean attacks by upending itself, embedding the spines on its shell in the ground, and spinning at incredible speeds.

PLANTS

ALBERO DI ANIMA
Lv. 38

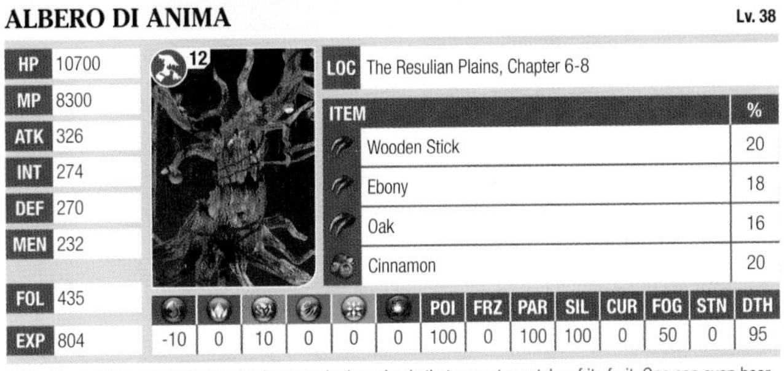

HP	MP	ATK	INT	DEF	MEN	FOL	EXP
10700	8300	326	274	270	232	435	804

LOC The Resulian Plains, Chapter 6-8

ITEM	%
Wooden Stick	20
Ebony	18
Oak	16
Cinnamon	20

						POI	FRZ	PAR	SIL	CUR	FOG	STN	DTH
-10	0	10	0	0	0	100	0	100	100	0	50	0	95

This itinerant tree practically inhales in one gulp the animals that come to partake of its fruit. One can even hear them scream as they digest.

BLIGHTCAP
Lv. 20

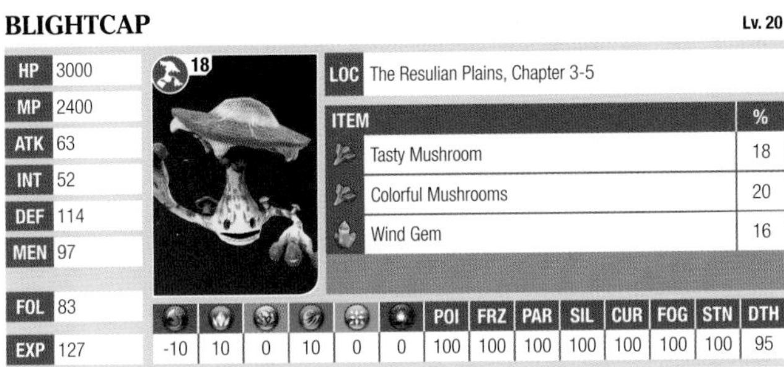

HP	MP	ATK	INT	DEF	MEN	FOL	EXP
3000	2400	63	52	114	97	83	127

LOC The Resulian Plains, Chapter 3-5

ITEM	%
Tasty Mushroom	18
Colorful Mushrooms	20
Wind Gem	16

						POI	FRZ	PAR	SIL	CUR	FOG	STN	DTH
-10	10	0	10	0	0	100	100	100	100	100	100	100	95

A myconid with a partially decayed cap. Though its wretched stench often induces vomiting, it is surprisingly edible once deodorized.

CARNIVOROUS PLANT
Lv. 26

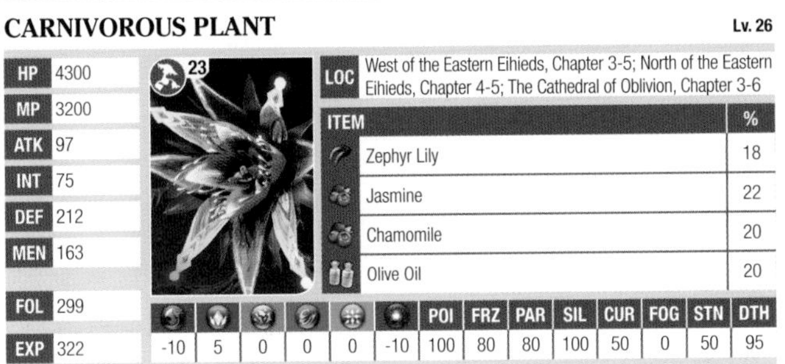

HP	MP	ATK	INT	DEF	MEN	FOL	EXP
4300	3200	97	75	212	163	299	322

LOC West of the Eastern Eihieds, Chapter 3-5; North of the Eastern Eihieds, Chapter 4-5; The Cathedral of Oblivion, Chapter 3-6

ITEM	%
Zephyr Lily	18
Jasmine	22
Chamomile	20
Olive Oil	20

						POI	FRZ	PAR	SIL	CUR	FOG	STN	DTH
-10	5	0	0	0	-10	100	80	80	100	50	0	50	95

A species of gargantuan flowering plant that populates Langdauq. It employs its lengthy vines and potent seeds to assay its enemies.

CHAOTIC CELL
Lv. 69

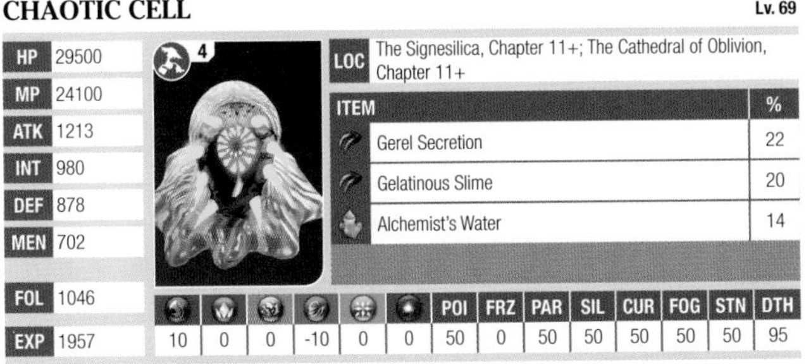

HP	MP	ATK	INT	DEF	MEN	FOL	EXP
29500	24100	1213	980	878	702	1046	1957

LOC The Signesilica, Chapter 11+; The Cathedral of Oblivion, Chapter 11+

ITEM	%
Gerel Secretion	22
Gelatinous Slime	20
Alchemist's Water	14

						POI	FRZ	PAR	SIL	CUR	FOG	STN	DTH
10	0	0	-10	0	0	50	0	50	50	50	50	50	95

A gerel that genetically mutated when exposed to a signet. As a result, it can no longer reproduce, but has an exceedingly long lifespan.

CORPULENT MAGVOR
Lv. 26

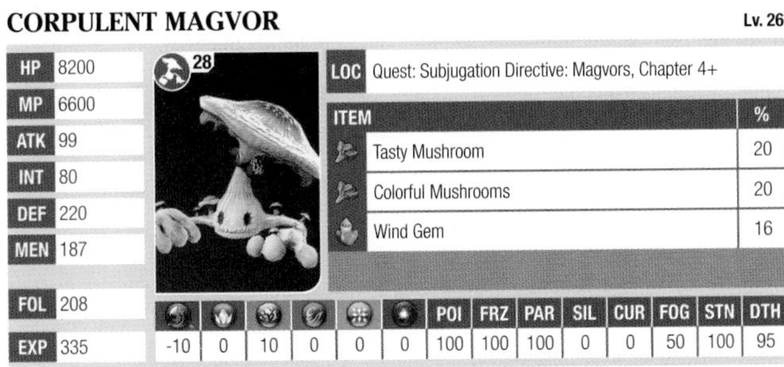

HP	MP	ATK	INT	DEF	MEN	FOL	EXP
8200	6600	99	80	220	187	208	335

LOC Quest: Subjugation Directive: Magvors, Chapter 4+

ITEM	%
Tasty Mushroom	20
Colorful Mushrooms	20
Wind Gem	16

						POI	FRZ	PAR	SIL	CUR	FOG	STN	DTH
-10	0	10	0	0	0	100	100	100	0	0	50	100	95

This foreign species of myconid, almost identical to native ones, multiplied rapidly in the few years since its spores alighted on Vestiel.

DIMINUTIVE FUNGUS
Lv. 34

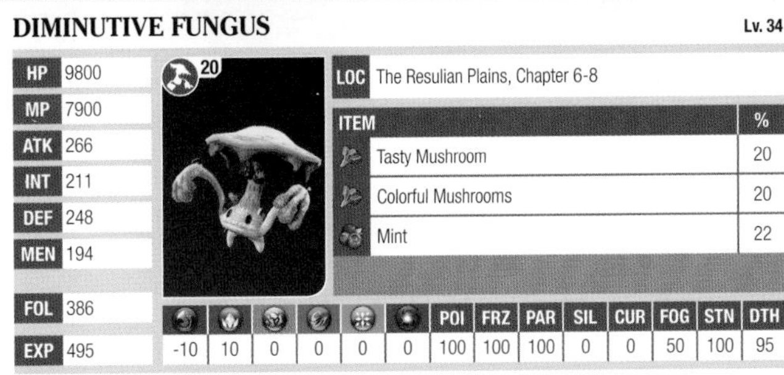

HP	MP	ATK	INT	DEF	MEN	FOL	EXP
9800	7900	266	211	248	194	386	495

LOC The Resulian Plains, Chapter 6-8

ITEM	%
Tasty Mushroom	20
Colorful Mushrooms	20
Mint	22

						POI	FRZ	PAR	SIL	CUR	FOG	STN	DTH
-10	10	0	0	0	0	100	100	100	0	0	50	100	95

This pin of a giant fungus protects itself by releasing the selfsame internal toxin into the air as its mature counterpart.

DISCORD GEREL
Lv. 7

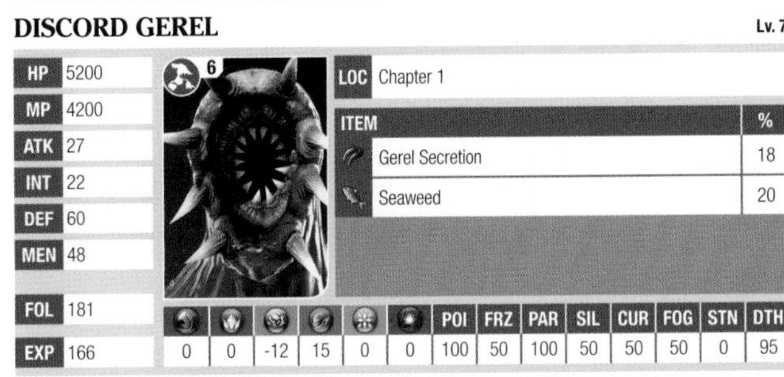

HP	MP	ATK	INT	DEF	MEN	FOL	EXP
5200	4200	27	22	60	48	181	166

LOC Chapter 1

ITEM	%
Gerel Secretion	18
Seaweed	20

						POI	FRZ	PAR	SIL	CUR	FOG	STN	DTH
0	0	-12	15	0	0	100	50	100	50	50	50	0	95

A monolithic mollusk that will occasionally appear on beaches. As it only leaves the shoals to feed, all who encounter it are potential prey.

DRYAD
Lv. 9

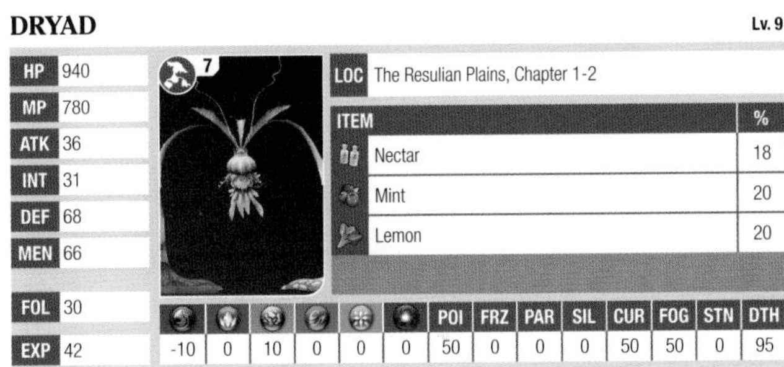

HP	MP	ATK	INT	DEF	MEN	FOL	EXP
940	780	36	31	68	66	30	42

LOC The Resulian Plains, Chapter 1-2

ITEM	%
Nectar	18
Mint	20
Lemon	20

						POI	FRZ	PAR	SIL	CUR	FOG	STN	DTH
-10	0	10	0	0	0	50	0	0	0	50	50	0	95

This ambulant plant uses its leaves and stems to migrate to more hospitable habitats. Only one year needs pass for it to attain this size.

ELDER TREANT
Lv. 54

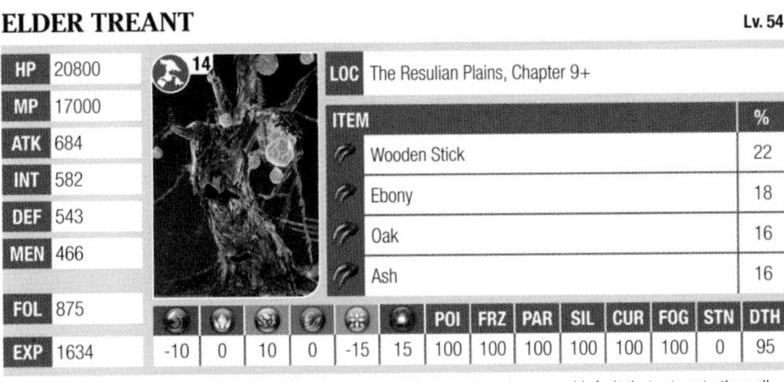

HP	MP	ATK	INT	DEF	MEN	FOL	EXP
20800	17000	684	582	543	466	875	1634

LOC The Resulian Plains, Chapter 9+

ITEM	%
Wooden Stick	22
Ebony	18
Oak	16
Ash	16

						POI	FRZ	PAR	SIL	CUR	FOG	STN	DTH
-10	0	10	0	-15	15	100	100	100	100	100	100	0	95

The bark of this sentient tree is laden with poisonous sap. Its branches also sag with fruit that return to the soil all who eat them.

EROSIVE CYKLA
Lv. 22

30

HP	MP	ATK	INT	DEF	MEN	FOL	EXP
3900	3300	91	81	187	159	106	263

LOC Quest: Corruption of the Land, Chapter 3+

ITEM	%
Zephyr Lily	16
Jasmine	20
Chamomile	18
Olive Oil	18

						POI	FRZ	PAR	SIL	CUR	FOG	STN	DTH
-10	5	0	0	0	-10	100	100	80	100	80	0	50	95

This signet-imbued plant was bred by a foolish noble who wished to win a flower contest, but instead created a murderous fiend.

FALLEN ARCEDIA

Lv. 68

HP	MP	ATK	INT	DEF	MEN	FOL	EXP
209700	162900	1443	1266	907	755	1448	2418

36

LOC Quest: Uprooting Families, Chapter 11+

ITEM	%
Wooden Stick	22
Ebony	20
Oak	18
Ash	16

						POI	FRZ	PAR	SIL	CUR	FOG	STN	DTH
-10	0	10	0	0	0	100	0	100	100	0	50	0	95

This plant was lovingly raised by an old woman looking for company, but its appearance is so horrific it brings childen to tears.

FECUND MAGVORLING

Lv. 26

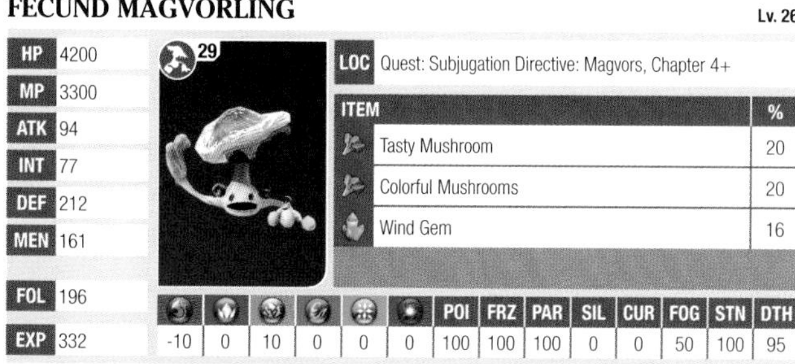

HP	MP	ATK	INT	DEF	MEN	FOL	EXP
4200	3300	94	77	212	161	196	332

29

LOC Quest: Subjugation Directive: Magvors, Chapter 4+

ITEM	%
Tasty Mushroom	20
Colorful Mushrooms	20
Wind Gem	16

						POI	FRZ	PAR	SIL	CUR	FOG	STN	DTH
-10	0	10	0	0	0	100	100	100	0	0	50	100	95

Though still immature by every other creature's standards, the young of magvors can already reproduce—at an alarming rate—soon after birth.

FRAN OF CONSTANT DECAY

Lv. 32

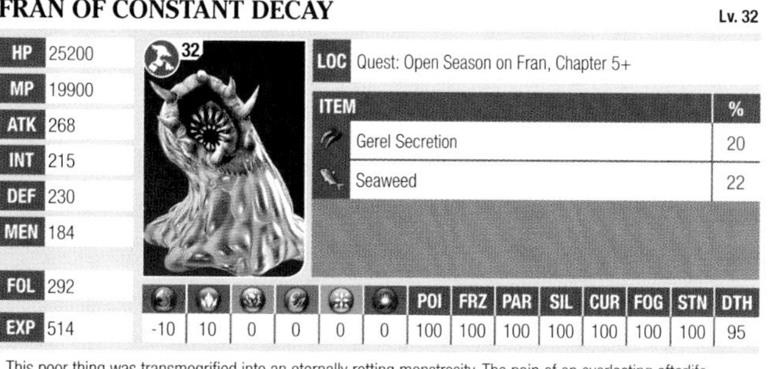

HP	MP	ATK	INT	DEF	MEN	FOL	EXP
25200	19900	268	215	230	184	292	514

32

LOC Quest: Open Season on Fran, Chapter 5+

ITEM	%
Gerel Secretion	20
Seaweed	22

						POI	FRZ	PAR	SIL	CUR	FOG	STN	DTH
-10	10	0	0	0	0	100	100	100	100	100	100	100	95

This poor thing was transmogrified into an eternally rotting monstrosity. The pain of an everlasting afterlife haunts her wherever she crawls.

GERALDINE

Lv. 63

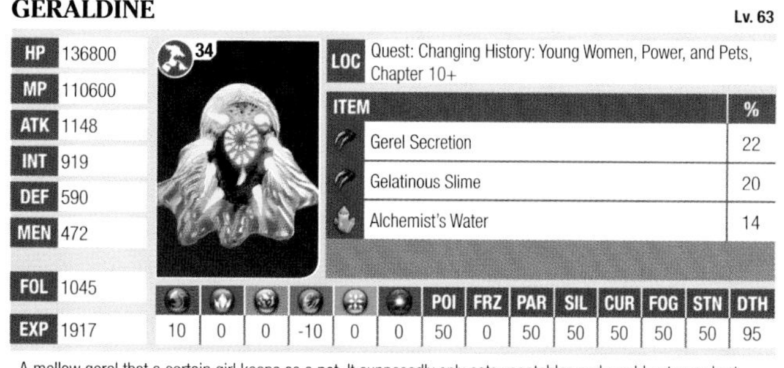

HP	MP	ATK	INT	DEF	MEN	FOL	EXP
136800	110600	1148	919	590	472	1045	1917

34

LOC Quest: Changing History: Young Women, Power, and Pets, Chapter 10+

ITEM	%
Gerel Secretion	22
Gelatinous Slime	20
Alchemist's Water	14

						POI	FRZ	PAR	SIL	CUR	FOG	STN	DTH
10	0	0	-10	0	0	50	0	50	50	50	50	50	95

A mellow gerel that a certain girl keeps as a pet. It supposedly only eats vegetables and would not even hurt a fly.

GEREL

Lv. 4

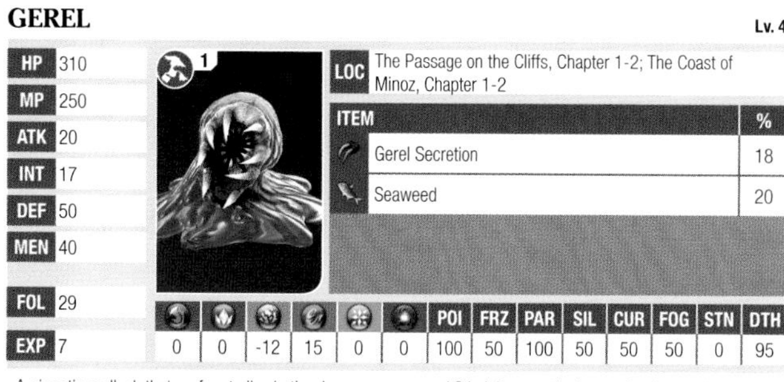

HP	MP	ATK	INT	DEF	MEN	FOL	EXP
310	250	20	17	50	40	29	7

1

LOC The Passage on the Cliffs, Chapter 1-2; The Coast of Minoz, Chapter 1-2

ITEM	%
Gerel Secretion	18
Seaweed	20

						POI	FRZ	PAR	SIL	CUR	FOG	STN	DTH
0	0	-12	15	0	0	100	50	100	50	50	50	0	95

A gigantic mollusk that prefers to live in the damp areas around Sthal. Its appetite is notoriously voracious, and it ingests all manner of things.

GIANT FUNGUS

Lv. 36

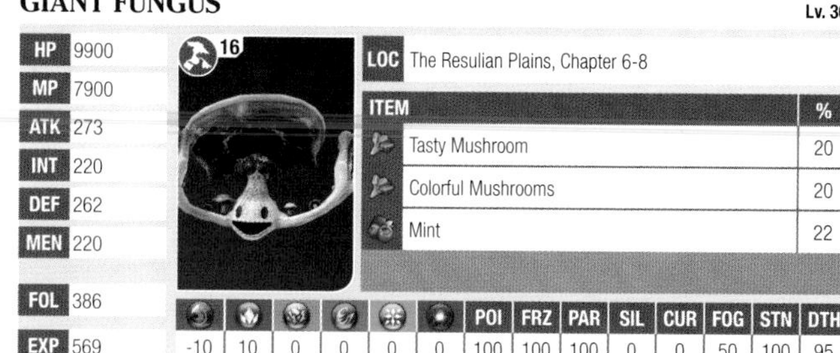

HP	MP	ATK	INT	DEF	MEN	FOL	EXP
9900	7900	273	220	262	220	386	569

16

LOC The Resulian Plains, Chapter 6-8

ITEM	%
Tasty Mushroom	20
Colorful Mushrooms	20
Mint	22

						POI	FRZ	PAR	SIL	CUR	FOG	STN	DTH
-10	10	0	0	0	0	100	100	100	0	0	50	100	95

The biology of this jumping Faykreedian mushroom is similar to that of the mist grave, but this subspecies possesses an internal toxin as well.

LAMIA RADIX

Lv. 54

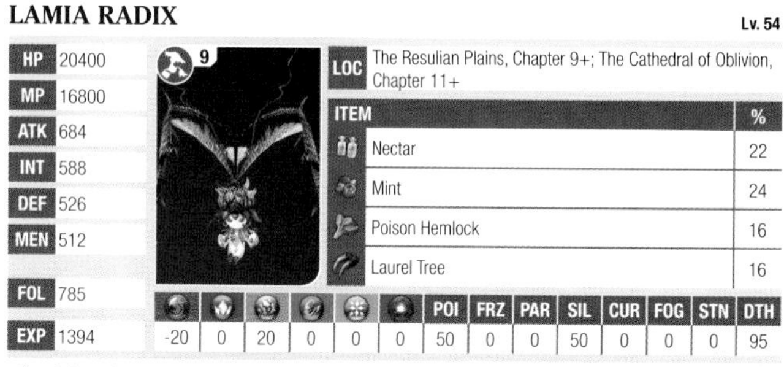

HP	MP	ATK	INT	DEF	MEN	FOL	EXP
20400	16800	684	588	526	512	785	1394

9

LOC The Resulian Plains, Chapter 9+; The Cathedral of Oblivion, Chapter 11+

ITEM	%
Nectar	22
Mint	24
Poison Hemlock	16
Laurel Tree	16

						POI	FRZ	PAR	SIL	CUR	FOG	STN	DTH
-20	0	20	0	0	0	50	0	0	50	0	0	0	95

Though it requires decades to grow, once it has, this creature becomes omniurnal and adept at signeturgy. It also has a habit of stargazing.

LANGUID PIJILLO

Lv. 68

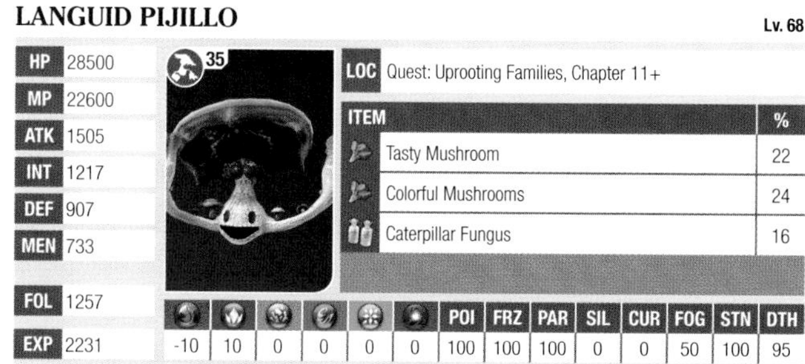

HP	MP	ATK	INT	DEF	MEN	FOL	EXP
28500	22600	1505	1217	907	733	1257	2231

35

LOC Quest: Uprooting Families, Chapter 11+

ITEM	%
Tasty Mushroom	22
Colorful Mushrooms	24
Caterpillar Fungus	16

						POI	FRZ	PAR	SIL	CUR	FOG	STN	DTH
-10	10	0	0	0	0	100	100	100	0	0	50	100	95

This plant species was lovingly raised by an old woman looking for companionship, but its spore dispersal has the neighborhood up in arms.

MAIDENLY BLOSSOM

Lv. 80

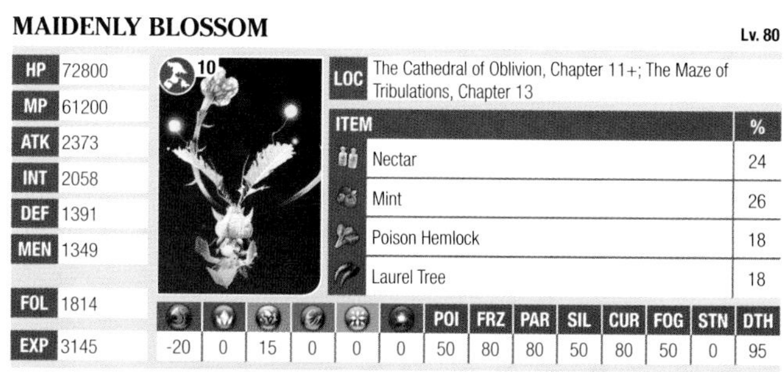

HP	MP	ATK	INT	DEF	MEN	FOL	EXP
72800	61200	2373	2058	1391	1349	1814	3145

10

LOC The Cathedral of Oblivion, Chapter 11+; The Maze of Tribulations, Chapter 13

ITEM	%
Nectar	24
Mint	26
Poison Hemlock	18
Laurel Tree	18

						POI	FRZ	PAR	SIL	CUR	FOG	STN	DTH
-20	0	15	0	0	0	50	80	80	50	80	50	0	95

The noctilucous liquid that courses through this plant causes it to glow, which becomes a true spectable when its kind assembles in droves.

MANDRAGORA

Lv. 19

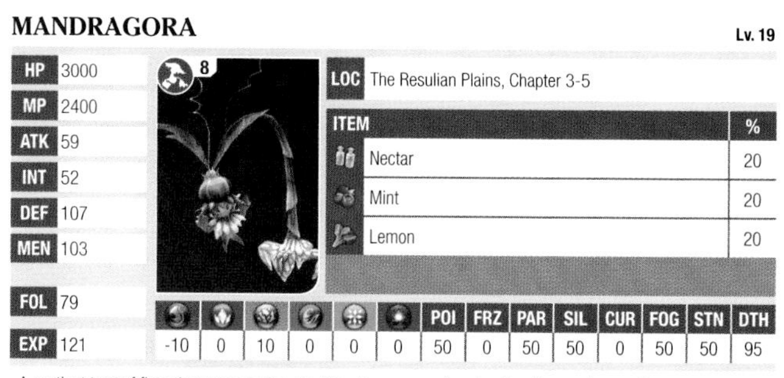

HP	MP	ATK	INT	DEF	MEN	FOL	EXP
3000	2400	59	52	107	103	79	121

8

LOC The Resulian Plains, Chapter 3-5

ITEM	%
Nectar	20
Mint	20
Lemon	20

						POI	FRZ	PAR	SIL	CUR	FOG	STN	DTH
-10	0	10	0	0	0	50	0	50	50	0	50	50	95

A sentient type of flora that grows in Resulia. After three years of maturation, it can release a fragrance so ambrosial it charms passersby.

MAN-EATING TREE

Lv. 22

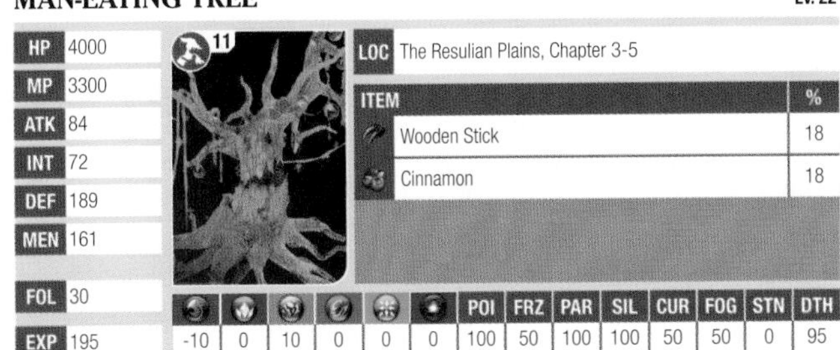

HP	MP	ATK	INT	DEF	MEN	FOL	EXP
4000	3300	84	72	189	161	30	195

LOC: The Resulian Plains, Chapter 3-5

ITEM	%
Wooden Stick	18
Cinnamon	18

						POI	FRZ	PAR	SIL	CUR	FOG	STN	DTH
-10	0	10	0	0	0	100	50	100	100	50	50	0	95

A sapling once, now it is an arboreal terror that roams the Resulian Plains, using its roots as feet and its branches as fists.

MAN TRAP

Lv. 61

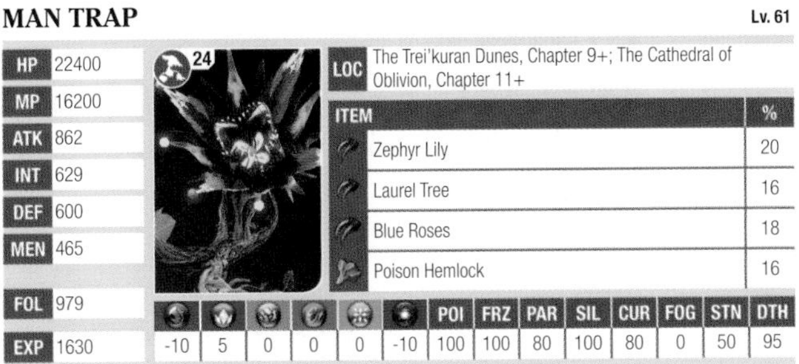

HP	MP	ATK	INT	DEF	MEN	FOL	EXP
22400	16200	862	629	600	465	979	1630

LOC: The Trei'kuran Dunes, Chapter 9+; The Cathedral of Oblivion, Chapter 11+

ITEM	%
Zephyr Lily	20
Laurel Tree	16
Blue Roses	18
Poison Hemlock	16

						POI	FRZ	PAR	SIL	CUR	FOG	STN	DTH
-10	5	0	0	0	-10	100	100	80	100	80	0	50	95

A giant, rotten flower that grows near Eastern Trei'kur. It lures prey in with a luscious fragrance, and then constricts its airways with vines.

MIST GRAVE

Lv. 10

HP	MP	ATK	INT	DEF	MEN	FOL	EXP
1700	1400	41	32	73	61	27	27

LOC: The Resulian Plains, Chapter 1-2

ITEM	%
Tasty Mushroom	18
Colorful Mushrooms	18

						POI	FRZ	PAR	SIL	CUR	FOG	STN	DTH
-10	0	10	0	0	0	100	100	100	0	0	50	100	95

A species of jumping mushroom found on Faykreed. It paralyzes victims with its spores, then attaches itself and sucks nutrients from them.

MYCONID

Lv. 53

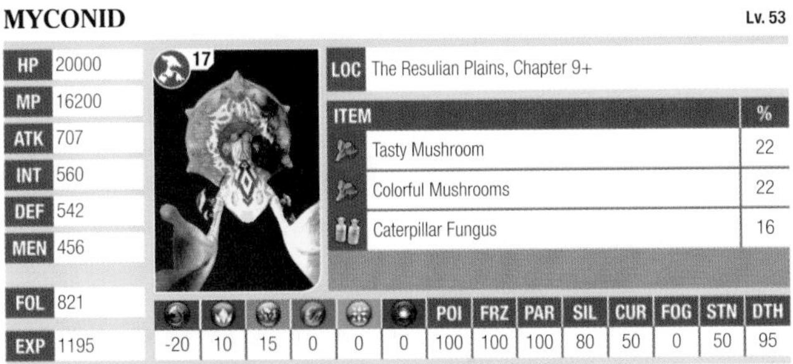

HP	MP	ATK	INT	DEF	MEN	FOL	EXP
20000	16200	707	560	542	456	821	1195

LOC: The Resulian Plains, Chapter 9+

ITEM	%
Tasty Mushroom	22
Colorful Mushrooms	22
Caterpillar Fungus	16

						POI	FRZ	PAR	SIL	CUR	FOG	STN	DTH
-20	10	15	0	0	0	100	100	100	80	50	0	50	95

Each bound this mushroom takes severs hyphae, thus shortening its lifespan. While it lives, though, the beast revels in its airborne freedom.

MYCONID SPORELING

Lv. 51

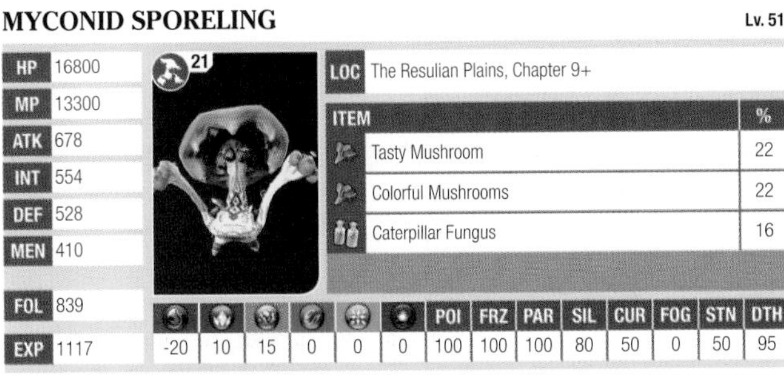

HP	MP	ATK	INT	DEF	MEN	FOL	EXP
16800	13300	678	554	528	410	839	1117

LOC: The Resulian Plains, Chapter 9+

ITEM	%
Tasty Mushroom	22
Colorful Mushrooms	22
Caterpillar Fungus	16

						POI	FRZ	PAR	SIL	CUR	FOG	STN	DTH
-20	10	15	0	0	0	100	100	100	80	50	0	50	95

The pin of a myconid. As if to challenge its fully grown form, it bounds about with utmost vigor, vexing people wherever it goes.

PYGMY GLAIVE

Lv. 8

HP	MP	ATK	INT	DEF	MEN	FOL	EXP
930	740	36	29	66	51	27	15

LOC: The Resulian Plains, Chapter 1-2

ITEM	%
Tasty Mushroom	18
Colorful Mushrooms	18

						POI	FRZ	PAR	SIL	CUR	FOG	STN	DTH
-10	0	10	0	0	0	100	100	100	0	0	50	100	95

Children constantly try to bring home these hypnotizingly adorable mist grave pins to keep as pets, but their parents know better.

STROPER

Lv. 47

HP	MP	ATK	INT	DEF	MEN	FOL	EXP
15200	12200	583	471	314	254	592	1119

LOC: The Trei'kuran Dunes, Chapter 6-8; The Cathedral of Oblivion, Chapter 7-10

ITEM	%
Gerel Secretion	20
Seaweed	22
Mercury	18

						POI	FRZ	PAR	SIL	CUR	FOG	STN	DTH
-10	10	0	0	0	0	100	100	100	100	100	100	100	95

The body of this gerel is colored in such a garish and ominous manner that it induces a flight reaction in its enemies almost instantly.

STUBBORN VEJHEERIT

Lv. 59

HP	MP	ATK	INT	DEF	MEN	FOL	EXP
20800	17400	975	813	573	550	952	1825

LOC: Quest: Subjugation Directive: Vejheerits, Chapter 9+

ITEM	%
Nectar	22
Mint	24
Poison Hemlock	16
Laurel Tree	16

						POI	FRZ	PAR	SIL	CUR	FOG	STN	DTH
-20	0	20	0	0	0	50	0	0	50	0	0	0	95

This species of flora originated by the slip of a tipsy signeturge's brush when imbuing a carrot. It pairs surprisingly well with beef stew.

THORAS THE ABOMINATION

Lv. 75

HP	MP	ATK	INT	DEF	MEN	FOL	EXP
1359700	1109300	2142	1645	947	813	0	27773

LOC: Chapter 12

ITEM	%
Wondrous Tincture	100

						POI	FRZ	PAR	SIL	CUR	FOG	STN	DTH
-10	5	0	0	0	-10	100	100	80	100	100	100	50	100

Thoras after fusing with a welwitschia. Now a blight on nature, he slithers around while expelling a miasma most foul.

THORAS THE ABOMINATION

Lv. 100

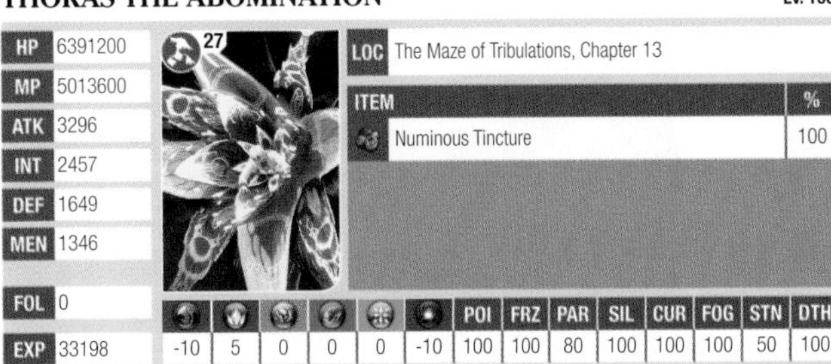

HP	MP	ATK	INT	DEF	MEN	FOL	EXP
6391200	5013600	3296	2457	1649	1346	0	33198

LOC: The Maze of Tribulations, Chapter 13

ITEM	%
Numinous Tincture	100

						POI	FRZ	PAR	SIL	CUR	FOG	STN	DTH
-10	5	0	0	0	-10	100	100	80	100	100	100	50	100

Thoras after fusing with a welwitschia. Now a blight on nature, he slithers around while expelling a miasma most foul.

TINYCAP
Lv. 18

HP	MP	ATK	INT	DEF	MEN	FOL	EXP
2900	2300	84	68	107	83	259	95

LOC: The Resulian Plains, Chapter 3-5

ITEM	%
Tasty Mushroom	18
Colorful Mushrooms	20
Wind Gem	16

						POI	FRZ	PAR	SIL	CUR	FOG	STN	DTH
-10	10	0	10	0	0	100	100	100	100	100	100	100	95

The pileus of this blightcap pin is only slightly rotten. Although its decaying, immature body is fragile, it continues to jump with zeal.

TREANT
Lv. 61

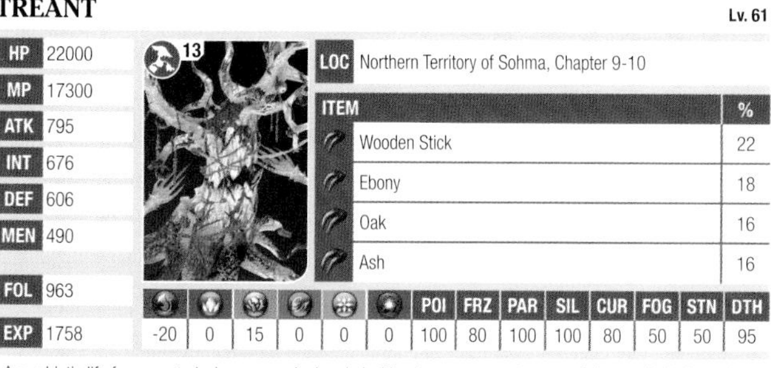

HP	MP	ATK	INT	DEF	MEN	FOL	EXP
22000	17300	795	676	606	490	963	1758

LOC: Northern Territory of Sohma, Chapter 9-10

ITEM	%
Wooden Stick	22
Ebony	18
Oak	16
Ash	16

						POI	FRZ	PAR	SIL	CUR	FOG	STN	DTH
-20	0	15	0	0	0	100	80	100	100	80	50	50	95

A symbiotic life form created when a parasite bonded with a tree over a century ago. It thoroughly believes that it is purely a tree.

VERDANT MUJA
Lv. 43

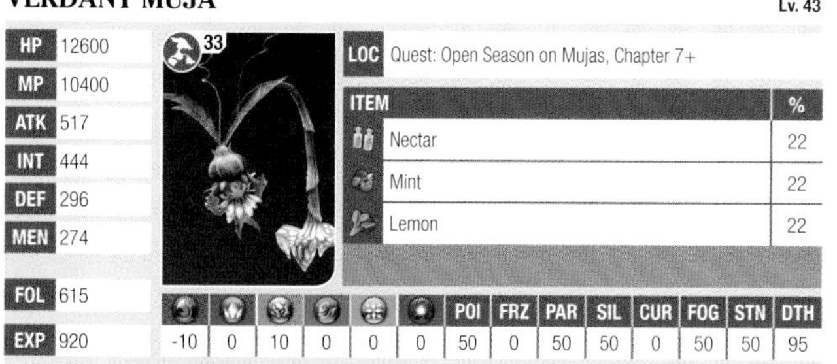

HP	MP	ATK	INT	DEF	MEN	FOL	EXP
12600	10400	517	444	296	274	615	920

LOC: Quest: Open Season on Mujas, Chapter 7+

ITEM	%
Nectar	22
Mint	22
Lemon	22

						POI	FRZ	PAR	SIL	CUR	FOG	STN	DTH
-10	0	10	0	0	0	50	0	50	50	0	50	50	95

This species of plant sprouted from the waste expunged from the royal institute, which is how it developed its taste for those with signets.

VISCOUS CLOD
Lv. 100

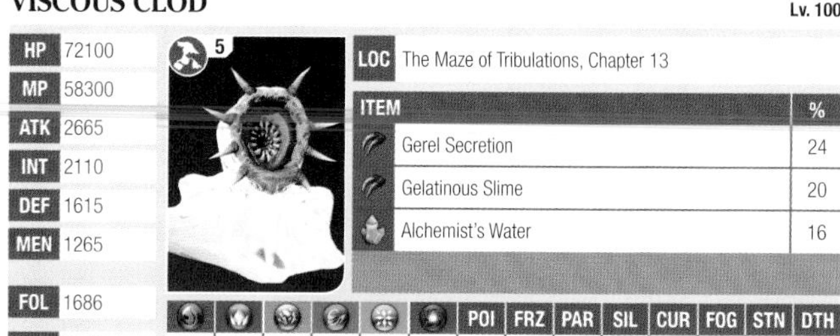

HP	MP	ATK	INT	DEF	MEN	FOL	EXP
72100	58300	2665	2110	1615	1265	1686	3242

LOC: The Maze of Tribulations, Chapter 13

ITEM	%
Gerel Secretion	24
Gelatinous Slime	20
Alchemist's Water	16

						POI	FRZ	PAR	SIL	CUR	FOG	STN	DTH
-20	0	0	0	0	10	100	100	100	100	100	100	100	95

A subspecies of gerel that gorged on yellow, acidic fruit for so long that it absorbed the fruit's genome and adopted those traits.

VOMITING GEL
Lv. 19

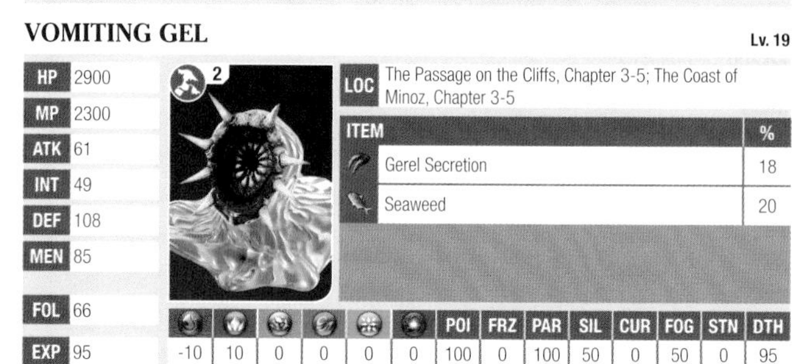

HP	MP	ATK	INT	DEF	MEN	FOL	EXP
2900	2300	61	49	108	85	66	95

LOC: The Passage on the Cliffs, Chapter 3-5; The Coast of Minoz, Chapter 3-5

ITEM	%
Gerel Secretion	18
Seaweed	20

						POI	FRZ	PAR	SIL	CUR	FOG	STN	DTH
-10	10	0	0	0	0	100	0	100	50	0	50	0	95

This mollusk prefers a dark, moist habitat. It expectorates digestive fluids, which react with the air to produce a thick, caustic brume.

WELWITSCHIA
Lv. 64

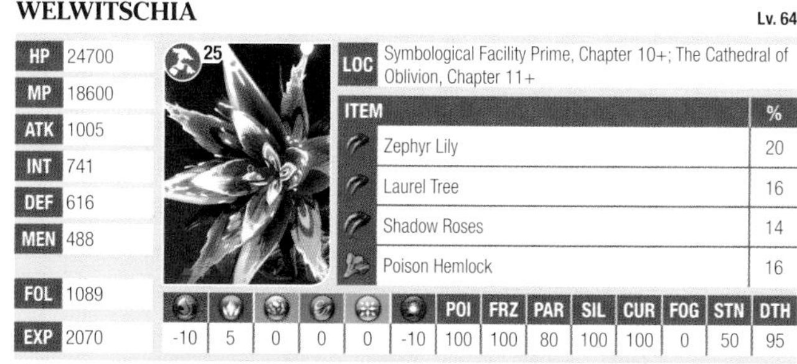

HP	MP	ATK	INT	DEF	MEN	FOL	EXP
24700	18600	1005	741	616	488	1089	2070

LOC: Symbological Facility Prime, Chapter 10+; The Cathedral of Oblivion, Chapter 11+

ITEM	%
Zephyr Lily	20
Laurel Tree	16
Shadow Roses	14
Poison Hemlock	16

						POI	FRZ	PAR	SIL	CUR	FOG	STN	DTH
-10	5	0	0	0	-10	100	100	80	100	100	0	50	95

A species of carnivorous plant reared at a Kronos research facility. Its tendrils are especially fibrous, and know no bounds when attacking.

CORRUPT

AMBER PRINCESS
Lv. 66

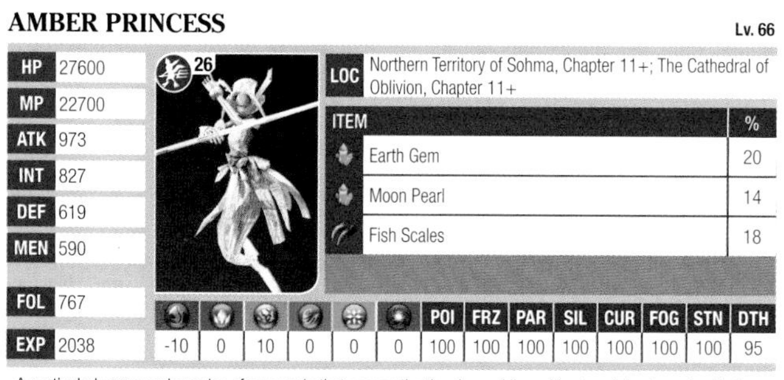

HP	MP	ATK	INT	DEF	MEN	FOL	EXP
27600	22700	973	827	619	590	767	2038

LOC: Northern Territory of Sohma, Chapter 11+; The Cathedral of Oblivion, Chapter 11+

ITEM	%
Earth Gem	20
Moon Pearl	14
Fish Scales	18

						POI	FRZ	PAR	SIL	CUR	FOG	STN	DTH
-10	0	10	0	0	0	100	100	100	100	100	100	100	95

A particularly smug subspecies of aquaregia that passes the time by cackling with glee while showering its foes with earthen boulders.

AQUAREGIA
Lv. 40

HP	MP	ATK	INT	DEF	MEN	FOL	EXP
10200	8600	340	280	276	263	373	598

LOC: The Passage on the Cliffs, Chapter 6-8; The Coast of Minoz, Chapter 6-8

ITEM	%
Ice Gem	18
Amber	14
Fish Scales	18

						POI	FRZ	PAR	SIL	CUR	FOG	STN	DTH
-10	0	0	0	0	0	100	100	80	80	100	100	50	95

This common mermaid may appear to be a single organism, but is really an amalgam of countless sentient water crystals that agreed to fuse.

AMORPHOUS DRYX
Lv. 22

HP	MP	ATK	INT	DEF	MEN	FOL	EXP
3900	3200	92	81	187	156	116	258

LOC: Quest: Corruption of the Land, Chapter 3+

ITEM	%
Rivets	18
Gunpowder	18

						POI	FRZ	PAR	SIL	CUR	FOG	STN	DTH
0	20	10	10	10	10	100	100	50	100	50	100	0	95

This subspecies of Corrupt was created and then promptly disposed of by an ignorant aristocrat looking for a momentary diversion.

BASKANIA
Lv. 80

HP	MP	ATK	INT	DEF	MEN	FOL	EXP
73500	58200	2398	2038	1435	1195	911	3501

LOC: The Maze of Tribulations, Chapter 13

ITEM	%
Mati	18
Scalestone	18
Philosopher's Stone	12
Alchemist's Water	16

						POI	FRZ	PAR	SIL	CUR	FOG	STN	DTH
0	0	0	0	0	0	100	100	80	100	100	50	0	100

A Corrupt that resembles massive floating eyeballs. Those who look it in ones of its eyes inevitably succumb to crippling bouts of fear and dread.

BLOODTHIRSTY FIEND

Lv. 140

33

HP	13155800
MP	10312000
ATK	5031
INT	3430
DEF	2689
MEN	2151
FOL	6337
EXP	97140

LOC: The Maze of Tribulations, Chapter 13

ITEM	%
Parchment	20
Fine Parchment	18
Bushy Fur	26
Orichalcum	18

						POI	FRZ	PAR	SIL	CUR	FOG	STN	DTH
-20	0	6	0	0	0	100	100	100	100	100	100	100	100

A manticore clad in armor emblazoned with signets and armed with a stinger made of crystal honed to the point where it could pierce stone.

BONE KNIGHT

Lv. 55

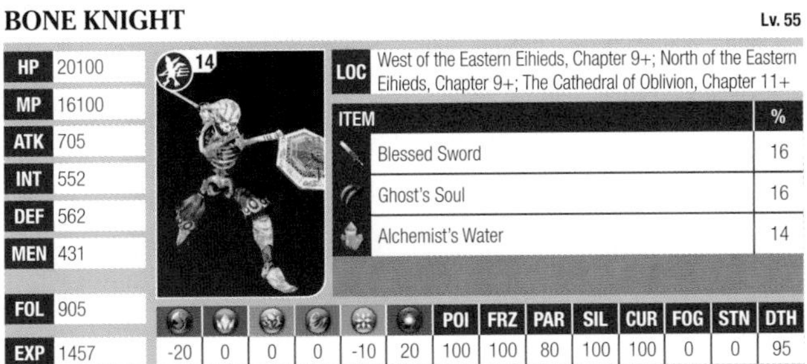

14

HP	20100
MP	16100
ATK	705
INT	552
DEF	562
MEN	431
FOL	905
EXP	1457

LOC: West of the Eastern Eihieds, Chapter 9+; North of the Eastern Eihieds, Chapter 9+; The Cathedral of Oblivion, Chapter 11+

ITEM	%
Blessed Sword	16
Ghost's Soul	16
Alchemist's Water	14

						POI	FRZ	PAR	SIL	CUR	FOG	STN	DTH
-20	0	0	0	-10	20	100	100	80	100	100	0	0	95

A knight who was reanimated by the gods so he could continue his quest. Every five steps, however, his purpose eludes him again.

CABRAKAN

Lv. 51

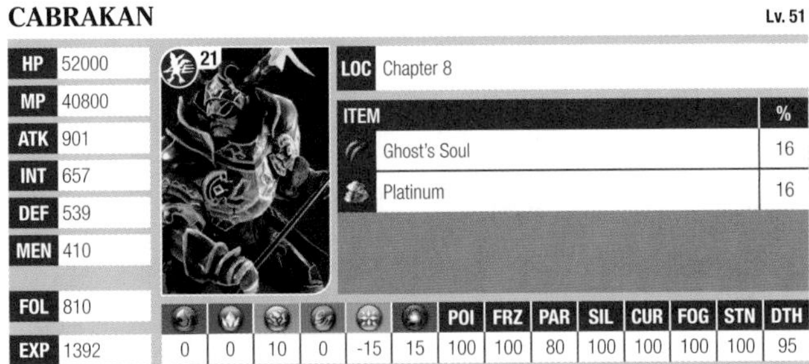

21

HP	52000
MP	40800
ATK	901
INT	657
DEF	539
MEN	410
FOL	810
EXP	1392

LOC: Chapter 8

ITEM	%
Ghost's Soul	16
Platinum	16

						POI	FRZ	PAR	SIL	CUR	FOG	STN	DTH
0	0	10	0	-15	15	100	100	80	100	100	100	100	95

An animated suit of armor that prowls the halls of the slaughtery. Its hammer can pulverize not only bones, but the dreams of its survivors.

CRYSTAL GUARDIAN

Lv. 71

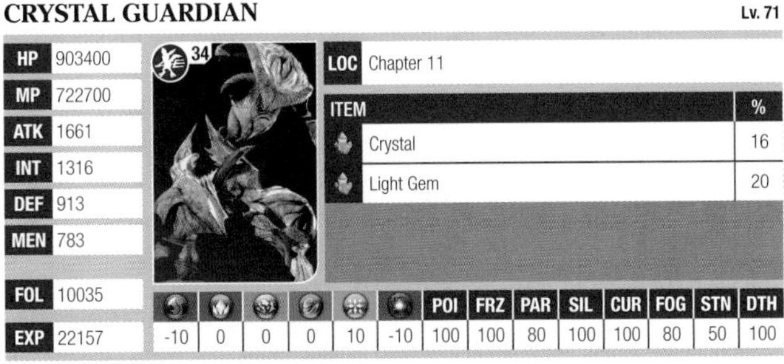

34

HP	903400
MP	722700
ATK	1661
INT	1316
DEF	913
MEN	783
FOL	10035
EXP	22157

LOC: Chapter 11

ITEM	%
Crystal	16
Light Gem	20

						POI	FRZ	PAR	SIL	CUR	FOG	STN	DTH
-10	0	0	0	10	-10	100	100	80	100	100	80	50	100

A chevalier carved from the most resilient of minerals. Its four tapered legs are regal and lithe—qualities that belie their shocking strength.

CUNNING ZURTAIL

Lv. 53

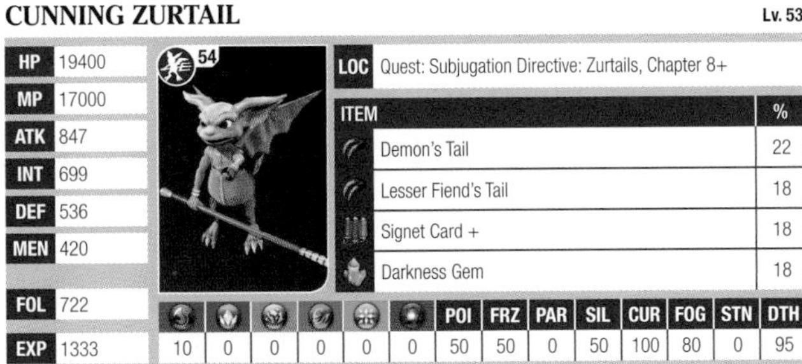

54

HP	19400
MP	17000
ATK	847
INT	699
DEF	536
MEN	420
FOL	722
EXP	1333

LOC: Quest: Subjugation Directive: Zurtails, Chapter 8+

ITEM	%
Demon's Tail	22
Lesser Fiend's Tail	18
Signet Card +	18
Darkness Gem	18

						POI	FRZ	PAR	SIL	CUR	FOG	STN	DTH
10	0	0	0	0	0	50	50	0	50	100	80	0	95

A critter obsessed with other people's possessions. Though many assumed demons had no use for money, these beasts' behavior suggests otherwise.

CURSED HORROR

Lv. 50

1

HP	16400
MP	13100
ATK	713
INT	531
DEF	500
MEN	430
FOL	721
EXP	1264

LOC: The Trei'kur Slaughtery, Chapter 8+; The Cathedral of Oblivion, Chapter 7-10

ITEM	%
Bloodstained Cloth	22

						POI	FRZ	PAR	SIL	CUR	FOG	STN	DTH
0	0	0	0	-20	10	100	100	0	100	100	0	0	95

A disembodied spirit that despises everything about the living. It uses a sickle to part victims' souls from their bodies, then feeds upon them.

DAMASCUS FORT

Lv. 39

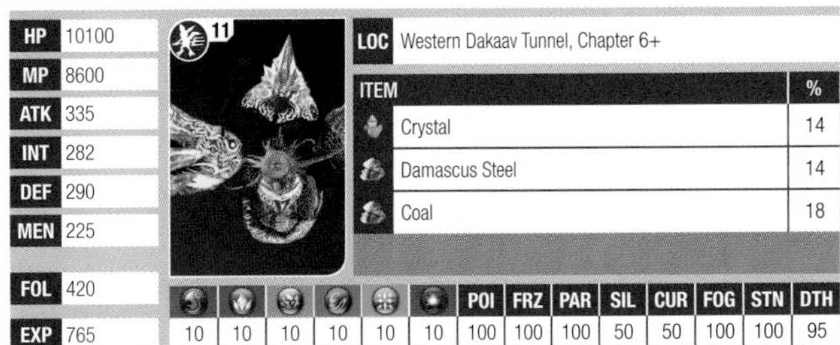

11

HP	10100
MP	8600
ATK	335
INT	282
DEF	290
MEN	225
FOL	420
EXP	765

LOC: Western Dakaav Tunnel, Chapter 6+

ITEM	%
Crystal	14
Damascus Steel	14
Coal	18

						POI	FRZ	PAR	SIL	CUR	FOG	STN	DTH
10	10	10	10	10	10	100	100	100	50	50	100	100	95

Every conceivable body part of this beast is outfitted with Damascus steel ore, making it a walking garrison that is nigh on invulnerable.

DANTE THE OBSTINATE

Lv. 69

56

HP	251400
MP	195000
ATK	1781
INT	1213
DEF	943
MEN	695
FOL	1489
EXP	2562

LOC: Quest: Subjugation Directive: Dante and Mateo, Chapter 11+

ITEM	%
Ghost's Soul	16
Mythril	14

						POI	FRZ	PAR	SIL	CUR	FOG	STN	DTH
0	0	10	0	-10	10	100	100	50	100	80	100	80	95

As no one knows the origin or identity of this prodigious armored man, people suspect him to be an ancient panoply animated by signets.

DARK MATERIAL

Lv. 68

9

HP	27900
MP	23300
ATK	1204
INT	983
DEF	916
MEN	725
FOL	454
EXP	1917

LOC: The Signesilica, Chapter 11+

ITEM	%
Darkness Gem	20
Crystal	16
Mythril	14
Platinum	16

						POI	FRZ	PAR	SIL	CUR	FOG	STN	DTH
0	0	0	0	-10	10	100	100	100	50	50	50	100	95

This mucoid organism has interred minerals that command darkness within its malleable frame, with which it attacks when not using spells.

DEK OF THE BOILING BLOOD

Lv. 20

44

HP	6300
MP	4900
ATK	67
INT	54
DEF	140
MEN	92
FOL	53
EXP	231

LOC: Quest: Subjugation Directive: Dek, Chapter 3+

ITEM	%
Iron	18

						POI	FRZ	PAR	SIL	CUR	FOG	STN	DTH
0	-10	0	0	0	0	100	100	100	100	100	100	100	95

A Corrupt that has raged for so long that he cannot even remember what angered him in the first place, yet doing so has become second nature.

DEMON IMP
Lv. 27

16

HP	6600
MP	5600
ATK	116
INT	95
DEF	215
MEN	165
FOL	148
EXP	344

LOC North of the Eastern Eihieds, Chapter 4-5

ITEM	%
Demon's Tail	20
Wolf Fang	24
Signet Card	20

						POI	FRZ	PAR	SIL	CUR	FOG	STN	DTH
10	0	0	0	0	0	0	50	0	50	80	50	0	95

A tiny and relatively cute demon that wields a trident. It can be found attacking journeymen in large groups outside Santeroule.

DEMON SERVANT
Lv. 56

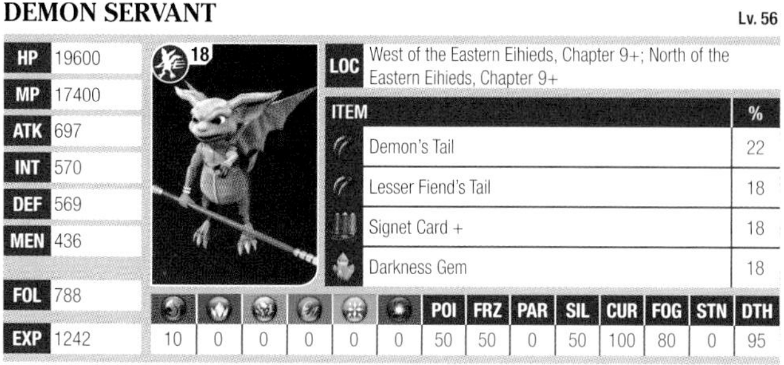

18

HP	19600
MP	17400
ATK	697
INT	570
DEF	569
MEN	436
FOL	788
EXP	1242

LOC West of the Eastern Eihieds, Chapter 9+; North of the Eastern Eihieds, Chapter 9+

ITEM	%
Demon's Tail	22
Lesser Fiend's Tail	18
Signet Card +	18
Darkness Gem	18

						POI	FRZ	PAR	SIL	CUR	FOG	STN	DTH
10	0	0	0	0	0	50	50	0	50	100	80	0	95

So pitiful is this lowest of the low-ranking demons that it only has wings to increas its apparent size as it stumbles about Langdauq.

DEVIL CHILD
Lv. 40

17

HP	10000
MP	8700
ATK	333
INT	272
DEF	284
MEN	221
FOL	362
EXP	518

LOC West of the Eastern Eihieds, Chapter 6-8; North of the Eastern Eihieds, Chapter 6-8; The Cathedral of Oblivion, Chapter 7-10

ITEM	%
Demon's Tail	20
Wolf Fang	24
Signet Card	20
Darkness Gem	18

						POI	FRZ	PAR	SIL	CUR	FOG	STN	DTH
10	0	0	0	0	0	50	50	0	50	80	50	0	95

The spawn of the most vile demon known to man. Though fine when left alone, it exhibits its sire's intractable temper when provoked.

DOLEFUL LORD BRAHMS
Lv. 70

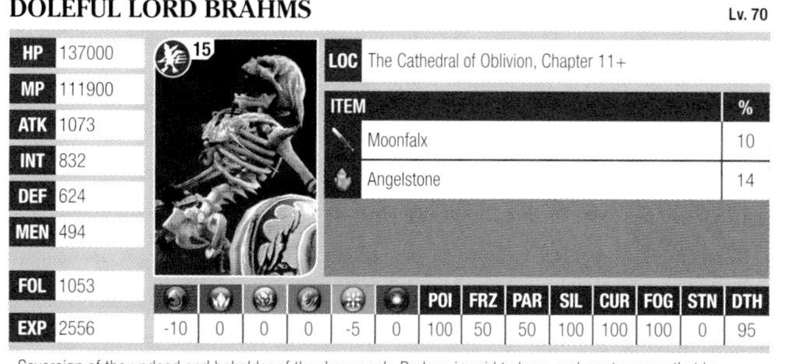

15

HP	137000
MP	111900
ATK	1073
INT	832
DEF	624
MEN	494
FOL	1053
EXP	2556

LOC The Cathedral of Oblivion, Chapter 11+

ITEM	%
Moonfalx	10
Angelstone	14

						POI	FRZ	PAR	SIL	CUR	FOG	STN	DTH
-10	0	0	0	-5	0	100	50	50	100	100	100	0	95

Sovereign of the undead and beholder of the dragon orb, Brahms is said to have such vast powers that he could easily transcend the gods.

DOUXRAH OF THE FROZEN TOUCH
Lv. 64

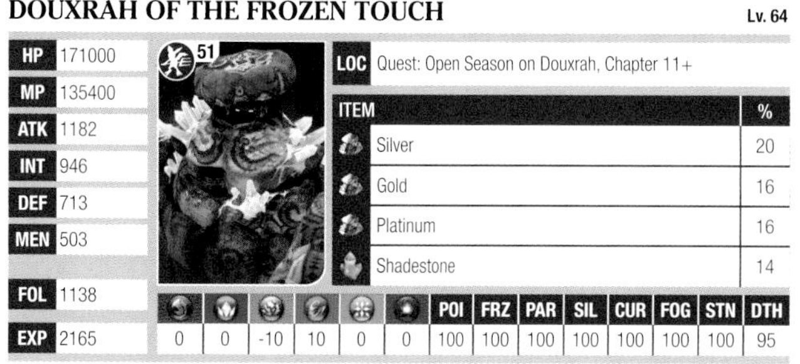

51

HP	171000
MP	135400
ATK	1182
INT	946
DEF	713
MEN	503
FOL	1138
EXP	2165

LOC Quest: Open Season on Douxrah, Chapter 11+

ITEM	%
Silver	20
Gold	16
Platinum	16
Shadestone	14

						POI	FRZ	PAR	SIL	CUR	FOG	STN	DTH
0	0	-10	10	0	0	100	100	100	100	100	100	100	95

A Corrupt thought to be a relic of the Signesilica. It surely had a purpose at one time, but is now nothing more than a lumbering fury.

EYEBALONE
Lv. 25

37

HP	41700
MP	32400
ATK	117
INT	97
DEF	207
MEN	168
FOL	4155
EXP	422

LOC The Cathedral of Oblivion, Chapter 3-6

ITEM	%
Earth Gem	16
Ice Gem	16

						POI	FRZ	PAR	SIL	CUR	FOG	STN	DTH
-10	0	0	0	0	0	100	100	80	100	100	50	0	100

Before its signet-catalyzed transformation, this creature was a shellfish. It emits beams from its triad of eyes and lashes foes with its tentacles.

EYEBALONE
Lv. 30

38

HP	70700
MP	55400
ATK	179
INT	152
DEF	227
MEN	193
FOL	4155
EXP	422

LOC The Cathedral of Oblivion, Chapter 3-6

ITEM	%
Fire Gem	16
Wind Gem	16

						POI	FRZ	PAR	SIL	CUR	FOG	STN	DTH
-10	0	0	0	0	0	100	100	80	100	100	50	0	100

Before its signet-catalyzed transformation, this creature was a shellfish. It emits beams from its triad of eyes and lashes foes with its tentacles.

EYEBALONE
Lv. 35

39

HP	101000
MP	78400
ATK	228
INT	186
DEF	259
MEN	209
FOL	4155
EXP	422

LOC The Cathedral of Oblivion, Chapter 3-6

ITEM	%
Light Gem	16
Darkness Gem	16

						POI	FRZ	PAR	SIL	CUR	FOG	STN	DTH
-10	0	0	0	0	0	100	100	80	100	100	50	0	100

Before its signet-catalyzed transformation, this creature was a shellfish. It emits beams from its triad of eyes and lashes foes with its tentacles.

FLYING ICE
Lv. 31

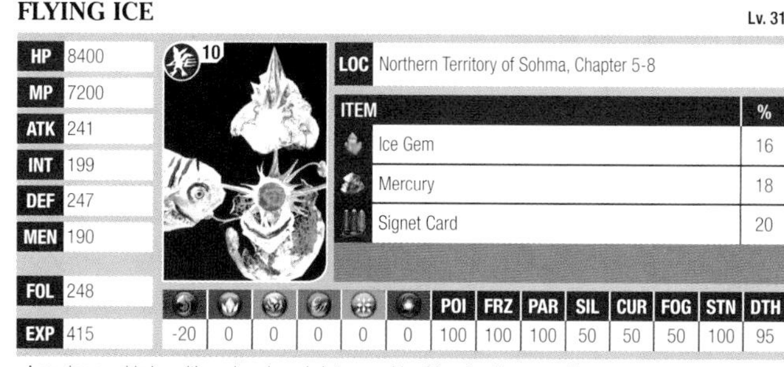

10

HP	8400
MP	7200
ATK	241
INT	199
DEF	247
MEN	190
FOL	248
EXP	415

LOC Northern Territory of Sohma, Chapter 5-8

ITEM	%
Ice Gem	16
Mercury	18
Signet Card	20

						POI	FRZ	PAR	SIL	CUR	FOG	STN	DTH
-20	0	0	0	0	0	100	100	100	50	50	50	100	95

A mucinous cnidarian with a mineral exoskeleton capable of freezing its surroundings.

GLACIATING LNKYRI
Lv. 14

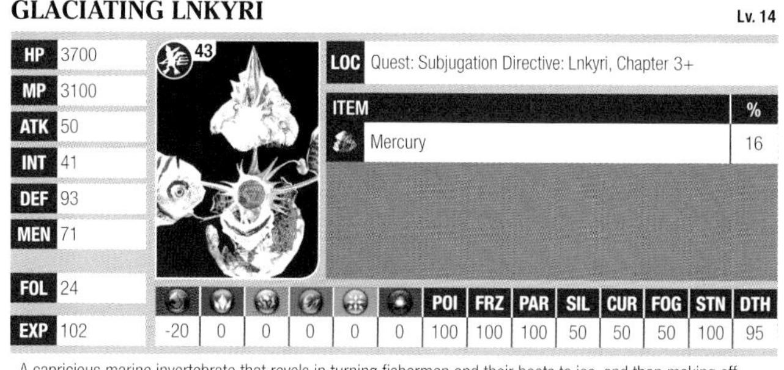

43

HP	3700
MP	3100
ATK	50
INT	41
DEF	93
MEN	71
FOL	24
EXP	102

LOC Quest: Subjugation Directive: Lnkyri, Chapter 3+

ITEM	%
Mercury	16

						POI	FRZ	PAR	SIL	CUR	FOG	STN	DTH
-20	0	0	0	0	0	100	100	100	50	50	50	100	95

A capricious marine invertebrate that revels in turning fishermen and their boats to ice, and then making off with their hard-earned catches.

GRENDELIAN KNIGHT-ERRANT

Lv. 51

HP	51500
MP	40800
ATK	998
INT	685
DEF	643
MEN	418
FOL	29
EXP	1469

23

LOC Chapter 8

ITEM	%
Ghost's Soul	16
Mythril	14

						POI	FRZ	PAR	SIL	CUR	FOG	STN	DTH
10	0	0	0	-15	15	100	100	80	100	100	100	100	95

A lone belligerent with a lavish suit of armor dyed like black cruor. A swing of its sword can fell a dozen men, and none get past its shield.

GRIM REAPER

Lv. 100

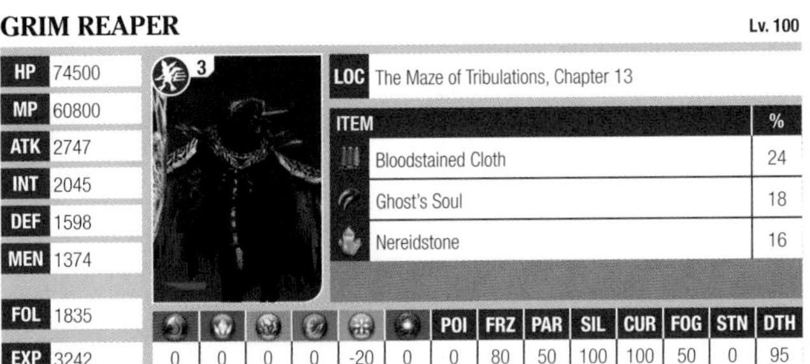

HP	74500
MP	60800
ATK	2747
INT	2045
DEF	1598
MEN	1374
FOL	1835
EXP	3242

3

LOC The Maze of Tribulations, Chapter 13

ITEM	%
Bloodstained Cloth	24
Ghost's Soul	18
Nereidstone	16

						POI	FRZ	PAR	SIL	CUR	FOG	STN	DTH
0	0	0	0	-20	0	0	80	50	100	100	50	0	95

This horrid apparition has devoted its afterlife to harvesting souls—not out of malice, nor hunger, nor a sense of duty, but for sport.

HARBINGER OF THE APOCALYPSE

Lv. 75

HP	129200
MP	103400
ATK	1071
INT	865
DEF	957
MEN	797
FOL	1470
EXP	2785

35

LOC Kronos's Sickle, Chapter 12

ITEM	%
Crystal	16
Light Gem	20
Meteorite	14

						POI	FRZ	PAR	SIL	CUR	FOG	STN	DTH
0	0	-10	0	0	0	100	100	80	100	100	80	80	100

A crystal guardian that dons armor redolent of twilight and wields its massive sword in defense of the parallel dimension Feria created.

HOODINI THE MOROSE

Lv. 59

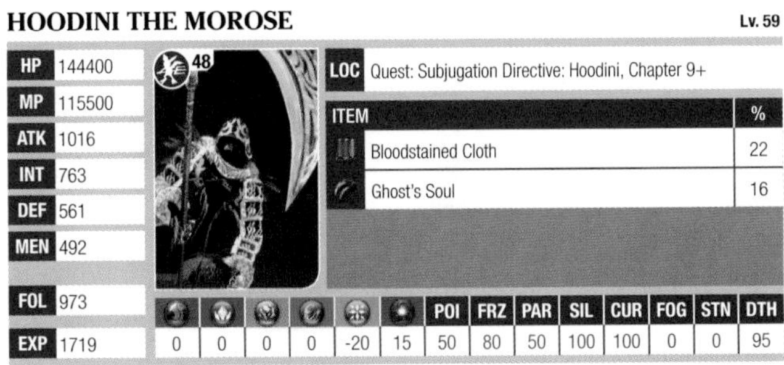

HP	144400
MP	115500
ATK	1016
INT	763
DEF	561
MEN	492
FOL	973
EXP	1719

48

LOC Quest: Subjugation Directive: Hoodini, Chapter 9+

ITEM	%
Bloodstained Cloth	22
Ghost's Soul	16

						POI	FRZ	PAR	SIL	CUR	FOG	STN	DTH
0	0	0	0	-20	15	50	80	50	100	100	0	0	95

The vengeful ghost of an amateur mage who liked fiddling with spells, but one day imbued a signet that caused his own flesh to fall off.

ILLUSTRIOUS MANTICORE

Lv. 66

HP	300000
MP	222871
ATK	1756
INT	1229
DEF	658
MEN	522
FOL	9706
EXP	17294

32

LOC Chapter 10

ITEM	%
Parchment	100
Moonlight Signets, Vol. 3	100

						POI	FRZ	PAR	SIL	CUR	FOG	STN	DTH
-20	0	6	0	0	0	100	100	100	100	50	50	50	100

A Corrupt with the ferocious snout and elegantly flowing, fearsome mane of a lion. It takes three pairs of wings to keep it off the ground.

IVOR OF THE LUSTFUL LOOK

Lv. 59

HP	154900
MP	115500
ATK	1005
INT	845
DEF	591
MEN	492
FOL	1109
EXP	1843

58

LOC Quest: A Peeping Golem!, Chapter 9+

ITEM	%
Mati	16
Coal	18

						POI	FRZ	PAR	SIL	CUR	FOG	STN	DTH
0	0	0	0	0	0	100	100	80	100	100	50	0	100

This curious baskania simply cannot help but peer at those who bathe in desert oases. Young, old, man, woman—all are equal in his eyes.

JADE GOLEM

Lv. 56

HP	20800
MP	16200
ATK	720
INT	576
DEF	638
MEN	450
FOL	924
EXP	1591

7

LOC West of the Eastern Eihieds, Chapter 9+; North of the Eastern Eihieds, Chapter 9+

ITEM	%
Silver	18
Gold	16
Platinum	16
Shadestone	14

						POI	FRZ	PAR	SIL	CUR	FOG	STN	DTH
0	0	-10	10	0	0	100	100	100	100	100	100	100	95

A stone automaton crafted by a signeturege who refused to stop improving upon the metal golem until his design was consummate.

LAVA GOLEM

Lv. 62

HP	22400
MP	16800
ATK	929
INT	743
DEF	720
MEN	481
FOL	1100
EXP	1774

6

LOC The Trei'kuran Dunes, Chapter 9+

ITEM	%
Silver	18
Platinum	16
Ruby	16
Gnomestone	14

						POI	FRZ	PAR	SIL	CUR	FOG	STN	DTH
0	-10	0	0	0	0	100	100	100	100	100	100	100	95

This animate amalgamation of minerals lumbers about the desert near Eastern Trei'kur, heating metals in its vicinity with its igneous core.

LITTLE SATAN

Lv. 68

HP	27100
MP	23000
ATK	1179
INT	973
DEF	907
MEN	696
FOL	1032
EXP	1776

19

LOC The Signesilica, Chapter 11+

ITEM	%
Shadow Roses	16
Lesser Fiend's Tail	20
Signet Card +	18
Darkness Gem	20

						POI	FRZ	PAR	SIL	CUR	FOG	STN	DTH
10	0	0	0	0	0	100	80	100	50	100	100	100	95

Unlike devil children, this type of demon got its name from its innate turpitude. Though it may be small, this terror is destined for big things.

MALICE COALESCED

Lv. 64

HP	23900
MP	20300
ATK	1145
INT	1015
DEF	604
MEN	524
FOL	1099
EXP	2061

42

LOC Quest: Keys to the Present in the Past, Chapter 10+

ITEM	%
Micro Circuit	18
Gunpowder	22
Reinforced Gunpowder	20
High-Power Generator	12

						POI	FRZ	PAR	SIL	CUR	FOG	STN	DTH
0	20	10	10	10	10	100	100	50	100	50	100	0	95

After falling to Daeus, this soldier became so enraged that his contempt for the swordsman was made manifest as a brightly burning Corrupt.

MATEO OF THE SLOW WIT

Lv. 69

HP	254000
MP	197100
ATK	1578
INT	1163
DEF	1074
MEN	724
FOL	1475
EXP	2610

LOC: Quest: Subjugation Directive: Dante and Mateo, Chapter 11+

ITEM	%
Ghost's Soul	16
Mythril	14

						POI	FRZ	PAR	SIL	CUR	FOG	STN	DTH
10	0	0	0	-10	10	100	100	50	100	80	100	80	95

None know from whence this heavily armored swordsman came or even what he looks like, so it is likely a suit that moves of its own accord.

NIFLHEIM, THE ARMOR THAT ROAMS

Lv. 41

HP	109400
MP	83200
ATK	393
INT	290
DEF	329
MEN	232
FOL	29
EXP	3847

LOC: Chapter 6

ITEM	%
Ghost's Soul	14

						POI	FRZ	PAR	SIL	CUR	FOG	STN	DTH
10	0	0	0	-10	10	100	100	50	100	80	100	80	95

A cryptic suit of armor that contains a phantasmal horror and walks the Dakaav Tunnels. Releasing its specter is likely to call forth a flood.

METAL GOLEM

Lv. 40

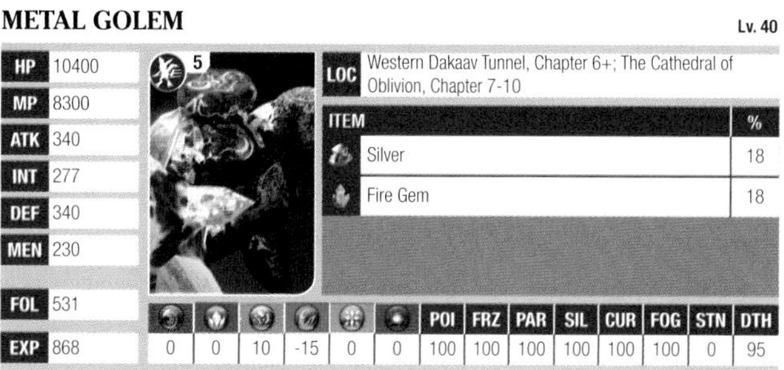

HP	10400
MP	8300
ATK	340
INT	277
DEF	340
MEN	230
FOL	531
EXP	868

LOC: Western Dakaav Tunnel, Chapter 6+; The Cathedral of Oblivion, Chapter 7-10

ITEM	%
Silver	18
Fire Gem	18

						POI	FRZ	PAR	SIL	CUR	FOG	STN	DTH
0	0	10	-15	0	0	100	100	100	100	100	100	0	95

A golem created to live forever. Its body still functions properly, but its soul has wasted away over the years, leaving naught but a machine.

NIFLHEL, THE ARMOR THAT WALKS

Lv. 41

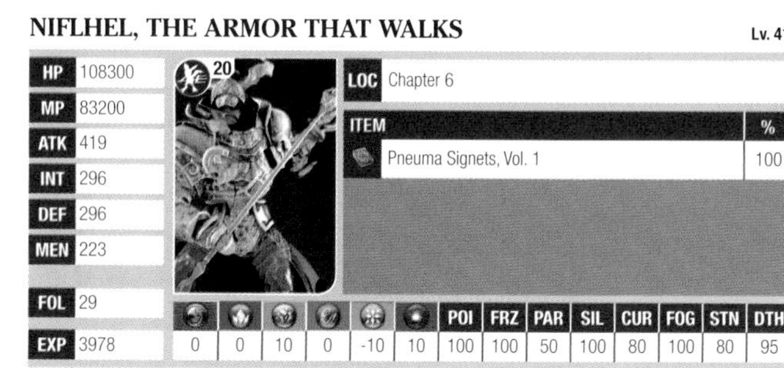

HP	108300
MP	83200
ATK	419
INT	296
DEF	296
MEN	223
FOL	29
EXP	3978

LOC: Chapter 6

ITEM	%
Pneuma Signets, Vol. 1	100

						POI	FRZ	PAR	SIL	CUR	FOG	STN	DTH
0	0	10	0	-10	10	100	100	50	100	80	100	80	95

A cryptic suit of armor that contains a phantasmal horror and walks the Dakaav Tunnels. Releasing its specter is likely to engulf all in flames.

MISFORTUNER

Lv. 60

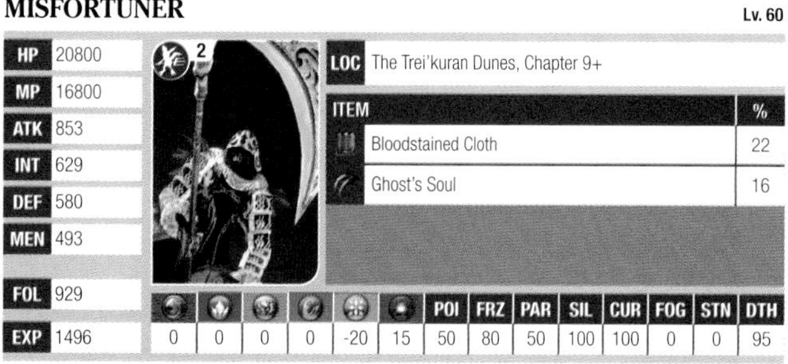

HP	20800
MP	16800
ATK	853
INT	629
DEF	580
MEN	493
FOL	929
EXP	1496

LOC: The Trei'kuran Dunes, Chapter 9+

ITEM	%
Bloodstained Cloth	22
Ghost's Soul	16

						POI	FRZ	PAR	SIL	CUR	FOG	STN	DTH
0	0	0	0	-20	15	50	80	50	100	100	0	0	95

A terrifying specter that swings a titanic sickle. Having never received a corporeal form when reborn, it savagely culls the living out of spite.

PANDORA'S CUBE

Lv. 64

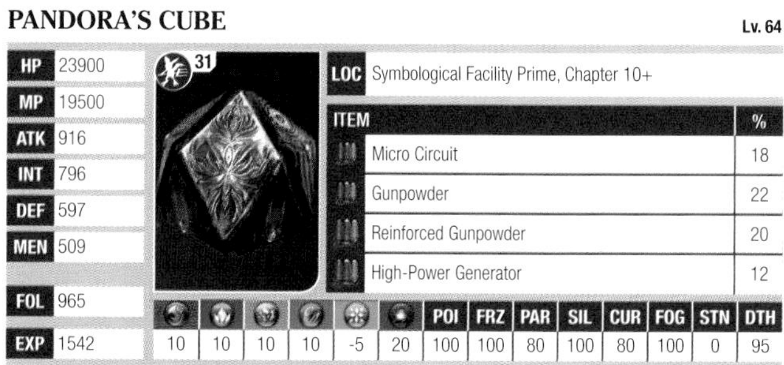

HP	23900
MP	19500
ATK	916
INT	796
DEF	597
MEN	509
FOL	965
EXP	1542

LOC: Symbological Facility Prime, Chapter 10+

ITEM	%
Micro Circuit	18
Gunpowder	22
Reinforced Gunpowder	20
High-Power Generator	12

						POI	FRZ	PAR	SIL	CUR	FOG	STN	DTH
10	10	10	10	-5	20	100	100	80	100	80	100	0	95

An accidental byproduct of Kronos's research on the seventh core. It is as full of ill portent as the mythological artifact its name references.

NAPTO THE STALWART

Lv. 35

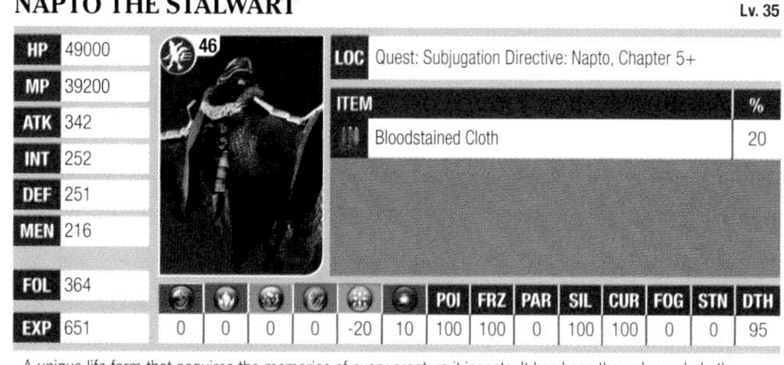

HP	49000
MP	39200
ATK	342
INT	252
DEF	251
MEN	216
FOL	364
EXP	651

LOC: Quest: Subjugation Directive: Napto, Chapter 5+

ITEM	%
Bloodstained Cloth	20

						POI	FRZ	PAR	SIL	CUR	FOG	STN	DTH
0	0	0	0	-20	10	100	100	0	100	100	0	0	95

A unique life form that acquires the memories of every creature it ingests. It has been through much, both vicariously and directly.

PARCHED ORIZON

Lv. 50

HP	16200
MP	12800
ATK	805
INT	631
DEF	527
MEN	400
FOL	848
EXP	1188

LOC: Quest: Open Season on Orizons, Chapter 8+

ITEM	%
Crest Mail	16
Ghost's Soul	16

						POI	FRZ	PAR	SIL	CUR	FOG	STN	DTH
-10	0	0	0	-5	0	100	100	100	100	100	100	100	95

A type of sword-wielding signeturge who has risen from the grave. He would still be alive if his signet was not mistakenly inscribed.

NETHERPHANTOM

Lv. 100

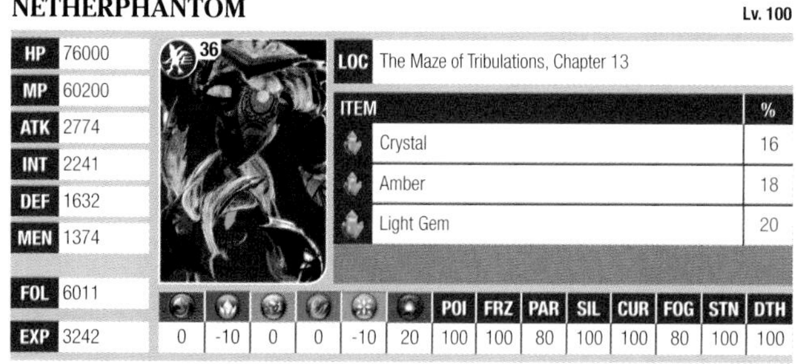

HP	76000
MP	60200
ATK	2774
INT	2241
DEF	1632
MEN	1374
FOL	6011
EXP	3242

LOC: The Maze of Tribulations, Chapter 13

ITEM	%
Crystal	16
Amber	18
Light Gem	20

						POI	FRZ	PAR	SIL	CUR	FOG	STN	DTH
0	-10	0	0	-10	20	100	100	80	100	100	80	100	100

A wraith draped in flames who guards the gates to the underworld. It is said this apparition takes the form of whatever its beholder fears most.

PILLAGING MOJANGO

Lv. 64

HP	23400
MP	19500
ATK	1157
INT	955
DEF	616
MEN	483
FOL	975
EXP	1936

LOC: Quest: Subjugation Directive: Mojangos, Chapter 10+

ITEM	%
Demon's Tail	22
Lesser Fiend's Tail	20
Signet Card +	18
Darkness Gem	20

						POI	FRZ	PAR	SIL	CUR	FOG	STN	DTH
10	0	0	0	0	0	50	50	0	50	80	50	0	95

A tiny, adorable, and vicious creature that hunts in packs, surrounding and then tearing at its prey from all sides until only scraps remain.

POLYHEDRON

Lv. 34

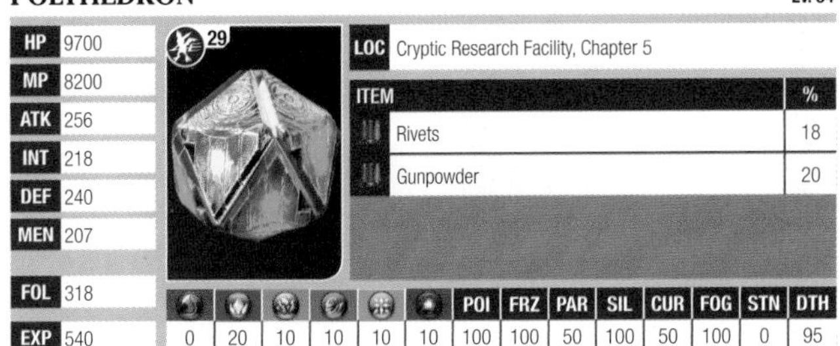

HP	9700
MP	8200
ATK	256
INT	218
DEF	240
MEN	207
FOL	318
EXP	540

29

LOC Cryptic Research Facility, Chapter 5

ITEM	%
Rivets	18
Gunpowder	20

						POI	FRZ	PAR	SIL	CUR	FOG	STN	DTH
0	20	10	10	10	10	100	100	50	100	50	100	0	95

Though not the most foreboding, its icosahedral form provides a very stable center of gravity while it spins and charges forward to attack.

REVENANT SWORDMASTER DAEUS

Lv. 64

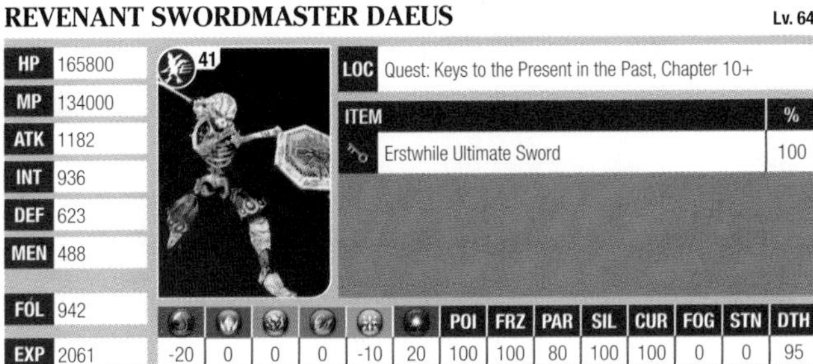

HP	165800
MP	134000
ATK	1182
INT	936
DEF	623
MEN	488
FOL	942
EXP	2061

41

LOC Quest: Keys to the Present in the Past, Chapter 10+

ITEM	%
Erstwhile Ultimate Sword	100

						POI	FRZ	PAR	SIL	CUR	FOG	STN	DTH
-20	0	0	0	-10	20	100	100	80	100	100	0	0	95

The ghostly remains of the preeminent swordsman from a bygone era. He intently wanders the continent in search of his long-dead nemesis.

ROCK HERMIT

Lv. 31

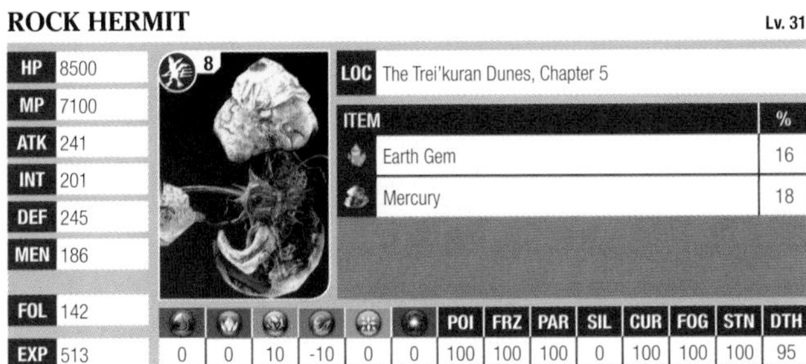

HP	8500
MP	7100
ATK	241
INT	201
DEF	245
MEN	186
FOL	142
EXP	513

8

LOC The Trei'kuran Dunes, Chapter 5

ITEM	%
Earth Gem	16
Mercury	18

						POI	FRZ	PAR	SIL	CUR	FOG	STN	DTH
0	0	10	-10	0	0	100	100	100	0	100	100	100	95

A mucoid invertebrate that fashioned an exoskeleton out of boulders. It may not have a spine, but it does have brains and can use signets.

RUPHIN THE IMPERIOUS

Lv. 50

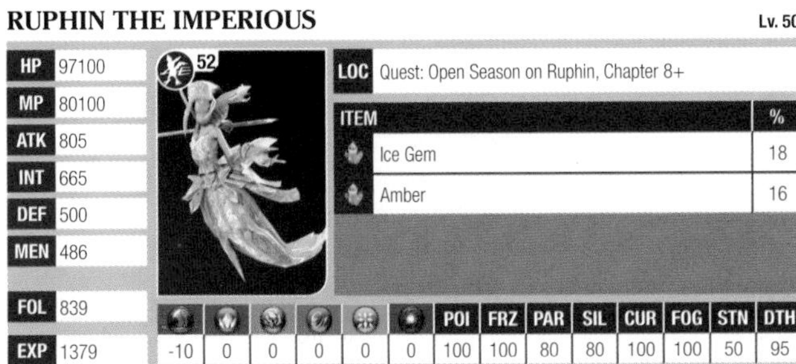

HP	97100
MP	80100
ATK	805
INT	665
DEF	500
MEN	486
FOL	839
EXP	1379

52

LOC Quest: Open Season on Ruphin, Chapter 8+

ITEM	%
Ice Gem	18
Amber	16

						POI	FRZ	PAR	SIL	CUR	FOG	STN	DTH
-10	0	0	0	0	0	100	100	80	80	100	100	50	95

This aquaregia inherited not only her master's signeturgical skills when he bestowed his knowledge upon her, but his haughty attitude as well.

SANDRA THE MAJESTIC

Lv. 53

HP	141600
MP	117900
ATK	874
INT	728
DEF	531
MEN	492
FOL	803
EXP	1548

53

LOC Quest: Subjugation Directive: Sandra, Chapter 8+

ITEM	%
Earth Gem	18

						POI	FRZ	PAR	SIL	CUR	FOG	STN	DTH
-10	0	10	0	0	0	100	100	100	100	100	100	100	95

The phantom of a female warrior from ages past. She stalks the desert, seeking vengeance upon Trei'kur for wiping her homeland off the map.

SEVENTH CORE

Lv. 45

HP	15700
MP	13100
ATK	510
INT	439
DEF	308
MEN	257
FOL	636
EXP	1006

30

LOC The Trei'kuran Dunes, Chapter 7-8; Symbological Facility Prime, Chapter 7-9; The Cathedral of Oblivion, Chapter 7-12

ITEM	%
Wire	18
Gunpowder	20
Reinforced Gunpowder	18

						POI	FRZ	PAR	SIL	CUR	FOG	STN	DTH
10	10	20	0	10	10	100	100	50	100	50	100	0	95

This experimental polyhedron weapon, developed by Kronos, utilizes the "seventh sense" that lies dormant within the human subconscious.

SHROUDED GAZE

Lv. 73

HP	938800
MP	713800
ATK	1584
INT	1293
DEF	949
MEN	798
FOL	14382
EXP	26263

28

LOC Chapter 12

ITEM	%
Mati	18
Coal	80
Alchemist's Water	14

						POI	FRZ	PAR	SIL	CUR	FOG	STN	DTH
0	0	0	0	0	0	100	100	100	100	100	50	0	100

A subspecies of baskania that shrouds itself in gloom. Its mournful gaze causes all who lock eyes with it to completely lose their sense of self.

SKELETON ARMOR

Lv. 38

HP	10000
MP	8000
ATK	333
INT	261
DEF	270
MEN	214
FOL	425
EXP	698

13

LOC Western Dakaav Tunnel, Chapter 6+

ITEM	%
Crest Mail	14
Ghost's Soul	14

						POI	FRZ	PAR	SIL	CUR	FOG	STN	DTH
-10	0	0	0	-5	0	100	100	100	100	100	100	100	95

The wandering remains of a man whose flesh was said to be devoured by some monstrosity. Exactly when killed him, though, may never be known.

SKELETON SOLDIER

Lv. 65

HP	28000
MP	21900
ATK	974
INT	747
DEF	624
MEN	489
FOL	96
EXP	1704

12

LOC Northern Territory of Sohma, Chapter 11+; The Cathedral of Oblivion, Chapter 11+

ITEM	%
Falchion	18
Ghost's Soul	16
Alchemist's Water	14
Nereidstone	14

						POI	FRZ	PAR	SIL	CUR	FOG	STN	DTH
-10	0	0	0	-5	0	100	50	50	100	100	100	0	95

A fallen conscript who has forgotten all his worldly desires, and now finds solace only in the arrant slaughter of the living.

SNOW MERMAID

Lv. 30

HP	6900
MP	5700
ATK	215
INT	175
DEF	225
MEN	216
FOL	240
EXP	437

24

LOC Northern Territory of Sohma, Chapter 5-8

ITEM	%
Ice Gem	16
Fish Scales	18

						POI	FRZ	PAR	SIL	CUR	FOG	STN	DTH
-10	0	0	0	0	0	80	100	50	50	50	50	0	95

A mermaid with skin as frigid and frosted as a Sohman windowsill in winter. It freezes everyone it meets so that they can share in its misery.

PART 06

STONE GOLEM
Lv. 25

HP	4300
MP	3200
ATK	92
INT	74
DEF	247
MEN	162
FOL	160
EXP	268

4

LOC: West of the Eastern Eihieds, Chapter 3-5; North of the Eastern Eihieds, Chapter 4-5; The Cathedral of Oblivion, Chapter 3-6

ITEM	%
Iron	18
Fire Gem	16

						POI	FRZ	PAR	SIL	CUR	FOG	STN	DTH
0	0	10	-10	0	0	100	100	100	100	100	100	0	95

A humanoid figure carved from stone and able to cast signeturgy. It mistakes people for its master, killing them when it realizes the truth.

TINAT OF THE DAWNING LIGHT
Lv. 22

HP	12000
MP	9500
ATK	94
INT	76
DEF	219
MEN	153
FOL	137
EXP	265

40

LOC: Quest: The End of Welch's Laboratory!?, Chapter 3+

ITEM	%
Discarded Silver Spoon	100

						POI	FRZ	PAR	SIL	CUR	FOG	STN	DTH
0	0	10	-15	0	0	100	100	100	100	100	100	0	95

A metallic being that had survived for countless generations before becoming a Corrupt. It is no longer nearly as strong as it once was.

UNDERHANDED PARGYN
Lv. 40

HP	10000
MP	8300
ATK	399
INT	333
DEF	287
MEN	223
FOL	449
EXP	847

47

LOC: Quest: Subjugation Directive: Pargyns, Chapter 6+

ITEM	%
Demon's Tail	20
Signet Card	20
Darkness Gem	18

						POI	FRZ	PAR	SIL	CUR	FOG	STN	DTH
10	0	0	0	0	0	0	50	0	50	80	50	0	95

A particularly troublesome breed of fledgling demon that, when it matures, will likely bring ruin upon the entirety of civilization.

VLAD THE UNSULLIED
Lv. 60

HP	166100
MP	134300
ATK	1066
INT	770
DEF	568
MEN	484
FOL	983
EXP	1887

55

LOC: Quest: Subjugation Direction: Vlad, Chapter 9+

ITEM	%
Bloodstained Cloth	22
Ghost's Soul	16
Nereidstone	14

						POI	FRZ	PAR	SIL	CUR	FOG	STN	DTH
0	0	0	0	-20	0	0	80	50	100	100	50	0	95

Executed in the tower he built, the ghost of this former duke does not take kindly to Trei'kur—especially since they destroyed his own country.

MACHINES

ANCIENT GUARD
Lv. 100

HP	79100
MP	60200
ATK	2638
INT	2110
DEF	2006
MEN	1319
FOL	2091
EXP	3242

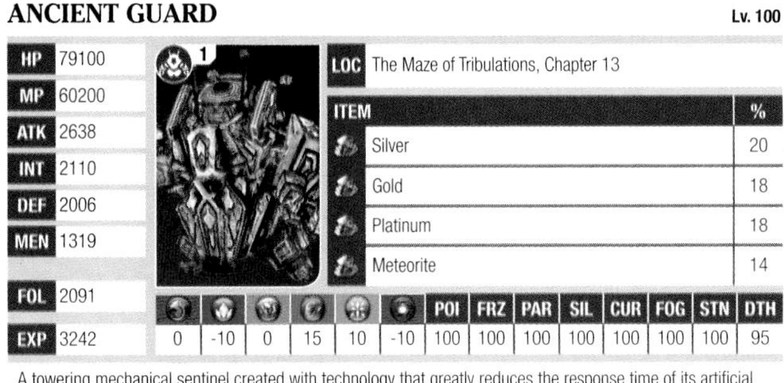

1

LOC: The Maze of Tribulations, Chapter 13

ITEM	%
Silver	20
Gold	18
Platinum	18
Meteorite	14

						POI	FRZ	PAR	SIL	CUR	FOG	STN	DTH
0	-10	0	15	10	-10	100	100	100	100	100	100	100	95

A towering mechanical sentinel created with technology that greatly reduces the response time of its artificial nervous system.

ARMED DRAGOON
Lv. 100

HP	564700
MP	403900
ATK	1712
INT	1216
DEF	1734
MEN	1306
FOL	416
EXP	3242

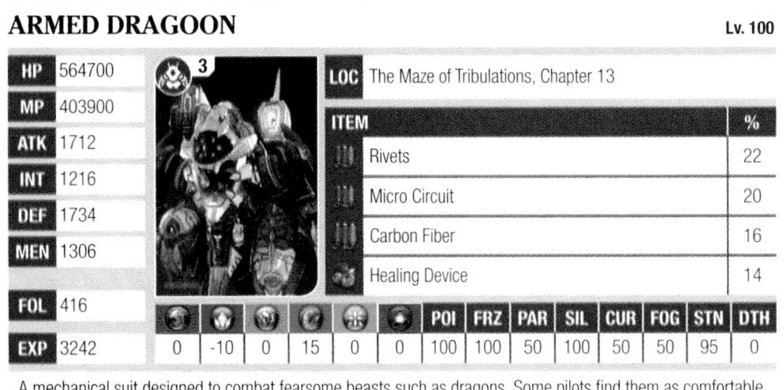

3

LOC: The Maze of Tribulations, Chapter 13

ITEM	%
Rivets	22
Micro Circuit	20
Carbon Fiber	16
Healing Device	14

						POI	FRZ	PAR	SIL	CUR	FOG	STN	DTH
0	-10	0	15	0	0	100	100	50	100	50	50	95	0

A mechanical suit designed to combat fearsome beasts such as dragons. Some pilots find them as comfortable as a second home and never leave.

AVENGER
Lv. 72

HP	47700
MP	36300
ATK	1527
INT	1197
DEF	950
MEN	752
FOL	1424
EXP	2395

12

LOC: The Alcazar of the Golden Age, Chapter 12; The Cathedral of Oblivion, Chapter 11+

ITEM	%
Diffusion Device	18
Quantum Processor	14
High-Power Generator	12
Blank Disk	10

						POI	FRZ	PAR	SIL	CUR	FOG	STN	DTH
15	-10	0	0	0	0	100	100	50	100	100	50	0	95

A special sentinel equipped with superb enemy detection software. It mercilessly pelts intruders until they are as porous as sponges.

BLUTGANG
Lv. 73

HP	49700
MP	35300
ATK	1629
INT	1144
DEF	968
MEN	759
FOL	1758
EXP	2755

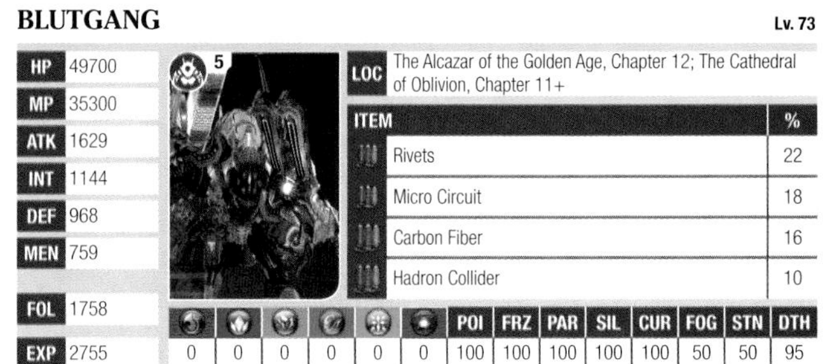

5

LOC: The Alcazar of the Golden Age, Chapter 12; The Cathedral of Oblivion, Chapter 11+

ITEM	%
Rivets	22
Micro Circuit	18
Carbon Fiber	16
Hadron Collider	10

						POI	FRZ	PAR	SIL	CUR	FOG	STN	DTH
0	0	0	0	0	0	100	100	100	100	100	50	50	95

True to its namesake's meaning of "blood fetcher," this armored bipedal weapon uses its advanced AI and swift speed to spill enemy cruor.

DESTROYER
Lv. 46

HP	322000
MP	249800
ATK	858
INT	665
DEF	338
MEN	254
FOL	724
EXP	10951

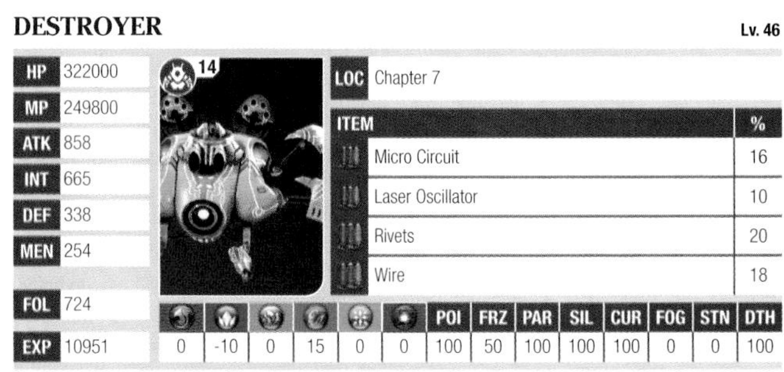

14

LOC: Chapter 7

ITEM	%
Micro Circuit	16
Laser Oscillator	10
Rivets	20
Wire	18

						POI	FRZ	PAR	SIL	CUR	FOG	STN	DTH
0	-10	0	15	0	0	100	50	100	100	100	0	0	100

This quadrupedal weapon manufactured by Kronos sports a multitude of maneuvers that enable it to leave nothing but stumps of its foes.

ELIMINATOR
Lv. 62

HP	22600
MP	16800
ATK	978
INT	759
DEF	639
MEN	486
FOL	1078
EXP	1614

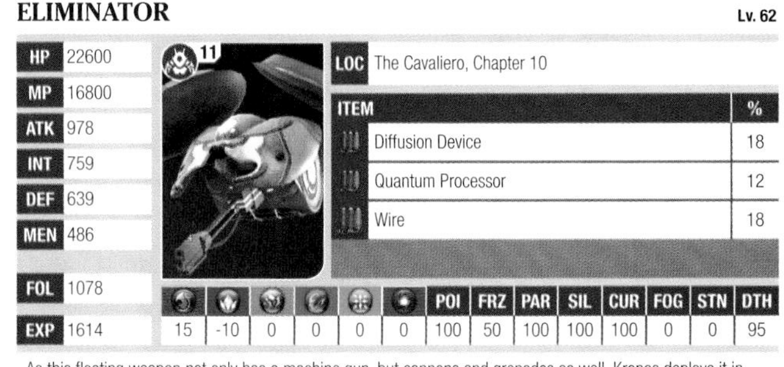

11

LOC: The Cavaliero, Chapter 10

ITEM	%
Diffusion Device	18
Quantum Processor	12
Wire	18

						POI	FRZ	PAR	SIL	CUR	FOG	STN	DTH
15	-10	0	0	0	0	100	50	100	100	100	0	0	95

As this floating weapon not only has a machine gun, but cannons and grenades as well, Kronos deploys it in especially sensitive localities.

FAFNIR
Lv. 65

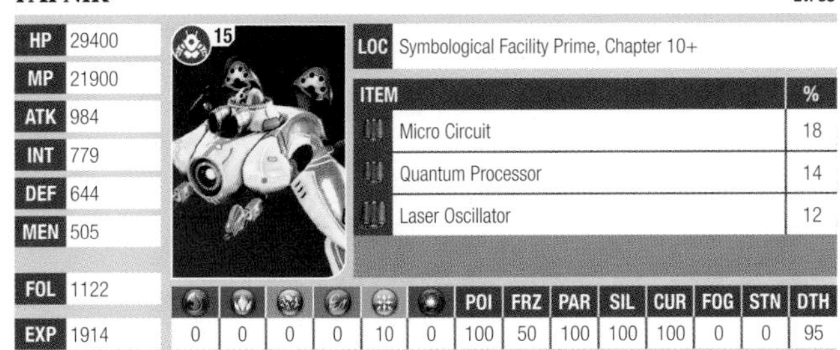

HP	MP	ATK	INT	DEF	MEN	FOL	EXP
29400	21900	984	779	644	505	1122	1914

LOC Symbological Facility Prime, Chapter 10+

ITEM	%
Micro Circuit	18
Quantum Processor	14
Laser Oscillator	12

						POI	FRZ	PAR	SIL	CUR	FOG	STN	DTH
0	0	0	0	10	0	100	50	100	100	100	0	0	95

A peculiar type of Kronos sentinel optimized for tracking enemies. Thus, it can move without hindrance, no matter how small the space.

MELUSINE
Lv. 80

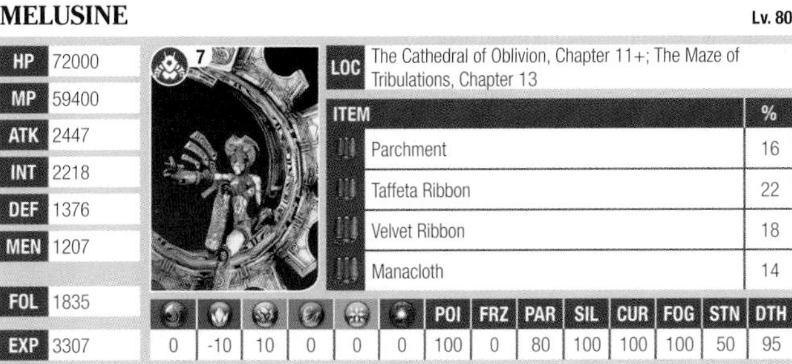

HP	MP	ATK	INT	DEF	MEN	FOL	EXP
72000	59400	2447	2218	1376	1207	1835	3307

LOC The Cathedral of Oblivion, Chapter 11+; The Maze of Tribulations, Chapter 13

ITEM	%
Parchment	16
Taffeta Ribbon	22
Velvet Ribbon	18
Manacloth	14

						POI	FRZ	PAR	SIL	CUR	FOG	STN	DTH
0	-10	10	0	0	0	100	0	80	100	100	100	50	95

The demonic spawn of human experimentation. While it never seeks out conflict, any who approach it are doomed to a life of despair.

METAL SCUMBAG
Lv. 100

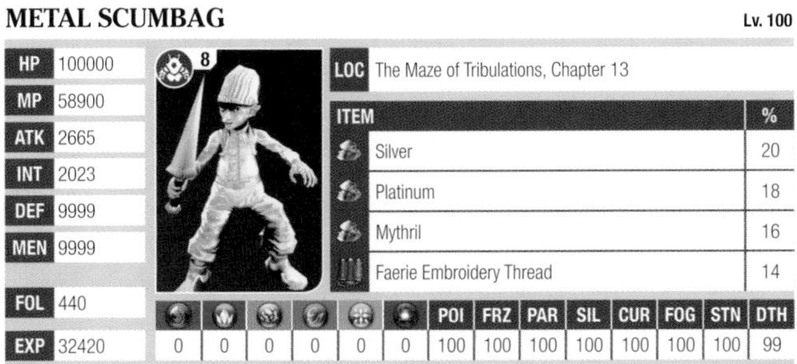

HP	MP	ATK	INT	DEF	MEN	FOL	EXP
100000	58900	2665	2023	9999	9999	440	32420

LOC The Maze of Tribulations, Chapter 13

ITEM	%
Silver	20
Platinum	18
Mythril	16
Faerie Embroidery Thread	14

						POI	FRZ	PAR	SIL	CUR	FOG	STN	DTH
0	0	0	0	0	0	100	100	100	100	100	100	100	99

Having attained larcenist's enlightenment, this brigand has become what he covets. Those who best him before he flees will surely be rewarded.

PHANTOM DRAGOON
Lv. 46

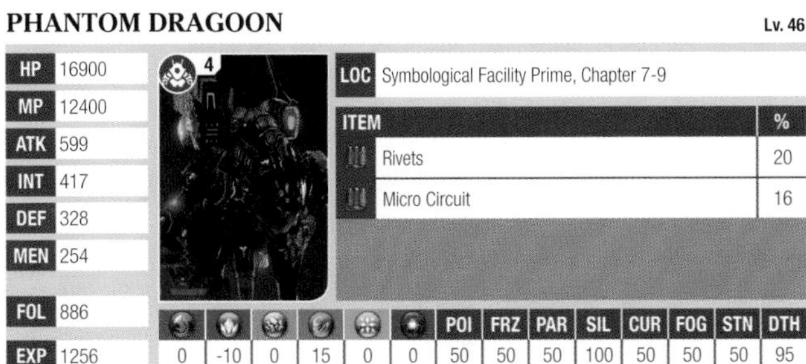

HP	MP	ATK	INT	DEF	MEN	FOL	EXP
16900	12400	599	417	328	254	886	1256

LOC Symbological Facility Prime, Chapter 7-9

ITEM	%
Rivets	20
Micro Circuit	16

						POI	FRZ	PAR	SIL	CUR	FOG	STN	DTH
0	-10	0	15	0	0	50	50	50	100	50	50	50	95

Despite its hulking size, this mechanized weapon moves with the celerity of a ghost, seemingly appearing before its enemies out of thin air.

ROBO GUNNER
Lv. 36

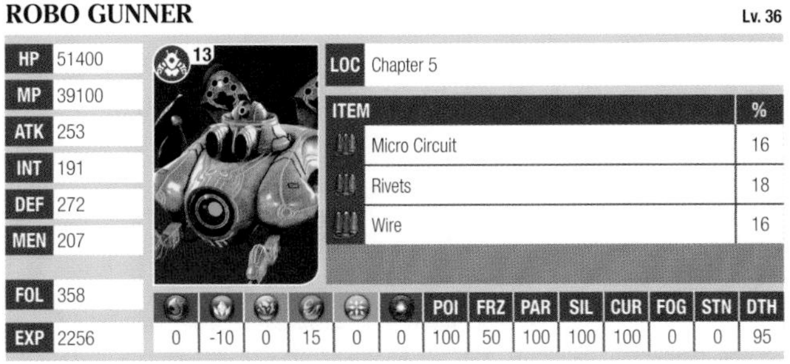

HP	MP	ATK	INT	DEF	MEN	FOL	EXP
51400	39100	253	191	272	207	358	2256

LOC Chapter 5

ITEM	%
Micro Circuit	16
Rivets	18
Wire	16

						POI	FRZ	PAR	SIL	CUR	FOG	STN	DTH
0	-10	0	15	0	0	100	50	100	100	100	0	0	95

A quadrupedal mechanized defense unit that Kronos originally built to repair space stations, but now lays waste to infiltrators.

SACRED GUARD
Lv. 69

HP	MP	ATK	INT	DEF	MEN	FOL	EXP
32400	24900	1200	960	1064	717	1403	1935

LOC The Signesilica, Chapter 11+; The Cathedral of Oblivion, Chapter 11+

ITEM	%
Silver	20
Gold	16
Platinum	16
Mythril	14

						POI	FRZ	PAR	SIL	CUR	FOG	STN	DTH
0	-10	0	15	-10	10	100	100	100	100	100	100	100	95

Programmed to devalue life while prioritizing killing efficiency, this robot was devised solely for the purpose of eradicating intruders.

SENTINEL
Lv. 35

HP	MP	ATK	INT	DEF	MEN	FOL	EXP
10200	7800	279	217	264	207	351	586

LOC Cryptic Research Facility, Chapter 5

ITEM	%
Diffusion Device	16
Wire	16

						POI	FRZ	PAR	SIL	CUR	FOG	STN	DTH
15	-10	0	0	0	0	100	50	100	100	100	0	0	95

An airborne defense unit constructed by Kronos. It employs an ultramodern machine gun to pelt intruders with a torrent of ammunition.

TOY SOLDIER
Lv. 61

HP	MP	ATK	INT	DEF	MEN	FOL	EXP
21300	16600	812	636	575	480	910	1518

LOC The Cavaliero, Chapter 10; The Cathedral of Oblivion, Chapter 11+

ITEM	%
Quantum Processor	12
Carbon Fiber	14
Diffusion Device	18

						POI	FRZ	PAR	SIL	CUR	FOG	STN	DTH
0	0	0	0	0	0	100	100	100	100	100	100	100	95

This mechanized soldier was built to keep Kronos ships safe, but was modeled on Faykreed's backstabbing scumbags—not the best of ideas.

VALIANT CONSCRIPT
Lv. 73

HP	MP	ATK	INT	DEF	MEN	FOL	EXP
44600	36400	1506	1144	930	736	1307	1947

LOC The Alcazar of the Golden Age, Chapter 12; Kronos's Sickle, Chapter 12; The Cathedral of Oblivion, Chapter 11+

ITEM	%
Quantum Processor	14
Laser Oscillator	12

						POI	FRZ	PAR	SIL	CUR	FOG	STN	DTH
-10	0	0	0	-5	0	100	100	100	100	100	100	100	95

A mechanized skeletal warrior with a decimating swing despite its frail frame. One blow from this colossus is enough for a lifetime.

DIVINITIES

The Divinities category of monsters is brief and contains special endgame bosses, so it isn't reordered alphabetically.

TRANSMOGRIFIED ALMA

Lv. 77

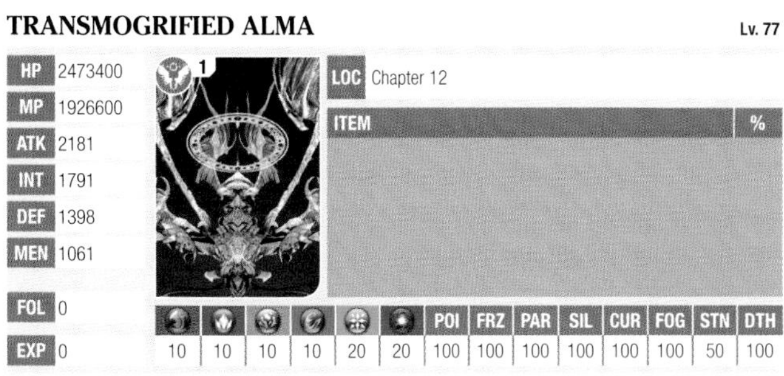

HP	2473400
MP	1926600
ATK	2181
INT	1791
DEF	1398
MEN	1061
FOL	0
EXP	0

LOC: Chapter 12

ITEM	%

						POI	FRZ	PAR	SIL	CUR	FOG	STN	DTH
10	10	10	10	20	20	100	100	100	100	100	100	50	100

The product of Alma using spacetime symbology to fuse with Feria. Innumerable symbols float around this new, monstrous form of theirs.

TRANSMOGRIFIED ALMA

Lv. 140

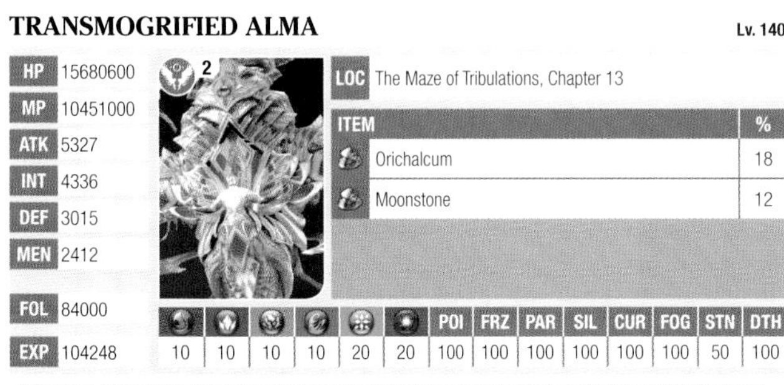

HP	15680600
MP	10451000
ATK	5327
INT	4336
DEF	3015
MEN	2412
FOL	84000
EXP	104248

LOC: The Maze of Tribulations, Chapter 13

ITEM	%
Orichalcum	18
Moonstone	12

						POI	FRZ	PAR	SIL	CUR	FOG	STN	DTH
10	10	10	10	20	20	100	100	100	100	100	100	50	100

Alma's and Feria's symbology resonate even more strongly to cocoon the two in a simultaneously brilliant and portentous light.

GABRIEL CELESTE

Lv. 120

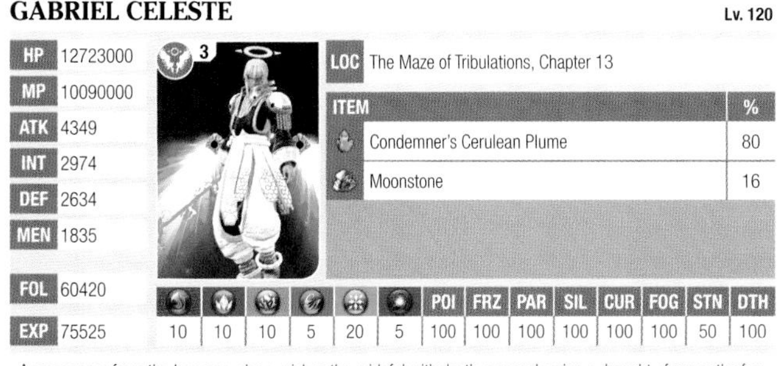

HP	12723000
MP	10090000
ATK	4349
INT	2974
DEF	2634
MEN	1835
FOL	60420
EXP	75525

LOC: The Maze of Tribulations, Chapter 13

ITEM	%
Condemner's Cerulean Plume	80
Moonstone	16

						POI	FRZ	PAR	SIL	CUR	FOG	STN	DTH
10	10	10	5	20	5	100	100	100	100	100	100	50	100

A messenger from the heavens who punishes the prideful with death, never showing a draught of sympathy for those at the end of his lance.

GABRIEL CELESTE

Lv. 160

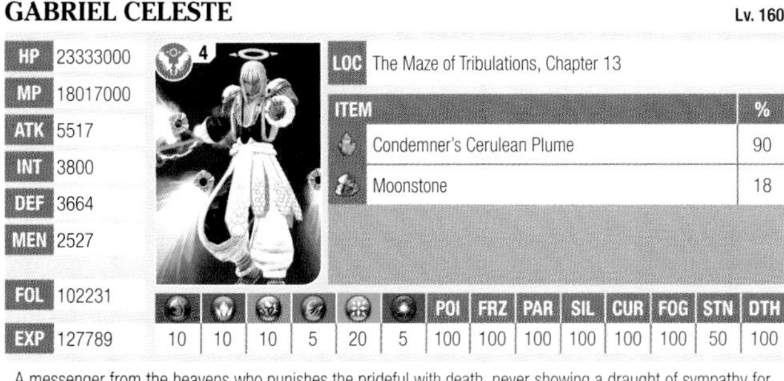

HP	23333000
MP	18017000
ATK	5517
INT	3800
DEF	3664
MEN	2527
FOL	102231
EXP	127789

LOC: The Maze of Tribulations, Chapter 13

ITEM	%
Condemner's Cerulean Plume	90
Moonstone	18

						POI	FRZ	PAR	SIL	CUR	FOG	STN	DTH
10	10	10	5	20	5	100	100	100	100	100	100	50	100

A messenger from the heavens who punishes the prideful with death, never showing a draught of sympathy for those at the end of his lance.

GABRIEL CELESTE

Lv. 200

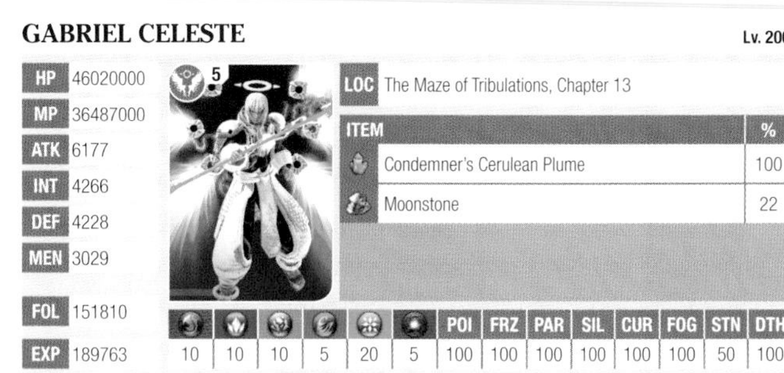

HP	46020000
MP	36487000
ATK	6177
INT	4266
DEF	4228
MEN	3029
FOL	151810
EXP	189763

LOC: The Maze of Tribulations, Chapter 13

ITEM	%
Condemner's Cerulean Plume	100
Moonstone	22

						POI	FRZ	PAR	SIL	CUR	FOG	STN	DTH
10	10	10	5	20	5	100	100	100	100	100	100	50	100

A messenger from the heavens who punishes the prideful with death, never showing a draught of sympathy for those at the end of his lance.

ETHEREAL QUEEN

Lv. 180

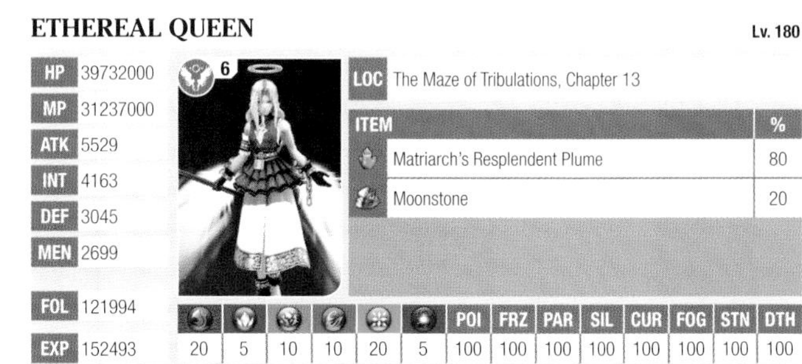

HP	39732000
MP	31237000
ATK	5529
INT	4163
DEF	3045
MEN	2699
FOL	121994
EXP	152493

LOC: The Maze of Tribulations, Chapter 13

ITEM	%
Matriarch's Resplendent Plume	80
Moonstone	20

						POI	FRZ	PAR	SIL	CUR	FOG	STN	DTH
20	5	10	10	20	5	100	100	100	100	100	100	100	100

This herald of utter ruin comes wrapped in a mantle of baleful flame. Her scythe has razed whole cities in one stroke with its resultant gales.

ETHEREAL QUEEN

Lv. 220

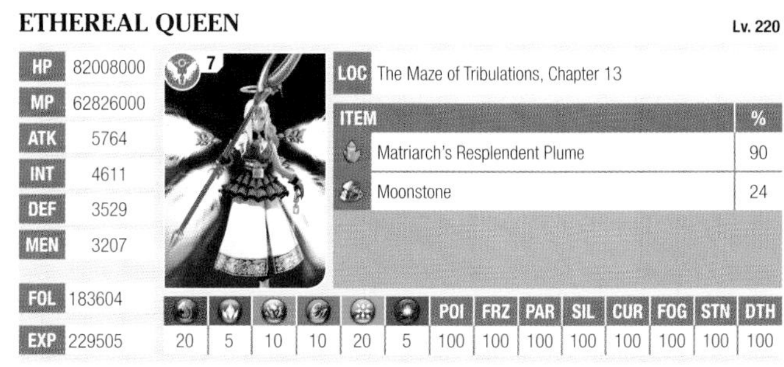

HP	82008000
MP	62826000
ATK	5764
INT	4611
DEF	3529
MEN	3207
FOL	183604
EXP	229505

LOC: The Maze of Tribulations, Chapter 13

ITEM	%
Matriarch's Resplendent Plume	90
Moonstone	24

						POI	FRZ	PAR	SIL	CUR	FOG	STN	DTH
20	5	10	10	20	5	100	100	100	100	100	100	100	100

This herald of utter ruin comes wrapped in a mantle of baleful flame. Her scythe has razed whole cities in one stroke with its resultant gales.

ETHEREAL QUEEN

Lv. 255

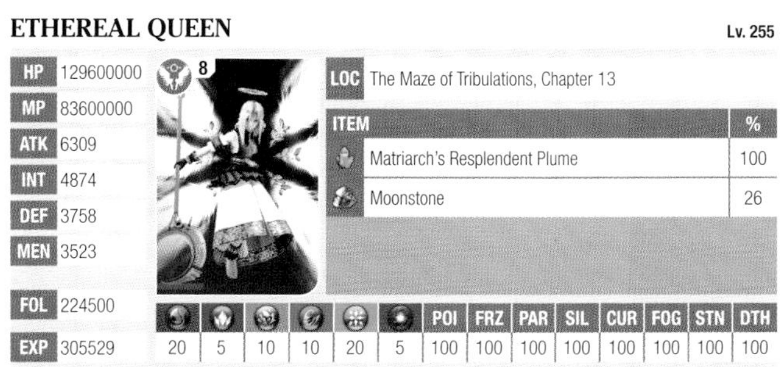

HP	129600000
MP	83600000
ATK	6309
INT	4874
DEF	3758
MEN	3523
FOL	224500
EXP	305529

LOC: The Maze of Tribulations, Chapter 13

ITEM	%
Matriarch's Resplendent Plume	100
Moonstone	26

						POI	FRZ	PAR	SIL	CUR	FOG	STN	DTH
20	5	10	10	20	5	100	100	100	100	100	100	100	100

This herald of utter ruin comes wrapped in a mantle of baleful flame. Her scythe has razed whole cities in one stroke with its resultant gales.

BATTLE AND SYSTEM TROPHIES

BATTLE TROPHIES

Battle trophies are small, in-game accomplishments that track progress in various ways. Ongoing tallies of victories, hits, and various battle abilities are kept, along with all-time highs in damage dealt, chains, enemies finished off at once, and so on. Cleared Battle Trophies can be viewed in the Main Menu, under Resources.

Many objectives simply unlock during the course of normal gameplay, but others require focused effort. Battle Trophies for blocking consecutive attacks are best tackled immediately at the beginning of the game, where it's possible to get away with blocking continuously for a long time without getting badly hurt, or having allies take out enemies prematurely. On the other hand, some objectives clearly have to wait until the party is considerably powerful indeed, like the Battle Trophy for scoring a single 99,999 damage hit. A few objectives require that a particular character be used, like for hitting many foes with a particular battle skill, or finishing off so many enemies in a row using a given ally.

A handful of Battle Trophies, once completed, open access to special roles for dictating ally behavior in combat. There are also system trophies unlocked by collecting battle trophies—the bronze Stalwart Veteran system trophy for accomplishing half the battle trophy objectives, and the silver Consummate Combatant system trophy for finishing all of them.

One-Time Events

NUMBER	TITLE	DESCRIPTION
1	1 Attack / 500 Damage	Inflict 500 or more damage with 1 hit.
2	1 Attack / 1,000 Damage	Inflict 1,000 or more damage with 1 hit.
3	1 Attack / 5,000 Damage	Inflict 5,000 or more damage with 1 hit.
4	1 Attack / 10,000 Damage	Inflict 10,000 or more damage with 1 hit.
5	1 Attack / 25,000 Damage	Inflict 25,000 or more damage with 1 hit.
6	1 Attack / 50,000 Damage	Inflict 50,000 or more damage with 1 hit. Completing this Battle Trophy unlocks the **Eccentric** role.
7	1 Attack / 99,999 Damage	Inflict 99,999 damage with 1 hit.
8	Defeat 2 Foes at Once	Defeat 2 enemies at once.
9	Defeat 3 Foes at Once	Defeat 3 enemies at once.
10	Defeat 4 Foes at Once	Defeat 4 enemies at once. Completing this Battle Trophy unlocks the **Instigator** role.
11	Defeat 5 Foes at Once	Defeat 5 enemies at once.
12	3 Hits with Death Palm	Hit 3 enemies with Fidel's Death Palm. Hitting the same enemy twice doesn't count.
13	4 Hits with Explosion	Hit 4 enemies with Miki's Explosion. Hitting the same enemy twice doesn't count.
14	3 Hits with Flying Guillotine	Hit 3 enemies with Victor's Flying Guillotine. Hitting the same enemy twice doesn't count.
15	4 Hits with Dark Devourer	Hit 4 enemies with Fiore's Dark Devourer. Hitting the same enemy twice doesn't count.
16	3 Hits with Sound Spike	Hit 3 enemies with Emmerson's Sound Spike. Hitting the same enemy twice doesn't count.
17	3 Hits with Hammer of Might	Hit 3 enemies with Anne's Hammer of Might. Hitting the same enemy twice doesn't count.
18	Miki's Brute Force	Defeat an enemy with Miki by delivering either a weak or strong attack, or by counterattacking.
19	Mistress Brunelli's Punishment	Defeat an enemy with Fiore by using a counterattack.
20	Defeat with Reserve Rush	Defeat an enemy with a reserve rush.
21	Defeat with Battle Skill	Defeat an enemy with a battle skill.
22	Defeat with Item	Defeat an enemy with an attack item.
23	Kill It with Ice	Use an ice-based attack with Fidel to defeat an enemy vulnerable to them.
24	Kill It with Earth	Use an earth-based attack with Miki to defeat an enemy vulnerable to them.
25	Kill It with Fire	Use a fire-based attack with Victor to defeat an enemy vulnerable to them.
26	Kill It with Darkness	Use a darkness-based attack with Fiore to defeat an enemy vulnerable to them.
27	Kill It with Light	Use a light-based attack with Emmerson to defeat an enemy vulnerable to them.
28	Kill It with Wind	Use an air-based attack with Anne to defeat an enemy vulnerable to them.
29	Flawless Victory	Win a battle without anyone in your party taking damage.
30	30-second Victory	Eliminate all enemies in under 30 seconds.
31	20-second Victory	Eliminate all enemies in under 20 seconds.
32	10-second Victory	Eliminate all enemies in under 10 seconds.
33	3-second Victory	Eliminate all enemies in under 3 seconds.

Chains

NUMBER	TITLE	DESCRIPTION
34	10-hit Combo	Chain 10 hits together with an attack.
35	50-hit Combo	Chain 50 hits together with an attack.
36	100-hit Combo	Chain 100 hits together with an attack.
37	250-hit Combo	Chain 250 hits together with an attack. Completing this Battle Trophy unlocks the **Stun Supporter** role.
38	500-hit Combo	Chain 500 hits together with an attack.

NUMBER	TITLE	DESCRIPTION
39	Long Range 10-hit Combo	Chain 10 hits together from long range with a normal attack. Attacks that do not land do not count.
40	Long Range 50-hit Combo	Chain 50 hits together from long range with a normal attack. Attacks that do not land do not count.
41	Long Range 100-hit Combo	Chain 100 hits together from long range with a normal attack. Attacks that do not land do not count. Completing this Battle Trophy unlocks the **Betrayer** role.
42	Long Range 250-hit Combo	Chain 250 hits together from long range with a normal attack. Attacks that do not land do not count.
43	Block 5 Consecutive Attacks	Defend against 5 consecutive enemy attacks. Counter resets if you fail to guard during that time.
44	Block 10 Consecutive Attacks	Defend against 10 consecutive enemy attacks. Counter resets if you fail to guard during that time.
45	Block 30 Consecutive Attacks	Defend against 30 consecutive enemy attacks. Counter resets if you fail to guard during that time. Completing this Battle Trophy unlocks the **Pacifist** role.
46	Block 50 Consecutive Attacks	Defend against 50 consecutive enemy attacks. Counter resets if you fail to guard during that time.
47	5 Consecutive Critical Hits	Land 5 consecutive critical hits. Counter resets if a hit is not critical.
48	10 Consecutive Critical Hits	Land 10 consecutive critical hits. Counter resets if a hit is not critical.
49	25 Consecutive Critical Hits	Land 25 consecutive critical hits. Counter resets if a hit is not critical. Completing this Battle Trophy unlocks the **Critical Combatant** role.
50	50 Consecutive Critical Hits	Land 50 consecutive critical hits. Counter resets if a hit is not critical.
51	5 Foes in a Row with 1 Blow	Defeat 5 consecutive enemies at full health with 1 blow each. Counter resets if you attack an injured enemy.
52	10 Foes in a Row with 1 Blow	Defeat 10 consecutive enemies at full health with 1 blow each. Counter resets if you attack an injured enemy. Completing this Battle Trophy unlocks the **Warmonger** role.
53	20 Foes in a Row with 1 Blow	Defeat 20 consecutive enemies at full health with 1 blow each. Counter resets if you attack an injured enemy.
54	5 Consecutive Finishing Blows	Have the character you control finish off the last enemy 5 times in a row. Counter resets if an ally lands a finishing blow.
55	10 Consecutive Finishing Blows	Have the character you control finish off the last enemy 10 times in a row. Counter resets if an ally lands a finishing blow. Completing this Battle Trophy unlocks the **Evasionist** role.
56	20 Consecutive Finishing Blows	Have the character you control finish off the last enemy 20 times in a row. Counter resets if an ally lands a finishing blow.
57	5 Consecutive Finishes with Miki	Finish off the last enemy as Miki 5 times in a row. Counter resets if an ally lands a finishing blow.
58	5 Consecutive Finishes with Victor	Finish off the last enemy as Victor 5 times in a row. Counter resets if an ally lands a finishing blow.
59	5 Consecutive Finishes with Fiore	Finish off the last enemy as Fiore 5 times in a row. Counter resets if an ally lands a finishing blow.
60	5 Consecutive Finishes with Emmerson	Finish off the last enemy as Emmerson 5 times in a row. Counter resets if an ally lands a finishing blow.
61	5 Consecutive Finishes with Anne	Finish off the last enemy as Anne 5 times in a row. Counter resets if an ally lands a finishing blow.

Cumulative Accomplishments

NUMBER	TITLE	DESCRIPTION
62	1,000 Total Hits	Exceed a total of 1,000 hits.
63	10,000 Total Hits	Exceed a total of 10,000 hits. Completing this Battle Trophy unlocks the **Gritty Warrior** role.
64	100,000 Total Hits	Exceed a total of 100,000 hits.
65	1,000,000 Total Hits	Exceed a total of 1,000,000 hits.
66	Deal 99,999 Total Damage	Inflict a total of 99,999 damage on enemies.
67	Deal 9,999,999 Total Damage	Inflict a total of 9,999,999 damage on enemies.
68	Deal 99,999,999 Total Damage	Inflict a total of 99,999,999 damage on enemies.
69	Deal 999,999,999 Total Damage	Inflict a total of 999,999,999 damage on enemies.
70	Take 1,000 Total Damage	Take more than 1,000 damage in total from enemies.
71	Take 10,000 Total Damage	Take more than 10,000 damage in total from enemies.
72	Take 100,000 Total Damage	Take more than 100,000 damage in total from enemies. Completing this Battle Trophy unlocks the **Hothead** role.
73	Take 1,000,000 Total Damage	Take more than 1,000,000 damage in total from enemies.
74	100 Total Critical Hits	Land a total of 100 critical hits.
75	1,000 Total Critical Hits	Land a total of 1,000 critical hits.
76	10,000 Total Critical Hits	Land a total of 10,000 critical hits.
77	Poison 100 Foes	Poison a total of 100 enemies.
78	Paralyze 100 Foes	Paralyze a total of 100 enemies.
79	Silence 100 Foes	Silence a total of 100 enemies.
80	Stun 100 Foes	Stun a total of 100 enemies.
81	Freeze 100 Foes	Freeze a total of 100 enemies.
82	Cloud 100 Foes' Vision	Cloud the vision of a total of 100 enemies.
83	Curse 100 Foes	Curse a total of 100 enemies.
84	Defeat 100 Total Foes	Defeat a total of 100 enemies.
85	Defeat 1,000 Total Foes	Defeat a total of 1,000 enemies.
86	Defeat 10,000 Total Foes	Defeat a total of 10,000 enemies.
87	Fight in 100 Battles	Take part in a total of 100 battles.
88	Fight in 500 Battles	Take part in a total of 500 battles.
89	Fight in 1,000 Battles	Take part in a total of 1,000 battles.
90	10 Victories	Be victorious in a total of 10 battles.
91	100 Victories	Be victorious in a total of 100 battles.
92	500 Victories	Be victorious in a total of 500 battles. Completing this Battle Trophy unlocks the **Master Tactician** role.
93	1,000 Victories	Be victorious in a total of 1,000 battles.
94	100 Counterattacks	Counterattack 100 times.
95	100 Reserve Rushes	Activate 100 reserve rushes.

NUMBER	TITLE	DESCRIPTION
96	Use Special Arts 1,000 Times	Use special arts 1,000 times.
97	Use Signeturgy 1,000 Times	Use signeturgy 1,000 times.
98	Use Items 100 Times	Use items 100 times in battle.
99	Use Items 500 Times	Use items 500 times in battle. Completing this Battle Trophy unlocks the **Item Expender** role.
100	Use Items 1,000 Times	Use items 1,000 times in battle.

SYSTEM TROPHIES

System trophies are unlocked with various actions throughout the game, from story progression to optional tasks like item creation, synthesis, and quests. Pop-up notifications appear to announce system trophy acquisition (unless trophy notifications are disabled at the console level). System trophies are compiled here. This list isn't spoiler-saturated, but it is sprinkled with some names perhaps best left as surprises for long-time fans of this series.

Trophies are mostly self-explanatory. Apart from standard progression in the story and the normal course of playing, most trophies can be collected by exploring as much content as possible." One trophy will unlock halfway through bestiary/item/quest/battle trophy collection, and another trophy for total completion in each category. There are also trophies for reaching the apex of item creation and synthesis in each item category, and for true completionist tasks like repeat playthroughs and completions on higher difficulties.

The capstone platinum trophy is acquired by collecting all other trophies.

System Trophies

ICON	TITLE	QUALITY	DESCRIPTION
	Warden of the Stars	Platinum	Obtain all trophies.
	The Hero Sthal Needs	Bronze	Eradicate Eitalon. Chapter 2 progress.
	Pavine Pummeler	Bronze	Defeat Pavine in the Eihied Mountains. Chapter 5 progress.
	Der-Suul Deposer	Bronze	Defeat Der-Suul in the Slaughtery. Chapter 8 progress.
	Thoras Thrasher	Bronze	Defeat Thoras in the parallel dimension. Chapter 12 progress.
	Alma Annihilator	Bronze	Defeat General Alma in the throne room. Chapter 12 progress.
	Archnemesis of the Heavens	Silver	Defeat Gabriel Celeste. Maze of Tribulations progress.
	Slayer of Divine Beings	Gold	Defeat Ethereal Queen. Maze of Tribulations progress.
	Together Forever	Silver	View Miki's ending.
	His Will Lives On	Silver	View Victor's ending.
	Straightened Priorities	Silver	View Fiore's ending.
	Traverse the Stars	Silver	View Emmerson's ending.
	All Alone with Anne	Silver	View Anne's ending.
	Relia Finds Happiness	Silver	View Relia's ending.
	The Legend Begins	Bronze	Start a second playthrough.
	Call for Backup	Bronze	Activate a reserve rush.
	Right Back Atchya	Bronze	Make a riposte.
	He Who Runs Away Lives to Fight Another Day	Bronze	Flee from a battle.
	My Reaction When	Bronze	Use an emote during a cutscene.
	Supernal Aspirations	Silver	Ascend to level 255.
	Universally Renowned	Silver	Beat the game on Universe difficulty.

ICON	TITLE	QUALITY	DESCRIPTION
	Survivor of Chaos	Gold	Beat the game on Chaos difficulty.
	Please Be Gentle	Bronze	Create an item.
	Successor to the Vineyard Throne	Silver	Unlock all item creation recipes.
	Apothecary Extraordinaire	Bronze	Create the most valuable medicinal item.
	Culinary Virtuoso	Bronze	Create the most valuable edible item.
	Alchemical Artisan	Bronze	Create the most precious metal.
	Nature's Blessing	Bronze	Create the most valuable naturally-occurring item.
	Seeker of Sorcerous Knowledge	Bronze	Create the most valuable sorcerous item.
	Master Machinist	Bronze	Create the most valuable mechanical item.
	Learn from Your Mistakes	Silver	Create an item that you shouldn't.
	Full Arsenal	Bronze	Obtain all battle skills and signeturgical spells.
	Hail to the Chief	Silver	Obtain the vast majority of the roles.
	Stalwart Veteran	Bronze	Obtain half of the battle trophies.
	Consummate Combatant	Silver	Obtain all battle trophies.
	Biology Buff	Bronze	Encounter half of all enemies.
	Boss of the Bestiary	Silver	Encounter every enemy.
	Item Identifier	Bronze	Catalogue half of all items.
	Compendium Completionist	Silver	Catalogue every item.
	Helping Hand	Bronze	Complete half of all quests.
	Quid Pro Quest	Silver	Complete all quests.

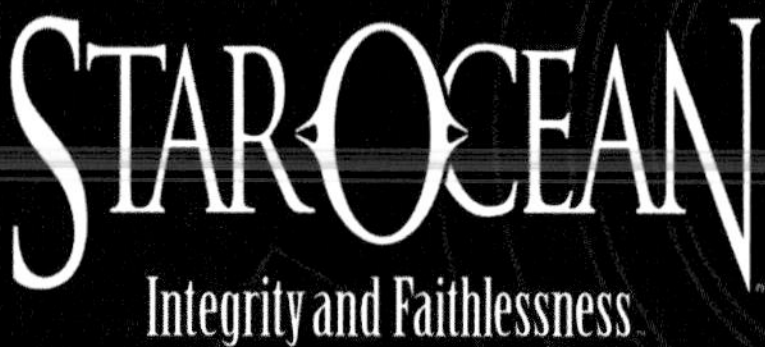

Written by Long Tran and Joe Epstein

DK/Prima Games, a division of Penguin Random House LLC
6081 East 82nd Street, Suite #400
Indianapolis, IN 46250

ISBN: 978-0-7440-1742-7
Printing Code: The rightmost double-digit number is the year of the book's printing; the rightmost single-digit number is the number of the book's printing. For example, 16-1 shows that the first printing of the book occurred in 2016.

19 18 17 16 4 3 2 1

001-300305-Jun/2016

Printed in the USA.

CREDITS

Senior Development Editor
Chris Hausermann

Book Designer
Dan Caparo
Brent Gann

Production Designer
Julie Clark

Production
Angela Graef

Copy Editor
Angie Mateski

PRIMA GAMES STAFF

VP & Publisher
Mike Degler

Editorial Manager
Tim Fitzpatrick

Design and Layout Manager
Tracy Wehmeyer

Licensing
Christian Sumner
Paul Giacomotto

Marketing
Katie Hemlock

Digital Publishing
Julie Asbury
Tim Cox
Shaida Boroumand

Operations Manager
Stacey Ginther

ACKNOWLEDGEMENTS

LONG TRAN

The construction of this book would not have been possible without the aid of copious amounts of caffeine, so big shout-outs to caffeine and caffeine-related consumables. Of course, just as important to the creation of this magnificent beast of a strategy guide are several terrific people from Square Enix and Prima Games. Thanks to Mat Clift, David Carillo, and the rest of the SE QA crew for their incredibly helpful game research. You guys really understand and care about your game. Thanks to Tyler Wissler and Jeffrey Winternheimer for meticulously double-checking my game-related content. Thanks to Joe Epstein for introducing me to this business and supporting me throughout my learning experience. Thanks to Brent Gann, Dan Caparo, and Julie Clark for being able to decipher all of my scatterbrained callouts in documents and putting together an amazingly vibrant layout. Also, a huge appreciation goes out to Angie Mateski for her editing expertise. Last but not least, thanks to Chris Hausermann for trusting in me to take on a larger role for this book. I learned so much working on this guide and I hope we can team up again in the future!

JOE EPSTEIN

Thanks to everyone at tri-Ace and Square-Enix who helped make another great, gorgeous RPG, and to everyone at Prima who helped assemble this guide. In particular, thanks to Long Tran, Chris Hausermann, Dan Caparo, Brent Gann, Julie Clark, and Angie Mateski. Thanks also to Mat Clift, David Carillo, and our other contacts at Square, who are always beyond helpful.